SEVENTH EDITION

Government and Politics in the Lone Star State

Theory and Practice

L. Tucker Gibson, Jr.
Trinity University

Clay Robison

Longman

Boston   Columbus   Indianapolis   New York   San Francisco
Upper Saddle River   Amsterdam   Cape Town   Dubai   London   Madrid   Milan
Munich   Paris   Montreal   Toronto   Delhi   Mexico City   São Paulo   Sydney
Hong Kong   Seoul   Singapore   Taipei   Tokyo

Editor-in-Chief: Eric Stano
Editorial Assistant: Elizabeth Alimena
Marketing Manager: Lindsey Prudhomme
Supplements Editor: Donna Garnier
Senior Media Supplements Editor: Regina Vertiz
Production Manager: Denise Phillip
Project Coordination, Text Design, and Electronic Page Makeup: Pre-PressPMG
Cover Designer/Manager: Wendy Ann Fredericks
Cover Photo: © Lee Snider/Photo Images/Corbis
Senior Manufacturing Buyer: Roy Pickering
Photo Researcher: L. Tucker Gibson, Jr.
Printer and Binder: R. R. Donnelley & Sons/Harrisonburg
Cover Printer: R. R. Donnelley & Sons/Harrisonburg

Library of Congress Cataloging-in-Publication Data

Gibson, L. Tucker.
Government and politics in the Lone Star state : theory and practice / L. Tucker Gibson, Jr., Clay Robison.—7th ed.
  p. cm.
Includes bibliographical references and index.
ISBN-13: 978-0-205-77902-4 (alk. paper)
ISBN-10: 0-205-77902-6 (alk. paper)
1. Texas—Politics and government—1951-I. Title.
JK4816.G53 2011
320.4764—dc22

2010000296

2 3 4 5 6 7 8 9 10—DOH—13 12 11 10

Longman
is an imprint of

www.pearsonhighered.com

ISBN-13: 978-0-205-77902-4
ISBN-10:   0-205-77902-6

Contents

CHAPTER 8
The Texas Legislature 229

CHAPTER 9
The Texas Executive 278

Preface

For almost twenty years, the authors have worked together, organizing their thoughts and presenting their views on Texas government and politics. During these years, there have been numerous changes, which we have tracked and reported in successive editions. Statewide, the one-party Democratic system has been transformed into a system dominated by the Republican Party. Texas's population continues to grow at a faster rate than the nation's. Sometime during the year in which this book was published, the combined minority population of the state surpassed 50 percent. The urban characteristics of the state are more evident than twenty years ago. Growth and diversification in the economy continue. So does urban sprawl. There has been a massive highway construction program, and budgets and expenditures have increased at all levels of government, accompanied by increased government employment. Water, once an inexpensive resource, is now becoming the center of intense regional conflict over how it should be allocated. New markets for water are emerging with competition between the public and private sectors. Public school enrollment has increased, presenting additional demands for funding. New institutions of higher education have been created to serve a growing student population. New federal and state environmental laws have been enacted, and demands for social services, especially medical care, have increased.

These changes were anticipated more than twenty years ago by scholars, policymakers at all levels of government, think tanks, advocacy groups, and others concerned about the quality of life in Texas and the ability of governments and the private sector to respond and adapt to new economic, demographic, and political realities. We have watched closely the response of public officials and political institutions to these changing conditions. We have observed the political behavior of the general public in the selection of leaders and the articulation of concerns and expectations about public policy.

Sometimes, public officials and institutions "get it right" when they enact new policies. Sometimes, they adopt only partial solutions. Some policy initiatives have been underfunded, misdirected, or based on faulty assumptions that have failed to produce real solutions. Other policy initiatives have benefited a few at the expense of the many, and at other times, nothing has been done about serious problems.

In an earlier edition, we noted that the authors might be "excessively cranky, reflecting the many long hours we have spent observing, studying, and writing about government and politics." In some respects, we may be crankier and more impatient today than we were in the past. While we may be cranky, we are not cynical.

We have a passion for democracy, citizen participation, open government, responsive leadership, fairness in the distribution of public services, protection of those with limited political and economic resources, informed and civil public discourse, and balancing the needs and interests of individuals with those of the general society. A commitment to democratic values does not preclude critical analysis of our institutions and political leaders. It also does not preclude our criticism of the citizenry when there is apathy or indifference to the state's public life.

Democracy is usually defined and articulated in terms of its broad ideals, and very few political systems meet these ideals. There are people who are excluded from participating in a significant way in the decisions of government. There are political leaders whose behavior is self-serving, arrogant, and sometimes criminal. There are individuals or groups who attempt to impose their "will" on others with little consideration for the interests or needs of key segments of the state's population. And there are instances of public policies that produce harmful consequences for some people.

Political philosophers and scholars have been dealing with these issues for centuries, and we like to think of ourselves as political realists. People are capable of doing bad things, and it takes power to balance or control the abuses of power. Democratic societies depend on an informed and engaged citizenry that gives attention to the actions of their leaders. Individuals function in terms of their self-interests, but a democracy depends on "interests well understood" that lead to a concern for others and a willingness to subordinate narrow self-interests to the common good.

We present a great deal of factual material in the chapters that follow. Facts are the building blocks necessary to understand state and local government. We place these facts within a general conceptual framework that will help you organize information and move your analysis to broad generalizations and comparisons. Facts become dated, and you should strive to look at the bigger picture that is presented. For example, Texas has an identifiable political culture rooted in its historical experience. With changing demographics, how might this political culture change or assimilate the values and views of new populations? In the chapter on political parties, we emphasize realignment theory that provides perspectives on the conditions and causes of party change. The state has recently experienced realignment, and more realignment is anticipated in the future. The legislative chapter is constructed around the theory of institutionalization, which provides a conceptual perspective on the development of the Texas legislature.

Both authors have their political biases, but we have attempted to suppress these. Our job is not to convert you to a particular philosophical or partisan position. We encourage you to grapple with the materials presented. Argue with the authors when you disagree. Engage your instructor in a critical assessment of the conclusions we draw. Finally, work on formulating your own views about government, politics, and your role in the Texas political system.

One author is trained as an academic in the theories and concepts that apply to state and local government. If there are parts of the narrative that appear excessively pedantic, blame him. After forty-plus years in the classroom, he still enjoys a robust class discussion of the basic principles of government. Despite his academic orientation, he has considerable experience in business, consulting with governments across the state, and party politics. He also served on the San Antonio Civil Service Commission.

The second author is a journalist. He brings to the subject a forty-year career of covering state, local, and national politics. His position as the Austin Bureau Chief of the *Houston Chronicle* and the *San Antonio Express-News* placed him in proximity to the state institutions and political actors who are interspersed throughout this book. His job was to "tell the story," crafting the analysis in language engaging to the reader. He has also edited and eliminated most of the arcane words of the first author.

NEW TO THIS EDITION ──────────────────────────●

This is our seventh go at this book. We hope we are getting better over time. Just as musicians and athletes must practice and practice until they get it write (oops, right), so must the student of politics and government.

We continue to update information throughout. There are some new stories as well as ones that we just couldn't let go because they speak directly to the concepts that we advance. There are new players in the political arena, and there are some who have exited. As we look back over the past two decades, we see a few new issues, such as homeland security, but most of the issues that are woven into the narrative are the recurring issues or problems of state politics.

That being said, there are new features and updates we have added to this edition that we think are worthy of note:

- New "Questions to Guide Your Reading" appear at the beginning of every chapter to highlight and reinforce concepts that will be developed in the chapter
- Tables and graphs have been updated throughout the text to include the most current data available.
- New coverage of recent economic developments analyzes why the economic downturn arrived later and with less negative consequences in Texas than in other states across the country.
- Updated and expanded issue coverage takes an in-depth look at the state's policies on welfare, education, and global warming.
- Analysis of state-federal relationships examines the impact of the George W. Bush presidency and the early initiatives of the Obama administration on Texas.
- An expanded discussion of immigration—both legal and illegal—looks at changes in laws providing public services to new immigrants and the impact of immigration on the state's public education system.
- Projections of future population increases in the Texas Urban Triangle have been developed using updated information on the urbanization of Texas.
- An expanded discussion of drug-related violence looks at its impact on Texas and its spill-over into other areas of the U.S.
- Changes in campaign technology are discussed, including the tools of communication that are now used by party activists to reach the general electorate.
- A synopsis of the leadership changes in the Texas House of Representatives analyzes the effects of the coalition of Republicans and Democrats in the House.
- A discussion of job opportunities provides an inside look into the workings, performance, and overall effectiveness of state agencies.

We hope that this book assists you in your lifelong journey as a citizen and participant in the political process. If we help you understand the governmental institutions and politics of Texas, we will feel that we have been successful.

ACKNOWLEDGMENTS ──────────────────────────●

A note of thanks goes to those who reviewed the previous edition and made helpful suggestions for changes and improvements. Joe Tognetti served as our research assistant in the early stages of this project. Thomas Bell helped bring our work to closure through his work on data sources, photographs, and editing. Pearson Longman's editorial staff deserves a special kudo.

In our attempt to tell the story of Texas government and politics, a number of our political science colleagues serving in other institutions have reviewed our work. Their comments have been invaluable in addressing the strengths as well as deficiencies in earlier editions. They have helped us keep our work relevant, focused, and engaging. And if there are any errors, they are ours. A special note of appreciation go to Mary Barnes, Blinn College; Jeffrey C. Herndon, Texas A&M University—Commerce; Alan Lehmann, Blinn College; J. D. Phaup, Texas A&M University at Kingsville; Blayne Primozich, El Paso Community College; John David Rausch, Jr., West Texas A&M University; Jimmie F. Strain, Mountain View College; and Reed Welch, West Texas A&M University.

L. Tucker Gibson, Jr.

Clay Robison

About the Authors

L. TUCKER GIBSON, JR., is professor of political science at Trinity University, where he teaches introductory courses in American national and state governments as well as courses on U.S. legislatures, political parties, and interest groups. He has served on the Civil Service Commission of the city of San Antonio, assisted local governments across central and south Texas in redistricting their governmental bodies, and conducted public opinion research for political candidates, businesses, and corporations. Gibson is the coauthor of *Politics in America: Texas Edition.*

CLAY ROBISON covered state government and politics in Texas for almost 40 years as a journalist, first for the *San Antonio Light,* and then for the *Houston Chronicle* and the *San Antonio Express-News.* He covered many of the personalities and events that significantly impacted Texas government. Robison is the coauthor of *Politics in America: Texas Edition.*

The Social and Economic Milieu of Texas Politics

Questions to Guide Your Reading

1. What impact will continued demographic changes have on the state's political culture?

2. Do race and ethnicity continue to play a major role in the politics of the state?

3. Does the state have the resources and public policies in place to absorb large numbers of residents?

4. How has the state's economy changed and adapted to the global economy?

Life is too short not to live it in Texas.

—Bumper sticker seen on a car in San Antonio

It is therefore necessary, if we would become acquainted with the legislation and the manners of a nation, to begin by the study of its social condition.

—Alexis de Tocqueville[1]

With a colorful history of vast open spaces, cowboys, Texas Rangers, and oilmen, Texas has a rugged, bigger-than-life mystique that annoys or amuses many non-Texans. In many obvious and not-so-obvious ways, Texans continue to manifest this legacy of the frontier in their speech, their "can-do" attitude, their celebration of their "Texan-ness," and their actions (see "Perpetuating the Myths of Texas: The Cowboy President and the 'Secessionist Governor'"). In what other state do you find the pervasive display of the state's flag or the pilgrimage of so many to the state's "holy shrine"—the Alamo? Behaviors and language with which others take umbrage and often misunderstand are viewed by most Texans to be simply part of the rich culture and legacy of the state.

The twenty-first century wasn't very old, however, before it became obvious that Texas also had oversized problems. Houston-based Enron Corp., a symbol of how to transform unbridled confidence into seemingly unlimited corporate wealth, came tumbling down, taking thousands of jobs and pensions with it. The Enron debacle damaged public confidence in corporate America and was a precursor to the near-collapse a few years later of the financial industry, which precipitated a recession in the United States and throughout the world in 2008. Texas didn't fare as poorly as many other states, but many Texans lost their jobs and their homes as credit markets dried up and the stock market plummeted.

The terrorist attacks on the World Trade Center and the Pentagon on September 11, 2001, challenged Texans' and other Americans' long-held assumptions about the basic security of our country and our state. Within a few years, Texas was thrust into the center of renewed debate over illegal immigration, including concerns over how to improve the security of the border with Mexico and deal with hundreds of thousands of undocumented workers seeking better lives for themselves and their families.

Back-to-back hurricanes in 2005 challenged Texas' ability to provide education, health care, and other social services for thousands of Katrina refugees from Louisiana, many of whom stayed in Texas—and then help thousands of residents of southeast Texas rebuild their lives following Hurricane Rita. Many of those victims were still recovering when Hurricane Ike struck Galveston and other coastal communities with a devastating blow in 2008.

Although some Texans think Texas can go it alone with little outside help, the realities of the global economy link Texas to the fortunes of people and governments throughout the world. The state's population will continue to be transformed by immigration and other changing demographic patterns, even though a legacy of individualism and limited government makes it difficult for some Texans to adjust to a changing economy, a changing society, and a changing political landscape.

The frontier, rural society, characterized by the cowboy, is long gone. The "Oil Patch," where wildcatters and roughnecks once prevailed, has been replaced by what one author dubbed the "Silicon Prairie . . . where venture capitalists and software engineers roam."[2] Texas is now urban, with more than 80 percent of the population living in cities or suburban areas, largely in the central Texas urban triangle. The state

Perpetuating the Myths of Texas

The Cowboy President and the "Secessionist Governor"

During his administration, President George W. Bush was described by some as the "cowboy president." At least two of his predecessors, Theodore Roosevelt and Ronald Reagan, were also portrayed as cowboys, either in cartoons, photos, or prose. The cowboy mythology resonates with most Americans, and it can be used by presidents to symbolize their style of leadership. At the beginning of the invasion of Iraq, Bush branded former Iraqi leader Saddam Hussein an "outlaw" and declared that he wanted terrorist Osama Bin Laden "dead or alive." At a conference in Aqaba on the Red Sea, Bush said that he was going to appoint a coordinator to "ride herd" on Middle East leaders along the peace trail. Many in his audience had no idea what he was talking about.

Bush owns a 1,600-acre ranch in Texas, which he purchased during his governorship, but he didn't grow up or work on a ranch. He has been reported to be afraid of horses. While visiting the former president of Mexico, Vicente Fox, on his ranch, he was offered the opportunity to ride a horse but reportedly backed away from the animal.

It was later reported that Fox referred to him as a "windshield cowboy."

Bush wore a stylish Stetson and a large belt buckle. He conveyed an "aw shucks" demeanor, scrambled his words in a folksy manner, staged photo-ops on his ranch, and seemed to enjoy driving his guests around in his Jeep. While these activities irritated many, his cowboy imagery made for good press. Some observers, particularly his critics, thought a lot of this was orchestrated by his staff and consultants.

The president's characterization as a cowboy in thousands of articles, newscasts, and cartoons fed the perception many have of the frontier culture of Texas and its style of politics.

Bush's gubernatorial successor, Rick Perry, in opposing the "strings" attached to federal stimulus money in 2009, even went so far as to suggest that Texas had the right to secede from the Union. He didn't advocate secession, but his remarks were greeted with derision across the nation, and, once again, the "goofy" remarks of a Texas officeholder provided fodder for the state's critics (see Chapter 9).

includes three of the ten largest cities in the United States—Houston, San Antonio, and Dallas.

Texans, just as most citizens of other states, are woefully ignorant of their state and local governments and the public officials who make important decisions affecting their daily lives. Many view government as something in Austin or at the courthouse, where people do things to us, not for us. Government is often described in terms of red tape, inefficiency, and anonymous or rude bureaucrats. Political campaigns are perceived as a form of organized mud wrestling in which candidates characterize each other as despicable, immoral, incompetent, or whatever, and this perception results in large numbers of Texans tuning out politics. Many people distrust government—a traditionally strong sentiment in Texas—and hope it interferes with their lives as little as possible. Most Texans don't vote in elections, leaving the selection of public leaders to a few people.

But, like most Americans, Texans assume there will be potable water flowing through their kitchen taps, streets and highways on which to drive their cars, quality public schools to which they can send their children, parks for family outings, and police officers to help protect their lives and property. And many people have come to believe that they can have all of this without paying higher taxes, an attitude perpetuated by many politicians who promise more services but refuse to address their costs.

We all have a stake in what governments do because these institutions have a daily impact on our livelihoods and our quality of life. We pay taxes for a multitude of programs and services and would like to feel that the benefits we receive are worth what we pay. People generally don't get excited or concerned about government, however, until it fails to meet their demands or expectations. Such indifference and ignorance can be harmful to the people's interests, particularly today, as Texas undergoes changes that will determine what kind of state it will be for years to come and, consequently, how well or how poorly the public's needs will be met. Our past, marked by good times as well as bad, is a prelude to our future, and decisions that we make about our politics, governments, and public policies will determine how well we can adapt to change.

CHALLENGES OF THE TWENTY-FIRST CENTURY ———————⬤

Sustained population growth; the continued transformation of the state's economy; environmental, transportation and water problems; security needs; and increased demands for public services pose tremendous challenges to the resources, capabilities, and the very structure of Texas's governments. Federal mandates and reductions in federal funds have forced state and local governments to scramble to develop more effective and efficient means of assisting low-income people. Public officials also are challenged by a regressive and outdated tax system, high rates of unemployment and underemployment in various areas of the state, the influx of immigrants from Mexico and other countries, an aging population that requires long-term nursing care, large numbers of people who have no health insurance, an inadequate highway system, and changes in welfare law. Inequities in public education pose a challenge for developing a workforce that can compete in the global economy. And the state's growth has aggravated environmental problems, including water use and air pollution, that affect everyone's health and well-being.

These problems and issues are the ingredients of contemporary Texas politics. They reflect the fundamental conflicts between competing interests and the way Texans decide "who gets what, when, and how."[3] Government and our form of politics are the systems that we have developed to structure conflict, develop an orderly and stable process by which competing interests can be expressed, and, finally, decide who will benefit and who will pay the bill.

As we begin our analysis of Texas government and politics, we ask why Texans and their public officials make the political choices they do. Why, for example, do expenditures for public education rank low in comparison to other states? How do we account for Texas's highly **regressive tax** system, which requires low-income citizens to pay a higher proportion of their income in state and local taxes than do the wealthy? Why are Texans so willing to fund the construction of highways, roads, and prisons while letting their state rank near the bottom of all the states in expenditures for public welfare?[4]

These policy issues are directly linked to a variety of other questions about government and the political system. Why are Texans content to live under a state constitution that most scholars regard as obsolete? Why, until recently, was Texas a one-party Democratic state? Why are state politics now dominated by Republicans? And does this make any difference in public policies? Does a small group of powerful individuals make the primary policy decisions for the state, or are there various competitive centers of power? Do Texans feel they are paying more but getting less for their tax dollars? Are Texans increasingly disenchanted with government?

Most of these issues affect Texans personally. They pay the costs, even though they may not receive the benefits of every policy decision. The actions of governmental leaders can have an immediate and direct effect on people's lives, and, from time to time, those holding positions of power have made decisions that have cost Texans dearly. For example, the Enron debacle and the manipulation of energy markets were the result, in large part, of the failure of state and federal governments to regulate the energy industry adequately. And cuts in governmental services—or increases in tuition at state-supported universities—often result from the refusal of the Texas legislature to increase taxes.

Each generation has to address fundamental questions of the role of government, the relationship of the people to that government, and what can be done to make government more responsive and responsible. When one hears or reads of many of the contemporary policy debates or policy failures, there is a real sense of *deja vu*—we have seen these problems and issues before. Funding of public education, a major problem now, was also an issue during the Texas revolution of 1836, the Reconstruction era after the Civil War, and throughout much of the state's history. There are also new issues, such as the regulation of genetic engineering, the changing international economy, the environment, and the health and social problems posed by AIDS. But many of today's issues are enduring issues of government and politics.

The fundamental changes in the social, economic, and political structure of the state require new solutions. Funding public education in the days of the one-room schoolhouse was one thing. Funding today's educational system in a way that provides equity among the state's 1,000-plus school districts is much more complex.

The demographics, or population characteristics, of the state have changed dramatically since the 1940s, when Texas was still predominantly rural. Texas is now an urban state with urban problems. With more than 24 million residents, Texas is second only to California in population. Its ethnic and racial composition has changed, and it is now home to a large number of individuals who were born and reared in other parts of the United States or outside the country—people who have a limited sense of Texas history and politics. Although oil and natural gas are still important to the state's economy, **economic diversification** is the dominant theme promoted by business leaders, government officials, and economists. Change places heavy demands on the state's governmental institutions, and Texans will need to give increased attention to modernizing and adapting government to new realities.

This chapter will introduce you to the people of Texas, the views they have of themselves, the state's political subcultures, and its economy. We refer to these factors generally as the political environment, a concept developed by political scientist David Easton to refer to the milieu, or context, in which political institutions function.[5] While much of our discussion focuses on broad patterns or characteristics of the political environment, individual and collective behavior of groups will determine how our governments respond to changing conditions.

THE MYTHS OF TEXAS'S POLITICAL CULTURE ●

Although most Texans have only a cursory knowledge of their state's governmental institutions, political history, and contemporary public policy, they do have views—often ill defined—of the state, its people, and its culture. Key elements of these views, shared by millions of Texans, are described by some scholars as **political myths**.

In recent years, serious scholarship has focused on myths as ways to assess the views people have of their common historical and cultural experiences. A myth can be regarded as a "mode of truth that codifies and preserves moral and spiritual values" for a particular culture or society.[6] Myths are stories or narratives that are used to describe past events, explain their significance to successive generations, and provide an interpretive overview and understanding of a society and its culture.[7] Myths provide a world picture or, in our case, a picture of the state of Texas. Myths serve, in part, to affirm the values, customs, and beliefs of Texans.[8] The relevance of a myth depends, in part, on the degree to which it approximates the events it is describing and its pervasiveness in the literature, symbols, rituals and popular culture of the state.

Texas has produced its own myth of origin, which continues to be a powerful statement about the political system and the social order on which it is based. For many Texans, the battle of the Alamo clearly serves to identify the common experiences of independence and the creation of a separate, unique political order.[9] No other state was a **republic** prior to joining the Union, and several scholars argue that independence and "going at it alone" from 1836 to 1845 resulted in a cultural experience that distinguishes the Texas political system from that of other states. The state's nickname—the Lone Star State—is a constant reminder of this unique history. A set of heroes came out of the formative period of Texas history, including many who fought and died at the Alamo or secured Texas independence on the San Jacinto battlefield.

Pulp Fiction. The dime novel helped create the myth of Texas individualism by popularizing and exaggerating the image of the cowboy.

Hero or Villain? The Texas Rangers played an important (but sometimes controversial) role in taming the Texas frontier.

Texas schoolchildren are introduced to these heroes at a very early age with field trips, or "pilgrimages," to the Alamo in San Antonio and visits to the San Jacinto monument in Houston.

The Texas mythology also includes the Texas Ranger and the cowboy. There is considerable lore of the invincible, enduring ranger defeating overwhelming odds. Newspapers and dime novels in the nineteenth century introduced readers throughout the United States to the cowboy, who was often portrayed as an honest, hardworking individual wrestling with the harsh Texas environment. The cowboy's rugged **individualism**, with strong connotations of self-help and independence, symbolizes a political culture in Texas that doesn't like to look to government as a solution to many of its problems.[10] It is the kind of individualism that continues to be exploited by political candidates in campaign ads and by the state legislature in limited appropriations for welfare, health care, and other public-assistance programs. This legacy of individualism and risk taking is further reinforced by the stories of "wildcatters" who made and lost fortunes in the early days of oil exploration in the state.

The frontier to which the Texas Ranger and the cowboy belong is part of a cultural myth of limited government and unlimited personal opportunity. The Texas frontier experience also perpetuates the myth of "land as wilderness and land as garden."[11] The hostile Chihuahuan desert of the far southwestern part of the state eventually gives way to the more edenic green of the Piney Woods of East Texas. But space, distance, and size are pervasive in a great deal of literature on the state. Literally thousands of books written about Texas provide varied perspectives on the geography and typology of the land. One might argue that the "wide open spaces" of the frontier shaped Texans' views of their autonomy, independence, vulnerability, and interdependence. It has clearly shaped attitudes toward land and the legal rights to use land as one sees fit.

The Texas myths, however, have been primarily the myths of the white (Anglo) population and have limited relevance to the cultural and historical experiences of many African-American and Hispanic Texans. From the 1840s to the mid-1960s, these latter groups were excluded from full participation in Texas politics and the state's economic and social life. To many Hispanics, for example, the Texas Ranger is not a hero, but a symbol of ruthless suppression.

Over the past twenty years, African Americans, Hispanics, and Asian Americans have made significant political and economic gains. Their share of the population has been increasing as well, and these three groups combined now constitute a majority of the state's population.

As this shift occurs, Hispanic and African-American historical experiences are likely to be incorporated into the mythology of the state, and some components of the contemporary mythology will be challenged and redefined. These revisions may already be under way, as demonstrated by heated debate over what actually took place during the battle of the Alamo. According to one recently published account, some of the Alamo's heroes surrendered to Mexican soldiers and were executed, rather than fighting to the death, as was long believed. African Americans in Texas have been successful, after several years of trying, in getting the state legislature to make Martin Luther King, Jr.'s birthday a state holiday. June 19, the day slaves in Texas learned of their emancipation in 1865, also has significant meaning for the state's African Americans and is celebrated as the Juneteenth holiday. For Hispanics, the *Cinco de Mayo* and *Diez y Seis* celebrations speak to common cultural and historical experiences with Mexico.

New Elements of the Political Culture. Cinco de Mayo is celebrated by Texas Hispanics in commemoration of Mexico's defeat of French troops at Puebla, Mexico, in 1862.

Free at Last. Juneteenth or Emancipation Day in Texas, a state holiday since 1980, celebrates the day (June 19, 1865) African Americans first heard that 'all slaves are free.'

THE POLITICAL CULTURE OF TEXAS ⎯⎯⎯⎯⎯⎯⎯⎯⎯⎯●

Texas shares the common constitutional, institutional, and legal arrangements that have developed in all fifty states, including a commitment to personal liberties, equality, justice, the rule of law, and popular sovereignty with its limitations on government. But there are cultural differences among the states and even among regions within individual states. Texas is a highly diverse state, with racial and ethnic differences from one region to another and divergences in political attitudes and behavior that are reflected in the state's politics and public policies.

The concept of **political culture** helps us compare some of these differences. Political culture has been defined as the "set of attitudes, beliefs, and sentiments which give order and meaning to a political process and which provide the underlying assumptions and rules that govern behavior in the political system."[12] The political culture of the state includes fundamental beliefs about the proper role of government, the relationship of the government to its citizens, and who should govern.[13] These complex attitudes and behaviors are rooted in the historical experience of the nation, shaped by the groups that immigrated to the United States, and carried across the continent to Texas.

One authority on American political culture, Daniel Elazar, noted that three political subcultures have emerged over time in the United States: the individualistic, the moralistic, and the traditionalistic. All three draw from the common historical legacy of the nation, but they have produced regional political differences. Sometimes they complement each other, while at other times they produce conflict.[14]

The Individualistic Subculture

The political view of the **individualistic subculture** holds that politics and government function as a marketplace. Government does not have to be concerned with creating a good or moral society but exists for strictly "utilitarian reasons, to handle those functions demanded by the people it is created to serve."[15] Government should be limited, and its intervention in the private activities of its citizens should be kept to a minimum. The primary function of government is to ensure the stability of a society so that individuals can pursue their own interests.

In this view, politics is not a high calling or noble pursuit but is like any other business venture in which skill and talent prevail and the individual can expect economic and social benefits. Politics is often perceived by the general public to be a dirty business that should be left to those willing to soil their hands in the political arena. This tradition may well contribute to political corruption, and members of the electorate who share this view may not be concerned when government corruption is revealed. New policies are more likely to be initiated by interest groups or private individuals than by public officials, and it is assumed that those elected to public office will pursue their self-interests.[16]

The Moralistic Subculture

The **moralistic subculture** regards politics as one of the "great activities of man in his search for the good society."[17] Politics, it maintains, is the pursuit of the common good. Unlike the attitude expressed in the individualistic subculture that governments are to be limited, the moralistic subculture considers government a positive instrument with a responsibility to promote the general welfare.[18] Politics, therefore, is not to be left to the few but is a responsibility of every individual. Politics is a duty and possibly a high calling. This cultural tradition has a strong sense of service. It requires a high standard for those holding public office, which is not to be used for personal gain. Politics may be organized around political parties, but this tradition has produced nonpartisanship where party labels and organizations are eliminated or play a reduced role.[19] This tradition produces a large number of "amateur" or "nonprofessional" political activists and officeholders and has little toleration for political corruption. From the moralistic perspective, governments should actively intervene to enhance the social and economic interests of their citizens. Public policy initiatives can come from officeholders as well as from those outside the formal governmental structure.[20]

The Traditionalistic Subculture

The **traditionalistic subculture** holds the view that there is a hierarchical arrangement to the political order. This hierarchy serves to limit the power and influence of the general public, while allocating authority to a few individuals who comprise self-perpetuating elites. The elites may enact policies that benefit the general public, but that is secondary to their own interests and objectives. Public policy reflects the interests of those who exercise influence and control, and the benefits of public policy go disproportionately to the elites.

Family, social, and economic relationships, not mass political participation, form the basis for maintaining this elite structure. In fact, in many regions of the country where traditionalistic patterns existed, there were systematic efforts to reduce or eliminate the participation of the general public. Although political parties may exist in such a subculture, they have only minimal importance that is often subject to manipulation or control by elites. Many of the states characterized by the traditionalistic subculture were southern states in which two-party politics was replaced by factionalism within the Democratic Party.[21]

HISTORICAL ORIGINS OF POLITICAL SUBCULTURES

The historical origins of these three subcultures can be explained, in part, by the early settlement patterns of the United States and by the cultural differences among the groups of people who initially settled the eastern seaboard. In very general terms, the New England colonists, influenced by Puritan and congregational religious groups, spawned the moralistic subculture. Settlers with entrepreneurial concerns and individualistic attitudes tended to locate in the Mid-Atlantic States, while the initial settlement of the South was dominated by elites who aspired, in part, to recreate a semifeudal society.

As expansion toward the western frontiers progressed, there were identifiable migration patterns from the initial three settlement regions. Texas was settled primarily by people holding the individualistic and traditionalistic views of a political system. The blending of these two views, along with the historical experience of the Republic and frontier, contributed to the distinct characteristics of Texas's political culture.[22]

These two political subcultures have merged to shape Texans' general views of what government should do, who should govern, and what constitutes good public policy. Given the characteristics of these two traditions, one might well conclude, as have many scholars, that the Texas political culture is conservative. Politics in Texas tends to minimize the role of government, is hostile toward taxes—especially those that are allocated toward social services—and is often manipulated by the few for their narrow advantages at the expense of the general population. During much of its history, Texas was one of the least democratic states, with restrictions on voting rights, limited party competition, and low rates of voter participation.[23]

Some scholars have reservations about the concept of political subcultures because the theory is difficult to test. Their reservations are legitimate, but we know of no other single theory that presents such a rich historical perspective on the relationship of settlement patterns in the state and the evolution of political attitudes and behavior.

THE PEOPLE OF TEXAS —————————————————————●

The politics and government of Texas can be understood, in part, from the perspective of the people living in the state. What follows is an assessment of a select number of demographic, or population, characteristics of Texans. In subsequent chapters, we examine the relationship of race, ethnicity, and other demographic characteristics to partisan behavior, public opinion, institutional power, and public policy.

Native Americans

There are only three small Native-American groups (Alabama-Coushatta, Tigua, and Kickapoo) living on reservations in Texas, and the Native-American population is less than one-half of 1 percent of the state's total population. Unlike Native Americans in Oklahoma, New Mexico, and Arizona, those in Texas have little influence on governmental institutions, politics, or public policy.

In the early nineteenth century, there were at least twenty-three different Native-American groups residing in Texas (see "Tejas Means Friendship").

During the period of the Republic (1836–1845), President Sam Houston attempted to follow a policy of "peace and friendship" with the Native Americans, but he was followed by President Mirabeau B. Lamar, who set out to "expel, defeat, or exterminate" them. Statehood did not improve the conditions for Native Americans, and the period between annexation in 1845 and the Civil War (1861–1865) was "one of devastation, decimation, and dislocation" for many of the state's tribes.[24] As the European populations expanded to lands traditionally claimed by various Native-American tribes, conflict ensued, and most of the Native-American population was eventually eliminated or displaced to other states.

In recent years, Native American tribes have cooperated with officials in many states in establishing gambling casinos on tribal reservations. Such casinos are allowed under federal law, but some casino gambling comes into conflict with Texas law. The Kickapoos operate a limited casino outside of Eagle Pass, but the Tiguas and Alabama-Coushattas have been denied the right to run casinos on their reservations. Some Native American leaders consider casinos a major potential source of revenue, jobs,

---

Tejas Means Friendship

The Native-American legacy of Texas remains in the state's name. The word "Texas" is derived from *tejas*, which means "friends" or "allies" in Spanish. As Spanish explorers and missionaries moved across Texas, they confronted a Native-American confederacy, the Hasinai. It was to this particular group that they applied the term, and, eventually, the Anglo form of the name became the permanent name of the region and then the state.[25]

In 1989, the Texas Department of Transportation proposed changing the state's vehicle license plates to include the phrase "The Friendship State." The public reaction, however, was immediate and generally hostile, and the proposal was quickly dropped. Some Texans apparently found the phrase incompatible with the state's rugged frontier image. The irony is that the common nomenclature for the state, which means friendship, is used almost every day by these same people.

Betting on the Future. The Kickapoo tribe has staked its economic development on a limited gambling casino located on its reservation outside of Eagle Pass.

and economic development for their people, but recent efforts to change state law have been unsuccessful.

Hispanics

In the eighteenth and nineteenth centuries, neither Spain nor Mexico was very successful in convincing Hispanics to settle in the Tejas territory of Mexico. The Spanish regarded it as a border province of relatively little value, except as a strategic buffer between Spanish colonies and those held by the British and the French. By the time Mexico declared its independence from Spain in 1821, the total Texas population under Spanish control was estimated to be approximately 5,000 people. With the rapid expansion of Anglo-American immigration to Texas in the 1820s and 1830s, Hispanics became a small minority of the population.[26]

Some Hispanics were part of the Texas independence movement from Mexico, and, after independence in 1836, men such as Jose Antonio Navarro and Juan Seguin were part of the Republic's political establishment. But the Anglo migration rapidly overwhelmed the Hispanic population and greatly reduced its political and economic power. There was even an effort at the Constitutional Convention of 1845 to strip Hispanics of the right to vote. The attempt failed, but it was an early indication of Anglo hostility toward the Hispanic population.[27]

"Sworn to be a Texan" Jose Antonio Navarro (1795–1871) played a central role in the colonization and independence of Texas. Largely self-educated, he was a lawyer, merchant, and the only Hispanic or Tejano to serve as a delegate to the 1845 Texas Statehood Convention.

By 1887, the Hispanic population had declined to approximately 4 percent of the state's population. In 1930, it was 12 percent and was concentrated in the border counties from Brownsville to El Paso (Figure 1–1). Modest increases in the Hispanic population continued until it reached 18 percent of the state's population in 1970, after which it grew at a more rapid rate. By 1990, it had reached 25 percent, spurred by immigration from Mexico and other Latin American countries, as well as by higher birth rates among Hispanic women. These growth patterns continued in the 1990s, and by 2008, Hispanics comprised 36.5 percent of the state's population.[28] In addition to their traditional concentrations in the Rio Grande Valley and South-Central Texas, large Hispanic populations are found in most metropolitan areas. Except for the Asian population, which is considerably smaller, the Hispanic population is growing at a significantly higher rate than other populations in Texas.

Hispanics will continue to increase at a higher rate than most other populations, and around 2030, Hispanics are likely to exceed 50 percent of the state's total.[29] This growth in population is being translated into political power and influence. Six Hispanics have been elected to statewide office. And, after successful redistricting and legal challenges to city, county, school board, and state legislative districts, Hispanics held some 2,435 elected positions in Texas in 2009, the highest number of any state.[30]

The regions of the state where Hispanics were concentrated (South Texas and along the Mexican border) before their more widespread migration to cities were areas heavily influenced by the traditionalistic subculture. Extreme poverty, low levels of education, and local economies based on agriculture contributed to the development of political systems dominated by a few Anglos, who often considered Hispanics second-class citizens. Hispanics' increasing political clout, however, has produced major political and governmental changes in those regions.

African Americans

Relatively few African Americans lived in Texas during the colonization period, and the modern story of African-American settlement did not begin until after independence in 1836. When Texas was part of Mexico, Mexican law restricted slavery within the territory. During the period of the Republic and early statehood prior to the U.S. Civil War, there

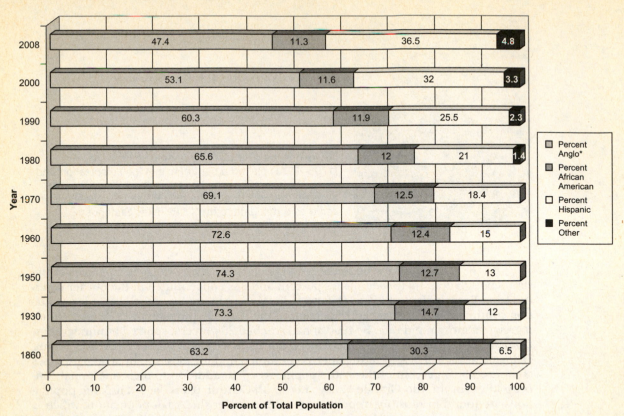

FIGURE 1–1   Ethnic and Racial Composition of Texas 1860–2008

Note: Data for Asian and other populations not tabulated by the Bureau of the Census prior to 1980. Spanish total for 1970 based on "Persons of Spanish language or surname."

*White, not of Hispanic origin (2000 Census)

Sources: Terry G. Jordan with John L. Bean, Jr., and William M. Holmes, *Texas: A Geography* (Boulder, CO: Westview, 1984), pp. 81–83; and U.S. Census Bureau, U.S. Censuses, 1860–2000; U.S. Census Bureau, *National and State Population Estimates,* July 1, 2008.

was a significant increase in the African-American population as Americans settling in Texas brought cotton cultivation and the slavery system with them. At the time of the Civil War, 30 percent of the state's residents were African American, but that percentage declined after the war. By 1960, it had leveled off at 12 percent, about the same level counted in the 2000 census (see Figure 1–1). African Americans are expected to represent between 11 and 12 percent of the state's population through the 2020 census.

There is a large concentration of African Americans in East Texas, where white southerners and their slaves originally settled. African Americans are also concentrated in the urban areas of Dallas, Fort Worth, Houston, and Austin. Relatively few African Americans live in the western counties or in the counties along the Mexican border. The increased number of African-American state legislators, city council members, county commissioners, and school board trustees representing urban communities is an indication of the political power of the African-American population in selected areas. In 2002,

Successful Despite the Hostile Environment. Norris Wright Cuney (1846–1898), born to a slave mother and white planter father, became an influential African American political leader during Reconstruction. Active in the Texas Republican Party, he was selected national committeeman in 1886 and derived much of his power from his ties with the national Republican Party, appointed offices, and as a dispenser of political patronage.

the most recent year for which data were available, there were 466 African-American elected officials in Texas. Four African Americans have been elected to statewide office.[31]

The slaveholding whites who migrated to Texas from the lower southern states brought with them the dominant values of the traditionalistic political subculture. Although slaves were freed after the Civil War, continued political and economic discrimination against African Americans was commonplace in the eastern part of Texas into the 1960s. As in South Texas, the politics of East Texas served the interests of the white elites by reducing or eliminating African American participation in the political process through restrictive election laws and outright physical intimidation.

Anglos

In the vernacular of Texas politics, the white population is referred to as "Anglos," although there is no census designation by that name. The term includes Jews, the Irish, Germans, Poles, and just about any other individual who is designated by the Bureau of the Census as "non-Hispanic white."

Scholars have identified two distinct early patterns of Anglo migration into Texas from other states. These patterns, as well as population movements through much of the late nineteenth and early twentieth centuries, largely explain the regional locations of the state's two dominant political subcultures.

In the early nineteenth century, the first Anglos moving to Texas were from the upper South—Tennessee, Kentucky, Arkansas, and North Carolina—a region significantly influenced by the individualistic subculture that emphasized limited government. The earliest settlements were primarily in what is now northeast Texas, in the Red River Valley. After Mexican independence from Spain, there was a second wave of immigration from the upper South. Few of these early colonists were plantation slaveholders from the lower South.

After Texas gained its independence, slavery was legalized, and settlers from the lower South began arriving. By the outbreak of the Civil War, Anglos who had moved to Texas from the lower South were roughly equal in number to those from the upper South. Arrivals from the slaveholding lower South initially settled in southeastern Texas, near Louisiana, but soon they began to move northward and westward.

A line between Texarkana and San Antonio in effect divides Texas subcultures. Most of those Anglos who settled north and west of this line were from the upper South and heavily influenced by the individualistic subculture. Anglos who settled south and east of the line were by and large from the lower South and shaped by the traditionalistic subculture. While the characteristics of these two subcultures were somewhat different, they merged to create a political system that was conservative, limited the scope of government, and often served the interests of elites.

This pattern of immigration and settlement continued after the Civil War. It was primarily those populations from the upper South who pushed westward to the Panhandle and West Texas. This expansion introduced into the western part of the state the cultural experience of those who resisted the notion that government existed to solve all of society's ills. To this day, West Texas is still one of the most politically conservative areas of the state.[32]

In 1860, Anglos constituted approximately 63 percent of Texas's population (see Figure 1–1). The Anglo population increased until it reached 74 percent in 1950. But by 1990, the stabilization of the African-American population and the increase in the Hispanic population had reduced the Anglo share to 60 percent. Anglos accounted for only 53 percent of Texas's population by the year 2000 and 47.4 percent in 2008. Although the number of Anglos will continue to increase with Texas's projected growth, their share of the total population will continue to decrease.

The Anglo population is diverse, as exhibits in the Institute of Texan Cultures in San Antonio remind us. Towns throughout Texas are identified with immigrants of national origin other than Anglo-Saxon, and these national groups brought with them a rich heritage. Castroville, for example, is identified with the Alsatians; New Braunfels and Fredericksburg, the Germans; Panna Maria, the Poles; and West and Halletsville, the Czechs.

Asian Americans

In 1980, Asian Americans accounted for 0.8 percent of Texas's population. By 2008, this group had grown to 3.3 percent of the population and was projected to increase to 4.2 percent by 2020. This rapid increase parallels national trends. Changes in immigration policy and the dislocation of Asians due to war and political persecution have resulted in larger numbers of Asian immigrants entering the United States and Texas since the 1970s. Moreover, the Asian population is increasingly diverse and includes individuals from Vietnam, China, Iraq, Iran, Pakistan, South Korea, and a number of other countries.

The largest concentration of Asian Americans in Texas is in Houston, where several Asian Americans have been elected to major public offices. Among them, community activist Martha Wong was elected to the Houston City Council in 1993 and then to the Texas House of Representatives in 2002. Wong apparently was the second Asian American to serve in the Texas House. Tom Lee of San Antonio, who served in the 1960s, was believed to be the first. Another Houstonian, Hubert Vo, a Vietnamese American, was elected to the Texas House in 2004. Asian Americans hold or have held public offices in several other Texas cities as well.

Politics, Race, and Ethnicity

Today, few Texans go running around the state wearing Ku Klux Klan robes, burning crosses or marching in support of white supremacy. But there still are occasions of extreme racial violence and cruelty, such as the murder of James Byrd, Jr., an African American who was dragged to death by three white men in a pickup truck in early 1999 near Jasper in

An Emerging Political Force. The rapid increase in the Asian-American population has produced circumstances in which members of this population can now win public office. Hubert Vo, a Houston businessman, took his seat in the Texas House of Representatives in 2005 as the first Vietnamese American ever to be elected to the legislature. Vo was reelected in 2006 and 2008.

East Texas. Despite such incidents, the state has made progress in creating a more equitable society. A state law barring African Americans from voting in party primaries was declared unconstitutional in the 1940s, and many other laws that were intended to reduce the political participation of African Americans and Hispanics have been eliminated. The federal Voting Rights Act, which was enacted in 1965 and extended to Texas in 1975, has also helped open up state and local electoral systems to minorities. There is still evidence of employment and housing discrimination, and opposition to the desegregation of a public housing project in Vidor received national publicity in 1993. But restrictive codes prohibiting a specific group of people from buying residential property have been declared unconstitutional, and federal and state laws have given minorities greater access to jobs.

Nonetheless, race and ethnicity are implicit in many contemporary political and policy issues. Throughout the ongoing debate on restructuring the school finance system, the protagonists are identified as the "rich" and the "poor" school districts of the state. But, in large part, these are alternative terms for "nonminority" and "minority" school systems. There have been bitter legal battles about redistricting of political districts to increase Hispanic and African-American representation on city councils, school boards, special districts, the state legislature and the U.S. Congress. And although many poor Anglos live in Texas, the disproportionately high poverty rates among minority groups often influence discussions about social services.

The state's budget crisis of 2003 produced a particularly contentious legislative session, when funding was reduced for many of the state's health and social programs. Many state and local elections show evidence of polarized voting along ethnic lines. Race and ethnicity also emerge in jury selection, employment patterns, contracts with state and local governments, and expenditures for public health and social service programs. Admissions policies of Texas colleges and universities resulted in a succession of legal challenges that centered on affirmative action and reverse discrimination.

More than forty years ago, V. O. Key, a Texan scholar of American politics, concluded that Texas politics was moving from issues of race to issues of class and economics. He argued that voters in Texas "divide along class lines in accord with their class interests as related to liberal and conservative candidates."[33] In part, he was correct in that unabashed racial bigotry and public demagoguery are no longer acceptable. In part,

Are There Any More Seats? Some school districts are experiencing declines in enrollment, but many of the urban districts are seeing a rapid rise in school enrollment, making it difficult for these districts to provide permanent classrooms. Sandra Day O'Connor High School, located in the northern part of Bexar County, had inadequate space the day it opened in 1998 and now houses students in some 30 temporary portable buildings.

though, he was incorrect and much too optimistic. If the state divides on economic issues, this division often puts the majority of Anglos on one side and the majority of Hispanics and African Americans on the other.[34]

GROWTH AND CHANGING DEMOGRAPHICS ———————●

Population Growth

Over the past fifty years, the population of Texas has increased much faster than the national average. According to the 2000 census, the state's population was 20,851,820, an increase of approximately 4 million people in ten years. This growth rate of 22.8 percent was significantly higher than the national growth rate of 13.2 percent.[35] In the first eight years of this century, the population increased by another 4 million people, or more than 16 percent, a rate also higher than the national average of 8 percent. With a population exceeding 24 million, Texas is now the second most populous state, second only to California.[36]

High birthrates explain part of the population increase, but migration from other states also has been a significant factor. In recent decades, demographers (those who study populations) have described a nationwide shift in population from the Northeast and

Midwest to the South and West. For each census from 1940 to 1970, in-migration from other areas accounted for less than 10 percent of Texas's growth. But in-migration jumped to 58.5 percent of the total growth between 1970 and 1980, the period in which demographers identified massive shifts of population from the "frostbelt" to the "sunbelt." Between 1980 and 1990, it contributed 34.4 percent to the state's growth.[37] In-migration slowed down somewhat between 1990 and 2000, but at the beginning of this decade, approximately 23 percent of Texas residents reported other states as their place of birth.[38]

Although it is expected to become less significant in the future, in-migration from other states has already contributed to the restructuring of Texas's traditional one-party, Democratic political system into a Republican-dominated system. Many new residents came from states with strong Republican Party traditions and brought their party affiliation with them. In the long run, in-migration is likely to affect elements of the state's political culture.

Texas also attracts individuals from other countries. Approximately 2.9 million, or 14 percent, of Texas residents were identified as foreign born in the 2000 census, and this number increased to 3.8 million, or 16 percent, in 2007. More than 75 percent of Texans born in other countries come from Latin America. There are some 1.2 million foreign-born persons who have become U.S. citizens, but approximately 11 percent (or 2.6 million) of all Texas residents are not U.S. citizens, a fact that has several implications.[39]

Citizenship is directly related to political participation, and noncitizens, while counted in the census for reapportionment of congressional seats, cannot vote. The overwhelming majority of noncitizens are Hispanic, thus reducing the number of eligible Hispanic voters in relation to their population.

Under current federal policy, noncitizens have been denied access to some public social services that are funded in whole or in part by the national government. Needy immigrants are especially affected by such policies, and in some instances, the state has found it necessary to use its own funds to provide services.

Some 7.4 million, or one third of Texans older than five, speak languages other than English at home, and 43 percent of this group report they don't speak English well.[40] Some states have adopted English as their official language, but there has not been a significant English language movement in Texas. Nonetheless, language is a policy issue for Texas in terms of bilingual education, official documents and publications, translators for court proceedings, and a host of related language issues in the workplace.

The increase in population places demands on all levels of government, and many local governments throughout Texas are hard pressed to provide adequate services. Many Texas cities, for example, are running out of landfill space. Environmental laws make it difficult to obtain new licenses for garbage and waste disposal, and without additional dumpsites, new population growth cannot be served. The increased population also has raised questions about the adequacy of water supplies throughout the state with different cities, regions and industries competing intensely for the resources now available. These water battles will only intensify in the future. Streets and highways in urban and suburban areas are clogged with traffic. A survey, released in the fall of 2007 by the Texas Transportation Institute, indicated continued increases in daily commute time in metropolitan areas. This means additional gasoline consumption, pollution, and costs of time.[41] Building new roads is one solution, but it's impossible to build enough new roads to keep up with the state's population growth. Other possible solutions include managing road systems more efficiently, restructuring demand, relieving chokepoints, diversifying development patterns, and increasing use of public transportation.[42]

The Aging Population

Texans, along with other Americans, are aging. The national median age in 1900 was 22.9 years. In 2007, the median age in Texas was 33.2 years, compared to 36.7 years for the entire country.[43] Approximately 10 percent of the state's population was older than sixty-five in 2007, and that group was expected to increase to 17 percent by 2030.[44] This aging population will place unprecedented demands on the public and private sectors for goods and services, including expanded health care and long-term care. In recent years, increasing state expenditures under the Medicaid program for long-term nursing care have strained the state's budget and forced a shift in priorities in public programs.

Younger Texans will be asked to pay increased taxes to support the needs of the projected aging population. These intergenerational obligations, critical to a stable political system, are often overlooked in debates over funding public services. Younger Texans need older voters to support public education through their tax dollars, and older voters need younger Texans to support health care services. If push comes to shove and comity disappears, the older population has significantly more political clout than do younger voters, who are less informed about politics and who vote at rates much lower than the older population.

Urban Texas

Although Texas was a rural state during the first 100 years of its history, 83 percent of the state's population in 2000 resided in areas classified by the Bureau of the Census as urban, and one estimate put the urban population in 2008 at 87.7 percent (see Table 1–1).[45] **Urbanization** and suburban sprawl now characterize Texas's settlement

TABLE 1–1   Urban–Rural Population of Texas, 1850–2008

Year	Urban Percentage	Urban Population	Rural Percentage	Rural Population	Total
1850	4%	7,665	96%	204,927	212,592
1860	4%	26,615	96%	577,600	604,215
1870	7%	54,521	93%	764,058	818,579
1880	9%	146,795	91%	1,444,954	1,591,749
1890	16%	359,511	84%	1,886,016	2,245,527
1900	17%	520,759	83%	2,527,951	3,048,710
1910	24%	938,104	76%	2,958,438	3,896,542
1920	32%	1,512,689	68%	3,150,539	4,663,228
1930	41%	2,389,148	59%	3,435,367	5,824,715
1940	45%	2,911,389	55%	3,503,435	6,414,824
1950	63%	4,838,050	37%	2,873,134	7,711,194
1960	75%	7,187,470	25%	2,392,207	9,579,677
1970	80%	8,922,211	20%	2,274,519	11,196,730
1980	80%	11,333,017	20%	2,836,174	14,229,191
1990	80%	13,634,517	20%	3,351,993	16,986,510
2000	83%	17,204,073	17%	3,647,747	20,851,820
2008*	88%	21,344,461	12%	2,982,513	24,326,974

*Estimate based on Office of Management and Budget June 2003 classification of urban and rural.

Source: U.S. Census Bureau, U.S. Censuses, 1850–2000; and United States Department of Agriculture, Economic Research Service, State Fact Sheets: Texas, Update June 30, 2009.

The Texas Urban Triangle

About 80 percent of the state's population lives within or near a triangular area (often referred to as the central Texas triangle or the Texas urban triangle) formed by linking the metropolitan areas of Dallas-Fort Worth, Houston, and San Antonio. Population from the core cities is expected to continue expanding into neighboring counties. This area dominates the state's economy and is projected to play a greater role in the future. The area has major research and educational institutions, investment capital, an ample supply of low-cost labor, available energy, a pro-business tax structure, affordable housing, medical facilities, cultural venues, and other amenities. Each of the metropolitan areas has its own distinct characteristics, but there will be increased integration and interdependence in their economies.[46]

patterns, and many urban corridors and suburban areas cross county boundaries (see "The Texas Urban Triangle"). Residents of these areas often encounter problems that cut across political jurisdictions, and local governments sometimes find it difficult to resolve them.

The dramatic growth of Texas's largest cities is shown in Table 1–2. From 1960 to 2008, the populations of Houston, San Antonio, El Paso, and Laredo more than doubled. Dallas increased by 84 percent. Arlington had a population of only 44,775 in 1960, but in 2008 its population was 374,943, an increase of more than 730 percent. During this forty-year period, Austin's population increased from 186,545 to 736,172, and in 2008, the Austin-Round Rock metropolitan area ranked with Raleigh, North Carolina, as the fastest growing metropolitan area in the nation.[47]

Three of the ten largest cities in the United States are in Texas, and, like urban areas throughout the country, Texas's largest cities increasingly are home to minority and lower income populations. This trend results from higher birth rates among minority populations, urban migration patterns, and what is often referred to as "white

TABLE 1–2   Ten Largest Texas Cities, 1920–2008

City	1920	1940	1960	1980	1990	2000	2008
Houston	138,276	384,514	838,219	1,595,138	1,630,553	1,953,631	2,149,948
San Antonio	161,379	253,854	587,718	785,880	935,933	1,144,646	1,336,040
Dallas	158,976	294,734	679,684	904,078	1,006,877	1,188,580	1,248,184
Austin	34,876	87,960	186,545	345,496	465,622	656,562	736,172
Fort Worth	106,482	177,662	356,268	385,164	447,619	534,694	688,222
El Paso	77,560	96,810	276,687	425,259	515,342	563,662	609,327
Arlington	3,031	4,240	44,775	160,113	261,721	332,969	374,943
Corpus Christi	10,522	57,301	167,690	231,999	257,453	277,454	285,600
Plano	1,715	1,582	3,695	72,331	128,713	222,030	279,607
Garland	1,421	2,233	38,501	132,857	180,650	215,768	222,007

Sources: U.S. Census Bureau, U.S. Censuses, 1920–2000; and Texas State Data Center, *Population Estimates and Projections, 2008.*

flight" from the cities to suburban areas. Minority groups now account for the majority of the population in five of Texas's ten largest cities (Houston, San Antonio, Dallas, El Paso, and Corpus Christi). These minority residents include Hispanics, African Americans, and Asian Americans—groups that do not always constitute a cohesive bloc of interests. As minority growth continues, there will be areas of potential conflict among these groups.

Population density refers to the number of people per square mile in a specific political jurisdiction, and it provides another measure of urbanization. As people crowd into smaller areas living in close proximity to each other, problems are inevitable. Noise, land use, property maintenance, traffic patterns, and numerous other issues must be addressed. The 2000 census reported the greatest population density in the Dallas–Fort Worth Metroplex and in Houston. Demographers also detect the evolution of an extremely dense corridor along Interstate 35 running from north of Dallas to San Antonio.

There are marked differences in the population and density of Texas's 254 counties. Loving County in West Texas has a population of about 62 living in an area of 677 square miles. The most populous county is Harris County (Houston), with more than 3.9 million people living within 1,777 square miles.[48] Clearly, the problems and issues that Loving County faces are significantly different from those faced by Harris County, yet both counties function with the same form of government that was created by the state's constitution of 1876.

Texas politics has often divided along urban–rural lines, creating conflict, a trend compounded by suburban areas of the state taking on more importance. Redistricting battles and a host of other public policy issues are evidence of that. Until recently, the Texas legislature was dominated by rural lawmakers, many of whom were often insensitive to urban needs. To make matters more difficult, suburban legislators with a different constituency base and interests often pursue policies in conflict with both the central city and rural legislators. Moreover, many of urban Texas's problems are aggravated by constitutional restrictions written when Texas was still a rural state.

Wealth and Income Distribution

There is a wide disparity in the distribution of income and wealth across the state. In 2007, the median household income was $47,548 and the median family income was $55,742, both below national income levels (see Table 1–3). Approximately 26 percent of Texas households reported incomes less than $25,000 per year. By contrast, 18.5 percent of Texas households reported incomes in excess of $75,000.

Income disparities are evident among the different regions of the state, ethnicity, and race. The median household income for Collin County, north of Dallas, was $79,657 in 2007, and only 6.5 percent of the population fell below the poverty line. In sharp contrast, the median household income for Hidalgo County on the border with Mexico was $30, 295 with 34.3 percent of the population falling below the poverty level. Some of the poorest counties in the state as well as the nation are along the Texas–Mexico border.[49]

On all measures of income, Hispanics and African Americans fall significantly below the Anglo and Asian populations. According to the 2007 *American Community Survey*, 34.3 percent of Hispanic households and 37.5 percent of African-American households in Texas reported incomes below $25,000, but only 19 percent of Anglo households and a similar portion of the Asian-American population reported incomes below that level.

TABLE 1–3   U.S. and Texas Income Figures, 2007

	U.S.	TEXAS				
	All Persons	All Persons	Anglos	Hispanics	African American	Asian American
Median Income						
Household	$50,740	$47,548	$59,532	$35,709	$33,843	$62,389
Families	61,173	55,742	73,882	37,410	40,619	72,258
Per Capita Income	26,688	23,938	33,161	13,698	17,307	27,148
Percent of Persons below Poverty Level	13.0%	16.3%	8.4%	24.8%	23.8%	11.4%

Source: U.S Census Bureau, *2007 American Community Survey*.

By contrast, 39 percent of Anglo households but only 16 percent of Hispanic households and 17.6 percent of African-American households reported incomes above $75,000.[50]

Many Texans live in severe poverty. Some of the nation's poorest counties are in Texas. These are border counties (Dimmit, Hidalgo, Maverick, Starr, Willacy, Zapata, and Zavala) with large Hispanic populations and unemployment rates that are more than twice the state average. The per capita income (total state income divided by the population) for Texas was $23,938 in 2007. For the Anglo population, it was significantly higher, $33,161, but for African Americans, the figure was $17,307, and for Hispanics, $13,698.

This Ain't Luxury. There are some 1,200 colonias or settlements along the Texas-Mexico border with sub-standard housing and little or no access to running water, sewer lines, or paved roads. The state has allocated funds for improvements, but much more needs to be done.

In 2007, the poverty level guidelines used in Texas to establish eligibility for many federal and state assistance programs were $21,027 for a family of four with two children under the age of 18 and $10,787 for one person under 65 years of age. According to the U.S. Bureau of the Census, 16.3 percent of the state's population, or 3.8 million people, fell below the poverty level. Nationally, 13.0 percent, or 38.8 million persons, fell below the poverty level in 2007. The impact of poverty disproportionately affected children, particularly those living in a one-parent household, and those who were Hispanic or African American. In the seven counties mentioned above, some 30 percent or more of the population fell below the poverty level in 2007, with 40 percent or more of all children living in families below the poverty line.[51] Many of these families don't have adequate housing or health care and depend on food stamps or charities for food. Some 25 percent of Texans do not have health insurance, including some individuals who can afford it but choose not to purchase coverage.

The recession that emerged in 2008–2009 slowed the state's economy and increased unemployment rates. The full impact of those conditions had not been measured at the time this book was completed. But the higher unemployment was expected to increase poverty and limit incomes even further.

Although many Texans are suffering economically, others make large salaries and have significant assets, including those on the annual *Forbes* 400 list of the richest Americans. Thirty-nine Texans made the list in 2008, with a reported net worth ranging from $1.3 billion to $23.2 billion.[52] The vast majority of Texans, however, have incomes or assets that are nowhere near those of the super wealthy.

Although the state's economic growth over the past decade has reduced poverty somewhat, scholars who study demographic trends fear that poverty is likely to worsen in Texas if several policy issues are not addressed. Without significant changes in educational levels and expanded economic opportunities, it is possible that approximately 20 percent of the state's households will fall below the poverty level by 2030, and income disparity will be especially problematic for minorities.[53]

Financial resources can be translated into political power and influence through campaign contributions, funding one's own campaign for public office, access to the mass media, and active support for policy think tanks, interest groups, and lobbying activity. Wealth is not the only dimension of political power, but some Texans obviously have the potential for much greater clout than others.

Education and Literacy

Public education has been a dominant issue in state politics for many years. Litigation has forced the legislature to struggle with changes in the funding of public schools, and education will be a primary factor in determining whether Texas can successfully compete in the global economy.

Over the next decade, a large proportion of the new jobs created in Texas will be in service industries. Most of these jobs will require increased reading, writing and math skills, and high-school dropouts will find fewer and fewer opportunities for decent paying jobs. Across the nation, millions of low-skilled jobs have been outsourced to other countries, and most of the higher paying jobs now require a college education. Texas faces a crisis in public education, and the state's ability to resolve it will directly affect the financial well being of many Texans.

According to the 2007 *American Community Survey*, 79.1 percent of Texans age twenty-five and older had completed high school, and 25.2 percent had completed college

TABLE 1–4   Educational Attainment by Race and Ethnicity, 2007

	United States		Texas	
	High School Diploma	College Degree	High School Diploma	College Degree
Anglo*	89.4%	30.5%	90.7%	33.3%
Hispanic	60.6	12.5	56.6	10.6
African American	80.1	17.2	83.4	17.9
Asian	85.8	49.5	86.8	52.8
All Persons	84.5	27.5	79.1	25.2

*White, not of Hispanic origin

Source: U.S. Census Bureau, 2007 American Community Survey.

(see Table 1–4). Educational attainment has improved over the past twenty years with positive changes reported for all racial or ethnic groups in the state.[54] But there are still wide disparities in the educational levels of the three major ethnic-racial groups, and some of these differences are directly linked to the number of residents born in other countries (see Chapter 3). In 2007, 91 percent of the Anglo population reported that they had completed high school, and one-third had college degrees. By contrast, 56.6 percent of the Hispanic population had high school diplomas and only 10.6 percent reported having college degrees. Some 83 percent of African Americans graduated from high school, with 18 percent indicating they had college degrees. Particularly noteworthy is the Asian population, which reported that 53 percent of those 25 and older had college degrees.

Education not only helps determine a person's employment and income potential but also affects his or her participation in politics. Individuals with high educational levels are much more likely to believe they can influence the actions of policymakers, be informed about politics, and participate in the political process.

The Size and Geographic Diversity of Texas

Texas is a big state. Covering 261,797 square miles, it is second only to Alaska in land mass. Although Texans appear to have adjusted to long distances—they don't seem to mind driving fifty miles for a night out—visitors from out-of-state often are overwhelmed by Texas's size and diversity. The distance from Texarkana in Northeast Texas to El Paso in far West Texas is about 800 miles, which makes a person living in Texarkana closer to Chicago than to El Paso. Brownsville in South Texas is closer to Mexico City than it is to Texline in the Texas Panhandle.[55]

Many would argue that perceptions of the state's size have helped shape political attitudes and concepts, and size obviously has affected state policy. Roads and highways, for example, historically have received a significant—and, some would argue, a disproportionate—share of the state's budget. Economic development in such a large and diverse state required a commitment to highway construction because roads were regarded as essential to the development of an integrated economy. Size also contributes to the economic diversity of the state. While some parts of the state will be experiencing economic growth, other areas may experience economic downturns.

One scholar argued that the great distances in Texas were politically important because they made it difficult for a politician to develop a statewide following, such as could be cultivated in many southern states. Size works against the organizational strategies and continued negotiations necessary to sustain a statewide political machine similar to those that developed in Virginia and Louisiana in the 1920s and 1930s. Although there have been regional or local political machines, such as the now-defunct Parr machine in South Texas, none of these was extended statewide.[56]

Size also contributes to the high costs of political campaigns. Candidates in the 2002 gubernatorial race spent more than $100 million to communicate with and mobilize Texas voters. There are twenty separate media markets in the state, and the cost of communicating with the voters on a statewide basis continues to increase.

If Texas were still an independent nation, it would be the thirty-seventh largest in geographic area. The state has one-twelfth of the total coastline of the United States. It has 23 million acres of forest and more than 4,790 square miles of lakes and streams. A traveler driving across Texas is struck by the diversity in topography, climate, and vegetation. The state's "landforms range from offshore bars and barrier beaches to formidable mountains, from rugged canyons, gorges, and badlands to totally flat plains."[57] The western part of the state is dry and semiarid, while the east is humid and subtropical, producing extremes in precipitation. South Texas often enjoys a tropical winter, while North Texas experiences cold winters with snowfall.[58] The growing seasons in the south are virtually year round, while those in the north are approximately 180 days. East Texas is characterized by its piney woods, semiarid South Texas by its brush country.

Geography shaped historical migration and land use in Texas. Although we are capable of partially compensating for climate and geography through modern technology, geography continues to shape the economy and population patterns of the state.

The Economy of Texas

Politics, government, and economics are inextricably linked. An economy that is robust and expanding provides far more options to government policymakers than an economy in recession. A healthy tax base is dependent on an expanding economy, and when the economy goes through periods of recession, state and local governments are confronted with the harsh realities of having to increase taxes or cut back on public services, usually at a time when more people are in need of governmental assistance.

Historically, the health of the Texas economy had been linked to oil and natural gas, but by the last decade of the twentieth century, the state's economy had experienced significant diversification. In 1981, for example, 27 percent of the state's economy was tied to energy-related industries. The decade started with rapid increases in the world price of oil, and there was an economic boom throughout the financial, construction, and manufacturing sectors of the state's economy.[59]

Changes in international fuel markets, particularly a big drop in oil prices in the 1980s, staggered the Texas petroleum industry. Natural gas prices also fell. Thousands of energy-related jobs were lost, and many exploration and drilling companies went out of business. Cheaper foreign oil replaced the demand for Texas oil, and a decline in recoverable reserves further reduced the importance of fossil fuels to the state's commerce. Within two decades, oil- and gas-related industries were contributing only 10 percent to the Texas economy.[60] As oil approached $150 a barrel in midsummer of 2008, there was a significant increase in exploration and production, moving the industry's share of the state economy to 15 percent, but many industry experts predicted it would be a short-lived boom.[61]

The recession of 2008–2009 reminded many Texans of the 1980s, when a combination of factors, including plummeting oil prices, put the state economy into a tailspin. Mexico's peso also experienced a precipitous decline, which had a negative impact on the economies of border cities and counties. In 1983, a harsh freeze in South Texas and a severe drought in West Texas had serious adverse effects on the agricultural sector. There also was a worldwide slump in the electronics industry. These events hurt the construction and real estate sectors of the economy and, in turn, manufacturing and retail trade. For sixteen straight months in 1986 and 1987, the state's employment dropped, with a loss of an estimated 233,000 jobs.[62]

These reversals had disastrous effects on Texas's banks and savings and loan institutions. "In 1987 and 1988, more Texas financial institutions failed than at any other time since the Great Depression," the state comptroller's office reported. And the pattern of bank failures continued through 1990. The federal government developed a plan to bail out institutions that were covered by federal deposit insurance, and the state's banking system ultimately was restructured. But as the magnitude of the problem became clearer, there was a bitter debate over its causes, including the deregulation of the savings and loan and banking industries, inadequate government scrutiny of banking practices, a frenzy of speculation with questionable or unsecured loans, and outright fraud and malfeasance.[63]

State and local governments consequently suffered declines in revenues. With falling property values, local governments that depended on the property tax were particularly vulnerable. The legislature convened a special session in 1986 to pass an $875 million tax bill and cut the state budget by about $580 million in an attempt to "patch up" the widening holes in projected state revenues. In 1987, the legislature, mandated by the constitution to a "pay as you go" system of government and denied the option of deficit financing, enacted a $5.6 billion tax bill, including an increase in the sales tax, a **regressive tax** that most adversely affects low-income people.[64]

With the exception of three years, the Texas economy outpaced the overall national economy from 1990 through 2008. There have been ups and downs, including the recession of 2001, which was short-lived at the national level. But the recession did not end in Texas until the summer of 2003, and unlike previous recessions linked to energy production, this recession reflected the structural changes in the Texas economy. As Texans worked to diversify the economy, high-tech industries took on more significance. From 1990 through 2001, employment grew at higher rates than the national average, and many of these new jobs were in high-tech companies.

The "bust" in the high-tech industry nationwide had a disproportionate impact on the Texas economy with an estimated loss of 100,000 jobs. The recessionary pressures were compounded by the terrorist attacks of September 11, with a direct impact on the state's transportation industry. In effect, the extended 2001 recession in Texas was due to a "high-tech bust, not an oil price shock."[65]

Several good years followed, but the "Great Recession" that broke across the nation in the summer of 2008 had arrived in Texas by the late winter of 2009.[66] The worldwide crisis in financial and credit markets was linked to subprime lending, accounting scandals, overextended credit to consumers, dramatic declines in manufacturing and trade, and a loss of confidence on the part of the consumer. With massive federal intervention, a concerted effort was being made to stop the slide, but the final story on this period was yet to be written. We can anticipate a significant decline in personal wealth due to declines in the stock markets and housing values. Just as previous recessions produced a restructuring of the economy, we can expect a similar impact of this recession. And, local governments across Texas were beginning to feel a recessionary impact on their budgets.

In 2008, Texas had a gross state product of $1.2 trillion in current dollars, or $925.5 billion "chained" to the value of 2000 dollars. By comparison, the gross domestic product of the United States in 2008 was $11.5 trillion in 2000 dollars or $14.2 trillion in current dollars.[67] The Texas economy was the third largest among the states, following California and New York. If Texas were a nation, its economy would rank twelfth in the world.[68]

Several lessons can be drawn from the state's recent economic history. The health of the state's economy for much of the twentieth century was directly tied to the price of oil. Even during national recessions, high oil prices served to insulate Texas from their effects. In effect, the Texas economy grew or contracted in relationship to the price of oil.

Initiatives to diversify the state's economy, which began some 50 years ago, have transformed the economy's basic structure. With economic diversification paralleling the structure of the national economy, Texas is in a much stronger position to minimize the impact of economic downturns. One or more core sectors of the economy may be in recession while other sectors are experiencing growth.

The core economic sectors are not distributed uniformly across the state, and growth and recession are not experienced in the state's varied economic regions in the same way. Only certain areas of the state, for example, will suffer the brunt of low beef or other agricultural commodity prices.

Economic diversification has been directly tied to high-tech industries, including companies that produce semiconductors, microprocessors, computer hardware, software, telecommunications devices, fiber optics, aerospace guidance systems, and medical instruments.[69] High tech also includes biotechnology industries that produce new medicines, vaccines, and genetic engineering of plants and animals. The state and local governments developed aggressive recruitment programs that included economic development bonds and tax breaks for high-tech companies.

Texas's restructured economy is heavily oriented to exports with approximately 35 percent of the state's employment "in industries that can be classified as basic, or exportable."[70] Approximately 22,000 companies exported goods from their Texas locations in 2006.[71] Just as we can speak of the **globalization of the economy** nationally, a similar pattern has developed in Texas. In 1999, Texas exported some $83 billion in merchandise to other countries. By 2008, total exports were $192 billion with approximately 33 percent ($62 billion) going to Mexico.[72] The North American Free Trade Agreement (NAFTA) among the United States, Mexico, and Canada (see Chapter 3) has produced changes in the economic relationships among these countries with more economic interdependence anticipated.

It also is critical to recognize the relationship of the Texas economy to the Mexican economy. In earlier periods, economic declines in Mexico were felt primarily in the counties along the Mexican border. But NAFTA and the *maquiladora* program have linked most areas of the state to the Mexican economy (see Chapter 3).

Economic Regions of Texas

The economic diversity of Texas can be described in terms of twelve distinct economic regions (Figure 1–2). There are marked differences among these areas.[73] One may be undergoing rapid economic growth, while another may be experiencing stagnation. Regions vary in population, economic infrastructure, economic performance, and rates of growth. One region's economy may be heavily dependent on only two or three industries. If one

1. High Plains
2. Northwest Texas
3. Metroplex
4. Upper East Texas
5. Southeast Texas
6. Gulf Coast
7. Central Texas
8. Capital
9. Alamo
10. South Texas
11. West Texas
12. Upper Rio Grande

FIGURE 1–2   Economic Regions of Texas, 2009. *Source:* Texas Comptroller of Public Accounts.

or two of those industries suffers an economic downturn, that region may have a more severe recession than the state overall. There also are marked differences in personal income, poverty levels, and geography among the areas. All regions, meanwhile, share in one economic sector—significant levels of government employment.

The economic factors at play in a region help shape the priorities of local governments and the priorities of state legislators elected from that area. The following descriptions of three of the twelve regions offer a sampling of the economic differences encountered throughout Texas.

The *High Plains Region* is made up of forty-one counties and includes Amarillo, Lubbock, the XIT Ranch, and Palo Duro Canyon. Agricultural production, whose major source of water is the Ogallala Aquifer, is a dominant industry. Related businesses include agricultural services, food processing, and the manufacturing of feed, fertilizers, and farm machinery and equipment. Oil and gas production also is still an important component of the region's economy, but employment in the energy industry has declined from earlier periods. The region's population grew by only 6 percent, a rate significantly lower than the state's growth, from 2000 to 2007—to 800,000 people. Solid job growth is projected through 2012 in health care, education, government, leisure and hospitality, construction, financial activities, and professional and business services.[74]

The *South Texas Border Region* encompasses 28 counties, including the cities of Corpus Christi, Brownsville, Laredo, Del Rio, McAllen, Eagle Pass, and Harlingen. Eight of its counties share their borders with Mexico, and a significant amount of commerce ($125 billion in 2007) flows through border crossings within these counties. It has five seaports, including the Port of Corpus Christi, which was ranked in 2006 as the nation's sixth-largest port in total cargo tonnage. This area is identified with agriculture, including cattle, cotton, sugarcane, citrus, table produce, and food processing. Oil and gas extraction and processing also are a key part of the area's economy. Over the past decade, this area has received a significant boost from the construction of manufacturing plants in Mexico and trading benefits from the North American Free Trade Agreement (NAFTA). Some structural changes are occurring in this region's economy with education and health care projected to experience the most significant growth through 2012.

Approximately 81 percent of the population in this region is Hispanic. The region's growth rate has exceeded the state average and is projected to continue to do so. It has a relatively young population when compared to the state as a whole. Educational attainment and income are below the state average, and it has a large population that falls below the poverty level.[75]

The *Upper East Texas* Region, which includes 21 counties, is located in the northeast corner of the state. It includes the cities of Longview, Texarkana, and Tyler (the "City of Roses"). Since 2000, its growth rate has been significantly lower than the statewide average. While more than 80 percent of the state's population resides in urban areas, approximately 50 percent of this region's population is classified as urban. The average population of this region is older than the state's and is predominately Anglo (71%).

Agriculture—including horticulture, timber and the dairy industry—is a key component of the region's economy, as are food processing and food distribution. Transportation-related industries—including the manufacture of railroad rolling stock and motor vehicle bodies—have a strong presence. So do distribution, warehousing, and storage. Oil and gas production also can be found in this region.[76]

SUMMARY AND CONCLUSIONS

1. Texas is a highly diverse state with a rapidly expanding population and a rich cultural legacy.
2. The traditional, conservative politics of the state were shaped by several historical factors. They included the state's dominant political subcultures, a political ethos based on individualism and traditionalism, the aftermath of the Civil War, the systematic exclusion of minorities from the political process, one-party politics, and the dominance of conservative economic elites.
3. Expanding populations place additional burdens and responsibilities on governments, and during the twenty-first century, the decisions of leaders in both the public and private sectors will directly impact the standard of living and the quality of life for Texans.

4. Politics in Texas has been characterized as the politics of race and class, and although Hispanics and African Americans now participate in the political process, marked disparities in income and wealth related to ethnicity and race have produced political dividing lines on policy priorities.
5. Texas is now the second most populous state and has the third largest state economy. Once dependent on oil and natural gas, the state's economy has demonstrated a rapid diversification, structured, in part, by a dramatic expansion in service and high-tech industries and an increase in manufacturing and service exports to other countries.
6. The state's economy is, in fact, a composite of twelve diversified regional economies. Based on the experiences of the past thirty years, these

regions are affected in markedly different ways by national and international economic trends.

7. For much of the 1980s, the state's economy lagged behind the national economy, but this pattern was reversed in the early 1990s, when the state's economy outpaced national economic growth. And, it is expected to continue to do so.

KEY TERMS

Regressive tax   4
Economic diversification   5
Political myths   5
Republic   6
Individualism   7

Political culture   8
Individualistic subculture   9
Moralistic subculture   9
Traditionalistic subculture   10

Urbanization   21
Population density   22
Globalization of the
   economy   28

FURTHER READING

Articles

Chilton, Stephen, "Defining Political Culture," *Western Political Quarterly* 41 (September 1988), pp. 419–45.

Fitzpatrick, Jody L., and Rodney E. Hero, "Political Culture and Political Characteristics of the American States: A Consideration of Some Old and New Questions," *Western Political Quarterly* 41 (March 1988), pp. 145–53.

Miller, David Y., David C. Barker, and Christopher J. Carman, "Mapping the Genome of American Political Subcultures: A Proposed Methodology and Pilot Study," *Publius: The Journal of Federalism* 36 (Winter 2006), pp. 303–15.

Rice, Tom W., and Alexander F. Sumberg, "Civic Culture and Government Performance in the American States," *Publius: The Journal of Federalism* 27 (Winter 1997), pp. 99–114.

Books

Buenger, Walter L., and Robert A. Calvert, eds., *Texas Through Time: Evolving Interpretations.* College Station: Texas A & M University Press, 1991.

Calvert, Robert A., and Arnoldo DeLeon, *The History of Texas.* Arlington Heights, IL: Harlan Davidson, 1990.

Elazar, Daniel J., *American Federalism: A View from the States.* New York: Thomas Y. Crowell, 1966.

———, *The American Mosaic: The Impact of Space, Time, and Culture on American Politics.* Boulder, CO: Westview, 1994.

Fehrenbach, T. R., *Lone Star: A History of Texas and the Texans.* New York: Collier, 1968.

Flood, Christopher G. *Political Myths.* New York, NY: Garland, 1996.

Hill, Kim Quaile, *Democracy in the Fifty States.* Lincoln, NE: University of Nebraska Press, 1994.

Jordan, Terry G., with John L. Bean Jr., and William M. Homes, *Texas: A Geography.* Boulder, CO: Westview, 1984.

Montejano, David, *Anglos and Mexicans in the Making of Texas, 1836–1986.* Austin: University of Texas Press, 1987.

Murdock, Steve H., Md. Nazrul Hogue, Martha Michael, Steve White, and Beverly Pecotte, *The Texas Challenge: Population Change and the Future of Texas.* College Station, TX: Texas A & M University Press, 1997.

Murdock, Steve H., Steve White, Md. Nazrul, Beverly Pecotte, Xuihong You, and Jennifer Balkan, *The New Texas Challenge: Population Change and the Future of Texas.* College Station, TX: Texas A&M University Press, 2003.

O'Conner, Robert F., ed., *Texas Myths.* College Station, TX: Texas A & M University Press, 1986.

Richardson, Rupert, Ernest Wallace, and Adrian N. Anderson, *Texas: The Lone Star State,* 7th ed. Upper Saddle River, NJ: Prentice-Hall, 1988.

Websites

State of Texas   http://www.texasonline.com/portal/ The state's webpage provides links to state agencies, local and county governments, and councils of states, where a wide array of data for the state is to be found.

U.S. Bureau of the Census   http://www.census.gov/ Population and economic data for the state are provided by the Bureau of the Census, which conducts the decennial census and a wide range of population studies between censuses.

Office of the Comptroller   http://www.cpa.state.tx.us/ The comptroller's office maintains a database for the Texas economy.

Texas State Data Center   http://www.txsdc.utsa.edu/ The Texas State Data Center provides "ready access to Texas census information and other information on the population of Texas."

ENDNOTES ●

1. Alexis de Tocqueville, *Democracy in America*, with an introduction by Joseph Epstein (New York: Bantam Dell, 2004), p. 51.
2. Allen R. Meyerson, "A New Breed of Wildcatters for the 90's, *New York Times*, November 30, 1997, Section 3, p. 1.
3. Harold Lasswell, *Who Gets What, When, and How* (New York: Meridian, 1958).
4. Texas Comptroller of Public Accounts, *Fiscal Notes,* June 1998, p. 6; Texas Comptroller of Public Accounts, *Texas—Where We Stand,* February 2006; and Institute on Taxation and Economic Policy, "Texas Taxes Hit Poor and Middle Class Far Harder than the Wealthy," January 7, 2003.
5. David Easton, *A Framework for Political Analysis* (Englewood Cliffs, NJ: Prentice Hall, 1965), Chapter 5.
6. Louise Cowan, "Myth in the Modern World," in *Texas Myths,* edited by Robert F. O'Conner (College Station, TX: Texas A & M University Press, 1986), p. 4.
7. Joseph Campbell, *Thou Art That* (Novato, CA: New World Library, 2001), pp. 1–9.
8. Christopher G. Flood, *Political Myth* (New York: Garland, 1996), Chapter 2. The author also links political myths to political ideology.
9. Cowan, p. 14. For an excellent analysis of the concept of the "myth of origin" as integrated into the American mythology, see Robert N. Bellah, *The Broken Covenant: American Civil Religion in Time of Trial* (New York: Seabury, 1975).
10. T. R. Fehrenbach, "Texas Mythology: Now and Forever," in *Texas Myths*, pp. 210–17.
11. Robin Doughty, "From Wilderness to Garden: Conquering the Texas Landscape," in *Texas Myths,* p. 105.
12. Lucian W. Pye, "Political Culture," in *International Encyclopedia of the Social Sciences,* Vol. 12 (New York: Crowell, Collier and Macmillan, 1968), p. 218.
13. Ellen M. Dran, Robert B. Albritton, and Mikel Wyckoff, "Surrogate Versus Direct Measures of Political Culture: Explaining Participation and Policy Attitudes in Illinois," *Publius: The Journal of Federalism* (Spring 1991), p. 17.
14. Daniel Elazar, *American Federalism: A View from the States* (New York: Thomas Y. Crowell, 1966), p. 86. Elazar's three subcultures closely parallel observations made in 1835 by Alexis de Tocqueville in *Democracy in America.*
15. Ibid., p. 86.
16. Ibid., pp. 86–89.
17. Ibid., p. 90.
18. Ibid., p. 90.
19. Ibid., p. 91.
20. Ibid., p. 92.
21. Ibid., pp. 92–94.
22. Ibid., pp. 97, 102, 108.
23. Kim Quaile Hill, *Democracy in the Fifty States* (Lincoln, NE: University of Nebraska Press, 1994), Chapter 5.
24. Ellen N. Murray, "Sorrow Whispers in the Winds," *Texas Journal* 14 (Spring–Summer 1992), p. 16.
25. Rupert N. Richardson, Ernest Wallace, and Adrian Anderson, *Texas: The Lone Star State,* 5th ed. (Englewood Cliffs, N.J.: Prentice Hall, 1988), p. 1.
26. Terry G. Jordan, with John L. Bean, Jr., and William M. Holmes, *Texas: A Geography* (Boulder, CO: Westview, 1984), pp. 79–86.
27. David Montejano, *Anglos and Mexicans in the Making of Texas, 1836–1986* (Austin: University of Texas Press, 1987), p. 38.
28. U.S. Census Bureau, *National and State Population Estimates, Annual Population Estimates,* July 1, 2008. Hispanics can be of any race.
29. Texas State Data Center, *Population Estimates and Projections Program, 2008.* This conclusion is based on Scenario 1.0 and Scenario 2000–2007.
30. National Association of Latino Elected and Appointed Officials, *2009 National Roster of Hispanic Elected Officials.*
31. Joint Center for Political Studies, *National Roster of Black Elected Officials, 2002.*
32. Jordan, et al., *Texas: A Geography,* pp. 71–77.
33. V. O. Key, *Southern Politics in State and Nation* (New York: Vintage, 1949), p. 261.
34. For an excellent analysis of Key's projections for political change in Texas, see Chandler Davidson, *Race and Class in Texas Politics* (Princeton, NJ: Princeton University Press, 1990).
35. U.S. Census Bureau, *2000 Census of the Population.*
36. U.S. Census Bureau, *Population Estimates,* July 1, 2008.
37. Office of the Governor, Texas 2000 Commission, *Texas Trends,* pp. 5–6; Office of the Governor, Texas 2000 Commission, *Texas Past and Future: A Survey,* p. 6.
38. U.S. Census Bureau, *2000 Census of the Population.*
39. Ibid.; U.S. Census Bureau, *American Community Survey,* 2007.
40. U.S. Census Bureau, *American Community Survey, 2007.*
41. Texas Transportation Institute, Texas A & M University, *2007 Urban Mobility Study,* September 2007.
42. Ibid.
43. U.S. Census Bureau, *American Community Survey,* 2007.
44. Steve H. Murdock, Md. Nazrul Hoque, Martha Michael, Steve White, and Beverly Pecotte, *The Texas Challenge:*

Population Change and the Future of Texas (College Station, TX: Texas A & M University Press, 1997), p. 29.

45. United States Department of Agriculture, Economic Research Service, *State Fact Sheets: Texas,* data updated June 30, 2009.

46. Federal Reserve Bank of Texas, "Houston Business—A Perspective on the Houston Economy," April 2004; and James P. Gaines, "Looming Boom: Texas Through 2030," *Tierra Grande,* January 2008 (published by the Real Estate Center at Texas A&M University).

47. U.S. Census Bureau, *Population Estimates,* July, 2008.

48. U.S. Census Bureau, *2000 Census of the Population, Census 2000;* Texas State Data Center, *Population Estimates and Projections Program,* 2008.

49. U.S. Census Bureau, *American Community Survey, 2007.*

50. Ibid.

51. U.S. Census Bureau, *Small Area Income and Poverty Estimates: State and County Estimates for 2007.*

52. *Forbes,* "The Four Hundred Richest Americans," Special Edition, September 2008, http://www.forbes.com/richest/.

53. Murdock, et al., *The Texas Challenge,* pp. 64–65.

54. U.S. Census Bureau, *2000 Census of the Population;* U.S. Census Bureau, *American Community Survey, 2007.*

55. Rupert N. Richardson, Ernest Wallace, and Adrian Anderson, *Texas: The Lone Star State,* 5th ed. (Englewood Cliffs, NJ: Prentice Hall, 1988), p. 2.

56. Key, *Southern Politics in State and Nation,* p. 260.

57. Jordan, et al., *Texas: A Geography,* p. 7.

58. Ibid., pp. 18–21.

59. For an expanded analysis of the Texas economy and the dominant role played by corporations, see James W. Lamare, *Texas Politics: Economics, Power and Policy,* 7th ed. (St. Paul, MN: West, 2001), Chapter 2.

60. Texas Comptroller of Public Accounts, "Texas Economic Outlook," *Texas Economic Quarterly,* (December 1996), p. 2.

61. Bruce Wright, "Weathering the Storm," *Fiscal Notes,* March 2009.

62. "Boom, Bust and Back Again: Bullock Tenure Covers Tumultuous Years," *Fiscal Notes* (December 1990), pp. 6–7.

63. "Road to Recovery Long and Bumpy, but Positive Signs Begin to Appear," *Fiscal Notes* (March 1989), p. 4.

64. "Boom, Bust and Back Again," p. 7.

65. Mine Yucel, "Texas in the Most Recent Recession and Recovery," in Federal Reserve Bank of Dallas, *The Face of Texas: Jobs, People, Business, Change,* October 2005.

66. Ali Anari and Mark G. Dotzour, "Monthly Review of the Texas Economy—May 2009," Real Estate Center at Texas A&M University, Technical Report 1862.

67. U.S. Bureau of Economic Analysis, "Economic Slowdown Widespread Among States in 2008," June 2, 2009.

68. Texas Comptroller of Public Accounts, *Texas Ahead,* "Comptroller's Economic Outlook,", http://www.texasahead.org/economy/outlook.html (June 5, 2009).

69. Harry Hurt, "Birth of a New Frontier," *Texas Monthly* (April 1984), pp. 130–35.

70. Laila Assanie and Mine Yucel, "Industry Clusters in Texas," in Federal Reserve Bank of Dallas, *The Face of Texas: Jobs, People, Business, Change,* October 2005.

71. U.S. Department of Commerce, International Trade Administration, "Texas: Exports, Jobs, and Foreign Investment," February 2009, http://ita.doc.gov/td/industry/otea/state_reports/texas/html.

72. Ibid.

73. The following discussion of the twelve economic regions is based on a series of reports produced by the Texas Comptroller of Public Accounts. The reports are part of a series entitled *Texas in Focus* that commenced with a statewide summary published in 2008. Reports for four of the regions were available by June of 2009.

74. Texas Comptroller of Public Accounts, *Texas in Focus: The High Plains,* April 2008.

75. Texas Comptroller of Public Accounts, *Texas in Focus: South Texas,* August 2008.

76. Texas Comptroller of Public Accounts, *Texas in Focus: Upper East Texas,* October 2008.

CHAPTER 2

The Texas Constitution

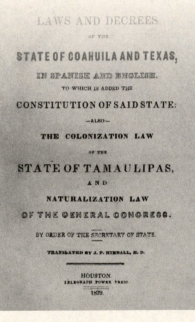

Questions to Guide Your Reading

1. Do constitutions reflect the core values of a political system?

2. How does the Texas Constitution differ from the U.S. Constitution?

3. Does the Texas Constitution adequately serve the needs of the urbanized areas of the state?

4. How do you account for the resistance to modernizing the Texas Constitution?

*Humbly invoking the blessings of Almighty God, the people of the
State of Texas, do ordain and establish this Constitution.*

—Preamble to the Constitution of Texas 1876

*If men were angels, no government would be necessary. If angels were to govern
men, neither external nor internal controls on government would be necessary. In
framing a government which is to be administered by men over men, the great difficulty lies in this: you must first enable the government to control the governed;
and in the next place oblige it to control itself.*

—James Madison[1]

The year was 1874, and unusual events marked the end of the darkest chapter in Texas history—the Reconstruction era and the military occupation that followed the Civil War. Texans, still smarting from some of the most oppressive laws ever imposed on American citizens, had overwhelmingly voted their governor out of office, but he refused to leave the Capitol and hand over his duties to his elected successor. For several tense days, the city of Austin was divided into two armed camps of people—those supporting the deposed governor, **Edmund J. Davis**, and those supporting the man who defeated him at the polls, Richard Coke. Davis finally gave up only after the Texas militia turned against him and marched on the Capitol.

That long-ago period bears little resemblance to modern Texas, but the experience still casts a long shadow over state government. The state constitution, written by Texans at the close of Reconstruction, was designed to put strong restraints on government to guard against future abuses, and most of those restraints remain in place today. The Texas Constitution, adopted in 1876 and amended many times since, is so restrictive that many scholars and politicians believe it is counterproductive to effective, modern governance. They believe the document, which is bogged down with statutory detail, is a textbook example of what a constitution should not be. State government functions despite its constitutional shackles: a weak chief executive, an outdated, part-time legislature, a poorly organized judiciary, and dedicated funds that limit the state's budgetary options. But a total rewrite of the constitution has been elusive thanks to numerous special interests who find security in the present document—from holders of obsolete offices to beneficiaries of dedicated funds and bureaucrats who fear change. Public ignorance and indifference to the problems created by the restrictive constitutional provisions also thwart an overhaul of the document.

It is our position, shared by others who study state governments, that one cannot develop a clear understanding of Texas government or its politics without some familiarity with and understanding of the Texas Constitution.[2] Constitutions are more than the formal frameworks that define the structure, authority, and responsibilities of governmental institutions. They also reflect fundamental political, economic, and power relationships as determined by the culture, values, and interests of the people who create them and the events of the period in which they were written.[3]

The constitution of Texas is not an easy read, and the casual reader can quickly get bogged down in details that seem to make little sense. But a careful study of the document provides insights into the distribution of power among competing groups and regions within the state. The constitution outlines the powers of the state and local

TABLE 2–1   The Seven Texas Constitutions

1827: Constitution of Coahuila y Tejas
Adopted in 1827 while Texas was still part of Mexico, this constitution recognized Texas as a Mexican state with Coahuila.

1836: Constitution of the Republic
The constitution of March 16, 1836, declared independence from Mexico and constituted Texas as an independent republic.

1845: Constitution of 1845
Texas was admitted to the Union under this constitution.

1861: Civil War Constitution
After the state seceded from the Union and joined the Confederacy in 1861, Texans adopted this constitution.

1866: Constitution of 1866
This was a short-lived constitution under which Texas sought to be readmitted to the Union after the Civil War and before the Radical Reconstructionists took control of the U.S. Congress.

1869: Reconstruction Constitution
Power was centralized in the state government and local governments were significantly weakened under this constitution, which reflected the sentiments of Radical Reconstructionists, not of most Texans.

1876: Texas Constitution
Adopted at the end of Reconstruction and amended 467 times since, Texas currently functions under this constitution. Highly restrictive and antigovernment, this constitution places strict limitations on the powers of the governor, the legislature, and other state officials.

governments, and it also defines the limitations imposed on these governments. From the perspective of political economy, the constitution also speaks to "the relation of the state to economic activity, including both the extent of direct governmental support for enterprise and the appropriate balance between promotion and regulation of economic development."[4]

Texas has had seven constitutions, and understanding that legacy is critical to understanding contemporary Texas politics and public policy (see Table 2–1). The first constitution was adopted in 1827, when the state was still part of Mexico. The second was drafted when Texas declared its independence from Mexico in 1836 and became a republic. The third was adopted in 1845 when the state joined the Union. The fourth constitution was written when Texas joined the Confederacy in 1861, and the fifth was adopted when the state rejoined the Union in 1866. The sixth constitution was adopted in 1869 to satisfy the **Radical Reconstructionists'** opposition to the 1866 constitution, and the seventh constitution was adopted in 1876 after the termination of Reconstruction policies.

CONSTITUTIONALISM ●

The Functions of a Constitution

A **constitution** defines the principles of a society and states or suggests what political objectives that society is attempting to achieve. It outlines the specific institutions that the people will use to achieve their objectives, and it defines who can participate in collective decisions and who can hold public office. It also defines the relationship between those people who govern and those who are governed and sets limits on what each group can and cannot do. Because of the stability of the American political system and a general commitment to the rule of law, we often overlook the fact that a constitution also reflects the way a society structures conflict through its institutional arrangements.[5]

The Texas Constitution in a Comparative Perspective

Constitutions do not lend themselves to easy reading. The formal, legal language often obscures the general objectives of the document and its relevance to contemporary issues of political power and public policy. Scholars believe, first, that constitutions should be brief and should include general principles rather than specific legislative provisions. In other words, constitutions should provide a basic framework for government and leave the details to be defined in **statutory law**. Second, experts say, constitutions should grant authority to specific institutions, so as to increase the responsiveness and the accountability of individuals elected or appointed to public office. Scholars also believe that constitutions should provide for orderly change but should not be written in such a restrictive fashion that they require continual modifications to meet contemporary needs.[6]

Amended only twenty-seven times since its adoption in 1789, the U.S. Constitution is a concise, 7,000-word document that outlines broad, basic principles of authority and governance. No one would argue that the government of the twenty-first century is comparable to that of the 1790s, yet the flexibility of the U.S. Constitution makes it as relevant now as it was in the eighteenth century. It is often spoken of as "a living constitution" that doesn't have to be continually amended to meet society's ever-changing needs and conditions. Its reinterpretations by the courts, the Congress, and the president have produced an expansion of powers and responsibilities within the framework of the original language of the document.

By contrast, the Texas Constitution—like those of many other states—is an unwieldy, restrictive document. With more than 90,000 words, it has been on a life-support system—the piecemeal amendment process—for most of its lifetime (see Figure 2–1). It is less a set of basic governmental principles than a compilation of detailed statutory language, often referred to as "constitutional legislation," reflecting the distrust of government that was widespread in Texas when it was written and the fact that the national constitution says so very little about state government.[7] In effect, it attempts to diffuse political power among many different institutions. As drafted in 1875, it also included restrictions on elections and civil rights that were later invalidated by the U.S. Supreme Court. Those early provisions were efforts to limit the power of minority groups to fully participate in state government.[8]

The historical constitutional experiences of Texas parallel those of many southern states that have had multiple constitutions in the post–Civil War era. The former Confederate states, Texas included, are the only states whose constitutions formally acknowledge the supremacy of the U.S. Constitution, a provision required by the Radical Reconstructionists for readmission to the Union.

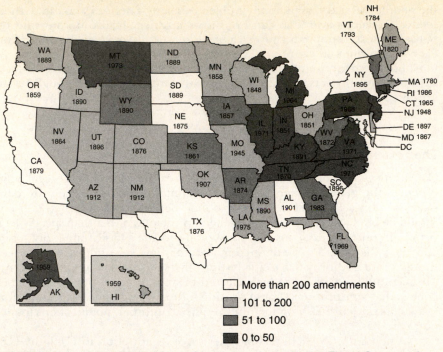

FIGURE 2–1   Frequency of State Constitution Amendment: Texas Compared with Other States as of January 2009. *Source: The Book of the States, 2009 Edition,* vol. 41 (Lexington, Ky: Council of State Governments, 2009), Table 1.1.

THE CONSTITUTIONAL LEGACY

Each of Texas's seven constitutions was written in a distinct historical setting. And though there are significant differences—as well as similarities—among these documents, each contributed to the state and local governments that we know today.

The Constitution of Coahuila y Tejas (1827)

Sparsely populated Texas was part of Mexico when that country secured its independence from Spain in 1821, about the time that Stephen F. Austin and others began the Anglo colonization of Texas. Initially, Anglo Texans appeared willing to be incorporated into the Mexican political system as long as there was limited intrusion by the Mexican government into their daily affairs. In 1824, the new Republic of Mexico adopted a constitution for a federal system of government that recognized Texas (Tejas) as a single state with Coahuila, its neighbor south of the Rio Grande. Saltillo, Mexico, was the state capital.

The constitution of *Coahuila y Tejas,* completed in 1827, provided for a **unicameral** congress of twelve deputies, including two from Texas, elected by the people. Most of the legislators were from the more populous and Spanish-speaking Coahuila and the laws were published in Spanish, which few Texas colonists understood. The executive department included a governor and a vice governor. The governor enforced the law, led the state militia, and granted pardons. The constitution made Catholicism the state religion, although that requirement was not enforced among Texas's Anglo settlers. Additionally, Anglo Texans were not subject to military service, taxes, or custom duties. In effect, Texas served as a buffer between Mexico and various Native American tribes—and the United States.

But with increased Anglo immigration and the perceived threat of U.S. imperial or expansionary policies, Mexico soon attempted to extend its control over Texas. This effort reinforced cultural differences between the Anglo and Spanish populations and would eventually lead to revolution by Anglo Texans.[9]

This formative period produced some enduring contributions to the Texas constitutional tradition. Elements of the Mexican legal system are still to be found in property and land laws, water laws and water rights, and community property laws. One justification for the revolution of 1836 was the failure of the Mexican government to provide for sufficient funding for public education. But while there were expectations of funding by the central government, a "concept of local control over school development was firmly established."[10] This issue of local control has been a continuing constitutional question and is central to the current issue of funding public education.

The Constitution of the Republic of Texas (1836)

During the late 1820s and the early 1830s, increased immigration from the United States into the territory of Texas heightened the tension and conflict between the Anglo settlers and the Mexican government. Mexico's efforts to enforce its laws within Texas produced conflicts between cultures, legal traditions, and economic interests that resulted in open rebellion by the colonists.

At the same time, Mexico was embroiled in its own internal dissension. It struggled to stabilize its political system but didn't have the legacy and social and political institutions to assure a successful democratic system. In many respects, the events in Texas were a footnote to the power politics in Mexico. Had the autonomy of Texas that was mandated in the Mexican Constitution of 1824 been maintained, the history of this region might well have been different.

Increased internal conflict among competing Mexican interests resulted in the seizure of power by the popular general, Antonio Lopez de Santa Anna Perez de Lebron. Santa Anna began to systematically suspend the powers of the Mexican Congress and local governments and, in October 1835, the national Constitution of 1824 was voided. Mexico adopted a new constitution providing for a **unitary system** with power centralized in the national congress and the presidency. The principle of **federalism**, which divided power and authority between the national government and the states, was repudiated. This major change intensified conflict between the national government and the Mexican states. Texas was not the only area of Mexico where the principles of federalism were highly regarded, and although Texas was eventually successful in establishing its autonomy, several other Mexican states were subjected to harsh military retaliation.

As the Mexican government under Santa Anna attempted to regain control over Texas, colonists who initially supported the national government and those who expressed ambivalence were only slowly converted to the cause of independence. Stephen F. Austin had consistently supported the position that Texas was a Mexican state, and he represented a large part of the Anglo population living in Texas. But when Mexican troops moved across the Rio Grande into Texas in the fall of 1835, Austin sent out a call for resistance.

Birth of the Republic. Faced with the advancing Mexican armies, fifty-nine Texans met in the small settlement of Washington-on-the-Brazos in this building, declaring their independence on March 2, 1836. A constitution was written for the Republic of Texas and adopted on March 16, 1836.

The numerous special interests that later were to obstruct the course of constitutional development in Texas were missing at the small settlement of Washington-on-the-Brazos in 1836. The fifty-nine male colonists who convened to declare Texas's independence from Mexico on March 2 and to adopt a constitution for the new republic two weeks later had two overriding interests: the preservation of their fledgling nation and the preservation of their own lives. By the time they had completed their work, the Alamo—only 150 miles away—had fallen to a large Mexican army under Santa Anna, and a second Mexican force was also north of the Rio Grande. Accordingly, the constitution writers wasted little time on speechmaking.

Consequently, the Constitution of the Republic, adopted on March 16, 1836, was not cluttered with the details that weaken the present Texas Constitution. It drew heavily from the U.S. Constitution and, because forty-four of the fifty-nine delegates were from the South, from the constitutions of several southern states. The document created an elected **bicameral** Congress and provided for an elected president. Members of the clergy were prohibited from serving as president or in Congress, and there was no official, state-preferred religion. Slavery was legal, but importation of slaves from any country other than the United States was illegal. Free African Americans had to have the Congress' permission to leave Texas.

Approximately six weeks after the disastrous defeat at the Alamo, the Texas army, under the command of Sam Houston, defeated Santa Anna's army at the battle of San Jacinto on April 21, 1836. The war of independence had been relatively short and

Opposition to Succession Cost Him the Governorship.
Governor Sam Houston, who played a pivotal role throughout
the formative period of Texas history, opposed the state's
secession from the Union and was replaced on March 16, 1861,
by Governor Ed Clark.

involved limited casualties, but the problems of creating a stable political system under
the new constitution were formidable. There was no viable government in place, no
money for paying the costs of government, and no party system.[11] And, although
defeated, Mexico did not relinquish its claims to Texas and was to demonstrate in subsequent actions that it wanted to regain this lost territory. Nevertheless, the "transition
from colony to constitutional republic was accomplished quickly and with a minimum
of disorganization."[12]

The experience of independence and national autonomy from 1836 to 1845 contributed significantly to the development of a sense of historical uniqueness among
Texans. Although the effects on the state's political psyche may be difficult to measure,
the "Lone Star" experience has been kept alive through school history texts, the celebration of key events, and the development of a mythology of the independence period.

The Constitution of 1845

During the independence movement and immediately thereafter, there were overtures
by some Texans to the United States to annex Texas, but they were initially blocked by
the issue of slavery and its relationship to economic and regional influence in U.S. politics. Increased immigration to Texas in the late 1830s and early 1840s, more interest
among Texans in joining the Union, and expansionist policies of the U.S. government
stepped up pressures for annexation. It was a major issue in the U.S. presidential campaign of 1844, and the election of James K. Polk accelerated the move toward Texas's
admission to the United States in 1845 (see "Five 'Lone' Stars?").

The annexation bill approved by the U.S. Congress included a compromise that
allowed slavery to continue in Texas.[13] Racial issues that emerged from this period continue to shape contemporary politics and public policy in the state. Texas still struggles
with voting rights issues, inequities in funding of education, and the maldistribution of
economic resources that directly affect the quality of life for many minorities.

Five "Lone" Stars?

The terms of Texas's admission into the Union provided that Texas could divide itself into as many as five states, a provision largely forgotten until state Representative David Swinford, a Republican from Dumas, made such a proposal in 1991. The idea attracted some newspaper headlines and some interest in the Panhandle, which is geographically isolated from most of Texas, but it wasn't given serious consideration.

The state constitution drafted to allow Texas's annexation was about twice as long as the Constitution of 1836. It borrowed not only from its predecessor but also from the constitutions of other southern states, particularly from Louisiana.

The Constitution of 1845 created an elected legislature that met biennially and included a house of representatives and a senate. It provided for an elected governor and an elected lieutenant governor, and it empowered the governor to appoint a secretary of state, attorney general, and state judges, subject to senate confirmation. The legislature chose a comptroller, treasurer, and land commissioner. In 1850, however, Texas voters amended the constitution to make most state offices elective. In this respect, Texas was following a national pattern of fragmenting the powers of the executive branch of state government. Today, Texas still has a plural executive system under which practically all statewide officeholders are elected independently of the governor, a system that contrasts sharply with the appointive cabinet system of executive government enjoyed by the president of the United States.

The 1845 constitution protected private homesteads from foreclosure, guaranteed separate property rights for married women, and established a permanent fund for the support of public schools—provisions also found in the present constitution. The 1845 charter also recognized slavery, prohibited anyone who had ever participated in a duel from holding public office, and prohibited state-chartered banks. This constitution "worked so well that after several intervening constitutions, the people of Texas recopied it almost *in toto* as the Constitution of 1876."[14]

The Civil War Constitution (1861)

When Texas seceded from the Union in 1861, just before the outbreak of the Civil War, the state constitution was again revised. Although most of the provisions of the 1845 document were retained, significant changes were made in line with Texas's new membership in the Confederacy. Public officials were required to pledge their support of the Confederate constitution, greater protection was given to slavery, and the freeing of slaves was prohibited.

Any semblance of a two-party system had been destroyed by the issues of slavery and secession during the 1850s, and state politics was dominated by personalities, factions, and war-related issues. Factionalism within the Democratic Party persisted for more than 100 years, until the emergence of a two-party system in the 1980s.

The Civil War era also contributed to a legacy of states' rights, which was to persist well into the next century and was to spark an extended struggle for desegregation. Theoretically, the constitutional issue of the Civil War was whether a state, once having joined the Union, could leave the Union. The southern states subscribed to a view of the

Transition President. Anson Jones was the last president of the Republic of Texas, serving from December 1844 to February 1846.

national government as a **confederacy**, and it was their position that a state could withdraw, or secede. Although the northern victory dispelled this interpretation, Texas, along with other southern states, found ways to thwart national policy through the 1960s. Their efforts were based, in part, on their continued arguments for states' rights.

The Constitution of 1866

After the Civil War, Texas government was subject to national control, first through a military government, and then through a provisional government headed by A. J. Hamilton, a former U.S. congressman who had remained loyal to the Union. These were dark days for Texans. Although the state had witnessed relatively few battles and had not suffered from the scorched-earth tactics used by Union generals elsewhere, the economy was in disarray. Many Texas families had lost loved ones, and many surviving

Confederate veterans had been wounded physically or psychologically. Although the national government developed policies to assist the newly freed slaves, these policies were never fully funded and were halfheartedly—and often dishonestly—carried out. And the presence of an occupation army heightened tensions and shaped subsequent political attitudes.

The Reconstruction plan initiated by President Abraham Lincoln but never fully implemented envisioned a rapid return to civilian government for the southern states and their quick reintegration as equals in the national political system. Requirements were modest: the abolition of slavery, the repudiation of the Secession Ordinance of 1861, and the repudiation of all debts and obligations incurred under the Confederacy.[15]

Texas voters revived the Constitution of 1845 and amended it to include the stipulations required by the national government. But while slavery was eliminated and the freed slaves were given the right to hold property and were accorded legal rights before a jury, no black people could testify in any court case involving whites. And African Americans were denied the right to vote.[16] The new constitution was adopted in June 1866, a new government was elected, and on August 20, 1866, President Andrew Johnson "declared the rebellion in Texas at an end."[17]

In short order, however, the mild Reconstruction policies of Johnson were replaced by the severe policies of the Radical Reconstructionists who captured control of Congress in 1866. The new Texas Constitution was invalidated by Congress, which passed, over the president's veto, the Reconstruction Acts, which established military governments throughout the South. The civilian government initiated by the state constitution of 1866 was short-lived, and Texas functioned for two years under a reinstituted military government.

This period had an enduring impact on Texas constitutional law and politics. In a broad sense, it prolonged the full reintegration of Texas into the national political system. In specific terms, it transformed the constitutional tradition of Texas into one of hostility and suspicion toward government.

The Constitution of Reconstruction (1869)

The Reconstruction Acts required a Texas Constitution that would grant African Americans the right to vote and include other provisions acceptable to Congress. A Republican slate of delegates to a new constitutional convention produced a new charter in 1869. It did not reflect the majority Texas sentiment of the time, but it conformed to Republican wishes. Centralizing more powers in state government while weakening local government, the charter gave the governor a four-year term and the power to appoint other top state officials, including members of the judiciary. It provided for annual legislative sessions; gave African Americans the right to vote; and, for the first time, provided for a centralized, statewide system of public schools. Texans were unhappy enough with their new constitution, but the widespread abuses of the document that followed under the oppressive and corrupt administration of Radical Republican Governor Edmund J. Davis would soon produce shackles on state government that are still in place today.

In the 1869 election, the first under the new constitution, large numbers of former slaves voted, whereas Anglos who had volunteered during the war to fight for the Confederacy were not allowed to cast ballots. The entire process was supervised by Radical supporters of Davis, a former Union Army officer. The military governor certified that Davis beat Conservative Republican A. J. Hamilton by 39,901 to 39,092 votes. This outcome was allowed despite widespread, flagrant incidents of voter fraud, which

Detested by Many. A Union general and later governor of Texas (1870–74), Edmund J. Davis conducted one of the most oppressive administrations in U.S. history. Texas reacted to such practices by building restrictions on the governor's power into the Constitution of 1876.

also were ignored by President Ulysses S. Grant and Congress. A radical majority in the new Texas legislature then approved a series of authoritarian—and, in some respects, unconstitutional—laws proposed by Davis. They gave the governor the power to declare martial law and suspend the laws in any county and created a state police force under the governor's control that could deprive citizens of constitutional protections. The governor also was empowered to appoint mayors, district attorneys, and hundreds of other local officials. Another law that designated newspapers as official printers of state documents in effect put much of the press under government control.

Davis exercised some of the most repressive actions ever imposed on United States citizens. And Texans responded. First, in 1872, they elected a Democratic majority to the legislature that abolished the state police and repealed other oppressive laws. Then, in 1873, they elected a Confederate veteran, Democrat Richard Coke, governor by more than a 2–1 margin over Davis. Like the Radical Republicans in the previous gubernatorial election, the Democrats were not above abusing the democratic process, and, once again, voting fraud was rampant. "Democrat politicos bluntly indicated that power would be won depending on who outfrauded whom. No practice was ignored. There was terror, intimidation, and some murders on both sides," wrote historian T. R. Fehrenbach.[18]

As was described earlier in this chapter, Davis initially refused to leave office and appealed to President Grant for federal troops to help him retain power. Grant refused, and Davis finally gave up after the Texas militia turned against him and marched on the Capitol in January 1874. Bloodshed was avoided, Reconstruction was ending, and the Constitution of 1869 was doomed.

The Constitution of 1876: Retrenchment and Reform

The restored Democratic majority promptly took steps to assemble a new constitutional convention, which convened in Austin on September 6, 1875. The delegates were all men. Most were products of a rural and frontier South, and still smarting from Reconstruction abuses, they considered government a necessary evil that had to be heavily restricted. Many, however, had previous governmental experience. Initially, seventy-five Democrats and fifteen Republicans were elected delegates, but one Republican resigned after only limited service and was replaced by a Democrat.[19]

The vast majority of the delegates were white, and some disagreement remains over how many African Americans served in the convention. Some historians say there were six. According to one account, however, six African Americans were elected but one

Members of the 1875 Convention.
Ninety delegates, including six recently emancipated African Americans, were elected to the Constitutional Convention of 1875.

resigned after only one day of service and was replaced in a special election by a white delegate. All of the African-American delegates were Republicans.[20]

Only four of the delegates were native Texans. Most had immigrated to Texas from other southern states, including nineteen—the largest single group—from Tennessee, which one author called the "breeding ground" of Texas delegates. Their average age was forty-five. The oldest was sixty-eight; the youngest was twenty-three.[21] Eleven of the delegates had been members of previous constitutional conventions in Texas, but there is disagreement over whether any had participated in drafting the Reconstruction Constitution of 1869. In any event, the influences of the 1869 constitution were negative, not positive.

At least thirty of the delegates had served in the Texas legislature, two others had served in the Tennessee and Mississippi legislatures, two had represented Texas in the U.S. Congress, and two others had represented Texas in the Confederate Congress. Delegates also included a former attorney general, a former lieutenant governor, and a former secretary of state of Texas; and at least eight delegates had judicial experience. Many delegates had been high-ranking Confederate military officers. One, John H. Reagan, had been postmaster general of the Confederacy.[22] Reagan later would become a U.S. senator from Texas and the first chairman of the Texas Railroad Commission.

Another delegate who epitomized the independent, frontier spirit of the time was John S. "Rip" Ford, a native of South Carolina who had come to Texas in 1836 as a physician. He later became a lawyer, journalist, state senator, mayor of Austin, and Texas Ranger captain. In 1874, he was a leader of the militia that marched on the Capitol and forced Edmund J. Davis to relinquish the governor's office to his elected successor. Ford had been a secessionist delegate to the 1861 convention and, during the Civil War, had commanded a makeshift cavalry regiment that fought Union soldiers along the Texas–Mexico border.[23]

According to one account, delegates to the 1875 convention included thirty-three lawyers, twenty-eight farmers, three physicians, three merchants, two teachers, two editors, and one minister. At least eleven other delegates were part-time farmers who also pursued other occupations.[24] Other historians have suggested slightly different breakdowns, but all agree that the influence of agricultural interests was substantial in the writing of the new Texas charter.

About half the delegates were members of the Society of the Patrons of Husbandry, or the **Grange.** An organization formed to improve the lot of farmers, the Grange became politically active in the wake of national scandals involving abuses by big business and government. The Grange started organizing in Texas in 1873, and its influence was directly felt in constitutional provisions limiting taxes and governmental expenditures and restricting banks, railroads, and other corporations.

The delegates did not try to produce a document that would be lauded as a model of constitutional perfection or mistaken for a literary classic. They faced the reality of addressing serious, pressing problems—an immediate crisis that did not encourage debate over the finer points of academic or political theory or produce any prophetic visions of the next century.

The Civil War, Reconstruction, and the Radical Republican administration had plunged the state into economic ruin and state government into deep debt, despite the heavy taxation of Texas citizens, particularly property owners. The bottom had fallen out of land prices, a disaster for what was still an agricultural state. Governmental corruption had been pervasive under the Davis administration, and the dictatorial powers that Davis had exercised, particularly the abuses of his hated state police, had left deep scars. Moreover, the national political scene under President Grant's two administrations (1869–1877) had also been plagued by corruption and scandal.

The framers of the Texas Constitution of 1876 reacted accordingly. In seeking to restore control of their state government to the people and restore economic stability, they fashioned what was essentially an antigovernment charter. Centralization was replaced with more local control, strict limits were placed on taxation, and short leashes were put on the legislature, the courts, and especially the governor.[25]

Texas's traditional agricultural interests, which had been called upon to finance industrial development and new social services during Reconstruction, were once again protected from onerous governmental intrusion and taxation. The retrenchment and reform embodied in the new charter soon would hamper the state's commercial and economic development. But the post-Reconstruction Texans applauded the multitude of restrictive details that the new constitution carried. They ratified the new document in February 1876 by a vote of 136,606 to 56,052.

GENERAL PRINCIPLES OF THE TEXAS CONSTITUTION

A relatively short preamble and the first two sections of the Bill of Rights express the underlying principle of the Texas Constitution of 1876 (see Table 2–2). It is a social compact, formed by free men (no women participated in its drafting), in which "all political power

TABLE 2–2   Comparison of the U.S. Constitution and the Texas Constitution

	U.S. Constitution	Texas Constitution
General principles	Popular sovereignty Limited government Representative government Social contract theory Separation of powers	Popular sovereignty Limited government Representative government Social contract theory Separation of powers
Context of adoption	Reaction to weakness of Articles of Confederation—strengthened national powers significantly	Post-Reconstruction—designed to limit powers of government
Style	General principles stated in broad terms	Detailed provisions
Length	7,000 words	90,000-plus words
Date of implementation	1789	1876
Amendments	27	467
Amendment process	Difficult	Relatively easy
Adaptation to change	Moderately easy through interpretation	Difficult; often requires constitutional amendments
Bill of Rights	Amendments to the Constitution—adopted in 1791	Article 1 of the Constitution of 1876
Structure of government	Separation of powers, with a unified executive based on provisions of Articles I, II, III	Separation of powers with plural executive defined by Article 2
Legislature	Bicameral	Bicameral
Judiciary	Creation of one Supreme Court and other courts to be created by the Congress	Detailed provisions creating two appellate courts and other state courts
Distribution of powers	Federal	Unitary
Public policy	Little reference to policy	Detailed policy provisions

is inherent in the people ... founded on their authority, and instituted for their benefit."[26] These brief sections are based on the principles of **popular sovereignty** and **social contract** theory, both of which were part of a legacy of constitutional law in the United States. Although the language articulates the noble aspirations of a free and just society, it was limited in scope and application. Women and minorities were initially denied full citizenship rights. And although women gained the right to vote in 1920, it has taken years for African Americans and Hispanics to receive the full protection implicit in these statements.

A third major principle is **limited government**. The Bill of Rights and other provisions throughout the constitution place limits on governmental authority and power. The constitution spells out the traditional rights of religious freedom, procedural due process of law, and other rights of the citizen in relation to the government.

A fourth major principle is **separation of powers**. Unlike the U.S. Constitution, in which this principle emerges through powers defined in the three articles related to Congress, the president, and the judiciary, Article 2 of the Texas Constitution specifically provides for it.

The Constitution of 1876 created three branches of government—legislative, executive, and judicial—and provided for a system of checks and balances that assured that no single branch would dominate the others. This principle originated with the U.S.

Constitution, whose drafters were concerned about the so-called mischief of factions.[27] They feared that groups or special interests would be able to capture governmental institutions and pursue policies that were not in the national interest. So institutional power was fragmented to guard against that potential problem. In some respects, this was an issue of even greater concern to the framers of the Texas Constitution. Reacting to the highly centralized authority and abuses of the Davis administration, they took the separation of powers principle to its extreme.

Lawmaking authority is vested in an elected legislature that includes a 150-member House of Representatives and a 31-member senate and meets in regular sessions in odd-numbered years and in special sessions of limited scope and duration when called by the governor. The sixty-five sections of Article 3 spell out in detail the powers granted and the restrictions imposed on the legislature.

An elected governor shares authority over the executive branch with several other independently elected, statewide officeholders. The governor can veto bills approved by the legislature, and a veto can be overridden only by a two-thirds vote of the house and the senate.

Also elected are members of the judiciary—from justices of the peace, with limited jurisdiction at the county level, to the highest statewide appellate courts. This provision reflects the strong sentiment of post-Reconstruction Texans for an independent judiciary and is a major difference from the federal government, in which judges are appointed by the president. Also unlike the federal system, in which the U.S. Supreme Court is the court of last resort in both civil and criminal appeals, Texas has two courts of last resort. The Texas Supreme Court has jurisdiction over civil matters, and the Texas Court of Criminal Appeals has final review of criminal cases.

WEAKNESSES AND CRITICISMS OF THE CONSTITUTION OF 1876

Executive Branch

Many experts believe that the Texas Constitution excessively fragments governmental authority and responsibility, particularly in the executive branch. Although there is a natural disposition for the public to look to the governor to establish policy priorities, the governor does not have control over other elected state executives, but rather shares both authority and responsibility for policy with them. This situation can be problematic, as when former Republican Governor Bill Clements, for example, shared executive responsibilities with Democrats who sharply disagreed with his priorities. Even when the governor and other elected officials are of the same party, differences in personality, political philosophy, and policy objectives can produce tension and sometimes deadlock. Political divisiveness and feuding at the highest levels of state government became particularly strident in 2006, when Comptroller Carole Keeton Strayhorn, a Republican, became an independent candidate to unsuccessfully challenge Republican Governor Rick Perry's reelection.

The governor's power has been further diffused by the creation over the years of numerous boards and commissions that set policy for executive agencies not headed by elected officials. Although the governor appoints most of those board members, they serve staggered six-year terms that are longer than a governor's term. And a newly elected governor—who cannot fire a predecessor's appointees—usually has to wait through most of his or her first term to gain a majority of appointees to most boards.

Fragmented authority and responsibility also are found in county governments, which are administrative agents of the state (see Chapter 12). Various elected county officials often clash over public policy, producing inefficiencies or failing to meet public needs. And just as the voters are faced with a long ballot for statewide offices, they also must choose among a long, often confusing list of county officers. Because a long ballot discourages many people from voting, this obstacle reduces public accountability, an end result that the framers of the Constitution of 1876 certainly never intended.

Legislative Branch

The constitution created a low-paid, part-time legislature to ensure the election of citizen-lawmakers who would be sensitive to the needs of their constituents, not of professional politicians who would live off the taxpayers. Unwittingly, however, the constitution writers also produced a lawmaking body easily influenced by special interest groups. And the strict limitations placed on the legislature's operations and powers slow its ability to meet the increasingly complex needs of a growing, modern Texas.

In 1972, voters approved a constitutional change to lengthen the terms of the governor and other executive officeholders from two to four years. This change gave the governor more time to develop public policies with the prospect of seeing them implemented. But voters repeatedly have rejected proposals to provide for annual legislative sessions, and legislative pay remains among the lowest in the country.

Judicial Branch

The Texas Constitution also created numerous locally elected judicial offices, including justice of the peace and county and district courts. Although there are appeal procedures, these judges derive a great deal of autonomy, power, and influence through their local constituencies.

Public Education

Another example of decentralization is the public school system. The centralized school system authorized under the Constitution of 1869 was abolished, and local authorities were given the primary responsibility of supervising public education. The concept of "local control" over their schools is important to many Texans, but decentralization and wide disparities in local tax bases have produced an inequitable public education system.

Budgeting and Finances

The Texas Constitution, including key amendments adopted after 1876, requires a balanced state budget, but also heavily restricts the legislature's choices over state spending. The dedication of large amounts of revenue to specific purposes has made it increasingly difficult for lawmakers to address changing state needs (see Chapter 13).

Individual Rights

Although articulating a general commitment to democracy and individual rights, the constitution was used for many years to retard democratic development in Texas.[28] Like many other southern states, Texas had restrictive laws on voter participation. It levied a poll tax, which reduced the voting of minorities and poor whites until 1966, when an amendment to the U.S. Constitution and a decision by the U.S. Supreme Court outlawed

Rick Noriega. Minority participation at all levels of Texas government has increased significantly since the 1980s as a result of the Voting Rights Act and federal court decisions that declared state laws unconstitutional that kept minorities from registering and voting. Democratic senatorial nominee Rick Noriega, a former member of the Texas House, is shown campaigning in 2008.

poll taxes. Federal courts struck down a Texas election system that excluded African Americans from voting in the Democratic primary, which was where elections were decided when Texas was a one-party state. The elimination of significant numbers of people from participating in elections helped perpetuate the one-party political system for approximately 100 years.[29]

Excessive Details

The Texas Constitution is also burdened with excessive detail. Although few individuals are disposed to read the 90,000-plus word document, a person casually perusing it can find language, for example, governing the operation of hospital districts in Ochiltree, Castro, Hansford, and Hopkins counties (see "Who Needs All This Trouble?"). There also is a provision dealing with expenditures for relocating or replacing

Who Needs All This Trouble?

Roberts County Judge Vernon H. Cook was convinced that his rural county near the top of the Texas Panhandle did not need a constable. He believed the sheriff provided enough law enforcement for the county's 1,500 residents. For years, the county had not had a constable, but the office, which was created in the Texas Constitution, remained on the books. Unexpectedly, in 1992, a write-in candidate ran for constable and was elected. The office then became an extra expense for county taxpayers, as county commissioners felt obliged to pay the new officeholder a $600-a-month salary plus a $200-a-month car allowance and health insurance benefits.

Convinced they were not getting their money's worth—"As near as we can tell, he served two official papers in his first year in office," Cook complained—commissioners later reduced his salary,

and the constable left town[30]. To avoid a recurrence of the problem, commissioners had to ask the state legislature to put a constitutional amendment abolishing the Roberts County constable's office on a statewide ballot so all the state's voters could decide the issue. Thus voters in Houston—600 miles away—would have a greater say in abolishing the office than Roberts County's own taxpayers, because Houston's 1.6 million residents cast many more votes. Although that may not seem fair—Houston taxpayers, after all, did not pay the Roberts County constable's salary—it is just one of many obstacles and inconveniences imposed on modern government by a nineteenth-century constitution. Most amendments abolishing obsolete county offices, however, are approved by Texas voters, including amendments abolishing the constables' offices in Roberts County and two other rural counties in 1995.

sanitation sewer laterals on private property. Whereas the 7,000-word U.S. Constitution leaves the details for implementation to congressional legislation, the Texas Constitution often spells out the authority and power of a governmental agency in specific detail. Most experts would argue that many constitutional articles are of a legislative nature and have no business in a constitution.[31] The excessive detail limits the adaptability of the constitution to changing circumstances and places undue restrictions on state and local governments.

Consequently, there are obsolete and contradictory provisions in the constitution that create confusion in its interpretation and application. Constitutional amendments have been periodically approved to "clean up" such deadwood, but the problem persists.[32]

The Amendment Process

Another important criticism of the Texas Constitution focuses on amendments and the amendment process. Alabama has had more constitutional amendments than any other state (see Table 2–3), but Texas ranked third, with 467 amendments from 1876 through 2007. In contrast, the U.S. Constitution has been amended only twenty-seven times since 1789, and ten of those amendments were adopted as the Bill of Rights immediately after

TABLE 2–3   Ten Shortest & Ten Longest State Constitutions

State	Number of Constitutions	Effective Date of Current Constitution	Estimated Number of Words	Amendments Submitted to Voters	Amendments Adopted
Ten Shortest State Constitutions					
New Hampshire	2	1784	9,200	287	145
Vermont	3	1793	10,286	211	53
Indiana	2	1851	10,379	78	46
Rhode Island	2	1986	10,908	11	10
Iowa	2	1857	11,500	58	53
Minnesota	1	1858	11,740	215	120
Kansas	1	1861	12,296	123	93
Tennessee	3	1870	13,300	61	38
Montana	2	1973	14,028	55	30
Illinois	4	1971	15,751	17	11
Ten Longest State Constitutions					
New York	4	1895	51,700	293	218
Oregon	1	1859	54,083	484	243
California	2	1879	54,645	879	518
Florida	6	1969	57,017	148	115
Arkansas	5	1874	59,500	193	95
Louisiana	11	1975	69,773	221	154
Oklahoma	1	1907	74,075	344	179
Colorado	1	1876	74,522	329	154
Texas	7	1876	90,000	642	467
Alabama	6	1901	365,000	1,103	807

Source: The Book of the States, 2009 Edition, Vol. 41, Table 1.1 (Lexington, KY: Council of State Governments, 2009).

the government organized. The numerous restrictions and prohibitions in the Texas Constitution require excessive amendments to enable state government to adapt to social, economic, and political changes.

CONSTITUTIONAL CHANGE AND ADAPTATION ●

Amendments

Although the drafters filled the constitution with a multitude of restrictive provisions, they also provided a relatively easy method of amending it. This piecemeal amendment process has enabled state government to meet some changing needs, but it has also added thousands of words to the document.

Proposed constitutional amendments can be submitted only by the legislature. Approval by two thirds of the house and the senate puts them on the ballot, where adoption requires a majority vote. Although voters had approved 467 amendments through 2009, they had rejected 175 others. The first amendment was adopted on September 2, 1879. A record twenty-five amendments were on the November 3, 1987, ballot. Seventeen were adopted, and eight were defeated.

Some amendments are of major statewide importance, but many have affected only a single county or a handful of counties or have been offered simply to rid the constitution of obsolete language (see "Adding a Cup of Java to the Constitution"). One amendment approved by voters in 1993 affected only about 140 families, two church congregations, and one school district in Fort Bend and Austin counties. It cleared up a title defect to their land.

Unlike voters in many other states, Texas citizens cannot force the placement of constitutional amendments or binding referenda on the ballot because Texas does not have **initiative** or **referendum** on a statewide level. On taking office in January 1979 as Texas's first Republican governor since Reconstruction, Governor Bill Clements made the adoption of initiative and referendum a priority. But the process could not be provided without a constitutional amendment, and the legislature—which did not want to give up such a significant policy prerogative to the electorate—ignored Clements.

Adding a Cup of Java to the Constitution

Many people may enjoy a cup of coffee with a chocolate dessert. But do such treats belong in the state constitution? Most Texas voters said they did. One of nineteen propositions approved on the 2001 ballot exempted from property taxes raw coffee beans and cocoa imported through the Port of Houston. The proposal was promoted by business people seeking to increase imports of those commodities through Houston. More imports, they hoped, would increase the need for more warehouses, create more jobs, and boost business profits. The tax exemption met a condition necessary for the New York Board of Trade to award "exchange port" status to the Port of Houston, a key requirement for import growth.

There was no organized opposition to the amendment, which also was endorsed by city and county officials in Houston, who believed it offered a potential boost to the area's overall economy. But the proposal was approved by a relatively close margin—52 percent—perhaps because many non-Houstonians viewed it as a special-interest favor for the state's largest city and didn't like the way it tasted.

At times, however, the legislature has demonstrated a tendency to seek political cover by selectively letting the voters decide particularly controversial issues, such as a binding referendum in 1987 on the legalization of pari-mutuel betting on horse and dog racing. In 1993, the legislature proposed a constitutional amendment, which voters overwhelmingly endorsed, to prohibit a personal income tax in Texas without voter approval.

Constitutional Convention

The constitution also provides for revision by constitutional convention, which the legislature can call with the approval of the voters. Delegates to such a convention have to be elected and their terms subject to voter approval. Proposed changes adopted by a constitutional convention must also be approved by the voters. In 1919, voters overwhelmingly rejected a proposal for a constitutional convention.[33] There were subsequent efforts, including an attempt by Governor John Connally in 1967, to initiate reforms using a constitutional convention, but they also were defeated.[34] Connally's efforts, however, did result in adoption of a "cleanup" amendment in 1969 that removed many obsolete provisions from the constitution, and it laid the groundwork for a constitutional convention in 1974.

The Constitutional Reform Efforts of 1971 to 1975

The **constitutional convention of 1974**, the only one ever held under the present charter, ended in failure. Its delegates were the 181 members of the legislature. It had its beginning in 1971, when state Representative Nelson Wolff of San Antonio and several other first-term legislators won the leadership's backing for a full-scale revision effort. In 1972, voters approved the necessary constitutional amendment that specified that the convention would comprise house members and senators elected the same year.

In 1973, the legislature created a thirty-seven-member Constitutional Revision Commission to hold public hearings around the state and make recommendations to the convention. The constitutional convention, or "con–con," as it came to be called by legislators and members of the media, was convened on January 8, 1974. House Speaker Price Daniel, Jr., was elected president, and Lieutenant Governor Bill Hobby, in an address to delegates, offered a prophetic warning: "The special interests of today will be replaced by new and different special interests tomorrow, and any attempt to draft a constitution to serve such interests would be futile and also dishonorable."[35]

Hobby's plea was ignored. Special interests dominated the convention, which finally adjourned in bitter failure on July 30, failing by three votes to get the two-thirds vote necessary to send a new constitution to Texas voters for ratification.

The crucial fight was over a business-backed attempt to lock the state's **right-to-work law** into the constitution. The right-to-work law prohibits union membership as a condition of employment, so the effort was bitterly fought by organized labor. Then as now, business was politically stronger than labor in Texas, but the two-thirds vote necessary to put a new constitution on the ballot was too great an obstacle.

Other factors also worked against the revision effort. One was Governor Dolph Briscoe's refusal to exercise any significant leadership on behalf of a new state charter. Except for opposing proposals that he thought would further weaken the authority of the governor, he provided little input to the convention and did not attempt to twist delegates' arms to get enough votes to send the document to the electorate. Louisiana voters approved a new state constitution in 1974, and Governor Edwin Edwards' strong

Final Days of the 1974 Convention. After three years of preparation and deliberations, the proposed constitution of 1974 failed by three votes in the final hectic session of the constitutional convention, when the gallery was filled with interested onlookers, including many representatives of labor and other interest groups.

support had been considered instrumental. Gubernatorial leadership in other states also appears to have been critical to successful constitutional conventions.

Another major obstacle was the convention's makeup. The 181 members of the legislature constituted the constitutional convention. Soon after the convention began its work, many of them were facing reelection campaigns in the party primaries, which diverted their attention from the business of the convention.

Additionally, a minority of legislators—dubbed "cockroaches" by President Daniel—did not want a new constitution and attempted to delay or obstruct the convention's work at every opportunity. Most legislators, even those who wanted a new constitution, reacted to their own political fears and ambitions. They were very susceptible to the influence of special interests, far more susceptible than most private-citizen delegates likely would have been. And special interests were legion at the convention. In addition to various business and professional groups and organized labor, many county officeholders whose jobs—protected by the Constitution of 1876—were suddenly in jeopardy put pressure on the delegates.

During its next regular session in 1975, the legislature, with the strong support of House Speaker Bill Clayton and Lieutenant Governor Bill Hobby, resurrected the constitutional revision effort. Lawmakers voted to present to Texans the basic document that the convention had barely rejected the previous summer in the form of eight separate constitutional amendments. The first three articles dealing with the separation of powers and the legislative and executive branches were combined into one ballot proposition. Each of the remaining seven propositions was a separate article, each to be independently approved or rejected by the voters. The most controversial issues that the

1974 convention had debated, such as right-to-work, were excluded. The streamlined amendments would have considerably shortened the constitution and provided some major changes, including annual legislative sessions, a unified judicial system, and more flexibility in county government. It would have been a much more flexible, modern constitution than the 1876 document and had cost several million tax dollars and countless hours to produce. But voters rejected all eight propositions on November 4, 1975, some by margins of more than 2 to 1.

A stock fraud scandal in the Legislature in 1971 (see Chapter 8) and the Watergate scandal that forced the resignation of President Richard Nixon in 1974 had raised Texans' distrust of government, and the proposed new constitution had been drafted by state officials, not by private citizens.

Nelson Wolff, who years later would be elected mayor of San Antonio and then county judge of Bexar County, also had noted an earlier, general lack of citizen interest in the work of the constitutional convention. In his book, *Challenge of Change,* he wrote: "The constitutional revision effort in Texas had attempted to use every means known to get citizen participation in the process. A toll-free telephone had been set up for the convention. Committees of the convention met at night and on weekends to provide working people an opportunity to testify. We provided to the best of our ability optimum conditions for testimony. Yet many people avoided participation in the revision process."[36]

Most people are not attentive to the details and nuances of constitutional revisions, and it is a difficult task translating these complexities into arguments that make sense to the average voter.[37] The voter distrust and apathy played right into the hands of numerous special interests, who did not want to give up the protections that the old constitution afforded them.

Efforts to enact these proposals were further thwarted by Governor Dolph Briscoe. Although he had never taken an active role in the revision effort, three weeks before the 1975 election, he openly opposed the eight propositions and suggested that the existing constitution had served the state well and would continue to be adequate for the future.[38]

Further Piecemeal Reforms

So it was back to piecemeal constitutional changes. Between 1975 and 2009, 246 amendments were approved by Texas voters, and 39 were rejected. Propositions winning approval included the creation of the state lottery in 1991, the 1993 amendment to ban a personal income tax without voter approval, and a series of propositions authorizing $3 billion in tax-backed bonds for a huge prison expansion program (see Chapter 13). In 1985, voters approved an amendment to give the governor and legislative leaders authority to deal with budgetary emergencies between legislative sessions. In 1995, they approved an amendment to abolish the state treasurer's office and transfer its duties to the comptroller. During its 1999 session, the legislature rejected a proposal—the first of its kind in more than twenty years—to rewrite the constitution. But legislators approved an amendment, which voters also approved, to remove more obsolete language from the document. One of the more controversial amendments in recent years, Proposition 12, ratified new limits on some monetary damages in medical malpractice lawsuits. It was narrowly approved by voters in 2003 (see "Political Controversy: Should Constitutional Amendments Be Submitted to the Voters in Special Elections?").

Political Controversy: Should Constitutional Amendments Be Submitted to the Voters in Special Elections?

Proposition 12, The constitutional amendment concerning civil lawsuits against doctors and health care providers, and other actions, authorizing the legislature to determine limitations on noneconomic damages (Special Constitutional Amendments Election, September 2003).

Supporters said Proposition 12 was a cure for high medical malpractice insurance premiums that were forcing some doctors, particularly in rural areas, to close their practices. Opponents argued that medical malpractice coverage was high because state regulators weren't effectively clamping down on bad doctors, and they warned that Proposition 12 was instead an effort by business and insurance interests to further restrict access to the courts for injured or aggrieved consumers. In any event, Texas voters narrowly approved the constitutional amendment in 2003 after a multimillion-dollar advertising war. Doctors, hospitals, nursing homes and other business interests primarily financed the campaign promoting the amendment. Plaintiffs' lawyers—who make their living suing doctors, hospitals and businesses on behalf of injured consumers—picked up most of the tab for the media campaign against it, although numerous consumer advocacy groups also opposed the proposal.

The amendment did two things. First, it ratified a 2003 law enacted by the legislature to put new limits on non-economic damages—money awarded for such things as pain, suffering and disfigurement—in medical malpractice suits. Such damages, which are in addition to medical costs and other actual economic losses that could be awarded a patient who suffered from a botched medical procedure, were capped at $750,000 for each case. Of that amount, only $250,000 can be recovered from physicians or other medical personnel. The remainder would come from hospitals, nursing homes or other health care facilities that may be involved. Additionally—and potentially more far-reaching—Proposition 12 included language clearing the way for future sessions of the legislature to enact new limits on damages in other civil lawsuits.

Legislative sponsors of Proposition 12 also were accused of trying to sneak the proposal past the voters by scheduling the constitutional amendments election for September 13, rather than November 4, the general election date on which constitutional amendments were traditionally set for voter review. Supporters of the amendment said it was important to win voter approval earlier than normal to remove any legal uncertainty over the new malpractice limits. But opponents argued that the early election, with no other issues to attract voters, was designed to avoid the higher voter turnout that would be generated by a hotly contested mayoral race in Houston on November 4. Voters in Houston, the state's largest city, usually are a major factor in determining statewide elections, and a high voter turnout there could prove to be pivotal in determining the fate of Proposition 12. According to this argument, the higher the voter turnout in Houston, the higher the likelihood that the amendment would be defeated, because Democrats and plaintiffs' lawyers still had some clout over elections in that city. Opponents of Proposition 12, as it turned out, had reason to fear the early election date. The proposal narrowly passed statewide, but 58 percent of Houston voters—turning out in far fewer numbers than would vote two months later in the mayor's race—cast ballots against it. "It (the statewide result) would have been a real horse race if it had been held in conjunction with the Houston mayor's race," said University of Houston political scientist Richard Murray.[39]

Protecting Marriage Or Promoting Discrimination?

Texas became the eighteenth state to add a ban on same-sex marriage to its constitution when voters overwhelmingly approved Proposition 2 in 2005. The amendment had the strong support of Governor Rick Perry and many church leaders, who argued that it was necessary to guard against any legal challenges to an already existing state law that defined marriage as a union of one man and one woman. Opponents, however, contended the measure was unnecessary and, intentionally or not, promoted hostility toward homosexuals, a minority group.

"I'm not sure the right to desegregate schools, the freedom to marry another race or even access to contraception in many states would exist if those issues were put up for a vote," said Matt Foreman, executive director of the National Gay and Lesbian Task Force.

But Garrett Booth, pastor of Grace Community Church in Clear Lake and a supporter of the amendment, had a different viewpoint.

"It's important we do not sit idly by and let an extreme minority set aside what God has set in place. We are living in a day when the things that you and I hold precious are being redefined," Booth said. The proposition, one of nine amendments on the ballot, was approved by a three-to-one margin.[40]

Tackling another controversial issue, voters overwhelmingly approved a constitutional amendment in 2005 to ban same-sex marriages in Texas (see "Protecting Marriage or Promoting Discrimination?"). In 2007, voters—encouraged by Governor Rick Perry and cycling champion Lance Armstrong, a cancer survivor—approved $3 billion in bonds to boost state funding for cancer research.

Constitutional Provisions, Interest Groups, and Elites

Only a small percentage of registered voters—often less than 10 percent—participate in elections when constitutional amendments are the only issues on the ballot (Table 2–4). When amendments are submitted to the voters along with gubernatorial or presidential elections, the turnout is much higher. But in many instances, a relative handful of Texans ultimately decide on fundamental changes in government, which enhances their influence over the constitutional revision process.

Interest groups, which historically have been strong in Texas, work diligently to protect their concerns and objectives. They develop strategies to get provisions into the constitution that would benefit them or to keep provisions out that they fear would hurt

TABLE 2–4   Turnout for Constitutional Amendment Elections, 1970–2009

Type of Election	Number of Elections	Percent of Registered Voters	Percent of Voting Age Population
Special*	18	12.5	8.5
General (Gubernatorial)	10	42.7	28.2
General (Presidential)	10	62.8	45.3

*Only constitutional amendments on the ballot.
Source: Texas Secretary of State, Elections Division.

them. Because most amendments represent nonpartisan issues, a well-financed public relations campaign is likely to produce public support for an amendment.[41]

Interest groups are able to kill many proposed constitutional changes in the legislature, where the two-thirds vote requirement works to their advantage. Only a small fraction of constitutional amendments proposed by legislators get put on the ballot. The amendments that are put on the ballot usually have the support of one or more special interest groups, which often finance publicity campaigns to promote the propositions to the voters. Few amendments attract organized opposition after being put on the ballot, but there have been exceptions. In 2003, doctors, insurance companies, and business interests heavily promoted Proposition 12, the ratification of new medical malpractice limits. They were successful, despite a media campaign against the amendment financed primarily by plaintiffs' lawyers.

Many recent constitutional changes have reflected a pro-industry and economic development push that contrasts sharply with the antibusiness sentiment of the original constitutional framers. Recent amendments also have helped build up a public-bonded indebtedness that the nineteenth-century writers would have been unable to comprehend. Texas was rural then. It is now the country's second most populous state, is largely urban, and is working to diversify and expand its economy as well as provide the infrastructure required to support the large increases in population. Business has repeatedly turned to state government for tax breaks and other economic incentives and has found receptive ears in the legislature and the governor's office.

Nine of the record twenty-five amendments on the November 1987 ballot were actively promoted as an economic development package by the Build Texas Committee, a bipartisan group of business and civic leaders. Voters approved most of the amendments, including bonds for new water projects and prisons.

Industry, with the unusual support of organized labor and environmental groups, won a major tax break through a constitutional amendment approved by Texas voters in November 1993. It requires local governments to grant property-tax exemptions for expensive pollution-control equipment that businesses are required by state or federal law to install in their plants and other facilities. The business community supported the amendment because it represented untold millions in potential tax savings. Labor supported it because money not spent on taxes could mean more money spent on jobs. And environmentalists viewed it as an antipollution measure. Some local officials were fearful of the potential loss of huge amounts of revenue to counties, school districts, and other local governments, but they were clearly overpowered. Sometimes, however, relief can turn into heartburn, as it did in 2001 when lawmakers and Texas voters accidentally put a new tax law into the constitution when they thought they were repealing one.

It has been argued that the Texas Constitution serves the interests of a small number of elites—those individuals who control businesses and other dominant institutions in the state. This argument suggests that the severe constraints built into the constitution limit the policy options of state government and have historically thwarted the efforts of public interest groups to restructure or improve the tax system, education, social services, health care, and other policies that would benefit low- and middle-income Texans. Power is so fragmented that these groups have had to turn to the courts to force change. This same argument, incidentally, has often been made about the U.S. Constitution.

If this interpretation is accurate, it is ironic that those who framed the Texas Constitution of 1876 directed much of their wrath against railroads, banks, and other institutions that are today considered elitist. The tumultuous last quarter of the nineteenth century witnessed high levels of class and economic conflict with the emergence of the

Greenback and the Populist political parties, which articulated the interests of the lower income groups. But moneyed business interests eventually were able to use the state constitution and subsequent legislation to reestablish their dominance over Texas government. Although the elite structure of the state has changed since 1876, some scholars argue that there has been a gradual transfer of power and control to new elites, who continue to exercise enormous influence over public policy.

Change Through Court Interpretation

Some evidence indicates that Texas courts are now prepared to play a more expansive role in interpreting the constitution and, in turn, effect major changes in state policy. The best-known example is the Edgewood school finance case, in which the courts invalidated the system of funding public education and ordered the legislature to provide more equity in tax resources among the state's 1,000-plus school districts. Wide disparities in spending on students between rich and poor districts—the result of wide disparities in local property values—violated the state constitution's requirement for an "efficient" system of public schools, the Texas Supreme Court ruled.

Prospects for Future Change

Experts can point out the many flaws of the Texas Constitution, but attempts at wholesale revision have not been successful. Numerous piecemeal changes have been made, but they have not addressed the fundamental criticisms of the charter. What is to be made of all this?

First, Texas has a long history of suspicion of government, and this tradition continues. Most people fear governmental abuses and excesses more than they worry about government's inability to respond quickly and efficiently to the needs of its citizens. In the vernacular of the layperson, "If it ain't broke, don't fix it." And it is not clear that the layperson regards the constitution to be "broke." Moreover, if something needs fixing, it can be done by tinkering through constitutional amendments. Also, many groups and interests which have learned how to use the amendment process to advance their priorities benefit from the existing constitution, and they have demonstrated a collective resolve to minimize change. Finally, most Texans, as demonstrated by their participation in special constitutional elections, give little thought to changing the constitution because they are ill prepared to deal with the complexities of the document. Enormous problems must be overcome if citizens are to be educated and motivated to press for constitutional revision. It takes a statewide effort by reform advocates to mobilize the political resources and develop a successful strategy to produce an overhaul of a state constitution.[42]

SUMMARY AND CONCLUSIONS ────────────────●

1. In addition to defining the formal institutional structure of governments, constitutions reflect the primary values and political objectives of a state. A constitution defines the relationships between those who govern and the general population and ultimately structures political power. A constitution limits the power and authority of government and provides basic protection for the citizen from excesses and abuses of those who hold power.

2. A constitution should spell out broad powers and general principles and leave it to the legislature and state agencies to fill in the details with statutory laws and regulations.

3. Texas, like most other states, has functioned under a series of constitutions. Each is appropriately

understood from the perspective of the period in which it was adopted.

4. Texas currently operates under a constitution that was adopted following the Civil War and the Radical Reconstruction era. Events of that period left an enduring legacy of suspicion of government, limited government, and fragmented governmental institutions. The 1876 Constitution was predicated on the theory that governmental excesses could be minimized by carefully defining what governments could or could not do.

5. The framers failed to anticipate that the limitations they imposed on governmental institutions would ultimately allow major economic interests within the state to dominate the policymaking process, often to the detriment of the lower socioeconomic groups.

6. What the delegates to the Constitutional Convention of 1875 regarded as the strengths of the constitution—fragmented authority, detailed limitations on the power of governmental institutions, and decentralization—have served to limit the ability of state and local governments to adapt effectively to economic and demographic changes. The perceived solutions to many of the problems of 1875 have compounded the problems of state and local governments in the 2000s.

7. Efforts to overhaul the Texas Constitution have failed. Consequently, the state has been forced to amend the document continually on a piecemeal basis. This process has produced some success in modernizing the charter, but many structural problems of state government require major institutional changes that cannot be resolved through this amendment process.

8. In many ways, the Texas Constitution reflects the values of the state's conservative political culture, which continues to be suspicious of far-reaching constitutional changes. Moreover, constitutions and the debates that surround them are complex, and most people pay little attention to these issues. Consequently, it is much easier to mobilize public opinion against rather than for wholesale change.

9. Over the years, numerous groups have attempted to protect their interests through constitutional amendments. But the same groups usually oppose any proposed changes that threaten their influence, power, or benefits. Consequently, the interests of small segments of the state's population often prevail over the interests of the majority.

KEY TERMS

Edmund J. Davis 35
Radical Reconstructionists 36
Constitution 36
Statutory law 37
Unicameral 38
Unitary system 39
Federalism 39

Bicameral 40
Confederacy 43
Grange 47
Popular sovereignty 48
Social contract 48
Limited government 48
Separation of powers 48

Initiative 53
Referendum 53
Constitutional convention
of 1974 54
Right-to-work law 54

FURTHER READING

Articles

Bruff, Harold H., "Separation of Powers under the Texas Constitution," *Texas Law Review* 68 (June 1990), pp. 1337–67.

Harrington, James C., "Free Speech, Press, and Assembly Liberties under the Texas Bill of Rights," *Texas Law Review* 68 (June 1990), pp. 1435–67.

Hirczy, Wolfgan, "Texas Equal Rights Amendment: Twenty Years and a Few Surprises Later," *Texas Journal of Political Studies* 16 (Fall 1993), pp. 22–46.

Keyser, David R., "State Constitutions and Theories of Judicial Review: Some Variations on a Theme," *Texas Law Review* 63 (March–April 1985), pp. 1051–80.

Lutz, Donald S., "The Purposes of American State Constitutions," *Publius: The Journal of Federalism* 12 (Winter 1982), pp. 27–44.

Maltz, Earl M., "The Dark Side of State Court Activism," *Texas Law Review* 63 (March–April 1985), pp. 995–1023.

Mauer, John Walker, "State Constitutions in a Time of Crisis: The Case of the Texas Constitution of 1876," *Texas Law Review* 68 (June 1990), pp. 1615–47.

Nice, David C., "Interest Groups and State Constitutions: Another Look," *State & Local Government Review* 20 (Winter 1988), pp. 21–7.

Parker, Allan E., "Public Free Schools: A Constitutional Right to Educational Choice in Texas," *Southwestern Law Journal* 45 (Fall 1991), pp. 825–976.

Watts, Mikal, and Brad Rockwell, "The Original Intent of the Educational Article of the Texas Constitution," *St. Mary's Law Journal* 21 (1990), pp. 771–821.

Books

Braden, George D., et al., *The Constitution of the State of Texas: An Annotated and Comparative Analysis.* 2 vols. Austin, TX: Texas Advisory Commission on Intergovernmental Relations, 1977.

Braden, George D., *Citizens' Guide to the Texas Constitution.* Austin: Texas Advisory Commission on Intergovernmental Relations and the Institute for Urban Studies, University of Houston, 1972.

Cnudde, Charles F., and Robert E. Crew, Jr., *Constitutional Democracy in Texas.* St. Paul, MN: West Publishing Company, 1989.

Dinan, John J., *The American State Constitutional Tradition.* Lawrence, KS: University Press of Kansas, 2006.

Gardner, James A., *Interpreting State Constitutions.* Chicago, IL: The University of Chicago Press, 2005.

Lutz, Donald S., *Principles of Constitutional Design.* New York: Cambridge University Press, 2006.

May, Janice C., *The Texas Constitution Revision Experience in the 70s.* Austin, TX: Sterling Swift, 1975.

_____, *The Texas State Constitution: A Reference Guide.* Westport, CN.: Greenwood Press, 1996.

McKay, Seth Shepard, *Debates in the Texas Constitutional Convention of 1875.* Austin, TX: University of Texas Press, 1930.

_____, *Seven Decades of the Texas Constitution of 1876.* Lubbock, TX: Texas Tech College, 1943.

Texas Legislative Council, *Amendments to the Texas Constitution Since 1876.* Austin, TX: Texas Legislative Council, 2008.

Tarr, G. Alan, *Constitutional Politics in the States.* Westport, CN: Greenwood Press, 1996.

Tarr, G. Alan, *Understanding State Constitutions.* Princeton, NJ: Princeton University Press, 1998.

Wolff, Nelson, *Challenge of Change.* San Antonio, TX: The Naylor Co., 1975.

Websites

Texas Legislature on Line   http://www.legis.state.tx.us/ The entire text of the Texas Constitution can be downloaded from this site (see Search). It also provides an index to the constitution and allows the text of the constitution to be searched using key words. The site also provides access to legislative resolutions providing for constitutional amendments as well as legislative histories of these resolutions.

Secretary of State   http://www.sos.state.tx.us/ This office is responsible for compiling state election returns, including constitutional amendments. County-level returns for constitutional amendments since 1993 can be accessed from this site.

League of Women Voters   http://www.lwvtexas.org/ The Texas League of Women Voters is a nonpartisan organization committed to increasing political participation, improving state and local government, and increasing public understanding of major policy issues. When constitutional amendments are submitted to voters, the league usually publishes information about the purpose and effects of the amendments.

Cornell University Law   http://www.law.cornell.edu/statutes.html. If you are interested in the constitutions of other states, this is one of several sites that provide you access to these documents.

ENDNOTES

1. James Madison, "Federalist 51," in *The Federalist Papers,* by Alexander Hamilton, James Madison, and John Jay with an introduction by Clinton Rossiter (New York: New American Library, 1962), p. 322.

2. G. Allan Tarr, *Understanding State Constitutions* (Princeton, NJ: Princeton University Press, 1998), p. 3.

3. Daniel Elazar, "The Principles and Traditions Underlying American State Constitutions," *Publius: The Journal of Federalism* 12 (Winter 1982), p. 23.

4. Tarr, pp. 4–5.

5. Donald S. Lutz, "The Purposes of American State Constitutions," *Publius: The Jounalism of Federalism* 12 (Winter 1982), pp. 31–36.

6. David Saffell, *State Politics* (Reading, MA: Addison-Wesley, 1984), pp. 23–24.

7. Tarr, pp. 6–11.

8. Elazar, pp. 20–21.

9. T. R. Fehrenbach, *Lone Star: A History of Texas and Texans* (New York: Macmillan, 1968), pp. 152–73.

10. Richard Gambitta, Robert A. Milne, and Carol R. Davis, "The Politics of Unequal Educational Opportunity," in *The Politics of San Antonio,* edited by David R. Johnson, John A. Booth, and Richard J. Harris (Lincoln, NE: University of Nebraska Press, 1983), p. 135.

11. Joe B. Frantz, *Texas: A Bicentennial History* (New York: W.W. Norton, 1976), p. 73.

12. Ibid., p. 76.

13. Fehrenbach, *Lone Star,* p. 265.

14. Frantz, *Texas,* p. 92.

15. Fehrenbach, *Lone Star,* p. 396.

16. Ibid., pp. 398–99.

17. Ibid., p. 401.

18. Ibid., p. 429.

19. J. E. Ericson, "The Delegates to the Convention of 1875: A Reappraisal," *Southwestern Historical Quarterly* 67 (July 1963), p. 22.

20. Ibid., p. 23.

21. Ibid.

22. Ibid., pp. 25–26.

23. Fehrenbach, *Lone Star,* pp. 374, 431, 434.

24. Ericson, "The Delegates to the Convention of 1875: A Reappraisal," pp. 24–25.

25. Fehrenbach, *Lone Star,* p. 435.

26. *Texas Constitution,* Art. 1, Sec. 2 and 3.

27. See James Madison, "Federalist 10," in *The Federalist Papers,* by Alexander Hamilton, James Madison, and John Jay with an introduction by Clinton Rossiter (New York: New American Library, 1962), p. 77.

28. Janice May, "Constitutional Revision in Texas," in *The Texas Constitution: Problems and Prospects for Revision* (Arlington, TX: Texas Urban Development Commission, 1971), p. 82.

29. Ibid.

30. *Houston Chronicle,* November 6, 1995.

31. David Berman, *State and Local Politics,* 6th ed. (Dubuque, IA: Wm. C. Brown, 1991), p. 61.

32. May, "Constitutional Revision in Texas," p. 76.

33. John E. Bebout, "The Problem of the Texas Constitution," in *The Texas Constitution: Problems and Prospect for Revision,* p. 9.

34. Ibid., p. 11.

35. *Houston Chronicle,* January 8, 1974.

36. Nelson Wolff, *Challenge of Change* (San Antonio, TX: Naylor, 1975), pp. 45–46.

37. Bebout, "The Problem of the Texas Constitution," pp. 45–46.

38. *Houston Chronicle,* October 15, 1975.

39. *Houston Chronicle,* September 16, 2003, p. 13A.

40. *Houston Chronicle,* November 7, 2005, p. B1; and *Houston Chronicle,* November 9, 2005, p. A1.

41. Lewis A. Froman, Jr., "Some Effects of Interest Group Strength in State Politics," *American Political Science Review* 60 (December 1966), pp. 952–63.

42. See Tarr, *Understanding State Constitutions* for an extensive discussion of the distinctive features of state constitutions, state constitutions within the federal context, and an analysis of state constitutional development.

CHAPTER 3

Intergovernmental Relationships

Questions to Guide Your Reading

1. What explanations can you offer for the increased role of the national government in the federal system?

2. In recent years, a number of presidents have talked about the devolution or return of significant powers and responsibilities to the states. What are the obstacles to devolution?

3. What is the role of Texas and its local governments in the formulation and implementation of policies enacted by the national government?

4. Will increased trade between Texas, the United States, and Mexico stimulate sufficient economic development in Mexico to reduce illegal immigration?

*In the compound republic of America, the power surrendered by the people
is first divided between two distinct governments, and then the portion
allotted to each sub-divided among distinct and separate departments.*

—**James Madison**[1]

*American federalism was born in ambiguity, it institutionalizes ambiguity
in our form of government, and changes in it tend to be ambiguous too.*

—**Martha Derthick**[2]

Texans, like most American citizens, are subject to the authority of an array of governments. If you live in a large metropolitan area in Texas, you may be under the jurisdiction of as many as ten or more different governments or taxing authorities. A person living within the corporate limits of San Antonio is subject to the laws, regulations, and taxes of the federal government, the state of Texas, Bexar County, the city of San Antonio, the Alamo Community College District, one of sixteen independent school districts, the Edwards Aquifer Authority, the San Antonio River Authority, the Bexar County Hospital District, and a public transportation authority.

There are more than 89,000 governmental units in the United States, with approximately 500,000 persons serving on their governing bodies. According to a 2007 census of governments (Table 3–1), Texas had 4,836 individual governments, including 254 counties, 1,209 municipalities, and 3,372 school districts and other special districts. What's more, the total number of governments in Texas increased by some 1,400 between 1967 and 2007. Most of the additional ones were special districts.

The jurisdictional structure of governments in this country is complex and confusing, and people are often frustrated when they try to identify the government that has the authority or responsibility to address one of their specific needs or concerns. Governments in the United States share many responsibilities, and it is quite possible for individuals to find themselves enmeshed in jurisdictional disputes between agencies of different governments.

From our very beginnings, Americans have been leery of highly centralized government.[3] So these diverse and complex jurisdictional arrangements were created to limit government, especially the federal government. Moreover, the enormous size of

TABLE 3–1   Governments in the United States and Texas, 2007

	U.S.	Texas
U.S. Government	1	—
State Government	50	1
Counties	3,033	254
Municipalities	19,492	1,209
Townships and Towns	16,519	—
School Districts	13,051	1,081
Special Districts	37,381	2,291
Total	89,527	4,836

Source: U.S. Department of Commerce, Bureau of the Census, *2007 Census of Governments, Government Organizations,* vol. 1, Table 3.

the country and the great distances between settlements during the nation's formative period made it extremely difficult for a centralized government at either the national or state level to serve and control political subdivisions. This contributed to the proliferation of smaller governmental units. Regional differences in religion, economics, and political cultures also encouraged decentralization and the development of local governments.

STRUCTURING REGIONAL AND NATIONAL INTERESTS

Governments around the world are struggling to find ways to coordinate local and regional interests with national interests. The former Soviet bloc, for example, has struggled with institutional arrangements to integrate diverse racial, cultural, and ethnic groups within a single political system. Canada, which already has a stable political system, continues to seek political and institutional solutions to the movement for French separatism. In the effort to rebuild Iraq, there is extensive debate over the geographical distribution of power and authority among the Sunnis, Shiites, Arabs, and Kurds. Many similar issues confronted the constitutional framers during the United States' formative period, and their solution was to structure federal–state relationships on the federal principle.

There are three fundamental systems—unitary, confederal, and federal—used in structuring the relationship of a central government to its constituent parts. Over the history of our nation, all three organizational principles have been used at one time or the other.

In some countries, democratic as well as authoritarian, ultimate power is vested in a national or central government. Under such a **unitary system,** local or regional governments are created by the national government, have only the power and authority granted to them by the national government, and serve "only to implement policies established by the national government."[4]

A **confederation** is based on the principle that each component government is sovereign in its own right, and the powers of the national government are limited to those powers delegated to it by the member governments. The United States experimented with a confederal system prior to the adoption of the present Constitution in 1789, and the southern states used the confederal principle during the Civil War. There are inherent weaknesses in such a system, including the ability of member governments to nullify the acts of the national government and withdraw from the relationship. Citizenship in and loyalty to the component governments precede citizenship in and loyalty to the central government.

Delegates to the U.S. Constitutional Convention of 1787 rejected the confederal principle in favor of **federalism**, which balances the power and sovereignty of the state governments with that of the national government. Both the states and the national government derive their authority directly from the people, and the states have considerable latitude and autonomy within their areas of defined power and responsibility. In many respects, federalism is a middle ground between a confederal system and a unitary system of government.

The unitary principle, however, is the basis for the relationship between state and local governments under the Texas Constitution and state laws (see Chapter 12). Counties, cities, and special districts have only those powers granted to them by the state. There is no such thing as the sovereignty of local government in Texas. Local governments are primarily administrative subdivisions of the state. The prevailing constitutional theory regarding local governments in the United States, which has been incorporated into Texas law, was articulated in the **Dillon rule,** which held that if a state could create local governments, it could also destroy or eliminate them.[5] Political and practical considerations, however, usually preclude the elimination of local governments.

DEFINING FEDERALISM

Although the U.S. Constitution outlines federalism in broad terms, it does not clearly specify the governmental relationships that should be established. For more than 200 years, scholars, politicians, judges, and bureaucrats not only have been debating the complexities of the federal system, they also have been trying to figure out how to define federalism.[6] One scholar has identified 267 definitions and concepts relating to the term.[7] The problem is compounded by the fact that the relationships among federal, state, and local governments have changed over the past two centuries. And, these relationships continue to change.

If scholars cannot agree on a definition of federalism and the current elements of these complex governmental relationships, how is the student to understand contemporary federalism? First, it is important to assess federalism over time. There are periods in our political history when the pendulum of power shifted from the states to the national government. At other points, there was a decentralizing tendency in federal–state relationships. Our discussion attempts to provide a broad overview of these historical patterns.

As we assess broad historical periods, there is a tendency to over-generalize and to simplify. In any given period, the three branches of the federal government do not speak with a unified voice on federal issues. A Congress and the president may pursue policies that centralize power in Washington; the federal judiciary may pursue a different course of action through its decisions in cases involving federal issues. Moreover, different subunits within the executive and congressional branches of the national government may pursue different courses on federal–state relationships.

Finally, the policy process relating to federalism is so complex with so many different actors that it is often difficult to measure the exact impact of the national government's actions on the states. The complex "policy networks" discussed later involve many participants, including elected officials, administrators, political parties, interest groups, and private organizations. In some policy arenas, there is a tendency for centralization of public goods and services. In others, participants favor decentralization.[8]

Federal–State Relationships from a Constitutional Perspective

We tend to think of federalism as a division of power between the states and the national government, and we look to the U.S. Constitution to specify the powers and responsibilities of each. However, the Constitution is vague on these points, and "all efforts to define the distribution of authority among governments have been unsuccessful."[9] The structure and operation of our federal system of government confuse many individuals. It is a system of many shared functions and responsibilities that often make it difficult to identify a single person or institution as having the ultimate responsibility for addressing a specific issue or problem.

Ambiguous constitutional provisions have helped produce jurisdictional conflicts throughout the nation's history. We even fought a war among ourselves to determine what were the powers and authority of the states and national government. Although the Civil War resolved the issue that a state could not withdraw from the federal union, a large number of other questions continue to be debated. These ambiguities and changes in political and economic conditions make the relationships among governments subject to further change in the future. Over the past three decades, there has been a lot of debate at all levels of government over **devolution**, or the return of power to the states. But any action has been put on hold, in large part because of the responses to the terrorist attacks on the Pentagon and the World Trade Center in 2001 and more recently, the deep recession that began in 2008.

The enumerated or **delegated powers**, of the national government are outlined primarily in Article 1, Section 8, of the U.S. Constitution. They include the powers to tax, to borrow and coin money, to declare war, and to regulate interstate and foreign commerce.

The first seventeen paragraphs of Section 8 are rather specific, apparently because the constitutional framers, apprehensive about potential abuses, intended to limit the powers of the national government. But they did not close the door to unforeseen events. In paragraph 18 of Section 8, they further provided that Congress shall have the power "to make all Laws which shall be necessary and proper for carrying into Execution the foregoing Powers."[10] This provision is the **implied powers** clause, which has been used to justify the subsequent expansion of the federal government's powers.

To further compound the jurisdictional question, Article 6 states that the U.S. Constitution and the laws made in pursuance "shall be the supreme Law of the Land."[11] This **supremacy clause** suggests that when a conflict develops between the powers of the states and the national government, the federal law prevails.

Although the Constitution does not spell out the authority of the states and their subdivisions in detail, the states have assumed a formidable array of powers and responsibilities in domestic affairs. Most governmental actions affecting our daily lives are taken by state or local governments. The policy, regulatory, and taxing powers of the state affect us daily, and most litigation in the country takes place in state or local courts, not in federal courts.

The absence of specific constitutional language spelling out many powers of the state was of concern to many state governments. The Tenth Amendment, adopted in 1789 by Congress and ratified by the states in 1791, was intended to address these concerns. This clause states, "The powers not delegated to the United States by the Constitution, nor prohibited by it to the States, are reserved to the States respectively or to the people."[12]

In addition to these **reserved powers**, there are **concurrent powers** held by the states and the national government. Both have the power to raise taxes, develop and implement public policies, spend money, borrow money, and establish their own court systems.

There also are certain constitutional guarantees to the states. Texas is assured a republican form of government, protection against invasion and domestic violence, and the power to maintain a militia. If a person is accused of a federal crime in Texas, the trial is to be held in Texas. Texas cannot be divided into another state without its permission and is assured two members in the U.S. Senate and membership in the U.S. House of Representatives based on its population in relation to the other states. After the 1990 census, Texas had thirty members of the U.S. House but gained two seats after the 2000 census. The state also has a role in ratifying amendments to the U.S. Constitution and controls many aspects of federal elections.[13]

Reflecting its drafters' concerns about governmental excesses, the Constitution also limits the powers of both the states and the national government. These prohibitions, or **denied powers**, are interspersed throughout the document and are enumerated, in particular, in the first ten amendments—the Bill of Rights. The original intent of the Bill of Rights was to limit the powers of the national government. But since the Civil War, the federal courts have gradually incorporated the Bill of Rights into the Fourteenth Amendment, which was intended to restrict the powers of the state governments. This expansion of the Bill of Rights to the states has been described by some as the nationalization of the Bill of Rights.

The broad and often ambiguous language of the U.S. Constitution lends itself to controversy and interpretation, and over the years, Congress, the states, and the courts have attempted to resolve conflicts over powers and jurisdiction. In many instances, the Supreme Court has played an instrumental role in redefining the relationship between the states and the federal government.

Relationships among the States

The federal system is not limited to the relationship between the states and the national government (vertical federalism). It also includes the relationship of the states to each other (horizontal federalism). Many of these constitutional–legal obligations were included in the Articles of Confederation, which established the first system of national government in the United States. Conflict as well as cooperation among the states during that period provided the rationale for defining the obligations and responsibilities of the states to each other.

The Constitution states, "Full Faith and Credit shall be given in each State to the public Acts, Records, and judicial Proceedings of every other state."[14] To eliminate chaos and to stimulate cooperation, this **full faith and credit clause** assures that official governmental actions of one state are accepted by other states. A marriage of a heterosexual couple in Texas is recognized as legal in other states. So are business contracts. This also means that a person cannot flee to another state to avoid an adverse court judgment. But this obligation is not absolute, as demonstrated by the enactment of the federal Defense of Marriage Act (1996). This law, which denies federal recognition of marriages or civil unions between homosexuals, has allowed states to refuse to recognize civil unions of same-sex couples performed in other states. But the divisive issue is still unresolved.

By the summer of 2009, same-sex unions, domestic partnerships, or marriages had been legitimized in some form in fourteen states and Washington, D.C.[15] But given the constitutional language and application of the "full faith and credit" provision, what law is to be applied when same-sex couples move to states that do not recognize the legality of their unions? Can they obtain a divorce in those states? If there are children, how is custody determined? What law prevails over the separation of property? The U.S. Supreme Court eventually may be called upon to determine if congressional action in the Defense of Marriage Act or other legislation "trumps" a constitutional

Federalism Without Washington

In addition to interstate compacts, joint action among the states has included the enactment of uniform state laws, reciprocal or contingent legislation, and interstate administrative cooperation. These actions permit the states to work together in dealing with common issues or problems, such as water pollution, drug abuse, radioactive waste, economic development, and higher education.

And, it is believed that the use of these resources has been expanded. To achieve what Morton Grodzins, an authority on American federalism, termed "federalism without Washington," the states have organized a number of cooperative organizations, including the Council of State Governments and a variety of groups of state elected officials.[16]

provision or how this constitutional provision is to be reconciled with divergent state action.

As a person travels from one state to another, the Constitution entitles that person to the **privileges and immunities** of the states where he or she is going. A person can acquire property in another state, establish residency and eventually citizenship, and be assured of access to the legal system of that state. But there are certain exceptions that have been established by court interpretation. States, for example, can charge nonresidents higher college tuition or higher fees for hunting and fishing licenses.

The Constitution also provides for the return of a person accused of a crime. If a person who has been charged with manslaughter or another offense in Texas attempts to avoid trial by fleeing to Oklahoma, he or she can be returned to Texas by a process called **extradition**. States routinely handle hundreds of these cases each year. Once the accused has been located, the state seeking the individual will request that the second state arrest and return him. The governor is responsible for granting extradition requests.

Until fairly recently, governors used an 1861 court decision to maintain that they had the discretion to refuse another state's extradition request.[17] This was the prevailing view for 125 years, until Puerto Rico challenged the discretionary powers of the governor in a 1987 case.[18] The Supreme Court held that the "duty to extradite is mandatory, and the federal courts are available to enforce that duty."[19]

The Constitution writers also anticipated the need for structuring more formal, long-term, cooperative relationships among the states. Article I, Section 10 allows the states, with the approval of Congress, to enter into **interstate compacts**. There are more than 100 of these, some affecting only two states, whereas others include all fifty states. Texas now belongs to several interstate compacts, including the Interstate Oil and Gas Compact, the Interstate Mining Compact, and the Low Level Radioactive Waste Compact.

Although cooperation is desired, states often find themselves involved in disagreements that only lawsuits can resolve (see "Get Off Our Land, You Varmints!"). Boundary disputes, control or use of water resources, and licensing fees that affect interstate shipping are among issues that are litigated in the federal judiciary, where the Supreme Court has original jurisdiction in all "controversies between two or more states."[20]

Get Off Our Land, You Varmints!

During the contentious 2003 sessions of the Texas legislature, one had to look for humor wherever it could be found. For a few days, the atmosphere at the capitol in Austin was provided limited relief with news that a New Mexico legislator had filed a bill in that state's senate to recover some 603,485 acres—a three-mile strip along the Texas–New Mexico border—which had been wrongly assigned to Texas in 1859 as a result of a surveyor's error. For whatever reason, the issue periodically has been resurrected over the years by New Mexican officials.

No one in Texas expected the latest claim to go anywhere, and it didn't. But as the issue churned around in the corridors of the New Mexico legislature and the newsrooms of state papers, an element of absurdity emerged. New Mexico papers began to pick up on the potential humor and demanded that Texans vacate the disputed area. An *Albuquerque Tribune* headline ordered: "Waltz off our land, you Texas varmints."

About the same time, Texas Land Commissioner Jerry Patterson challenged his New Mexican counterpart, Patrick H. Lyons, to a duel. According to one account —the information is quite sketchy— the duel took place in early 2004 in Austin. The weapons of choice were vintage flintlocks. We don't know if shots were fired, but both officials claimed the honor of their respective states had been served.[21]

GENERALIZED VIEWS OF FEDERALISM

The constitutional–legal descriptions of federalism outlined above can leave one with the idea that the federal, state, and local levels of government are autonomous and function independently, a view often linked to dual federalism. Morton Grodzins, an authority on federalism, has argued that this perspective, which is now inaccurate, was analogous to a "layer-cake" theory of intergovernmental relations.

Grodzins suggested that intergovernmental relations can be more accurately symbolized by a "marble cake." Rather than possessing distinct and separate powers and responsibilities, governments have shared responsibilities. In describing federalism, Grodzins wrote:

> Whenever you slice through it [marble cake] you reveal an inseparable mixture of differently colored ingredients. There is no neat horizontal stratification. Vertical and diagonal lines almost obliterate the horizontal ones, and in some places there are unexpected whirls and imperceptible merging of colors, so that it is difficult to tell where one ends and the other begins. So it is with federal, state, and local responsibilities in the chaotic marble cake of American Government.[22]

Public functions are not neatly divided among the different levels of government. In virtually every area of public policy, governments coordinate, collaborate, and cooperate to meet shared goals and objectives. This view reflects, in large measure, governmental relationships associated with **cooperative federalism**, which we discuss later in this chapter.

A third metaphor, the "picket-fence" theory of federalism, builds on Grodzins's notions of shared powers and responsibilities but focuses on specific policy arenas that cut across each level of government. This metaphor suggests that we look at a specific policy arena (e.g., highways, education, or welfare), identify the primary participants at each level of government, and map out their patterns of interaction. While the concept is an oversimplification, it does suggest complex institutional and political relationships that cut across all levels of government.[23]

As might be expected, the complexity of federalism has generated much discussion about how to best describe and assess the relationships among governments. The problem, of course, is compounded by the fact that governmental relationships are shaped by changes in the political parties, presidents, the composition of Congress, the courts, prevailing economic and social conditions, and the public's expectations of their governments.

CHANGING PATTERNS IN FEDERAL RELATIONSHIPS

Federal relationships have changed over the nation's history, generating some of the confusion in reaching conclusive descriptions and definitions of federalism. We can assess broad patterns of federal–state relationships by historical periods, although relationship patterns don't start or stop in specific years but can continue over multiple eras. Various scholars have developed different classifications, but there has been a general pattern of increased centralization and federal authority.

State-Centered and Dual Federalism

In both theory and practice, federal relationships from 1790 to the 1930s usually are defined in terms of dual federalism. During the early decades of our political history, the primary responsibility for domestic policy fell to the states and local governments with very little involvement or intervention by the federal government. Yet, there were domestic policies that generated conflict, and both the national and state governments were continually engaged in legal and policy issues that attempted to define the lines of demarcation between their respective powers. There was a continued saga of "sorting out roles and specifying clear boundaries."[24] Conflicts usually were resolved through court cases and statutory laws, but the federal–state issues centering on slavery erupted into the Civil War. The dual federalism of this era was marked by adversarial, if not antagonistic, relationships at various levels of government.

One of the first instances when the U.S. Supreme Court addressed the issue of state–federal relationships was in 1819 in the case of *McCulloch v. Maryland*.[25] The state of Maryland had levied a tax on the Baltimore branch of the Bank of the United States. McCulloch, the bank's cashier, refused to pay the tax, thus precipitating a lawsuit. The case raised a fundamental issue regarding federalism. Did the national government have the power to create a bank that, in fact, would compete with state banks? The Supreme Court, then headed by Chief Justice John Marshall, an advocate of central power, ruled that the implied powers clause of the Constitution, linked to the delegated or enumerated powers, gave the federal government this authority.

A second issue was whether a state could tax the branch bank, an institution of the national government. The court again ruled in favor of the U.S. government. It held that the states do not have the power to tax the national government because, if this were to be permitted, the states could destroy national institutions, and federal laws would be subordinate to those of the states, thus undermining the supremacy clause of the Constitution.

Hundreds of federal–state issues have been litigated in the federal courts since McCulloch, and those cases making it to the Supreme Court demonstrate the role of the court to arbitrate disputes between state and federal authority.[26] Along with political and economic changes, these cases have been central to redefining federal–state relationships over the past 200 years, although the principles outlined in McCulloch remain intact.

Cooperative Federalism

The economic hardships produced by the Great Depression of the 1930s resulted in demands for a greater role of the federal government in domestic policy. States and cities simply were unable to provide many basic services or address the personal needs of large numbers of people who were unemployed. The states did not have the economic resources to deal with problems that extended beyond their borders, and many lacked the political or institutional will to implement new policies. Moreover, the increased economic interdependency of the states and the national scope of economic problems were compelling arguments for federal intervention. Although there were precedents for greater federal–state cooperation prior to the 1930s, the New Deal expanded dramatically the role of the federal government in relation to the states and local governments.[27]

V. O. Key, who wrote extensively on state government, summarized the extent of these changes:

> The federal government underwent a radical transformation after ... 1932. It had been a remote authority with a limited range of activity. It operated the postal system, improved rivers and harbors, maintained armed forces on a scale fearsome only to banana republics, and performed other functions of which the average citizen was hardly aware. Within a brief time, it became an institution that affected intimately the lives and fortunes of most, if not all, citizens.[28]

Those supporting the development of cooperative federalism rejected the notion of dual federalism, where each level of government had virtual or exclusive authority in select areas of domestic policy. The commerce and the supremacy clauses of the Constitution were used to support an expanded role of the federal government. Many of the new programs engaged local, state, and federal policymakers in cooperative efforts—from program development to program implementation. Cooperative federalism assures that all three levels of government share the responsibility for domestic programs "by making the larger governments primarily responsible for raising revenues and setting standards and the smaller ones primarily responsible for administering the programs."[29] Another way to conceptualize this relationship is Deil Wright's concept of the "overlapping authority model," in which "the three levels have independent, interdependent, and overlapping authority with both cooperation and competition and a large degree of bargaining among the governments and levels involved."[30]

Over the past fifty years, the federal government has used various devices to shape and implement domestic programs, but the primary vehicle has been the provision of federal funds for public programs through **categorical grants-in-aid**. There are more than 400 of these grant programs, through which approximately 80 percent of federal aid to states and local governments is allocated. Money allocated under a specific program can be spent only for that purpose or category. Federal laws also include specific standards or requirements that recipients must meet, such as prohibitions against racial or sex discrimination or prohibitions against nonunion pay scales.

There are two types of categorical grants. The first is the **project grant**, which requires a state or local government to apply for a grant to the appropriate federal agency and compete against other state or local governments for the funds. The money is awarded on the merits of an application. The second type of categorical grant is the **formula grant**. As the name implies, federal funds are allocated to states and local governments on the basis of a prescribed formula. These formulas vary from program to program, but might include income or poverty levels of a state's residents or its population figures. Congress determines the formulas for specific programs, and the federal dollars are then distributed on the basis of the statutory criteria. Many of these federal grants require **matching funds** from the governments that receive the money. The percentage of costs borne by the federal government varies from program to program, with the state or local governments picking up the balance. One reason for requiring such matches is to encourage state and local governments to have a strong commitment to the funded program and its policy objectives.

In 2008, the federal government spent $461 billion on these grants and was projected to spend $568 billion in 2009 and $652 billion in 2010. These increases, largely due to the 2009 Recovery Act, were designed to stimulate the nation's economy.[31]

Centralized Federalism

The domestic programs initiated by President John F. Kennedy (1961–1963) and subsequently expanded by President Lyndon B. Johnson in the Great Society programs resulted in a dramatic expansion of the federal government's role to virtually every area of domestic policy. The number of identifiable grant programs increased in eight years from 132 to 379; federal funding for grant programs more than tripled within ten years, and the federal share of state and local budgets increased from 17 percent in 1960 to 23 percent in 1970. Many of these programs targeted specific populations for assistance and were intended to redistribute resources primarily to lower income groups. Moreover, there were several federal programs that virtually bypassed state governments and went directly to local governments, thus eroding the legal relationship of local governments to the states.[32] Some scholars suggest that this massive extension of federal initiatives in domestic policy transformed cooperative federalism into coercive federalism or regulatory federalism, a relationship in which state power was subordinated to federal power in a wide range of policy arenas.[33]

The Multiple Phases of New Federalism

Organized opposition to cooperative federalism can be detected from its origins in the 1930s. As federalism was transformed to the more centralized programs of the 1960s during the Democratic administrations of Kennedy and Johnson, conservatives, who are often Republicans, intensified their criticism of this shift of power to the national government, and the Republican Party began to stake out what has become a rather consistent rhetorical theme of decentralization and devolution.

Opposition to the increased role of the national government in domestic policy is based on many factors. Some argue that the Constitution never provided for the expanded powers claimed by the national government. The new programs, coupled with mandates and preemptions, placed a heavy financial burden on states and local governments. Moreover, these policies often encouraged governments to pursue federal dollars even when funded programs were not their most pressing issues. The expansion of the federal bureaucracy was deemed to be directly related to the new programs.

Inefficiencies were built into the programs, and some were mismanaged. Finally, federal programs placed restrictions on how monies could be spent, and it was argued that no one size fit all of the local conditions or needs.

For the Republican Party, there was a subtle political issue. As grant programs had evolved, various groups and individuals—that is, stakeholders—developed vested interests in maintaining them. Members of Congress viewed many of these programs as "pork" for the folks back home, and administrators at all levels of government justified their jobs and their agencies' existence on the basis of these programs. Many of the constituencies that benefited from federal grants traditionally supported the Democratic Party, and if the Republican Party were to become the majority party, it would have to break up the implicit alliances built on federal funding of state and local programs.

The Nixon Years (1969–1974)

Republicans, beginning with President Richard Nixon (1969–1974), defined their views of federal–state relationships using the term "**new federalism**." In fact, there have been several iterations of "new federalism," reflecting the philosophical differences among Republican presidents. The details of presidential proposals varied, but the general objective was to return responsibilities for many domestic policies to the state and local governments. Presidential proposals were also based on a desire to reduce federal spending for many domestic programs and reduce the federal budget, a policy that had widespread appeal among many Republican constituents.

When Richard Nixon was elected president in 1968, he, like many other conservatives, criticized the expanded role of the federal government and advocated a reversion of program responsibilities to the states. Nixon argued that his "new federalism" was designed to "rationalize the intergovernmental system by restructuring the roles and responsibilities of governments at all levels."[34] At the same time, Nixon wanted to reduce the role of the federal government and largely decentralize federal programs. His strategy included four key components. He proposed management changes to expedite and coordinate the grant application process and the consolidation of many categorical grants into a few large **block grants**, which would give state and local governments greater discretion over the use of funds. He also proposed the replacement of many categorical grants with **revenue sharing** dollars, which could be used by the recipient government for virtually any purpose—with "no strings attached." Finally, Nixon advocated a restructuring of the nation's welfare system. He unsuccessfully proposed replacing Aid to Families with Dependent Children, the existing grant program, with the Family Assistance Plan, a federal income payment based on family size.[35]

After almost six years of program initiatives and changes that were supposed to increase state and local powers, policies enacted during Nixon's administration produced results that appeared to be just the opposite. Many believe that "Nixon left behind what was probably a more centralized federal system than the one he inherited."[36] Federal expenditures for many domestic programs had increased dramatically, and the regulatory powers of the federal government had been expanded.

The Ford (1974–1977) and Carter (1977–1981) Years

Nixon was followed by Presidents Gerald Ford (1974–1977) and Jimmy Carter (1977–1981). President Ford, who took over the White House after Nixon's humiliating resignation, also called for a greater balance between the national and state governments, and initiatives enacted during his administration were similar to that of his predecessor.

There was an extension of revenue sharing and two block grants—community development and manpower programs—during his short time in office.[37]

President Carter, a Democrat who had served as governor of Georgia, attempted to expand the federal role to assist local governments. His budgets reduced revenue sharing dollars to the states, and he attempted to redirect those funds to cities with several new policy initiatives. There was a great deal of planning and consultation with mayors and other local officials during his administration, but little of his urban program made its way through Congress.[38]

The Reagan (1981–1989) and Bush I (1989–1993) Years

President Ronald Reagan (1981–1989), a Republican who is often given credit for initiating what some call the "Reagan Revolution," also expressed a commitment to reducing federal programs—especially welfare programs—and the revitalization of the powers of state and local governments. Though he used some of the same tactics and resources as Nixon, he clearly had a different agenda. Reagan was particularly critical of welfare assistance, and beginning with his 1981 legislative agenda, he attempted to reduce federal support of social programs and eliminate categorical grants through their consolidation into block grants. In 1981, Reagan "convinced Congress to consolidate seventy-six categorical grant-in-aid programs and a block grant program into nine new or reconstituted block grants."[39] He also attempted to consolidate additional grant programs during subsequent congressional sessions, but had little success.

Reagan also opposed revenue sharing, which the federal government ended in 1986. The program was attacked for contributing to the federal budget deficit, funding governments that did not need the money, funding programs of questionable merit, and producing a reliance on revenue-sharing dollars for the operating budgets of many governments.

Reagan's effort to reduce federal funding of social services was particularly harsh on state and local governments, which had taken on many of the responsibilities for the administration of public assistance. One strategy initiated by the Reagan administration in 1982 was to turn back welfare (Aid to Families with Dependent Children) and the food stamp programs to the states in return for the federal government assuming responsibility for the Medicaid program, which provided health care for many low-income individuals. Although this proposal was rejected by Congress, Reagan (as well as his successor, George H. W. Bush) attempted on numerous occasions to return programs to state governments.[40]

Presidential and congressional rhetoric about reducing federal powers and returning authority to the states, however, often does not correspond to what actually takes place. During the Reagan and first Bush administrations, there was no restructuring of the federal system in the direction of dual federalism. Although some efforts were made, primarily through executive orders and administrative initiatives, to increase the discretionary powers of the states, the **mandates** and **preemptions** enacted by Congress as well as court decisions affecting federal relations during this period (1981–1993) worked against the transfer of power to the states. Moreover, some argue that Reagan's "New Federalism was a general philosophy favoring a smaller federal role but not necessarily a larger state and local role in the governance system."[41]

From 1789 to 2005, Congress enacted 535 laws preempting state or local authority. Some 368, or more than 65 percent, were enacted after 1965, a period in which Republicans dominated control of the presidency.[42] Only a limited number of laws during this period provided relief from federal preemptions.[43] Many preemptive restrictions were adopted with Reagan's approval and appear to reflect Reagan's commitment to marketplace economics and a reduced role for all government.[44]

Under constitutional law, statutory law, or federal regulations, the federal government also can require states or local governments "to undertake a specific activity or provide a service meeting minimum national standards."[45] Throughout the 1980s, while decentralization and return of power to the states were major themes of the Reagan and first Bush administrations, Congress enacted numerous statutes that imposed additional mandates and regulations on the states.[46] There is no question that the costs imposed by federal "mandates and restraints on state and local governments total in the billions of dollars and force these governments to divert funds from many worthy projects to finance the national policies."[47] According to data from the Congressional Budget Office, federal regulations adopted between 1983 and 1990 imposed cumulative estimated costs of between $8.9 billion and $12.7 billion on states and localities, depending on how mandates are defined. These costs increased at a pace faster than overall federal aid.[48] In 1994, the Texas Legislative Budget Board reported that increases in mandates and other federal programs had accounted for $13 billion, or 65 percent, of a $20 billion increase in the Texas budget since 1990–1991.[49] Moreover, mandates aren't limited to state and local governments. Private institutions, for example, are required to bring their facilities into compliance with the Americans with Disabilities Act. Both public and private hospitals with emergency rooms cannot turn away patients who are unable to pay for services. These requirements impose real costs for which there are no reimbursements.

President George H. W. Bush was perceived as sensitive to state and local problems during his administration (1989–1993), but the huge federal deficit and agreements to cap federal expenditures provided no prospects for additional financial assistance to the states. Congress, with his approval, continued to impose mandates that added to the financial burdens of states and cities while preempting more and more authority over programs from the states.[50] During Bush's administration, Congress passed the Americans with Disabilities Act in 1990. The act prohibits discrimination against persons with disabilities and requires governments to make extensive and costly changes in public facilities to accommodate disabled individuals.[51] During 1990, Congress also passed three other major pieces of legislation (the Clean Air Act Amendments, the Education of the Handicapped Act Amendments, and the Fiscal 1991 Budget Reconciliation Act), which imposed additional requirements on the states and local governments.

The Clinton (1993–2001) Years

Democrat Bill Clinton assumed the presidency in 1993 after serving six terms as governor of Arkansas, and many expected him to be more responsive to the impact of mandates and other issues facing the states. But, like his predecessor, Clinton failed to provide a coherent theory of federalism in the wide range of proposals he initially submitted to Congress. Under the leadership of Vice President Al Gore, Clinton's emphasis on "reinventing government" led to the elimination of some 400,000 positions in the federal bureaucracy and a similar reduction in the military. This led to a considerable increase in governmental contracting with private firms for services previously provided by government employees or the military. Clinton's policies reduced the size of the federal bureaucracy, but with the exception of welfare reforms, there was no significant devolution of powers to the states.[52]

    Committed to deficit reduction, Clinton and Congress left little leeway to provide financial relief or expand funding to states and local governments. The Motor Voter Bill (i.e., National Voter Registration Act) enacted in 1993 encouraged the registration of more voters but also expanded federal authority in state elections. The Family and Medical Leave Act, enacted the same year, requires firms with fifty or more employees and state and local governments to provide up to twelve weeks of unpaid personal leave to employees. Congress passed the Goals 2000: Educate America Act in 1994, which expanded the federal role in public education through the development of national curriculum content and student performance standards.

    Republicans gained control of both houses of Congress in 1994, and their "Contract with America" raised several issues that had a potential impact on federal relationships. These included term limits for elected officials, a balanced budget, restrictions on punitive damages in civil lawsuits, the line-item veto for the president, regulatory relief, and welfare reform. Many of the newly elected Republicans were clearly committed to restricting the powers of the national government. And, in response to state demands, Congress enacted the Unfunded Mandates Reform Act (1995). Any legislation that would impose $50 million or more in costs to state and local governments would be subject to a parliamentary procedure that requires a vote to waive the prohibition on unfunded mandates. In effect, it requires members of Congress to go on record that they are voting to impose more costs on the state and local governments. The act did nothing to remedy mandates that were already on the books, and since its enactment, it has had very little effect on reducing costs to the other governments in the federal system.[53]

    Deficit reduction in 1995 was directly linked to devolution of powers to the states. Debate over spending limits for Medicare and Medicaid, tax reductions, and a cash assistance program for the poor demonstrated the intentions of Republicans to shrink the national budget and give states additional control over domestic programs.[54]

    Congress enacted a major welfare reform bill in 1996 that eliminated the entitlements under the sixty-one-year-old Aid to Families with Dependent Children program. It was replaced by a new program, Temporary Assistance for Needy Families, which is funded by block grants to the states and gives the states a wide range of options for establishing their own welfare programs.[55] Under waivers permitted by federal law, states also are experimenting with a variety of managed health care reforms in the Medicaid program, which serves low-income people. States, supported by new federal funds, expanded the medical insurance coverage of low-income children in 1997 and obtained relief from some of the regulations of the Environmental Protection Agency. In 1998, Congress enacted a $216 billion public works program which was designed to help states and local governments build roads, bridges, and mass transit systems.[56] Despite the Unfunded Mandates Act of 1995, additional requirements and preemptions in health care, telecommunications, immigration reform, securities reform, and minimum wages were enacted by Congress in 1997.[57]

    In 1996, Congress passed the Defense of Marriage Act, which was a response to the state Supreme Court in Hawaii upholding the legality of gay marriages. For fear that the "full faith and credit clause" of the U.S. Constitution would require other states to recognize gay marriages, Congress, with Clinton's encouragement, defined marriages as heterosexual unions and permitted states to refuse to recognize homosexual marriages.[58]

    Some argued that the "devolution revolution" of 1996 has transformed the federal system into a "new federal order," in which the "federal government intrudes less into the affairs of states and also offers less financial assistance."[59] Additionally, others concluded that congressional action gave states and local governments greater "flexibility" in carrying out federally funded programs because of waivers included in several pieces of legislation.

But there were skeptics. John Kincaid, a specialist in federalism, argued that "devolution (was) plodding along at a turtle's pace while centralization (was) still racing ahead at a rabbit's pace."[60] While there has been considerable symbolic rhetoric and some federal legislation that point to greater state and local responsibility and authority, a closer assessment suggests minimal changes in federal relationships. There is also some evidence of the national government actually increasing its influence in select policy areas.[61] In the early years of the twenty-first century, "the federal government provides about 25 percent of the states' general-fund revenues through its approximately 608 categorical grants and 17 block grants."[62]

Bush II (2001–2009) and Post–9/11 Federal Relationships

In the initial months of his administration, President George W. Bush (2001–2009) gave few clues of how his domestic policy objectives would affect state–federal relationships. He established an Interagency Working Group on Federalism in February 2001, but there is no evidence that it met.[63] Some government watchers expected him to outline and pursue policies similar to his Republican predecessors, but the September 11, 2001, terrorist attacks sidetracked the development of any initiatives that he may have been considering. Homeland security took priority.

Historically, the federal government had played a very limited role in police functions or domestic security. America has never had a national police force because that responsibility was—and still is—allocated to the states and local governments. But the magnitude of the terrorist threat to domestic security prompted President Bush to call for the creation of a new national agency charged with coordinating security programs of federal, state, and local agencies. The Department of Homeland Security, created by Congress in November 2002, represented a comprehensive realignment of federal agencies with functions relating to security, including everything from commercial air travel to patrols along U.S. borders. The new department also developed collaborative programs with states and local governments. With greater emphasis on domestic security, it is argued that these initiatives tipped "the federal system—in matters of politics, police functions, and the law—towards Washington to an unprecedented degree."[64]

With President Bush's support, Congress also enacted the USA Patriot Act soon after the September 11 attacks. That measure increased government surveillance powers in investigations of espionage or terrorism. Supporters contended the legislation was essential in combating terrorists. But civil libertarians, among other critics, feared that the changes it made in federal law enforcement tactics could be abused. By the end of 2003, more than 170 cities and counties around the country had passed resolutions criticizing the law, and several state legislatures passed resolutions expressing concern about excesses in how it was enforced.[65] Sixteen of the law's 150 provisions were to expire at the end of 2005 unless reauthorized by Congress. The debate over reauthorization was extremely contentious, reflecting deep divisions over the relationship of national security and civil rights. With some modifications, these 16 provisions were reauthorized in March 2006.

As more and more of the states' National Guard troops were federalized to fight the wars in Iraq and Afghanistan, states began to resist, and the issue came to a head when Louisiana Governor Kathleen Blanco "refused to accede to the president's request that Guard troops be placed under federal command in the immediate response to Hurricane

Katrina."[66] Congress passed legislation in 2006 that increased "the president's ability to federalize Guard troops without gubernatorial consent."[67] Congress also enacted the REAL ID Act in 2005 as part of the nation's security policy. This act required the Department of Homeland Security to establish federal standards for state driver's licenses, which were to be used for boarding airplanes or admission to federal facilities. States, which estimated the requirements would cost some $14 billion, were to comply with the REAL ID Act by May 2008. But changes in the regulations, pressed by the states, extended the time period for full implementation and reduced the costs.[68]

A significant piece of legislation passed during the second Bush presidency, which was unrelated to the fight against terrorism, was the No Child Left Behind (NCLB) Act of 2002. As governor of Texas, Bush had prided his record on education, which was intended to bring accountability into the public schools while expanding state support for local school districts. Education reform was a cornerstone of his presidential campaign and his legislative agenda. His education initiatives as president were significant to state–federal relationships because, historically, education had been primarily a function of state and local governments. Federal aid to public education had been limited and often targeted toward specific groups of students, such as the disabled or those from low-income families. The impact of NCLB was enormous because it included new federal mandates for reading and math proficiency. Test scores were to be used to evaluate the progress of a school or a school district. If schools failed to meet specified standards, they would suffer repercussions, including loss of funding and loss of students, who would be allowed to transfer to better performing schools.[69]

Issues of federalism played little role in the 2004 presidential election, but federal–state issues came rushing to the center stage of domestic policy debate in 2005, and they continue to generate considerable public attention. The chaotic emergency response to Hurricane Katrina in late summer of 2005 demonstrated the confusion and ineptitude of federal, state, and local governments, with President Bush and the federal government bearing the brunt of the criticism.

State and local governments, meanwhile, increased their criticism of the No Child Left Behind Act. Utah, a conservative Republican state, enacted a law asserting that state education law took precedence over the federal act, and several lawsuits were filed against the funding provisions of the federal education law. Issues related to Medicaid, including funding for health care insurance for low income children, and more stringent work requirements under federal welfare laws also increased states' demands for new directions in national policy.

Across the political spectrum, there has been agreement that the power of the states was diminished during the Bush administration. Bush said relatively little about federalism, nor did he develop an explicit federalism agenda.[70] As noted, his homeland security and education policies expanded the presence of the federal government in domestic programs. Without significant legislative approval and often asserting that the president cannot be restrained by laws enacted by Congress, his administration compiled a record replete with attacks on the fundamental provisions of the Bill of Rights.[71] Preemptions, mandates and other "centralizing statutes" continued at a significant rate; tax policy, especially tax cuts and the phasing out of the federal estate tax, hurt state finances; and federal rule-making, with limited waivers, constrained state discretion.[72]

It is ironic that conservative Republicans, who have long decried centralization, helped lead the country in the direction of centralization. As far as we know, Bush never used the term "new federalism," but if his administration coined a new term for federalism, it would be "big government conservatism" in which the powers of the "federal government and the executive branch were expanded" to achieve a social and economic policy agenda.[73]

It is critical that the student of politics does not simply listen to the rhetoric or symbolism of policy initiatives. The reality is in the details, which may not correspond to the rhetoric.

The nation's attention was focused on national security during Bush's first term. But as the details of his administration's policies became clear, states began a counteroffensive against the increased centralization and his conservative economic and social objectives. Through effective lobbying and political maneuvering, states were successful during Bush's second term "in securing relief from burdensome federal directives regarding the National Guard, homeland security, education, and welfare policy"[74] Several state legislatures passed measures vowing they would not cooperate with the federal government and demanding repeal of a variety of federal directives. And some federal officials became more cooperative with state governments, producing a number of significant waivers in federal programs. In the absence of federal action, meanwhile, states took the initiative on a number of immigration issues. States also were at the forefront of debates about climate change, universal health care, election reform, eminent domain, social policy, capital punishment, and water allocation.[75]

Obama (2009–) and New Directions in Federalism?

When this book was completed, it was much too early to draw conclusions from President Barack Obama's public statements about his position on federalism. In May 2009, the White House issued a memorandum on preemptions, stating that the general policy of Obama's administration was "that preemption of state law by executive departments and agencies should be undertaken only with full consideration of the legitimate prerogatives of the States and with a sufficient legal basis for preemption."[76] Some pundits viewed this as an indication of the new president's movement toward "progressive federalism," a new iteration of cooperative federalism.[77] But some Obama critics alleged that the corporate bailouts and economic stimulus package he supported to deal with the recession would lead to increased centralization of government. The American Recovery and Reinvestment Act of 2009 was estimated to cost $787 billion over the next few years with $280 billion to be administered by states and local governments. Texas's initial share was estimated at $14.4 billion with some 70 percent going to education, transportation, and health and human services.[78] Moreover, if debates initiated in 2009 led to a major overhaul of health care programs, some observers predicted a further expansion of the powers of the national government.

The Role of the U.S. Supreme Court in Defining Federalism

The federal courts have played a central role in defining power, authority, and jurisdiction in the federal system. In looking to the courts to provide the definitive theory of federalism, we might expect a conservative Supreme Court to be more concerned with states' rights and to reconsider the doctrines underlying mandates and preemptions. But this has not always been the case.

In a 1985 Texas case, *Garcia v. San Antonio Metropolitan Transit Authority,* the U.S. Supreme Court held 5–4 that states could not claim immunity from federal regulation over functions that have been defined as "integral" or "traditional."[79] This case, which involved municipal employees and their coverage by the Fair Labor Standards Act, had far-reaching implications for federal–state relationships.[80] In the extreme, the case suggested that Congress, not the courts interpreting the Constitution, would define federalism. The case also suggested that there were no "discrete limitations on the objects of federal authority" other than those provisions of the Constitution that give the states a role in the selection of the president and members of Congress.[81]

By 1995, the court, under the leadership of Chief Justice William Rehnquist, had become much more concerned with the expansion of federal powers and was reasserting itself in cases that involved federal issues. The court ruled 5–4 in the case of *United States v. Lopez* that "the Congress had overreached its constitutional power to regulate interstate commerce when it passed the Gun-Free School Zones Act of 1990."[82] In *Bush v. Vera,* the court struck down a Texas political redistricting plan, suggesting that it was less likely to support redistricting that was designed primarily to benefit minority groups. Other cases soon followed challenging race and ethnicity as criteria for redistricting, and the court's position was clarified somewhat in a 2001 decision (*Easley v. Cromartie*) in which it held that race is not an unconstitutional consideration in redistricting as long as it is not the "dominant and controlling" factor.[83] In another case, the court held that federal laws did not preempt state laws that penalized negligent manufacturers.[84]

A Texas case, *City of Boerne, Texas v. Flores* (1997), also demonstrated the Supreme Court's disposition to place limits on congressional powers.[85] In this case, the high court ruled that the Religious Freedom Restoration Act of 1993 was unconstitutional because it was too broad in its protection of religious freedom. The court ruled that provisions of the act infringed on state powers and also threatened "the authority of the court to determine the constitutionality of federal and state laws."[86] The ruling was handed down after a Roman Catholic parish in Boerne used the law to challenge the city's decision to deny it a permit to enlarge a church in a historic district. The court also struck down provisions of the Brady Handgun Violence Prevention Act, which required background checks on gun purchasers, in *Printz v. United States.*[87]

The court has not been single-minded in its efforts to restrain the powers of the national government.[88] In 1996, the court handed down several civil rights decisions that imposed limits on state powers. It also struck down a 1992 Colorado constitutional amendment that prohibited governments from defining homosexuals as a protected class. In another case, Virginia, on the basis of the Fourteenth Amendment, was required to permit women to attend Virginia Military Institute, which had been an all-male school.[89] In the *Seminole Tribe v. Florida* case, the Supreme Court concluded that Congress had virtually all "authority to legislate in the area of Indian affairs and states had none."[90]

Although not all of its recent decisions reflect a pro-state position, the Supreme Court does appear to have pursued an agenda of redefining or clarifying federal–state relationships, and through its decisions the "allocation of powers in the federal system are still evolving."[91] The high court has continued to receive a number of cases involving federal issues, giving some evidence of curbing congressional intrusion on state powers.[92] But decisions beginning in 2003 appear to have moderated the court's position in restraining federal powers, and it is still not clear which direction the court ultimately will take.

THE IMPACT OF FEDERALISM ON STATE FINANCES

Federal taxes paid into the national treasury from Texas in 2007 totaled approximately $225 billion, or approximately $9,428 per person. Only California and New York paid larger amounts. Federal expenditures in the state were $171.8 billion or $7,185 per

TABLE 3–2   Sources of Revenue for the 2008–2009 Biennium

Source of Revenue	Dollar Amount	Percent of Budget
General Revenue Funds	$79,951,500,000	47.7
Federal Funds	*50,963,000,000*	*30.4*
Other Funds	30,564,300,000	18.2
General Revenue Dedicated Funds	6,308,400,000	3.8
Totals	$167,787,200,000	100

Source: Texas Legislative Budget Board, "Legislatitve Budget Board Fiscal Size-Up: 2008–2009 Biennium," March 2008.

capita. Texas ranked forty-second among the states in per capita federal government expenditures. These expenditures include federal government payroll, defense and other procurement, direct payments to residents under programs such as Social Security and Medicare, and grants to state and local governments.[93] Grants and other payments to Texas's state and local governments totaled $28.1 billion in 2007, placing Texas forty-third among the states in per capita payments.[94]

For years, state officials have complained about the disparity between federal taxes collected in Texas and the distribution of federal funds in the state. The state has long attempted through its congressional delegation and the Office of State-Federal Relations to obtain more equitable formulas as Congress amends or reauthorizes grant programs.

Federal funds accounted for approximately $51 billion, or about 30 percent, of the $168 billion state budget for the 2008–2009 biennium (see Table 3–2). Health and human services, including a wide range of social services for millions of low-income Texans, received some 61 percent of all federal funds allocated to the state for this period. Business and economic development programs received 17 percent, and education programs received 17 percent.[95]

State government, through the Office of State–Federal Relations, and many of the larger cities in Texas have full-time staffers working to obtain additional federal dollars. Like other states, Texas also lobbies the federal government for additional programs, changes in existing programs, relief from mandates and preemptions, and adjustments in funding formulas that adversely affect the state.

Many of the grants that come to Texas are formula grants, based on population, levels of poverty, or some other criteria written into the federal act. Others are competitive and must be sought out by Texas governments. Some state agencies and local governments are aggressive and often successful in obtaining competitive grants, but others are not. Governments with limited staff often find it difficult to reallocate employees' time to the complex grant application process. Available programs must be identified through publications such as the *Federal Register,* and applications must be submitted in a timely manner. Some assistance is available to local governments through their regional councils of governments, and some consultants provide grant-writing services. Some local governments may not apply for grants because of disinterest, political opposition, or other reasons.

State agencies are required to look at their specific programs and aggressively pursue relevant federal grants. Within the governor's office, there is a State Grants Team whose "mission is to increase Texas's access to available federal funds." This group helps in the identification of grant programs, informs other state and local agencies of grant availability, assists in the writing of grant applications, and monitors agency activities in pursuing grants.[96]

REACTIONS TO THE EXPANDED ROLE
OF THE FEDERAL GOVERNMENT

Many citizens argue that economic, environmental, and social issues are national in scope, and it is impossible for states, singularly or collectively, to address these problems adequately. The complexity of these problems requires a coordinated national effort with common standards and objectives. Not all governments have the financial resources to deal with many of these problems, and without federal assistance, some significant segments of our society would simply do without or suffer. From a philosophical perspective, these individuals are inclined to ask why some parts of our population should be neglected.

Others have taken the view that many governments would not address such issues if they were not required to do so by federal mandates. Others argue the federal system potentially brings expertise and support to those governments that don't have adequate resources. Still others look at the long history of discrimination in the United States and argue that changes would not have occurred if the federal government had not taken the lead through legislation and public policy.

From our origins as a nation, there has been an expressed fear of government centralization. In the ratifying debates over the U.S. Constitution, the anti-Federalists made many of the arguments against a strong national government that are still heard today. In addition to a general fear of tyranny, corruption, and abuses, there are concerns that people in one area of the country could impose their will on others. Is it possible for officials in Washington to understand the issues and problems facing citizens at the local level across the country? The ever-increasing number of mandates and preemptions constrains state and local governments, often bringing significant budgetary costs. There are strings attached to taking federal grant monies, and some state agencies and communities across Texas resist taking federal dollars because of these restrictions. Communities have their own needs and priorities, and some argue that federal grants entice governments to rearrange their priorities. But it is very difficult for most public officeholders to pass up these available dollars.

Several federal grant programs have cross-over provisions that link one policy area to a totally different one. For example, the Texas legislature raised the minimum legal drinking age from eighteen to twenty-one in 1986. Although some Texans had lobbied for the older drinking age, a major impetus for the change came from federal legislation that linked the drinking age to federal grants for road construction. Texas could have refused to adopt the higher age, but it would have lost 10 percent of its federal highway dollars after 1988.

Many of the federal assistance programs were designed to redistribute resources from the wealthier segments of the population to lower income groups, a practice that some people oppose. Moreover, this redistribution is linked in Texas to issues of race and ethnicity because minority groups constitute a disproportionate segment of the state's low-income population. Some political leaders have resisted federal grant programs for fear that funding projects would enhance the political position of minority groups.

Some suggest that the increased use of fiscal federalism (federal grants linked to preemptions and mandates) has produced a mindset that the federal government should assume more responsibility for domestic programs, both in terms of program development and funding.[97] They fear that federal dominance undermines the creative capacity of states and local governments to deal with many local and regional problems. Moreover, many would argue that the states are now much more innovative than the federal government in policy implementation and streamlining the administrative processes.

TRANSNATIONAL REGIONALISM

Texas shares a 1,200-mile border with Mexico, and common problems and interests that bond the two neighbors, called **transnational regionalism,** have taken on increased importance since the mid-1980s.

Historically, relations between the United States and Mexico were often strained. The United States fought a war against Mexico from 1846 to 1848, and on subsequent occasions, American troops entered Mexican territory, ostensibly to protect U.S. economic and national security interests. Apprehension about U.S. objectives resulted in Mexican policies on trade, commerce, and foreign ownership of property that were designed to insulate the country from excessive foreign influence and domination. Nevertheless, the interests of the two countries have long been bound by geopolitical factors, economics, and demographics. One Mexican author has compared the interdependence of the two countries to Siamese twins, warning that "if one becomes gangrenous, the other twin will also be afflicted."[98]

Maquiladoras

Changes in the economic relationship between Mexico and the United States began with the **maquiladora program**, an initiative under Mexico's 1964 Border Industrialization Program to boost employment, foreign exchange, and industrial development. It was also designed to transfer technology to Mexico, help train workers, and develop managerial skills among Mexican nationals.[99]

The concept was to develop twin plants, one in the United States and one in Mexico, under a single management. The plant in the United States would manufacture parts, and its Mexican counterpart would assemble them into a product, which, in turn, would be sent back to the United States for further processing or for shipping to customers.[100] Parts shipped into Mexico would not be subject to the normal tariffs, and the tax imposed on the assembled product would be minimal. In 1984, Mexico changed its laws to permit the United States and other foreign countries to establish these relationships throughout Mexico, rather than just on the border, and to permit 100 percent foreign ownership of the assembly plants in Mexico. The latter step was a radical departure from previous Mexican law, which prohibited such foreign ownership.[101]

The maquiladora program has not resulted in the construction of a significant number of manufacturing plants on the Texas side of the border because American companies have used existing plants throughout the United States to produce parts to be assembled in Mexico. Nevertheless, Texas's border counties have benefited through the creation of thousands of support jobs in transportation, warehousing, and services.[102] Some 4,100 maquiladora plants were in operation in 2007, providing hundreds of thousands of jobs but also contributing to increased population density along the Mexican side of the border, where most of the Mexican assembly plants are located.[103]

The maquiladora program continues to play a major role in transnational economic development. American organized labor opposes the program, arguing that the maquiladoras drain jobs from the United States. But the program provides a source of inexpensive labor for American businesses, which have complained for years that they cannot compete against cheap foreign labor costs.

The North American Free Trade Agreement (NAFTA)

Negotiations on a free trade agreement in 1991 marked another significant change in the relationship between Mexico and the United States. The negotiations were precipitated, in part, by world economics and the emergence of regional trading zones. But the administration of Mexican President Carlos Salinas de Gortari was also reacting to the failure of Mexico's economic policies of the 1980s and a fear of economic isolation. The end of the Cold War, a reduction in Central American conflicts, and internal population pressures also were factors.[104]

The convergence of interests of the United States, Mexico, and Canada produced the North American Free Trade Agreement (NAFTA) to reduce tariffs and increase trade among the three countries. It created the world's largest trading bloc, which had a combined population of approximately 452 million in 2009 and a combined gross national product of more than $17.2 trillion in 2008.[105] Other regions of the world have recognized the value of creating large trading blocs, and the European Union, now comprised of 27 nations, is estimated to have a combined population of 492 million and a combined GDP of $14.8 trillion.[106]

Approved by the U.S. Congress in late 1993, NAFTA has increased trade among the three countries, strengthened previous economic ties and created new ones. Texas has experienced significant economic changes from these new relationships, but the benefits have not been uniformly distributed throughout the state.

Continued Concerns about NAFTA

Some people on both sides of the U.S.–Mexico border believe that NAFTA is harming their respective countries. Labor unions in the United States are particularly concerned that cheap labor costs in Mexico have moved jobs from the United States. Some manufacturers argue that labor and capital costs in Mexico threaten their American markets. Some Texas officials and many Texas residents fear that opening up the state's highways to Mexican trucks will create safety problems, and American trucking interests, including owners and drivers, oppose competition from Mexican trucks. Mexican trucks still were not allowed unlimited movement in all fifty states, despite treaty provisions to the contrary.

In Mexico, there is concern that American corporations will dominate and reduce Mexico's control over its own economy since approximately 80 percent of Mexico's exports are going to the United States. Human rights advocates have expressed concerns about working conditions, workers' benefits, and the broader social impact of the plants on the lives of hundreds of thousands of Mexican citizens.

Environmentalists on both sides of the border have argued that increased manufacturing and commerce worsen the air, water, and waste pollution problems in the area. Both countries have environmental laws, and the treaty calls for collaboration on environmental issues, but there have been allegations that U.S. manufacturers have shipped their dirty plants to Mexico, which, as an emerging country, is less inclined or able to crack down on polluters.

Trade Patterns between Texas and Mexico

The United States and Texas do a lot of business with Mexico. U.S. exports to Mexico were $12.4 billion in 1986 and $151 billion in 2008 (see Table 3–3). Imports from Mexico, now the United States' third largest trading partner, were $216 billion in 2008. Mexico accounted for 8.5 percent of all goods imported into the U.S. in 2008 and 8.2 percent of U.S. exports.[107] Texas exported more than $62 billion worth of goods, accounting for 38 percent of U.S. exports to Mexico in 2008.

The sheer volume of goods, services, and people is obvious on the highways leading into Mexico and in the long lines of people on foot and in autos and trucks at border crossings in Brownsville, Laredo, and El Paso. There were 97.5 million legal border crossings between Texas and Mexico in 2008. There were more than 57 million small vehicle crossings, 33 million pedestrian crossings, and 6 million truck crossings. More than 33,000 pedestrians crossed the border at El Paso each day, and more than 8,600 trucks crossed the border each day at Laredo, the nation's largest inland port.[108] Billions of dollars are required to upgrade and expand the roads, highways, bridges, water and sanitation systems, and other facilities on both sides of the border. Some initiatives have been taken by both countries, but many of these facilities will not be completed for years, contributing to delays and gridlock in both countries at border crossings. The North American Development Bank was created to help address these needs.

TABLE 3–3   **Texas and U.S. Exports to Mexico, 1993–2008**

Year	Texas Exports to Mexico (in billions of dollars)	U.S. Exports to Mexico (in billions of dollars)	Texas Exports as a Percent of U.S. Exports
1993	20.4	41.6	49%
1994	23.8	50.8	47%
1995	21.9	46.3	47%
1996	27.0	56.8	48%
1997	31.2	71.4	44%
1998	36.3	79.0	46%
1999*	37.9	87.0	44%
2000	47.8	111.7	43%
2001	41.6	101.5	41%
2002	41.6	97.5	43%
2003	41.6	97.5	43%
2004	45.7	110.8	41%
2005	50.1	120.0	42%
2006	54.9	134.2	41%
2007	56.0	136.5	41%
2008	62.1	151.2	38%

*The Massachusetts Institute for Social and Economic Research applied a more advanced algorithim to data beginning in 1999. Thus, the post-1998 export figures more accurately account for unreported exports by states and, therefore, more accurately reflect actual export revenue than do pre-1999 figures.

Source: Massachusetts Institute of Social and Economic Research and the U.S. Census Bureau (based on "origin of movement to port" state-level data series); Texas Department of Economic Development, April 2000; and International Trade Administration, *TradeStats* program.

It sometimes looks like a train coming. Many of the 8,600 trucks that cross the border each day at Laredo travel on Interstate 35, often giving the impression that there is a 'train' on the highway.

Border crossings declined between 2007 and 2008, and some reasons are still unknown. Both countries were impacted by the recession in 2008, resulting in less commerce along the border and reductions in imports and exports. In the aftermath of the 9/11 terrorist attacks, crossing the border is now more difficult with new security measures in place. American citizens, for example, are now required under the Western Hemisphere Travel Initiative to present a passport or some other document proving citizenship, and similar provisions apply to nationals of other countries coming into the United States.

Illegal Immigration

Population growth in Texas has always been affected by migration from other states and foreign countries. But the proximity of Texas to Mexico has put the state in the center of a long-running dispute over the illegal immigration of large numbers of Mexicans and other Latin Americans. And the dispute erupted anew in 2005 as President George W. Bush and the U.S. Congress debated changes in immigration law.

The federal government, not the states, has the authority to determine immigration laws and policies.[109] Congress enacted the Nationalization Act of 1790, which limited naturalization to "free white persons" of "good moral character" and established residency requirements for citizenship. Other laws of modest scope were enacted in the early nineteenth century. They established reporting procedures for immigrants, created a commissioner for immigration, placed centralized control over immigration with the Secretary of State, and excluded prostitutes and convicts. The Chinese Exclusion Act (1882) was the first major law restricting immigration into the United States.

It limited Chinese immigration and denied this population naturalization rights. The law later was extended and expanded to include the mentally ill, persons with certain illnesses, contract labor, and polygamists. Quotas based on national origin were central to national immigration policy until 1965 and gave preference to immigrants from northern European countries. Piecemeal legislation dealing with immigration was consolidated in the Immigration and Nationality Act of 1952, which maintained the quota system, established preferences for skilled labor and relatives of U.S. citizens, and enhanced screening and security procedures.

The quota system discriminated against Asians, eastern Europeans, African Americans, and Latin Americans. But during World War II, the United States faced a labor shortage and negotiated a *Bracero Program* with Mexico, which made it possible for temporary workers from Mexico to enter the United States. This program was terminated in 1964.

The Immigration and Nationality Act of 1965 eliminated national quotas but set limits on the number of immigrants from different regions of the world. The law produced a dramatic shift in immigration patterns with large numbers of Asians now entering the country. As war and political instability affected developing countries, additional immigrants began entering the United States.

The nation's robust economy after World War II, coupled with economic problems, political instability, and persecutions in many developing countries, generated a surge and a huge backlog in applications for legal immigrant status. Consequently, a massive influx of illegal immigration began. If arrested, illegal immigrants were deported; but until 1986, it was not illegal for American employers to hire them.[110] Moreover, large portions of the Texas and American economies are built on the availability of cheap, low-skilled foreign labor, and businesses and individuals were willing to ignore the illegal status of millions of immigrants, particularly from Mexico and other Latin American countries.[111]

As the scale of the problem became more evident, the U.S. Congress enacted the Immigration Reform and Control Act in 1986. That law imposed fines on employers who hired illegal immigrants and provided jail sentences for flagrant violators. Potential employees had to provide documentation, and employers had to verify their employees' citizenship. Since there was no practical way to deport millions of illegal immigrants, the law also provided a means for giving legal status, or amnesty, to illegal immigrants who had moved to the United States before January 1, 1982. It also provided for temporary status for agricultural workers who could satisfy specific residency requirements.[112]

But illegal immigration continued and public pressure mounted for more rigorous action. Additional legislation was passed in 1996 to increase funds for border guards and inspectors, to increase penalties for smuggling people into the United States and using fraudulent documents, to construct fences along the border, and to make it easier to detain and deport illegal immigrants.[113] The U.S. Congress also passed major changes in welfare laws in 1996, cutting off most public assistance to both legal and illegal immigrants in the United States.

Critics of the previous welfare system had argued that the accessibility of public funds and services was a strong attraction to immigrants, many of whom are poverty stricken. They argued that American taxpayers had no obligation to support anyone who entered the country illegally or even legal immigrants who couldn't support themselves. Children of illegal immigrants represent a heavy financial burden for many school districts and taxpayers throughout the country. Undocumented workers also increase demands on public health care and welfare programs.[114] Some citizens, particularly unskilled workers, view the illegal arrivals as a threat to their jobs and standard of living.

With some exceptions for medical emergencies, the 1996 welfare law barred illegal immigrants from receiving benefits provided by a federal agency or by federal funds, including welfare, retirement, health, disability, food assistance, or unemployment benefits. States are also prohibited from providing state or local benefits to illegal immigrants unless state officials pass specific laws making immigrants eligible for aid from state or local funds.

Most legal immigrants, even those already in the country when the law was changed, are now ineligible for federal supplemental security income and food stamps until they become citizens. Those who have come to the United States legally since the law was passed will be denied most federal welfare benefits for five years. States, however, can assist legal immigrants with benefits funded entirely by state or local funds. The law also places additional financial responsibilities on people who sponsor immigrants. But several years after the 1996 law was enacted, there was considerable evidence that the welfare restrictions weren't deterring illegal immigration nor reducing immigrants' use of public services.[115]

Immigration reform was a centerpiece of President George W. Bush's domestic program. But border security became a greater concern after the terrorist attacks of September 11, 2001. The creation of the Department of Homeland Security in 2002 combined and realigned a number of existing agencies to increase controls on the borders. Meanwhile, political debate increased over the competition for jobs between U.S. citizens and illegal immigrants and a host of other immigration-related issues.

In late 2005, the U.S. House approved a bill to improve border security and make criminals of undocumented immigrants, ignoring a proposal by Bush to provide illegal immigrants already in the country a way to become citizens. The U.S. Senate rejected the House bill and approved legislation providing a so-called "pathway" to citizenship for illegal immigrants who paid fines, learned to speak English, and met certain other requirements. Meanwhile, the controversy also played out in peaceful, but noisy, demonstrations in many American cities, including Dallas, Houston, and San Antonio, and in numerous political campaigns. Thousands of immigrants, their descendants and supporters took to the streets to wave American and Mexican flags for their cause.

Although immigration reform legislation failed, Congress in 2005 authorized a border wall or fence along the U.S.–Mexico border by attaching it as a rider to the REAL ID ACT, a law requiring states to develop a standard driver's license for use as identification. When the details of the fence became public in 2007, there was another round of intense political controversy on both sides of the border. More fuel was added to the political fire in 2008, when the Department of Homeland Security announced it would pursue construction despite potential conflicts with some 34 existing laws. Given the physical barrier that the Rio Grande presents to vehicles, most fences built on the Texas border are pedestrian fences.[116]

President Bush also ordered several thousand National Guard troops to the border to help the Border Patrol in 2006. It was widely believed the president took this additional step to "secure" the border in order to boost support for his proposal to allow immigrants already in the country illegally to earn citizenship and to help members of his party in the 2006 congressional elections. As drug-related violence increased on the border, President Barack Obama announced in March 2009 that he was considering deploying National Guard troops to contain the violence."[117]

Of the more than 300 million Americans in 2007, some 38 million were foreign born.[118] We don't know how many illegal immigrants are in the United States, but the best estimates range from 11.3 to 11.9 million people. Most are from Mexico and Central America.[119] Many enter through Texas and continue on to other areas of the country, but others remain in the state. Of the 3.8 million foreign born persons living in Texas in 2007, approximately 1.7 million, or almost half, were in the state illegally.[120]

It is virtually impossible to stop all illegal immigration, and divided public opinion over the issue makes enforcement even more difficult. Some immigrants violate the law for economic reasons. They are willing to take the risk they will be caught, knowing that the worst thing that can happen is that they will be deported or receive limited jail time. Others have binational families, with relatives who are U.S. citizens. One also could argue that the federal government was complicit through lax enforcement with those who believed that cheap foreign labor was critical to the health of the economy.

The federal government's failure to address the immigration problem has prompted many states and local communities to enact their own restrictions. Since 2005, states have enacted more than 600 laws dealing with immigration, including restrictions on drivers' licenses, requiring documents for employment, punitive action against companies that hire illegal immigrants and restrictions on access to higher education and public services.[121] Similar bills have been introduced in the Texas Legislature but failed.

President Obama emphasized immigration reform during his campaign for the White House and the early months of his administration. "I'm committed to passing comprehensive immigration reform as President of the United States," he said, with vague references to clarifying the status of those here illegally, requiring them to pay a penalty and taxes if they want to become citizens, learn English, and "go to the back of the line behind those who played by the rules."[122] But other issues, including economic recovery and health care reform, took precedence during his first year in office.

Other Border Controversies

Many Americans also are concerned about other issues affecting the United States' relationship with its neighbor to the south, including increased drug violence and smuggling, political corruption, the stability of the country, the long-term effects of the domination of Mexican politics by the Institutional Revolutionary Party (PRI), its commitment to democratic values, and human rights violations.

Drug-related violence and alleged collusion between high-ranking Mexican officials and the drug cartels have raised questions about Mexico's ability to fight the drug problem, and some recent reports about conditions in Mexico have gone so far as to conclude that Mexico is fast moving to the status of a "failed state."[123] An estimated 5,300 persons were murdered in Mexico in 2008 in drug-related violence.[124] Several Mexican government officials responsible for enforcing drug laws have been murdered, as have members of the Mexican press who have reported on the drug cartels. In many areas, local police forces have been corrupted, and the Mexican government has turned to the military and the federal police to deal with the cartels. Americans also fear that violence among the competing drug cartels in Mexico's border cities could spill over into the United States. The enormous amount of money linked to the illegal drug trade increases the potential for the corruption of public officials in the United States as well.[125]

The potential for political instability in Mexico surfaced dramatically with the uprising on January 1, 1994, of the Zapatistas, a peasant-based guerrilla movement centered in Chiapas. Although some efforts were made to address the Zapatistas' grievances, the

Most of these Come from Texas. From all indications, the vast number of weapons used by Mexican drug cartels to carry out their violent activities in Mexico come from the United States. These weapons were seized by U.S. Immigration and Customs Enforcement in its efforts to stem the tide of weapons flowing into Mexico.

massacre of 45 people in late December of 1997 by gunmen with alleged links to the ruling party cast more shadows on Mexico's political system.

Presidential candidate Luis Donald Colossi was assassinated in March 1994, and José Francisco Ruiz Massieu, secretary general of the ruling party, was murdered in September of that year. There are still widespread suspicions in the United States and Mexico that officials of PRI, the then-ruling party, were involved in these murders.

When Vicente Fox Quesada, a candidate of the largest opposition party, the National Action Party (PAN), captured the Mexican presidency in 2000, ending the 70-year domination by the Institutional Revolutionary Party (PRI), there was hope that he would initiate widespread reforms in the economy, the bureaucracy, the military, and law enforcement. Some changes have occurred, but the task he faced was daunting, with formidable entrenched opposition. PAN's presidential nominee, Felipe Calderon, won the presidency in 2006 in a highly contentious election that produced an election challenge by his opponent, Andres Manuel Lopez Abrader. For two months, Abrader's supporters took to the streets of Mexico City in an effort to influence the decision of the Federal Electoral Tribunal, but on September 6, 2006, Calderon was declared the winner.

President Fox and President George W. Bush developed a cooperative relationship when they served as governors of their respective states, and initially their cooperation extended into their presidencies. But their relationship soured in 2003 when Mexico, along with most other members of the United Nations, refused to endorse America's military action against Iraq. Relations between the two countries further eroded because of the renewed debate over immigration, a dispute over water allocations from the Rio Grande, and the perception that the Bush administration was giving little attention to the interests of Mexico and other Latin American countries.

Common Borders, Common Problems

To anyone living on the border, the economic interdependence of the United States and Mexico is evident every day. Tens of thousands of pedestrians, cars, and trucks move across the international bridges, to and from the commercial centers on both sides of the Rio Grande. When the Mexican economy suffered a precipitous decline in 1982, the peso devaluation severely disrupted the Texas border economy, causing unemployment to skyrocket and a considerable number of U.S. businesses to fail.

Much of the effort toward improving relations between the United States and Mexico has focused on potential economic benefits, but other complex problems confronting both countries also merit attention. One is health care. On both sides of the border, many children have not been immunized against basic childhood diseases. On the Texas side are more than 1,200 *colonies*—rural, unincorporated slums that have substandard housing, roads, and drainage and, in many cases, lack water and sewage systems. These conditions have contributed to severe health problems, including hepatitis, dysentery, and tuberculosis. Higher than normal numbers of both Texan and Mexican children along the border also have been born with serious birth defects. Public health facilities in Texas report that Mexican women come across the border to give birth to their children in American facilities. This practice, which has the effect of creating "binational families," increases the burden on public hospitals—and taxpayers— in Texas. Children born in the United States are U.S. citizens and are entitled to various public services.[126]

Industrial development and population growth along the border also increase environmental problems. U.S. antipollution laws have been more stringent than those of Mexico, but air and water pollution generated in Mexico does not stop at the border. The side agreements to NAFTA provide a basic framework for addressing these problems, but some have argued that a country such as Mexico, under enormous pressure to industrialize rapidly, is less likely to be concerned with environmental issues. In addition, U.S. efforts to impose its environmental standards on Mexico could be interpreted as another American effort to dominate the country.[127] In June 1994, several maquiladora plants in Matamoros, across the border from Brownsville, settled lawsuits alleging that pollution caused rare birth defects in children born in Texas.

Regional interdependence, though perhaps not recognized by most people on both sides of the border, has taken on greater importance in the press and in academic, business, and labor communities in the United States. Transnational public policies are emerging, creating legal issues in product liability, insurance, copyrights, and patents that must still be resolved. The governors of Mexican and U.S. border states have their own association, the Border Governors Conference, which meets regularly to discuss such issues as free trade, the environment, education, and tourism.[128]

SUMMARY AND CONCLUSIONS ●

1. Government and politics in Texas are shaped by the federal system, a complex structure of overlapping authority and shared responsibilities among different levels of government. Federal relationships have changed over the country's history through the actions of Congress, the

president, the federal courts, and state and local governments.

2. Many argue that the federal government has encroached excessively on the powers of the state and local governments through mandates and pre-emptions, thus limiting the policy options available to the states.

3. The dynamics of federalism appear to shift between coercion and cooperation, depending on multiple factors, including the conditions of a specific period, policies pursued by the president and Congress, and decisions of the Supreme Court. State and local governments aggressively lobby the national government to address their needs and interests. Members of Congress, who have close relationships with the communities within their states, make continuous efforts to obtain funding for local projects or changes in federal policies or regulations that adversely impact community interests.

4. The ongoing debate over devolution, or the return of powers to the states, has been a rhetorical component of the varied views of "new federalism" advanced by Republican presidents since Richard Nixon. But, despite the antifederal rhetoric, Republican presidents have contributed to a shift of power to Washington. This shift was more extensive during George W. Bush's administration. While historically it has been the role of the Supreme Court to provide the definitive interpretation on state–federal powers, some of the court's recent decisions have created some ambiguity.

5. Relationships under the federal system are both vertical (state–federal) and horizontal (state to state), both of which are outlined by the U.S. Constitution. Issues and problems facing states do not stop at their borders, and states have joined numerous cooperative efforts, including inter-state compacts, uniform laws, and collaboration on shared problems.

6. The politics, economy, and social system of Texas are now inextricably linked to Mexico. Transnational regionalism can be used to explain and assess the complex interdependency that exists between the two countries.

7. While there has been an enormous increase in trade between the U.S. and Mexico, Mexico's economic growth has been insufficient to absorb a large part of its population, which is attracted to employment opportunities in the U.S. Many sectors of the American economy also depend on the low-wage labor provided by the Mexican immigrants.

8. Immigration from Mexico and other parts of Latin America contributes significantly to the demographic transformation of the state. Both legal and illegal immigration present an array of policy issues, including education, social services, and health care.

9. The federal government has failed to enact immigration policies addressing the dilemma that Texas and other states face. So some states have enacted their own immigration-related laws. Texas so far has not, although many residents think it should.

10. There are common border problems, including education, health care, the environment, and drugs. With the almost daily reports of murder, violence, corruption in Mexico, and the perception that Mexico's drug problems are now becoming America's problem, some suggest that Mexico is a "failed state," which will produce negative reverberations for Texas and the United States.

KEY TERMS

Unitary system 66
Confederation 66
Federalism 66
Dillon rule 67
Devolution 68
Delegated powers 68
Implied powers 68
Supremacy clause 68
Reserved powers 68
Concurrent powers 68

Denied powers 69
Full faith and credit clause 69
Privileges and immunities 70
Extradition 70
Interstate compacts 70
Cooperative federalism 71
Categorical grants-in-aid 73
Project grant 74
Formula grant 74
Matching funds 74

New federalism 75
Block grants 75
Revenue sharing 75
Mandates 76
Preemptions 76
Transnational regionalism 85
Maquiladora program 85
North American Free Trade
    Agreement (NAFTA) 86

FURTHER READING ●

Articles

Center for the Study of Federalism, *Publius: The Journal of Federalism*. This journal is an excellent source of information on a wide variety of topics centered on federalism and federal relationships.

Drinan, John, and Dale Krane, "The State of American Federalism, 2005: Federalism Resurfaces in the Political Debate," *Publius: The Journal of Federalism* 36 (May 2006), pp. 327–74.

McGuinn, Patrick, "The National Schoolmarm: No Child Left Behind and the New Educational Federalism," *Publius: The Journal of Federalism,* 35 (Winter 2005), pp. 41–68.

Books

Dye, Thomas R., and Susan McManus, *Politics in States and Communities,* 12th ed. Upper Saddle River, NJ: Prentice Hall, 2007.

Grodzins, Morton, *The American System,* edited by Daniel J. Elazar. Chicago: Rand McNally, 1966.

Hanson, Russell L., ed., *Governing Partners: State-Local Relations in the United States.* Boulder, CO: Westview, 1998.

Martin, Roscoe C., *The Cities and the Federal System.* New York: Atherton, 1965.

Martinez, Oscar J., *Troublesome Border.* Tucson: University of Arizona Press, 1988.

Metz, Leon C., *Border: The U.S.–Mexico Line.* El Paso, TX: Mangan, 1989.

Peterson, Paul, *Evolving Federalism: The Intergovernmental Balance of Power in America and Europe.* Syracuse, NY: Campbell Public Affairs Institute, Maxwell School of Citizenship and Public Affairs, 2003.

Posner, Paul, *The Politics of Unfunded Mandates.* Washington, DC: Georgetown University Press, 1998.

Scheberle, Denise, *Federalism and Environmental Policy.* Washington, DC: Georgetown University Press, 1997.

Stephens, G. Ross, and Nelson Wikstrom, *American Intergovernmental Relations: A Fragmented Polity.* New York: Oxford University Press, 2007.

Teske, Paul, *Regulation in the States.* Washington, DC: Brookings Institution Press, 2004.

Walker, David B., *The Rebirth of Federalism,* 2nd ed. New York: Chatham House, 2000.

Zimmerman, Joseph F., *Congressional Preemption: Regulatory Federalism.* Albany, NY: State University of New York Press, 2005.

Zimmerman, Joseph F., *Interstate Disputes: The Supreme Court's Original Jurisdiction.* Albany, NY: State University of New York Press, 2006.

Zimmerman, Joseph F. *Contemporary American Federalism: The Growth of National Power,* 2nd ed. Albany, NY: State University of New York Press, 2008.

Websites

Council of State Governments http://www.csg.org/ This site provides links to other organizations of state officials as well as information on policies affecting states, publications, suggested legislation, and state information centers.

Nelson A. Rockefeller Institute of Government http://www.rockinst.org/ This institute is located at the State University of New York and is actively involved nationally in research and special projects on the role of state governments in American federalism. In addition to providing links to other public policy websites, this site references numerous studies related to federalism.

Urban Institute http://www.urban.org/ The Urban Institute focuses on a range of social and economic policies that are directly shaped by the dynamics of the federal system.

ENDNOTES ●

1. James Madison, "Federalist 51," *The Federalist Papers,* by Alexander Hamilton, James Madison, and John Jay with an Introduction by Clinton Rossiter (New York: New American Library, 1962), p. 323.
2. Martha Derthick, *Keeping the Compound Republic: Essays on American Federalism* (Washington, DC: Brookings Institution Press, 2001), p. 154.
3. See Alexis de Tocqueville's highly informative assessment of the American experience with centralized authority.

Alexis de Tocqueville, *Democracy in America,* with an introduction by Joseph Epstein (New York: Bantam Dell, 2004).
4. David C. Nice, "The Intergovernmental Setting of State-Local Relations," in *Governing Partners: State-Local Relations in the United States,* edited by Russell L. Hanson (Boulder, CO.: Westview, 1998), p. 17.
5. For a discussion of the Dillon Rule, see Anwar Syed, *The Political Theory of American Local Government* (New York: Random House, 1966), Chapter 3.

6. Thomas J. Anton, *American Federalism and Public Policy* (New York: Random House, 1989), p. 3.

7. See William H. Stewart, "Metaphors, Models, and the Development of Federal Theory," *Publius: The Journal of Federalism* 12 (Winter 1982), pp. 5–24; and William H. Stewart, *Concepts of Federalism* (Lanham, MD: Center for the Study of Federalism and University Press of America, 1984).

8. William T. Gormley, Jr., "Money and Mandates: The Politics of Intergovernmental Conflict," *Publius: The Journal of Federalism* 36 (May 2006), pp. 523–540. This is an excellent article that provides a method for disaggregating broad trends in federal–state relationships.

9. Anton, *American Federalism and Public Policy,* p. 19.

10. U.S. Constitution, Article I, Section 8, Paragraph 18.

11. U.S. Constitution, Article VI.

12. U.S. Constitution, Amendment X.

13. For an excellent summary of the guarantees to and limitations on state governments defined by the U.S. Constitution, see Thomas Dye, *American Federalism* (Lexington, KY: D. C. Heath, 1990), pp. 9–11.

14. U.S. Constitution, Article IV, Section 1.

15. National Conference of State Legislatures, "Same Sex Marriage, Civil Unions and Domestic Partnerships: Quick Facts on Key States," June 2009.

16. Morton Grodzins, *The American System,* edited by Daniel J. Elazar (Chicago: Rand McNally, 1966), pp. 151–53.

17. *Commonwealth of Kentucky v. Denison, Governor,* 65 U.S. (24 How.) 66 (1861).

18. *Puerto Rico v. Branstad,* 483 U.S. 219 (1987).

19. Kenyon Bunch and Richard J. Hardy, "Continuity or Change in Interstate Extradition? Assessing *Puerto Rico v. Branstad,*" *Publius: The Journal of Federalism* 21 (Winter 1991), p. 59.

20. U.S. Constitution, Article III, Section 2.

21. Patrick H. Lyons, New Mexico State Land Office, Press Release, March 14, 2003; Ray Cooklis, "Border Dispute: Texas Strip Stake," *Cincinnati Enquirer,* March 14, 2003; and Texas General Land Office, Press Release, January 7, 2004.

22. Morton Grodzins and Daniel Elazar, "Centralization and Decentralization in the American Federal System," in *A Nation of States,* 2nd ed., edited by Robert A. Goldwin (Chicago: Rand McNally, 1974), p. 4.

23. Deil S. Wright, *Understanding Intergovernmental Relations,* 2nd ed. (Monterey, CA: Brooks/Cole, 1982), pp. 60–68.

24. Ibid., p. 46.

25. *McCulloch v. Maryland,* 4 Wheaton 316 (1819).

26. Thomas R. Dye, *Politics in States and Communities,* 8th ed. (Englewood Cliffs, NJ: Prentice Hall, 1994), p. 67.

27. Timothy Conlan, with an introduction by Samuel H. Beer, *New Federalism* (Washington, DC: The Brookings Institution, 1988), p. 5.

28. V. O. Key, *The Responsible Electorate* (Cambridge, MA: Harvard University Press, 1966), p. 31. (font size)

29. Daniel J. Elazar, *American Federalism: A View from the States,* 2nd ed. (New York: Harper & Row Publishers, 1972), p. 47.

30. Deign S. Wright, *Understanding Intergovernmental Relations* (North Scituate, NH: Duxbury Press, 1978; and G. Ross Stephens and Nelson Wikstrom, *American Intergovernmental Relations: A Fragmented Federal Polity* (New York: NY: Oxford University Press, 2007), p. 32.

31. Office of Management and Budget, *Analytical Perspectives: Budget of the U.S. Government, Fiscal Year 2010,* http://www.budget.gov/.

32. Conlan, *New Federalism,* p. 6.

33. Dye, *Politics in States and Communities,* p. 83.

34. Conlan, *New Federalism,* p. 3.

35. Ibid., pp. 3, 19–30, 77–81.

36. Ibid., p. 90.

37. Richard P. Nathan, Thomas L. Gais, and James W. Fossett, "Bush Federalism: Is There One, What is It, and How Does It Differ?" Paper presented at the Annual Research Conference Association for Public Policy Analysis and Management, November 7, 2003, Washington, DC, p. 5.

38. Ibid., p. 6.

39. Joseph F. Zimmerman, "Federal Preemption under Reagan's New Federalism," *Publius: The Journal of Federalism* 21 (Winter 1991), p. 11.

40. Michael A. Pagano, Ann O'M. Bowman, and John Kincaid, "The State of American Federalism, 1990–1991," *Publius: The Journal of Federalism* 21 (Summer 1991), p. 1.

41. Zimmerman, "Federal Preemption under Reagan's New Federalism," p. 26.

42. Joseph F. Zimmerman, "Congressional Preemption and the States," in *The Book of the States 2006,* vol. 38 (Lexington, KY: Council of State Governments, 2006), p. 26; see also Joseph F. Zimmerman, *Congressional Preemption: Regulatory Federalism.* Albany, NY: State University of New York Press, 2005.

43. Robert B. Hawkins, "Pre-Emption: The Dramatic Rise of Federal Supremacy," *The Journal of State Government* 63 (January–March 1990), p. 10.

44. Zimmerman, "Federal Preemption under Reagan's New Federalism," p. 26.

45. Ibid., p. 27.

46. Timothy J. Conlan, "And the Beat Goes On: Intergovernmental Mandates and Preemption in an Era of Deregulation," *Publius: The Journal of Federalism* 21 (Summer 1991), p. 52.

47. Joseph F. Zimmerman, "Preemption in the U.S. Federal System," *Publius: The Journal of Federalism* 23 (Fall 1993), p. 9.

48. Timothy J. Conlan and David R. Beam, "Federal Mandates: The Record of Reform and Future Prospects," *Intergovernmental Perspective* 18 (Fall 1992), p. 9.

49. State of Texas, Legislative Budget Board, *Analysis of Federal Initiatives and State Expenditures,* June 15, 1994.

50. Pagano, et al., "The State of American Federalism, 1990–1991," p. 1.

51. Conlan, "And the Beat Goes On: Intergovernmental Mandates and Preemption in an Era of Deregulation," pp. 44–46.

52. Stephens and Wikstrom, *American Intergovernmental Relations,* pp. 40–1.

53. Paul L. Posner, "Unfunded Mandates Reform Act: 1996 and Beyond," *Publius: The Journal of Federalism* 27 (Spring 1997), p. 53.

54. Carol S. Weissert and Sanford F. Schram, "The State of American Federalism, 1995–1996," *Publius: The Journal of Federalism* 26 (Summer 1996), p. 6.

55. Sanford F. Schram and Carol S. Weissert, "The State of American Federalism, 1996–1997," *Publius: The Journal of Federalism* 27 (Spring 1997), pp. 5–8.

56. Alan K. Ota, "Highway Law Benefits Those Who Held Purse Strings," *Congressional Quarterly Weekly* 56 (June 13, 1998), pp. 1595–1596.

57. Schram and Weissert, "The State of American Federalism, 1996–1997," p. 8.

58. Weissert and Schram, "The State of American Federalism, 1995–1996," p. 14.

59. Schram and Weissert, "The State of American Federalism, 1996–1997," p 1.

60. John Kincaid, "The Devolution Tortoise and the Centralization Hare," *New England Economic Review* (May–June 1998), pp. 36, 38.

61. Richard L. Cole, Rodney V. Hissong, and Enid Arvidson, "Devolution: Where's the Revolution?" *Publius: The Journal of Federalism* 29 (Fall 1999), pp. 99–112.

62. John Kincaid, "Trends in Federalism: Is Fiscal Federalism Fizzling?" *The Book of the States 2003,* vol. 35 (Lexington, KY: Council of State Governments, 2003), p. 27.

63. George W. Bush, "Memorandum on the Interagency Working Group on Federalism," February 26, 2001; and Joseph Francis Zimmerman, *Contemporary American Federalism,* 2nd ed. (SUNY University Press, 2008), p. 127.

64. Daniel Henniger, "Homeland Security Will Reshape the Homeland," *Wall Street Journal,* November 22, 2002, p. 16.

65. *Austin American-Statesman,* September 26, 2003, p. B1.

66. John Dinan, "The State of American Federalism 2007–2008: Resurgent State Influence in the National Policy Process and Continued State Policy Innovation," *Publius: The Journal of Federalism* 38 (May 2008), p. 383.

67. Ibid.

68. Ibid., pp. 384–5.

69. Wright, "Federalism and Intergovernmental Relations," p. 23.

70. Sidney M. Milkis and Jesse H. Rhodes, "George W. Bush, the Party System, and American Federalism," *Publius: The Journal of Federalism* 37 (May 2007), p. 483.

71. Gene Healy and Timothy Lynch, *Power Surge: The Constitutional Record of George W. Bush* (Washington, DC: Cato Institute, 2006).

72. Tim Conlan and John Dinan, "Federalism, the Bush Administration, and the Transformation of American Conservatism," *Publius: The Journal of Federalism* 37 (April 2007), pp. 283–8.

73. Milkis and Rhodes, "George W. Bush, the Party System, and American Federalism," p. 478.

74. John Dinan, "The State of American Federalism 2007–2008: Resurgent State Influence in the National Policy Process and Continued State Policy Innovation," *Publius: The Journal of Federalism* 38 (May 2008), p. 381.

75. Ibid., pp. 382–401.

76. Barack Obama, "Memorandum for the Heads of Executive Departments and Agencies," May 20, 2009.

77. John Schwartz, "Obama Seems to be Open to a Broader Role for States," *New York Times,* January 30, 2009.

78. U.S. General Accounting Office, "Recovery Act: As Initial Implementation Unfolds in States and Localities, Continued Attention to Accountability Issues is Essential," GAO-09-580, April 23, 2009; and "Texas Comptroller of Public Accounts, American Recovery and Reinvestment Act: A Texas Eye on the Dollars," *Window on State Government.*

79. *Garcia v. San Antonio Metropolitan Transit Authority,* 105 S. Ct. 1005 (1985).

80. Anton, *American Federalism and Public Policy,* pp. 14–16.

81. Dye, *American Federalism,* pp. 8–12.

82. *U.S. v. Lopez,* 115 S. Ct. 1624 (1995); and Schram and Weissert, "The State of American Federalism, 1996–1997," p. 10.

83. *Bush v. Vera,* 116 S. Ct. 1941 (1996); *Easley* v. *Cromartie,* 121 S. Ct. 2239 (2001); and *New York Times,* April 19, 2001, p. 1.

84. Weissert and Schram, "The State of American Federalism, 1995–1996," p. 12; and *Medtronic, Inc.* v. *Lohr et vir.,* 116 S. Ct. 2240 (1996).

85. *City of Boerne, Texas v. Flores,* 117 S.Ct. 2157 (1997).

86. Schram and Weissert, "The State of American Federalism, 1996–1997," p. 26.

87. *Printz v. U.S.,* 117 S.Ct. 2365 (1997).

88. Weissert and Schram, "The State of American Federalism, 1995–1996," p. 13.

89. Ibid., p. 10; *Romer et al.* v. *Evans, et al.,* 116 S. Ct. 1620 (1996); and *U.S. v. Virginia et al.,* 116 S. Ct. 2264 (1996).

90. Ibid.; and *Seminole Tribe v. Florida,* 116 S. Ct. 1941 (1996).

91. Sanford F. Schram and Carol S. Weissert, "The State of U.S. Federalism: 1998–1999," *Publius: The Journal of Federalism* 29 (Spring 1999), p. 34.

92. Dinan and Krane, "The State of American Federalism, 2005: Federalism Resurfaces in the Political Debate," p. 26.

93. Internal Revenue Service, *Internal Revenue Service Data Book 2007,* Table 5; and U.S. Census Bureau, *Consolidated Federal Funds Report for Fiscal Year 2007,* Table 10.

94. U.S. Census Bureau, *Federal Aid to States for Fiscal Year 2007,* Figure 5.

95. Legislative Budget Board, *Fiscal Size-Up, 2008–2009* (Austin, TX: Legislative Budget Board, 2008), Figure 10.

96. Office of the Governor, State Grants Team, http://www.governor.state.tx.us/divisions/stategrants.

97. Hawkins, "Pre-emption: The Dramatic Rise of Federal Supremacy," p. 12.

98. M. Delal Baer, "North American Free Trade," *Foreign Affairs* 70 (Fall 1991), p. 138.

99. Joan B. Anderson, "Maquiladoras and Border Industrialization: Impact on Economic Development in Mexico," *Journal of Borderland Studies* 5 (Spring 1990), p. 5.

100. Michael Patrick, "Maquiladoras and South Texas Border Economic Development," *Journal of Borderland Studies,* IV (Spring 1989), p. 90.

101. Martin E. Rosenfeldt, "Mexico's In Bond Export Industries and U.S. Legislation: Conflictive Issues," *Journal of Borderland Studies* 5 (Spring 1990), p. 57.

102. Patrick, "Maquiladoras and South Texas Border Economic Development," p. 90.
103. Mexico's Maquila & Pitex Online Directory 2008, **www.maquiladirectory.com/index/htm**. United States, International Trade Data System, *Importing/Exporting Resources,* http://www.itds.teas.gov/maquiladora.html.
104. Baer, "North American Free Trade," pp. 132–49.
105. Central Intelligence Agency, *The World Factbook—2009,* http://www.cia/publications/factbook/.
106. Ibid.
107. International Trade Administration, "U.S. Total Imports from Individual Countries, 1998–2004," *Industry, Trade and the Economy,* April 4, 2005, Table 7, http://ita.doc.gov/td/industry/otea/usfth/aggregate/ 04T07.html.
108. Texas Center for Border Economic and Enterprise Development, Texas A&M International University, *Border Crossings,* http://texascenter.tamiu.edu/texcen_services/border_crossings.asp.
109. This discussion of the history of immigration laws is based on Clarke E. Cochran, Lawrence C. Mayer, T.R. Carr, and N. Joseph Cayer, *American Public Policy,* 9th ed. (Boston: Wadsworth, 2009), pp. 400–6; Federation for American Immigration Reform, "History of U.S. Immigration Laws," January, 2008; and Cornell University Law School, "Immigration Law: An Overview."
110. Robert W. Gardner and Leon F. Bouvier, "The United States," in *Handbook on International Migration,* edited by William J. Serow, Charles B. Nam, David F. Sly, and Robert H. Weller (New York: Greenwood Press, 1990), p. 342.
111. James F. Pearce and Jeffery W. Gunther, "Illegal Immigration from Mexico: Effects on the Texas Economy," *Federal Reserve Bank of Dallas Economic Review* (September 1985), p. 4.
112. "Congress Clears Overhaul of Immigration Law," *Congressional Quarterly Almanac,* 1986 (Washington, DC: Congressional Quarterly, 1987), pp. 61–67.
113. Dan Carney, "Law Restricts Illegal Immigration," *Congressional Quarterly Weekly Report* 54 (November 16, 1996), p. 3287.
114. Steven A. Camarota, "Immigrants in the United States, 2007: A Profile of America's Foreign-Born Population," Center for Immigration Studies, November 2007.
115. Jeffrey L. Katz, "Welfare Overhaul Law," *Congressional Quarterly Weekly Report* 54 (September 21, 1996),

pp. 2696–2705; and Stephen A. Camarota, "Back Where We Started: An Examination of Trends in Immigrant Welfare Use Since Welfare Reform," Center for Immigration Studies, March 2003.
116. U.S. Customs and Border Protection, Secure Border Initiative, "Pedestrian Fence 225," November 2008.
117. Mario Recio, "Obama: Troop Move to Mexican Border Under Consideration," *MClatchy Newspapers,* March 11, 2009.
118. Pew Hispanic Center, "Statistical Portrait of the Foreign-Born Population in the United States, 2007."
119. Camarota, "Immigrants in the United States, 2007"; and Jeffrey S. Passel and D'Vera Cohn, "A Portrait of Unauthorized Immigrants in the United States," Pew Hispanic Center, April 14, 2009.
120. Ibid.
121. National Conference of State Legislators, Immigration Policy Project, "2009 Immigration-Related Bills and Resolutions in the States," April 2009.
122. White House, Office of the Press Secretary, "Obama Remarks at Esperanza National Hispanic Prayer Breakfast," June 19, 2009.
123. Barry R. McCaffrey, "Memorandum for Colonial Michael Meese," December 29, 2008.
124. Ken Ellingwood, "Calderon seeks to Dispel Talk of 'failing state,'" *Los Angeles Times,* January 25, 2009.
125. James Pinkerton, "Equal-opportunity Corruption in the Valley," *San Antonio Express-News,* January 2, 2007, p. 1A. From March 2004 to the end of 2006, 19 public officials in the valley were convicted of taking bribes and kickbacks.
126. Joan Anderson and Martin de la Rosa, "Economic Survival Strategies of Poor Families on the Mexican Border," *Journal of Borderland Studies* 6 (Spring 1991), p. 51.
127. Howard G. Applegate, C. Richard Bath, and Jeffery T. Trannon, "Binational Emissions Trading in an International Air Shed: The Case of El Paso, Texas and Ciudad Juarez," *Journal of Borderland Studies* 4 (Fall 1989), pp. 1–25.
128. See the Border Governors Conference website at http://www.bordergovernorsconference.com.

Interest Groups and Political Power in Texas

Questions to Guide Your Reading

1. Are the decisions of Texas governments controlled by a small elite or are power and influence distributed across many sectors of society?

2. Throughout our history, there has been a persistent pattern of associational or group membership. Why are people so inclined to join groups, and how does this contribute to a democratic political system?

3. What are the key elements in a group's success in the policymaking process?

4. If people are not linked to the political process through groups, who speaks for their interests?

In America there is no limit to freedom of association for political ends.

—Alexis de Tocqueville[1]

*The Citizens shall have the right, in a peaceable manner, to assemble for
their common Good, and apply to those invested with the powers of
government for redress of grievances or other purposes by petition, address
or remonstrance.*

—Texas Constitution, Article 1, Section 27

The business community, through endorsements and political contributions, was influential in Republicans capturing a majority of Texas House of Representative seats in 2002, giving the GOP control of that body for the first time since Reconstruction and leading to the election of the first Republican House speaker of modern times. The Texas Association of Business, or TAB, an umbrella group representing many businesses, was one of the most visible backers of Republican candidates who supported business priorities, including more restrictions on civil lawsuits, fewer governmental regulations and holding the line on state taxes. In pursuit of its policy agenda, TAB took the unusual—and controversial—step of spending $2 million in corporate contributions on political advertising in twenty-four state legislative races. Most of the candidates supported by TAB won, but the tactic prompted a criminal investigation of the business group and precipitated a debate over free speech versus undue corporate influence over elections.

State law allows officers and employees of corporations to make personal contributions to political candidates or to contribute through political action committees established for that purpose. But it is illegal for corporate funds to be given directly to a candidate, and soon after the election, Travis County District Attorney Ronnie Earle began investigating TAB's contributions. TAB argued that the corporate donations were legal because they weren't given directly to candidates but instead were used to purchase advertising that educated voters on issues important to the group. The ads didn't directly advocate the election or defeat of any candidates, although they obviously influenced election results.

TAB fought the investigation with a series of legal maneuvers, arguing that the ads amounted to constitutionally protected free speech. National business groups also rallied to TAB's defense, claiming that Earle, a Democrat, was letting politics influence his investigation. But Earle argued that he was merely investigating "allegations of crime."[2]

The organization was later indicted by a Travis County grand jury on charges of violating state campaign finance laws. The investigation resulted in related charges against then–U.S. House Majority Leader Tom DeLay of Sugar Land and two associates, who also had been active in securing the Republican takeover of the Texas House. TAB eventually pleaded to a misdemeanor charge of unlawful campaign expenditures and paid a $10,000 fine. None of the other defendants had come to trial by late-2009, but the controversy prompted DeLay's resignation from Congress.

TAB's ad campaign was one of the more visible examples of an interest group's influence in Austin in recent years. The objectives of the association were clear and unambiguous—defeat Democratic candidates who were deemed hostile to the group's interests. But much of the influence of interest groups and their lobbyists is subtle, elusive to public scrutiny, and reflects complex relationships among interest groups, elected public officials, and those who administer the law.

TABLE 4–1   State Lobbying Expenditures in 2004–2006: The Top Ten

State	2004 Total Expenditures	2005 Total Expenditures	2006 Total Expenditures
California	$212,695,872	$227,940,496	$271,680,365
New York	144,000,000	149,000,000	151,000,000
Florida	No total	No total	121,760,708
Texas	162,111,407	173,594,357	120,215,500
Massachusetts	31,052,702	70,955,161	78,960,743
New Jersey	25,126,328	28,922,559	55,321,166
Pennsylvania	No total	124,813,732	54,090,812
Minnesota	50,217,111	54,718,363	53,287,186
Washington	34,996,252	37,049,691	38,717,055
Connecticut	27,629,998	No total	38,419,882

Source: Center for Public Integrity, "State Lobbying Totals, 2004–2006," December 1, 2007.

Political candidates often claim to be running against "the special interests" and promise to be responsive to all the people rather than to a few well-financed business, trade, or union groups. But most successful candidates freely accept campaign contributions from interest groups, and many Texans, along with other Americans, feel that governments are dominated by a few big interests looking out for themselves. National election surveys conducted by the University of Michigan for more than thirty years indicate a clear pattern of increased public distrust of government. In 1964, 28 percent of those surveyed felt that government was run by a few big interests, but during most of the years since 1974, more than 60 percent of Americans expressed this sentiment.[3]

Two other studies, conducted more than forty years apart, placed Texas among states with strong pressure-group systems.[4] Powerful pressure groups usually evolve in states with weak political parties, which has always been the case in Texas.[5] During the many years that Texas was a one-party Democratic state, the Republican Party posed no serious challenge to the Democratic monopoly, and the Democratic Party was marked by intense factionalism. Although the conservative Democratic wing generally dominated state politics through the 1970s, interest groups often played a greater role in the policymaking process. Subsequent Republican growth has changed Texas's party system (see Chapter 6), but interest groups remain strong in the state and spend millions of dollars trying to elect favored candidates and influence governmental decisions (see Table 4–1). More often than not, these interest groups still have a greater impact on the policymaking process than do the political parties.

INTEREST GROUPS DEFINED

An **interest group** may be defined as "an organized collection of individuals who are bound together by shared attitudes or concerns and who make demands on political institutions in order to realize goals which they are unable to achieve on their own."[6] Members of an interest group share common interests or goals, organize to pursue those goals collectively because they cannot achieve them individually, and focus some of their efforts on influencing governmental decisions.[7] These characteristics, particularly the political and policy objectives, distinguish these groups from other organizations.

We do not know exactly how many groups or organizations there are in the United States or even in Texas. The *Encyclopedia of Associations* has identified approximately 22,000 associations of national scope. Across the country at the regional, state, and local level, some 115,000 associations have been documented.[8] Comparing these totals with earlier estimates, it is clear that there has been an "explosion" of group activity since the 1950s.[9] There are thousands in Texas. Some have long histories, while others are formed to address a specific need, interest, or problem and disappear after a relatively short period. Although most organizations have the potential to participate in the policymaking process, many will not. In our attempt to define the pressure-group system in Texas, we focus on those groups that can be identified as continuous active players.

Most organizations are not formed for political purposes. One scholar has suggested that only 10 percent of the people participate in organizations active in the pressure group system.[10] People usually don't join a chess club or a fraternal order, for example, to have an impact on public policy. Participation in church-related activities is usually based on spiritual or personal needs, although church groups can become involved in the political process (see Chapter 6).

We also should distinguish between categorical groups and interest or pressure groups. Women collectively constitute a categorical grouping of the female population; senior citizens, African Americans, and Hispanics also comprise categorical groups. Although these are often spoken of as groups of people with similar political objectives, individuals within each group hold a wide diversity of interests, concerns, and goals. By contrast, an interest group is a segment of the population that organizes for specific purposes and objectives in the policymaking process.

GROUP MEMBERSHIP

It is estimated that 75 percent of Americans belong to some type of organization. Church membership is the single largest category, with more than 40 percent of the population claiming weekly attendance at religious services. Americans also join a wide array of civic, sports, service, fraternal, hobby, economic, and professional groups and organizations. Close to 50 percent of the country's population reported membership in two or more groups.[11]

At first glance, it would appear that the overwhelming majority of Americans have potential access to the policymaking process by way of their group memberships. Closer inspection, however, raises serious questions about the distribution of political power and resources. The argument that the policy playing field is tilted to benefit some groups or interests to the exclusion of others has some validity.[12] And, if part of the population has limited potential to affect the decisions of government, there are serious questions about the very nature of a democratic society and the role of groups within this political structure.

Those who study organizations generally agree that persons with higher incomes, better educations, higher status occupations, and higher standards of living are more likely than other people to belong to groups.[13] Historically, men have joined at a higher rate than have women; older people join at higher rates than do younger people; Anglos are more likely to be members than are Hispanics or African Americans; and people with established community ties are more likely to participate. Not only do these people join more groups, but they also are more likely to be active participants. These findings suggest that there is a class bias in the interest group system in Texas. People from higher socioeconomic classes are more easily organized and are more likely to maintain their support for these organizations.[14] Lower socioeconomic groups, minorities, and diffused constituencies, such as consumers, find it very difficult to compete on an equal footing with business, industrial, and professional groups, who also can better afford lobbying expenses and the financial contributions to political campaigns that usually guarantee access to officeholders.

WHY PEOPLE JOIN INTEREST GROUPS ●

Individuals join groups for a variety of reasons, which may change over time. One is the number of personal and material benefits that can be derived from interest groups.[15] A teacher, for example, may join the Texas State Teachers Association (TSTA) because it lobbies for higher teacher salaries, better fringe benefits and working conditions, and general educational issues. But TSTA also offers its members publications, insurance programs, potential legal assistance, discounts for travel, and valuable professional information.

People also realize social benefits from joining groups. Membership and participation provide them with a sense of personal identification with larger organizations and institutions that are likely to be more visible and potentially effective in the policymaking process than an individual would be if acting alone.[16] They may believe their personal status and prestige also are enhanced by group membership.[17]

Finally, there is the personal satisfaction or sense of purpose that a person receives from belonging to a group that he or she believes has a worthwhile cause or objective. There are people who join groups to try to make the world a better place.[18] One motivation for joining such groups as Common Cause or the League of Women Voters, for example, may be a commitment to improving the election system in Texas. For many people, reform of the election system provides broad, but intangible, benefits that go well beyond the group or organization.

INTEREST GROUPS, PLURALISM, AND DEMOCRATIC THEORY ●

The issue of interest groups and political power in American politics has been debated since the Constitutional Convention of 1787. Writing in the *Federalist Papers* at a time when there were no political parties or interest groups as we know today, James Madison argued that it was inevitable that people would organize into groups, or "factions," and attempt to impose their will on others and use governments for their specific purposes. Madison also recognized two basic problems: there was a potential for the majority to tyrannize or impose its will on others, and a potential for the majority, in its pursuit of narrow self-interests, to harm the long-term interests of society as a whole.[19]

The cure for this **mischief of factions** was both institutional and socioeconomic. If the number of factions or groups increased, there would be greater competition and less likelihood that any one group could dominate the policymaking process. Competitors would have to find compromises. And, institutional power would be fragmented among three branches of government and a federal system, in which powers would be further divided between the national government and the states. Elections for different offices are staggered in different years, and there are significant variations in electoral constituencies. The effect of the variations in national, state, and local elections is to make it even more difficult to construct large, permanent coalitions that could exercise absolute control over all institutions and subsequently dominate all policies.

Drawing in part on this tradition established by Madison, David Truman, an American political scientist, argued in his classic study, *The Governmental Process,* that American politics can be understood primarily in terms of the way groups interact with each other.[20] Expanding on Truman's theories, other scholars have attempted to develop a general understanding of politics organized around groups. These scholars often are referred to as *pluralists* and their theories as **pluralism**. They believe that significant numbers of diverse and competing interest groups share political influence in a way that limits the power of any single group.

Although there are differences in emphasis among the pluralists, they have established the following general characteristics of a pluralistic society:

- Groups are the primary actors in the policymaking process. They provide the individual with political resources and link a person to governmental institutions.
- Politics is basically group interaction, in which groups come into conflict with each other over the limited resources of society, and public policy is ultimately the resolution of group conflict and differences.
- There are so many groups that no one group can dominate the political process. Although some groups have more resources than others, a group always has the potential to influence policy. If there is no group to address a particular concern or problem, one can be organized.
- Although most people do not actively participate in the policymaking process, they have access to the process through the leaders of the groups to which they belong. There are numerous leadership opportunities within groups for individuals who want active roles.
- Most group leaders are committed to democratic values, and competition makes them responsive to other members and serves to check or constrain their actions.[21]

Pluralism is appealing because it gives credence to our general views of a democratic society and offers potential solutions, or at least hope, for those people who are excluded from full political participation or benefits.

One can find evidence in Texas to support the pluralist view. There are thousands of different groups organized on a statewide or community level. Hundreds of lobbyists are registered in Austin to represent a wide variety of economic, social, civic, and cultural organizations. A growing state population and a diversifying economy have significantly increased the number of interest groups over the past three decades.

David Truman has suggested that there are periods, or "waves," in American political history in which there are rapid proliferations of groups in response to economic, social, or political change.[22] To compensate for imbalances in the political system, additional groups will be organized and attempt to reestablish an equilibrium.

Groups can be formed for any number of reasons. Concerns over economic changes, public school funding, environmental protection, medical care for low-income Texans, and other pressing issues have generated additional interest groups in Texas in recent years. Movements focusing on the interests of Hispanics, African Americans, women, and homosexuals led to the creation of interest groups lobbying to advance their concerns. Still other organizations have emerged to protect existing interests, or the status quo, and some groups have been formed in response to new governmental policies and regulations.[23]

With the elimination of historic discriminatory practices, minority Texans have made significant economic, social, and political gains. In addition to having increased access to mainstream groups, minorities have formed their own professional and economic organizations. It is not uncommon to find Hispanic chambers of commerce or African American bar associations in many Texas cities.

Advocates of pluralism use the foregoing arguments and examples to support their view. Despite the earlier periods in Texas history, when large segments of the population were excluded from the political and policymaking processes, they argue that the political system is now open and accessible to new groups. They believe that those holding public office are responsive to the needs and interests of a greater diversity of Texans than ever before.

THE ELITIST ALTERNATIVE

Other political scientists, however, insist that the pluralist theories simply do not describe the realities of power and policymaking in Texas or the United States. They say the pluralists have not given enough attention to the fact that a few individuals still control enormous resources. Although there are thousands of groups, they are neither equal in political resources nor can they equally translate their interests or demands into public policy. These scholars believe the political system in Texas can be more accurately described in terms of **elitism**.

According to this view, the ability to influence the most important policy decisions is monopolized by a few individuals who derive power from their leadership positions in large organizations or institutions, particularly those with great financial resources. From the elitist perspective, power is not an individual commodity or resource but an attribute of social organizations.[24]

People who subscribe to this theory also believe that the existence of elites within any society is inevitable. Robert Michels, a European social scientist writing during the first part of the twentieth century, argued that any organization, no matter how structured, will eventually produce an "oligarchy," or rule by a few individuals. Michels' **iron rule of oligarchy** was applicable to any organization and was a universal law applied to all social systems.[25]

Beginning with C. Wright Mills in his book, *The Power Elite,* many American scholars have been proponents of the elitist theory.[26] Although there has been rigorous intellectual debate between elitist and pluralist theorists, a number of generalizations can be derived from the elitist school of thought:

- Power is held by a few individuals and is derived from their positions in large institutions. In addition to economic institutions, these include the government, the mass media, and civic organizations.
- Historically, political elites constituted a homogeneous group drawn primarily from the upper and upper middle classes. They were older, well-educated, primarily white, Anglo-Saxon males.
- Although there is competition among elites and the institutions they represent, there is considerable consensus and cohesion among elites on primary values, interests, and the rules of the game.
- Elites are linked by a complex network of interlocking memberships on the governing bodies of corporations, financial institutions, foundations, and civic and cultural organizations.

- Policy decisions are made by a few individuals and primarily reflect the interests of the dominant institutions. The interests of the dominant elites are not necessarily opposed to those of other classes of society.
- The vast majority of people are passive spectators to the policymaking process. Voting has been the primary means by which the general population can participate in governmental decisions, but other than selecting governmental officials, elections have limited effects on policy decisions.[27]

A number of students of Texas government and politics have argued from the elitist perspective. George Norris Green, writing about the period from 1938 to 1957, concluded that Texas was "governed by conservatives, collectively dubbed **the Establishment**."[28] This was a "loosely knit plutocracy comprised mostly of Anglo businessmen, oilmen, bankers and lawyers" that emerged in the late 1930s, in part as a response to the liberal policies of the New Deal.[29] They were extremely conservative, producing a "virulent" strain of conservatism marked by "Texanism" and "super-Americanism."[30]

The "traditionalistic–individualistic" political culture described in Chapter 1 was especially conducive to the dominance of the conservative establishment, which had little interest in the needs of the lower socioeconomic groups within the state. The exclusion of minorities from participation in elections and the low rates of voter turnout resulted in the election of public officials who were sympathetic to the views of the conservative elites. In addition, public opinion was manipulated by "unprincipled public relations men" and "the rise of reactionary newspapers."[31]

In a more recent study of Texas politics, Chandler Davidson argues that there is a group of Texans, extraordinarily wealthy or linked to large corporations, who constitute "an upper class in the precise meaning of the term: a social group whose common background and effective control of wealth bring them together politically."[32] While warning against a hasty conclusion that an upper class is a ruling class, Davidson describes their shared values, group cohesiveness, and interlocking relationships.[33] The upper class has enormous political power. When united on specific policy objectives, its members usually have prevailed against "their liberal enemies concentrated in the working class."[34] Moreover, the institutional arrangements of the state's economic and political structure work to produce an upper-class unity that contributes to their successes in public policy.[35]

The sharply contrasting views of political power in Texas have produced an ongoing debate. To a large extent, the issue of who controls Texas politics has not been resolved because of insufficient data to support one position over the other. There also is evidence suggesting that power relationships have changed over time. Historically, Texas government and public policy were dominated by an upper class or a conservative establishment. But with the enormous social, economic, and political changes that have taken place over the past twenty years, Texans may well be moving from an elitist system to some variation of pluralism.

HYPERPLURALISM, POLICY SUBSYSTEMS, AND SINGLE-ISSUE INTEREST GROUPS

Some scholars believe that the rapid expansion of interest groups in Texas and the nation has produced a system of **hyperpluralism**. In effect, hyperpluralism is the interest group system out of control.[36] Historically, political stability was achieved by competition and bargaining among interest groups. Public policy that had some degree of coherence and reflected shared views of the general interest was developed.

But as groups proliferate there is a potential for the policy process to degenerate into a series of subsystems. This problem has been compounded by the notion that the demands of all interest groups are legitimate and governments should attempt to respond to as many groups as possible. This theory of interest group liberalism is developed at length by Theodore Lowi in *The End of Liberalism*.[37]

Governments respond to the demands of various groups by enacting laws and regulations or appropriating funds to address their priorities. In many cases, additional governmental agencies may be created to carry out the new laws. Legislative committees also may be given control over new programs. Eventually, the interactions among the interest groups, the administrative agencies, and the legislative committees produce permanent relationships that have been described as the **iron triangles of government** (see Chapter 13).

Lowi's concerns about the excesses of pluralism may be valid. Some state agencies are closely tied to the industries they regulate. Sometimes, interest groups even lobby for dedicated sources of funding for their programs, thus assuring they will benefit from specific taxes year after year, regardless of other state needs.

Hyperpluralism also can lead to deadlock. Lobbying, described in the next section, has become increasingly sophisticated. Often, lobbyists representing a single influential group can block policy initiatives for which there is widespread support but which threaten the group's priorities. Considering the difficulties in addressing the problems facing state and local governments in recent years, one can conclude that it is easier to block solutions than enact policies addressing pressing needs for change.

In recent years, a number of scholars have identified another threat to the stability of the political system—the **single-issue groups**. These are highly ideological groups that attempt to push on the public agenda a single issue or cause without regard for the views or attitudes of other groups. These groups often are reluctant to compromise and often engage in tactics and strategies designed to extract concessions upon threat of policy deadlock. Their position on an issue leaves no grounds for accommodation or compromise. These groups also base their support for or opposition to a political candidate on a single issue with little regard for the candidate's other policy positions.

RESOURCES OF INTEREST GROUPS ●

Some interest groups are extremely powerful and exercise considerable influence over the formation of public policy, while others are ineffectual and weak. The differences can be explained by a number of factors.

One is the size of a group, the number of members and voters it can potentially influence. There are numerous teachers' and educational groups within the state, for example, representing a significant number of people. The promise of support or the threat of retaliation by such groups will be assessed by a legislator as he or she decides to support or oppose the groups' policy proposals. As will be discussed later in this chapter, individual educational groups don't always agree on legislation, but their numbers are difficult to ignore. Teachers who had been instrumental in the 1982 election of Governor Mark White withdrew that support in 1986 in a dispute over some of White's education reforms; the loss of that support contributed to his defeat.

The size of a group alone, however, does not guarantee power or influence. A large group internally divided, with no clear policy focus, is less likely to be successful than a smaller group with a fixed goal. Other major factors in a group's success are its cohesiveness and the ability of its leaders to mobilize its membership in support of policy objectives.

Another key factor is the distribution of a group's membership across the state. A group concentrated in one geographic area has less potential impact on the election of a large number of legislators than does a group with members distributed across the state. Organized labor, for example, has its greatest membership strength in the Houston and Beaumont areas in Southeast Texas. On the other hand, teachers and small business owners are plentiful throughout the state and have the potential to affect more local and district elections.

A group's power also is determined by its financial resources. Groups that represent low-income people have difficulty raising the dollars necessary to mount effective lobbying or public relations campaigns. By contrast, organizations representing large corporations or high-income professional groups are in a much better position to raise funds for the campaign contributions and lobbying expenditures necessary to assure access to policymakers.

A group's influence is affected also by its reputation, both within the legislature and among the general public. A major function of interest groups is to provide information to policymakers, and the reliability and accuracy of this information are critical. If a group lies, unduly distorts information, or is less than forthright in its dealings with other actors in the policymaking process, its reputation can be irreparably damaged.[38]

The leadership of a group and its hired staff also contribute to its success. As policy issues develop, a competent staff will conduct research, provide position papers, draft specific proposals, contact key decision makers and the press, maintain communication with the membership, and develop public relations strategies to mobilize the membership to bring pressure on policymakers.

THE DOMINANT INTEREST GROUPS IN TEXAS ●

Throughout much of our history, state government was dominated by large corporations and banks, oil companies, and agricultural interests that backed the conservative Democratic officeholders who had a stranglehold on the legislature, the courts, and the executive branch.[39] Big business still carries a lot of weight in Austin and can purchase a lot of influence with major political contributions and the sophisticated skills of public affairs strategists. State officials who want to build public support for new policy proposals usually solicit the support of the business community first.

Beginning in the 1970s, however, influence began to be more diffused. Single-member districts (see Chapter 8) increased the number of minorities, Republicans, and liberal Democrats elected to the legislature. Consumer, environmental, and other public advocacy groups emerged. Organized labor, which had been shut out by the corporate establishment, found some common interests with the trial lawyers, who earn fees suing businesses on behalf of consumers and other plaintiffs claiming damages or injuries caused by various companies or products. The decline of oil and gas production and the emergence of high-tech service industries also helped diffuse the business lobby into more competitive factions.

Business

The diverse business interests in Texas organize in several ways to influence the policy-making process. First, broad-based associations, including the Texas Association of Business (TAB) and the Texas Taxpayers and Research Association, represent business and industry in general. Their overall goal is to maintain and improve upon a favorable business climate by seeking favorable tax and regulatory policies.

The business community also organizes through trade associations that represent and seek to advance the interests of specific industries. Some of the more active associations include the Texas Bankers Association, the Texas Association of Realtors, the Wholesale Beer Distributors of Texas, the Texas Independent Producers & Royalty Owners Association, the Texas Chemical Council, the Texas Automobile Dealers Association, and the Texas Restaurant Association.

Many individual companies also retain their own lobbyists to represent them before the legislature and administrative agencies. A lobbyist may be a salaried employee of a company or a professional, freelance lobbyist—or "hired gun"—who is retained by several clients. Some wealthy individuals, such as Ross Perot, the Dallas billionaire computer magnate and former presidential candidate, even hire their own lobbyists.

Finally, a group representing a broad range of business members can be organized to pursue a single issue. Perhaps the best-known example of this is Texans for Lawsuit Reform, which for several years has doggedly lobbied for a series of limitations on civil lawsuits and damage awards against businesses and their insurance companies.

Business groups form coalitions in opposition to organized labor, consumer advocates, and trial lawyers on major political and philosophical issues, such as limits on consumer lawsuits. But the business lobby is far from monolithic. There are numerous issues, including tax policy and utility regulation, on which different companies or trade associations differ. During the 1999 legislative session, for example, lawmakers had to perform a delicate balancing act to put together an electric deregulation bill allowing petrochemical plants and other heavy industrial users of electricity to generate and sell power in competition with utility companies. And government has been frequently confronted in recent years with rivalries in the expanding telecommunications industry.

For many years, the interest groups associated with oil and natural gas played a dominant role among the business and industry lobbies. At one time, oil and natural gas accounted for 30 percent of the state's economic output. But this contribution has sharply declined since the 1980s recession, and the oil and gas lobby, though still effective, now has to work with political leaders who are focused on economic diversification. Other sources of traditional political power in Texas—the financial and real estate industries—also were at the center of Texas's economic downturn in the 1980s but have recovered and remain an effective lobbying force.

Professional Groups

A number of professional groups have played dominant roles in Texas politics and the policymaking process. One of the better known is the Texas Medical Association (TMA), which in recent years has joined forces with business against trial lawyers to push for laws putting limits on malpractice suits and other damage claims against physicians and the business community. The TMA's political action committee (TEXPAC) is a major contributor of campaign dollars to candidates for the legislature, the Texas Supreme Court, and other state offices. It won a major victory in 2003, with legislative and voter approval of a constitutional amendment imposing new limits on monetary damages in medical malpractice cases.

Litigation over medical malpractice, product liability, and workers' compensation also has raised the profile of trial lawyers, who make their living representing injured persons, or plaintiffs. Trial lawyers are compensated with a share of the damages awarded their clients by a court or negotiated in a settlement with the defendant or the defendant's insurance company. A defendant can be a doctor accused of malpractice in the handling of an individual's care, a manufacturer accused of making a faulty product that caused an injury, a city whose truck was involved in an auto accident, an employer whose worker suffered an injury on the job, or just about any legal entity deemed responsible for causing harm to someone. Individually and through their political action committee, trial lawyers have contributed millions of dollars to judicial, legislative, and other selected candidates since the 1970s. In the early 1980s, they succeeded in electing several Texas Supreme Court justices who shared their viewpoint, and the court issued precedent-setting opinions making it easier for plaintiffs to win large damage awards. The business and medical communities retaliated by boosting their own political contributions and lobbying efforts and, by 1990, had succeeded in tipping the state Supreme Court's philosophical scale back to its traditional business-oriented viewpoint (see Chapter 11).

Although the war over tort law, as these types of damage suits are called, continued to rage—before the courts and in the legislature–trial lawyers usually were on the defensive in the new era of Republican statehouse control.

Education

A variety of educational interests are very visible in the policymaking process in Austin. The changing global economy and increased technology have enhanced the importance of education in developing the state's future, and there is widespread public support for improving the public schools and expanding access to colleges and universities. Some education groups have been more successful than others, and lobbying for higher education has been particularly effective.

Most university regents, chancellors, and presidents are well connected politically. Universities also are capable—through the use of donations and other nontax funds—of hiring a well-paid cadre of legislative liaisons, or lobbyists. Another effective lobbying source for universities, particularly the larger ones, are the armies of alumni, many of them politically influential, ready to make phone calls, send e-mails, or write letters on behalf of their alma maters when the need arises. The business community also is a strong supporter of higher education. The influence of the University of Texas System, in particular, was instrumental in the legislature's enactment of a law in 2003 giving university governing boards the authority, for the first time in Texas, to raise student tuition independently of legislative control.

The struggle for equity and quality in public elementary and secondary education in Texas, a major issue for many years, has been complicated by more than two dozen groups representing various—and often conflicting—interests within the educational community. There are at least four different teachers' associations, one for school boards, a separate lobby group for school administrators, and still others for elementary school principals and secondary school principals. Separate groups also have been formed for urban school districts, suburban districts, rural districts, and districts with large numbers of special-needs students. Many of the associations are well financed, and some indirectly receive taxpayer money through dues paid by member school districts. Virtually all the groups have paid lobbyists, and although all claim to support educational quality, their primary goals are to protect the specific interests of their members, which often dilute their effectiveness in the policy process.

Public Interest Groups

Most of the **public interest groups** represented in Austin are concerned primarily with protecting consumers and the environment from big business, promoting stronger ethical standards for public officials, and increasing funding for health and human services programs for the poor, the elderly, the young, and the disabled. Many have full time lobbyists and some staff, but nowhere near the financial resources of the business and professional groups. Grassroots volunteer efforts and the effective use of the mass media are crucial to their success. The most active include the Sierra Club, Texas Watch, the Gray Panthers, Americans Disabled for Attendant Programs Today (ADAPT), and Public Citizen, a Texas affiliate of the national public interest group founded by consumer advocate Ralph Nader.

Although public interest lobbyists concentrate most of their attention on the legislature, some consumer groups are also active before state regulatory agencies, particularly the Public Utility Commission, which has oversight over telephone and electric utilities, and the Department of Insurance, which regulates insurance rates and practices. Among the more militant groups is ADAPT, which has staged highly visible demonstrations by wheelchair-bound Texans—including an overnight occupation of the governor's reception room—to demand more money for community-based facilities and attendant services for the disabled.[40]

Public interest advocates usually play more defense—trying to keep anticonsumer legislation from becoming law—than they do offense whenever lawmakers meet. But they scored a rare, significant victory during the 2003 regular session, when lawmakers enacted one of their priorities—a strengthened ethics law for public officials and political candidates. Among other things, the new law required officeholders to list the occupations and employers of their political contributors and imposed new, financial reporting requirements on mayors and city council members.[41]

Minorities

The advent of single-member, urban legislative districts in the 1970s significantly increased the number of African-American and Hispanic lawmakers and strengthened the influence of minority interest groups. These groups often have found that the courthouse can still be a shorter route to success than the statehouse, but the legislature has become increasingly attentive to their voices.

The League of United Latin American Citizens (LULAC) and the Mexican American Legal Defense and Educational Fund (MALDEF) are two of the better known Hispanic organizations. LULAC, founded in 1929, is the oldest and largest Hispanic organization in the United States and continues to be particularly influential in causes such as education and election reform in Texas. It was a plaintiff in a federal lawsuit that sought to replace the countywide system of electing urban trial judges in Texas with district elections so as to boost the election of minorities to the bench. LULAC lost the suit but focused much public attention on an important policy issue (see Chapter 11).

MALDEF, formed in San Antonio in 1968, fights in the courtroom for the civil rights of Hispanics. It has been successful in numerous battles over the drawing of political boundaries for governmental bodies in Texas and in lengthy litigation over public school finance. MALDEF represented the property-poor school districts that won a unanimous landmark Texas Supreme Court order (*Edgewood v. Kirby*) in 1989 for a more equitable distribution of education aid between rich and poor districts. The victory eventually led to major legislative changes in the school finance system (see Chapter 13).

The National Association for the Advancement of Colored People (NAACP) is a leader in promoting and protecting the interests of African Americans. The NAACP initiated many of the early court attacks on educational inequality and the disfranchisement of minorities. While the organization has long pursued employment issues such as increasing opportunities for African Americans in state agencies, a strategy that has produced some successes, it recently has directed attention to financial issues, such as predatory lending in the mortgage industry.

A coalition of minority groups in the early 1990s prevailed on the legislature to encourage all state agencies to make a "good faith effort" to improve minority contracting by establishing a program under which historically underutilized businesses (HUBs)— companies owned by minorities or women—received special notification of contracts and work available from the state. The HUBs, however, had to compete with other companies for the contracts. By 1996, women- and minority-owned businesses received $936 million in contracts from the state, or about 16 percent of the total contracts the state awarded that year.[42] But the share began steadily dropping after that year, slipping to 9.7 percent in 2002, much to the concern of minority groups and minority legislators.[43]

In recent years, the Industrial Areas Foundation (IAF), a collection of well-organized, church-supported community groups, also has been a strong and effective voice for low-income minorities. Member groups include Valley Interfaith in South Texas, Communities Organized for Public Service (COPS) in San Antonio, The Metropolitan Organization (TMO) and the Fort Bend Interfaith Council in the Houston area, and the El Paso Interreligious Sponsoring Organization (EPISO).

The first IAF chapter in Texas, San Antonio's COPS, developed an early reputation for being confrontational and raucous in demanding better drainage facilities and other improvements for the city's impoverished neighborhoods. COPS members would surround city council members in city hall offices and hallways, yell their demands, and refuse to take "no" or "maybe" for an answer. The group began to moderate its tactics as it matured politically and developed influential friends. At the state level, it has lobbied for health care for the poor, more equity in school funding, and water and sewer service for the *colonias,* or unincorporated slums, along the Texas-Mexico border.

Minority groups were confronted with perhaps their biggest challenge in decades when then–Attorney General Dan Morales, interpreting a federal court order in 1997, banned universities in Texas from using racial preferences in deciding admissions and granting student aid. Supporters of affirmative action had considered those preferences crucial to reversing the effects of historic discrimination against African Americans and Hispanics. The ban was lifted after the U.S. Supreme Court, ruling in a case from Michigan in 2003, held that affirmative action could be a factor in university admissions (see Chapter 13).

Labor

Organized labor has traditionally taken a back seat to business in Texas, a strong "right-to-work" state in which union membership cannot be required as a condition of employment. Antilabor sentiment ran particularly high in the 1940s and 1950s, at the height of the conservative Democratic establishment's control of Texas politics. Labor-baiting campaigns in which unions were portrayed as evil communist sympathizers were not uncommon then.[44]

Today, about 450,000 Texans, or 4.5 percent of the workforce, are members of labor unions.[45] Among the largest unions in the state are the Communications Workers of America (CWA); the Texas Federation of Teachers (TFT); the American Federation of State, County, and Municipal Employees (AFSCME); and the United Auto Workers (UAW).

Unions can provide grassroots support for political candidates through endorsement cards, phone banks, and other get-out-the-vote efforts, and this support has historically gone to Democratic candidates. With Republican and conservative gains in recent years, many labor-backed candidates have not fared well in Texas, especially in statewide elections.

Labor generally sides with the trial lawyers on such issues as workers' compensation, worker safety, and business liability for faulty products. One of labor's major victories in Texas politics was the defeat of a proposal to lock the right-to-work law into the state constitution. That dispute helped scuttle the Constitutional Convention of 1974, and labor prevailed only because of a convention rule that required proposals to receive a two-thirds vote (see Chapter 2).

Governmental Lobbyists

Local governments are significantly affected by state laws and budgetary decisions. The stakes are particularly high now because governments are finding revenue harder to raise—especially with the federal government passing the cost of numerous programs on to the state, and the state issuing similar mandates to local governments. As a result, counties, cities, prosecutors, metropolitan transit authorities, and various special districts are represented by lobbyists in Austin.

Many local governments belong to umbrella organizations such as the Texas Municipal League, the Texas Association of Counties, and the Texas District and County Attorneys Association, which have full-time lobbyists. Several of the larger cities and counties also retain their own lobbyists, and mayors, city council members, and county judges frequently travel to Austin to visit with legislators and testify for or against bills.

Some legislators complain that Houston and Harris County, the state's largest city and county, take up a disproportionate amount of the legislature's time with perennial fights over fire and police civil service regulations, mass transportation, and other local issues. One reason is because political unanimity is seldom achieved among Harris County's large, diverse legislative delegation. Another reason is restrictive state laws, such as those governing fire and police civil service, which may better be left to local discretion.

Agricultural Groups

Although Texas is now predominantly urban, agriculture is still an important part of the state's economy, and a number of agricultural groups are represented in Austin. Their influence is obviously strongest among rural legislators. But the Texas Farm Bureau, the largest such group, was instrumental in the 1990 electoral defeat of liberal Democratic Agriculture Commissioner Jim Hightower, who had angered many agricultural producers and the chemical industry with tough stands on farm worker rights and pesticide regulation.

Other producer groups include the Texas and Southwestern Cattle Raisers Association, the Texas Nurseryman's Association, and the Texas Corn Producers Board.

The United Farm Workers Union has been a strong advocate of better conditions for workers and has frequently been at odds with agricultural producers. Represented in court by the Texas Civil Liberties Union and Texas Rural Legal Aid attorneys, farm workers won major lawsuits and legislation in the 1980s on such issues as unemployment compensation, picketing rights, the right to be informed about dangerous pesticides used in fields, and a higher minimum wage.

Religious Groups

Influenced in part by their views of separation of church and state, many people think religious groups have little or no legitimate role in the political process. Nevertheless, religious groups have helped influence policy in Texas, and the abortion issue and other social and economic issues have increased the presence of religious groups in Austin.

A number of religious groups have emerged since the 1940s, with an identifiable right-wing orientation. These groups, predecessors of what is now known as the "Religious Right," combined Christian rhetoric and symbols with anticommunism, antilabor, anti-civil rights, antiliberal, or anti–New Deal themes. Although these groups were often very small, they were linked to the extreme right wing of the Texas establishment, and they were the precursors to many of the conservative ideological groups that have emerged in American politics in the past twenty years.[46] Many of these organizations have gravitated toward the Republican Party.[47] With a strong organizational effort, religious conservatives were influential in a right-wing takeover of leadership positions in the Texas Republican Party in 1994 (see Chapter 6).

The Texas Freedom Network, founded in 1995, provides an alternative voice to the Christian right. It now claims a membership of some 30,000 people supporting religious freedom and individual liberties. The organization claims success in "defeating initiatives backed by the religious right in Texas, including private school vouchers, textbook censorship, and faith-based deregulation."[48]

Many religious denominations have boards or commissions responsible for monitoring governmental action. One well-known religious interest group is the Christian Life Commission of the Baptist General Convention of Texas, a strong advocate of human services programs and an outspoken opponent of gambling.

Churches across the state, particularly the Catholic Church, whose policies on social action have been shaped by papal encyclicals and Vatican II, have established links to community-based organizations that address the social and economic needs of the poor. In many regards, this is a redefinition of the Social Gospel, a church-based political movement of the late nineteenth and early twentieth centuries.

Who Are the Lobbyists?

During each regular session of the Texas legislature, hundreds of individuals representing businesses, trade associations, and other interests register as lobbyists with the Texas Ethics Commission. They run the gamut from well-dressed corporate lobbyists with generous expense accounts to volunteer consumer and environmental advocates in blue jeans and sneakers. Most are male, although the number of female lobbyists has increased in recent years, and many women now hold major lobbying positions. Most lobbyists came to their careers by way of other occupations and jobs, but they have, on the whole, an acute understanding of the policymaking process and the points of access and influence in that process (see "How I See It: Long-Term Survival Assessments for Lobbyist-to-Be").

How
I See It | # Long-Term Survival Assessments for Lobbyist-to-Be

Jack W. Gullahorn

Jack Gullahorn, who operates his own public issues consulting firm, has a wealth of experience as a lobbyist and governmental insider. His current activities include serving as president and general counsel to the Professional Advocacy Association of Texas (http://www.texasadvocacy.com), a trade association for contract lobbyists in Texas, which Gullahorn founded in 2002. He is a former senior vice president of Public Strategies, an Austin-based national public affairs and policy development firm, and is a former partner with the national law firm of Akin, Gump, Strauss, Hauer, and Feld, LLP.

A native Texan, Gullahorn graduated from Trinity University with a degree in political science. He received his Doctor of Jurisprudence degree from the University of Texas Law School. Gullahorn began his career in government service in 1973, serving in the office of Texas State Representative Bill Clayton. When Clayton was elected speaker of the Texas House in 1975, he became his executive assistant. Gullahorn was both an independent attorney and lobbyist in Austin prior to his association with Akin, Gump. He also was involved in making recommendations that led to the creation of the Texas Ethics Commission.

Lobbying *is* a career.

It seems, however, that most people accept it as a vocational choice somewhat akin to prostitution, deciding to engage in the activity after acknowledging that selling your body for immoral purposes is the prevalent public view of the lobbyist's job description.

It doesn't have to be that way. Those who choose the profession can either change the perception or fulfill the public's low expectations. What follows is a suggested template for what could become a career type. How well suited are you to the key elements of the profession that could allow you to survive and at the same time enhance the image of a lobbyist to the public?

1. ***Ego Subjugation***

    How impressed are you with yourself? Nothing wrong with that (as a matter of fact, you shouldn't be considering this as a lifestyle if you don't think that you were pretty much able to handle any situation extemporaneously). But if you want to succeed at this game, be prepared to mask that superior intellect and ability. Most policymakers actually believe that they are there as a fulfillment of a mission. Your role is to make them feel as if you are there to help them fulfill that destiny, not to mold the world through your brilliance, using them as your tool. One of the reasons that the majority of former legislators and officeholders make such lousy lobbyists is that they just aren't able to make the ego transition—from imperious to supplicant.

2. ***Political Addiction***

    If you don't love politics, go do something else. A disdain for the system will show through. As your cynicism grows, unless you have a real passion for the game, your patience and willingness to play the part (see #1) won't cut it. This means staying current, knowing the players

(Continued)

as well as understanding the system. And it means that you are always thinking further ahead of the political consequences of every action than is the policymaker with whom you are dealing.

3. ***Ethics***

Don't leave home without it. Knowing the law is a big part of it, but your personal morality in how you handle your business is what will show through to your audience. Assume that every phone conversation, every e-mail, every memo will be on the front page of the *New York Times*. Over-report when in doubt—no one ever got in trouble for disclosing too much.

4. ***Truth or Consequences***

Never, never lie to a policymaker. Know that if you are going to be doing this job for a while, you will be back in front of that policymaker again, and your reputation for shooting straight (or not) will precede you. Once you develop the reputation for bending the facts, start preparing for mediocrity.

5. ***Relationships***

It's not who you know, it's how you know them. The key maxim of lobbying is the realization that policymakers come and go, but lobbyists stay around a lot longer and, as a result, meeting and learning about those you seek to convince is a continuing art form. If you are an introvert, focus on one-on-one opportunities. If you like receptions, bars, and crowds, great, but don't lose sight of the fact that building trust requires a substantive relationship beyond the "friendship" veneer of the "social lobbyist." Relationships build trust. Trust inspires action. Action is what you get paid for.

6. ***Pay Your Dues***

Don't expect to walk into the lifestyle of a successful lobbyist without earning the right to be there. Government is a great training ground for lobbyists because it allows you to experience firsthand the system and the ego glorification of the process. So are campaigns because the same lessons are taught: fidelity, loyalty, friendship, and the importance of relationships. Also, you make acquaintances that will survive a lifetime. Both of these are better done when young— when you can afford it, monetarily and physically, especially the wear and tear on your mind, body, and soul.

7. ***Staying Fresh***

You are only going to be as good as your last creative strategy. Tomorrow, everyone else will be doing the same thing, and you better be figuring out a new and improved way to move your message so it will stand out from the masses. Read and reserve a special time for yourself dedicated to shutting your eyes and actually thinking. On top of all that, learn who are the best thinkers on substance and process and study them.

8. ***Ideas Have Consequences***

Subscribe to the belief that for every action there will be a reaction, a consequence. That can be either positive or negative, but count on the fact that you should be prepared to deal with whichever consequence you are dealt so you can make the most of every situation. As you think, plan for the consequences. Most people act, realize that something will happen from that action, and then decide how to react, continuing the cycle and never getting ahead of the curve.

9. ***Life Is Easier if You Believe Your Own BS***

To thine own self be true. Sometimes the engagement may be tempting: the profile, the money, the players. But if you can't believe in the issue, pass on the opportunity. If your standard is to at least not represent issues and clients with which/whom you disagree personally, your credibility will be much easier to maintain. Think about it: You are trying to convince a decision maker to act based on the wisdom of following your advice. If you don't believe it, it will show, eventually. It is the same song for representing different sides of the same issue because your client has changed. Bottom line, remember that how you spend your days is how you spend your life.

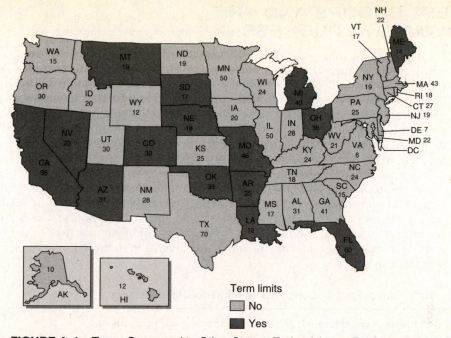

FIGURE 4–1   Texas Compared to Other States: Ex-Legislators Registered to Lobby, 2005
Source: Center for Public Integrity, "Statehouse Revolvers," October 12, 2006.

Many lobbyists are former legislators (see Figure 4–1). They bring to the process their legislative skills, personal relationships with former legislative colleagues, and expertise in substantive policy areas. A number of other lobbyists are former legislative staffers.

Many of the trade and professional associations, labor unions, and public interest groups have fulltime staffs in Austin who function as their lobbyists. Many corporations also use their own employees to lobby. Some companies have governmental affairs departments or offices staffed by employees with experience in government or public affairs. In large corporations that do business across the country, the governmental affairs staffs may be rather large because such companies will attempt to follow the actions of numerous state legislatures, city councils, and the U.S. Congress.

A number of lawyers have developed very successful lobby practices. Some of these professional freelancers—or "hired guns"—specialize in specific policy areas, whereas others represent a wide array of clients. Some may be identified as "super lobbyists" because of their ability to exercise considerable influence in the policymaking process. Many work for the state's largest law firms, which have established permanent offices in Austin. Some of the topnotch freelancers aren't attorneys, but they have a strong knowledge of the governmental process.

Some public relations firms also offer their services to interest groups. These companies specialize in "image creation" or "image modification."[49] Although they may not handle direct lobbying efforts, they often are retained to assist in indirect lobbying campaigns. They are responsible for developing relationships with the press, developing media campaigns, and assisting in political campaigns.

INTEREST GROUPS AND THE
POLICYMAKING PROCESS ●

For many people, the term **lobbying** may suggest shady characters lurking in the halls of the state Capitol, attempting to bribe legislators with money, sex, or booze. That perception was reinforced, especially before a new ethics law in 1991, by published reports of legislators being treated to trips, golf tournaments, and concerts by lobbyists (see Chapter 8). Though such tactics are questionable, they are only part of the complex relationships between interest groups and policymakers. Lobbying is central to a pluralistic society, and the legal foundations of lobbying activity are found in the U.S. and Texas constitutions, which provide for the right to petition "the governments for a redress of grievances."[50]

In the broadest sense, lobbying is "simply the practice of attempting to influence the decisions of government."[51] Most scholars take this view. Lobbying is both indirect and direct and includes, but is not limited to, electoral activities, public relations campaigns, protests and demonstrations, and direct contact with policymakers (Table 4–2). According to political scientist Carol Greenwald, "Lobbying may thus be defined as any form of communication, made on another's behalf, and intended to influence a governmental decision."[52]

TABLE 4–2   Techniques Used by Lobbyists to Influence Policymakers

1. Conduct and maintain relevant research and information pertaining to policy issues
2. Provide reliable research results or technical information supporting a group's policy interests to decision makers, the press, and other audiences
3. Contact government officials or their key staff members directly to present the organization's point of view on policy
4. Testify at hearings of committees and subcommittees
5. Engage in and maintain informal contacts with legislators and other policymakers at conventions, over lunch, on the golf course, and so on
6. Communicate by e-mail or newsletter with members of the organization to inform them about organizational activities on public policy issues
7. Enter into coalitions with other organizations to support or block policy initiatives
8. Establish and cultivate media contacts to advance a group's policy position
9. Consult with government officials to plan and execute legislative strategies
10. Help draft legislation
11. Work with group's members, allies, or the general public in letter writing, e-mail or telephone campaigns to influence policymakers' decisions
12. Mount grassroots lobbying efforts to encourage members and the general public to contact public officials
13. Mobilize influential constituents to contact their representatives' offices
14. Help formulate and draft administrative regulations, rules, or guidelines
15. Serve on advisory commissions and boards
16. Inform legislators of the effects of a bill on their districts
17. Make campaign contributions to political candidates
18. Endorse candidates running for office
19. File lawsuits or otherwise engage in litigation to impact policy

Sources: From Kay Lehman Scholzman and John T. Tierney, *Organized Interests and American Democracy.* New York: Harper and Row, 1986; and Rogan Kersh, "The Well-Informed Lobbyist: Information and Interest Groups Lobbying," in *Interest Group Politics,* 7th ed., edited by Allan J. Cigler and Burdett A. Loomis (Washington, DC: CQ Press, 2007), pp. 389–411.

Indirect Lobbying

Effective lobbying starts with the election of officeholders supportive of a group's viewpoint on key issues and the building of general public support for a group and its objectives.

Electoral Activities.　　Although the electoral activities of interest groups are similar to those of political parties, there are some significant differences. Political parties are broad coalitions of voters concerned with a wide range of issues, whereas most interest groups are focused on only a limited set of issues. Parties function not only to contest elections but also to govern once elected. Interest groups primarily are concerned with influencing and shaping only those policies that directly affect them. Most interest groups also cross party lines in supporting candidates.

Interest groups must decide which candidates they will back through campaign contributions, organizational support, and public endorsements. Most groups are not interested in political ideology or philosophy but primarily are concerned with electing their "friends" and defeating their "enemies."

Most interest groups spend their money selectively, contributing to those legislators who serve on the committees that have jurisdiction over their industry or areas of concern. (See the discussion of the "iron triangles" of government earlier in this chapter and in Chapter 13.) The Texas legislature's highly centralized leadership encourages groups to concentrate their resources on a small number of key lawmakers.

In some cases, interest groups will use promises of financial campaign support to recruit opponents for incumbent legislators who consistently vote against them. In other instances, incumbents and potential challengers will approach interest groups for support. Although this process has become a permanent fixture of contemporary elections, it still can present an unsavory image of a mutual shakedown. Although a candidate cannot legally promise a specific vote for financial or other campaign support, an interest group will make every effort to assure that a potential recipient of campaign contributions is "sympathetic" and will be "accessible" to the group.

Under state and federal laws, interest groups and many corporations are able to form political action committees (PACs) for raising and distributing campaign funds. Money is contributed to a PAC by individual members of a group or employees of a corporation and then distributed among selected candidates. In most instances, a PAC is managed by the professional staff of the interest group, and the campaign contributions are a key part of the organization's overall lobbying strategy.

Federal campaign finance restrictions and reporting requirements are stricter than the state's. Federal law limits individual contributions to $2,400 per candidate for each election and PAC contributions by corporations, labor unions, trade associations, and other organizations to $5,000 per candidate per election. After several years of debate, the U.S. Congress in 2002 enacted the Bipartisan Campaign Reform Act, which banned the previously unlimited "soft money" contributions that businesses and special interest groups had been increasingly making to political parties to support candidates and campaign activities. The new federal law also restricted political television advertising by corporations and labor unions. The law was challenged in court by a diverse array of groups, including the United States Chamber of Commerce, the National Rifle Association, and the American Civil Liberties Union, which contended it unconstitutionally restricted free speech. A three-judge federal district court in Washington struck down parts of the law in 2003, putting the issue in the hands of the United States Supreme Court, which upheld its constitutionality during its 2003–2004 term.[53]

Texas law prohibits corporations or labor unions from making direct contributions to state and local political candidates, but sets no limits on the amount of money a PAC or an individual can give to candidates for nonjudicial offices. There have been instances in which PACs and wealthy individuals have given several hundred thousand dollars to a single candidate.

Interest groups sometimes provide in-kind support for political candidates. A group may make its phone banks available to a candidate, it may conduct a poll and provide the candidate with the results, or it may provide office space and equipment to a candidate's campaign. Some organizations may even "loan" the services of their staffers to a campaign or provide postage, cars for travel, printing services, and other types of assistance. State law requires such in-kind contributions to be publicly reported to the Texas Ethics Commission, just as financial donations are. Some groups, depending on how they are organized under federal tax laws, cannot make in-kind contributions directly, but can do so through their political action committees.

Groups also endorse candidates and publicize their endorsements in newsletters, news releases, press conferences, or conventions. Some groups maintain phone banks during election campaigns to inform their members of their endorsements and encourage them to get out and vote for their chosen candidates. Public endorsements often are sought by candidates when a group's size, prestige, and influence are considered valuable, and candidates use these endorsements in their advertising campaigns.

Public Opinion.   Interest groups also may try to cultivate favorable public opinion about themselves through media campaigns. One objective is to "develop a reservoir of good will in the minds of the citizenry that can be drawn upon when political battles over specific issues occur."[54] Although this practice is more pronounced at the national level, state organizations in Texas that are associated with national interest groups often participate in national campaigns.

Public relations campaigns also are used to mobilize public support for a group's position on a specific issue being debated in Austin.[55] Voters may be encouraged to write, call, fax, or send e-mail to their legislators. The Texas Medical Association, for example, has sought public support for restrictions on medical malpractice awards by distributing cards to doctors' waiting rooms that attempt to explain how the high cost of malpractice insurance can affect the costs and quality of health care.

Interest groups may sponsor advertising campaigns featuring emotional language and imagery. They may use press conferences and informal media contacts to encourage favorable editorials or put their "spin," or viewpoint, on news coverage. For years, Texas legislators resisted pari-mutuel horserace betting and the lottery. But groups supporting those proposals continued to wage strong media campaigns, insisting that gambling would boost state revenue. Eventually, during economic downturns when the legislature was struggling to find new sources of revenue, they won the fight.

Public interest advocates, in their efforts to protect consumers and the environment, cannot match the financial firepower that utilities, insurance companies, and other big industries can muster. Their success depends on their ability to stir up public concern—or outrage—over pocketbook issues and the relationships between monied special interests and government. Quality research that focuses on political issues such as campaign contributions or policy issues is one of the more effective resources available to public interest groups. Using this research, they avidly work the news media, which are crucial to their ability to spread their message. They seldom can afford paid advertising campaigns, but they hold frequent news conferences, issue a stream of press releases, and readily return reporters' phone calls. They also recognize strength and efficiency in numbers and sometimes issue joint statements or hold joint news conferences on issues of mutual concern.

Protests and Marches.   Staged demonstrations against governmental decisions or inaction have long been used by individuals or groups attempting to influence public policy. Although many people have mixed feelings about such tactics, protests and marches can be effective in capturing public attention. Television coverage of such events, in particular, can convey powerful and intense images. The civil rights movement capitalized on this resource, and that movement's success, in large measure, turned on the ability of minority leaders to show the nation that discriminatory policies were incompatible with the values of a democratic society.

In recent years, both antiabortion groups and abortion rights activists in Texas have marched in support of their positions. Animal rights groups have picketed stores that sell fur coats. Gay and lesbian groups have held vigils to protest incidents of "gay bashing," and a variety of other groups have used public demonstrations to dramatize their particular issues or concerns. It is not clear what effects these tactics have. But many groups that use them have limited resources and recognize their value in gaining free media attention.

Direct Lobbying

Although interest groups may spend much time and money electing "friendly" candidates and building public support for their objectives, their work has only begun. The next crucial step is direct lobbying, or the communication of information and policy preferences directly to policymakers. Lobbying is often associated with legislatures, but it is directed to other governmental institutions as well. Public officials depend on the information provided by interest groups, and many policy initiatives, including proposed legislation, come from lobbyists. Interest groups also attempt to use the courts to advance their policy goals. They file lawsuits to challenge existing laws or regulations—and force changes—or file briefs supporting or opposing other groups' positions in pending litigation.[56]

Lobbyists engage in a wide range of activities. Most groups understand the necessity of pursuing their legislative agendas at every conceivable opportunity, and they also realize it usually is easier to block policy initiatives than to enact new policies.[57]

Drafting Legislation.   Interest groups often will draft proposed laws for formal introduction into the legislature. In any given legislative session, hundreds of bills are drafted by the legal or technical staffs of interest groups. The groups usually work closely with legislative sponsors or their staffs in the drafting process, and they may consult staffers from the agencies that would be affected by the legislation.

Planning and Implementing a Legislative Strategy.   Interest groups supporting a bill will usually work closely with the bill's sponsor, committee chairs, and other legislative leaders at every stage of the process. Strategy will be planned from the introduction of the legislation through committee hearings and then through final action by the House and the Senate. Potential opposition will be assessed, and ways of diffusing that opposition and building support for the bill will be mapped out.

Personal Contacts and Communications.   If one were to ask most interest groups why they contribute to political candidates and what they expected in return, the overwhelming response would be "access." The interest group system revolves around communication and the exchange of ideas and information with policymakers. To have some prospects of success, a group must have access to lawmakers, something that often is no small task to achieve.

With thousands of bills considered during each regular legislative session, interest groups have to compete for the opportunity to discuss their programs with lawmakers. Lobbyists are denied direct access to legislators on the floor of the House and the Senate while legislators are in session, but there are numerous other opportunities for direct or indirect contact.

During House and Senate sessions, many lobbyists will wait outside the chambers to stop legislators who pass by. Or they will have the doorkeepers send messages asking individual lawmakers to step outside the chambers for brief meetings in the lobby—hence the term, "lobbyists." It is not unusual for several dozen lobbyists to be gathered at one time outside the House or the Senate chamber on the second floor of the Capitol,

That's Why It is Called Lobbying. Lobbyists and visitors, who are denied access to the floor of the Senate or House while they are in session, are seen mingling outside of the House chamber waiting for the opportunity to "chat" with a legislator. Many of those shown in this photo taken on the day Governor Perry gave his State of the State Address to a joint session of the legislature are from ADAPT, a grassroots disability rights group.

particularly on days when major bills are being debated. Lobbyists also sit in the House and Senate galleries. In some instances, a lobbyist's presence in the gallery is simply a matter of minor interest or a way to kill some time before a committee meeting. But sometimes special interest groups will pack the gallery in a show of force to threaten recrimination against lawmakers who don't vote their way.

Effective lobbyists, however, do most of their work long before a bill reaches the House or the Senate floor for a vote. They will stop by legislators' offices to present information and solicit support for or against specific legislation. If they can't meet personally with a legislator, they will meet with his or her staff. In many cases, lobbyists will provide lawmakers with written reports, summarizing the highlights of an issue and their position on it. Many interest groups will back up the personal efforts of their lobbyists with letter-writing, e-mail or telephone campaigns directed at legislators by the groups' members.

Much of the personal lobbying is done away from the Capitol, sometimes far away—over lunch and dinner tables, at cocktail parties, and on golf courses. Although these occasions involve a great deal of socializing, they also provide lobbyists with golden opportunities to solidify friendships with lawmakers and make pitches for or against specific legislative proposals. A five- or ten-minute business conversation reinforced with a few hours of social camaraderie can work wonders, as many interest groups and their lobbyists very well know. Such entertainment, however, is expensive—lobbyists have spent well in excess of $1 million during a regular legislative session entertaining lawmakers—and it can easily be used to abuse the policymaking process. Repeated news accounts of extravagant and questionable lobby spending finally convinced the legislature in 1991 to ban many lobby-paid trips for lawmakers and to limit lobby expenditures on entertainment to $500 per year per legislator (see Chapter 8).

Many lobbyists and legislators were concerned that the 1991 ethics law also may have outlawed that most sacred and basic of lobby handouts—the free lunch. Their uncertainty prompted the legislature to pass a bill in 1993 to make sure that it remained legal for lawmakers to dine at lobbyists' expense.

Testifying at Hearings. During each regular legislative session, House and Senate committees and subcommittees hold hundreds of hearings on bills that have to win committee approval before they can be considered by the full House and Senate. Interest groups can use committee hearings to present information formally to legislators or to help mobilize public support for or against a bill. Testifying at public hearings is often symbolic and secondary to the personal communications with legislators and their staffs.

Coalitions of Interest Groups. Sometimes, a group will not have sufficient resources to influence the outcome of a contested issue, or a legislative or regulatory proposal may affect many different groups. Groups thus sometimes find it advantageous to form coalitions to coordinate their electoral and direct lobbying activities. These coalitions are informal, tenuous, or short-lived, based on current common interests or objectives and a desire to maximize resources and share costs and expenses.[58]

In 1991, some consumer advocates teamed up with the Texas Trial Lawyers Association to defeat a products-liability bill that would have made it more difficult for consumers injured by defective products to sue manufacturers and retailers. But two years later, consumers learned how tenuous that alliance was when trial lawyers and key legislators negotiated a products-liability compromise with the business community. Consumer groups, which opposed the legislation, were excluded from the negotiations.

SUMMARY AND CONCLUSIONS ————————————————●

1. Political power in Texas is essentially structured around organizations, whether they be corporations, professional associations, or interest groups. The interaction and conflict among these groups in the policymaking process help decide who gets what, when, and how. The great disparity in the distribution of resources among these institutions raises a fundamental question: Does everyone in the political system have equal access and influence in the decision-making process?

2. Pluralists, while recognizing the inequities in political resources, argue that individual interests are adequately represented through membership in interest groups. They contend that with thousands of groups competing, no one group can dominate the policy process. New groups are constantly being formed to provide new leadership opportunities and greater access to the decision-making process for people who have been historically denied influence. With the political mobilization of minorities and public interest groups, the decline of the oil and gas industry, and the emergence of new economic interests, the interest group structure in Texas now bears little resemblance to the restricted interest group system of the 1950s. Moreover, pluralists believe that leaders of groups are generally committed to democratic values and faithfully represent the concerns, needs, and expectations of their membership.

3. The elitist theory emphasizes the marked differences in the resources and subsequent political influence of groups and contends that relatively few corporations and other institutions with great financial resources dominate the policy process in Texas. Over much of the state's political history, the most influential institutions have been dominated by white, Anglo-Saxon men from Texas's higher socioeconomic levels. Although there is some competition among these leaders, they agree on most public policy issues and the underlying functions of government. Historically, this Texas "establishment" has expressed indifference, if not hostility, toward the interests of labor, minorities, and the lower socioeconomic groups. These wealthy institutions are tied together through complex interlocking relationships, and access to leadership positions in them is limited.

4. There is evidence suggesting that the source of political power and influence lies somewhere between the elitist and pluralist positions. Sometimes, the narrow, limited interests of a few groups prevail, but public policy at other times is responsive to the needs and interests of broad segments of the population.

5. The effectiveness of an interest group in the policymaking process is determined by its size, the geographical distribution of its membership, its economic resources, its reputation, and its leadership and staff.

6. Interest groups and other organizations use a variety of techniques to communicate their wants and needs to policymakers. Although lobbying has a negative connotation for many Texans, it is essential to elected and appointed policymakers, who depend on the information, coalition building, and public support of groups for their decisions and actions.

7. Interest groups engage in indirect and direct lobbying. Indirect lobbying includes campaign financing and other efforts to elect candidates who share a group's views. It also includes efforts to shape public opinion to favor the group's objectives. Direct lobbying involves a variety of strategies and techniques to shape the decisions of policymakers. Effective lobbyists know how to gain access to legislators and other policymakers, to build and maintain coalitions with other interests, and to follow policy decisions at every step of the process.

8. Interest groups are the fundamental building blocks of the Texas political system. Policymakers must resolve the fundamental conflicts among these competing interests with sound public policy that serves specific and general interests. But the excessive influence that comes through large campaign contributions and the limited resources of many groups challenge the concept of equity and fairness.

KEY TERMS

FURTHER READING

Articles

Coombs, Kathryn, Mark Reilly, and Robert Stone, "Grassroots Lobbying and the Internet Explosion," *Campaigns & Elections*, February 1999, pp. 26–33.

Thomas, Clive S., and Ronald J. Hrebenar, "Who's Got Clout? Interest Group Power in the States," *State Legislatures*, April 1999, pp. 30–34.

Books

Bachrach, Peter, *The Theory of Democratic Elitism: A Critique.* Boston: Little, Brown and Company, 1967.

Berry, Jeffrey M., and Clyde Wilcox, *The Interest Group Society,* 4th ed. New York: Longman, 2007.

Davidson, Chandler, *Race and Class in Texas Politics.* Princeton: Princeton University Press, 1990.

Domhoff, G. William, *Who Really Rules?* Santa Monica, CA: Goodyear Publishing Company, Inc., 1978.

———, *Who Rules America Now?* Englewood Cliffs, NJ: Prentice Hall, Inc., 1983.

Dye, Thomas R., *Who's Running America? The Bush Era,* 5th ed. Englewood Cliffs, NJ: Prentice Hall, Inc., 1990.

Green, George Norris, *The Establishment in Texas Politics, 1938–1957.* Westport, CT: Greenwood Press, 1979.

Hrebenar, Robert J., and Clive S. Thomas, eds., *Interest Group Politics in Southern States.* Tuscaloosa, AL: University of Alabama Press, 1992.

Hrebenar, Robert J., and Ruth K. Scott, *Interest Group Politics in America,* 2nd. ed. Englewood Cliffs, NJ: Prentice Hall, Inc., 1990.

Lowi, Theodore J., *The End of Liberalism,* 2nd ed. New York: W. W. Norton, 1979.

Nownes, Anthony J., Clive S. Thomas, and Ronald J. Hrebenar, "Interest Groups in the States," in *Politics in the American States: A Comparative Analysis,* 9th edition, edited by Virginia Gray and Russell L. Hanson. Washington, DC: Congressional Quarterly Press, 2007.

Pittman, H. C., *Inside the Third House.* Austin, TX: Eakin, 1992.

Rogers, Mary Beth, *Cold Anger: A Story of Faith and Power Politics.* Denton, TX: University of North Texas Press, 1990.

Rosenthal, Alan, *The Third House: Lobbyists and Lobbying in the States.* Washington, DC: Congressional Quarterly Press, 1993.

———, *The Decline of Representative Democracy: Process, Participation, and Power in the State Legislatures.* Washington, DC: Congressional Quarterly Press, 1998.

Websites

National Institute on Money in State Politics   http://www.followthemoney.org/   This nonpartisan organization is "dedicated to accurate, comprehensive and unbiased documentation and research on campaign finances at the state level." Data are provided for most statewide and legislative races in Texas.

Texans for Public Justice   http://www.tpj.org/   "A non partisan, non profit organization which tracks the influence of money and corporate power in Texas politics."

Texas Ethics Commission   http://www.ethics.state.tx.us/   Under Texas law, organizations that lobby the legislature are required to file with the Ethics Commission. This source provides names of registered lobbyists and their clients, as well as lobbyists organized by legislative subject matter. Candidates and political action committees are also required to file their financial statements with this agency.

The Center for Public Integrity   http://www.publicintegrity.org/   This is a nonprofit, nonpartisan organization located in Washington, D.C. Its purpose is to "produce research about significant public issues to make institutional power more transparent and accountable." The center has produced reports on state lobbyists, lobbying expenditures, and party finance and expenditures.

ENDNOTES ─────────────────────────────────────●

1. *Democracy in American,* translated by George Lawrence and edited by J. P. Mayer. (Garden City, NY: Anchor, 1969), p. 191. Copyright for the English translation by Harper & Row, Publishers, 1966.

2. Janet Elliott, "Execs Lose Appeal in Campaign Donation Case,"*Houston Chronicle,* October 2, 2003, p. 19A.

3. See Robert S. Erikson, Norman R. Luttbeg, and Kent L. Tedin, *American Public Opinion,* 3rd ed. (New York: Macmillan Publishing Company, 1988), p. 118; and Robert L. Lineberry, George C. Edwards III, and Martin P. Wattenberg, *Government in America,* 5th ed. (New York: HarperCollins Publishers, 1991), p. 341.

4. Belle Zeller, *American State Legislatures* (New York: Thomas Y. Crowell, 1954), and Clive S. Thomas and Ronald J. Hrebenar; "Interest Groups in the States," in *Politics in the American States,* 6th ed., edited by Virginia Gray and Herbert Jacob (Washington, DC: Congressional Quarterly Press, 1996), p. 152.

5. Harmon L. Zeigler and Hendrik van Dalen, "Interest Groups in State Politics," in *Politics in the American States,* 3rd ed., edited by Herbert Jacob and Kenneth N. Vines (Boston: Little, Brown, 1976).

6. Dennis S. Ippolito and Thomas G. Walker, *Political Parties, Interest Groups, and Public Policy* (Englewood Cliffs, NJ: Prentice Hall, 1990), p. 271.

7. Ibid., pp. 270–71.

8. Encyclopedia of Association, *Encyclopedia of Associations Bluesheet,* October 1, 2009, http://library.dialog.com/bluesheets/html/bl0114.html.

9. Kay Lehman Schlozman and John T. Tierney, *Organized Interests and American Democracy* (New York: Harper & Row, 1986), p. 75.

10. See E. E. Schattschneider, *The Semi-Sovereign People* (Hinsdale, IL: Dryden Press, 1975); and Ronald J. Hrebenar and Ruth K. Scott, *Interest Group Politics in America,* 2nd ed. (Englewood Cliffs, NJ: Prentice Hall, 1990), p.29.

11. Robert Salisbury, "Overlapping Memberships, Organizational Interactions, and Interest Group Theory." Unpublished paper presented at the annual meeting of the American Political Science Association, Chicago, 1976; see also Carol S. Greenwald, *Group Power* (New York: Praeger, 1977), pp. 38–40.

12. Schlozman and Tierney, *Organized Interests and American Democracy,* pp. 73–74.

13. Hrebenar and Scott, *Interest Group Politics in America,* p. 29.

14. Ippolito and Walker, *Political Parties, Interest Groups, and Public Policy,* p. 278.

15. For an extended summary of these incentives, see Jeffrey M. Berry, *The Interest Group Society,* 3rd ed. (New York: Longman, 1997), pp. 70–77. See also Robert H. Salisbury, "An Exchange Theory of Interest Groups," *Midwest Journal of Political Science* 13 (February 1969), pp. 1–32.

16. Greenwald, *Group Power,* pp. 32–35.

17. Ippolito and Walker, *Political Parties, Interest Groups, and Public Policy,* pp. 279–80.

18. Berry, *The Interest Group Society,* p. 73.

19. Lawrence J. R. Herson, *The Politics of Ideas* (Prospect Heights, IL: Waveland, 1990), p. 68.

20. David B. Truman, *The Governmental Process,* 2nd ed. (New York: Alfred A. Knopf, 1971).

21. For a succinct summary of the elitist-pluralist debate, see Thomas R. Dye and Harmon Zeigler, *The Irony of Democracy,* 7th ed. (Monterey, CA: Brooks/Cole, 1987), Chapter 1.

22. David Truman, *The Governmental Process,* Chapter 4.

23. Ippolito and Walker, *Political Parties, Interest Groups, and Public Policy,* pp. 275–76.

24. Thomas R. Dye, *Who's Running America: The Bush Era,* 5th ed. (Englewood Cliffs, NJ: Prentice Hall, 1990), p. 4.

25. Robert Michels, *Political Parties: A Sociological Study of the Oligarchical Tendencies of Modern Democracy,* translated by Eden Paul (1915, reprint, New York: Free Press, 1962), p. 70.

26. C. Wright Mills, *The Power Elite* (New York: Oxford University Press, 1956).

27. See Dye and Zeigler, *The Irony of Democracy,* Chapter 1.

28. George Norris Green, *The Establishment in Texas Politics: 1938–1957* (Westport, CT: Greenwood, 1979), p. 1.

29. Ibid., p. 17.

30. Ibid., p. 1.

31. Ibid., p. 10.

32. Chandler Davidson, *Race and Class in Texas Politics* (Princeton, NJ: Princeton University Press, 1990), p. 54.

33. Ibid., Chapter 4 and 5.

34. Ibid., p. 83.

35. Ibid., p. 108.

36. Lineberry, et al., *Government in America,* p. 342.

37. See Theodore J. Lowi, *The End of Liberalism,* 2nd ed. (New York: W. W. Norton, 1979).

38. Schlozman and Tierney, *Organized Interests and American Democracy,* p. 103.

39. See Green, *The Establishment in Texas Politics,* Chap. 1.

40. *Houston Chronicle,* September 15, 1991.

41. *Houston Chronicle,* June 20, 2003, page 29A.

42. *Austin American–Statesman,* November 4, 1997.

43. *El Paso Times,* February 18, 2003, page 7B.

44. See George Norris Green, *The Establishment in Texas Politics,* for an excellent analysis of the labor-bashing techniques used by Texas business in the 1940s and 1950s.

45. United States Department of Labor, Bureau of Labor Statistics, "Economic News Release: Union Affiliation of Employed Wage and Salary Workers by State," January 28, 2009.

46. Green, *The Establishment in Texas Politics,* Chapter 5.

47. See Davidson, *Race and Class in Texas Politics,* Chapter 10.

48. Texas Freedom Network, "About Us," *TFN.org,* http://www.tfn.org/site/PageNavigator/aboutus/AboutUs.

49. Hrebenar and Scott, *Interest Group Politics in America,* p. 83.

50. *U.S. Constitution,* First Amendment; *Texas Constitution,* Article 1, Section 27.

51. Alan Rosenthal, *Third House: Lobbyists and Lobbying in the States* (Washington, DC: Congressional Quarterly Press, 1993), p. 1.

52. Greenwald, *Group Power,* pp. 61–62.

53. Linda Greenhouse, "The Supreme Court: Arguments-Justices Hear Vigorous Attacks on New Campaign Finance Law, *New York Times,* September 9, 2003, page 1A.

54. Ippolito and Walker, *Political Parties, Interest Groups, and Public Policy,* p. 323.

55. Hrebenar and Scott, *Interest Group Politics in America,* pp. 114–15.

56. Ippolito and Walker, *Political Parties, Interest Groups, and Public Policy,* pp. 364–65.

57. The following section draws from the research of Scholzman and Tierney, *Organized Interests and American Democracy,* Chap. 7.

58. Hrebenar and Scott, *Interest Group Politics in America,* pp. 148–53.

The Mass Media in Texas Politics

Questions to Guide Your Reading

1. There are more sources of news now than in the past. But are Texans better informed about politics and public policy?

2. Texans now have access to a broad array of news sources. Which of these sources do you perceive to be most thorough in their coverage of the state's governments and politics? Most independent and objective? Most trustworthy?

3. Does the media shape or influence the outcomes of elections in the state?

4. What is the role of the media in the policymaking process?

When the right of every citizen to cooperate in the government of society is acknowledged, every citizen must be presumed to possess the power of discriminating between the different opinions of his contemporaries, and of appreciating the different facts from which inferences may be drawn.

—**Alexis de Tocqueville**[1]

The people, in delegating authority, do not give their public servants the right to decide what is good for the people to know and what is not good for them to know.

—**Texas Legislature, 1973**

Officeholders can communicate directly with their constituents, relaying their own subjective accounts of their accomplishments through personal contact, public speeches, newsletters, websites and blog postings on the Internet, e-mail messages, twittering, or paid television commercials. Political parties and special interest groups regularly disseminate governmental information through their membership networks. But most of the information that people have about their government—particularly on the state and federal levels—comes directly or indirectly through the mass media. An individual reads a newspaper or magazine article, sees a television newscast, hears a radio summary of a particular event, reads an e-mail or a blog posting on a particular news media story, or otherwise hears the news from a newspaper or magazine reader, television viewer, or radio listener.

In adopting First Amendment guarantees of press freedom more than 200 years ago, the framers of the U.S. Constitution recognized that a free press was an independent conduit of information essential to making a representative democracy work. It was to provide a public forum for the exchange of ideas and a means of scrutinizing the actions of public officials so as to establish accountability. The mass media has not always been impartial, and in many cases, it has not been as independent as the Constitution's drafters probably envisioned. But the unofficial fourth branch of government, for all its flaws, has served as a check and balance on the legislative, executive, and judicial branches.

It will continue to perform that role, although the extent of future media coverage of the Texas statehouse and the media's future influence on state government have been brought into serious question by the recent financial struggles of the newspaper industry and reductions in political and governmental coverage. Even before the recession of 2007, newspapers in Texas and across the country were losing readers and millions of dollars in crucial advertising revenue to information sources on the Internet. The recession compounded those losses, prompting several Texas papers to make large reductions in reporting staffs, including reporters assigned to Austin. Major television stations already had cut back on legislative coverage. Internet bloggers, meanwhile, were expanding their presence in the political arena, but blogging is a mixed bag. Most bloggers represent distinct political viewpoints, and few do any original reporting, raising questions about who was going to fill the gap left by the reductions in traditional news gathering.

Some observers feared that the reductions in the traditional **capitol press corps** would make it easier for special interest groups to dictate governmental decisions with most taxpayers being none the wiser. Optimists believed that newspapers and other traditional news sources would survive the economic and technological shakeout but with major changes. Online presentations, rather than print, would play a greater role in future news dissemination, it was predicted. But it remained to be seen how thorough and independent the news reporting of the future would be and how strong an impact it would have on political decisions affecting millions of Texans.

Traditionally, the media has played a significant role in setting public policy by influencing the outcome of elections in which policymakers are chosen and by contributing to the public debate over policy alternatives. The media also has been a watchdog over officialdom, evaluating the competency of public officials and attacking their ethical lapses. The media informs, educates, and often angers its audience and, like the political figures and issues it covers, is itself constantly subjected to public scrutiny and questions of fairness.[2]

Subjective decisions by a newspaper editor or television news producer can affect the final news product and determine whether it is perceived as fair. Should a paper, for example, publish a story about a minor indiscretion by a political candidate? Or should a story be run that suggests a major indiscretion that is based on circumstantial, largely undocumented evidence? How about a story about a suggestive joke that a political candidate utters in an informal setting? If any of these stories are published or broadcast, should they be on the front page, used to lead the evening newscast, or posted prominently on a newspaper or television website? How much space or time should be given to a particular issue, event, or personality? Editors' and producers' answers to these questions, which can help determine who is elected to public office and influence government policymaking, are influenced by the competitive nature of the news business.

The media has become a major institution linking governments to their constituents. Ironically, however, in the current, so-called **information age**—when it has become easier than ever before to be informed—millions of Americans, particularly young adults, are ill-informed and indifferent to the actions and decisions of their leaders and governmental institutions. This disturbing development threatens the foundations of a democratic society, because democracy depends on an informed and involved public.

THE MASS MEDIA AND THE POLICY AGENDA ———————●

The media has an impact on public policy, although it doesn't dictate policy to elected officials. Some scholars and media experts believe one of the major contributions of the media to politics is **agenda setting**. By choosing which events and issues to cover and how extensively to cover them, they say, the media helps define what is important for the public and, by omission, what is not important. Maxwell McCombs and Donald Shaw, recognized authorities on the mass media, argued that "the idea of agenda setting asserts that the priorities of the press to some degree become the priorities of the public. What the press emphasizes is in turn emphasized privately and publicly by the audiences of the press."[3]

The media uses five basic criteria to select what events and subjects to cover. First, a story must have a significant impact on its audience, such as a legislative proposal to increase taxes or to change the public education system. Second, it needs to be something that generates considerable interest. That may be an act of violence or conflict, a natural disaster, a political scandal, or legislation to ban assault rifles. A third component is familiarity—the public identifies with well-known individuals or familiar situations. A reported event also should occur in some proximity to readers and viewers, and, finally, a news story should be timely. Conflict, proximity, and timeliness often appear to be the more critical elements of a story's newsworthiness.[4] Yet, public policymaking is complex and often highly technical and doesn't always produce the kinds of stories necessary to sustain general public interest.

In cases in which the public interest is aroused, some experts extend the agenda-setting role of the media to **agenda building**. The media's coverage of specific issues creates a climate for political action by shaping the atmosphere in which these issues will be debated and their solutions developed.[5] By helping to make an issue relevant, the media gives people reasons for taking sides and converting the problem into a serious political issue. From this perspective, "the public agenda is not so much set by the media as built up through a cycle of media activity that transforms an elite issue into a public controversy."[6] Issues and concerns of a few individuals now become the concerns of many, and the dynamics of the policymaking process are changed.[7]

The most consistent readers and viewers of governmental and political news are the business, community, and political leaders who actively influence and work on policy formation. Most key public officials and their staffs spend a lot of time keeping up with media coverage of public issues. Clipping and filing news stories and checking newspaper websites and blog postings on the Internet are important parts of the routine in many state offices.

But some people familiar with the workings of Texas government believe that the policy-building role of the press is overstated. This view suggests that the media merely mirrors what others think about public issues.

This passive view is supported by the argument that the Texas press was largely reactive in reporting some of the most crucial issues facing Texans in recent memory, including educational equality, criminal justice, and care of the mentally ill and the mentally retarded. Although newspapers were influential in prompting the legislature to make improvements in all three of these areas in the years following World War II, deterioration set in, and the media and the legislature later took back seats to the judiciary. The media had largely ignored a recurrence of substandard conditions in state prisons and Department of Mental Health and Mental Retardation facilities—and, consequently, so had the legislature—until after the federal courts had stepped in with landmark reform orders. Disparities in property wealth and educational opportunities between rich and poor school districts had been growing wider for years, worsening a dropout problem that, in turn, helped keep the prisons crowded. But educational disparities received only occasional attention from news reporters until after the Mexican American Legal Defense and Educational Fund had won a state court judgment declaring the school finance system unconstitutional. Once the courts had forced the issues, however, the media devoted extensive coverage to them, keeping the problems, their causes, and potential solutions in the public eye.

The media's attention to public problems and officialdom's response form something of a never-ending cycle. In the early 1980s, for example, the deaths of several elderly patients at a nursing home in Galveston prompted changes in state law designed to tighten oversight of such facilities. By the early 1990s, however, the *Houston Chronicle* and other newspapers again were reporting widespread deficiencies in state regulation of the nursing home industry. Those reports and a hard-hitting, national network television exposé of abuse and neglect at Texas nursing homes—complete with nauseating glimpses shot by a hidden camera—put pressure on Governor Ann Richards, the legislature, and the Texas Department of Health to address the problem again. The media reports suggested that the lax attitudes of some state regulators may have been partly to blame, but inadequate funding of nursing home regulation also may have been a factor.

If so, it was an all-too-typical conflict of two governmental policies: a policy to protect vulnerable members of society, but to do so within the confines of a broader policy to limit costs and taxes.

Anthony Downs describes these phases of news coverage and public interest in terms of an **issue-attention cycle**.[8] There is a pre-public phase in which a problem, such as poor nursing home conditions, quietly affects numerous individuals. Someone, perhaps a relative of a nursing home resident, then attempts to transform the issue into a public concern through the media. Press coverage starts slowly but rapidly intensifies, prompting more and more outraged citizens to discuss the problem. But initial enthusiasm for solutions gives way to the "realization that significant progress will be costly not only in terms of money but social stability," and many people begin to lose interest. After the enactment of policies to address some of the problems, governmental responses tend to become institutionalized, and many of the initial changes are ignored or become ineffective. Although press coverage may continue intermittently, it has limited effect in renewing public opinion or prompting further governmental action—until someone, usually several years later, restarts the cycle.[9]

The media's degree of influence over specific governmental actions can vary considerably, depending on the media's own interest in an issue and the public's reaction to what they read and hear. All too often, an apathetic public and indifferent public officials—or strong differences in opinions between the media and policymakers—minimize the media's role in agenda setting or agenda building. During the 2003 regular legislative session, for example, when the state faced a $10 billion revenue shortfall, most of the state's newspapers repeatedly wrote editorials urging Governor Rick Perry and lawmakers to minimize budget cuts—particularly for health and human services programs—with a modest increase in state taxes. But Perry and the Republicans in control of the legislature ignored the pleas and chose deep cuts over any tax increase. They insisted that most Texans didn't want higher taxes. They also may have been influenced by the fact that Hispanics, who benefit disproportionately from health and human services programs, weren't a significant factor in the 2002 election, when Perry defeated a Hispanic Democratic challenger.

THE MASS MEDIA AND THE ELECTORAL PROCESS

Candidates for public office in Texas still attend rallies in the park and salute the flag at Fourth of July parades. Some legislative and local candidates, particularly those with more shoe leather than money, still rely heavily on door-to-door campaigning. But in races for statewide offices, and many local and district offices as well, the campaign stump has long since been replaced by the **sound bite**, the press conference, and the contrived pseudo-event developed by the campaign consultant. Campaigning is now constructed around the mass media, particularly paid television advertising, and the media, in effect, has displaced the political party as the major information link between the voters and those in government (see Chapter 6).

Journalists and political scientists repeatedly debate the effects of news coverage on elections. Most journalists believe their job is to be as objective as possible in outlining the issues and reporting and evaluating the backgrounds, philosophies, activities, and policy proposals of candidates. The news media tries to determine what issues should be important in a campaign, although journalists are being increasingly challenged by television ads with which the candidates themselves seek to dictate what the electorate should consider important.

News media reports, paid political advertising and, increasingly, political bloggers all play roles in shaping voters' decisions. Studies have indicated that party identification helps determine voters' choices in general elections—there is a lot of straight-ticket, one-party voting—but long ballots in primaries and general elections force many voters to seek other sources of information about the candidates as well. These voters may rely on news reports, political blogs and television advertising to clarify the candidates' characteristics, campaign issues, policy positions, and electoral prospects. Newspaper editorial endorsements of candidates also provide additional cues to many voters. Candidates, of course, welcome editorial endorsements and often feature them in political advertising. But favorable exposure on the news pages and on television screens often is more crucial to a candidate's electoral success.

Covering the "Horserace"

The media has been criticized for covering campaigns much as it would a horserace. Some critics argue that reporters often neglect candidates' positions on substantive policy issues in favor of stories about campaign strategies, tactics, and personalities, which usually are easier to develop. Numerous national studies indicate that policy issues receive only a small part of campaign coverage, and a cursory review of campaign reporting in Texas leads to a similar conclusion.

The "horserace" approach includes the publication of poll stories indicating candidate voter strength in trial heats at different stages of a campaign. Some polls are leaked to the press by the candidates who commission them—if the polls make a candidate look strong or his opponent appear weak. Other polls are conducted periodically by media organizations and other independent groups. While some of these surveys also attempt to measure public opinion on selected issues, their primary focus is on who is winning and who is losing.

Campaigning for Television

Most candidates for major offices plan their daily campaign appearances with television newscasts in mind. They participate in activities—such as visits to schools or high-tech plants—that look good in a thirty-second news segment. Unfortunately for the viewers, however, such superficial coverage doesn't even begin to shed light on the complex issues in a race or the candidate's position on them. Neither does a candidate's paid television advertising.

During campaigns, reporters in Austin are frequently given videotapes or e-mail attachments of a candidate's latest television advertisement. It may be a positive, "feel good" spot, portraying the candidate in the best possible light—playing with children, visiting a hospital, or shaking hands with the president of the United States. Or it may be a negative, "attack" advertisement, charging an opponent with a weakness or an indiscretion unworthy of the public trust or deliberately misrepresenting the opponent's record or position on an issue. Reporters often write reviews of the ads, usually getting reaction from the candidate's opponent or the opponent's campaign consultant.

Some media organizations analyze paid television spots for accuracy and report their findings. Before their recent staff cutbacks, major Texas newspapers—while often preoccupied with the horserace—also devoted considerable resources to coverage of candidates and issues, attempting to provide the in-depth perspective missing in the electronic media. It remains to be seen whether newspapers will continue that level of coverage in the future. In any event, though, most Texas voters will continue to become acquainted with candidates through televised images, and television will continue to dominate the political process.

Television has allowed a candidate with enough money to "buy" an election legally. Bill Clements, who had never previously held elective office and was a stranger to most Texans, spent millions of dollars of his own fortune on television advertisements in 1978 to become the first Republican to capture the governor's office in modern times. But not every multimillionaire candidate has been so successful. In 1990, Clayton Williams, another wealthy businessman and political neophyte, spent more than $21 million, including $8.4 million from his own pocket, to create an attractive, 30-second television image but lost by a whisker to Democrat Ann Richards. And Laredo businessman Tony Sanchez, a Democrat making his first statewide race, spent $59 million of his own fortune on a 2002 gubernatorial campaign, only to lose to Republican Rick Perry.

Political scientists, reporters, many voters, and even some candidates loudly criticize what television has done to campaigns for public office, putting style over substance and orchestrated events over thoughtful debate of the issues. But the creators of superficial television ads know they have a large audience. Since candidates are in the race to win office and not to reform the system, they spend millions of dollars perpetuating the political problem, which is actually part of a larger social problem.

Particularly susceptible to the image creators and media manipulators are the young adults who, according to recent studies, are less likely to read newspapers, watch television news programs, and otherwise keep up with current events than their parents or grandparents. "The 30-second commercial spot is a particularly appropriate medium for the MTV generation," noted one study. "Sound bites and symbolism, the principal fuel of modern political campaigns, are well-suited to young voters who know less and have limited interest in politics and public policy. Their limited appetites and aptitudes are shaping the practice of politics and the nature of our democracy."[10] It isn't just curiosity, after all, that prompts presidential candidates to campaign on MTV and the late-night television circuit. But the long-term implications of the superficial, image-oriented campaign and an increasingly indifferent electorate are no less disturbing.

Television is now the main source of news for most Americans, but nationwide, more and more objective television coverage of political campaigns has given way in recent years to paid commercials, soft news, and "talking head" commentary with distinct political viewpoints, particularly on cable TV channels. Many opinion leaders fear the trend is further destroying Americans' interest in politics and urge the major television networks to voluntarily give free air time to presidential candidates. "Politics isn't going very well on television these days.... Campaigns unfold on all commercial television as a bread-and-circus blur of 30-second attack ads and eight-second sound bites. Citizens feel cheated. They grow cynical," wrote the late CBS News anchor Walter Cronkite.[11]

An estimated $2 billion-plus was spent on paid political advertising on television during the 2008 campaign cycle, including the presidential race, with special interest contributions to candidates picking up much of the tab.[12] But most local television stations and the national networks each broadcast an average of fewer than forty seconds a night of discussion or debate by candidates, according to reports by the University of Southern California and the Annenberg Public Policy Center. "Citizens are trapped in a system controlled by big-money candidates, special-interest donors and profit-hungry broadcasters," said Paul Taylor, chairman of the Alliance for Better Campaigns, which encourages broadcasters to offer candidates more free air time. "Increasingly, political campaigns have become a transfer of income from wealthy donors to wealthy broadcasters. Meantime, substantive issue discussion is disappearing from the public square of broadcast television."[13]

The 2003 gubernatorial recall election in California also generated much paid TV advertising, but unlike most campaigns it also received considerable coverage—in California and nationally—on TV news segments, thanks to the starring role played by action-film actor Arnold Schwarzenegger. According to an analysis by the Tyndall Report, which tracks national TV coverage, three major networks—ABC, CBS, and NBC—aired 169 minutes of stories about the October 7 recall between August 1 and October 3. That compared to only 40 minutes of news coverage on the same networks for all 36 gubernatorial races, including the one in Texas, in 2002. Moreover, more than one-third of the California recall stories, or 69 minutes' worth, focused exclusively on the candidacy of Schwarzenegger, a Republican who unseated Democratic Governor Gray Davis. "It's a shame that it takes a movie star candidate to get the media to pay attention to campaigns," said Meredith McGehee, president and executive director of the Alliance for Better Campaigns. "When it comes to covering elections, most broadcasters are AWOL. The 2002 gubernatorial campaigns were no less important to our democracy than this recall election. If money is the mother's milk of American politics, then celebrity must be its crack cocaine." McGehee also noted that most of the TV coverage of the recall focused on voter opinion polls or on "the circus-type atmosphere of the race," rather than on substantive issues. "That type of news does little to help citizens become informed, engaged voters," she said.[14]

Despite the national criticism, Ann Arnold, executive director of the Texas Association of Broadcasters, said that a "substantial number" of television and radio stations in Texas offered free air time to candidates. But many candidates don't accept the offers, she said. Arnold said the broadcasters' group also has sponsored seminars to help TV and radio stations find ways to make political news coverage more interesting and encourage more people to vote.[15]

Media Coverage of Recent Gubernatorial Campaigns in Texas

Some of the worst aspects of contemporary political campaigning occurred in the 2002 and 1990 Texas gubernatorial elections, which were characterized by **negative television ads**, personal attacks on the character and integrity of the candidates, and distortions of their public records. The races also demonstrated the dominance of well-financed campaigns and political advertising.

The news media's performance in covering both campaigns was mixed. The voters who followed the campaigns through the state's major daily newspapers—if they periodically wiped off the mud—were given more than enough information to compare the candidates' qualifications and personalities and evaluate their proposed solutions—or lack thereof—to the state's major problems. But many voters never got past the paid TV commercials.

Kicking off the 2002 political season with a large investment in a TV media campaign, multimillionaire Laredo businessman Tony Sanchez beat former Texas Attorney General Dan Morales in a mud-splattered fight for the Democratic gubernatorial nomination. Governor Rick Perry, who had succeeded former Governor George W. Bush in midterm after Bush was elected president, was unopposed in the Republican primary for his first full term as governor.

Perry later defeated Sanchez in the general election after both campaigns had spent a combined total of almost $100 million, much of it on negative TV advertising that became almost vicious. In one spot, Perry even tried to link Sanchez to the murder of a federal law enforcement officer. That ad was one of a series of commercials in which the Perry campaign attacked Sanchez over his previous ownership of Tesoro Savings & Loan, a thrift in Laredo that had failed during the recession of the 1980s. In his advertising and campaign statements, Perry repeatedly attacked Sanchez over $25 million in drug money that had been laundered through Tesoro. The deposits, made in 1983 and 1984, had been investigated by federal authorities, but no one at the financial institution was ever charged with a crime. Sanchez and other former Tesoro officials said they hadn't known the money belonged to drug dealers. Perry's Tesoro ads, nevertheless, continued, culminating in a commercial in which two former Drug Enforcement Agency agents blamed the drug lords who had laundered the money through Tesoro for the torture and slaying of a DEA agent. Sanchez called the attack sleazy, and his supporters said it was racist. Sanchez ran television commercials blaming Perry for high consumer electric bills. The Democratic nominee also sponsored a TV spot that featured video from a police camera, which had recorded Perry, then lieutenant governor, in a confrontation with a state trooper who had pulled over Perry's driver for speeding. But Sanchez couldn't counter the devastating effect of Perry's attack. Perry's Tesoro ads assured the Republican governor's election, said University of Houston political scientist Richard Murray. He said the ads were influential because Sanchez had never held elective office and many voters already were uncertain of his abilities.[16]

The Democratic gubernatorial primary of 1990 may have been even muddier than the 2002 campaign, and the media was in the middle of the fray. Before Ann Richards defeated then–Attorney General Jim Mattox in a runoff for the Democratic nomination, some media outlets even ran uncorroborated reports about Richards and Mattox using illegal drugs. Fearful of being beaten by a competitor in what had become a virtual feeding frenzy, some news people threw basic journalistic standards of substantiation and fairness out the window.

Businessman Clayton Williams, meanwhile, easily won the Republican gubernatorial nomination that year over three opponents, thanks to an effective television advertising campaign financed mainly by his own wealth. Williams received little critical media attention during his primary race. But almost immediately after he was nominated, he found himself thrust into the spotlight, beginning with negative news stories about a rape joke that he told several reporters in what he thought was an informal, off-the-record setting (see "Telling a Bad Joke").

Williams's campaign operatives then tried to restrict the media's access to him and to manage his public appearances more carefully. But Williams saw a gradual erosion of an early lead, with costly losses among Texas women. He also committed other major gaffes late in the campaign.

Only a few days before the November election, he admitted that he had paid no federal income tax in 1986 because of business losses, an admission that angered tax-weary voters of more modest means. In the fall, the *Houston Chronicle* also reported allegations that a bank, of which Williams was a director, had illegally required high-risk auto loan customers to purchase credit life insurance.[17]

The 1994 governor's race between Richards and her successful Republican challenger, George W. Bush, was much tamer, and the media's coverage reflected the difference. Richards received some criticism for referring to Bush as a "jerk" early in the campaign and for running television commercials attacking Bush's record as a businessman. Bush

Telling a Bad Joke

Clayton Williams, a rancher–oilman from Midland, took full advantage of Texas's television markets to swamp three opponents and win the 1990 Republican nomination for governor. Bankrolling his own campaign to the tune of $6 million for the March primary, Williams literally galloped to the nomination across the small screen. With paid television spots of himself riding horseback in cowboy duds across his ranch, he cultivated an image as an independent, successful businessman and governmental outsider with strong traditional roots who would mount a no-nonsense attack on the problems in Austin.

After the primary, however, Williams began to be subjected to closer and more critical scrutiny. His first encounter with increased media attention occurred in spectacular fashion when he invited reporters to his West Texas ranch for spring roundup. Sharing a cup of coffee around an early morning campfire with cowhands, campaign staffers, and three male reporters—R. G. Ratcliffe of the *Houston Chronicle,* Sam Attlesey of the *Dallas Morning News,* and John Gravois of the *Houston Post*—Williams saw no reason for caution. When he told an old joke comparing the morning's foggy weather to rape—"if it's inevitable, just relax and enjoy it"—he certainly had no idea it would become page one headlines in the next day's newspapers and an issue in the remainder of the campaign. But it did.

In the not-too-distant past, such remarks in an informal setting, where the candidate was hosting reporters, would have been treated as off-the-record and not been reported. But now every aspect of a public official's or candidate's life is subject to public scrutiny, as demonstrated on the national scene by the widespread reporting of sexual misconduct by President Bill Clinton. Reporters are making greater efforts to present voters with a candid view of a candidate, "warts" and all, something that viewers aren't going to see in the candidate's television commercials.

In reporting Williams's rape joke, the media also took into consideration society's increasing sensitivity to sexual abuse and harassment, the fact that a violent crime is no laughing matter, and the question of whether Williams, as governor, would be sensitive to issues of particular concern to half of Texas's population—women.

Communicating with the Voters. The press conference is a tool candidates and public officials use to communicate with voters. Former Agriculture Commissioner Jim Hightower with farm workers behind him is seen here holding a press conference.

contended the attacks on his business record were a "personal" assault. But Richards's supporters said they were fair because Bush, who had never held public office, had touted his business experience as proof of his leadership ability.

Reporters' access to both candidates was tightly controlled by their respective campaign organizations, while Bush and Richards both relied heavily on television advertising to carry their carefully crafted messages to the public. More than ever before, major newspapers, television stations, and the Associated Press analyzed the truthfulness of campaign advertising for their readers and viewers, a process requiring considerable time and research. But a *Texas Poll* published late in the campaign indicated that more people believed the TV ads than the news media's "fact checks." Fifty-four percent of the survey's respondents said they trusted what they saw and heard in both Bush's and Richards's commercials, while only 48 percent said they trusted the media's independent analyses of them. Forty-one percent of the respondents indicated the impressions they formed of the candidates from televised images affected how they voted more than published news accounts or the candidates' stands on the issues.

The 2006 gubernatorial campaign was relatively tame, even though Governor Rick Perry drew three major opponents and a Libertarian challenger. Republican Comptroller Carole Keeton Strayhorn and satirical author–musician Kinky Friedman, running as independents, pulled much of the media attention away from Democratic nominee Chris Bell, a former city councilman and former congressman from Houston. Friedman, in particular, attracted a disproportionate amount of free publicity with a campaign that featured an abundance of one-liners but a shortage of policy initiatives. Friedman was a colorful candidate who appealed to many political outsiders, but he was hurt by a poor performance in the only televised gubernatorial debate and by revelations of racially tinged, satirical remarks during his previous career as an entertainer. Friedman finished fourth behind Bell and Strayhorn, while Perry was reelected with 39 percent of the vote.

THE MASS MEDIA AND PUBLIC ETHICS ————————●

Perhaps the greatest potential for media influence in Austin is over the ethical conduct of legislators and other public officials, simply because of the potential embarrassment and political damage that can befall an elected official caught in an impropriety. But even that influence is sporadic because memories are short and, sooner or later, there will be another scandal. Seldom, too, is the relationship between reporters and governmental officials more adversarial than when the media is questioning the ethical behavior of officeholders or reporting on a prosecutor who is doing so.

Tension was particularly high in 1990 and 1991 when then–House Speaker Gib Lewis (D-Fort Worth) was fighting two misdemeanor ethics charges stemming from a grand jury investigation of his relationship with a tax-collection law firm. After Lewis was indicted on December 28, 1990—twelve days before the 1991 legislative session was to convene—the speaker mailed letters to newspapers across the state, urging editors to avoid a "rush to judgment" about his case. Maintaining his innocence, Lewis said, "All I ask is basic fairness—that I be given the time and opportunity to gather the facts and present my case before you judge me." The *Houston Chronicle* ran the letter at the top of its "Viewpoints," or letters-to-the-editor, column, accompanied by the mug shots, front and side views, taken of Lewis when he surrendered to law enforcement officers at the Travis County jail.[18]

Lewis was easily reelected speaker when the legislature convened, and he maintained a reasonable working relationship with the news media throughout the 1991 session. But there were some rough spots.

The controversy over Lewis's legal troubles was tame compared to the furor that erupted two years later when Travis County District Attorney Ronnie Earle, a Democrat, began investigating newly elected U.S. Senator Kay Bailey Hutchison, a Republican, for allegedly using state employees for political and personal chores while Hutchison was state treasurer. Hutchison, whose conduct had been questioned months earlier in a story in the *Houston Post,* was indicted by a Travis County grand jury in 1993. She was acquitted, however, in February 1994. Republican leaders had bombarded reporters with press releases and telephone calls accusing Earle of prosecuting the senator for political purposes. Republicans repeatedly pointed out that Earle had neglected to prosecute Land Commissioner Garry Mauro, a Democrat, for using state telephones and employees to campaign for then–presidential candidate Bill Clinton in 1992. Mauro, who had chaired Clinton's campaign in Texas, reimbursed the state after the *Houston Chronicle* reported the extent of the land office's political activity. Republicans also complained that Earle seemed reluctant to investigate Democratic Governor Ann Richards after her office had prematurely destroyed some state telephone records.

Although the Republicans' public relations campaign didn't influence Hutchison's acquittal, GOP officials said they were forced to attack Earle and try to influence public opinion in order to repair any political damage to the senator and other Republican candidates. Hutchison supporters met with newspaper editorial boards and spoke on radio talk shows. Her attorneys even sent grand jury members packets of news clippings about the case. Dr. John Todd, an associate professor of political science at the University of North Texas, told the *Dallas Morning News* that the Republicans had "surprising success in planting the idea that this has all been just a political enterprise undertaken against her [Hutchison]."[19]

Reporters were caught in another political firefight between Earle and Republicans when an investigation by the Democratic prosecutor led to campaign finance charges against then-U.S. Representative Tom DeLay of Sugar Land and two associates over donations made to several Republican legislative candidates in 2002. That was the year the GOP won a majority of seats in the Texas House. DeLay, then the Republican leader of the U.S. House, and his associates denied any wrongdoing, while Earle and his GOP detractors battled each other in the headlines. Thanks to a series of legal maneuvers, no one had come to trial by late 2009. But the controversy already had taken a political toll on DeLay, who had resigned from Congress in 2006 (see Chapter 4).

GUARDIANS OF OPEN GOVERNMENT

Since the soundness of any governmental policy or program is affected by the motives and capabilities of those officials who design and administer it, most members of the Capitol press corps take very seriously their role as watchdogs over the behavior and performance of elected officials and bureaucrats. Consequently, news people are persistent guardians of the public's access to governmental business through the state's **Open Meetings and Public Information acts**. These laws, which apply to state and local governments, basically provide that the public's business is to be conducted in public and that most records produced in the conduct of the public's business are to be made available to the public on demand. Each law provides for certain exceptions. Governmental bodies, for example, are allowed to hold closed-door meetings to consider personnel matters, to discuss lawsuits in which they are involved, and to consider real estate purchases, although all formal actions are to be taken in public. The Open Meetings Act requires a governmental body to post advance notices of all its meetings, even closed-door, executive sessions, and the Public Information Act establishes a procedure whereby the state attorney general's office decides disputes over whether specific governmental records can be kept confidential. But media representatives are engaged in a constant struggle against abuses and outright violations of the laws and attempts by school boards, city councils, and other governments to expand the list of exceptions that allow them to discuss business in private.

Several media organizations monitor and promote open government issues. The Freedom of Information Foundation of Texas, a nonprofit corporation that includes journalists, educators, and attorneys among its directors, maintains a telephone hotline to advise news people on open meetings and open-records rights and procedures and generally promotes openness in government. The Texas Daily Newspaper Association, the Texas Press Association, and the Texas Association of Broadcasters also lobby the legislature on open government issues. It's a difficult struggle because many public officials throughout Texas prefer to conduct the public's business in private. Numerous attempts usually are made each legislative session to weaken the open meetings and public information laws.

Media organizations are obviously in the business of disseminating information. But it is important to remember that they are not the only ones with a stake in strong open-government laws. Every Texan also has a right to know what his or her government is doing, to find open doors in city council chambers and school board meeting rooms, and to have ready access to public documents (see "Texas Reporters Get a 'Shield'").

Texas Reporters Get a "Shield"

Some reporters and news organizations in Texas, particularly in the broadcast media, advocated for years for a so-called reporter's **shield law** to protect journalists from having to reveal the names of confidential news sources when they are subpoenaed to appear in court. Often, the only way a reporter can learn of and develop stories of governmental corruption is through confidential sources, who in many cases are government employees or contractors who would lose their jobs if their names were made public. Without the protection of confidentiality, news organizations feared their sources would dry up and deprive the public of stories it needs to know.

After watching previous efforts fall short, reporters finally won at least a partial shield in 2009, when the Legislature passed and Governor Rick Perry signed the Free Flow of Information Act. With it, Texas joined 36 other states and the District of Columbia in offering limited protections for reporters and their news sources. The new law represented a compromise with prosecutors, who had opposed previous shield bills.

It provides that in criminal cases, reporters still could be required to disclose felony crimes and the identities of sources who admit to committing crimes. It also wouldn't protect reporters from having to testify as witnesses to crimes or when disclosure of a confidential source is necessary to prevent a likely death or substantial bodily injury. In civil cases, a judge can require a reporter to testify or produce notes if all reasonable efforts to obtain the information have been exhausted and the reporter's cooperation is essential to at least one of the sides in a lawsuit.

"I am pleased that lawmakers were able to strike a balance between protecting the rights of the people and the press," Perry said upon signing the bill.

Senator Rodney Ellis, a Democrat from Houston and sponsor of the bill, said, "Texas has finally stood behind the principle that the press plays a vitally important role in our democracy and must be protected from government intimidation."[20]

MEDIA BIAS ⎯⎯⎯⎯⎯⎯⎯⎯⎯⎯⎯⎯⎯⎯⎯⎯⎯⎯⎯⎯⎯⎯⎯⎯⎯⎯⎯⎯⎯⎯●

Most public officials are sensitive about what is written and broadcast about them, particularly if a controversial issue has thrust them into the spotlight. Consequently, they will often consider news stories slanted against them or their viewpoints. Complaints about alleged **media bias** are also made by readers and viewers, and the issue has sparked considerable debate and research. National studies have indicated that most reporters are more liberal than the general population in personal ideology and on many public policy issues, and conservatives have exploited these findings to support their contention of a liberal media bias.[21] But other people, including many liberals, have pointed to corporate media ownership and concluded that those who make the final decisions as to what news is covered and how it is covered reflect more conservative biases.

State capitol reporters in Texas normally attempt to present all sides of an issue. Most believe they are objective, dedicated to principles of fairness and balance, and report events as they happen. This view of the press as a mirror was summarized by Frank Stanton, former president of CBS, when he testified before a congressional committee that "what the media do is to hold a mirror up to society and try to report it as faithfully as possible." But news people and the organizations they represent sometimes have strong personal or corporate opinions about the issues or individuals they cover, and bias and the perception of bias are problems the media constantly has to fight.[22]

Subjective decisions—such as a reporter's own strong interest in an issue—may determine which news events are covered on a particular day or which angle is emphasized in a particular story. Unless they are personal friends, reporters seldom discuss their political preferences with each other, but their personal politics doubtlessly cover the spectrum—Democrats, Republicans, and independents; conservatives, moderates, and liberals.

More often than not, however, reporters eagerly provide a forum for the viewpoints of consumer advocates, environmentalists, and other individuals purporting to promote the public interest. One reason is that spokespersons for these groups are readily accessible, hold frequent news conferences, and actively cultivate media contacts. They depend on free media exposure to compensate for limited budgets in their battles against the business lobby for the tougher regulations and higher taxes that progressive programs often require. Another reason is that stories about the age-old struggle between the powerful and the powerless, the rich and the poor, attract considerable reader and viewer interest, centering as they do on controversy and conflict.

The prominence with which editors or news directors "play" stories—page one versus inside the paper, the lead item on the 10 o'clock news versus minor air treatment—is usually determined by the newsperson's perception of the public's interest in a given story. But an editor's or publisher's own opinion of an issue may also be a factor. Newspapers and broadcast stations often disagree with each other—and with their own reporters—on how stories should be played. Ultimately, a relatively few individuals decide which stories will be reported, how prominently they will be presented, and how much space or time will be allotted to them. And people alleging media bias will point out that fact.[23] Michael Parenti, a critic of institutional elites in the United States, concludes that "the very process of selection allows the cultural and political biases and class interests of the selector to operate as censor."[24] Other media watchers argue, however, that the media "gatekeepers"—those who decide what news to publish or broadcast—are constrained, at least in part, by their readers' or viewers' preferences, as determined through market research.

Stories about governmental scandals and political corruption are often displayed on the front pages of newspapers, at the top of evening television newscasts, or prominently on newspaper or television websites. Attempting to follow in the footsteps of the early muckrakers of American journalism, some Texas news people view themselves as crusaders and are determined to "clean up" government. In their eagerness, however, they can become susceptible to charges of unfair, personal bias against the public officials they are targeting. This is particularly true when haste to be the first with the latest development in an ongoing scandal produces reporting or editing mistakes.

Newspapers and radio and television stations in Texas are big businesses and, as such, sometimes have their own special interests to protect. Media opposition, for example, has played a major role in killing periodic attempts by legislators to put a sales tax on advertising. An advertising tax could raise millions of dollars for education, human services, and other programs that media outlets generally support, but media owners fear it would reduce advertising volume and deprive them of critical revenue.

Media bias will grow with the continued expansion of Internet information sources, including bloggers and other so-called "citizen journalists" who aren't bound by traditional journalistic ethics and make no pretense of objectivity. The digital environment is "more open to bias and to journalism for hire," warned Paul Starr, a professor of communications and public affairs at the Woodrow Wilson School at Princeton University. "Online there are few clear markers to distinguish blogs and other sites that are being financed to promote a viewpoint from news sites operated independently on the basis of professional rules of reporting," he wrote in the *New Republic.* "So the danger is not just more corruption of government and business—it is also more corruption of journalism itself."[25]

THE DEVELOPMENT OF THE MEDIA IN TEXAS ————●

Frontier Newspapers

Frontier Texans, isolated in their farmhouses and small settlements, lacked many creature comforts, but most had the opportunity to keep informed about the political sentiment of the day. The short-lived *Graceta de Tejas,* or the *Texas Gazette,* was established in Nacogdoches in 1812 long before Texas won its independence in 1836.[26] By 1860, according to historian T. R. Fehrenbach, there were seventy-one daily and weekly newspapers in Texas, with a total circulation of about 100,000. "Ninety-five percent of the white population could read and write and some publication reached virtually every family."[27] Like other early American newspapers, these publications were often highly partisan and primarily devoted to commentary on public issues—the local, state, and national political events of that turbulent period. Social calendars and stories about floods, fires, murders, and other everyday disasters were not yet standard journalistic fare. Editorial writing, however, had already developed into a backwoods art form. "This writing was often irate, biased, and misinformed—but much of it was clear and sound. It kept the freeholders of Texas fully aware of events; many farmers could quote Senator Stephen Douglas or Sam Houston at length. Texans were already keen political animals."[28]

Newspapers and "The Establishment"

Throughout much of the twentieth century, Texas's major newspapers were active members of the conservative, big-business, big-oil establishment that ran the statehouse and the state. During the pretelevision years of the 1940s and 1950s, in particular, publishers of some of the state's major newspapers, such as Amon Carter in Fort Worth and Jesse Jones in Houston, were oilmen and financiers who helped control local and state politics for the dominant conservative wing of the Texas Democratic Party. Another strong voice for the establishment was the *Dallas Morning News,* a tireless anticommunist, antilabor, antiliberal crusader. At various times, the *News* editorialized that "the presidency of Franklin Roosevelt was actually destructive of the Republic, the Senate's censure of Joe McCarthy [was] 'a happy day for Communists,' and the Supreme Court [was] 'a threat to state sovereignty second only to Communism itself.'"[29] There was little pretense of detached, neutral reporting, as the newspapers actively participated in the political process.

The establishment's close relationship with the Texas press was convincingly demonstrated in numerous election campaigns, including the 1954 Democratic gubernatorial runoff between Governor Allan Shivers, who had led conservative Texas Democrats in supporting Republican Dwight Eisenhower in the 1952 presidential race, and liberal challenger Ralph Yarborough, a party loyalist and strong supporter of organized labor. In the closing weeks of the campaign, ninety-five of the state's one hundred daily newspapers carried editorials endorsing Shivers, who won the runoff. Yarborough would later win election to the U.S. Senate, but the establishment's opposition to him was rabid. In its editorial endorsement of Shivers in 1954, the *Dallas Morning News,* however, was kind enough to concede that some of Yarborough's Texas supporters were not "reds ... radicals or goon squad supporters."[30]

Evolution of Texas Newspapers

News coverage has changed significantly during the past fifty years, and readers now will almost never find the kind of inflammatory, racist, demagogic writing that characterized much of the earlier Texas press. The media today is much more disposed to cover issues affecting the lower income populations, minorities, and others struggling against the power structure. Texas is still largely a conservative state, and a restructured business community is still influential in the setting of state policy. But the media—particularly the large newspapers and television stations—is much more eager to challenge the political and business establishment today.

For one reason, there is a high level of distrust of government now. A turning point in Texas was the Sharpstown stock fraud scandal that broke in 1971. It revealed that the legislature had given quick passage in 1969 to two banking regulation bills sought by Houston financier Frank Sharp and that high-ranking state officials had profited from insurance stock purchases financed with loans from Sharp's bank (see Chapter 8). That was soon to be followed by the Watergate scandal, which would force the resignation of President Richard Nixon and shake public confidence in government throughout the country, much as the bitter experience of the Vietnam War already had begun to do.

News people still depend on government officials for much of their information. But now they more readily question the motives of the governor, legislators, and other public officeholders and political candidates. The ethical behavior of officeholders and their relationship to the special interests that spend millions of dollars trying to influence state government came under closer scrutiny after the Sharpstown and Watergate scandals. The media also reexamined its own ethics. Most news organizations adopted policies prohibiting their reporters from accepting free airplane rides, junkets, and other "freebies" from state officials or candidates, practices that had been fairly common in Texas in the past.

Another significant factor in the evolution of the Texas press was the passing of the high-profile publishers who had been part of the conservative establishment. Many of their newspapers were subsequently sold to large national conglomerates with newspapers and broadcast holdings in many cities. Such purchases of major, once independently owned newspapers like the *Houston Chronicle,* the *Fort Worth Star–Telegram,* and the *Austin American–Statesman* were part of a consolidation of media ownership across the country, a development regarded as unhealthy by many within and outside the industry.

Such consolidations raised concerns that national owners, who had no personal ties to the local communities, were more concerned about profits and losses than the quality of news coverage—or diversity of editorial viewpoints—in their local outlets. And those concerns were renewed in the wake of recent technological advances, corporate mergers, downsizing of newspaper staffs, and newspaper closures.

But, perhaps paradoxically, national ownership can offer newspapers a greater degree of independence than was true in the past. Absentee corporate owners don't have sacred cows to protect in the Texas statehouse, the local courthouse, or city hall, and don't feel compelled to defend old provincial prejudices. If the *Austin American-Statesman,* for example, still had Texas owners, it may not have been so bold as to editorialize in the early 1990s for a state income tax when that proposal was still highly unpopular in Texas and opposed by most elected officials and business people. The *American-Statesman,* then owned by Atlanta-based Cox Enterprises, helped provoke a public debate over a critical issue that is becoming more difficult for the legislature to avoid. For the most part, Texas newspapers have maintained considerable **editorial autonomy** under national owners.

The *Dallas Morning News* is the only major metropolitan newspaper in the state still owned by a Texas-based corporation, and it still presents one of the most conservative editorial viewpoints on its opinion pages. It aggressively covers governmental and political institutions on its news pages, although it has scaled back its coverage in recent years following a series of financial setbacks and significant reductions in its news staff.

The 1970s and 1980s were turning points for many Texas newspapers. Many changed owners during this period, and the overall quality of Texas journalism began to improve noticeably. The most dramatic and most influential change occurred in Dallas, and it was brought about by the brief entry of one of the nation's media giants, the Times Mirror Company, into the Dallas newspaper market.

Times Mirror, publisher of the *Los Angeles Times,* one of the country's most respected newspapers, purchased the *Dallas Times Herald* from local owners in 1970. Within a few years, it precipitated a major newspaper war with its dominant competitor, the *Morning News.* Times Mirror brought in new editors, recruited reporters from all over the country, improved the quality and aggressiveness of its news coverage—"The Only Sacred Cow Here Is Hamburger," read a sign on the newsroom wall—and awakened the *Morning News* from what many media watchers had considered a long, provincial slumber. At one point, the *Times Herald* briefly passed the *Morning News* in Sunday circulation. But the *Morning News* responded by bringing in new editors of its own, expanding its news staff, and vastly improving its own product. During this period, both newspapers became major national award winners.

Initially, Times Mirror's foray into Dallas was extremely profitable, but with the precipitous decline in the Texas economy during the 1980s, the *Times Herald* began to lose money and was still second in advertising and circulation. The paper was sold in 1986 to a Texan, who was unable to reverse its financial position. It changed hands one more time before the *Morning News* purchased the struggling property and closed it in 1991.

Until its own recent financial downturn, the *Morning News* remained one of the nation's premier newspapers, thanks in large part to the swift kick administered by Times Mirror. Moreover, the higher journalistic standards that emerged in Dallas had positive effects on some of the state's other newspapers, which soon began undergoing transformations of their own. But journalistic improvements were soon to be replaced by financial decline in the newspaper industry.

Modern Newspapers, Modern Problems

Nowadays, the daily newspaper industry in Texas and the United States is fighting for its survival. Hundreds of newspapers in the U.S. have ceased publication since 1900, a reflection of declining circulation, corporate consolidations, the emergence of television, the proliferation of radio stations with targeted audiences, the development of specialized magazines, and, most recently, the development of the Internet as a major information and advertising source. The folding of the *Dallas Times Herald* was followed by the closing of the *San Antonio Light* in 1993, the *Houston Post* in 1995, and the *El Paso Herald-Post* in 1997, leaving all of the large cities in Texas with only one daily newspaper each. And by 2009, the survivors were reducing staff and news space and taking other cost-cutting steps to stay afloat in the face of a recession.

The Hearst Corporation, the *San Antonio Light*'s long-time owner, closed the paper after purchasing the rival *San Antonio Express–News,* which had gained the circulation lead in San Antonio. The *Light* had been published in San Antonio for 112 years, but lost a reported $60 million during its last six years of operation.[31] During its final years, the *Houston Post* also lost millions of dollars as it went through a succession of owners. Texas now has about ninety daily newspapers and about 450 weekly, biweekly, or monthly newspapers.

Most small-town weekly newspapers are oriented primarily to their local communities and carry little news of state government or politics. But most of the small towns served by weeklies also are in the circulation areas of daily newspapers. There are also a number of African American–oriented and Spanish-language papers in Texas, but they have limited circulations. The demise of major daily newspapers has raised the profiles of aggressive, alternative weeklies in some Texas cities. Two of the better known are the *Houston Press* and the *Dallas Observer.* And, statewide, the *Texas Observer,* a favorite of Texas liberals for more than fifty years, continues to publish every other week. In November 2009, a new online newspaper, the non-profit Austin-based *Texas Tribune* made its debut, specializing in state political coverage.

Newspapers can more thoroughly explain a pending issue, its history, and possible options for its resolution than can the electronic media. Newspapers also have their limits, primarily in the amount of space they can or will devote to governmental news. Responding to the popularity of television and its drain on available advertising revenue, newspapers already had reduced the proportion of space allocated to so-called "hard news." "Newspaper editors, like TV producers, have discovered the American public's insatiable hunger for 'fluff,'" one critic wrote.[32] Then news space was reduced even more following the Internet's raid on advertising dollars.

Newspapers now have their own webpages, which are updated with breaking news stories throughout the day. Some newspapers also post staff-produced audio reports, or podcasts, as well as video reports on their websites. They are posting blogs on politics, sports, and a variety of other subjects. They also are publishing blogs by readers and interactive polls to promote more online readership as circulation of their traditional print editions continues to decline. The Internet makes a newspaper's stories easily accessible to a national, or even international, audience well beyond its local or regional print circulation.[33] Most newspapers make their Web content available to readers free of charge, a business practice that many papers have come to regret. Newspapers sell advertising on their websites, but that revenue hasn't yet begun to replace the millions of dollars in print advertising revenue that the papers have lost to Internet competitors. Meanwhile, news coverage, including coverage of state government, is suffering.

The Electronic Media and the Internet

Television and the emergence of the Internet have had major impacts on the role of the media in government and politics. An estimated 98 percent of American homes have at least one television set, and most are linked to cable television systems. Television has replaced the newspaper as the public's primary source of news, but, like newspapers, it is getting increasing competition from the Internet.

Some 57 percent of American adults watched television news the previous day, compared to 40 percent who read a newspaper, 36 percent who listened to a radio newscast, and 23 percent who got their news from the Internet, according to a 2006 survey by the Pew Research Center for the People & the Press. The survey indicated that audiences for nightly network TV newscasts as well as local TV and radio news all had slipped during the previous two years but that the viewer losses were far less than TV news had suffered in the 1990s. Newspapers, the survey found, were using their online editions to help stem readership losses.[34]

In a follow-up survey by the Pew center in 2008, respondents saying they had read a newspaper the previous day had fallen from 40 percent to 34 percent, and most of that loss was among those who read the print newspaper. Only 27 percent of the respondents said they had read a print newspaper the previous day. The television news audience had generally remained stable since 2006, while online news consumption had grown. The proportion of Americans who said they got news online at least three days a week had increased from 31 percent to 37 percent during the previous two years. Daily online news use had increased from 18 percent to 25 percent.[35]

The 2008 survey identified "four distinct segments in today's news audience: Integrators, who comprise 23 percent of the public; the less populous Net-Newsers (13 percent); Traditionalists, the oldest (median age: 52) and largest news segment (46 percent of the public); and the Disengaged (14 percent), who stand out for their low levels of interest in the news and news consumption."[36]

Integrators get news from both traditional sources and the Internet and, according to the survey, are a "more engaged, sophisticated and demographically sought-after audience segment than those who mostly rely on traditional news sources."[37] Net-Newsers, who get most of their news online, are the youngest of the news user segments. They also are affluent and even better educated than the Integrators. Only 47 percent of Net-Newsers watch television news on a typical day and even fewer read a newspaper. Some 17 percent read an online newspaper, 8 percent read a printed newspaper, and 10 percent read both. Traditionalists are less affluent and less educated than Integrators and Net-Newsers, and television is their favored news source.[38]

With these changes, there has been increased concern about the role of television and the Internet in shaping our view of politics and setting the agenda for public policies. This concern is compounded by declining levels of news literacy among Americans, particularly the young. Although there has been a proliferation of news sources, a 1990 national survey concluded that "those under 30 know less than younger people once did, and they are less interested in what's happening in the larger world around them."[39] This decline, which has been re-emphasized in more recent surveys and will be discussed in more detail later in this chapter, has had its greatest impact on newspapers, but it also has implications for the broadcast media.

There are about 160 television stations in about twenty-three markets in Texas, ranging in size from Dallas–Fort Worth and Houston, which rank among the largest markets in the country, to numerous small cities. Some cable stations are now offering full-time news coverage. The first was established in Austin in 1999 by Time Warner Cable, which holds the cable TV franchise in Austin. Despite TV's emergence as Texans' primary news source, television coverage of state government and politics has become inconsistent in recent years, even in the larger cities. Austin TV stations regularly cover events at the state capitol, but no TV station from outside Austin has a full-time capitol bureau. Stations sometimes send news crews to Austin for special events, such as a gubernatorial inauguration or the opening day of a legislative session, but their overall coverage is spotty and inconsistent.

Even at its best, television is an inadequate substitute for newspaper coverage of government and politics. Most local television news programs provide only cursory reports on governmental issues and activities, and people who rely solely on television for news have little substantive information upon which to make critical and informed judgments. Television—which, of course, is visually oriented—is good at covering a protest demonstration on the capitol steps, getting a sound bite from the governor, or gathering interviews with citizens outraged over a tax increase. But the limited air time given to even the most important stories makes it difficult to explain why the protesters marched on the capitol or to explore the economic and political factors that produced the tax bill.

Most radio news also is of the headline variety, a quick summary of the day's news highlights. Many radio stations make no pretense of offering serious news coverage. Few have sufficient news staffs to cover major events or issues in Austin. They rely on wire stories or feeds from a news service such as the Texas State Network, which has an Austin bureau. A handful of news talk stations, however, offer more in-depth coverage and commentary on political events and public issues. This commentary includes talk show programs that offer primarily conservative viewpoints (see "Dan Patrick: Talking His Way into Office"). Although a large part of the population regularly tunes in to radio, the medium is a relatively minor source of state political news.

Dan Patrick: Talking His Way into Office

A long-time, outspoken radio host on a conservative station in Houston, Dan Patrick was a hero to many Republicans as he championed property tax cuts and other conservative causes. Along the way, he didn't hesitate to criticize public officials, including President George W. Bush and other fellow Republicans with whom he disagreed. When a Republican state senator chose to retire from a suburban Houston district in 2006, Patrick transformed his on-air personality and listener base into a successful race for the open Senate seat. His easy win over more politically experienced candidates in the Republican primary was a testimonial to the power of the airwaves and his ability to say what his audience wanted to hear.

Patrick headed to Austin, vowing to make changes. Some political observers doubted he would be able to keep all his promises, but no one doubted that he would continue to be heard.

Television and radio often take their cues about what to cover from the print media. Most stations don't have large enough reporting staffs to do the extensive background work required to develop many complex stories. But once a story broken by a newspaper has grabbed attention, the electronic media usually will join in pursuit.

Several Internet bloggers also have started covering and commenting on state government and politics in recent years. As noted earlier in this chapter, however, most offer a distinct political viewpoint and make no pretense of objectivity.

Growing Media Conglomerates and More Technological Changes

Just as there is national concern about growing chain ownership of newspapers, there is also concern about ownership patterns in the television industry. As an unsettling precedent, some media watchers cite the 1985 purchase of the National Broadcasting Company (NBC) by General Electric, a nonjournalistic conglomerate whose primary business had been "neither news nor entertainment but household appliances, airplane engines, nuclear reactors, and arms."[40] General Electric extended its reach into the entertainment sector in 2003, when it agreed to merge NBC with Vivendi Universal Entertainment, owner of Universal Pictures, Universal Television and a number of cable TV systems. The new company, NBC Universal, was to be 80 percent owned by General Electric. "With this merger, NBC will stay in the forefront of the fundamental changes taking place in television and other media," said Jeffrey Immelt, GE's chairman and chief executive.[41]

Several national media chains own newspapers or broadcast properties in Texas. Texas-based A. H. Belo Corp., owner of the *Dallas Morning News,* also owns television stations in Dallas, Houston, San Antonio, and Austin. San Antonio–based Clear Channel owned some 1,200 radio stations throughout the country in 2006 after an aggressive strategy of purchasing single stations and companies with several holdings. A merger that produced a high debt load for its holding company and the decline in advertising revenue due to the 2007 recession led to a sell-off of one-third of Clear Channel's stations by 2009 and speculation about the financial solvency of its holding company.[42]

Concerns over media ownership increased in 2003 after the Federal Communications Commission (FCC) voted to relax rules that restricted how many television stations one company could own nationally or in a local market and to ease regulations that prevented TV stations from merging with newspapers. Protests from public interest groups were so strong that Congress intervened and scaled back some of the FCC's changes. But the broadcast ownership issue is subject to periodic review—and renewed controversy.[43]

The recent technological changes suggest that we can anticipate a much greater range of news sources in the future. Some television stations carry their newscasts and even live coverage of major courtroom trials on their websites. Newspapers and broadcasters also have expanded their use of the Internet to collect and analyze statistical data for news stories.

Traditional broadcast owners, meanwhile, are facing increasing challenges from cable and satellite television, the emerging digital broadcast system, and other technological advances. There is a high-stakes war among the traditional—or "old media"—outlets, cable television and telephone companies, and Internet providers for the huge profits to be made in the high technology information age. That war reached a new level in early 2000 with the multibillion-dollar merger of America Online, the number one Internet provider, with Time Warner, the media and cable television giant.

A Dominant Force in the Radio Industry. Clear Channel Communications, headquartered in San Antonio, owned some 1,200 radio stations in 2006, and while it has sold off many stations, it continues to play a dominant role in the radio industry.

The AOL–Time Warner merger renewed debate over how much independence news outlets may be losing with corporate mergers, particularly since a relative handful of corporate owners with an array of business interests was now in ultimate control of most of those outlets. "The worry is not that there are fewer media outlets—the opposite is true—but that few people have ultimate control over them," the *New York Times* wrote. "Critics wonder if news judgments will be bent, with executives suppressing news deemed harmful to corporate interests. They wonder if companies will use their journalists to promote their other interests, be they movies, television shows or sports teams." Media experts interviewed by the newspaper, however, offered different opinions about those potential problems. "Defenders of the news divisions point out that plenty of media outlets would be eager to pick up on a story suppressed by a competitor. Top media executives also know and have argued to their corporate bosses that cheap or compromised journalism costs the enterprise both trust and profits," the newspaper noted.[44]

Many of the radio stations held by national conglomerates no longer provide local news. Some are basically remote facilities in which the programming is formatted in another city, and the reporters or disc jockeys are speaking from a studio miles away. Another potential source of local news is being lost to corporate consolidation. It is another step toward the homogenization of news.

Although it is difficult to foresee all the implications of the recent technological advances and high-stakes mergers, one can speculate that there will be major changes in the way the electorate receives information about politics and government—and the way the media will be exploited by officeholders and candidates.

THE CAPITOL PRESS CORPS ⎯⎯⎯⎯⎯⎯⎯⎯⎯⎯⎯⎯⎯●

The state's major newspapers, the Associated Press, and a radio network are represented at the Texas state capitol by reporters who cover state government and politics fulltime, but the capitol press corps has been shrinking in Austin, as has coverage of statehouses throughout the country. More than 50 reporters and television correspondents were assigned to the Texas capitol in 2000. By the end of the 2009 legislative session, that number had dwindled to approximately 40. Newspaper bureaus are smaller, and the only television stations that regularly cover events at the capitol are the Austin stations. Several "insider" subscriber newsletters and Internet bloggers focusing on state government also operate in Austin.[45] The muckraking *Texas Observer,* mentioned earlier, is still published fortnightly and still has a faithful following. The slick magazine *Texas Monthly* offers limited coverage of state government, including blogs and its ranking of what it considers the ten best and ten worst legislators after each regular session. The *Texas Lawyer,* a weekly newspaper specializing in the activities of the courts and other news of interest to the legal profession, also has an Austin-based reporter.

Individual news bureaus range in size from several staffers for the Associated Press to one-person operations for smaller organizations. The Associated Press is the only news organization with a full-time photographer on its capitol staff, although several freelance photographers are available to newspapers in Austin, and staff photographers are sent to the capitol from home offices for special assignments.

The small newspaper bureaus usually give priority to covering members of their local legislative delegations and events of particular interest to their communities, while the large papers and the wire service provide more general coverage. But even the large papers find it impossible to cover more than a fraction of state government activities, and that task has become even more difficult with the contraction of the newspaper industry and reductions in capitol staffs.

"The concern about statehouse coverage—indeed, about newspaper retrenchment in general—is not just the declining number of reporters, but deterioration in the quality of journalism," wrote Professor Paul Starr in the *New Republic.* "As the editorial ranks are thinned, internal checks on accuracy are being sacrificed. As reporters with years of experience are laid off, newspapers are losing the local knowledge and relationships with trusted sources that those reporters had built up, which enabled them to break important stories."[46]

The statehouse bureaus are generally considered prestigious assignments and attract capable and aggressive reporters. Nevertheless, in addition to the staff reductions, there has been considerable turnover on capitol news staffs in recent years. Only a dozen or so of the reporters covering the legislature in 2009 had more than ten years of experience on the capitol beat. This means many reporters have little historical perspective for comparing the administrations of different governors or the performance of the legislature over a sustained period.

There is no typical pattern to the careers of capitol reporters. Some were promoted from their organizations' local staffs, while others were hired from competing bureaus or from out-of-state newspapers. In recent years, relatively few capitol reporters have chosen to retire in those jobs, but only a handful have gone on to become editors or news directors in their home offices. Some have moved to news bureaus in Washington and jobs in other media markets, while others have become press secretaries or information specialists for elected officeholders or state agencies. Some have even left the news business for unrelated occupations.

Most news bureaus lease private office space near the capitol for their main offices and lease smaller, additional workspace from the state in an underground addition to the capitol building in Austin. With proper credentials, media representatives are granted access to the floors of the House and the Senate when the legislature is in session. Special worktables at the front of each chamber are provided for reporters, and the House and the Senate set standards for credentials under their respective rules.

Newspaper bureaus transmit their stories to their home offices via computer, and television correspondents use satellite transmissions. News organizations use the Internet and computerized databases to assist in researching and preparing stories, including, for example, articles detailing how many of a governor's appointees to state boards and commissions were political donors and how much money each gave.

Sound news judgment and perseverance are still the basic tools of the successful capitol reporter, just as they are for thousands of news people elsewhere. Statehouse reporters usually have to dig out the best stories, frequently using confidential sources to develop tips or hunches. Legislators, other elected officials, members of their staffs, bureaucrats, and lobbyists love to tell secrets about each other. Such sources, of course, often have their own political or personal agendas, and the smart reporter is wary. Campaigns for state office are notorious for whispered accusations or innuendoes directed against opposing camps. Sometimes a legislator, without allowing his or her name to be used, will leak a controversial proposal to a reporter as a trial balloon to see how other lawmakers and the general public react to the idea before deciding whether to actively promote it. Similar anonymous leaks, cast in a negative light, can

Keeping "Tabs" on the Legislature. Under the rules of the House and Senate, reporters have access to the floor while the two bodies are in session. Seen here are reporters covering the proceedings in the Texas House of Representatives.

be used to kill someone else's proposal before he or she has had a chance to gather support for it. Although reporters run the risk of being used in such situations, they also can be put on the trail of significant stories. A newsperson has to evaluate each tip on its own merits, although he or she often is pressured by the knowledge that competitors also get similar tips.

GOVERNMENTAL PUBLIC RELATIONS ———————————— ●

Most of the state's top elected officials and administrators of major agencies spend thousands of tax dollars each year on press secretaries and public relations operations to help disseminate public information and to promote themselves and their agencies. News releases, websites, press conferences, background briefings, slick reports, and videotapes are designed to maintain the visibility of state agencies, cultivate general goodwill, announce new programs, and anticipate budgetary attacks or program changes. In a dispute with the legislature or another state agency, a public official's media specialists often try to put a **spin** on a story that presents information in the best possible light for their boss.

The House and the Senate also provide media services for their members. Taxpayers pay for websites, written news releases, newsletters, and radio and television feeds to local stations. These resources can be used by a legislator to maintain a flow of information to constituents that, in effect, amounts to a continuous political campaign.

Some governors have used political funds to purchase statewide television satellite time to communicate directly with the public on major policy issues or proposals. And websites give governors and other officeholders an excellent opportunity—unfiltered by the media's critical eye—to promote their proposals directly to the public and tout what they claim to be their accomplishments.

Most of the Austin-based trade associations and other special interest groups have public relations specialists to promote their causes and keep their members informed of developments at the capitol. Interest groups are at the center of the policymaking process, and their proposals and efforts to get them enacted are inherently newsworthy. Lobbyists also provide a wealth of insider information to reporters, but news people must carefully evaluate it because of the large stakes that special interests have in the workings of state government.

HOW WELL INFORMED ARE TEXAS CITIZENS? ——————— ●

Despite the media's efforts, only a small percentage of Texans attempt to keep up with what their elected officials in Austin are doing. A few high-profile issues, such as taxes or the lottery, attract a lot of attention. But many taxpayers, particularly those who live in metropolitan areas that have numerous legislators, don't even know who their state representatives or state senators are, much less how they have voted on significant issues.

This may partly be the media's fault. Many small newspapers carry only brief wire service stories about news events in Austin, while others give an incomplete picture by concentrating primarily on issues of local interest. The major newspapers provide more complete coverage, but they seldom publish record votes of legislators within their readership areas. Most radio stations carry only cursory headline versions of statehouse news, and most television stations, through which most Texans get their news, don't do much better than that. Reporters don't always tell their readers and viewers how the actions of the legislature, the governor, the bureaucracy, and the courts are relevant to their lives and their futures.

But the uninformed and under informed state of many Texas citizens is only partly the media's fault. There are ample information sources by which anyone, with minimal effort, can stay informed of major developments in state government. The distractions and demands on a person's time are great in today's fast-paced world, and a person who wants to know what's going on in the governmental and political arena often has to juggle priorities. But the opportunities are there. It is up to the individual to make the time and the effort.

Ignorance among the general electorate plays right into the hands of the special interests, who not only stay abreast of developments in Austin, but also spend millions of dollars on political donations and legislative lobbying to influence those developments to their advantage, not to the benefit of the general public. Most governmental actions, whether taken by the legislature or a state regulatory board, eventually will affect the pocketbooks or quality of life of thousands, perhaps millions, of Texans, most of whom will be caught by surprise. If recent indications are correct, the influence of special interests over the public's business will become even greater in the future.

In one of the greatest ironies of the so-called "information age," Americans are consuming less news now than they did forty years ago. The continued decline over the past ten years is reflected in Table 5–1. Technology, of course, has changed media sources. Online news, for example, developed with the Internet and is now widely accessible. Its use is growing but is still limited. Surveys link news consumption patterns to political information and make it clear that there are large numbers of citizens who have limited knowledge for making informed judgments about politics and public policy. Moreover, one suspects that this political ignorance translates into a decline in political participation.

TABLE 5–1   Changing News Consumption Patterns, 1998–2008

	Trends in Regular News Consumption (%)						
	1998	**2000**	**2002**	**2004**	**2006**	**2008**	**Percent Change***
Regularly watch							
Local TV News	64	56	57	59	54	52	−12
Cable TV News	—	—	33	38	34	39	6
Nightly Network News	38	30	32	34	28	29	−9
Network Morning News	23	20	22	22	23	22	−1
Listened yesterday							
Radio News	49	43	41	40	36	35	−14
Read yesterday							
Newspaper (print and web)	48	47	41	42	40	34	−14
Three or more days a week							
Online News	13	23	25	29	31	37	24

*Calculated by comparing data for years available, 1998–2008.

Source: Pew Research Center for the People & the Press, *Pew Research Biennial News Consumption Survey*, August 17, 2008.

TABLE 5–2   The News Generation Gap, 2008

	18–24 (%)	25–34 (%)	35–49 (%)	50–64 (%)	65+ (%)
Consumed News Yesterday					
Watched TV News	34	50	55	64	74
Read Newspaper	15	24	31	40	55
Listened to Radio News	25	34	43	37	29
News Online	30	36	34	29	13
Newsless Yesterday	34	22	17	14	13

Source: Pew Research Center for the People & the Press, *Pew Research News Consumption Survey*, August 17, 2008.

The Pew Research Center for the People & the Press has regularly surveyed news consumption patterns in the United States. When surveyed in 2008, less than 25 percent of people younger than thirty-five said they had read a newspaper the previous day, compared to 40 percent of those 50–64 years of age and 55 percent of those 65 and older. Researchers also found growing disinterest among the young in other media venues. As age increased, news consumption increased across almost every news source, with the exceptions of call-in radio shows and online news (see Table 5–2).

Earlier studies also had determined that young Americans were less able than their parents to identify major newsmakers—except, perhaps, for sports figures—were much less critical of political leaders, and were less likely to vote. Only in coverage of sports and the abortion issue—which could directly affect the lives of many young persons—did young people match their parents' interest in news. "Abortion notwithstanding, an overall examination of the surveys conducted by Times Mirror (the predecessor to the Pew Center) reveals a younger generation with less curiosity about news of all sorts, and one with an especially small appetite for the most serious and complicated of issues," a 1990 survey concluded.[47] More recent studies of the civic literacy of young people continue to demonstrate low levels of knowledge about basic governmental institutions and contemporary public affairs, but civic illiteracy extends to a good part of the adult population as well.[48]

Researchers have suggested that the Vietnam conflict and the Watergate scandal, both of which damaged Americans' confidence in their government, may be partly to blame for such a large amount of indifference now. They also cite serious problems in public education—longtime classroom deficiencies that restrict young people's views of the world—which Texas and other states are still trying to resolve.[49] The increased number of entertainment alternatives now competing for young people's time is also a likely factor. Moreover, it has been suggested that many people believe that they can't make a difference. If so, many citizens have tuned out the political process.

Whatever the reason, the prospects for a quality state government sensitive to the public interest in the next generation are somewhat discouraging. If the surveys accurately reflect the news consumption patterns of young people, their levels of knowledge about government and politics, and attitudes toward participation and involvement in the political process, state and local governments will be controlled for years to come by special interests with only limited opposition or scrutiny by the general public.

SUMMARY AND CONCLUSIONS ————————————————●

1. The news media is the primary information link between those who govern and those who are governed. It affects the development of public policy by influencing the election of policymakers and informing and educating the public on policy alternatives. It can make the causes of a few individuals the concerns of many. This role has remained basically unchanged in this country since the adoption of the First Amendment to the U.S. Constitution more than 200 years ago, but vast changes in technology have transformed the media's preparation and transmission of information.

2. Texas newspapers, much improved in recent years, offer the most complete, thoughtful coverage of state government and politics, but they are struggling financially because of readership and advertising revenue lost to the Internet. Most Texans prefer the more abbreviated news summaries that television provides. Television has had a particularly strong impact on the elections process, in which wealthy or well-funded candidates can practically buy their elections through well-produced and highly effective paid advertising. The Internet also is growing as a news source, but it provides more immediacy than depth.

3. Thanks to major government scandals and the passing of former publishers who had helped run the conservative Texas establishment, the media today is much more independent of officialdom and much more eager to challenge those in power than it was forty years ago. Despite its greater independence, the media still must fight charges of bias in its presentation of the news, in part because the subtle, subjective decisions of a relatively few reporters, editors, and news directors have a major impact on which stories are covered and how prominently they are presented. Ironically, the fierce competition among media outlets has contributed to a "pack" mentality among reporters, who often pursue the same developments in the same major stories to avoid being beaten by a competitor.

4. Media organizations are persistent guardians of the public's access to governmental business through the state's Open Meetings and Public Information acts, but the fight against government secrecy is a never-ending battle.

5. One of the greatest ironies of the so-called "information age" is that young people apparently are paying less attention than their parents to governmental news and other substantive events occurring in the world around them. This dims the prospects for a quality state government in the next generation because ignorance among the general public plays right into the hands of the special interests who make it their business to influence public policy.

KEY TERMS ————————————————————————●

FURTHER READING ————————————————————●

Articles

Burka, Paul, "The Capitol Press Corpse," *Texas Monthly*, January 2008.

Denison, Dave, "Prime-Time Politics: Why TV News Doesn't Get the Picture," *Texas Observer*, December 21, 1990, pp. 4–8.

Glendening, Parris N., "The Public's Perception of State Government and Governors," *State Government* 53 (Summer 1980), pp. 115–20.

Books

Abramson, Jeffrey B., F. Christopher Arterton, and Gary R. Orren, *The Electronic Commonwealth*. New York: Basic Books, 1988.

Alger, Dean, *The Media and Politics*. Englewood Cliffs, NJ: Prentice Hall, 1988.

Ansolabehere, Stephen, and Shanto Iyengar, *Going Negative: How Political Advertisements Shrink and Polarize the Electorate*. New York: Free Press, 1995.

Arterton, F. Christopher, *Media Politics*. Lexington, MA: Lexington Books, 1984.

Bennett, W. Lance, *News: The Politics of Illusion*, 2nd ed. New York: Longman, 1988.

Christ, W. G., Harry Haines, and Robert Huesca, "Remember the Alamo: Late Night Local Newscasts in San Antonio, Texas," in *The Electronic Election: Perspectives on the 1996 Campaign Communication*, Vol. 1, edited by L. Kaid and D. Bystrom. Mahwah, NJ: Lawrence Erlbaum Associates, 1998.

Graber, Doris A., *Mass Media and American Politics*, 8th ed. Washington, DC: Congressional Quarterly Press, 2009.

Jamieson, Kathleen Hall, *Packaging the Presidency*. New York: Oxford University Press, 1984.

Jamieson, Kathleen Hall, *Eloquence in an Electronic Age*. New York: Oxford University Press, 1988.

Joslyn, Richard, *Mass Media and Elections*. Reading, MA: Addison-Wesley, 1984.

Nimmo, Dan, and James E. Combs, *Mediated Political Realities*. New York: Longman, 1983.

Parenti, Michael, *Inventing Reality: The Politics of the Mass Media*. New York: St. Martin's Press, 1986.

Websites

Freedom of Information Foundation of Texas   http://www.foift.org/   This organization "provides the leadership to ensure that the public's business is conducted in public and to protect individual liberties guaranteed by the First Amendment." It provides a range of services to its members in an effort to gain access to public information.

Stateline.org   http://www.stateline.org/   Funded by The Pew Charitable Trusts as a public service, it provides a daily survey of news developments in the fifty states. Reference materials are also published, including a State of the States report released every January.

Texas Association of Broadcasters   http://www.tab.org/   In addition to providing information about careers and jobs in the media, this site provides links to radio and television stations in Texas.

Texas Daily Newspaper Association   http://www.tdna.org/   This organization serves the interests of Texas newspapers. This site provides access to papers across the state, including university daily newspapers, and the organization's university journalism program.

Texas Press Association   http://www.texaspress.org/   The Texas Press Association provides a range of services to Texas newspapers, many of which require authorization to access. Internships and job opportunities in the print media can be found at this site.

The Pew Research Center for the People & the Press   http://www.peoplepress.org   This research center produces studies on the media habits of Americans. Surveys are conducted on a wide range of policy issues.

ENDNOTES •

1. *Democracy in America*, with an introduction by Joseph Epstein (New York: Bantam Dell, 2004), p. 210.
2. For an extended discussion of the role and functions of the mass media in politics, see Doris A. Graber, *Mass Media and American Politics*, 8th ed. (Washington, DC: CQ Press, 2009), Chapter 1.
3. Maxwell E. McCombs and Donald L. Shaw, "The Agenda-Setting Function of the Press," in *Media Power in Politics*, 2nd ed., edited by Doris A. Graber (Washington, DC: Congressional Quarterly Press, 1990), p. 75.
4. Doris A. Graber, *Mass Media and American Politics*, 2nd ed. (Washington, DC: Congressional Quarterly Press, 1984), pp. 78–79.
5. Ibid., pp. 268–69.
6. Gladys Engel Lang and Kurt Lang, *The Battle for Public Opinion: The President, the Press, and the Polls during Watergate* (New York: Columbia University Press, 1983), p. 58.
7. Larry N. Gerston, *Making Public Policy: From Conflict to Resolution* (Glenview, IL: Scott, Foresman and Company, 1983), pp. 55–56.
8. Anthony Downs, "Up and Down with Ecology—The Issue Attention Cycle," *Public Interest* 32 (Summer 1972), pp. 38–50.
9. See Barbara J. Nelson, *Making an Issue of Child Abuse: Political Agenda Setting for Social Problems* (Chicago: University of Chicago Press, 1984), pp. 51–75.
10. Times Mirror Center for the People and the Press, *The Age of Indifference: A Study of Young Americans and How*

They View the News (Washington, DC: Times Mirror Center for the People and the Press, 1990), p. 28.

11. Walter Cronkite and Paul Taylor, "To Lift Politics Out of TV Swamp," *Houston Chronicle,* March 10, 1996, p. 1E.

12. In the early part of President Obama's campaign, he relied on contributions of $1,000 or more. By election day, he raised some $750 million with approximately one-half coming from persons contributing $200 or less.

13. "Alliance for Better Campaigns," *Political Standard* 3, no. 5 (July 2000), p. 1.

14. Alliance for Better Campaigns press release, October 8, 2003.

15. Clay Robison, Interview with Ann Arnold, July 13, 2000.

16. John Williams, R.G. Ratcliffe, Rachael Graves, "Poll Puts Perry in Double-digit Lead; Cornyn Maintains Slim Advantage over Kirk for Senate," *Houston Chronicle,* November 3, 2002, p. 1A.

17. Bob Sablatura, "Williams' Bank Suspect in Car Loans," *Houston Chronicle,* September 12, 1990, p.1A.

18. Gibson D. "Gib" Lewis, "Media Rushed to Judgment," *Houston Chronicle,* January 6, 1991, Outlook, p. 3.

19. Sam Attlesey, George Kuempel, and Staff Writers of the *Dallas Morning News,* "DA Reveals Evidence Against Hutchison – Loyalists' Public Opinion Campaign Campaign Dividends, Party Leaders Say," *Dallas Morning News,* February 13, 1994, p. 1A.

20. "Texas Governor Signs Journalist Shield Law," *Associated Press,* May 14, 2009.

21. William Schneider and I. A. Lewis, "Views on the News," *Public Opinion* (August–September 1985), p. 7.

22. Edward Jay Epstein, *News from Nowhere* (New York: Random House), pp. 13–14.

23. Graber, *Mass Media and American Politics,* pp. 71–74.

24. Michael Parenti, *Democracy for the Few,* 5th ed. (New York: St. Martin's, 1988), p. 170.

25. Paul Starr, "Goodbye to the Age of Newspapers (Hello to a New Era of Corruption)," *New Republic,* March 4, 2009, http://www.tnr.com/article/goodbye-the-the-age-newspapers-hello-new-era-corruption-o.

26. Archie P. McDonald, "Anglo-American Arrival in Texas," in *The Texas Heritage,* 2e, edited by Ben Proctor and Archie McDonald (Arlington Heights, IL: Harlan Davidson, 1992), p. 28.

27. T. R. Fehrenbach, *Lone Star: A History of Texas and the Texans* (New York: Macmillan, 1968), p. 302.

28. Ibid., p. 303.

29. George Norris Green, *The Establishment in Texas Politics, 1938–1957* (Westport, CT: Greenwood, 1979), p. 10.

30. Ibid., p. 162.

31. Greg Hassell, "San Antonio Light Folds after 112 Years of Service," *Houston Chronicle,* January 28, 1993, p. 1A.

32. Vittorio Zucconi, "America's Media Empires," *World Press Review* (May 1986), p. 21. Excerpted from *La Republica* (Rome).

33. Erin Mulvaney, "Capitol Press Corps Adapts to Technology's Impact on Journalism," *Daily Texan,* March 2, 2009.

34. Pew Research Center for the People & the Press, "Pew Research Biennial News Consumption Survey," July 30, 2006.

35. "Key News Audiences Now Blend Online and Traditional Sources," Pew Research Center for the People & the Press, August 17, 2008.

36. Ibid.

37. Ibid.

38. Ibid.

39. Times Mirror Center for the People and the Press, *The Age of Indifference,* p. 1.

40. Zucconi, "America's Media Empires," p. 19.

41. "GE, Vivendi Universal Make Joint Plans Official," *Houston Chronicle,* October 9, 2003, p. 9C.

42. David Hendricks, "Is the Bell Tolling for Clear Channel?" *San Antonio Express News,* June 27, 2009, 1C.

43. *Los Angeles Times,* October 3, 2006, p. C1.

44. Felicity Barringer, "Does Deal Signal Lessening of Media Independence," *New York Times,* January 11, 2000, p. C12.

45. The three online newsletters—the *Quorum Report, Texas Weekly,* and *Capitol Weekly*—are available by subscription.

46. Starr, "Goodbye to the Age of Newspapers (Hello to a New Era of Corruption)."

47. Times Mirror Center for the People and the Press, *The Age of Indifference,* p. 9.

48. Intercollegiate Studies Institute, American Civic Literacy Program, "Our Fading Heritage," 2008.

49. Sara Lipka, "Freshmen Increasingly Discuss Politics, Worry About Money, Survey Finds," *Chronicle of Higher Education,* January 19, 2007, p. 21.

The Party System in Texas

Questions to Guide Your Reading

1. How critical are political parties to the development and maintenance of a democratic political system?

2. Through the 1970s, Texas was a one-party state dominated by the Democratic Party. Why?

3. How do you account for the recent transformation of the state's party system to a Republican dominated state?

4. What do you perceive to be the relationship of interest groups to political parties?

5. After a long decline or hiatus, is there any evidence of party revitalization?

*Political parties created democracy and modern democracy is
unthinkable save in terms of party.*

—E. E. Schattschneider[1]

*The common and continual mischiefs of the spirit of party are sufficient to make
it the interest and duty of a wise people to discourage and restrain it.*

—George Washington, Farewell Address to the People
of the United States, September 17, 1796

Much has been written in the media about Republican gains over the past three decades
that have transformed Texas from a one-party Democratic state into a Republican-
dominant state. But Democratic or Republican, political parties still do not get much
respect, esteem, or attention. In subtle and not-so-subtle ways, many Texans assert that
there is not a "dime's worth of difference between the two political parties." Others consider them a joke, and many cannot link the political parties to specific policy positions.
Parties have little relevance for many Texans, and media coverage of party-related activities often focuses on political patronage, questionable campaign contributions, negative campaigning, petty conflicts that lead to governmental deadlock, and instances of graft
or corruption. Many people don't give much thought to the role of parties in a democratic
political system. They know little of the origins, history, or structure of the political parties.
They don't identify parties with effective or responsive government. And many couldn't
care less about the health or viability of the state's party system. In sum, there is a significant segment of the state's population that holds clearly defined antiparty attitudes that
are often expressed in the simple statement, "I vote for the person and not the party."

Other people are ambivalent toward political parties. They don't know much about
their functions or activities and may not even be able to distinguish between the two
major parties. They do not hold contempt for political parties, nor do they regard them
to be a significant factor in decisions of governments. All they know about parties is that
they produce competition, and, if nothing else, the ability to "throw the rascals out" and
replace them with another set of rascals.

But some voters are intensely interested in political parties and are convinced that
parties are essential to developing and maintaining a democratic society. A political
party, these individuals believe, is one of the few mechanisms available to the general public for reviewing and possibly repudiating the actions of governmental leaders. With all
of their weaknesses, political parties provide a democratic process for choosing leaders.
They bring large numbers of people under an umbrella with some degree of consensus,
and they clarify policy alternatives.

For much of the century after the Civil War, Texas was a one-party Democratic
state. There was no organized opposition party available to mobilize the interests of
those who felt neglected or excluded from the Democratic Party. Electoral politics were
based on factions and personalities, and the interests of the lower socioeconomic classes,
especially minorities, were blatantly neglected. Over the past thirty years, however, Texas,
along with many other states that were part of the Confederacy, has witnessed the emergence of a strong Republican Party and the decline of the Democratic Party. During this
period of change, the electoral power of minorities also has increased dramatically, and
minority groups that once were excluded now play a significant role in Democratic Party
politics.

POLITICAL PARTIES AND A DEMOCRATIC SOCIETY

As long as a society is ruled by a few individuals and the interests or concerns of the general population have no political significance or influence, leaders have little reason to be concerned with what the masses think or want. But democratic societies are based on the principle that those who rule have a fundamental obligation to consider the preferences, interests, and opinions of those who are governed. Because it is impossible for every individual to participate in every public policy decision, we have chosen to construct representative governments in the United States. We choose individuals to act on our behalf, which makes it necessary for us to find mechanisms to assure that these individuals are selected fairly and are responsive and responsible. We try to accomplish this objective through several means, including elections, interest groups, and political parties.[2]

Although political parties share their representative roles with other institutions, scholars tend to agree that parties perform critical functions that other institutions cannot. There is considerable debate about formal definitions of parties, their characteristics, organizational and membership criteria, and the relationship of the parties to the governing institutions and the social system.[3] Our purpose is to focus on that part of the debate that would help us understand the political parties in Texas.

POLITICAL PARTIES IN PERSPECTIVE

Political parties are complex structures that relate to most other facets of government and politics. V. O. Key suggested that parties are social structures that are best understood from three perspectives: the party in the electorate, the party as an organization, and the party in government. The party in the electorate involves the party's relationship to voters and election activities. The party organization includes a wide range of activities from the precinct to the state level that are necessary to support the party's structure. The party in government covers the activities of those elected individuals who take office and carry out the functions of government (see Figure 6–1).

Definition of Political Parties

We find the party definition given by political scientist Leon D. Epstein to be best suited to Texas. A **political party** is "any group, however loosely organized, seeking to elect governmental officeholders under a given label."[4] Although we tend to think only in terms of Democrat and Republican, other political parties that meet this definition have emerged at both the state and local level in Texas history. Although political parties share some characteristics of other groups that function in the political arena, they are distinguished from these organizations by their primary preoccupation with contesting elections and the fact that "it is only parties that run candidates on their own labels."[5]

Parties and Interest Groups

At first glance, political parties and interest groups often appear indistinguishable, but there are differences, which were partially addressed in the earlier chapter on interest groups.

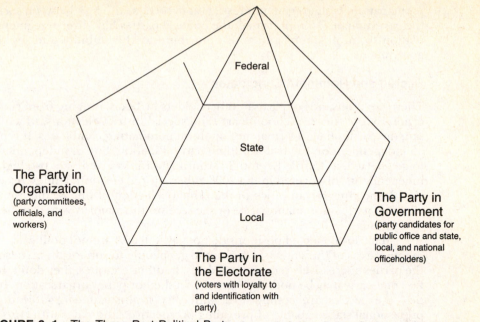

FIGURE 6–1   The Three Part Political Party. *Source:* V. O. Key, *Politics, Parties, and Pressure Groups* (New York: Cromwell, 1958); and Paul Allen Beck, *Party and Politics in America* (New York: Longman, 1997).

Interest groups are concerned with shaping public policy by influencing the actions and decisions of public officials, regardless of the officials' party affiliation. Political parties are structured under a "common label to recruit, nominate, and elect candidates for public office" under specific partisan labels.[6] An interest group usually focuses on a narrow range of policy issues. It can attempt to influence the outcome of elections, but it doesn't nominate candidates or take responsibility for the day-to-day management of government.[7] These are functions of the political parties and officials elected under their banners.

Studies conducted during the years of one-party Democratic domination in Texas concluded that the interest groups were especially powerful.[8] Some expect the relative power between interest groups and parties to change in two-party Texas, but that remains to be seen.

THE FUNCTIONS OF POLITICAL PARTIES: INTERMEDIARIES BETWEEN THE ELECTORATE AND GOVERNMENT ●

The over 24 million people who live in Texas have a wide range of interests and needs that they expect their governments to fulfill. Samuel Huntington, a modernization theorist, noted that political parties, though they share some characteristics with other social and political institutions, have a unique function in modern societies "to organize participation, to aggregate interests, and to serve as the link between social forces and the government."[9] Simply stated, the political parties link diverse segments of the population to government and thus contribute to the stability and legitimacy of the government.

Recruit and Nominate Candidates

There are thousands of partisan officeholders in Texas, ranging from constable to governor. Except for city, school board, and special district elections, which are nonpartisan, the parties have a virtual monopoly on nominating candidates. It is possible to get an independent on the ballot with no party affiliation, but an independent is not likely to get elected, as Carole Keeton Strayhorn and Kinky Friedman, two highly publicized independents, discovered in the 2006 gubernatorial election. Under Texas law, an individual who runs for an office in the primary election of one of the two major parties wins that party's nomination if he or she receives the majority vote in either the primary or a runoff.

Many local elected positions do not pay well and are not politically attractive and, in some areas of the state, it is difficult to get people to run for them. In some counties, the parties aggressively recruit candidates. In other counties, they don't. In some counties, one party may be nothing more than a shell or paper organization. In other counties, the parties are competitive, with very sophisticated organizations and paid professional staffs capable of providing prospective candidates with considerable campaign resources.

Parties have not always used the primary to nominate candidates. Prior to reforms enacted in the Terrell Election Laws of 1903 and 1905, candidates were nominated by party conventions that were attended by the party faithful.

Contest Elections and Mobilize Voters

Although candidate-centered campaigns built on modern media-oriented technology have reduced the role of the political parties in elections (see Chapter 7), parties are still the most important institutions for mobilizing voters for specific candidates. Even though most Texans aren't active in party affairs, approximately 60 percent of Texas voters identify with either the Republican or Democratic Party, which have a near monopoly on the votes cast. Given the size of the state, the number of people who participate in elections, the diversity of interests, and the variety of political subcultures within the state, the political parties have had considerable success in mobilizing voters in Texas.[10]

Organize and Manage the Government

Once elected, officeholders use their party affiliations in carrying out their public responsibilities, and with the development of a competitive party system in Texas, the parties have taken on a more significant role in the organization and management of government. Governor Ann Richards, a Democrat, appointed primarily Democrats to hundreds of positions on policymaking state boards and commissions and to vacancies on state courts. Her successors, Republicans George W. Bush and Rick Perry, appointed primarily Republicans.

After taking office in 1979 as Texas's first Republican governor in more than 100 years, Bill Clements appointed many Republicans to state boards, but he also named some Democrats, in part to encourage conservative Democrats to switch parties. His successful strategy was instrumental in adding to the strength and influence of the Republicans (often referred to as the Grand Old Party [GOP]) in Texas.

Despite the growth of the Republican Party and increased GOP representation in the legislature—Republicans captured their first majority of modern times in the state Senate in 1997 and in the Texas House of Representatives in 2002—the legislature's organizational structure remained bipartisan. In the last quarter of the twentieth century, Democratic leaders built coalitions by appointing Republicans as well as Democrats to major chairmanships. Republican leaders continued this bipartisan approach. Representative Joe Straus, a Republican from San Antonio, won the Texas House speakership in 2009 and resolved a contentious battle among Republican lawmakers by building a coalition between a handful of House Republicans and the majority of Democrats, who were united in unseating Straus' predecessor, Republican Tom Craddick.

Although the bipartisan tradition, shaped by political philosophy and local interests cutting across party lines, continues, party caucuses now appear to be more influential in defining policy positions and possibly legislative strategies. There has been increased voting along party lines in both the House and the Senate in recent legislative sessions (see Chapter 8). The ideological positions dividing the two parties in the legislature have been sharper, and there has been less willingness to compromise on selected, major issues. Some legislative battles also have become highly personalized. Trust that had crossed party lines consequently has suffered. If partisanship continues to increase, the majority party in the legislature may begin to use its organizational powers to further reduce the influence of the minority party.

Mediate the Effects of Separation of Powers

The political parties also help to bridge the inherent conflicts between the executive and legislative branches of government. The governor needs legislative support for key programs and, in turn, legislators often need the governor's support and assistance to get their bills enacted. The chances of such cooperation are enhanced if the governor and a majority of the legislature are of the same party. Republican Governor George W. Bush usually worked well with Democratic lawmakers and shared many of their priorities. But not too many years earlier, Republican Governor Bill Clements often had a stormy relationship with Democratic legislators. Bush had a more accommodating style than Clements, but Bush also had the added advantage of being governor as Republicans were nearing a legislative majority. Republican Governor Rick Perry has relied on the leadership of his party to help obtain approval for some of his legislative programs and has found it possible to marginalize Democratic influence in the legislative process.

Provide Accountability

One of the fundamental problems of a democratic government is how to keep public officeholders responsive and accountable to the people. Elected officials can abuse power. They can engage in graft and corruption. They can pursue policies that conflict with the interests of most of their constituents or pursue foolish or shortsighted policies that produce adverse results. The political parties, in their criticisms of each other and their electoral competitiveness, serve to inform the voters of the shortcomings and failures of elected officials. This process provides alternatives for the voters and gives them an opportunity to "turn the rascals out."

Manage Conflict and Aggregate Interests

The United States generally has had a stable political system that manages conflict among competing groups and interests, and the political parties have played a major role in that process. A party tries to find common ground among varied interests within the electorate so that successful coalitions of voters can be put together to support that party's candidates on Election Day. The Texas Democratic Party, for example, is built on a diverse coalition of African Americans, Hispanics, lower socioeconomic groups, labor, some professionals, and rural interests, to name a few. The Republican Party's base is markedly different than that of the Democrats, but party leaders and candidates also work to build stable coalitions of voters. To build durable support for its candidates, the party must find common interests, structure compromises, and develop accommodations among groups of voters. As interests within the party agree to support a variety of programs and common principles, the party succeeds in resolving conflict.[11]

Agenda Setting

Public policy doesn't just happen. It is the result of groups organizing around issues and keeping pressure on elected officials to respond. Some issues are longstanding problems that have produced sharp differences of opinion and will take years to resolve. Others emerge rapidly, perhaps as a result of a catastrophic event. A deadly school bus accident in the Rio Grande Valley, for example, produced an immediate outcry for safety barriers between public roadways and open, water-filled gravel pits like the one in which many young bus passengers drowned. Groups seeking change often try to build support for their programs through the political parties.

The parties also play a role in establishing policy priorities. Candidates running for public office under a party's banner announce their support or opposition to specific policies and, once elected, are expected to use the resources of their offices to try to achieve those objectives. In anticipation of future elections, officeholders will spend much time and energy trying to carry out policies that will solidify their support among the voters.

THE PARTY IN THE ELECTORATE ●

The Texas party system has been restructured by the social and economic changes that the state has experienced over the past thirty years. Texas now has a strong Republican Party, and although Democrats still hold on to many local offices, Republicans dominate statewide politics. But from the 1870s through the 1970s, Texas was a **one-party** Democratic state.

One-Party Democratic Politics

Texas's long domination by the Democratic Party can be traced to the period immediately after the Civil War, when the Republican Party was able to capture control of Texas government for a short period. Strong anti-Republican feelings were generated by the Reconstruction administration of Radical Republican Governor Edmund J. Davis, and the Republican Party was perceived by most Texans of that era to be the party of conquest and occupation. By the time the Constitution of 1876 was approved, the Republican

Party's influence in state politics was negligible. From 1874 to 1961, no Republican won a statewide office in Texas, and in only a few scattered areas were Republicans elected to local offices.

The state voted for Herbert Hoover, the Republican presidential candidate, in 1928. But for many Texans the key issue in that election was the fact that Al Smith, the Democratic nominee from New York, was a Catholic and favored the repeal of Prohibition. Anti-Catholicism and support for Prohibition had deep roots among many fundamentalist religious groups in Texas during that period.

The anti-Republicanism that evolved from the Civil War and Reconstruction, however, is only a partial explanation for the Democratic Party's longtime domination of Texas politics. V. O. Key, in his classic study, *Southern Politics*, presents the provocative thesis that Texas politics might be better understood in terms of "modified class politics."[12]

As Texas's conservative agricultural leaders attempted to regain control over the state's political system after Reconstruction, the postwar economic devastation divided Texas along class lines. Small farmers, African Americans, and an emerging urban labor class suffered disproportionately from the depression of this period. They turned their discontent into support for agrarian third parties, particularly the Populist Party, which began to threaten the monopoly of the traditional Texas power structure.

To protect their political power, the established agricultural leaders moved to divide the lower social groups by directing the discontent of the lower income whites against the African Americans. The rural elites, who manifested traditionalistic political values and wanted to consolidate power in the hands of the privileged few, also created alliances with the mercantile, banking, and emerging industrial leaders, who reflected the individualistic view of a limited government that served to protect their interests. These two dominant forces consolidated political power and merged the politics of race with the politics of economics. Then, for more than eighty years, the conservative Texas establishment pursued policies that best served its interests rather than those of the general population.

The elites were able to institutionalize their control through the adoption of constitutional restrictions and the enactment of legislation designed to reduce the number of voters. The effect of these actions was to reduce the potential of a popular challenge to the establishment's political monopoly.[13] Segregation legislation, called **Jim Crow laws**, stripped African Americans of many economic, social, and political rights and eliminated most of them from the political process. Restrictive voter-registration laws, including a poll tax, which also were designed to exclude African Americans, reduced the participation of low-income whites in the political process as well. And the costs of statewide political campaigns boosted the electoral prospects of candidates financed by the establishment.[14] The result of all this was a one-party Democratic system, dominated by influential conservatives.

Factionalism in the Democratic Party

The Texas Democratic Party, however, was not homogeneous. It was split by factions, regional differences, and personal political rivalries. Initially, there were no sustained, identifiable factions, as voting coalitions changed from election to election through much of the first third of the twentieth century. But the onset of the Great Depression in 1929, the election of President Franklin Roosevelt in 1932, and the policies of the New Deal reshaped Texas politics in the 1930s.

State party systems are linked to the national party system, and developments in the Texas party system must be understood as part of this relationship. During the period from the Civil War to Franklin Roosevelt's election, the national party system was dominated by the Republican Party. The elections from 1928 to 1936, however, produced a major national party realignment, and the Democratic Party, capitalizing on the devastation of the Great Depression, replaced the Republicans as the dominant national party.

Roosevelt's administrations articulated and developed a radically different policy agenda than that of the Republican Party. Government was to become a buffer against economic downturns as well as a positive force for change. Under Roosevelt, the regulatory function of the federal government was expanded to exercise control and authority over much of the nation's economy. The federal government also enacted programs such as Social Security, public housing, and labor legislation to benefit lower socioeconomic groups.

These national policies had a direct impact on many Texans and produced an active philosophical split within the Texas Democratic Party that was to characterize Texas politics for the next two generations. A majority of Texas voters supported Roosevelt in his four elections, and the Democratic Party maintained its monopoly over Texas politics. But competing economic interests clearly—and often bitterly—divided Texas Democrats along liberal and conservative lines.

A strong Republican Party didn't emerge at this time in Texas or any other southern state because "southern conservative Democratic politicians, who would have been expected to lead such a realignment, or any politicians for that matter, did not relish jumping from a majority-status party to one in the minority."[15] Furthermore, the restrictive voter-registration laws designed to reduce participation by minorities and poor whites continued to limit the electoral prospects of liberal Democrats and allowed conservatives to remain largely in control of the state party. "As long as the conservative Democrats remained dominant, they served as a check on the potential growth of the Republican Party."[16] There also were residual feelings from the Civil War and an antipathy toward the Republican Party that required generations to die off before new voters were willing to change party allegiances.

Despite some liberal successes under Governor James Allred, who was elected in 1934 and again in 1936, the conservative wing of the party prevailed in state elections from the 1940s to the late 1970s. Democratic presidential candidates carried Texas in 1944, 1948, 1960, 1964, 1968, and 1976, even though some of them were too liberal to suit the tastes of the state's conservative Democratic establishment.

By 1941, the conservative Democrats began to lay the groundwork for an all-out attack on the "New Deal," or liberal, Democrats in the 1944 presidential election. Roosevelt won the nomination and election for a fourth term; but in Texas there was a bitter intraparty battle between conservative Democrats and liberal Democrats (loyal to Roosevelt) for control of the party organization and delegates to the Democratic National Convention. This election was followed by three successive presidential elections in which conservative Democrats bolted the party to support either third-party candidates or the Republican nominee.[17]

The harbinger of this conservative—liberal split in a statewide political race—was the 1946 Democratic gubernatorial race between Homer Rainey and Beauford Jester. Rainey, a former University of Texas (UT) president who had been fired after a bitter fight over the UT governing board's censorship of books and efforts to force him to dismiss liberal faculty members, ran as a liberal, or progressive, candidate supporting academic freedom, labor legislation, and civil rights.

He was challenged by four conservatives who attacked him on the university issue, suggested there was rampant atheism at the university, and unleashed antilabor, anticommunist, and anti–African American attacks. Jester, in a well-financed campaign, eventually defeated Rainey 2 to1 in a runoff. Many of the allegations raised against Rainey were designed to inject demagoguery into the race and divert attention from the substantive social and economic issues of importance to the lower economic classes. The tactics served the economic and political objectives of the state's corporate establishment.

Similar volatile allegations emerged during many subsequent state elections, and the conservative Democrats were able to capitalize on them. In 1944, the U.S. Supreme Court had declared the white primary—party elections in which only whites could vote—unconstitutional in *Smith v. Allwright*. Subsequently, a number of candidates appealed to the sentiments of white supremacy. Texas also had its own brand of "McCarthyism" initiated by right-wing groups that alleged communist conspiracies throughout the state.[18]

Modified One-Party Democratic Politics

At first glance, it might appear that the **bifactionalism** in the Democratic Party partially compensated for the lack of a competitive two-party system in Texas. But in his study of southern politics, V. O. Key argued against that perception. He concluded that factionalism resulted in "no-party politics." Factionalism produces discontinuity in leadership and group support, so that the voter has no permanent reference point from which to judge the performance of the party or selected candidates. Because there are no clear distinctions between who holds power and who does not, the influence of pressure groups increases.[19] In one-party Democratic Texas, state government and public policy were conducive to control by wealthy and corporate interests.

This bifactional pattern of state Democratic politics was tested by a number of factors, including the national party's increased commitment after 1948 to civil rights and

Shivercrats. Governor Allan Shivers led conservative Democrats (called Shivercrats) in support of Republican Dwight D. Eisenhower in the 1952 presidential election.

social welfare legislation. These liberal developments alienated segments of the white population and eventually prompted many voters to leave the Democratic Party and to align with the Republicans.

Efforts by Texas oil interests to reestablish state control over the oil-rich tidelands off the Texas coast also played a key role in the demise of one-party politics and the development of a two-party system. President Harry Truman, concerned about national security and federal access to these offshore oil resources, refused to accede to state demands and vetoed legislation favorable to Texas oil interests in 1952. That veto prompted a series of maneuvers orchestrated by Democratic Governor Allan Shivers to move the support of conservative Democrats to the Republican Party.

Promising to support the Democratic Party, Shivers and his allies captured control of the Texas delegation to the 1952 Democratic National Convention. The Democrats nominated Adlai Stevenson for president, and the Republicans in their convention, Dwight Eisenhower. When the Texas Democratic Party convened its fall convention, Shivers succeeded in winning the party's endorsement of Eisenhower. The "Shivercrats," as they were called, were successful in carrying Texas for the Republican nominee. This election helped establish a pattern of Texas retaining its Democratic leanings at the state and local level but voting for Republicans for president.[20]

For years, the Republican Party's limited presence in Texas had been basically a patronage base for leaders who were more interested in an occasional appointment than in winning elections.[21] But the 1952 election marked a change in the party's state leadership and led to efforts to create a party capable of winning local and statewide elections.[22] It took years to develop the necessary organization, but the process would accelerate after the 1964 election.

In 1960, Democrat Lyndon B. Johnson ran both for vice president and for reelection to the U.S. Senate from Texas—a dual candidacy permitted under state law—and won both offices. His Republican opponent in the Senate race was John Tower, a relatively unknown college professor from Wichita Falls, who received 41 percent of the vote. After Johnson won the vice presidency and resigned from the Senate, a special election to fill the Senate seat was called in 1961. It attracted seventy-one candidates, including Tower, who defeated conservative Democrat William Blakely with 50.6 percent of the vote in a runoff.[23]

There is some evidence that liberal Democrats, in retaliation for having been locked out of the power centers of their party and in anticipation of an ideological realignment of the party system, supported Tower in this election.[24] The *Texas Observer,* an influential liberal publication, endorsed Tower with an argument for a two-party system. "How many liberals voted for Tower will never be known, nor will it be known how many 'went fishing,'" wrote Republican campaign consultant and author John R. Knaggs, who was a volunteer worker for Tower during the 1961 race. "But in reviewing Tower's razor-thin 10,343-vote margin out of 886,091 cast, it must be concluded that the liberal element was pivotal in electing the first Republican United States senator to represent Texas during the twentieth century."[25] Texas Republicans, incidentally, hadn't even held a primary in 1960.

Tower was reelected in 1966, 1972, and 1978, but no other Texas Republican won a statewide office until 1978, when Bill Clements was elected governor. Nevertheless, many students of Texas politics regard Tower's election in 1961 as a key factor in the development of the state's **two-party system**.[26]

Although Republicans made some gains in suburban congressional districts andlocal elections in the 1960s—including the election to Congress of a Houston

Early Beginnings of the Republican Era in Texas. John Tower's surprise election to the U.S. Senate in 1961 was the first statewide victory by a Republican since Reconstruction.

Republican named George Herbert Walker Bush—the numbers were inconsequential. Most significant election battles continued to take place for a while longer within the Democratic Party.

The only liberal Democratic candidate who was successful on a statewide basis during this period was Ralph Yarborough. After several losing campaigns, he was elected to the U.S. Senate in a special election in 1957 and held that office until his defeat in 1970 by conservative Democrat Lloyd Bentsen. Yarborough, who had a distinguished legislative career, was "the mainstay of the liberal wing until his primary defeat in 1970 and comeback failure in 1972."[27]

Despite some indications of an energized Republican Party and the increased mobilization of minorities in support of the liberal wing of the Democratic Party, conservative Democrats controlled state politics until 1978.

Conservatives were able to dominate the nominating process in the Democratic primaries through well-financed and well-executed campaigns. In the general elections, liberal Democrats had little choice but to vote for a conservative Democrat against what was usually perceived to be an even more conservative Republican.[28]

During this period of Democratic factionalism, Texas Democrats played a major role in the U.S. Congress and national politics. Sam Rayburn, the longtime speaker of the

U.S. House of Representatives and regarded as one of a handful of great speakers in U.S. history, came from a rural congressional district in northeast Texas. Before moving on to the vice presidency and then the White House, Lyndon B. Johnson was majority leader in the U.S. Senate. Other congressmen from Texas, as a result of the seniority system used in the selection of committee chairs in the U.S. Congress, had influential committee posts and used their positions to funnel large sums of federal dollars to the state.

Two-Party Politics in Texas

On the national level, **realignment** of political parties is often associated with a critical election in which economic or social issues cut across existing party allegiances and produce a dramatic, permanent shift in party support and identification.[29] Realignment did not occur in one single election in Texas, but over several decades. The early stages of this transformation are often hard to identify, but by the mid-1990s, it was clear that one-party politics had given way to a two-party system.

The civil rights movement was a major factor contributing to the transformation of the state's party system. African Americans and Hispanics went to federal court to attack state laws promoting segregation and restricting minority voting rights. Successful lawsuits were brought against the white primary, the preprimary endorsement, the poll tax, and racial gerrymandering of political districts (see Chapter 7). Then minorities turned to the U.S. Congress for civil rights legislation, a process that produced the 1965 Voting Rights Act, which Congress extended to Texas after 1975. African Americans and Hispanics challenged electoral systems throughout the state using federal law and a growing body of U.S. Supreme Court decisions prohibiting the dilution of minority voting power. Minorities were successful in their long, tortuous effort to increase electoral equity. But the creation of more political districts from which African Americans and Hispanics could win election also resulted in the creation of more districts from which Republicans could win public office. As the number of minority elected officials increased, the number of Republican elected officials also increased.

Economic factors also contributed to two-party development. African Americans and Hispanics are disproportionately low-income populations and generally support such governmental services as public housing, public health care, day care, and income support. These policies are associated by many with the liberal wing of the Democratic Party. Minority organizations made concerted efforts to register, educate, and mobilize the people in their communities. Approximately 90 percent of the African American vote in Texas is Democratic, and while there is less cohesion among Hispanic voters, approximately 75 percent of the Hispanic vote goes to Democrats. As the numerical strength of minorities increased, conservative Anglo Democrats found their position within the party threatened and began to look to the Republican Party as an alternative.

The large numbers of people who migrated to Texas from other states, particularly when the Sun Belt economy of the 1970s and early 1980s was booming and many northern industrial states were struggling, also contributed to the two-party system. Many of these new arrivals were Republicans from states with strong Republican parties, and many of them settled in high-income, suburban, Anglo areas in Texas.[30] Other significant factors were President Reagan's popularity in the 1980s and the 1978 election of Republican Governor Bill Clements, who encouraged many conservative Democratic officeholders to switch parties. Some scholars see an earlier outline of these changes in the so-called Southern strategy of Richard Nixon in 1968. Simply stated, the national

Republican Party made calculated efforts to peel off whites using wedge issues that were likely to resonate within the Southern political culture.[31]

During the 1970s, the Texas Republican Party had an organizational edge on the Democrats. As the minority party, the only way the GOP could successfully challenge the Democrats' numerical strength was to develop local party organizations capable of mobilizing membership, providing continuity between elections, and providing candidates with campaign resources. After the defeat of Republican presidential nominee Barry Goldwater in 1964, the national Republican Party began rebuilding using modern campaign technology. The national party assisted state parties, and Texas Republicans applied the new campaign technology to state and local elections. Moreover, Republican candidates appeared to more readily adapt technology to their campaigns. For a short period in the late 1980s and early 1990s, Texas Democrats tried to catch up by using money provided by the national party organization, but the Democratic leadership seemed incapable of making maximum use of these resources to reenergize state and local party organizations.

Other events of the 1970s and the 1980s demonstrated that the transformation of the Texas party system was well on its way. After the Sharpstown scandal (see Chapter 8), the Texas House elected a liberal Democrat, Price Daniel Jr., as speaker in 1973. Three other moderate-to-liberal Democrats were elected to statewide office in the early 1970s: Bob Armstrong as land commissioner in 1970, John Hill as attorney general in 1972, and Bob Bullock as comptroller in 1974. These men initiated and carried out policies that were more equitable in the treatment of lower socioeconomic Texans.[32]

In 1978, John Hill defeated Governor Dolph Briscoe, a conservative, in the Democratic primary, and Bill Clements, then a political unknown, defeated Ray Hutchison, a former state legislator who had the endorsement of most Republican state leaders, in the Republican primary. Hill neglected to mend fences with conservative Democrats, and Clements, a multimillionaire, used much of his own money on an effective media campaign to defeat Hill for governor by 17,000 votes in the general election. Four years later, Clements lost to Democratic Attorney General Mark White, but in 1986 he returned to defeat White in an expensive, bitter campaign (see Chapter 9).

In the 1982 election, Democratic candidates who were considered liberal won additional statewide offices. Ann Richards was elected state treasurer; Jim Mattox, attorney general; Jim Hightower, agriculture commissioner; and Garry Mauro, land commissioner.

The 1990 election further demonstrated how far the realignment process had gone. Democratic gubernatorial nominee Ann Richards defeated conservative businessman Clayton Williams, who had spent $6 million of his own money to win the Republican primary. But Republican Kay Bailey Hutchison was elected state treasurer, and Republican Rick Perry unseated Hightower to become agriculture commissioner. Republicans also retained one of the U.S. Senate seats from Texas when Phil Gramm easily won reelection to the seat once held by John Tower, and the GOP claimed eight of the 27 congressional seats that Texas then had in Congress.

In a special election in 1993 to fill the U.S. Senate seat vacated by Democrat Lloyd Bentsen when he was appointed secretary of the treasury by President Bill Clinton, Kay Bailey Hutchison defeated Democrat Bob Krueger to give the Republicans both U.S. Senate seats from Texas. Hutchison easily won reelection in 1994, despite a political and legal controversy over her administration of the state treasurer's office.

Also in 1994, Governor Ann Richards was unseated by Republican nominee George W. Bush, the son of former President George Bush and a future president himself. Republicans that year also captured four other statewide offices that had been held by Democrats, marking the most statewide gains by Texas Republicans in any single election since Reconstruction. Meanwhile, Republicans also were increasing their share of seats in the Texas legislature. In the same election, Republicans posted sweeping victories across the country, cashing in on anger over President Bill Clinton's policies, and gained control of both houses of Congress and a majority of the nation's governorships.

Toward Republican Dominance

The political transformation of Texas accelerated even more in 1996, when Republicans swept all statewide offices on the general election ballot and captured a majority of the state Senate for the first time since Reconstruction. Republican presidential nominee Bob Dole even carried the Lone Star State, despite a poor national showing against President Clinton. Republicans also increased their numbers in the Texas House and in the Texas congressional delegation. When the electoral dust had cleared, Republicans held twenty of Texas's twenty-nine statewide elected offices, including the top three. That number increased to twenty-one in 1997, when Presiding Judge Michael McCormick of the Texas Court of Criminal Appeals switched from the Democratic to the Republican Party.

Lieutenant Governor Bob Bullock and Attorney General Dan Morales, both Democrats, chose not to seek reelection or any other office in 1998, and Republicans cashed in on the opportunity. With Governor Bush winning reelection in a landslide, Republicans again swept all statewide offices. And a few weeks after the 1998 election, the GOP secured all statewide offices in Texas for the first time since Reconstruction when Texas Supreme Court Justice Raul A. Gonzalez, a Democrat, retired in midterm and was replaced by a Republican appointee of Bush. Republicans did not capture control of the Texas House, but picked up four seats to narrow the Democratic margin to six seats. In the governor's race, Bush won 69 percent of the vote against Democratic challenger Garry Mauro, the longtime land commissioner.

Democrats fielded candidates for only three of the nine statewide offices up for election in 2000. They lost all three but held their ground in state legislative races.

Republicans also swept all statewide races in 2002, including Governor Rick Perry's victory over Democratic nominee Tony Sanchez and former Texas Attorney General John Cornyn's victory over former Dallas Mayor Ron Kirk in a race to succeed retiring U.S. Senator Phil Gramm. Republicans also finally gained control of the Texas House of Representatives in 2002, capturing 88 of the 150 seats after the Legislative Redistricting Board in 2001 had drawn new districts that favored Republicans (see Chapter 8). Additionally, the GOP increased its margin in the state Senate by winning nineteen of the thirty-one seats. All statewide elected officials remained Republican.

The statewide losses in 2002 were particularly disappointing for Democratic leaders, who had carefully assembled a racially diverse ticket with an eye toward increasing minority turnout. Kirk, the U.S. Senate candidate, was African American, and Sanchez, a wealthy businessman from Laredo, was Hispanic. The Democratic nominee for lieutenant governor, John Sharp, a former state comptroller, was Anglo. Sanchez was unexpectedly challenged in the Democratic primary by former Texas Attorney General Dan Morales. The race was historic because it was the first gubernatorial contest in Texas between two Hispanics, and it was extremely contentious. Sanchez was supported by most party leaders because the party was banking on his wealth to help finance the Democrats' general election campaign.

Republicans achieved still another long-sought goal in 2004—a majority of Texas's congressional delegation—after the legislature, in a bitter partisan fight in 2003, redrew congressional district boundaries to favor GOP candidates (see Chapter 8).

Republican Governor Rick Perry was reelected in 2006 over three major opponents, including Democratic nominee Chris Bell, a former congressman and former city councilman from Houston. Republican Comptroller Carole Keeton Strayhorn and musician–author Kinky Friedman challenged Perry as independents. Republicans also won all other statewide offices against a Democratic ticket that was less experienced and more poorly financed than the party's slate of candidates in 2002. Barbara Ann Radnofsky, the Democratic nominee against U.S. Senator Kay Bailey Hutchison, was a Houston lawyer making her first race for elective office. Texas Republicans in 2006 also kept their majorities in the legislature and in the congressional delegation.

Republicans retained their control of all statewide elected offices in the 2008 general election. U.S. Senator John Cornyn turned back a challenge by Democrat Rick Noriega, a state representative from Houston and a veteran of the war in Afghanistan. Republicans also gained one congressional seat.

The GOP also has made significant gains across Texas at the county level. In 1974, Republicans held 53 county offices but had claimed 1,862 by 2008, paralleling the dramatic statewide realignment (see Table 6–1).

Although they lost all statewide races in 2006, Texas Democrats were showing signs of revival. They swept all Dallas County offices that year, including district attorney, county judge, and forty-two judgeships. Democrats also regained six seats in the Texas House to trim the Republican majority to 81–69. In 2008, Democrats picked up one seat in the state Senate and five seats in the Texas House to cut the Republican majority to a narrow 76–74.

TABLE 6–1   Growth of the Republican Officeholders in Texas, 1974–2008

Year	U.S. Senate	Other Statewide	U.S. Congress	Texas Senate	Texas House	County Offices*	District Offices**	Total
1974	1	0	2	3	16	53		75
1976	1	0	2	3	19	67		92
1978	1	1	4	4	22	87		119
1980	1	1	5	7	35	166		215
1982	1	0	5	5	36	191	79	317
1984	1	0	10	6	52	287	90	446
1986	1	1	10	6	56	410	94	578
1988	1	5	8	8	57	485	123	687
1990	1	6	8	8	57	547	170	797
1992	1	8	9	13	58	634	183	906
1994	2	13	11	14	61	734	216	1051
1996	2	18	13	17	68	938	278	1334
1998	2	27	13	16	72	1,108	280	1,518
2000	2	27	13	16	72	1,233	336	1,699
2002	2	27	15	19	88	1,443	362	1,956
2004	2	27	21	19	87	1,608	392	2,156
2006	2	27	19	20	82	1,814	379	2,343
2008	2	27	20	19	76	1,862	379	2,385

*County offices include: county judge, commissioners, constables, county attorneys, county clerks, district clerks, county judicial positions, treasurers, surveyors, justices of the peace, sheriffs, tax assessor/collectors, and other local offices.

**District offices include: court of appeals, district judges, and district attorneys.

Source: Republican Party of Texas.

Changing Party Identification

The changes in party affiliations over the past forty years illustrate Texas's political realignment. Belden Associates of Dallas reported in a 1952 survey that 66 percent of Texans called themselves Democrats, and only 6 percent claimed to be Republicans, a pattern that changed little from 1952 to 1964.[33] During the next decade, Republican Party identification increased to 16 percent and Democratic Party identification declined to 59 percent (see Figure 6–2).

Between 1975 and 1984, there was a dramatic decline in voter identification with the Democratic Party and a significant increase in Republican Party identification. By 2008, approximately 33 percent of Texas voters called themselves Republicans, and 30 percent identified as Democrats (see "Where Have All the Yellow Dogs Gone?"). The remainder called themselves independents, third-party affiliates, or undecided. This shift in party identification is further proof that Texas is now a Republican-dominant state on a statewide basis. But party identification does not always translate into winning elected offices at the county level.

A large number of voters identify themselves as independents. Independents don't have their own party, and their choices in most elections are limited to candidates from the two major parties. Further survey research, moreover, suggests that most self-proclaimed independents vote consistently for Republican candidates.

Ticket splitting, a practice associated with the realignment process, has been common in recent Texas elections. It explains, in part, why Democrats have been able to keep most local offices despite Republican sweeps statewide. Many Texans cast their votes selectively as they go down the general election ballot.

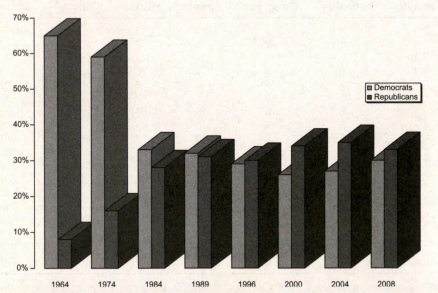

FIGURE 6–2 Changing Party Affiliation in Texas, 1964–2008. *Sources:* The Texas Poll, Summer 1993, Fall 1993, Winter 1996, Spring 1996, Fall 1996, Spring 1999, Summer 1999, Fall 1999, Winter 2000, Summer 2003, Fall 2003, Winter 2004, and Spring 2004; Pew Research Center, "Fewer Voters Identify as Republicans," March 20, 2008; 1,476 interviews were conducted in 2007 and 2008.

Where Have All the Yellow Dogs Gone?

For a long-time Democrat (that is, a person 50 or older), there is a bit of nostalgia when someone asks, "Where have all the yellow dogs gone?" To a newcomer to the state, this probably conjures up an image of a mangy, brownish, yellow mutt that is used for coon hunting or running the dogs at night while its keepers drink hard liquor around the campfire. But to a real Democrat, it is a code word for those Democrats, often white conservatives, who swore by the phrase, "I'd vote for a yellow dog if he ran on the Democratic ticket." Moreover, those "yellow dogs" also would encourage voters to "pull one lever"—that is, vote straight Democratic.

Yellow-dog, one-party voters are a dying breed. Historically, there were counties in Texas that had never elected a Republican to local office. Some had never had a Republican Party organization or seen a Republican challenge a Democrat in a local

election. With the transformation of the state to one-party Republican dominance, there are fewer and fewer yellow dogs. Franklin County, which is in deep East Texas, had not elected a member of the GOP from 1875 to 2000. But in 2002, three Republicans won elections to local offices.[34]

So, where have all the yellow dogs gone? The answer is rather clear. Many of them have died and passed over. Many others have converted to the Republican Party and are now voting the straight GOP ticket. Some of those yellow dogs have now become pedigree Republicans.

Voting differences and party identification sometimes are based on gender. Nationally, differences in the voting patterns of men and women have been significant. These differences usually are not as pronounced in Texas politics but on occasions, they have been. The gubernatorial election of 1990 produced one of the largest gaps between women and men in recent Texas political history. According to surveys of voters leaving the polls, Democrat Ann Richards enjoyed a lead of as much as 20 percent among women voters in some precincts in her defeat of Republican Clayton Williams. Part of that difference was believed to have been attributable to Williams's clumsy outspokenness, including a rape joke gaffe (see Chapter 5), which prompted a negative reaction among women across the state. Voter polls in the 1994 gubernatorial race indicated Richards held a more modest lead over Republican George W. Bush among women. Bush, who unseated Richards, obviously was more acceptable to women than Williams had been.[35]

There also is evidence suggesting that older and younger voters view the world in markedly different ways, a difference reflected in how people vote. On the basis of survey data, it is clear that younger voters, for example, are more tolerant of candidates who have experienced problems with alcohol or drug abuse. Many younger voters also are more tolerant of lifestyles, which can create problems for conservatives who campaign against homosexuality and gay rights. Unlike older voters, fewer 18–29 year olds express any party identification. Moreover, younger people vote at much lower rates than older citizens.

In 1992, Republican President George H. W. Bush carried Texas while losing his reelection bid to Democrat Bill Clinton. That election marked the first time a Democratic candidate won the White House without winning Texas's electoral votes, a feat that Clinton repeated in 1996 and Barack Obama accomplished in 2008. The 1992 and 1996 elections also included the independent candidacy of Ross Perot, a billionaire computer magnate from Dallas, who attracted a lot of attention but finished third in Texas each time, as he did nationwide.

DIFFERENCES BETWEEN REPUBLICANS AND DEMOCRATS

Social scientists make a lot of effort classifying voters according to party identification and voting patterns. When reviewing a survey or poll, it is critical to know the specific population from which the sample is drawn. A pollster could sample all Texans who are 18 and older or could focus on registered voters. If a pollster were trying to determine the relationship of party identification with actual voting, samples would be drawn from those who are likely to vote in an upcoming election. And, of course, one could use exit polling on Election Day to ascertain party identification and voting preferences. One is likely to reach a variety of conclusions about partisan preferences, depending on the group that is sampled.

As noted thus far, we have relied primarily on election results to support our conclusion that Texas has become a Republican-dominant state, but there have been recent Democratic gains as well. It is risky to predict the future, but in early 2009 the *Gallup Poll* published a state-by-state report on political party affiliation, which concluded that 43 percent of Texans identify with the Democratic Party while 41 percent identify with the Republican Party. What is one to make of this when Texas voters in 2008 cast 56 percent of their ballots for Republican presidential nominee John McCain and only 44 percent for Democratic winner Barack Obama?[36]

There are many exceptions in each party, but some broad generalizations about differences between Democrats and Republicans can be made. The Texas Republican Party is composed disproportionately of people who are college educated, higher income, Anglos, newcomers to Texas, and suburban residents. More men identify with the Republican Party than women, and support for the Republican Party increases with age. Republicans tend to classify themselves as conservative to moderate with significant numbers reporting frequent church attendance.

Democrats are more likely to have lower incomes, be younger, be African American, or Hispanic and be less educated. More women identify themselves as Democrats than do men. Democrats tend to classify themselves as moderate to liberal and attend church less regularly.[37]

A Caveat to Realignment

Although the party system has been transformed in Texas, there is considerable disagreement about what these changes will mean in the long run.

V. O. Key, writing in the 1940s, concluded that race was becoming less important and the electorate was dividing along liberal and conservative lines. He concluded that a "modified class politics seems to be evolving."[38] More than a half century later, the parties appear, in part, to be aligning around economic issues that are manifested in liberal and conservative philosophies, but issues involving race continue to shape attitudes.

Chandler Davidson argues that "the Republican Party's hard-line racial policy" attracted large numbers of conservative Democrats as well as supporters of George Wallace, the conservative American Independent Party's 1968 presidential nominee, and "strengthened the commitment of African Americans and Mexican Americans to the Democratic Party."[39] Some Texas African Americans and Hispanics, primarily well-educated, well-to-do individuals, have become Republicans. But the vast majority remain Democrats, and Sunday morning visits to African American churches in Houston and Dallas and appearances at South Texas *pachangas* (cookouts) are practically mandatory for Democratic candidates serious about winning statewide office.

Seeking to expand the Republican Party's base, Governor George W. Bush made a strong appeal to Hispanics during his 1998 reelection campaign and, according to some estimates, was rewarded with about 40 percent of the Hispanic vote. Some Republican strategists have been arguing for years that the GOP must strengthen its appeal to the growing Hispanic population—and chip away at Hispanics' traditional support for the Democratic Party—if the GOP is to continue to maintain its control over state politics. Anglo Protestants, who form the core of the Republican Party, are declining in proportion to the increased number of Hispanics in Texas. To maintain dominance, it has been argued, Republicans must embrace issues, such as improved health care and educational opportunities, which are central to Hispanic voting interests. And, according to this argument, they may need to develop a more tolerant attitude toward immigration than what was expressed in the 2006 Texas Republican Party platform, which advocated, among other things, a wall between Texas and Mexico. It is premature to conclude that there will be an erosion of Hispanic support from the Democratic Party, but both parties will be battling for the Hispanic vote over the next two decades. Republicans also have spoken about the need to appeal to African-American Texans who share their core values, but the GOP has had little success attracting African Americans from the Democratic Party.

An alternative view to realignment is that the party system is undergoing disintegration or **dealignment**[40] This view is supported by the decline of the parties' electoral functions, their general organizational weaknesses, and voter indifference toward partisan labels, as manifested in ticket splitting and the increasing numbers of people calling themselves independents. Since the 1980s, some 40 percent of Texans of voting age have not identified themselves as either Democrats or Republicans. According to these arguments, political parties no longer perform their traditional functions because other institutions—including interest groups, the media, and the candidates themselves—control the political process, and the number of persons who identify with neither party will continue to grow.

A well-financed candidate, for example, can ignore party leaders and still win a party's nomination by using effective campaign and media tactics in the primary. Interest groups, which offer sophisticated organizations to shape public policy, may provide more access to policymakers than do the parties. And the media play a much greater role in screening candidates and shaping public opinion. The dealignment arguments, however, were more prominent in the last two decades of the twentieth century. And although they may still have some validity, other evidence suggests that the party doomsayers were somewhat premature.

A contrary view in Texas is that the parties are undergoing a process of revitalization, attempting to reclaim basic party functions, especially in the areas of elections and campaigns.[41] **Party activists** are attempting to adapt modern campaign technology to the party organization. If the parties are able to provide strong support in fundraising, campaign advertising, phone banks, and other campaign functions, some candidates will likely become more dependent on the party organization. The massive infusion of "soft money" from corporations, labor unions, and other interest groups into the state and local party organizations by the national parties was one factor in this new vitality of state political parties. There also has been considerable collaboration between the state parties and the national parties in voter identification, voter mobilization, funding of campaigns, and organizational development. But campaign finance reforms enacted by Congress in 2002 restricted the use of soft money, and it is unclear what effects those changes will have on the Texas party system. Moreover, the dealignment argument is somewhat defused by a rather consistent pattern of independents identifying with a major political party.

THE PARTY ORGANIZATION

To carry out their functions, the two major parties in Texas have developed permanent and temporary organizations, structured by state law, state and national party rules, and a series of court decisions protecting voters' rights.

Party organizations are built around geographic election districts, starting with the **precinct**.[42] There is, however, no hierarchical arrangement to party organization. V. O. Key described the party structure as a "system of layers of organization," with each level—county, state, and federal—concentrating on the elections within its jurisdiction.[43] There is a great deal of autonomy at each party level, based on the limited sanctions that one level can impose on another, and the fact that each level of the party needs the others to carry out electoral functions.[44]

There are no membership requirements for either the Democratic or the Republican Party. Party members do not have to pay dues, attend meetings, campaign for candidates, or make contributions. When people register to vote in Texas, they are not required to state their party preference as they do in many other states. The right to participate in a party's electoral and nominating activities is based simply on voting in that party's primary election. When a person votes in one of the major party primaries, his or her voter registration card is stamped "Democrat" or "Republican."

The Permanent Organization

Election precincts—there were an estimated 8,400 in Texas in 2008—are created by the county commissioners of each of Texas's 254 counties. Population, political boundaries, and available voting sites help determine the number of precincts within a county. Voters in each precinct elect a **precinct chair** in the party primary (see Figure 6–3). Any eligible voter within the precinct can file for this position, and the names of write-in candidates can be added to the ballot. (One of this book's authors was elected a precinct chair with two write-in votes.)

Although there are many contested precinct chair elections, often no one runs for the office, leaving many precinct vacancies throughout the state. This problem has contributed to the parties' organizational decline. The chair calls the precinct convention (which is discussed below) to order and serves as a member of the county executive committee. Precinct chairs also can mobilize party supporters to vote. Many people do nothing with the position, while others contribute much time and energy and have successfully delivered the precinct for their party's candidates in the general election. In

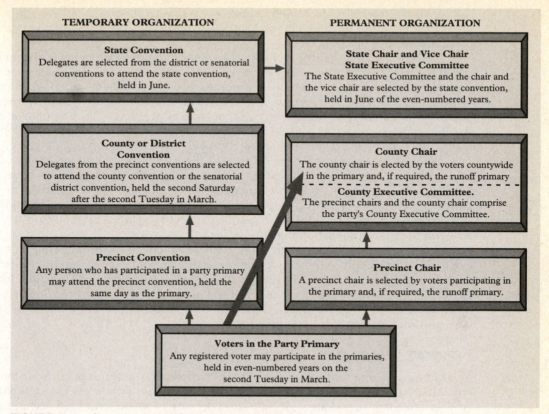

TEMPORARY ORGANIZATION

State Convention
Delegates are selected from the district or senatorial conventions to attend the state convention, held in June.

County or District Convention
Delegates from the precinct conventions are selected to attend the county convention or the senatorial district convention, held the second Saturday after the second Tuesday in March.

Precinct Convention
Any person who has participated in a party primary may attend the precinct convention, held the same day as the primary.

PERMANENT ORGANIZATION

State Chair and Vice Chair
State Executive Committee
The State Executive Committee and the chair and the vice chair are selected by the state convention, held in June of the even-numbered years.

County Chair
The county chair is elected by the voters countywide in the primary and, if required, the runoff primary

County Executive Committee.
The precinct chairs and the county chair comprise the party's County Executive Committee.

Precinct Chair
A precinct chair is selected by voters participating in the primary and, if required, the runoff primary.

Voters in the Party Primary
Any registered voter may participate in the primaries, held in even-numbered years on the second Tuesday in March.

FIGURE 6–3   Organization of Texas Political Parties.

some counties, the precinct chair is responsible for staffing the polling places on Election Day, but increasingly this is done by the county election administrator.

The second level of the party organization is the **county executive committee**, which includes each precinct chair and the **county chair**, who is elected to a two-year term by primary voters countywide. A major responsibility of the county chair and the executive committee is the organization and management of the primary election in their county. The county executive committee accepts filings by candidates for local offices and is also responsible for planning the county or district conventions. Funds for the management of primary elections are provided to the county party by the state through the secretary of state's office.

County committees may be well organized and actively work to carry out a wide range of organizational and electoral activities, or they may meet irregularly and have difficulty getting a quorum of members to attend. The county chair is an unpaid position. But party organizations in some counties have successful fundraising operations, and they support a party headquarters, retain professional staff, and are engaged in various party activities between elections.

The Texas Election Code provides for other district committees that correspond to a state senatorial, state representative, judicial, or congressional district. District committees that are solely within a county include precinct chairs, while multicounty district committees include representatives of all affected counties. These committees select candidates for vacancies in local and district offices if they occur between the primary and general election.

At the state level, a party's permanent organization is the **state executive committee**, which has sixty-four members, including the party's **state chair** and **vice chair**. When the parties meet in their biennial state conventions, two committee members—a man and a woman—are selected by delegation caucuses from each of the thirty-one state senatorial districts. The state chair and the vice chair, one of whom must be a woman, are also selected by the convention. The two top state party leaders and other executive committee members serve two-year terms and are unpaid.

Statewide candidates file for office with the executive committee, which also is responsible for planning and organizing the party's state convention and helps raise funds for the ongoing operations of the party. The committee serves to establish party policy, but day-to-day party operations are entrusted to the party's executive director and professional staff. The Texas Democratic Party and the Texas Republican Party have permanent staffs and headquarters in Austin.

Sometimes, the state committees are highly effective with strong, energetic leadership that carries over into the development and retention of a competent professional staff. At other times, however, the state committees have been divided along ideological, factional, or personal lines, producing conflict that sometimes has become open warfare. In those instances, a party finds it difficult to raise funds, maintain a highly qualified staff, and carry out its electoral functions.

Temporary Organization

The temporary organizations of the political parties are the series of conventions that are held every two years, beginning on the day of the party primaries. They are particularly significant in presidential election years because they—together with the presidential preference primary—help select the state's delegates to the national party conventions, which nominate the presidential candidates. The convention system also helps organize the permanent party structure and brings party activists together to share common political concerns and shape party policies. Most Texans, however, have little knowledge of the convention system, and few participate in it.

The Precinct Convention

Anyone who votes in a party primary, held on the first Tuesday in March of even-numbered years, is eligible to participate in that party's precinct convention, normally held in the same place as the primary after voting stops at 7 P.M. After the convention is organized and selects its permanent officers—chair, vice chair, and secretary—it begins its real business, the selection of delegates and alternate delegates to the county or senatorial district convention. Each precinct is assigned a specific number of delegates, based on the party's voting strength. Since 1972, the Democrats have used complex procedures designed to assure broad-based delegate representation by ethnicity, gender, and age. A precinct convention also can adopt resolutions to be submitted at the county or district conventions for possible inclusion in the party's **platform**.

In presidential election years, the presidential preference primary and the precinct conventions are the first steps in the selection of delegates to the national conventions. Before 1988, when Texas's participation in the first regional "Super Tuesday" presidential preference primary changed the delegate selection process, the precinct conventions

The Texas Two-Step. Any citizen who votes in a party's primary may participate in that party's precinct convention, held generally in proximity to where people voted, after the polls close on election day. Some conventions have only a handful of participants with little or no controversy, while others draw large numbers of party voters who will engage in long and intense debates over issues and candidates. These conventions are particularly significant during the presidential election years.

were extremely crucial to presidential candidates because a candidate had to have strong support among delegates at the precinct level to ultimately capture a significant number of Texas delegates to the national convention. Now, much of that luster has been stolen by the primary, although the conventions still play a role in the Democratic Party's presidential nominating process.

Precinct conventions held in nonpresidential election years are often poorly attended and, in many precincts, no one shows up. The precinct meeting may last 15 minutes, and those attending may not be able to get enough people to volunteer to be delegates to the upcoming county or senatorial convention. Such low participation rates are cited by those who conclude that the political parties are in decline.

In the past, highly motivated political and ideological movements have been able to capture precinct conventions and advance candidates who had little in common with mainstream party voters. Supporters of Barry Goldwater used this strategy in 1964 to help win the Republican presidential nomination for their candidate, as did supporters of Democrat George McGovern in 1972. But both men were soundly defeated in the general election. In recent years, the **Religious Right** has used a similar strategy to extend its influence in the Republican Party and was successful for the first time in Texas in

The Religious Right and the Republican Party

As the Republican Party expanded its support among Texas voters, it experienced sharp, often bitter, philosophical and ideological differences among its members. Overwhelmingly conservative, Republicans were split along lines of economic conservatism and the lifestyle conservatism advocated by the Religious Right. Conflict among Republicans over the abortion issue was a manifestation of the party's internal tension.

The Religious Right has long been part of the Texas political landscape. Although its influence was occasionally manifested in conservative Democratic politics, it has found far greater potential in the Republican Party for shaping electoral politics. It has strong religious overtones and draws considerable support from evangelical groups across the state. Some scholars attribute much of its success to its ability to mobilize voters who had traditionally been inactive and bring them into the Republican Party. The Republicans' difficulty in attracting minority groups gave the social conservative wing greater influence in the party.

Chandler Davidson concluded in 1990 that the Religious Right had not taken over the Republican Party, "but its influence is significant and gives the Texas Republicans their particular stridency and, at times, their appearance of a Know-Nothing movement.[45]" By 1994, however, the Religious Right was instrumental in a takeover by social conservatives of the Republican state convention and the party leadership.

Low voter turnout in the Republican primary had enabled well-organized social conservatives to gain control of the party's precinct conventions and elect a majority of delegates to the June state convention. Sensing defeat, Fred Meyer of Dallas, a traditional Republican who had guided the state party for six years during a period of growth and electoral success, stepped down as state GOP chairman and was replaced by Tom Pauken, a Dallas lawyer and former Reagan administration official who courted Christian activists. Delegates elected a new state party vice chair, Christian activist Susan Weddington of San Antonio, and put other members of the Religious Right on the State Republican Executive Committee.

The Religious Right also was instrumental in the election of Republican George W. Bush over Democrat Ann Richards in the 1994 gubernatorial race. According to an exit-poll of voters reported in the *Dallas Morning News*, 20 percent of the 4.4 million Texans who voted in that election identified themselves as white Christian fundamentalists. Of those, 84 percent said they voted for Bush. They also voted heavily for other Republican candidates.

The State Republican Executive Committee elected Susan Weddington state party chair after Pauken resigned in 1997 to run unsuccessfully for state attorney general. Weddington served in that post and was an outspoken advocate for social conservative causes until 2003, when she resigned to take a job directing a new state charitable foundation. She was succeeded by another conservative party activist, Houston attorney Tina Benkiser.

Governor Rick Perry actively courted the Religious Right as an important part of his electoral base. In 2005, on the eve of his 2006 reelection campaign, he successfully promoted a state constitutional amendment banning same-sex marriages in Texas, a proposition that attracted large numbers of social conservatives to the polls. He also visited a church school to sign a law requiring minors to have their parents' permission before obtaining abortions.

1994 (see "The Religious Right and the Republican Party"). And in 2008, the presidential campaigns of Democrats Barack Obama and Hillary Clinton went to great lengths organizing their support in the precinct conventions during their fight for the presidential nomination (see "Texas Democrats Dance the Two-Step").

Texas Democrats Dance the Two-Step

Democratic officials were delighted but also overwhelmed by the extraordinary response to the March 2008 Texas Democratic primary and related precinct conventions, the so-called "Texas Two-Step" that helped decide the tight race between Barack Obama and Hillary Clinton for the 2008 Democratic presidential nomination.

Texas wasn't even supposed to be in play in the presidential nominating campaign in 2008. Both Democratic and Republican nominations were expected to be all but decided by the time the March 4 Texas primary was held, following, as it did, the better-known caucuses in Iowa, the New Hampshire and South Carolina primaries, and a host of "Super Tuesday" contests stretching from New York to California. But the Democratic battle between Obama and Clinton was still wide open, focusing national attention on the Texas Democratic Party's bifurcated system of picking delegates that had been put to the test only once before—in 1988, when Michael Dukakis had won the nomination over the Rev. Jesse Jackson.

More than 2.8 million Texans (a record) voted in the 2008 Democratic primary, and about 1 million of them (also a record) returned after the polls closed for their precinct conventions. Clinton won the primary by about 101,000 votes over Obama and was awarded 65 delegates to Obama's 61. Another 67 delegates were awarded on the basis of support demonstrated in party caucuses, beginning with more than 8,000 precinct conventions held that evening after the primary vote had ended. A preliminary count of precinct convention results indicated that Obama would get most of those delegates, 37, and Clinton would get 30, a count that was made official at the State Democratic convention in June.

Both the primary and the caucuses drew criticism. Delegates based on the primary vote were allocated according to the 31 state senatorial districts. Furthermore, some districts were worth proportionately more delegates than others because they had had a higher Democratic turnout in the 2006 and 2004 elections. Senatorial districts, for example, in heavily Hispanic south Texas, where Clinton had a strong lead in the primary vote, didn't have as many delegates as some districts in Houston and Dallas, where Obama received more votes. Most of the criticism, however, was leveled at the caucus system. Some participants complained of long lines and confusion. Others said they had been locked out of their meeting places by delegates for the opposing candidate. Other people argued that it was "undemocratic" to allow caucus attendees to, in effect, vote twice for their candidates, once in the primary and again in the caucus.

The whole system was widely misunderstood, and the huge turnout slowed the delegate count. "The turnout was a tsunami. There's no other way to describe it," said Democratic consultant Ed Martin. Thousands of Texas voters were so confused and frustrated that party officials soon began examining ways to overhaul or replace the delegate selection process. But it wasn't clear whether significant changes would be made before the 2012 presidential campaign.

Adding to the confusion was the fact that Obama and Clinton supporters still had to compete a few weeks later at county and state senatorial conventions before the delegate allocation was finally ratified at the state convention.

The County or Senatorial District Conventions

County or senatorial district conventions are held two weeks after the precinct conventions. District conventions are held in the larger urban counties, such as Harris, Dallas, Tarrant, and Bexar, which include more than one state senatorial district. Delegates elected at the precinct conventions constitute the membership of this second level of the convention process, which, in turn, elects delegates to the state convention.

Conventions are about politics, selection of candidates, and control of the party apparatus. There have been intermittent periods of lackluster conventions. But during Texas's one-party, Democratic era, there were frequent, bitter convention fights between conservatives and liberals for control of the Democratic Party. And although those fights were most evident at the state convention, they also permeated the precinct, county, and district conventions. As Texas Republicans have increased in number and developed more diversified interests, similar intraparty struggles have surfaced.

State Conventions

The two major parties hold their state conventions in June of even-numbered years. Convention delegates certify to the secretary of state the names of those individuals who were nominated to statewide offices in the March primaries, adopt a party platform, and elect the state party chair, the vice chair, and the state executive committee.

In presidential election years, the state conventions also select delegates to their respective parties' national nominating conventions, elect members to their parties' national committees, and choose presidential electors. Electors from the party that carries Texas in the presidential race will formally cast the state's electoral votes for that party's candidate in December after the general election.

The allocation among the candidates of Texas delegates to the Republican National Convention is determined by the presidential primary, but the actual delegates are selected at the state convention. Texas delegates to the Democratic National Convention

The Party's Business is Conducted Here. State Party Conventions are held in June of even-numbered years in one of the major Texas cities. In addition to attending to the business of the party organization, these conventions are the critical final stage in delegate selection to the national nominating conventions. Seen here is the 2008 Texas Democratic Convention in Austin.

are determined through a more complicated process, based both on the primary vote and on candidate support from attendees at the series of party conventions, beginning at the precinct level.

The Party Activists

Texans participate in party politics for a wide variety of reasons, including some that are similar to reasons people join and participate in interest groups (see Chapter 4). Some see their participation in party organizational and campaign activities as a way to help shape or influence public policy.[46] Some are brought into party activities through issues or specific candidates running for office. Others, influenced by politically active families, have absorbed party loyalty and interest in the political process. Some hope that party activism will serve as a stepping stone to public office or political appointments. Political campaigns have a social component to them, and many activists enjoy the social contacts and friendships that come with actively working for the party or a candidate.

Texans who participate in the organizational activities of the political parties have characteristics that vary, to some extent, from other voters who support their respective political parties. In general terms, party activists tend to be more ideological than the voters who regularly support their party. Republican activists tend to be more conservative than most Republicans, and Democratic activists tend to be more liberal than most Democrats in the electorate. Activists tend to be better informed about candidates and issues than the general electorate, and they have "the time and financial resources to afford political activity, the information and knowledge to understand it, and the skills to be useful in it."[47]

Demographic and social characteristics of activists also differ between the two major parties. Democratic activists include more Hispanics, African Americans, union members, and Catholics. But despite differences in backgrounds and political views, activists of both parties tend to be better educated, to have higher incomes, and to hold higher status occupations than the general population.[48]

Approximately four decades ago, noted Washington columnist David Broder published *The Party's Over*, in which he linked the decline in party loyalties and weakened party organizations to the failure of governments in the United States to be more responsive in dealing with many social, economic, and political issues.[49] Broder noted that there was something fundamentally wrong with the American party system. As a debate emerged over realignment or dealignment of the party system, scholars turned their attention to the parties' loss of control over the nomination of candidates, the candidate-centered campaign, the development of an extensive campaign consulting industry, the expanded use of the mass media to inform and mobilize voters, candidate reliance on interest group contributions and resources, the high costs of campaigns, and the weakened party organization. Elections were now in the hands of the professionals, and there appeared to be little need for the party activists.

Other scholars focused on the decline in voting and its relationship to personal contacts by party workers or campaign volunteers. Study after study concluded that voter turnout increased with personal contacts, with numerous examples of voter turnout increasing by 5 to 10 percent because of organized grass roots efforts.[50] Obviously, party activists did not disappear, but it has taken a series of elections at all levels to reestablish an emphasis on the importance of grass roots or local campaign and party activity. The 2008 presidential campaign demonstrated how technology can be used to mobilize large numbers of volunteers in contacting voters effectively. Other parties and candidates can be expected to follow suit, and increased emphasis is likely to be given to the mobilization of the party activists.

The Party in Government

As part of V. O. Key's three-part perspective on political parties, we have begun our discussion of the political party in the electorate. In the next chapter, we will expand on this analysis by looking more closely at voting behavior, partisan attitudes, and the party activists. We also have presented a brief summary of the party organization. We will discuss the party in government in later chapters on the legislature, the executive branch, the bureaucracy, and the judiciary.

Political parties in Texas, however, do not produce cohesive, policy-oriented coalitions in government and have been unable to hold their elected officials accountable or responsive to those supporting the party. Under ideal circumstances, some students of government believe, the two major parties would lay out clearly defined political philosophies and policies they would pursue if their candidates were elected. Once elected, persons supported by the party would be committed to these programs, giving the voters a clear standard by which to evaluate their performance in office. This perspective is often referred to as the "responsible party model."

There are several reasons why Texas parties are incapable of functioning in this manner, none of which lessen the disenchantment and disgust that many voters have felt toward political parties and politicians. First, the political parties in Texas are highly decentralized and unable to discipline members who pursue goals that conflict with the parties' stated objectives. The large number of elected officials at both the state and the local level serves to diffuse party leadership.

Moreover, the coalitions that parties form with groups harboring different objectives, interests, and agendas make it next to impossible to develop clearly stated positions that would always differentiate one party from another. Philosophical, ideological, and programmatic differences among members and supporters of the same party result, for example, in ideological voting patterns in the legislature that cross party lines.

Another explanation for the lack of partisan accountability is the long-standing antiparty tradition of American politics. Many voters are ambivalent, even outright hostile, toward political parties and make little, if any, effort to become informed on political and public issues. And the parties make only limited efforts to include a large number of individuals in their organizational activities.

Third Parties in Texas

There has been a tradition of **third parties** in Texas, including Grangers, Populists, Progressives, Socialists, Dixiecrats, the American Independent Party, La Raza Unida, the Natural Law Party, and Libertarians. None has had statewide electoral success. But both the Populists in the 1890s and La Raza Unida in the early 1970s were perceived to be a significant threat to the established state party structure and those who controlled political and economic power.

Major third-party movements surfaced when Texas was still a one-party Democratic state and, in some respects, they suggested an alternative to the then-weak Republican Party. But both from a state and a national perspective, they were movements of crisis or discontent.[51] The Democratic Party, particularly its conservative wing, either co-opted these movements by making minor public policy concessions to them or by getting restrictive legislation, such as the poll tax, enacted to reduce their electoral base. In some instances, economic recriminations were the price individuals paid for participating in these third-party movements.[52]

La Raza Unida raised a particularly interesting prospect of a political party built upon an ethnic group. In the 1960s, young Hispanic leaders began to develop student organizations across the state that became the organizational framework on which this party was developed.[53] Low-income Hispanics historically had been excluded from any major role in the Democratic Party by restrictive voter registration laws, at-large elections, and racial gerrymandering designed to minimize Hispanic voting strength. An even more fundamental problem was that state public policy was not responsive to the educational and economic needs of Hispanics because conservative Democrats refused to enact legislation that would benefit that major part of the population.

La Raza Unida (People United), led by Jose Angel Gutierrez and Mario Compean, began in 1969 to organize in Crystal City in Zavala County and then extended its efforts to Dimmit, La Salle, and Hildago counties.[54] Overwhelmingly Hispanic and poor, these counties were characteristic of many South Texas counties, in which the Anglo minority controlled both the political and economic institutions and showed little sensitivity to the needs of low-income residents.

The struggle for access to the ballot box and fair elections in Zavala County parallels the experience of African Americans throughout the South. Manipulation of the election laws, economic reprisals, and intimidation by the police and Texas Rangers were used by the Anglo minority to try to retain control. La Raza Unida, however, won control of local and county offices in Crystal City and Zavala County in 1972, the same year that Ramsey Muniz ran as the party's gubernatorial candidate. During the general election campaign, there was considerable speculation in the press and apprehension among conservative Democrats that La Raza would drain a sufficient number of votes away from Dolph Briscoe, the Democratic nominee, to give Henry (Hank) Grover, a right-wing Republican, the governorship. Briscoe won the election, but without a majority of the votes.

The subsequent growth of liberal and minority influence within the Democratic Party, internal dissension within La Raza Unida, and legal problems encountered by Muniz contributed to the demise of this third party after 1978.

The most successful third party in Texas in recent years has been the Libertarian Party. Libertarians have qualified for a place on the ballot in every Texas general election since 1986 because the party has succeeded in winning at least 5 percent of the vote in at least one statewide race during each election year. But the party has never won an elected office in Texas.

In addition to statewide third parties, local political organizations connected to neither the Democratic nor the Republican Party have been influential in some cities. Elections for city offices are nonpartisan, and most are held during odd-numbered years when there are no state offices on the ballot. Cities such as San Antonio and Dallas developed citizens' associations, which had all of the characteristics of political parties. Many of these local organizations controlled city governments for decades and maintained a virtual monopoly over city elections, but these groups have disappeared in recent years.

Why a Two-Party System?

Why are there only two major political parties in Texas and the United States? Many other democratic countries have multiparty systems that function quite well. And, given the economic, regional, and social diversification of this nation and this state, one might conclude that multiple parties would be more capable of translating the interests of their members and supporters into public policy. Yet, the United States has a 200-year history of two-party politics.

By historical accident and certainly not by design, the first national party system in this country was configured around two identifiable coalitions of interests who articulated two alternative views of American government. Some have suggested that there was a natural dualism in American politics and parties aligned along these fundamental differences. By itself, that is not a very convincing argument, but subsequent generations have been politically socialized or educated to think that two parties are inevitable and preferred over any alternatives. Democrats and Republicans can fight over a wide variety of issues, but one will hear spokespersons of both parties extolling the virtues of two-party politics. Democrats and Republicans just don't talk about multiparty politics.

State election laws, which are written by Democratic and Republican legislators, also contribute to the persistence of a two-party system. Unlike the party primaries, where runoffs are held—if necessary—to select a nominee by majority vote, general elections are won by a simple plurality. The candidate who gets more votes than any other candidate, regardless of how many are in the race, is elected. There are no runoffs. Governor Rick Perry was reelected in 2006 with less than a majority over three major opponents—a Democrat and two independents. Governor Dolph Briscoe also won election with less than a majority in 1972, when La Raza Unida candidate Ramsey Muniz siphoned off traditional Democratic votes. Without a runoff, third-party candidates have little chance of winning office over major party nominees. Election laws also impose specific requirements that make it difficult for third parties to get their candidates listed on the ballot.

Most Texans do not have the intense ideological positions that may prompt the formation of a third party. Winning elections takes precedence over ideological purity, and only a relatively few individuals are "true believers" with a highly cohesive, systematic set of beliefs shaping their political behavior.[55] A conservative Republican may support marketplace economics and deregulation but oppose a ban on abortion. A liberal Democrat who is a Catholic may favor greater economic regulation and expanded social services but oppose government programs subsidizing family planning or sex education.

Although class and race shape politics and public policy debates, other issues and concerns cut across these groupings. There is a tendency of one party to attract more of one group of citizens than the other party, but no party has a monopoly on key segments of the electorate. There are Hispanics, Anglos, and African Americans in both major parties. Labor divides its support between the two parties, as do religious, economic, and educational groups. The multiclass and heterogeneous base of support for the two major parties minimizes the potential for third parties.[56]

SUMMARY AND CONCLUSIONS ●

1. Historically, Texans, along with most other Americans, have been indifferent toward political parties, giving little respect to the basic roles that parties play in a democratic society.

2. Political parties build electoral coalitions and serve as intermediaries between the voters and the government. They recruit and nominate candidates, attempt to mobilize voters, resolve conflicts among diverse groups, and set the political agenda.

3. Weak political parties allow special interest groups to play a more prominent role in policymaking. During much of its history, Texas had a weak one-party system, characterized by two competing factions within the Democratic Party. This weak party system, based in part on the systematic exclusion of many citizens through discriminatory election laws, contributed to a powerful interest group system. In Austin, as well as at the local level, the power of

interest groups is still seen in most aspects of the decision-making process, often to the detriment of the general public. It remains to be seen whether Texas's new two-party system will change the relative power between the political parties and interest groups.

4. Over the past thirty years, there have been significant changes in the state's party structure. One-party Democratic control has been transformed by complex economic, social, and political changes, and Texas is now a two-party state dominated by the Republican Party. Texas voters are divided among Democrats, Republicans, and independents, but the GOP has an edge. While some of these changes are appropriately discussed in terms of realignment, another view is that the state has finally become more integrated into the national party system, thus closely approximating the political alignments that exist outside the South. Historically, politics in Texas were configured around class and race, and despite all of the partisan changes these two factors are still significant in party alliances.

5. Some scholars argue that partisan realignment in Texas has been offset by the organizational weak-

nesses of the political parties and a decline in party identification among voters. The more pessimistic scholars believe that the parties are dealigning or disintegrating, with some of their primary functions being assumed by other institutions, including the media and interest groups.

6. A competitive, viable two-party system is directly related to the responsiveness of public officials and governing institutions. Public policy can be shaped through responsible and competitive political parties. But the continued neglect of the needs and interests of large segments of the state's population challenges the very premises upon which a democratic society is based. Moreover, the parties have rarely functioned as highly cohesive, disciplined organizations in the government. With candidate-centered campaigns, the parties have lost much of their control over those elected under party labels. Legislators and other elected officials are somewhat like free agents, taking sides on issues with little concern of recrimination from their political parties.

7. State laws outline the formal party structure, but the vitality and strength of local party organizations vary widely from one area of the state to another.

KEY TERMS

Political party 160
One-party politics 164
Jim Crow laws 165
Bifactionalism 167
Two-party system 168
Realignment 170
Ticket splitting 174

Dealignment 177
Party activist 177
Precinct 178
Precinct chair 178
County executive committee 179
County chair 179

State executive committee 180
State chair and vice chair 180
Platform 180
Religious Right 181
Third party 186

FURTHER READING

Articles

Bauer, John R., "Partisan Realignment and the Changing Political Geography of Texas," *Journal of Political Studies,* 12 (Spring/Summer 1990), pp. 41–66.

Dyer, James A., Arnold Vedlitz, and David B. Hill, "New Voters, Switchers, and Political Party Realignment in Texas," *Western Political Quarterly,* 41 (March 1988), pp. 155–67.

Stanley, Jeanie R., "Party Realignment and the 1986 Texas Election," *Texas Journal of Political Studies,* 9 (Spring–Summer 1987), pp. 3–13.

Stanley-Coleman, Jeanie R., and Candace Windel, "Gender Politics in the 1994 Elections," *Texas Journal of Political Studies* 18 (Fall–Winter 1995–1996), pp. 5–31.

Books

Anders, Evan, *Boss Rule in South Texas: The Progressive Era.* Austin, TX: University of Texas Press, 1982.

Black, Earl and Merle Black, *The Rise of Southern Republicans.* Boston: Harvard University Press, 2002.

Davidson, Chandler, *Race and Class in Texas Politics.* Princeton, NJ: Princeton University Press, 1990.

————, and Bernard Grofman, eds. *Quiet Revolution in the South: The Impact of the Voting Rights Act, 1965–1990.* Princeton, NJ: Princeton University Press, 1994.

Erikson, Robert S., Gerald C. Wright, and John P. McIver, *Statehouse Democracy: Public Opinion and Policy in the American States.* New York: Cambridge University Press, 1993.

Garcia, Ignacio, *United We Win: The Rise and Fall of La Raza Unida Party.* Tucson, AZ: Mexican American Studies and Research Center at the University of Arizona, 1989.

————, *Viva Kennedy Clubs: Mexican Americans in Search of Camelot.* College Station, TX: Texas A&M University Press, 2000.

Grantham, Dewey W., *The Life and Death of the Solid South: A Political History.* Lexington, KY: University Press of Kentucky, 1988.

Green, George Norris, *The Establishment in Texas Politics, 1938–1957.* Westport, CT: Greenwood, 1979.

Hershey, Marjorie Randon, and Paul Allen Beck, *Party Politics in America,* 10th ed. New York: Longman, 2003.

Hodges, Ed, *The Wins of Change: The Republican Tide in Texas.* Dallas, TX: Pinnacle Press, 1999.

Ivins, Molly, *Molly Ivins Can't Say That, Can She?* New York: Random House, 1991.

Key, V. O., *Southern Politics.* New York: Vintage Books, 1949.

Knaggs, John R., *Two Party Texas: The John Tower Era, 1961–1984.* Austin, TX: Eakin Press, 1986.

Maisel, L. Sandy, and Kara Z. Buckley, *Parties and Elections in America.* Lanham, MD: Rowman & Littlefield, 2005.

Morehead, Richard, *50 Years in Texas Politics: From Roosevelt to Reagan, From the Fergusons to Clements.* Burnet, TX: Eakin, 1982.

Quinones, Juan Gomez, *Chicano Politics.* Albuquerque, NM: University of New Mexico Press, 1990.

Smith, Oron. *The Rise of Baptist Republicanism.* New York: New York University Press, 1997.

Sundquist, James, *Dynamics of the Party System,* rev. ed. Washington, DC: Brookings Institution Press, 1983.

Tower, John G., *Consequences: A Personal and Political Memoir.* New York: Little, Brown, 1991.

Websites

Green Party of Texas   http://www.txgreens.org/   A third party committed to social justice, nonviolence, ecology, and grass-roots democracy, Greens have had limited impact on the state's electoral politics.

Libertarian Party of Texas   http://www.lptexas.org/ Libertarians tend to advocate a very limited role of governments, and they are particularly vocal in supporting "the right of individuals to live in whatever manner they choose, so long as they do not interfere with the rights of others."

Texas Democratic Party   http://www.txdemocrats.org/ This site provides a range of information on state party organization, county chairs, affiliate organizations, candidates, and policy issues.

Republican Party of Texas   http://www.texasgop.org/ In addition to information about the Republican Party and links to other state party organizations, this site provides information about Republican candidates, the party platform, and a calendar of party events.

ENDNOTES

1. E. E. Schattschneider, *Semisovereign People* (New York: Holt, Rinehart and Winston, 1960).
2. Dennis S. Ippolito and Thomas G. Walker, *Political Parties, Interest Groups, and Public Policy: Group Influence in American Politics* (Englewood Cliffs, NJ: Prentice Hall, Inc., 1980), p. 2.
3. John F. Bibby, *Politics, Parties and Elections in America* (Chicago: Nelson-Hall, 1987), pp. 3–4.
4. Leon Epstein, *Political Parties in Western Democracies* (New York: Praeger, 1967), p. 9.
5. Bibby, *Politics, Parties, and Elections in America*, p. 15.
6. Sarah McCally Morehouse, *State Politics, Parties and Policy* (New York: Holt, Rinehart and Winston, 1981), p. 118.
7. Ibid., pp. 118–19.
8. Ibid., p. 117.
9. Samuel Huntington, *Political Order in Changing Societies* (New Haven, CT: Yale University Press, 1980), p. 91.
10. Robert J. Huckshorn, *Political Parties in America,* 2nd ed. (Monterey, CA: Brooks/Cole Publishing Company, 1981), p. 23.
11. Bibby, *Politics, Parties and Elections in America*, p. 12.
12. V. O. Key, *Southern Politics* (New York: Vintage, 1949), p. 225.
13. Chandler Davidson, *Race and Class in Texas Politics* (Princeton, NJ: Princeton University Press, 1990), p. 21.
14. Ibid., p. 6.
15. Alexander P. Lamis, *The Two-Party South,* expanded edition (New York: Oxford University Press, 1988), p. 23.

16. Ibid., p. 194.
17. George Norris Green, *The Establishment in Texas Politics, 1938–1957* (Westport, CT: Greenwood, 1979), p. 57
18. Ibid., pp. 121–34.
19. Key, *Southern Politics*, pp. 302–10.
20. Green, *The Establishment in Texas Politics*, pp. 142–48.
21. Key, *Southern Politics*, pp. 294–97.
22. Green, *The Establishment in Texas Politics*, p. 148.
23. Lamis, *The Two-Party South*, p. 195.
24. Ibid., p. 195; Davidson, *Race and Class in Texas Politics*, p. 201.
25. John R. Knaggs, *Two-Party Texas: The John Tower Era, 1961–1984* (Austin, TX: Eakin, 1986), p. 15.
26. Davidson, *Race and Class in Texas Politics*, p. 199.
27. Lamis, *The Two-Party South*, p. 194.
28. Ibid., pp. 196–97.
29. For an excellent summary of realignment theory and conditions under which realignment is likely to take place, see James L. Sundquist, *Dynamics of the Party System*, rev. ed. (Washington, DC: Brookings Institution Press, 1983).
30. James A. Dyer, Arnold Vedlitz, and David B. Hill, "New Voters, Switchers, and Political Party Realignment in Texas," *Western Political Quarterly*, 41 (March 1988), p. 164.
31. See Kevin P. Phillips, *The Emerging Republican Majority* (New Rochelle, NY: Arlington House, 1969) and Richard M. Scammon and Ben J. Wattenberg, *The Real Majority* (New York: Coward-McCann, 1970).
32. Green, *The Establishment in Texas Politics*, p. 208.
33. Dyer and Vedlitz, "New Voters, Switchers, and Political Party Realignment in Texas," p. 156.
34. John Williams, *The Houston Chronicle Online*, November 17, 2002.
35. *Dallas Morning News*, November 9, 1994.
36. Jeffrey M. Jones, "State of the States: Political Party Affiliation," *Gallup Poll*, January 28, 2009.
37. Dyer and Vedlitz, "New Voters, Switchers, and Political Party Realignment in Texas," pp. 165–66; Scripps Howard, *Texas Poll*, Summer 2003, Fall 2003, Winter 2004, and Spring 2004; and *Rassmusen Reports*, "Election 2008: Texas Presidential Election," October 23, 2008.
38. Key, *Southern Politics*, p. 255.
39. Davidson, *Race and Class in Texas Politics*, p. 238.
40. Walter Dean Burnham, *Critical Elections and the Mainsprings of American Politics* (New York: W. W. Norton, 1970), Chapter 5; and Walter Dean Burnham, *The Current Crisis in American Politics* (Oxford: Oxford University Press, 1982).
41. See Robert Huckshorn, *Political Parties in America*, pp. 358–60.
42. John F. Bibby, "State Party Organizations: Coping and Adapting to Candidate-Centered Politics and Nationalization," in *The Parties Respond: Changes in American Parties and Campaigns*, 3rd ed., edited by L. Sandy Maisel (Boulder, CO: Westview, 1998), pp. 23–49.
43. V. O. Key Jr., *Parties, Politics and Pressure Groups*, 4th ed. (New York: Thomas Y. Crowell Company, 1958), p. 347.
44. Bibby, *Politics, Parties, and Elections in America*, p. 82.
45. Davidson, *Race and Class in Texas Politics*, Chapter 10; Green, *The Establishment in Texas Politics, 1938–1957* and *Dallas Morning News*, November 11, 1994.
46. This discussion of party activists draws from Marjorie Randon Hershey and Paul Allen Beck, *Party Politics in America*, 10th ed. (New York: Longman, 2003), Chapter 5; and Samuel J. Eldersveld and Hanes Walton, Jr., *Political Parties in American Society*, 2nd ed. (Boston: Bedford/St. Martin's, 2000), Chapter 8.
47. Hershey and Beck, *Party Politics in America*, p. 97.
48. Ibid.
49. David Broder, *The Party's Over: the Failure of Politics in America* (New York: Harper & Row, 1971), p. xvi.
50. Eldersveld and Walton, *Political Parties in American Society*, pp. 166–68.
51. Daniel Mazmanian, *Third Parties in Presidential Elections* (Washington, D.C.: Brookings Institution Press, 1974), p. 5.
52. George Rivera, "Building a Chicano Party in South Texas," *New South*, 26 (Spring 1971), pp. 75–78.
53. Ibid.
54. Juan Gomez Quinones, *Chicano Politics* (Albuquerque, NM: University of New Mexico Press, 1990), pp. 128–31.
55. John Crittenden, *Parties and Elections in the United States* (Englewood Cliffs, NJ: Prentice Hall, Inc., 1982), p. 11.
56. Huckshorn, *Political Parties in America*, p. 11.

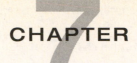

CHAPTER 7

Elections, Campaigns, and Political Behavior

Questions to Guide Your Reading

1. What explains the low rates of voter participation in many state and local elections?

2. How were minorities and women kept from full participation in Texas politics?

3. Do interest groups, PACS, and contributors with deep pockets threaten the integrity of elections in Texas?

4. Who are the people most likely to get involved in politics and run for office?

People never lie so much as after a hunt, during a war and before an election.

—**Otto von Bismarck**

Politics is show business for ugly people.

—**Bill Miller, political consultant.**[1]

At a time when millions of people around the world have eliminated authoritarian political systems and have made great sacrifices to win free and open elections, Texans congratulate themselves if one third of the eligible population votes. Such a poor turnout cannot be blamed on a lack of opportunity. After decades of denying voting rights to large parts of the population, Texas now has one of the more progressive voter registration laws in the United States. Contemporary political campaigns, especially those for national and statewide offices, have high media visibility. People are bombarded by sophisticated television advertising campaigns, direct mail, e-mail, phone bank solicitations for candidates, and daily news coverage. Yet something fundamental is disturbing Texas voters, as well as voters across the nation. Statewide election turnout rates in Texas are consistently low, and turnout rates in many local elections are downright appalling.

Some suggest that Texans do not care about what happens in government as long as their own selfish interests are being met. Other people argue that there is a sense of disenchantment, disillusionment, or alienation among Texas voters. Voters, they believe, feel disconnected from government and elected officeholders. They don't trust public officials to do what they said they were going to do in their election bids, and they believe politicians are using their offices to line their own pockets. Other Texans care about politics, government, and public policy but believe that a single vote will make no difference.

Elected officials, moreover, are perceived to be increasingly insulated from the popular will. Although they articulate a commitment to elections and political participation, many are not really interested in cultivating an electorate that is actively involved in the decisions of government. Some observers also have argued that elections staggered throughout the year, as they are in Texas and other states, are designed to reduce voter participation. The real brokers of politics and public policy, they believe, are the interest groups, lobbyists, political action committees, and the "fat cats" who contribute large sums of money to candidates and parties. And, with the decline of the political parties, many candidates become free agents who seem to sell their services to the highest bidders. When voters read or hear that candidates are taking hundreds of thousands of dollars from political action committees or individual donors, it is difficult to convince people that politicians aren't on the take or that they care about the average citizen.

Much has been written indicting contemporary elections in Texas and the United States. Elections were designed to give the people the opportunity to direct public policy through chosen officials who would then be held accountable at the next election, but the system will not work properly if people will not vote. Elections are clearly imperfect instruments, but we have found no other vehicle for translating the needs, interests, and expectations of the public into public policy.

THE FUNCTIONS OF ELECTIONS ●

For more than 200 years, we in the United States have been debating electoral issues. Who should participate? Should individuals who cannot read very well be permitted to vote? When should elections be held? What percentage of the popular vote is required to win an election—a majority or a plurality? What are the policy consequences of elections? Does it really make any difference who gets elected? Although these questions are significant, the most important issue is the relationship of elections to our definition of a democratic society. In the most fundamental terms, "elections are used to assure popular support and legitimacy for those who make governmental decisions."[2] A stable political system depends on popular support, and people freely participating in the process of choosing those who make public policy are more likely to accept and support policy without coercion or force.

Although elections provide broad statements of the voters' expectations for future public policy and a prospective judgment on the performance of elected officials, they seldom articulate or direct precise programs. Successful political parties and candidates build broad-based campaign coalitions, and the competing demands of the diverse groups courted by candidates make it difficult for candidates to specify in detail the policies they plan to pursue once elected. Most people seeking public office, therefore, prefer to speak in general concepts and try to avoid answering hypothetical "what if" questions posed by reporters, such as "What if there isn't enough money in the budget to raise teachers' pay or improve health care? Will you support a tax increase or cut back on other programs?"

Nevertheless, after an election, a successful candidate is likely to indicate that the people have spoken and claim a mandate to pursue specific public policies of his or her choosing. If there is a mandate, it is for the person elected, not for a specific program.[3]

Elections enable voters to replace public officials or force officeholders to change their policies.[4] They are, in effect, the one institution that a democratic society can use to control its leaders and provide a retrospective judgment of the past actions of elected officials. But this role is based on the assumptions that (1) there is universal **suffrage**, (2) voters are offered clear alternatives, (3) large segments of the population are informed about those aspiring to public office and public policy, and (4) there is significant voter participation. Throughout Texas history, elections often have been manipulated for the advantage and interests of the few.

Texas's political culture has unwritten rules as to how elections should be conducted and what candidates should and should not do. For example, we expect a candidate to shake the hand of his or her opponent even after a bitter defeat or attack. That is why Republican Clayton Williams's snub of the handshake offered by Democrat Ann Richards during one joint appearance in the 1990 gubernatorial campaign received much media attention. Candidates can attack, counterattack, make charges and countercharges against each other, and still be considered politically acceptable and civilized. Such election rituals are manifestations of the way in which we have institutionalized conflict.

Some would argue that elections and election rituals have only a symbolic function that serves to "quiet resentments and doubts about particular political acts, reaffirm belief in the fundamental rationality and democratic character of the system, and thus fix conforming habits of future behavior."[5] Although this position may be extreme, there is an implicit warning in the author's conclusions. The trivialization of elections may ultimately result in even more disenchantment, disdain, and disgust with politics and government. If the electorate is "fed a steady diet of buncombe, the people may come to expect and to respond with the highest predictability to buncombe."[6]

CHARACTERISTICS OF TEXAS ELECTIONS ────────●

Texans have numerous opportunities to vote, often as many as three or four times a year, in a variety of elections. Voters in Texas and other states, in fact, get to vote on more candidates and issues than citizens of any other democracy.[7] Turnout and interest is highest in the general election in presidential election years, but can be abysmally low in elections for constitutional amendments, school boards, and the governing bodies of single-purpose districts such as hospital and water districts.

Election Cycles

Except for some constitutional amendment elections, which are set by the legislature, and emergency elections set by the governor to fill vacancies in specific offices, elections are held at regular, predictable intervals mandated by state law. There has been a systematic effort to separate elections and thereby minimize the convergence of issues in state and local races.[8] Most city and school board elections are held in May of odd-numbered years to separate them from party primaries held in March of even-numbered years and general elections held in November. Many constitutional amendment elections are scheduled on the same day as the general election, but they can be held separately (see Chapter 2). There are all kinds of explanations and justifications for this election scheduling, but there is evidence to suggest that it contributes to "voter fatigue," reduced voter turnout, and the disproportionate influence of a few individuals in many of the local and special elections where voter turnout usually is the lowest. Some experts believe that many voters have tired of elections and tuned them out.

These election cycles also shape the policymaking process. A tax increase, for example, is likely to take place soon after an election, not immediately prior to one. Voter dissatisfaction, officeholders hope, would be dissipated by the time an election takes place after their tax vote. This is a double-edged sword. It insulates public officials from immediate public discontent when hard and unpopular decisions must be made. It also makes it difficult to punish elected officials for pursuing questionable or highly unpopular programs.

Primary Elections

Texas and most other states use the direct **primary election** to nominate major party candidates for public office. Prior to the adoption of the primary in 1903, the political parties used the party conventions to nominate their candidates, but changes were made for two basic reasons. Throughout the country during that era, a Progressive reform movement criticized the conventions as undemocratic, corrupt, and dominated by a few of the party elites. That movement advocated the party primary as an alternative. Second, the personal rivalries and factional disputes that erupted at nominating conventions threatened the monopoly that the Democratic Party had over Texas politics during that era, and the primary elections were a solution to excessive intraparty conflict. Under current law, any party that received 20 percent of the vote in the last gubernatorial election is required to nominate candidates by the primary. Other parties can continue to use the nominating convention.

Primaries are now held on the second Tuesday in March in even-numbered years, a change that was made in 1988 as part of the strategy of southern states to increase the region's influence in the presidential nominating process.

For practical purposes, the primaries in Texas are open because no party membership is designated on an individual's voter registration card. A voter does not register as a Republican or a Democrat. Only after a person has voted in a party's primary is the party's name stamped on the card, and that restricts a person to voting only in that party's runoff, if there is one.

Some students of Texas politics suggest that the structure of the state's primary delayed the development of the two-party system and contributed to the conservative establishment's long domination of state politics. Comparisons between earlier primary elections and general elections suggest that Republicans voted in the Democratic primaries and then voted for Republicans in the general election. Conservative candidates were usually nominated by both parties, so it was assured that conservatives would be elected in the general election.[9] During the period of one-party Democratic politics, the person who won the Democratic primary usually won the general election. One early student of the Texas primaries noted, "The only campaigning, therefore, to which the state is usually subjected comes in connection with the Democratic primaries, and it is largely taken up with personalities."[10]

Voter turnout in contemporary primary elections is significantly lower than in the general election, but this has not always been the pattern. From 1904, when the primary was first used for nominations, through 1950, turnout in the primary matched or exceeded that of the general election, except for the elections of 1924 and 1944. Yet, from the 1920s through 1970, the rate of turnout for the Democratic primary never exceeded 35 percent of the voting-age population.

There has been erosion in overall participation in the party primaries since the 1970s, due, in part, to partisan realignment, the weak party organization, and the candidate centered campaigns (see Chapter 6). About 28 percent of the voting-age population (persons 18 or older) voted in the hotly contested Democratic gubernatorial primary in 1972 (see Table 7–1). After that year, turnout in Democratic primaries fell

TABLE 7–1   Democratic and Republican Primary Turnout, 1970–2008*

Year	Race	Republican Primary Vote	Percent of Voting Age Population	Percent of Registered Voters	Democratic Primary Vote	Percent of Voting Age Population	Percent of Registered Voters
1970	Governor	109,021	1.5%	2.6%	1,011,300	**14.1%**	**24.4%**
1972	President/ Governor	114,007	1.5%	2.9%	2,192,903	**28.4%**	**56.63**
1974	Governor	69,101	0.8%	1.3%	1,521,306	**18.4%**	**28.4**
1976	President	356,307	4.0%	6.6%	1,529,168	**17.3%**	**28.47**
1978	Governor	158,403	1.7%	3.1%	1,812,896	**19.4%**	**35.76**
1980	President	526,769	5.3%	9.8%	1,377,767	**13.8%**	**25.67**
1982	Governor	265,794	2.5%	4.4%	1,318,663	**12.3%**	**21.64**
1984	President	336,814	3.0%	4.9%	1,463,449	**12.9%**	**21.34**
1986	Governor	544,719	4.6%	6.9%	1,096,552	**9.3%**	**13.79**
1988	President	1,014,956	8.3%	13.1%	1,767,045	**14.4%**	**22.78**
1990	Governor	855,231	6.8%	10.3%	1,487,260	**11.9%**	**17.95**
1992	President	797,146	6.2%	10.0%	1,482,075	**11.5%**	**18.56**
1994	Governor	557,340	4.3%	6.2%	1,036,944	**7.9%**	**11.47**
1996	President	1,019,803	**7.4%**	**10.5%**	921,256	6.7%	9.5
1998	Governor	596,839	4.2%	5.4%	664,532	**4.7%**	**5.95**
2000	President	1,126,757	**7.8%**	**9.7%**	786,890	5.4%	6.9
2002	Governor	622,423	4.0%	5.1%	1,003,388	**6.5%**	**8.2**
2004	President	687,615	4.3%	5.6%	839,231	**5.2%**	**6.8**
2006	Governor	655,919	**3.9%**	**5.2%**	508,602	3.1%	4
2008	President	1,362,322	7.7%	10.7%	2,874,986	**16.2%**	**22.54**

*Bold percentages note party with the largest turnout.

Source: Secretary of State, Elections Division.

below 20 percent with a low point of 3.1 percent of the voting age population in the 2006 gubernatorial primary.

But the battle between Hillary Clinton and Barack Obama for the 2008 Democratic presidential nomination sparked a record numerical turnout of more than 2.8 million voters in the Democratic primary that year. Almost 1.4 million voters cast ballots in the Republican primary for a record, total primary turnout of more than 4.2 million.

Prior to 1980, participation in the Republican primaries never exceeded 5 percent of the voting-age population or more than 7 percent of the registered voters.[11] That rate has increased somewhat since then, but the percentage of Texans voting in a Republican primary has never reached the levels of participation that the Democratic Party experienced when it dominated state politics. Since 1980, the Republicans' share of the voting-age population participating in their primaries has never exceeded 10 percent. One million voters, or 8.3 percent of voting-age Texans, cast ballots in the 1988 Republican presidential primary, when Texan George Bush was on the ballot. That is the highest turnout percentage in a Republican primary in Texas so far. More voters participated in the 2008 Republican primary, but the participation rate was lower as the total population and number of registered voters had increased.

A number of generalizations can be drawn from this data. Only a small percentage of the population normally participates in the selection of the political parties' nominees. And, those who participate in party primaries tend to be more ideological than the general population. This often prompts candidates to take more extreme positions on issues during their primary campaigns, only to try to move to the center in the general election campaign to appeal to more moderate voters.

A candidate must receive an absolute majority of votes cast for a specific state or local office in a primary to receive a party's nomination. If no candidate receives a majority in multi-candidate races, the two top vote getters must face each other in a **runoff election**. Voter turnout rates for runoffs are consistently lower than those for the first primary.

Minority groups have argued that the absolute majority requirement discriminates against African-American and Hispanic candidates. Although there has been no successful challenge to the requirement in the party primaries, runoff elections have been successfully challenged under the **Voting Rights Act** in many elections for local governments, where candidates usually are elected on a nonpartisan ballot. In cases where challenges have been successful, candidates receiving a plurality of votes (more votes than any other candidate) are elected.

Texas and a handful of other states give the political parties the responsibility of administering the primary elections. A party's county chairman and the county executive committee are responsible for printing the ballots, locating polling places, providing for voting machines, hiring the election judges and clerks, and canvassing the election returns. In recent years, however, the parties have had increasing difficulty managing their elections, prompting some joint administration of the primaries and contracts with counties for operating some elections.

Before 1972, the costs of the primaries were borne by the political parties, which paid for them primarily with filing fees paid by candidates running for office. Those fees could be extremely high. This system was perceived by many as a way of eliminating potential candidates from running for public office, and the system was successfully challenged in the federal courts in 1970.[12] Under current law, modest filing fees are still permitted, and the parties still conduct the primaries, but the state picks up most of the cost. Administrative costs for the 2008 primaries were more than $11.8 million, including about $1.25 million in Harris County (Houston) and $1.5 million in Dallas County.[13] A person can win a place on the primary ballot without paying a filing fee by submitting a designated number of registered voters' signatures on petitions to party officials.

While the primary has helped make the nominating process more democratic than the party conventions, some scholars and party advocates argue that the primary has contributed to the decline of the political parties. The parties no longer control the nomination process because any eligible individual can get on a primary ballot by paying the required filing fee or submitting the required petitions. Also, potential officeholders, organizing and funding their own campaigns, have little allegiance to the parties. A person who is even hostile toward the party's leadership, the party's platform, or its traditional public policy positions can win the party's nomination. A supporter of political extremist Lyndon LaRouche, for example, was elected chair of the Harris County Democratic Party in 1988. Not only was this person an embarrassment to the party, but the party regulars had to pass rules to bypass his authority in order to minimize potential political damage. Primary contests can be vicious with personal attacks that weaken the eventual winner, leading to a loss in the general election.

Parties function primarily to win elections, but the primaries may result in an unbalanced ticket and minimize the party's electoral strength. Bitter primary battles also can increase conflict within a party organization, and an expensive primary race can leave a candidate under-funded for a general election campaign. Moreover, a primary can nominate a weak candidate who will fare poorly in the general election.[14]

General Elections

General elections for state and federal offices are held on the first Tuesday after the first Monday in November in even-numbered years. Unlike the primaries, the administration and costs of the general election are the responsibility of the county. The names of the candidates nominated in the primaries by the two major parties are placed on a ballot, along with the names of third-party candidates who have submitted petitions bearing the names of registered voters equal to 1 percent of the vote in the last gubernatorial election.

Turnout in General Elections

In the election of 1896, the turnout rate was more than 80 percent of the eligible voting-age population, but only twelve years later in 1908, four years after the effective date of the poll tax, turnout had fallen to approximately 35 percent. During much of the period from 1910 to 1958, turnout rates in nonpresidential, general elections were less than 20 percent, mainly because the outcome already had been determined in the Democratic primaries. Presidential elections generated a somewhat higher turnout, but in very few instances did the turnout rate exceed 40 percent of eligible voters.[15]

But it was only $1.50. The poll tax, effective in 1904, was a requirement for voting until it was eliminated by a constituional amendment in 1996. The voter would register to vote by paying the tax yearly—$1.50 to $1.75—at the courthouse. Given the value of a dollar in 1904, the tax was hefty. Its effect was to keep minorities and low-income whites from voting.

TABLE 7–2   Turnout in Texas General Elections, 1970–2008

Year	Type of Election	Total Registered Voters	Total Votes Cast	Percent Turnout of Voting Age Population	Percent Turnout of Registered Voters
1970	Governor	4,149,250	2,235,847	31.1	53.9
1972	President	3,872,462	3,471,281	44.9	66.6
1974	Governor	5,348,393	1,654,984	20.0	30.9
1976	President	6,281,149	4,071,884	46.1	64.8
1978	Governor	5,681,875	2,369,764	25.3	41.7
1980	President	6,639,661	4,541,637	45.6	68.4
1982	Governor	6,414,988	3,191,091	29.8	49.7
1984	President	7,900,167	5,397,571	47.6	68.3
1986	Governor	7,287,173	3,441,460	29.1	47.2
1988	President	8,201,856	5,427,410	44.3	66.2
1990	Governor	7,701,449	3,892,746	31.1	50.6
1992	President	8,439,874	6,154,018	47.6	72.9
1994	Governor	8,641,848	4,396,242	33.6	50.9
1996	President	10,540,678	5,611,644	41.0	53.3
1998	Governor	11,538,235	3,738,078	26.5	32.4
2000	President	12,365,235	6,407,637	44.3	51.8
2002	Governor	12,563,459	4,553,979	29.4	36.2
2004	President	13,098,329	7,410,749	46.1	56.6
2006	Governor	13,074,279	4,399,068	26.4	33.6
2008	President	13,575,062	8,053,036	45.4	59.3

Source: Texas Secretary of State, Elections Division.

Turnout rates in presidential elections are considerably higher than in years when the governor and other statewide officials are elected. Since 1970, the average turnout in gubernatorial elections in Texas has been 28 percent of the voting age population and approximately 43 percent of registered voters. By contrast, average turnout in presidential elections has been 45 percent of the voting age population and 63 percent of registered voters. These turnout rates are significantly higher than turnout in the primaries, but it is evident, if not distressing, that so many Texans do not participate in the selection of their leaders (see Table 7–2).

State officials quoted in the news media often will refer to the voter turnout in terms of a percentage of registered voters. Turnout of registered votes will produce a higher rate and sounds better than percentage of the voting-age population, but it omits critical information about voter participation. If we compare voter registration figures with census data identifying the population eligible to vote, it is clear that a large part of the population doesn't even register to vote. Rates of participation are important to our efforts to establish the vitality of democratic values or norms.

Straight Ticket Voting

The ballot is styled in such a way as to permit straight party voting by pulling one lever, marking one block, punching one hole, or selecting the straight party ticket option.[16] In campaigns, candidates and political leaders often urge voters to "pull one lever" in support of one party's entire slate of candidates. Many voters claim to be independent, to vote for the individual, not the party. Yet, there is evidence that many Texas voters do not split their tickets. Even a casual review of voting returns points to a congruence in votes cast down ballot for the more obscure offices. There is a drop off in total number of votes cast down ballot, but the division of the party vote tends to be very consistent.

Ballot Security

Although some areas still use paper ballots and mechanical voting machines for elections other than the presidential election, many counties use punch cards, mark-sense ballots, or touch-screen voting that permit the election returns to be counted by computer.[17] In the aftermath of the ballot problems in Florida in the 2000 presidential election, ballot security and the accurate tabulation of votes have received more attention in Texas as well as the other states. Historically, there have been allegations of voter fraud, including "stuffing" ballot boxes, voting people who were dead or nonexistent, voting people more than one time, losing ballots, failing to count ballots, and various other accusations. Electronic voting does not eliminate these potential problems, and there are legitimate concerns that tabulation software can be hacked or electronic voting devices manipulated. In recent years, Republicans in the Texas Legislature have tried unsuccessfully to enact a law to require voters to have a form of photo identification, insisting the step would reduce voter fraud. But Democrats argue that the requirement would intimidate many minority and elderly voters who are likely to vote for Democratic candidates.

What type of requirements would assure that voters are U.S. citizens and eligible to cast ballots? And how can an election judge be assured that a person who shows up to vote is the person on the voter registration rolls without a photo ID or other form of documentation? Many people believe the answers to these questions can potentially impact the outcome of elections and provide partisan advantages to one side or the other.

City, School Board, Single-Purpose Districts

Most local elections, which are nonpartisan, are held in May in odd-numbered years to minimize the convergence of issues in national, state and local races. Across the state, there are wide variations in the competitiveness of these elections, campaign costs, and turnout.

Although turnout rates in **local elections** rarely match those in the general elections, competition for control of local governments became more intense in the 1970s and 1980s, partly because of the increased political mobilization of minority voters. More recently, however, participation seems to have declined. Contested local campaigns in large urban areas can be as expensive as state legislative and congressional races.

Most school board and single-purpose district elections, however, have abysmally low rates of voter participation. It is not uncommon for many seats to go uncontested, and turnout rates, even in large urban districts, can be as low as 2 to 5 percent. Candidates often spend little, if any, money on these elections, and their campaigns are usually informal. Recent legislation permits local governments to cancel an election if no offices are contested, and numerous communities in recent years canceled their elections for this reason.

Special Elections

The legislature can submit constitutional amendments to the voters in a general election or schedule them in a special statewide election, in which voter turnout is usually much lower.

In constitutional amendment elections since 1991, average turnout of registered voters has been 11.5 percent, but this was only 8.2 percent of the voting-age population. A few of those were **special elections**. Most, however, were held on the general election date in November of odd-numbered years, when the only other significant races on the ballot were races for mayor and city council in Houston. Consequently, the turnout in Houston is heavier than the rest of the state in constitutional amendment elections and usually is a major factor in determining the outcome. It is somewhat disturbing that, in most years, less than 10 percent of Texas citizens care enough to vote for constitutional amendments (see Chapter 2). The low turnout also means that special interest groups can mount well-organized campaigns to place provisions favoring them into the constitution with little public scrutiny or interest.

Local governments also conduct special elections for bond issues, local initiatives and referenda, and the recall of public officials. Although there are occasional high-interest, emotionally charged elections, turnout rates in these elections tend to be extremely low. People who do vote tend to be those with higher incomes and educational levels.

The governor also can call special elections to fill vacancies in certain offices, including legislative and congressional seats.

Extended Absentee Balloting

In 1988, Texas made a major change in the requirements for absentee voting. Prior to that time, if a voter was not going to be in the county on election day or was incapacitated, he or she could vote absentee in person at a designated polling place or by mail before election day. Now, anyone can vote early without having to state an excuse during an extended period for **absentee** (or in person early) **voting**. Urban counties, in particular, now maintain multiple voting places, including stations conveniently located in shopping malls, during the extended voting period, which runs from the twentieth day to the fourth day before the scheduled election day. Consequently, there has been a notable increase in the number of votes cast early—20 to 30 percent of all votes in some areas.

The extended early voting, now used in 31 states, has radically changed campaign strategies and tactics.[18] A candidate now has to communicate earlier to that part of the population that has a high likelihood of voting prior to election day. With a large portion of the vote cast early, a candidate might well carry the election day totals but lose the early vote and lose the election. A candidate also has to mobilize those voters who cast their votes on election day. Thus, a campaign must "peak" twice.

POLITICAL SUFFRAGE IN TEXAS: A STRUGGLE FOR MINORITIES AND WOMEN

Despite the rhetoric of democratic theory in the state's constitution and the somewhat venerable view that people have of elections and voting, Texas has a dark history of voter disfranchisement. For many years, African Americans, Hispanics, and low-income whites were systematically excluded from the political process. Texas had a political system in which the interests of a few could prevail over the interests of the majority. Many people paid a high price for this early legacy of discrimination.

After the Civil War, the state initiated efforts to organize a civilian government that would reestablish Texas's full statehood in the Union. The Constitutional Convention of 1866 accepted the supremacy of the national government and eliminated slavery, but it refused to adopt the Thirteenth Amendment, which gave African Americans the right to vote and hold public office.[19] This constitution was rejected by the Radical Reconstructionists in Congress in 1867, and subsequent Texas constitutions extended full voting rights to African Americans. Forty-one African Americans served in the Texas legislature from 1868 to 1894.[20] But while the Texas Constitution extended political rights to them, African Americans were threatened with physical violence and economic recriminations that reduced their political participation well into the twentieth century. In addition, several state laws were enacted to block their access to the ballot.

The Poll Tax

The conservative Texas establishment's reaction to the Populist movement and its potential for building a coalition between African Americans and low-income whites resulted in the legislature's adoption of a **poll tax**, which went into effect in 1904.[21] It was a tax of $1.50 to $1.75 that had to be paid each year before a person could vote. In the early 1900s, that was a large sum of money for low-income people. It was to be paid between October 1 and January 31, three months before the primaries were then held and nine months before the general elections, long before most people even began to think about voting. Consequently, the tax eliminated large numbers of voters who were likely to support the Populist Party and undermine the political establishment.[22]

The poll tax was in effect for more than sixty years in Texas. It was outlawed for federal elections by the Twenty-Fourth Amendment to the U.S. Constitution, adopted in 1964, but Texas retained the poll tax for state and local elections, thus requiring two sets of registered voters and separate ballots. In November 1966, Texas voters approved an amendment to the state constitution eliminating the poll tax for state elections and implementing annual voter registration. By that time, the U.S. Supreme Court had already ruled that the state poll tax was unconstitutional.[23]

The White Primary

Texas, along with several other southern states, also implemented the **white primary**, which was designed to eliminate African American participation in the elections that really counted.[24] Initially, the Texas legislature in 1923 enacted a law that denied African Americans the right to vote in the Democratic primary. That law was declared unconstitutional by the U.S. Supreme Court in 1927 on the basis of the Fourteenth Amendment.[25] But, almost immediately, the legislature authorized the state party executive committee to establish the qualifications for voting in the primaries, and the Democratic Party adopted a resolution that only whites could vote. This was challenged in the federal courts, and again, in 1932, the Supreme Court declared the white primary unconstitutional.[26]

Acting through its state convention and without legislative authorization, the Democratic Party then proceeded in May 1932 to exclude African Americans from the primary again. The issue was taken a third time to the Supreme Court, which this time ruled that the party, as a voluntary organization, had the authority to determine membership and the right of participation.[27] But African Americans continued to use the courts to attack the white primary, and, finally, in the case of *Smith v. Allwright* in 1944, the Supreme Court reversed its earlier decision and declared the white primary unconstitutional.[28]

Those who insisted on excluding African Americans from participation were extremely imaginative in their efforts to circumvent the court's decisions. They substituted a restrictive, preprimary selection process through the private Jaybird Democratic Association—open only to whites—to choose candidates, who then were formally

A "warrior" in the long battle to gain access to the ballot. Dr. Lawrence A. Nixon, a physician, an active Democrat, and charter member of the National Association for the Advancement of Colored People (NAACP), was part of the early efforts by African Americans to legally challenge the white primary in Texas.

nominated in the Democratic primary and subsequently elected in the general election. Finally, in 1953, the U.S. Supreme Court also declared this arrangement unconstitutional.[29]

Restrictive Registration Law

Until 1971, Texas had one of the most restrictive voter-registration systems in the nation. Voters had to register annually between October 1 and January 31. For voters who did not register in person at the county courthouse, deputy registrars could deliver or mail in only one registration form at a time, thus minimizing the possibilities of coordinated voter-registration drives. These restrictions discouraged voter registration across the state, especially among the African American, Hispanic, and low-income populations.[30]

More court intervention forced major changes in the voter-registration law in 1971.[31] The highly restrictive system was transformed, in a relatively short time, into one of the most progressive systems in the country. Annual registration was replaced with permanent registration. An individual now can register by mail or in person up to thirty days prior to an election. Persons working individually or with a political campaign can be deputized to register voters, and large voter-registration drives are encouraged. County voter registration officials now must send out cards to voters, automatically renewing their registrations, every two years. And there are restrictions on how soon officials can remove the names of voters who have moved from registration lists.

Property Ownership and the Right to Vote

From colonial times, one requirement for the right to vote was property ownership, a practice that continued in modified form through the 1970s in many states, including Texas. Property ownership was not required to vote in primaries and most other elections, but it was required in bond elections that were used by local governments to win financing of new buildings, roads, sewer systems, and other infrastructure needs. The exclusion of nonproperty owners from these elections was based on the argument that revenue from property taxes was used to repay these bonds, and if a person did not own property on which to pay a tax, he or she should not have the right to vote for the bonds.

Landlords, however, passed through their property taxes to renters, and many renters, therefore, had a direct interest in the outcome of bond elections. Many urban areas, moreover, had large amounts of rental property and many residents who were barred from participating in those elections. Eventually, the federal courts declared property ownership as a requirement for voting in bond elections unconstitutional.

Women and the Right to Vote

The national movement for women's suffrage, or the right to vote, was a long struggle fought in the state capitals as well as in Washington. In 1915, the Texas legislature considered a constitutional amendment extending the right to vote to women, but rejected it. In 1918, women were given the right to vote in primary elections and party conventions. Then, in 1919, Texas became the first Southern state to approve the Nineteenth Amendment to the U.S. Constitution, which, by late 1920, was approved by the required number of states to grant women's suffrage in all elections.[32]

Extension of the Vote to Those Eighteen Years of Age and Older

A long-standing debate over the age at which a person should be permitted to vote became more intense during the Vietnam War. Many people believed that individuals who were required to comply with the draft and risk death in battle should no longer be denied the right to vote. The Twenty-Sixth Amendment, which lowered the voting age from twenty-one to eighteen, was adopted in 1971, and the first election in which

Relishing the results of a long, arduous campaign for the right to vote. Mrs. L. W. Evans, President of the San Antonio Federation of Women's Clubs, casting a ballet at San Pedro Park Pavilion on November 4, 1924.

eighteen-year-olds could vote was in 1972. Perhaps because of the political activism of many college students during the Vietnam era, there were expectations that young people would vote at higher rates than older adults, but this has never materialized. The lowest voter turnout rates, in fact, are among voters eighteen to twenty-nine years old.

Other Discriminatory Aspects of Election Systems

Even after the most obvious discriminatory practices against minorities were eliminated, there were more subtle, but just as pervasive, techniques for reducing the political power and influence of these same groups.

One technique is racial **gerrymandering** of political boundaries. State legislators and many city council members are elected from **single-member districts**, each of which represents a specific number of people in a designated area. After the 2000 census, for example, each member of the Texas House ideally represented 139,012 people, and each member of the state Senate, 672,639 people. To minimize the possibilities of minority candidates being elected, policymakers could divide minority communities and attach them to predominantly nonminority communities—a tactic called *cracking*. Minority communities could also be consolidated into one district, a tactic called *packing*, with an 80 to 90 percent minority population, which would reduce the number of other districts in which minorities might have a chance of winning office. The federal Voting Rights Act forbids such practices, but minority groups continue to go to court to challenge redistricting plans.

At-large elections also have been used to reduce minority representation. At one time, members of the Texas House who came from urban counties were elected in multimember districts, which required candidates to win election in countywide races, a very difficult prospect for many minority candidates. The practice was eliminated in legislative races in the 1970s as a result of federal lawsuits. But many cities, school districts, and special districts across Texas continue to use at-large elections, requiring candidates to run for office citywide or districtwide. This system dilutes minority representation in most communities in which it is used. In addition to the increased costs of running in at-large elections, which discourage minority candidates, a minority group that may account for 60 percent of a city's total population and 52 percent of the voting-age population may account for only 45 percent of the registered voters. And, with the possibility of polarized voting, where minorities vote for the minority candidates and the nonminorities vote for the white candidates, there is a high likelihood that no minority could get elected in many at-large systems. At-large elections have come under increasing attack under the Voting Rights Act, and many local governments have adopted some form of single-member districting.

The Voting Rights Act

In 1965, the U.S. Congress passed the Voting Rights Act, which was extended to Texas in 1975. This law has been central to strategies by minorities in challenging discriminatory election systems and practices. Under the Voting Rights Act, minority groups can challenge state and local election systems in the federal courts. The burden of proof in such challenges is on the government. An election system that dilutes minority voting strength is illegal, even if there is no clear intent to discriminate against minorities. Furthermore, any changes in the election systems of state or local governments, including redistricting plans, must be reviewed and precleared by the U.S. Department of Justice, or must be approved by the U.S. District Court in Washington, D.C. This legislation has produced changes in election systems across the state and has helped increase minority representation in the Texas legislature and on local governing bodies.

By the mid-1990s, however, the Voting Rights Act was under attack by conservatives. And the U.S. Supreme Court, in "reverse discrimination" cases from Texas and Georgia, ruled that some congressional districts had been illegally gerrymandered to elect minority candidates. In the Texas case, three federal judges held that the Texas legislature had violated the U.S. Constitution by designing two districts in Houston and one in the Dallas area to favor the election of African American or Hispanic candidates. The court redrew thirteen congressional districts in Texas—the three minority districts and ten districts adjoining them—and ordered special elections to fill the seats.

Despite the redrawn boundaries, two incumbent African-American congresswomen in the affected districts were reelected. In effect, recent court cases have held that race or ethnicity can be considered in drawing legislative boundaries but cannot be the predominant factor. Representatives of minority groups fear that these recent cases will reduce the number of potentially winnable legislative districts for African-American and Hispanic candidates. They also are concerned that the Voting Rights Act will be significantly modified whenever temporary sections are scheduled to expire.

Motor Voter Registration

The **motor voter registration** law was passed by the U.S. Congress in 1993 and signed by President Bill Clinton, despite the opposition of Republicans, who apparently feared it would benefit the Democratic Party. An earlier version of the bill had been vetoed by President George Bush in 1992. The federal law, similar to a 1991 Texas law, requires states to provide eligible citizens the opportunity to register to vote when they apply for or renew a driver's license. The law also requires states to make voter registration forms available at certain agencies that provide welfare benefits or assist the disabled.[33] From 2006 through 2008, approximately 5 million registration applications were received by elections administrators in the state's 254 counties. Some 27 percent of these, or 1,352,012 applications, came from the Department of Public Safety's driver license offices.[34] The law has expedited the voter registration process for many Texans.

Facilitating Voter Participation

Over the past two decades, there have been efforts across the nation to reduce administrative barriers to political participation. Several states have adopted procedures for on-line registration. Other states have adopted "same day" registration, allowing people to register to vote on election day. Others have provided for on-line voting. Following the lead of Texas and a handful of other states, extended voting has been allowed. Some people advocate longer hours for voting, and others push for making election day a holiday, among other recommendations. Some of these proposals eventually may be adopted. Eliminating barriers can increase voter registration and increase turnout, but they won't resolve voter indifference, problems of transportation to the polls, and health issues that deter voting.

POLITICAL GAINS BY MINORITIES AND WOMEN ————●

Over the past thirty years, African Americans and Hispanics have made substantial gains in the electoral process. Elimination of restrictive voting laws, the adoption of a more liberal state voter registration system, and changes mandated by National Voter Registration Act of 1993 have contributed to an increase in minority voters across the state. Voter registration and mobilization drives coordinated by groups such as the National Association for the Advancement of Colored People and the Southwest Voter

Registration Education Project have contributed to increased participation, as has an increase in the number of minority candidates and elected officials. When minority candidates run and have a good chance of winning, minority voters have a stronger incentive to vote. Yet, it would be premature to conclude that the state's election system is now "color blind." The contentious debate over a Republican proposal to require a voter to present a photo identification card or two identifying documents is a case in point. Proponents argued that the requirement would reduce election fraud, while opponents argued that it would discourage minority voters from casting ballots. The proposal failed in both the 2007 and 2009 legislative sessions.

Hispanics

According to 2007 population estimates, Hispanics made up 36 percent of Texas's population. But the Hispanic population is younger than the Anglo and African-American populations, and Hispanics accounted for only 32.4 percent of Texans of voting age (see Table 7–3). Hispanics also include many immigrant noncitizens, thus reducing to approximately 25 percent the Hispanic portion of adults eligible to register and vote. And the percentage of Hispanics who actually register and vote is even smaller.

In the 2004 presidential election, the U.S. Census Bureau estimated that 22 percent of registered voters in Texas were Hispanic and 20 percent of those voting were Hispanic. By comparison, Anglos comprised 65 percent of those voting and African Americans, 12 percent.[35]

The 2008 presidential election produced a similar pattern of turnout and influence for the Hispanic population, with an estimated 20 percent of the Texas votes cast by Hispanic citizens. African Americans comprised 16.5 percent of the votes cast in the state.[36] Election studies conducted in the early 1990s concluded that Hispanics accounted for only 12 to 15 percent of Texans casting ballots.[37] The recent turnout shows improvement but certainly not the full potential for the state's Hispanic population.

Voter registration and turnout are not simply explained by racial or ethnic factors. Study after study of registration and turnout demonstrate a direct relationship between education and income. Across racial and ethnic groups, people with more education and higher incomes are more likely to vote than those at the lower end of the scales. Drawing from the demographic data in Chapter 1, it is evident that income and educational levels serve to deter voter participation among Hispanics.

Approximately 44 percent of Hispanic adults interviewed in the 2003 to 2004 *Texas Polls* identified with the Democratic Party, but the story is more complex.[38] Until

TABLE 7–3 **Population, Voting Age Population, and Eligible Population**

	Population	Percent of Total Population	Population 18+	Percent of Population 18+	Citizens 18+	Percent of Citizens 18+
Anglo	11,405,417	47.7%	8,933,154	51.7%	8,807,295	58.8%
Hispanic	8,600,385	36.0%	5,590,020	32.4%	3,686,677	24.7%
African American?	2,757,554	11.5%	1,940,453	11.2%	1,873,289	12.5%
Other	1,141,024	4.8%	811,306	4.7%	583,076	3.9%
Total	23,904,380	100.0%	17,274,933	100.0%	14,950,337	100%

Source: U.S. Census Bureau, 2007 *American Community Survey.*

Governor George W. Bush made substantial inroads into the Hispanic vote in 1998, Democratic candidates for president and governor consistently received more than 70 percent of the Hispanic vote in Texas.[39] Using state exit polls, the Pew Hispanic Center estimated that George W. Bush received 49 percent of the Hispanic vote in 2004. Barack Obama received 63 percent of the Hispanic vote in 2008.[40]

Hispanic voters dominated the 2002 Democratic primary, which for the first time featured two Hispanic gubernatorial candidates, Laredo businessman Tony Sanchez and former Attorney General Dan Morales. One of the three major candidates for the party's U.S. Senate nomination also was Hispanic—Victor Morales, a schoolteacher who had shocked party leaders by winning the 1996 senatorial nomination. The William C. Velasquez Institute, which specializes in Hispanic-related voting activity, reported that preliminary figures indicated that Hispanics cast a record 33 percent of the 2002 Democratic primary votes.[41] Spending heavily from his wealth on television advertising, Sanchez easily defeated Dan Morales for the gubernatorial nomination. And tapping into the Hispanic vote, Victor Morales got into a runoff for the Senate nomination with former Dallas Mayor Ron Kirk, an African American. Each received about one-third of the vote. But Kirk, who was supported by most party leaders, swamped Victor Morales in fundraising and won the Senate runoff, when Hispanic voter turnout had fallen off. Both Sanchez and Kirk later lost their general election races to Republicans.

The increased electoral strength of the Hispanic population is borne out in Table 7–4, which compares the number of elected Hispanic officials in Texas in 1974 to those holding office in 2009. Some 540 Hispanics held elected office in 1974. By 2009, there were 2,435 Hispanic elected officials, the highest in any state. The marked increase can be attributed to a more equitable apportionment of city, county, and school district political boundaries, the growth of the Hispanic population, and increased organizational efforts among Hispanics.

By 2009, only six Hispanics—Texas Supreme Court Justices Raul A. Gonzalez, Alberto R. Gonzales, and David M. Medina; Attorney General Dan Morales; and Texas Railroad Commissioners Tony Garza and Victor Carrillo—had been elected to statewide office in Texas. There have been other Hispanic candidates, such as Victor Morales and

TABLE 7–4   Latino Elected Officials in Texas, 1974–2009

	1974	1996	2001	2009
Federal	2	5	6	6
State	13	35	36	38
County	102	203	213	298
Municipal	251	536	555	621
Judicial/Law Enforcement	172	323	280	486
School Board	—	536	701	938
Special District	—	51	37	48
Total	**540**	**1,689**	**1,828**	**2,435**

Sources: Juan A. Sepulveda, Jr., *The Question of Representative Responsiveness for Hispanics,* Harvard College, Honors Thesis, March 1985; National Association of Latino Elected and Appointed Officials, *National Roster of Hispanic Elected Officials,* 1996, 2001; and NALEO Educational Fund, *2009 National Directory of Latino Elected Officials, Courtesy of Salvador Sepulveda.*

Tony Sanchez, who have made serious statewide races. With changing demographics and the increased political sophistication of the Hispanic population, Hispanics will win additional statewide and local offices in the future.

African Americans

African Americans constitute approximately 11 percent of the state's population, 11 percent of the voting-age population, and 10 to 12 percent of those who vote. Approximately 61 percent of Texas African Americans call themselves Democrats, but 80 to 90 percent of the African American vote is normally cast for Democratic candidates. Voting cohesively as a group, African Americans, like Hispanics, have considerable potential to influence the outcome of both primaries and general elections.

The increased political clout of the African-American population is also manifested in the number of African-American elected officials (Table 7–5). In 1970, there were only twenty-nine African Americans elected to public office in Texas. The number increased to 196 in 1980 and 466 in 2002. Only four African Americans have been elected to statewide office in Texas. They are Railroad Commissioner Michael Williams, Texas Supreme Court Chief Justice Wallace Jefferson, and Texas Supreme Court Justice Dale Wainwright, all Republicans, and former Texas Court of Criminal Appeals Judge Morris Overstreet, a Democrat. As noted earlier, former Dallas Mayor Ron Kirk, an African American, won the Democratic nomination for the U.S. Senate in 2002 but lost to Republican John Cornyn in the general election.

Women

Historically, the world of Texas politics has been dominated by men, but that is beginning to change. Prior to Ann Richards's election as state treasurer in 1982, there had been only two women elected to statewide office. Richards was elected governor in 1990, and Kay Bailey Hutchison, who had succeeded Richards as state treasurer, was elected to the U.S. Senate in 1993. As governor, Richards also appointed more women to key positions on state boards and commissions than her predecessors.

In 2009, eight women were holding statewide offices in Texas, including Hutchison, who was still in the U.S. Senate; state Comptroller Susan Combs; Railroad Commissioner Elizabeth Ames Jones; one member of the Texas Supreme Court; and four

TABLE 7–5   African-American Elected Officials in Texas, 1970–2002

	1970	1980	2002
Federal	—	1	2
State	3	14	17
County	—	5	21
Municipal	16	75	285
Judicial/Law Enforcement	—	21	47
School Board	10	78	94
Special District	—	2	—
Total	**29**	**196**	**466**

Source: Metropolitan Applied Research Center, Inc., and Voter Regional Council, Inc., *National Roster of Black Elected Officials*; and Joint Center for Political and Economic Studies, *National Roster of Black Elected Officials,* 1980, 1998, and 2002.

members of the Texas Court of Criminal Appeals. That same year, there were six women in the state Senate and thirty-seven in the state House, a significant increase over 1981, when the legislature included only one woman in the Senate and eleven in the House.

Women are playing an increased role in local government as well, and this pattern can be expected to continue. Over the past three decades, the state's three largest cities—Houston, Dallas, and San Antonio—had women mayors. A 2006 survey by the Texas Municipal League counted 198 women mayors (or 16 percent) in the state's 1,211 cities. The 6,021 council members in the cities included 1,588 women, or 26 percent of the total.[42] Of the 254 county judges in 2006, twenty-four (or 9.5 percent) were women, and women held sixty-five (or 6.4 percent) of 1,016 county commissioner posts.[43] There are a large number of other county offices, and women held a significantly high number of these positions. Of the 7,207 elected school board trustees in 2008, some 1,835 (or 25 percent) were women. There were 1,036 school superintendents in 2008, and 166 (or 16 percent) were women.[44]

THE NEW CAMPAIGN TECHNOLOGY

In Chapter 6, we discussed the long history of one-party Democratic politics in Texas. The only elections that counted then were the Democratic primaries, and they would often include five or six candidates for a single office. In statewide or local campaigns, candidates seldom ran as a ticket or coalition. Each candidate developed his or her own campaign organization, thus precluding the development of party campaign organizations. Individuals who became involved in a campaign were primarily motivated by their personal loyalties to a candidate and not to the political party.

With low rates of voter participation in the primaries and the absence of viable Republican challenges in the general elections, Democratic candidates were able to stumble through the election process with loose coalitions that often disintegrated after election day. Although there was competition in the Democratic primaries, conservative candidates, tied to the establishment, generally prevailed. Despite differences in personality and style, these conservative candidates were fundamentally committed to the policy agendas of the economic elites of the state.

By today's standards, political campaigns through the 1950s were amateurish and unsophisticated. Modern political campaigns have been reshaped by a number of factors, including an expanded electorate that is highly mobile, the growing dominance of the Republican Party, the organizational weaknesses of both political parties, the continuation of the candidate-centered campaign, the increased reliance on the electronic media for news and political information and the emergence of the Internet and social networking of the New Media.[45] Today's successful campaigns rely on sophisticated public opinion polling, slick campaign ads contrived by media experts, analyses of demographics, and targeting of selected populations through direct mail, phone banks, and a variety of increasingly sophisticated Internet techniques, most orchestrated by professional **campaign consultants**.

Such consultants have been around in Texas in some form or another for a long time. W. Lee "Pappy" O'Daniel, the owner of a flourmill that produced Hillbilly Flour and master of ceremonies of a daily radio talk show, ran for governor in 1938, exploiting a rustic image couched in religious, evangelical language that had a wide appeal in the rural areas of the state. His speeches were designed to create identification with the "common folks," but he was a wealthy businessman who had ties to Texas's corporate leaders. His homespun style was contrived, and O'Daniel relied heavily throughout his campaign on public relations expert Phil Fox of Dallas.[46] What is different about contemporary campaign consulting is that it is an identifiable industry with diversified expertise. More significantly, few candidates for statewide office or major local offices now run without utilizing the services of campaign consultants.

Public Opinion Polling

In a society based on mass consumption, it is no wonder that techniques were developed to measure public attitudes and opinions. The origins of the industry are usually linked to George Gallup, who conducted a statewide poll in 1932 for his mother-in-law, who ran for secretary of state in Iowa. Survey research or public opinion polling has a variety of applications, most of which are nonpolitical; market research is now a multibillion-dollar industry.[47]

Public opinion polling is used in political campaigns for a number of purposes (see "Who Am I?"). As would-be candidates consider running for office, they will often hire pollsters to conduct benchmark surveys of people who are likely to vote in the upcoming election. Using well-tested sampling techniques, the pollster will conduct either a telephone survey or a face-to-face survey of a representative sample of voters. The length and type of the survey usually is determined by available funds and the information desired by the candidate and those developing the campaign. Surveys are expensive. If the required number of completed interviews is 1,200 for a statewide race at a cost of $40 to $50 each, it is clear that polling can consume a hefty chunk of the campaign budget.

Surveys also are used to develop campaign strategy, monitor or track the progress of the campaign, and modify the campaign as changes take place in the attitudes, perceptions, or mood of the electorate. The benchmark survey, often taken some time before

Who Am I?

Statewide political candidates and officeholders often spend millions of dollars getting elected and reelected, but it seems that most of their constituents just are not paying any attention. According to a 1997 *Texas Poll*, most Texans—82 percent of those surveyed—knew then that George W. Bush was the governor. But after that there was a huge drop off in the public's ability to match the names of high-ranking state and federal officials with the offices they held.

The attorney general could be identified by name by only 30 percent; the comptroller and the land commissioner by 17 percent; the lieutenant governor by 16 percent, and the agriculture commissioner by 9 percent. Only 22 percent of the respondents could correctly name both U.S. senators from Texas.

Other, more recent surveys have indicated a similar lack of political awareness among the public. Surveys conducted from 2008 to 2009 for the University of Texas at Austin *Texas Politics Poll* indicated that approximately 23 percent of Texans thought President Obama was a Muslim. Some 36 percent could identify David Dewhurst as the Lieutenant Governor, and only 41 percent knew that the office was elected. Only 24 percent knew that the terms of the Texas House and Senate were two years and four years respectively. Fifty-seven percent knew that the Texas House was controlled by the Republicans, but more than 60 percent did not have an opinion of the job performance of the speaker and lieutenant governor.[48]

the official campaign gets underway, is rather lengthy and attempts to assess public opinion relating to the office a candidate is seeking. Issues are identified, perceptions of candidates are probed, and trial heats with potential opponents are tested. A wide range of demographic questions are included to permit the segmentation of the electorate into small groups whose specific interests or concerns can be identified and targeted.

As the campaign proceeds, tracking surveys are used to determine shifts in attitudes, perceptions, and support for the candidate. Does the candidate now have greater name identification? Do more people perceive the candidate positively and express their support with greater intensity? Is there a particular event or emerging campaign issue that might spell defeat? This information is used to adjust the campaign to changing conditions. Toward the end of the campaign, surveys are often taken nightly to permit further fine-tuning of the campaign in the final days.

A variation on the survey is the use of a focus group. As television advertisements are developed, the campaign staff may choose to test them before they are aired. A series of focus groups, each including eight to twelve persons recruited for specific demographic characteristics, will be asked to review these ads and provide their impressions and reactions. An experienced staff will watch these proceedings to identify subtle responses to the ads, the theme, or the message. On the basis of these qualitative assessments, the media consultants will decide which ads should be used and which should be discarded.

Some campaigns have resorted to "push polls," a practice that most scholars and reputable pollsters consider a violation of research ethics. The survey is presented to the voter as an effort to solicit perceptions and attitudes toward candidates, but as the interviewer moves through the questions, a controversial or negative position or attribute of a potential candidate is introduced. Finally, this attribute is linked to a specific candidate, and the voter is then asked if this fact would change her or his vote.

Segmentation and Targeting of the Electorate

A political campaign is fundamentally an organized effort to communicate with the electorate with the goal of convincing a majority of those who participate to vote for a specific candidate. But effective communication is difficult for a number of reasons. One is the low voter turnout in most elections. Voter turnout rates also vary among different ethnic, income, and education-level groups, and some of these voters will not support a particular candidate no matter what he or she says or does. In a partisan election, many people will vote for or against a candidate strictly on the basis of party identification. Obviously, not every voter shares a candidate's concerns and priorities.

Candidates use census data, surveys, and previous election returns with turnout and party voting patterns to divide voters into segments. Some research specialists are able to organize this information to permit the campaign to target its messages to small, well-defined populations. Psycho-demographics, a technique used by some opinion specialists, combines survey and census data to divide populations by lifestyles rather than party identification. Whether direct mail, television, radio, newspapers, phone banks, or block walking is used to reach its audience, the modern campaign will direct a specific, relevant message to these segmented populations based on sophisticated market research.

For example, survey data may suggest that a disproportionate number of women between the ages of forty-five and fifty-four have not heard of the candidate but are concerned about health care and medical insurance. Based on demographic data and television program ratings, the media specialist knows that a large number of these women watch daytime television programs. To get a specific message to these voters, television spots with a health care message oriented to the specific concerns of women from forty-five to fifty-four will be developed and aired during these times of the day. Most populations can be identified and targeted in this manner, increasing the likelihood that a desired message gets to the specific voters whose perceptions and attitudes the consultant wants to influence. The use of the Internet for political communications has made some aspects of segmentation and targeting even more sophisticated as large amounts of data on users can be captured and analyzed to determine what messages should be sent to specific populations.

The segmentation of the electorate may well lead to a fracturing of the political debate. Various segments of voters are exposed to narrow slices of the candidate's image, personality, and concerns. The campaign hopes that each group of voters will respond favorably to its own limited knowledge of the candidate, but some critics argue that this segmentation "further diminishes the importance of language, logic, and reason in the articulation of campaign issues."[49]

MEDIA AND ADVERTISING

It is easy to assume that a campaign can market a candidate much like a pack of cigarettes or a box of soap, and our increasing cynicism often leads to this facile conclusion. But voter response to candidates, the progress of the campaign, and the various ads and messages that voters receive form an extremely complex decision-making process. Scholars in various disciplines have attempted to unravel the effects of news reports, campaign advertising and campaign strategies and tactics on voter behavior. But the conclusions are only tentative because it is very difficult to demonstrate that a specific event, news story, or campaign ad results in the final decision of a voter.

Controlled Media

There are numerous media through which candidates can communicate their messages to the voters, and for those that can be purchased commercially, the only limitations are availability and finances. The media that is purchased by the candidate is often referred to as the **controlled media**. The candidate controls decisions concerning which media to use, when to purchase advertisements, and what message to convey. There are some technical and legal questions pertaining to campaign advertising, but the candidate has a wide range of options.

Billboards, bench signs, advertisements on buses and cabs, and electronic signs can be purchased to establish voter awareness and name identification. Although such ads are not likely to convert or mobilize voters, they establish the candidate's visibility.

Although candidates talk about "pressing the flesh" and making direct contacts with the voters, it is simply impossible to talk personally to the number of people necessary to win an election, particularly in a statewide or urban race. Candidates stage block walks and rallies in which they personally participate and meet with supporters, but many of these are **media events** they hope will be covered by the press. Campaigns still rely on block walking and phone banks, but in a sophisticated campaign, these tactics are coordinated with the media blitz and direct mail.

In many local elections across Texas, it is too costly or inefficient to use radio and television advertising. But it is almost impossible to run a viable statewide campaign without the use of the electronic media. Texas is large and diverse and has about twenty-three separate media markets. Candidates often spend half of the campaign budget for television and radio advertising, and the media specialists—ranging from the creative staff to the time buyers—have taken on increased importance in modern campaigns.

The thirty-second spot is now the standard for television advertising, and the candidate's consultants attempt to carefully craft advertisements that address concerns, perceptions, and expectations of varied segments of the electorate.[50] The media blitz usually picks up steam as the campaign moves closer to election day because it is assumed that it takes several exposures to a given ad for a voter to respond and, in many cases, allegations raised in an opponent's advertisements must be addressed.

Campaign advertising became an issue in the 1990 gubernatorial race, which was marked with what seemed to be an endless series of negative campaign ads and related tactics (see Chapter 5). "Gay-bashing" advertisements were used against Democratic nominee Ann Richards when she received the endorsement of groups alleged to be linked to lesbian rights, and a fundraising letter from the national Democratic chairman attempted to link Republican nominee Clayton Williams with neo-Nazism and racism.[51]

The negative advertisement wasn't new to Texas politics, but most observers agreed that advertisements in the 1990 gubernatorial race were more vitriolic, aired with more frequency, and were seemingly more irrelevant to the issues facing the state than most ads had been in the past. As the advertisements continued, newspapers began to analyze their themes and veracity, and voters indicated that they were displeased with them. But consultants continued to convince their clients that negative attacks worked and that people, while objecting to negative ads, had higher recall of them than many other television spots.

The 2002 gubernatorial race, in which Republican Rick Perry and Democrat Tony Sanchez spent almost $100 million, much of it bashing each other over the airwaves, was equally vicious. Sanchez tried to blame Perry for high electric bills and homeowners insurance rates. And Perry tried to link Sanchez, a wealthy Laredo businessman, to drug dealers. Perry's allegation was based on a federal investigation that had determined that a savings and loan owned by Sanchez in the 1980s had unwittingly been used to launder drug money. Sanchez never was implicated in any wrongdoing, and he and other officials of the savings and loan, which later folded, said they didn't know the depositors were connected to the illegal drug trade.

The computer is becoming a major vehicle for communicating with voters, reflecting a further extension of the controlled media. In addition to communicating with volunteers, supporters, and the news media through e-mail, many candidates and officeholders now maintain websites, which provide an additional tool for communicating large amounts of information to voters. Candidates also use e-mail to raise campaign funds and quickly respond to speeches or allegations raised by political opponents. Candidates and their consultants are also learning to use social networking sites on Facebook and Twitter for political communications.

Uncontrolled Media

Positive news stories about the candidate and campaign are potentially more valuable than paid advertising and don't cost the campaign money. Candidates and their handlers thus attempt to exploit the press by getting positive coverage and reducing as much as possible any negative slants in campaign stories. But the relationship between political candidates and the press is adversarial. The news media, ever alert for weaknesses in a candidate and tips spread by political opponents, can make or break a candidate by the coverage and slant given to the candidate's personality, reputation, view of the issues, and campaign activities.

Many campaigns hire press secretaries who specialize in media relations. One author has suggested that a successful media strategy entails the following: "Keeping the candidate away from the press; feeding the press a simple, telegenic political line of the day; and making sure the daily news line echoes [*magnifies* may be the better word] the images from the campaign ads, thus blurring the distinction between commercials and 'reality.'"[52] It is common to hear consultants speak of "staying on message" as they attempt to influence media coverage.

Members of the press are keenly aware of these efforts to manipulate them, and the best reporters are usually able to resist. But the hectic, irrational nature of statewide campaigns, the pressure of news deadlines, the propensity for pack journalism, and the fear of being beaten to a major story by a competitor often work against a reporter's sincere efforts to get the "straight skinny" on the candidate's abilities, leadership potential, and his or her stand on the issues.

Clayton Williams used his millions to win the 1990 Republican gubernatorial nomination with an effective paid television campaign that portrayed an attractive image of an independent, can-do, cost-conscious businessman. He lost the general election to Democrat Ann Richards after the uncontrolled news media painted a less attractive picture: that of a coarse, chauvinistic individual who had only the vaguest notion of what he would do as governor.

Direct Mail and Fundraising

People like to receive mail. Some people even like to receive junk mail, experts say, and direct mail has become a highly sophisticated component of modern campaigns. Direct-mail specialists provide campaigns with a technique for "persuasion and fundraising."[53] As a further refinement of the segmentation and targeting of voters, this technique permits the campaign to craft a specific message for a narrowly defined population and assure, with high probability, that households with the specified demographic or psychographic characteristics will receive the campaign message. In a sense, it is "narrow casting" a specific message to an identifiable audience.

Direct mail is big business in the United States, and it has been easily adapted to political campaigns. As new innovations are developed with direct Internet communications, we are seeing its increased use for communicating with voters and fundraising. In many instances, the campaign messages and appeals are very emotional, designed to push the voters' "hot buttons" on specific issues. They are crafted by specialists who have studied the emotional appeals of such communications, and the attention to detail often astonishes the uninitiated. The length of a letter, the color of the paper on which it is printed, the underlining and highlighting of specific words or phrases, and teasers on the envelope to get the recipient to open the letter receive critical attention by the specialist. Evidence indicates that people respond to direct-mail appeals, and, if the technique is integrated with phone banks, block walks, and the media campaign, it becomes an extremely valuable campaign tool.

Direct mail also has become a major tool in campaign fundraising. Massive mailing lists targeting virtually every population group in the state have been developed, and names of persons with probable political attitudes and beliefs are easily extracted from these files by computer. Successive mailings to probable supporters have a high likelihood of producing campaign dollars. The continued use and refinement of these lists increase the rate of return, and while campaigns still rely on large contributions, the more modest contributions received from direct-mail solicitation have taken on increased importance.

We have learned from some recent elections that huge amounts of money can be raised using the Internet.[54] A campaign that merges computer technology, the knowledge of segmentation and targeting, and well-developed appeals that speak to the interests or "hot buttons" of groups of voters can raise money from a vast number of small contributors giving less than $200 apiece. Greater amounts of information can be conveyed electronically. The potential contributor can be provided ongoing information about the direction and success of the campaign. And the campaign can go back again and again to those who demonstrate a predisposition to contributing.

Many down-ballot campaigns cannot afford the technologies discussed above. Nor do they have the technical staff available to develop and implement these new tools. Candidates do the best they can with what they have. As the new model of the "total campaign" becomes more visible, however, there will be innovative adaptations of these techniques to some of the more obscure offices.

Grassroots

During the last three decades of the twentieth century, the grass roots campaign was subordinated to the mass media. Candidates and consultants believed the mass media was more efficient because large numbers of voters could be contacted in a short period. If attacked by an opponent, a quick response could be aired. Repeated contacts also could be used to mobilize voters. Messages could be targeted to specific segments of the electorate. And the campaign did not have to engage in the time-consuming process of recruiting and managing volunteers. While grassroots campaigns never went away, they were often conducted on a shoestring with little careful thought as to how volunteers could be effectively integrated into the campaign.

Traditional grassroots activities include door-to-door campaigning (block walking), neighborhood gatherings, recruiting other volunteers, addressing and stuffing envelopes, making signs, staffing phone banks, staffing the polls on election day, and a host of other tasks. Whether the grass roots organization is paid or unpaid, a telephone call, letter, postcard, personal e-mail, or visit from a campaign worker who demonstrates an intense commitment to a candidate can still have a strong impact on voters. It takes a great deal of planning and resources to develop a grassroots campaign. And increasingly, sophisticated campaign software coupled with well-trained staff who understand the organization and dynamics of the grassroots campaign are understood to be critical to the campaign. As noted earlier, there is empirical evidence that such tactics can make a difference in the outcome of closely contested elections.

MONEY AND CAMPAIGNS ⸺⬤

Campaign Costs

No one knows precisely how much is spent on political campaigns in Texas because there is no single place where all this information is collected. Candidates for state office file campaign finance reports with the state Ethics Commission, but candidates for city councils, county offices, and school boards file reports with the jurisdictions in which they are running. There are wide variations in campaign costs among the different contested offices, but it is evident that costs, even at the local level, have increased significantly in recent years.

City council races in major cities such as San Antonio, Houston, Fort Worth, and Dallas can easily cost $50,000 to $100,000, and they can go higher. And, multimillion dollar races for mayor in the big cities are rather common. Bob Lanier spent $3 million getting elected mayor of Houston in 1991, and eight candidates spent more than $6.6 million in the 1997 race to succeed him. The 1997 winner, Lee Brown, spent more than $2.1 million alone, and the second-place finisher, businessman Rob Mosbacher, spent more than $3.5 million.[55] Those earlier figures, however, paled in comparison to the nearly $9 million that businessman Bill White spent to win the 2003 Houston mayor's race.[56] There have been reports of candidates for county commissioner spending $100,000 or more and of district judges in metropolitan counties spending more than $150,000. Historically, school board elections have been low budget, but it is not uncommon for slates of candidates in large urban school districts to spend $10,000 to $15,000 in low-turnout elections.

In the 2006 election cycle, candidates for state office reported contributions of more than $150 million (see Tables 7–6 and 7–7). Some $59.6 million was raised by candidates who ran for the Texas House of Representatives. Winners of House races raised, on average, $280,000 for a job that pays $7,200 a year. Some received $1 million or more in campaign donations.[57]

Some $27 million was contributed to state Senate candidates, including some who were not up for election. Senate winners received, on average, $917,000 and losers, $287,000.[58] Campaign contributions raised by the winners ranged from $530,000 to $1.9 million. Many of the losers raised inconsequential amounts, but there were at least three candidates who raised over $800,000 and still lost.

Candidates for governor in 2006 reported total campaign contributions of more than $42 million. The winner, incumbent Republican Rick Perry, received almost half of that—$21 million. His three major rivals spent more than $6 million each in the general election.[59] The most expensive gubernatorial race in the state's history was in 2002, when Perry and unsuccessful Democratic challenger Tony Sanchez spent more than $82 million. Sanchez's expenditures included more than $50 million from his own pocket.[60]

There are a number of explanations for the increased costs. The population has increased, requiring more money to be spent to reach more voters. Candidates increasingly rely on the electronic media, which is very costly. So is the increased use of consultants to organize and run political campaigns. Meanwhile, the growing number of interest groups and political action committees (PACs) has made more money available to candidates.

Unspent funds raised for a campaign can be carried over as a "war chest" for the successful candidate's next election. Even unopposed officeholders will attempt to raise large amounts of money to discourage potential opponents in the future. A significant question arising from a discussion of fundraising for the state Senate and House is why a person would go to such lengths to raise such huge sums of money to win an office that pays only $7,200 a year.

Fund Raising

Soaring campaign costs have raised considerable concern about campaign fundraising and contributions in Texas, as they also have nationally. There is concern that elections are being bought and that major campaign contributors are purchasing influence in

TABLE 7–6   Campaign Funds Raised in the 2006 Election Cycle

Economic Interests	Total Contributions by Individuals	Contributions by PACS/Business	Contributions by Sector	Rank
Lawyers and Lobbyists	$11,662,642	$11,709,686	$23,372,328	1
Miscellaneous Business	11,883,533	4,095,647	15,979,180	2
Finance	8,905,771	5,504,820	14,410,591	3
Ideological and Single Issue	262,267	13,320,758	13,583,025	4
Energy and Natural Resources	8,446,689	4,467,587	12,914,276	5
Construction	9,183,781	2,845,752	12,029,533	6
Health	5,600,420	5,921,329	11,521,749	7
Real Estate	5,613,614	2,509,340	8,122,954	8
Transportation	3,571,079	1,780,483	5,351,562	9
Communications	1,948,690	2,256,163	4,204,853	10
Other	1,557,589	2,123,959	3,681,548	11
Agriculture	2,165,505	1,425,626	3,591,131	12
Insurance	1,623,007	1,395,894	3,018,901	13
Labor	105,481	2,311,526	2,417,007	14
Computers and Electronics	1,437,552	471,454	1,909,006	15
Unknown	17,770,602	1,395,157	19,165,759	
Totals	**$91,738,222**	**$63,535,181**	**$155,273,403**	

Campaign Contributions by Individuals and Couples

	Total	Industry
Bob & Doylene Perry	$7,167,064	Construction
James & Cecilia Leininger	5,551,966	Health
Fred & Lisa Baron	2,100,821	Law
George & Amanda Ryan	1,390,354	Finance
Charles C. Butt	1,205,921	Food
John Herschell McCall	1,201,545	Miscellaneous
T. Boone Pickens, Jr.	1,200,348	Energy
Harold Simmons	1,129,400	Finance
John M. O'Quinn	1,116,556	Law
David & Martha Alameel	766,300	Health
Total	**$22,830,275**	

Source: Texans for Public Justice, "54 More Rich Donors Join the '$100,000 Club,'" *Lobby Watch*, April 19, 2007; and Texans for Public Justice, *Money in Politex: A Guide to Money in the 2006 Texas Elections*, September 2007.

the policymaking process. Some critics of contemporary campaigns have argued that current practices are a form of legalized bribery, implying that public officials are available to the highest bidder. Other critics have asserted that some officeholders engage in "shaking down" organizations for campaign contributions with implied threats.

Money is critical to most successful campaigns for public office because it permits the candidate to purchase advertising and other resources for communicating with the voters. But money is not the only factor affecting an election. Incumbency, existing party loyalties, the availability of party or campaign activists, the public's perceptions of a candidate, and a candidate's campaign skills or expertise also help determine electoral success. In numerous elections, well-financed candidates have been defeated by opponents with far fewer dollars. This may suggest that "there are genuine limits" on what money can accomplish in a campaign.[61]

Contributions are made to influence the outcome of an election and, subsequently, to shape public policy by electing persons who share similar political views with or who will be sympathetic or accessible to those making the contributions. Reports of large campaign contributions often prompt remarks that Texas has the "best Supreme Court that money can buy" or the "best legislature that money can buy." These remarks are given credence if key policy votes seem to be influenced by an officeholder's relationship to his or her political contributors.

Some people undoubtedly make contributions to candidates out of a sense of civic duty, general concern for good public policy, partisan loyalty, or personal friendship. But contributions of hundreds of thousands of dollars, either from individuals or political action committees, raise different questions about intent and purpose. For example, James Leininger, a wealthy businessman from San Antonio, is known for his support of conservative causes, particularly a proposal to spend tax dollars on private school vouchers. When a voucher proposal was defeated in the 2005 session of the legislature with the support of five Republicans, he then gave more than $2 million to their opponents in the 2006 Republican primaries.

Rarely will anyone admit publicly that he or she is attempting to buy a candidate. Individuals and PACs making large political contributions usually say they are doing so for the purpose of "gaining access" to elected officials.[62] Since officeholders have limited time to consider and assess competing interests, lobbyists representing interest groups and their PACs contend that campaign contributions are necessary to facilitate access and give them an opportunity to present their cases on specific legislation.

Political scientists and others have attempted to prove that there is a relationship between campaign contributions and public policy, but so far the research is inconclusive. Multiple factors shape the decisions of public policymakers, including an officeholder's personal views, the views of his or her constituents, legal and technical issues, and the merits of the requests made by specific individuals or groups.[63] Nevertheless, the strong appearance of a relationship between money and public policy is there and advocates of campaign finance reform can make strong arguments for change.

The Fat Cats, PACs and the Really Big Money

Just as they have nationally, **political action committees (PACs)** have increased their importance at the state and local level by bringing sophisticated fundraising skills to political campaigns. Representing special interest groups or individual companies, PACs collect money from their members and are a ready source of campaign dollars. They are in the business of influencing elections.

During the 2002 election cycle, candidates running for state offices raised $195 million. Of the total, $126.9 million came from individual donors, PACs, and party committees. Some $68.1 million came from the candidates themselves, either in personal contributions or loans.[64] Candidates reported more than 100,000 campaign contributions totaling a $155 million during the 2006 election cycle. Most contributors gave only modest amounts, but the lion's share of the money came from

PACs, party committees, and individuals associated with key sectors of the state's economy (see Table 7–6). Ten individuals or couples gave approximately $22.8 million—6.9 percent of all campaign contributions—in the 2006 election cycle.

Unlike the federal government, Texas places no limits on the amount of money an individual or political action committee can contribute to most political candidates. And there are no limits on how much a candidate can contribute to his or her campaign. The only exceptions in Texas are campaign contribution limits in judicial races, which were imposed by the legislature in 1995. Large contributions have long played a role in Texas politics and, over the years, most large contributions have gone to the conservative candidates, both Democratic and Republican. The role of large money may be mitigated in the future through the use of direct mail and the Internet to solicit small campaign donations. From the available data, however, it is still too early to discern such a pattern and, for the present, large donors, sometimes called **fat cats**, still dominate the contributions for Texas political campaigns (see "Bob Perry: Homebuilder and Big Donor").

Political action committees, as we discussed in Chapter 4, are an extension of interest groups. These committees, which collect money from their members for redistribution to candidates, have increased their importance at the state and local levels by bringing sophisticated fundraising skills to political campaigns. PACs are in the business of influencing elections, and they are key players in the fundraising game. Unlike PACs that are organized under federal law and contribute to national elections, PACs organized to influence state elections have few limitations on what they can contribute. Many PACs are organized by corporations and are a major source of business funding to political candidates in Texas. Corporations also can influence elections by spending money on issue advertising, provided they don't endorse a specific candidate. Many company executives also make individual contributions to candidates.

PACs and businesses contributed more than $50 million during the 2002 campaign season and $63 million in 2006. While there are many state PACs, the lion's share of campaign money is concentrated among a relative few. The top 50 PACs/businesses

TABLE 7–7   Campaign Contributions to Candidates Seeking State Offices, 2006 Election Cycle

Office	Totals for Winner in General Election	Totals for Loser in General Election	Totals for Primary Losers	Total Number of Candidates
Governor	$21,091,448	$21,223,785	$178,567	7
Lt. Governor	10,837,273	41,757	33,069	3
Comptroller	4,476,390	55,622	—	2
Attorney General	6,855,483	208,834	—	2
Land Commissioner	1,051,743	4,406	—	2
Railroad Commissioner	2,165,588	2,100	250	3
Agriculture Commissioner	2,203,298	81,522	—	2
House	42,009,324	10,720,172	6,850,313	309
Senate*	14,686,447	8,767,327	4,023,445	48
Totals	**$105,376,994**	**$41,105,525**	**$11,085,644**	**378**

Bob Perry: Homebuilder and Big Donor

Houston homebuilder Bob Perry tries to maintain a low public profile, but in recent years he has received significant publicity for emerging as one of Texas's most generous political contributors. In 2002, he was the biggest donor to state political candidates and causes, contributing at least $3.8 million during that election cycle, mostly to Republicans. Texas Land Commissioner Jerry Patterson, a former state senator and one of many candidates backed by Perry, said the homebuilder had never asked for favors. "He's a reserved, serious and principled guy who has never tried to influence my vote," Patterson said, according to the *Houston Chronicle* in 2002. "He truly is a philosophical contributor who wants to improve the Republican Party."[65]

But Perry's voice obviously is heard. He was believed to be influential in the legislature's creation in 2003 of a new state agency, the Residential Construction Commission, to develop performance standards for builders and discourage lawsuits against builders by unhappy homebuyers. Governor Rick Perry (who isn't related to the homebuilder) appointed an executive of Bob Perry's company to the new agency's board, less than one month after the governor had received a $100,000 contribution from Bob Perry. The homebuilder had contributed more than $500,000 to Rick Perry since 1997. The governor's office said the appointment wasn't influenced by the contributions, but by the appointee's experience in the homebuilding industry.

During the 2006 cycle, Perry and his wife contributed approximately $7.2 million to candidates, including approximately $1.3 million to four statewide candidates. The Perrys also gave large sums of money to many legislators and legislative candidates. Some observers suspected the homebuilder was trying, among other things, to convince lawmakers not to abolish the Residential Construction Commission, which was up for sunset review in 2009. The agency, opposed by many consumer advocates, nevertheless was abolished.

contributed $47,586,261 in 2002 to candidates and the political parties. One of the biggest contributors was Texans for Lawsuit Reform, which gave almost $2 million and played a leading role in a successful lobbying effort that produced more restrictions during the 2003 legislative session on damage lawsuits filed against doctors and businesses. Other major donors included the Texas Association of Realtors, the Texas Trial Lawyers Association, the Texas Medical Association, the Texas Dental Association, and the Texas State Teachers Association.

The fight over civil justice restrictions, or tort reform, has been a divisive issue—and a major source of campaign contributions—in the Texas legislature for years. Several major PAC contributors have been involved in the controversy. The trial lawyers were major opponents of further restrictions, whereas the Texas Medical Association was a major ally of Texans for Lawsuit Reform in winning the new limits in 2003 (see Chapters 2 and 11).

Since money is the mother's milk of politics, the above data suggest a disturbing pattern. The really big money stands out. Moreover, it is often hard to trace the movement of money from a corporation to a PAC to a party committee and then to a candidate. Campaign costs are not likely to be reduced, nor are Texans likely to support public financing of campaigns. What is needed, though, is more information to make it easier to identify the trail of funds to elected officials.

Attempts at Reform

On the heels of the Sharpstown scandal, in which high-ranking state officials were given preferential treatment in the purchase of stock in an insurance company (see Chapter 8), the legislature enacted a major campaign finance disclosure law in 1973. This law, with some changes, is now administered by the state Ethics Commission. Although the law did not limit the size of political contributions, for the first time it required candidates to list the addresses as well as the names of donors and the amounts and dates of contributions. It also required PACs contributing to candidates or officeholders to report the sources of their donations, which in the past had usually been hidden. Also for the first time, officeholders were required to file annual reports of their political contributions and expenditures—even during years when they were not seeking reelection—and candidates were required to report contributions and other financial activity that occurred after an election. A candidate also had to formally designate a campaign treasurer before he or she could legally accept political contributions. Campaign finance reform, however, remains a difficult and seemingly endless struggle as officeholders, individuals and organizations resist efforts to reduce the influence of money and require the fundraising process to be more transparent.

POLITICAL PARTICIPATION ●

Several years ago, a small group of protesters pitched tents and erected a series of crude displays outside the offices of what then was known as the Texas Water Commission in Austin. They came from a small town south of Dallas where, they claimed, an industrial plant was polluting the environment with cancer-causing agents. People living in the community had experienced disproportionately high cancer rates and immunity and respiratory problems. These were middle-aged Texans who had never before participated in, much less organized, a demonstration. They appeared to be uncomfortable, but there was a sense of desperation as they talked about their families and friends.

A month or so later in San Antonio, several thousand antiabortionists organized a three-mile-long demonstration along a major highway. The demonstration took place after church on a Sunday, and many of the well-groomed protesters carried Bibles and had their young children in tow. Waving placards, singing songs, and praying, they used tactics that have been used across the nation by other antiabortion groups.

On any given day, Texas newspapers publish hundreds of "letters to the editor" addressing a wide range of state and local political issues. People contact public officials every day about stop signs, public facilities, garbage collection, and a multitude of governmental functions and responsibilities. Thousands of people are involved in politics as they attempt to shape the actions of public officials.

Voting or running for office are the first two activities that may come to mind when we think of political participation. But they are just a small part of the ongoing process necessary to sustain a democratic political system, translate the interests and demands of the public into specific policies, and assure governmental responsiveness.

Most people who participate in politics engage in what scholars call conventional political behavior. This includes voting, running for office, contributing to and campaigning for candidates, writing letters, gathering petitions, participating in other **grassroots** activities, and lobbying.

Fewer individuals participate in what is considered unconventional political behavior. These are acts that may offend many people. They can include boycotts, protest marches, and other nonviolent demonstrations, although many individuals consider any lawful, peaceful demonstration a very conventional means of exercising their constitutional rights. To virtually everyone, however, destruction of property, personal injury, assassination, and other forms of violence are totally unacceptable forms of political behavior.[66]

Not everyone, of course, participates in politics at the same level. Why some people get actively involved in politics and public life while others seem totally uninterested in government, current events, or public policy is a question that has challenged scholars, candidates, journalists, and reform groups for years. And it has generated much research.

From the day a person is born, he or she is subject to a socialization or learning process. The process is complex, lifelong, and structured by the interaction of the individual with the environment in which he or she lives. As the person approaches adulthood, the process includes the shaping of political attitudes, beliefs, and behavior.

Political socialization, the process by which people learn to behave politically, "transmits a broad array of values and opinions, from general feelings about trust in government to specific opinions" about the economy, political leaders, and institutions.[67] The agents of political socialization include the family, where the young child first learns of the views and attitudes of parents and relatives toward government, the political process, and leaders. The process is expanded through the schools, where children are exposed to national and state history, government, heroes, and values. Civics lessons and courses are taught to further shape commitment to the dominant values of the society. Other institutions, such as the church and the mass media, also contribute to this molding process. So do a person's peers and life experiences. Individuals tend to validate their perceptions and attitudes through the opinions of friends and acquaintances, and a major life experience, such as a tour of duty in the military or extended unemployment, has a potential effect on one's political behavior.

Political behavior is complex and changes over time. The limited space dedicated to this topic here is insufficient to flesh out its nuances and complexities, and we warn you to avoid drawing hard-and-fast conclusions. But a few broad generalizations about political behavior are in order.

A number of scholars have developed classifications of political behavior that run from high levels of involvement in a wide range of activities to virtual passivity. Sidney Verba and Norman H. Nie, well-known American political scientists specializing in political socialization, identified six categories of political participation. At one end of the spectrum are the complete **activists** (approximately 11 percent of the population), who are engaged in all types of political activity. Not only are these individuals involved in political campaigns, but they also participate in almost every other arena of community life. At the other end are the *inactives* (22 percent), who participate rarely, if at all, in the political life of the community. Some scholars refer to the first group as *political gladiators* and the second group as *apathetics*.

Another group that is relatively inactive and shares many of the characteristics of the inactives are the *voting specialists* (21 percent). These individuals vote regularly in presidential and local elections but seldom engage in other organizational activities or attempt to contact policymakers personally.

There are a small number of *parochial participants* (4 percent) who vote but do not engage in collective activity or campaigns. Nevertheless, they do contact policymakers over specific issues that affect their personal lives.

Another group, the *communalists* (20 percent), demonstrates a high rate of participation in community life but a low level of campaign activity. These people participate in community activities such as church, PTA, and neighborhood associations but rarely engage in the high-conflict game of political campaigns.

The *campaigners* (15 percent) are just the opposite. They participate regularly in political campaigns but rarely in community activities. This group appears to be attracted to the conflict of campaigns.[68]

Although we have limited survey data for Texas, some generalizations emerge from national studies to provide insights into the patterns of political participation in the state:

1. **Income.** Individuals with higher income levels are more likely to be active participants in a wider range of political activities than those with low incomes. Affluent people have more time and resources to engage in political activities. They have a better understanding of the process, and they are acquainted with other participants and public officials.

2. **Education.** Participation increases as the level of education increases. People with college degrees are more likely to participate in politics than those less educated. Education also is correlated with income. Knowledge of political issues, public policies, the political process, and public officials makes a person aware of the importance and potential benefits of political participation.

3. **Gender.** Historically, men had participated in politics at higher rates than women. But in recent years women and men have been participating at comparable levels, and in some areas of the country, women now participate at higher rates than men. More women are now running for and winning public office. In recent years, there has been evidence of differences between men and women in support of the major political parties, which is often referred to as the "gender gap."

4. **Age.** Young people are far less likely to engage in politics than older people. The highest rates of participation are among middle-aged people. Younger adults tend to be in a transitory stage of their lives in which they don't identify with the issues or politics of the communities in which they live. Younger voters are engaged in a wide range of volunteer activities, but these tend not to be political.

5. **Race and ethnicity.** Rates of participation among Anglos are highest. But African Americans, despite historical patterns of discrimination, are now moving toward the Anglo level of participation. Hispanics tend to participate at much lower rates than either Anglos or African Americans. Explanations for these variations include educational and income differences, citizenship status, and the degree to which Hispanics have been assimilated into the political culture.

6. **Political efficacy.** Complex psychological attributes contribute to one's sense of having an impact on others or on political events. Political activists believe that they can influence the outcome of events. The more intense this sense of efficacy, the more likely one is to become involved politically.

In Texas and elsewhere, there is a great deal of concern about decreased political participation. Election turnout has declined, and it is often difficult to get strong candidates to run for public office. Public discourse has lost its civility, and citizens do not seem to have learned the lessons of the benefits and "logic of collective action." Surveys indicate much distrust of elected officials, and many people believe that government is for sale to the highest bidder. Moreover, some people just don't care. These findings lead many to conclude that there has been an erosion of democratic practices in the state and the nation.

SUMMARY AND CONCLUSIONS ●

1. Elections provide the general population with an opportunity to shape public policy indirectly, through the selection of leaders. For elections to achieve their ideal purpose under democratic theory, voters must be well informed, attentive to the actions of their leaders, and care about the outcome of elections.

2. One of the most disturbing aspects of the contemporary Texas political system is the low voter turnout in most elections, despite the elimination of discriminatory election laws, the creation of an extended voting period, and easy voter registration. Many people apparently are too uninformed about governmental actions to care to vote. Other people may be turned off by a feeling that public officials put their own interests and special interests before the public interest. Stories of governmental corruption and negative advertising in many political campaigns also disillusion voters. And frequent elections may contribute to voter fatigue.

3. Historically, political parties played a central role in elections, but now candidates increasingly rely on paid campaign consultants, who have taken over many of the traditional party functions. The consultants' primary objective is to win campaigns, and they appear to give little consideration to the subsequent effects of campaigns on governance and policymaking.

4. From the Civil War through the 1960s, state election law was highly discriminatory towards minorities and low income whites. These discriminatory practices—the poll tax, the white primary, and restrictive periods of registration—have been eliminated through court challenges and federal law.

5. Over the past thirty years, Hispanics and African Americans have realized substantial gains in the electoral process and increased success in winning election to public office. There also has been a dramatic increase in the number of women elected to public office.

6. The costs of statewide campaigns, as well as many regional and local campaigns, have escalated over the past three decades. Candidates receive much of their money in large campaign contributions from political action committees and wealthy individuals. Although money may not buy public officials, it certainly buys access to them, and it creates the impression that well-organized interests, corporations, or wealthy individuals have a disproportionate influence on policymakers.

7. Political participation includes a number of activities in addition to elections. People in the higher socioeconomic groups are more likely to participate in a wider range of political activities and have more influence on the policymaking process than people in the lower socioeconomic groups.

KEY TERMS ●

Suffrage 194
Primary election 195
Runoff election 197
Voting Rights Act 197
General election 198
Local election 200
Special elections 201
Absentee (or in person early) voting 201

Poll tax 202
White primary 202
Gerrymandering 205
Single-member districts 205
At-large election 205
Motor voter registration 206
Campaign consultant 210
Public opinion polling 211

Controlled media 213
Media events 213
Political action committee (PAC) 219
Fat cat 220
Grassroots 222
Political socialization 223
Activists 223

FURTHER READING ●

Articles

Beiler, David, "The Eyes of America Were Upon Him," *Campaigns and Elections,* July 1999, pp. 48–53.

Carrington, Paul O., "Big Money in Texas Judicial Elections: The Sickness and Its Remedies," *SMU Law Review* 53, Winter 2000, pp. 263–75.

Garcia, John A., "The Voting Rights Act and Hispanic Political Representation in the Southwest," *Publius: The Journal of Federalism* 16, Fall 1986, pp. 49–66.

Books

Ansolabehere, Stephen, and Shanto Iyengar, *Going Negative: How Political Advertisements Shrink and Polarize the Electorate.* New York: Free Press, 1997.

Asher, Herbert, *Polling and the Public: What Every Citizen Should Know,* 7th ed. Washington, DC: CQ Press, 2007.

Baker, Ray J., *I Wouldn't Do It Any Other Way: Lessons I Learned from Vote Getting Texas Style for the High and Mighty.* Wilsonville, Oregon: Book Partners, 1998.

Bennett, W. Lance, *The Governing Crisis: Media, Money, and Marketing in American Elections.* New York: St. Martin's, 1992.

Bryson, Conrey, *Dr. Lawrence A. Nixon and the White Primary,* rev. ed. El Paso, TX: Texas Western Press, 1992.

David, Chandler, and Bernard Grofman, eds., *Quiet Revolution in the South: The Impact of the Voting Rights Act, 1965–1990.* Princeton, NJ: Princeton University Press, 1994.

Diamond, Edwin, and Stephen Bates, *The Spot: The Rise of Political Advertising on Television,* rev. ed. Cambridge, MA: MIT Press, 1988.

Erikson, Robert S., Norman R. Luttberg, and Kent L. Tedin, *American Public Opinion,* 4th ed. New York: Macmillan, 1991.

Erikson, Robert S., Gerald C. Wright, and John P. McIver, *Statehouse Democracy: Public Opinion and Policy in the American States.* New York, NY: Cambridge University Press, 1993.

Flanigan, William H., and Nancy H. Zingale, *Political Behavior of the American Electorate,* 11th ed. Washington, DC: CQ Press, 2006.

Maisel, L. Sandy, *Parties and Elections in America, 2nd ed.* New York: McGraw-Hill, 1993.

Olien, Roger M., *From Token to Triumph: The Texas Republicans since 1920.* Dallas, TX: SMU Press, 1982.

Rosenstone, Steven J., *Mobilization, Participation, and Democracy in America.* New York: Macmillan, 1993.

Scher, Richard K., *The Modern Political Campaign.* Armonk, NY: M. E. Sharpe, 1997.

Sorauf, Frank J., *Money in American Elections.* Glenview, IL: Scott Foresman, 1988.

Traugott, Michael W., and Paul J. Lavrakas, *The Voter's Guide to Election Polls.* Chatham, NJ: Chatham House, 1996.

Wattenberg, Martin P., *Is Voting for Young People?* New York: Pearson Longman, 2007.

———, *The Rise of Candidate-Centered Politics.* Cambridge, MA: Harvard University Press, 1991.

Websites

American University, Center for Congressional and Presidential Studies http://www.spa.american.edu/ccps/links.php Links to a wide range of sites dealing with elections, campaign finance, campaign consulting, and interest groups.

National Institute on Money in State Politics http://www.followthemoney.org/ This nonpartisan organization is "dedicated to accurate, comprehensive and unbiased documentation and research on campaign finances at the state level." Data are provided for most statewide and legislative races in Texas.

Project Vote Smart http://www.vote-smart.org/ Project Vote Smart is a national nonpartisan organization that tracks the performance of approximately 40,000 national and state elected officials and candidates. Information on policy positions, campaign finances and expenditures, and job performance is provided about the governor and state legislators.

Secretary of State http://www.sos.state.tx.us/ In addition to compiling county election data for state offices, this office provides information on election law, election procedures, county officials, and a program for voter education (Project V.O.T.E.).

Texans for Public Justice http://www.tpj.org/ "A nonpartisan, nonprofit organization which tracks the influence of money and corporate power in Texas politics."

ENDNOTES

1. This quote was reported in Sam Attlesey, "Politicians Sometimes Say the Funniest Things," *Dallas Morning News*, October 13, 1991, p. 44A.
2. L. Sandy Maisel, *Parties and Elections in America* (New York: Random House, 1987), p. 1.
3. Gerald Pomper, *Elections in America* (New York: Dodd, Mead and Company, 1968), p. 12.
4. Herman Finer, *The Theory and Practice of Modern Government* (New York: Holt, 1949), p. 219.
5. Murray Edelman, *The Symbolic Uses of Politics* (Urbana, IL: University of Illinois Press, 1964), p. 17.
6. V. O. Key Jr. with the assistance of Milton C. Cummings Jr., *The Responsible Electorate* (Cambridge, MA: Harvard University Press, 1965), p. 7.
7. Maisel, *Parties and Elections in America*, p. 1.
8. Ibid., p. 3.
9. Frank J. Sorauf, *Party Politics in America*, 5th ed. (Boston: Little, Brown, 1984), p. 213; and George Norris Green, *The Establishment in Texas Politics* (Westport, CT: Greenwood, 1979), p. 164.
10. Douglas O. Weeks, "The Texas Direct Primary System," *Southwestern Social Science Quarterly*, 13, September 1932, p. 99.
11. Davidson, *Race and Class in Texas Politics*, p. 24.
12. *Carter v. Dies*, 321 F. Supp. 1358, 1970.
13. Office of the Secretary of State, Elections Division, telephone conversation on July 30 (2009).
14. Frank Sorauf, *Party Politics in America*, p. 220.
15. Davidson, *Race and Class in Texas Politics*, p. 24.
16. Robert S. Lorch, *State and Local Politics*, 3rd ed. (Upper Saddle River, NJ: Prentice Hall, 1989), p. 63; and Bexar County Elections Administration, phone conversation, November 26, 2003.
17. Office of the Secretary of State, Elections Division, telephone conversation on July 30, 2009.
18. National Association of Secretaries of State, "Engaging the Energized Electorate: NASS Survey on State Preparations for the 2008 Presidential Election," September 2008, Appendix D.
19. Rupert Richardson, Ernest Wallace, and Adrian Anderson, *Texas: The Lone Star State*, 5th ed. (Englewood Cliffs, NJ: Prentice Hall, 1988), p. 231.
20. See Merline Pitre, *Through Many Dangers, Toils and Snares: Black Leadership in Texas, 1868–1890* (Austin, TX: Eakin, 1985).
21. Richardson, et al., *Texas: The Lone Star State*, p. 312.
22. Wilbourn E. Benton, *Texas Politics: Constraints and Opportunities*, 5th ed. (Chicago: NelsonHall, 1984), pp. 72–73.
23. *Harper v. Virginia State Board of Elections*, 86 S. Ct. 1079 (1966).
24. Benton, *Texas Politics*, pp. 67–72.
25. *Nixon v. Herndon, et al.*, 273 U.S. 536 (1927).
26. *Nixon v. Condon*, 286 U.S. 73 (1932).
27. *Grovey v. Townsend*, 295 U.S. 45 (1935).
28. *Smith v. Allwright*, 321 U.S. 649 (1944).
29. *John Terry, et al., Petitioners v. A. J. Adams, et al.*, 345 U.S. 461; and National Voting Rights Institute, "'Wealth Primary'-Legal Theory," *NVRI.org*, http://www.nvri.org/about/wealth1.shtml.
30. Beryl E. Pettus and Randall W. Bland, *Texas Government Today: Structures, Functions, Political Processes*, 3rd ed. (Homewood, IL: Dorsey, 1984), pp. 85–86.
31. *Beare, et al. v. Preston Smith, Governor of Texas*, 321 F. Supp. 1100 (1971).
32. Benton, *Texas Politics*, p. 65.
33. *Congressional Quarterly Weekly* Report 51 (September 1993), p. 2318.
34. U.S. Election Assistance Commission, "The Impact of the National Voter Registration Act of 1993 on the Administration of Elections for Federal Office, 2007–2008," June 30, 2009, Table 2a.
35. U.S. Census Bureau, "Voting and Registration in the Election of November 2004," *Current Population Reports*, P20-556, March 2006.
36. U.S. Census Bureau, "Voting and Registration in the Election of November 2008," *Current Population Reports*, Supplement, April 6, 2009, Table 4b.
37. Telephone conversation with Robert R. Brischetto, Southwest Voter Research Institute, Inc., November 1, 1991.
38. *Texas Poll*, Spring 2003, Summer 2003, Fall 2003, Winter 2004 (Austin, TX: Scripps Howard, 2004).
39. Telephone conversation with Robert Brischetto; and Robert R. Brischetto, *The Political Empowerment of Texas Mexicans, 1974–1988* (San Antonio, TX: Southwest Voter Research Institute, Inc., Latino Electorate Series, 1988), p. 5.
40. Pew Hispanic Center, "The Hispanic Vote in the 2008 Election," November 7, 2008, p. 11.
41. William C. Valasquez Institute, news release, March 13, 2002.
42. Texas Municipal League, *Texas Municipal League Directory of City Officials*, 2006 (Austin, TX: Texas Municipal League, 2006).
43. Data courtesy of Richard O. Avery, Director of the V. G. Young Institute of County Government, Texas A&M University. Survey completed in 2006.
44. Texas Association of School Boards, data provided by the courtesy of the association.
45. For an excellent analysis of the early development of campaign professionals, see Larry J. Sabato, *The Rise of the Political Consultants* (New York: Basic Books, Inc., 1981).
46. Norris, *The Establishment in Texas Politics*, pp. 24–25.
47. For a general introduction to polls and polling techniques, see Herbert Asher, *Polling and the Public: What Every Citizen Should Know*, 7th ed. (Washington, DC: CQ Press, 2007).

48. *Texas Poll*, Fall 1997, conducted for Scripps Howard by the Office of Survey Research of the University of Texas; and Department of Government, University of Texas at Austin, *Texas Politics Poll*, 2008–2009.

49. W. Lance Bennett, *The Governing Crisis: Media, Money and Marketing in American Elections* (New York: St. Martin's Press, 1992), p. 32.

50. See Edwin Diamond and Stephen Bates, *The Spot: The Rise of Political Advertising on Television*, rev. ed. (Cambridge, MA: MIT Press, 1988).

51. *Texas Observer*, September 28, 1990, p. 8.

52. Bennett, *The Governing Crisis*, pp. 33–34.

53. Sabato, *The Rise of the Political Consultants*, p. 220.

54. Moveon.org—Democracy in Action and the campaign of President Obama are two cases that merit further attention for their fundraising strategies.

55. Allen Berstein, "Election '97—The Race for City Hall— Record Spent on Mayoral Election Despite Limits," *Houston Chronicle*, December 2, 1997, p. 1A.

56. John Williams, Salatheia Bryant, and Rachel Graves, "Election 2003—It's White in a Rout—Parker Wins Controller Post," *Houston Chronicle*, December 7, 2003, p. 1A.

57. Texans for Public Justice, *Money in Politex: A Guide to Money in the 2006 Texas Elections*, September 2007.

58. Ibid.

59. Ibid.

60. Texans for Public Justice, *Money in Politex: A Guide to Money in the 2002 Texas Elections*, November 2003.

61. Sorauf, *Money in American Elections*, pp. 298–307.

62. Larry Sabato, *PAC Power* (New York: W. W. Norton, 1985), pp. 126–28.

63. Sorauf, *Money in American Elections*, pp. 306–17.

64. Texans for Public Justice, pp. 7, 10, 11.

65. John Williams and Janet Elliott, "Top Donor Spends Big, Stays in the Background," *Houston Chronicle*, December 22, 2002, p. 1A; and Janet Elliott, "Perry Homes Executive Named to Commission—Houston Builder Governor's Top Contributor," *Houston Chronicle*, September 30, 2003, p. 15A.

66. Samuel H. Barnes and Max Kaase, *Political Action* (Beverly Hills, CA: Sage, 1979), Chapter 2.

67. Lance T. LeLoup, *Politics in America*, 2nd ed. (St. Paul, MN: West Publishing Co., 1989), p. 156.

68. Sidney Verba and Norman H. Nie, *Participation in America* (New York: Harper & Row, 1972) pp. 79–80, 118–19. Seven percent of the sample was not classified.

CHAPTER 8

The Texas Legislature

Questions to Guide Your Reading

1. Would Texas be better served by a highly professional, full-time legislature?

2. Would the interests of Texans be better served if redistricting were done by a nonpartisan board or commission?

3. What skills are required of the presiding officers to be effective?

4. Where is the "real" or substantive work of the legislature done?

5. With thousands of legislative items introduced each session, how does a legislator know what is good or bad policy?

*Leadership by encouragement can be more successful than
leadership by full frontal force.*

—**Joe Straus, Speaker of the Texas House of Representatives, 2009[1]**

The Republican takeover of the Texas House of Representatives in 2003 was a watershed event in state politics. It marked the first GOP majority of that body since the 1870s and ensured the election of veteran lawmaker Tom Craddick of Midland as the first Republican House speaker since Reconstruction. Craddick quickly imposed an autocratic style of leadership over the House and—with the help of Republican Governor Rick Perry and a Republican majority in the state Senate—advanced a conservative GOP agenda. Republican leaders closed a $10 billion revenue shortfall that year by imposing deep cuts in health care and other public services and, in a bitter partisan fight, redrew congressional district lines to give Republicans a majority of the Texas delegation elected to the United States House of Representatives.

But Craddick's heavy-handed tactics soon began to erode his support, even among Republicans. In subsequent elections, Democrats reclaimed several House seats from Republicans who had been loyal to Craddick. It was believed that Craddick had pressured some of the unseated GOP lawmakers to vote against the interests of their own districts on such critical issues as public education. Craddick survived a leadership challenge from a fellow Republican in 2007 but was unseated by Republican Joe Straus of San Antonio in 2009 after Democrats, in the 2008 elections, had narrowed the Republican majority in the 150-member House to 76–74.

Straus had served in the House for only two terms and had never been a committee chairman but emerged as the choice of eleven anti-Craddick Republicans shortly before the 2009 session convened. His election as speaker resulted when 64 Democrats also endorsed his selection. Straus had a much more relaxed leadership style than Craddick, was criticized by some Republicans for securing pivotal support from Democrats, and failed to secure House passage of a key Republican priority—a bill to require voters to have photo identification before casting ballots. But he received mostly positive assessments at the end of the session and claimed to have enough support to be reelected speaker in 2011. His leadership, however, could be cut short if Democrats reclaimed a House majority in the 2010 elections.

The leadership turnover and other recent legislative experiences have reflected some of the enormous social, political, and economic changes that have occurred in Texas during the past generation. Forty years ago, a rural-dominated legislature showed little concern for the problems of urban areas and minority groups. Operating within the context of one-party Democratic control and an interest group system dominated by oil, finance, and agriculture, legislative leaders tied to conservative factions in the Democratic Party pursued selected policies that benefited those sectors of the Texas economy.

Today, Texas is the country's second most populous state and is more than 80 percent urban. The ethnic and racial characteristics of its population have changed, and still more changes are projected in its social composition. Texas is now dominated by the Republican Party, its economy is diversifying, and there are more demands today on the legislature than in the past. The issues and policy questions that confront lawmakers are more complex, and the special interests demanding attention are more numerous and diverse.

Despite these major demographic and political changes, however, lawmakers still have to operate under outdated constitutional restrictions—including strict limits on when they can meet—that were written for a rural state in a bygone era.

LEGISLATIVE FUNCTIONS

The legislature, whose members are elected from districts throughout Texas, is the chief policymaking branch of state government. Its basic role is similar to that of the U.S. Congress at the federal level, though there are major differences between the two institutions. The Texas legislature performs a variety of functions, but its primary task is to decide how conflicts between competing groups and interests are to be resolved. Although often taken for granted, this orderly, institutionalized process of conflict management and resolution is critical to a stable political system.[2]

Enacting Laws

Every two years, the legislature enacts several hundred laws governing our behavior; allocating resources, benefits, and costs; and defining the duties of those institutions and bureaucrats responsible for putting these laws into effect. From local legislation that affects one city or county to general statewide policies and proposals for constitutional amendments, there are literally thousands of ideas advanced for new laws every legislative session. The legislative arena includes a wide range of players in addition to legislators, and lawmaking requires compromise and accommodation of competing ideas and interests.

Budgets and Taxes

The legislature establishes programs providing a variety of public services and sets priorities through the budgetary process. It sets the budgets for the governor, the bureaucracy, and the state courts. It decides whether state taxes should be increased, how high they should be increased, and how the tax burden should be distributed. Indirectly, its actions affect local tax rates as well.

Overseeing State Agencies

Hundreds of laws are passed each legislative session, and the legislature assigns specific state agencies and local governments the responsibility of carrying out the laws on a day-to-day basis. It is ultimately the legislature's responsibility to make sure agencies and bureaucrats are doing what they are charged with by law, and this review, or "oversight," process is achieved through legislative budget hearings, other committee investigations, and program audits.

The Senate further influences policy by confirming or rejecting the governor's appointees to hundreds of state boards and commissions that administer public programs.

Educating the Public

The 181 members of the Texas legislature certainly do not speak with one voice, and on major policy issues, it is inevitable that there will be a variety of opinions and proposed solutions. Individual lawmakers try to inform the public about their own actions and the collective actions of the legislature. They use speeches, letters to constituents, news releases, telephone calls, newsletters, websites, e-mails, and other techniques to explain the legislative process and substantive policy issues.

Representing the Public

The legislature is a representative body whose members are chosen in free elections. This process provides legitimacy to legislative actions and decisions. People may disagree over how "representative" the legislature is in terms of race, ethnicity, gender, or class. Furthermore, many Texans may be indifferent toward or ignorant about public policy. But successful lawmakers must demonstrate concern for the attitudes and demands of their constituents. Legislators use many methods to learn how their constituents feel, including public opinion polls, questionnaires, phone calls, town hall meetings, and personal visits.

INSTITUTIONALIZATION OF THE TEXAS LEGISLATURE

As noted at the beginning of this chapter, the Texas Legislature has undergone significant institutional changes over the past 130 years. Some changes have been due to external factors, such as the development of a two-party system in Texas, changes in the state's interest group system, and complex social and economic problems. Other changes were internal. They included the increased tenure of the legislative membership, changing career and leadership patterns, expanded workload, the development and enforcement of complex rules and procedures, the evolution of professional staffs, and the emergence of partisan divisions. Political scientists describe these developments as **institutionalization**.[3]

Institutionalization varies throughout the fifty states. Some state legislatures are highly professional, while others are not.[4] In some states, salaries are high, turnover is limited, and legislators think in terms of legislative careers. Similarly, some legislatures have developed sophisticated staff and support services. By contrast, in other legislatures members are poorly paid, turnover is high, legislative service is regarded as a part-time activity, and support services are limited. The Texas legislature falls somewhere between those state legislatures that can be classified as highly professional and those that can be classified as amateur or citizen lawmaking bodies (see Table 8–1). The institutionalization process has produced a more professional legislature in Texas, and this development is likely to continue in the future.

Although it is generally assumed that a "professional" state legislature is a more effective policymaking body, there are some indications that this is not always true. In recent years, California, Pennsylvania, New York, and Illinois—states with professional legislatures—have witnessed ugly partisan confrontations, ethical violations, and the decline of civility among legislators.

THE ORGANIZATION AND COMPOSITION OF THE TEXAS LEGISLATURE

Following the oppressive efforts of Governor Edmund J. Davis and the Radical Reconstructionists to centralize power and authority in Texas after the Civil War, the rural delegates who dominated the constitutional convention in 1875 were distrustful,

Professional—Full Time, Large Staff, High Pay, Low Turnover

Alaska	Massachusetts^	Ohio*
California*	Michigan*	Pennsylvania
Florida*	New Jersey	Wisconsin
Illinois	New York	

Professional-Citizen—Moderate Pay, Staff, Turnover, and Time

Alabama	Kentucky	Oregon^
Arkansas*	Louisiana*	South Carolina
Arizona*	Maryland	Tennessee
Colorado*	Minnesota	Texas
Connecticut	Missouri*	Virginia
Delaware	Nebraska*	Washington^
Hawaii	North Carolina	
Iowa^	Oklahoma*	

Citizen—Part-Time, Low Pay, Small staff, High Turnover

Georgia	Montana*	South Dakota*
Idaho	New Hampshire	Utah^
Indiana	New Mexico	Vermont
Kansas	Nevada*	West Virginia
Maine*	North Dakota	Wyoming^
Mississippi	Rhode Island	

*States currently with term limits (fifteen total).
^States in which term limits have been repealed by legislative or court action (six total).

TABLE 8–1   Texas Compared to Other States: Professionalism in the 50 State Legislatures.
Source: National Conference of State Legislatures, unpublished report, 1998; U.S Term Limits, "State Legislative Term Limits," *TermLimits.org,* http://www.termlimits.org/content.asp?pl=18&sl= 19&contentid=19; National Conference of State Legislatures, "The Term Limited States," *NCSL.org,* February 2006, http://www.ncsl.org/Default.aspx? Tabld=14844; National Conference of State Legislatures, "Three Kinds of State Legislatures," *State Legislatures,* 30 (July-August 2004), p. 7; and James D. King, "Changes in Professionalism in U.S. State Legislatures," *Legislative Studies Quarterly* 25 (May 2000), pp. 327–43.

even fearful, of the excesses and abuses of big government. They created a part-time, **bicameral legislature** that included a 31-member Senate and a 150-member House of Representatives. All other states also have bicameral legislatures, except Nebraska, which has a unicameral system with only one lawmaking body of forty-nine members. The sizes of other state senates range from twenty in Alaska to sixty-seven in Minnesota, whereas houses of representatives vary in size from forty in Alaska to 400 in New Hampshire.[5]

Legislative Sessions

To curb lawmakers' power, the Texas constitutional framers limited the **regular legislative session** to a maximum of 140 days every two years but gave the governor the authority to call special sessions when necessary. Lawmakers convene in regular session on the second Tuesday of January in odd-numbered years. **Special sessions** are limited to thirty days each and to subjects submitted by the governor, but there is no limit on the number of special sessions that a governor can call.

There have been periods of frequent special sessions. From midsummer of 1986 through midsummer of 1987, for example, during a lingering budgetary crisis spawned by a depressed oil industry, the legislature convened for its regular 140-day session and four special sessions, two of which lasted the maximum thirty days. The seventy-first legislature in 1989–1990 held six special sessions to deal with school funding and medical expenses for workers injured on the job. The seventy-second legislature had two special sessions in the summer of 1991 to write a new budget, pass a tax bill, make changes in the criminal justice system, and redraw the boundaries of congressional districts. And, as noted earlier, the seventy-eighth legislature had three special sessions in the summer and early fall of 2003 in a protracted, partisan fight over congressional **redistricting**. Governor Rick Perry called one special session in the spring of 2004 and two more in the summer of 2005 to try to lower school property taxes and change the education funding system, but all three were unsuccessful. The legislature finally met those goals in still another special session in the spring of 2006, but only after the Texas Supreme Court had declared the school finance system unconstitutional and given lawmakers a deadline.

Some state officials and government experts believe the Texas legislature should have annual regular sessions, at least for budgetary purposes (see Chapter 13). Only six other state legislatures do not. The change, however, would require a constitutional amendment.

Terms of Office and Qualifications

Article III of the Texas Constitution establishes the structure, membership, and selection of the Texas Legislature. Representatives serve two-year terms, while senators are elected to four-year, staggered terms. A senator has to be a qualified voter, at least twenty-six years old, a resident of Texas for five years preceding his or her election, and a resident of the district from which elected for at least one year. A representative must be a qualified voter, at least twenty-one years old, a Texas resident for two years, and a resident of the district represented for one year.[6] There is no limit on the number of terms an individual can serve in the legislature.

Pay and Compensation

Members of both the House and the Senate and their presiding officers have a base pay of $7,200 per year. This figure is set by the state constitution and can be raised only with voter approval. This is one of the lowest legislative pay levels in the country and was last increased in 1975 by a constitutional amendment that also set lawmakers' per diem, or personal expense allowance, at $30 a day while the legislature is in session.

Legislators proposed a constitutional amendment in 1989 to increase their salaries to more than $20,000 a year, but the voters turned the proposal down by a 2-to-1 margin. The amendment also would have removed voter control over legislative pay and given lawmakers the power to give themselves raises by setting their pay at one-fourth the governor's salary, which the legislature sets and periodically increases.

In 1991, Texas voters approved a constitutional amendment creating a state Ethics Commission that could recommend legislative pay raises to the voters and change per diem on its own. The commission set per diem at $139 per day for the 2009 legislative session.

By 2008, only Alabama, Texas, New Hampshire, and Rhode Island had limits on legislative pay that could be changed only by constitutional amendment. Compensation commissions now recommend legislative pay levels in some states, while legislatures in other states set their own salaries, often with the approval of the voters. In 2008, legislative pay ranged from a high of $116,208 in California, where lawmakers set their own salaries and are considered a fulltime legislature, to a low of $200 a year in New Hampshire, which has annual sessions but a constitutional limit on salaries.[7]

Advocates of higher legislative pay in Texas say it is only fair because legislative service has become much more than a part-time job for many lawmakers, particularly during periods of frequent special sessions. They argue that the present low compensation level restricts legislative service to wealthy individuals or those who have law practices or own businesses in which partners or employees can help take up the slack while they are in Austin. They believe higher pay would broaden the potential pool from which legislators are drawn—and perhaps improve the prospects for quality—by encouraging more salaried working people to run for legislative office. A broader pool of candidates also could broaden the perspectives from which policy issues are viewed and addressed.

The outside personal income of many legislators obviously does suffer while they are in office, but legislative service can also enhance business and professional connections. Critics of higher legislative pay also note that candidates, many of whom spend thousands of dollars to get elected to the legislature, know the pay level before they run for the office. Texas lawmakers also have provided themselves one of the best legislative retirement plans in the country. And they can increase their retirement benefits without voter approval.

Retirement benefits are computed on the basis of state district judges' salaries, which legislators raise periodically, thereby increasing their own retirement benefits as well. Many former legislators receive pensions that are much larger than their paychecks were while they were in office. In 1991, legislators sweetened their retirement plan even more by quietly amending a state employee retirement bill to allow former legislators to receive full retirement benefits at age fifty instead of fifty-five, as set in earlier law, and reduce the required time for service in office. The sponsor of the amendment, Representative Nolan "Buzz" Robnett, a Republican from Lubbock, who, incidentally, was fifty at the time, helped make himself eligible for $1,780 a month in retirement pay, almost triple his legislative salary.[8]

Physical Facilities

The House chamber and representatives' offices have been traditionally located in the west wing of the Texas State Capitol, and the Senate chamber and senators' offices are in the east wing (see Figure 8–1). The pink granite building was completed in 1888, but the growth of state government and periodic renovations created a hodgepodge of cramped legislative offices. After one visitor died in a fire behind the Senate chamber in 1983, it also became obvious that the building had become a firetrap. So the state launched a $187 million capitol building restoration and expansion project in 1990 that included a four-story underground addition to the building. Legislative committee hearing rooms and many lawmakers' offices were relocated from the main building to the underground extension, which is connected to the original capitol and nearby office buildings by tunnels.

When the legislature is in session, access to the floor of each chamber on the second floor of the capitol building is restricted to lawmakers, certain other state officials, some

Oh, how it has changed! The capitol complex (looking north) has expanded over the years to include underground office space, the Supreme Court building to the left, the State Library and Archives to the right, and state office buildings to the north along Congress Avenue.

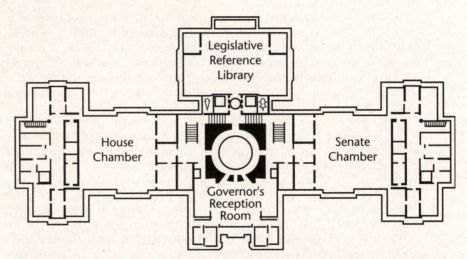

Legislative Reference Library

House Chamber

Senate Chamber

Governor's Reception Room

FIGURE 8–1 Corridors of Power in the Texas Capitol. The second floor of the Texas Capitol, shown here, houses the Senate and House chambers, the Legislative Reference Library, and the Governor's Reception Room.

staff members, and accredited media representatives. The galleries, to which the public is admitted, overlook the chambers from the third floor of the capitol.

In both the House and Senate chambers, members have desks facing the presiding officer's podium, which is flanked by desks of the clerical staff. Unlike the U.S. Congress, where seating is arranged by party affiliation, seats are assigned to state legislators by seniority.

Membership

In 1971, the Texas legislature was overwhelmingly white, male, and Democratic. There were two African Americans in the 150-member House and one in the thirty-one-member

TABLE 8–2   Comparative Profile of Texas Legislators, 1971–2009

	House				Senate			
	1971	**1981**	**2001**	**2009**	**1971**	**1981**	**2001**	**2009**
Democrats	140	112	78	74	29	24	15	12
Republicans	10	38	72	76	2	7	16	19
Males	149	139	120	113	30	30	27	25
Females	1	11	30	37	1	1	4	6
Hispanics	11	17	28	31	1	4	7	6
African Americans	2	13	14	14	1	0	2	2
Asian Americans				1				
Anglos	137	120	108	104	29	27	22	23

Sources: Texas House and Senate rosters, 1971, 1981, 2001, 2009.

Senate. The one African-American senator was also the only woman in the Senate. She was Barbara Jordan of Houston who, two years later, would begin a distinguished career in Congress. Frances Farenthold of Corpus Christi was the only woman in the House. She was a reform-minded lawmaker who was often referred to as the "Den Mother of the Dirty Thirty," a coalition of liberal Democrats and conservative Republicans who challenged the power of House Speaker Gus Mutscher while a major stock fraud scandal involving the speaker was unfolding. In 1972, Farenthold ran a strong race for governor in the Democratic primary but lost a runoff election to Uvalde rancher Dolph Briscoe. There was only one Hispanic senator and eleven Hispanic members of the House. Only twelve legislators were Republicans—ten in the House and two in the Senate.

By 2009, changing political patterns and attitudes, redrawn political boundaries, and court-ordered single-member districts for urban House members had significantly altered the composition of the legislature (see Table 8–2). That year, Republicans had a 19–12 majority in the Senate. The Senate also had two African-American members, six Hispanics, and six women.

House in 2009 had a 76–74 Republican majority, a smaller Republican majority than the 88–62 margin the GOP had in 2003, when it gained its first majority of modern times. The 150 House members in 2009 included fourteen African Americans, thirty-one Hispanics, one Asian American and thirty-seven women. Representation from the urban and suburban areas of the state had grown, reflecting the population shifts accommodated by redistricting.

Business has been the dominant occupation of legislators serving in recent years, followed by law. The House in 2009 included one pharmacist, one dentist, two physicians, one automobile dealer and three restaurant owners. The Senate included one physician, one pharmacist, a retired firefighter and a radio talk-show host.

Legislative Careers

Various career patterns lead to election to the Texas legislature.[9] Lawmakers include former members of city councils and school boards, former prosecutors, former legislative aides, and long-time Democratic and Republican Party activists. Twenty of the thirt... senators in 2009 had previously served in the House. Many first-term legislato... arrive in Austin with relatively little political experience.

Deliberating legislation. With the hundreds of decisions that legislators make on a routine basis, their actions bring together a complex network of communications and influences.

Legislative Turnover

Compared to other states, turnover in the Texas legislature is relatively low.[10] Yet few individuals who serve can be considered career legislators. Only six senators and nine House members entered the 2009 regular session with twenty or more years of legislative service. The average legislative experience in the Senate was thirteen years, while House members had served an average of eight years.

In addition to the effects of redistricting of legislative seats every ten years, turnover is due to the low pay and the personal costs involved in running for public office. While in session, many legislators lose income from their regular sources of employment. Political ambition also is a factor. Many lawmakers who want to move up the political ladder serve only a few terms in the Texas House before running for the Texas Senate, the U.S. Congress, or other state or local offices. Other legislators quit after a few sessions to become lobbyists.

Five senators, including three of the chamber's more senior members, ended their legislative careers in 2006, taking with them a cumulative 112 years of experience in the House and the Senate. Democrats Ken Armbrister of Victoria, Gonzalo Barrientos of Austin, and Republican Jon Lindsay of Houston voluntarily retired. Democrat Frank Madla of San Antonio was unseated in his party's primary, and Republican Todd Staples of Palestine ran for state agriculture commissioner. In the House, former Speaker Pete Laney, a Democrat, also retired after 34 years in the legislature. In addition, twenty-six other House members did not return for the 2007 legislative session. Madla died in a house fire in San Antonio a few months after leaving office, and Armbrister joined Governor Rick Perry's staff as legislative liaison for the 2007 session.

REPRESENTATION AND REDISTRICTING

Many European legislatures use a system called proportional representation, in which legislative seats are allocated on the basis of each party's vote. By contrast, the Texas legislature and most other American legislatures allocate seats geographically on the basis of single-member districts. The long legal and political battles over apportionment and redistricting address some of the fundamental questions of who should be represented and how they should be represented.

The Texas Constitution of 1876 provided that the legislature redraw state representative and senatorial districts every ten years, "at its first session after the publication of each United States decennial census," to reflect changing population patterns. Despite this requirement, members of earlier rural-dominated legislatures were reluctant to apportion the legislative seats equitably to reflect the increased urbanization of the state, and inequities grew. In 1948, Texas voters approved a constitutional amendment creating the Legislative Redistricting Board to carry out redistricting responsibilities if the legislature failed to do so during the required session. The board includes the lieutenant governor, the speaker of the House, the attorney general, the comptroller, and the commissioner of the General Land Office.

But for many more years, the urban areas of the state still were denied equality in representation. In 1960, the House districts ranged in size from 23,602 to 155,393 persons, and Senate districts, 131,970 to 1,243,158.[11] With those disparities in population, it was possible for approximately 33 percent of the state's population to elect a majority of both the Texas House and the Senate.[12] And rural legislators tended to neglect urban problems.

Court Intervention in Redistricting

Equality in redistricting finally came to Texas as a result of federal court intervention. In 1962, the U.S. Supreme Court, in the case of *Baker v. Carr*, applied the principle of equality to congressional redistricting. Then, in the case of *Reynolds v. Sims*, the court held that state legislative districts had to be apportioned on the "one person, one vote" principle. Litigation in 1965 (*Kilgarlin v. Martin*) extended this ruling to Texas, and the "reapportionment revolution" produced dramatic changes in the composition of the Texas legislature.[13] To a large degree, the increased representation of minorities and Republicans in Texas's lawmaking body is a result of the legal and political redistricting battles.

The Texas Senate has always been elected by single-member districts, and after the 1970 census, the application of the equality principle to the Senate resulted in districts that were comparable in size. The issues of racial and partisan gerrymandering—the practice of drawing lines to favor a particular individual or group—were still to be resolved through subsequent litigation and federal legislation.

Rural members of the Texas House also were elected from single-member districts, but in the urban counties that had been allocated more than one representative, the elections were held in multimember districts. Each candidate for a House seat in an urban area had to run for election countywide, a practice that put ethnic and political minorities at a disadvantage because their votes were diluted by the dominant Anglo and Democratic populations.

In 1972, a three-judge federal court ruled that multimember districts in Dallas and Bexar counties were unconstitutional because they diluted the voting strength of African Americans in Dallas and Hispanics in Bexar. Coincidentally, they also diluted the voting strength of Republicans in both counties.

Despite the fact that 50 percent of Bexar County's population was Hispanic, under the countywide, or at-large, election system only one Hispanic from Bexar had served in the Texas House in 1971. Dallas County, which had a large African-American population, had only one African-American House member. Single-member districts in Harris County had been drawn by the Legislative Redistricting Board in 1971, and after the U.S. Supreme Court upheld the lower court's decision regarding Dallas and Bexar Counties, multimember legislative districts were soon eliminated in all other urban counties.

After 1975, Congress put Texas under the provisions of the federal Voting Rights Act, which prohibits the dilution of minority voting strength, requires preclearance of redistricting plans by the Department of Justice, and gives African Americans and Hispanics a strong weapon to use in challenging a redistricting plan in court.

At the beginning of the twenty-first century, however, minorities believed their fight for equal representation was still far from over because the Voting Rights Act was under attack by conservatives. The U.S. Supreme Court, in "reverse discrimination" cases from Texas and Georgia, had ruled that some congressional districts had been illegally gerrymandered to elect minority candidates. And, in another case from Georgia, the high court held in 2003 that states have the right to determine how best to draw legislative and congressional districts to protect minority voters.[14]

Texas Republicans scored huge redistricting victories in 2001, after the legislature failed to redraw its own districts during that year's regular session. Under the state constitution, the task then fell to the five statewide elected officials, four of whom were Republicans, on the Legislative Redistricting Board. The panel drew new legislative maps that helped increase Republican strength in the thirty-one-member Senate to nineteen GOP senators. It also enabled Republicans to capture their first majority of modern times in the 150-member Texas House. With legislative candidates running under the new plan in the 2002 elections, the GOP increased its strength in the House from 72 seats to 88 seats, a margin that cleared the way for state Representative Tom Craddick of Midland, a Republican, to be elected speaker after the regular session convened in 2003. The GOP takeover of the Texas House also gave Republicans the opportunity to redraw the lines for Texas's congressional districts later that year. Republicans prevailed after a bitter partisan fight that included two walkouts by Democratic legislators. The new congressional map gave Republicans a 21–11 majority among members of the U.S. Congress elected from Texas in 2004, ending the congressional careers of several Democratic incumbents. Most of the plan was later upheld by the U.S. Supreme Court. The court, however, ordered the redrawing of some district lines in South Texas to protect minority voting rights. Those changes led to the unseating of a Republican incumbent in 2006, trimming the GOP majority to 20–12 (see "Legislative Redistricting: A Partisan Drama").

Legislative Redistricting: A Partisan Drama

The contentious, nationally publicized fight over congressional redistricting in 2003 was not the Texas legislature's finest hour. But the drama of Democratic lawmakers fleeing across state lines to shut down legislative business in Austin, the bitter partisan rhetoric, and the persistence of the eventual Republican victors vividly illustrated the huge political stakes that were involved.

The Republican takeover of the Texas House in 2003 gave the GOP control of state government, but Democrats still held a 17–15 edge among members of the U.S. Congress elected from Texas. The lines for congressional districts had been redrawn to reflect new census data in 2001 by a federal court, not by the legislature because the Texas House, which still had a Democratic majority in 2001, couldn't agree on a new map with the Republican-dominated Senate. Once Republicans had control of both legislative chambers, the Republican leader of the U.S. House, Congressman Tom DeLay, began urging Texas Republican leaders to redraw the congressional lines to favor more Republican candidates and help their party maintain its narrow majority of the U.S. House. But a redistricting bill died late in the regular legislative session that spring when more than 50 Democratic members of the Texas House fled to Ardmore, Oklahoma, to break a House quorum and prevent the body from conducting business for four days—long enough to miss a deadline for action on the redistricting measure. The Democrats, outnumbered 88–62, didn't have enough votes in the House to defeat the bill outright, but they had enough members to shut down work because a quorum required two-thirds of the members to be present. The Democrats left the state in order to avoid being arrested by state troopers and forced to return to the Capitol. In their absence, Speaker Tom Craddick and the remaining members had placed a "call" on the House, authorizing the sergeant-at-arms to enlist the aid of law enforcement officers to round up the missing members.

Republican leaders, most notably DeLay and Governor Rick Perry, didn't give up. Perry called the legislature back into a 30-day special session

in June to tackle redistricting again. This time, Democrats didn't bolt, and the House easily approved the bill. But the measure died in the Senate, where Democratic senators used the "two-thirds rule" to block action on it. That traditional procedure required two-thirds of the senators to approve debate on any legislation, and Republicans, although they were in the majority, didn't constitute two-thirds of the body. At the end of the first special session, Lieutenant Governor David Dewhurst, a Republican who earlier had been reluctant to force a vote on redistricting, announced that he would bypass the two-thirds rule during a second special session. That prompted eleven Democratic senators to fly to Albuquerque, N.M., breaking a Senate quorum, only minutes before Perry issued a proclamation calling the second special session. The Democrats remained holed up in New Mexico for more than a month, outlasting the entire second session. The only Democratic senator who didn't flee was Ken Armbrister of Victoria, who represented a strongly Republican district.

While the national media listened and watched, the Democrats in Albuquerque and the Republicans in Austin exchanged a barrage of partisan charges and countercharges. The dissident Democrats—who included nine minorities and two Anglos who represented predominantly minority districts—accused the Republicans of trying to redraw congressional districts to dilute the voting strength of Hispanics and African Americans. "This is a shameful return to the days of the Jim Crow laws designed to prevent electoral participation of minorities in the South," said state Senator Leticia Van de Putte of San Antonio, chair of the Senate Democratic Caucus. Dewhurst and the Republican senators denied the charges. They said redistricting would enhance minority voting strength. And they argued that Republicans, with a majority in Texas, were entitled to a majority of congressional seats from the state.[15]

The stalemate finally ended when one of the Democrats, state Senator John Whitmire of

(Continued)

Houston, returned to Texas, announcing that he would continue the fight on the Senate floor. Because Whitmire's return restored the Senate's two-thirds quorum, the remaining dissidents returned as well. Perry called a third special session in September, and Republican majorities in the House and the Senate approved different versions of a redistricting map. Final approval, however, was delayed for several days because House and Senate Republicans, ironically, continued to fight among themselves over a handful of districts. The main hangup was over West Texas, where Craddick insisted that his hometown, Midland, get a congressional district it could dominate. In the end, Craddick got his wish, but not before DeLay visited Austin to personally help negotiate between House and Senate members of the conference committee that drew the final map.

The third special session ended on October 12, and Perry quickly signed the new redistricting plan. Democrats filed suit in federal court to block the law, but a three-judge federal panel approved it in time for the 2004 elections, which gave Republicans 21 of Texas's 32 congressional seats. Ruling in 2006, the United States Supreme Court upheld most of the plan. The high court, however, held that one South Texas district was unconstitutional because it didn't protect the voting rights of Hispanics. Subsequent revisions in the plan led to the defeat of one Republican congressman in 2006, trimming the Republican edge in the Texas congressional delegation to 20–12.

LEGISLATIVE LEADERSHIP

The highly institutionalized leadership structure found in the U.S. Congress is only now beginning to emerge in the Texas legislature—and only to a limited extent. The Texas legislature is a part-time institution that, until recently, was dominated by a small group of Democratic lawmakers. With no significant party opposition or minority representation until recent years, legislative leadership was highly personal and dependent on the political relationships between the presiding officers and key legislators. Recent Republican growth in the statehouse, however, is forcing changes.

House Leadership

The presiding officer of the House of Representatives is the **speaker**, who is elected by the House from among its membership. With the long tenures of Gib Lewis and his immediate predecessor in the speaker's office, Bill Clayton, there wasn't a contested speaker's race between 1975 and 1991 (see Table 8–3). Lewis's decision not to seek reelection in 1992 prompted several House members to announce for the post. But veteran Democratic Representative James E. "Pete" Laney, a farmer–businessman from Hale Center, secured the support of the necessary majority of House members several weeks before the 1993 legislature convened, and his election on the opening day of the session was unopposed.

Laney served five terms as speaker and, although he was a Democrat, enjoyed the support of many Republican House members. Continuing a bipartisan tradition, he appointed several Republicans to chair House committees. But Republicans, after winning a strong majority of House seats in the 2002 elections, elected state Representative Tom Craddick, a Republican from Midland, to succeed Laney as presiding officer in 2003. Craddick, a House member since 1969, became the first Republican speaker of modern times. Laney, who had won re-election to his West Texas district in 2002, remained in the House, becoming the first former speaker in years to return to a seat on the House floor after having been presiding officer. Laney also was reelected from

TABLE 8–3   Presiding Officers of the Texas Legislature, 1951–2009

Lieutenant Governors	Party	When Served	Home
Ben Ramsey	Democrat	1951–1961*	San Augustine
Preston Smith	Democrat	1963–1969	Lubbock
Ben Barnes	Democrat	1969–1973	DeLeon
Bill Hobby, Jr.	Democrat	1973–1991	Houston
Bob Bullock	Democrat	1991–1999	Hillsboro
Rick Perry	Republican	1999–2000	Haskell
Bill Ratliff	Republican	2000–2003	Mt. Pleasant
David Dewhurst	Republican	2003–	Houston

Speakers	Party	When Served	Home
Reuben Senterfitt	Democrat	1951–1955	San Saba
Jim T. Lindsey	Democrat	1955–1957	Texarkana
Waggoner Carr	Democrat	1957–1961	Lubbock
James A. Turman	Democrat	1961–1963	Gober
Byron M. Tunnell	Democrat	1963–1965	Tyler
Ben Barnes	Democrat	1965–1969	DeLeon
Gus Mutscher	Democrat	1969–1972	Brenham
Rayford Price	Democrat	1972–1973	Palestine
Price Daniel, Jr.	Democrat	1973–1975	Liberty
Bill Clayton	Democrat	1975–1983	Springlake
Gib Lewis	Republican	1983–1993	Fort Worth
James E. "Pete" Laney	Republican	1993–2003	Hale Center
Tom Craddick	Republican	2003–2009	Midland
Joe Straus	Republican	2009–	San Antonio

*Ben Ramsey resigned as lieutenant governor on September 18, 1961 upon his appointment to the Railroad Commission. The office was vacant until Preston Smith took office in 1963.
Sources: Texas Legislative Council, *Presiding Officers of the Texas Legislature*, 1846–1982 (Austin, TX: Texas Legislative Council, 1982); and Texas Legislature Online, http://www.legis.state.tx.us/.

his district in 2004 but didn't seek reelection in 2006, ending a thirty-four-year legislative career.

It is illegal for a speaker candidate to make outright promises in return for members' support. But, continuing a tradition, Craddick gave his key supporters choice leadership positions when the new speaker exercised one of his most significant formal powers and made his committee assignments. Legislators know that the earlier they hop onto a winning bandwagon in a speaker's race, the better chance they will have at getting their preferred committee assignments or the opportunity to advance their legislative programs. Sometimes, however, choosing the winning candidate is difficult because the campaigning is largely conducted behind the scenes with candidates making personal pleas to individual House members.

Until the 1950s, it was unusual for a speaker to serve more than one two-year term. The position was circulated among a small group of legislators who domina[...] House. Clayton, a lawmaker from Springlake in West Texas, set what was [...] by serving four consecutive terms before retiring in 1983. Lewis of Fort Wo[...] each surpassed Clayton's record by serving five terms.

Assisting in the heavy workload. As the legislative workload has become increasingly complex, legislators have expanded their capitol and district staff. Senator Jeff Wentworth (R-San Antonio) meets with a legislative aide in the Senate chamber.

Unlike most of their predecessors, recent speakers have devoted long hours to the job and kept large fulltime staffs. With the complexities of a growing state putting more demands on the legislative leadership, recent Senate leaders (lieutenant governors) also have made their jobs virtually fulltime and also have hired large staffs of specialists to research issues and help develop legislation. The presiding officers also depend on key committee chairmen to take the lead in pushing through their legislative priorities.

During Laney's speakership, the state completed a multibillion-dollar expansion of its prison system, overhauled criminal justice laws, and enacted a school finance law that addressed a Texas Supreme Court order for more equity in education spending. In a bipartisan endeavor, Laney actively supported then-Governor George W. Bush's unsuccessful effort to replace a large chunk of local school property taxes with higher state taxes in 1997. He also encouraged opposing sides to find common ground on other major issues, but one of his own priorities was to improve the way the House conducted its business. Laney won significant changes in House rules that produced, in the view of many House members, a more democratic lawmaking process than under previous speakers. But Craddick, his successor, exercised a more authoritarian style of leadership.

Backed by a Republican majority, Craddick was a key figure in the legislature's tight-fisted approach to drafting the new state budget in 2003, which cut spending in many areas to bridge a $10 billion revenue shortfall. He was a strong opponent of raising state taxes, although he insisted the legislature enact a separate law allowing university governing boards to raise college tuition. Craddick also was a key figure in the legislature's enactment of the redistricting bill to increase the number of Republicans elected to Congress from Texas. He was a consistently tough negotiator. "He's the toughest, hardest trader I've ever met. When you start trading with the speaker, it's tough trading," said state Senator Steve Ogden, a Republican from Bryan and a longtime friend of Craddick's.[16]

Craddick continued to deal a difficult hand with the Senate and Lieutenant Governor David Dewhurst in prolonged attempts during 2005 to draft a new school funding system. During the regular session and two special sessions that year, the House and the Senate repeatedly failed to agree on how to trade higher state taxes for reductions in local school property taxes. Finally, faced with a Texas Supreme Court order for school funding changes during a 2006 special session, Craddick endorsed a plan promoted by Governor Rick Perry and helped win enactment of an expanded business tax and a higher cigarette tax to help pay for school tax reductions. He also led the House in reaching agreement with Dewhurst and the Senate on a teacher pay raise and other educational improvements.

By 2007, Craddick's speakership was under attack from some Republicans as well as Democrats. His iron-fisted style was partly blamed for the defeat of several incumbent Republican House members in 2006. Critics said the speaker had forced the lawmakers to vote against the best interests of their districts on such important issues as education, thus making them vulnerable to challengers. Craddick survived a challenge at the beginning of the 2007 session, when he was reelected to a third term as presiding officer. In the closing days of the session, however, he faced an open rebellion on the House floor, hanging on to the speaker's post by refusing to recognize motions to depose him. By the time the session adjourned in late spring, several Republican and Democratic House members had announced they would challenge Craddick for speaker when the next regular session convened in January 2009.

Craddick's tenure was effectively ended when Democrats won additional House seats in the 2008 elections, trimming the Republican House majority to 76–74. Several weeks later, eleven anti-Craddick Republicans, meeting behind closed doors, selected Republican Joe Straus of San Antonio as their choice for speaker. Straus promptly won the endorsement of sixty-four Democrats and easily won election as speaker when the 2009 session convened.

From the outset, Straus, then forty-nine, faced two major obstacles. Beginning only his third term in the House, he was the most inexperienced speaker in recent Texas history—and he was a Republican who owed his election primarily to Democrats. The House's work got off to a slower-than-normal start that session, thanks to the leadership turnover and Straus' inexperience and more-relaxed leadership style. The new speaker appointed Democrats to leadership positions, but some Democrats complained because he named Republicans to chair most of the major committees. Outmaneuvered by Democrats in a late-session parliamentary fight, Straus failed to win House approval of the Republicans' top legislative priority, a bill that would have required voters to have photo identification cards.

Straus nevertheless was well liked personally by his House colleagues, both Democrats and Republicans, and received generally favorable marks when the session ended. Despite the loss of the voter ID bill, Straus helped unite the House's Republican caucus, said Representative Byron Cook, Republican of Corsicana, an ally of the new speaker. "He has now proven himself to Republican members," Cook said.[17] But questions about his leadership style, particularly among members of Craddick's former team, lingered. "I like Joe personally. I just am not sure a total hands-off leadership style works,"

A bipartisan speaker? Joe Straus (R-San Antonio) challenged Tom Craddick for speaker at the beginning of the 2009 legislative session. His election was atypical in that the majority of his support came from Democratic members of the House.

said Representative Beverly Woolley, Republican of Houston, who had chaired a major committee under Craddick. "Somebody's got to be looking at the big picture and making sure it's all coordinated."[18]

Assessing his own leadership at the end of the session, Straus said he believed he had restored civility to the House. "There may be a few voices out there who want to rewind the clock," he said. "They miss the point that leadership by encouragement can be more successful than leadership by full frontal force. Members (legislators) who sit in their seats waiting to be told what to do will never be happy in my administration."[19]

Straus claimed enough pledges of support from House members to win reelection as speaker in 2011. Nevertheless, Democrats, despite their key support in 2009, were expected to challenge him if they won a majority of House seats in the 2010 elections.

The speaker appoints a speaker pro tempore, or assistant presiding officer, who is usually a close ally. In 1981, Speaker Clayton named the first African American, Representative Craig Washington of Houston, to the post. Although Clayton was a rural conservative and Washington was an urban liberal, Washington proved to be a critical member of the speaker's team. He also exercised considerable influence in the House on a wide range of issues of importance to minorities. Ten years later, Gib Lewis named another African-American legislator, Representative Wilhelmina Delco of Austin, as the first woman speaker pro tempore. Speaker Joe Straus, who owed his election in 2009 to the key support of Democrats, appointed Democratic Representative Craig Eiland of Galveston to the post.

The membership of most House committees is determined partly by seniority. The speaker has total discretion, however, in naming committee chairs and vice chairs and in appointing all the members of procedural committees, including the influential Calendars Committee, which will be described in more detail later in this chapter. Under a rules change in 2003, Craddick also had total discretion—without regard for seniority—in appointing the budget-writing House Appropriations Committee, and he bumped some senior Democratic members from the panel. Seniority was restored to Appropriations appointments in 2009 in a rules change under Straus.

The Lieutenant Governor

The lieutenant governor is chosen by the voters in a statewide election to serve a four-year term as presiding officer of the Senate. Unlike the vice president of the United States—his or her counterpart in the federal government, who has only limited legislative functions—the lieutenant governor has traditionally been the Senate's legislative leader. This office, which is elected independently of the governor, has often been called the most powerful office in state government because of the lieutenant governor's opportunity to merge a statewide electoral base into a dominant legislative role.[20] Lieutenant governors, however, get most of their power from rules set by the senators, not from the constitution.

The lieutenant governor's power is based in part on the same coalitional strategies that are used by the speaker through committee assignments and relationships with interest groups. But the lieutenant governor has traditionally had more direct control over the Senate's agenda than the speaker has over the House's. Under longstanding Senate rules, the lieutenant governor determines when—and if—a committee-approved bill will be brought up for a vote by the full Senate. In the House, the order of floor debate is determined by the Calendars Committee. Although that key panel is appointed by the speaker and is sensitive to the speaker's wishes, it represents an intermediate step that the lieutenant governor doesn't have to encounter.

The lieutenant governor also has had more formal control over the membership of Senate committees than the speaker has over House panels. Under its rules, the Senate has allowed the lieutenant governor to appoint members of all standing committees without regard to seniority or any other restrictions.

The Senate has a president pro tempore, or assistant presiding officer, who is chosen by senators from among their membership. This position is rotated among the senators on a seniority basis. It is held for a limited period, and the holder of the position is third in line of succession to the governorship. There is a tradition that the governor and the lieutenant governor both allegedly "leave" the state on the same day so that the president pro tempore can serve as "governor for a day" at one point during his or her term.

Bill Hobby, a quiet-spoken media executive who served a record eighteen years as lieutenant governor before voluntarily leaving the office in January 1991, patiently sought consensus among senators on most major issues and rarely took the lead in promoting specific legislative proposals. One notable exception occurred in 1979, when Hobby tried to force Senate approval of a presidential primary bill opposed by most Democratic senators. After Hobby served notice that he would alter the Senate's traditional operating procedure to give the bill special consideration, twelve Democratic senators, dubbed the "Killer Bees," hid out for several days to break a quorum and keep the Senate from conducting business. They succeeded in killing the bill and reminding Hobby that the senators set the rules.

Hobby's successor, Bob Bullock, had demonstrated strong leadership and a mercurial personality during sixteen years as state comptroller. On taking office as lieutenant governor, he had major policy changes in mind for state govern.

impatient to see them carried out by the legislature. Unlike Hobby, Bullock took the lead in making proposals and then actively lobbying for them. During his first session in 1991, he reportedly had shouting matches with some lawmakers behind closed doors and one day abruptly and angrily adjourned the Senate when not enough members were present for a quorum at the scheduled starting time. But his experience and knowledge of state government and his tireless work habits won the respect of most senators and their support for most of his proposals.

Bullock, a Democrat, strengthened his leadership role during the 1993 and 1995 sessions and was actively involved in every major issue that the Senate addressed. Recognizing that increases in Republican strength after the 1992 and 1994 elections made the Senate more conservative than it had been in several years, and eager to strengthen his support in the business community, Bullock saw to it that compromises on major issues—including some long sought by business—were reached behind closed doors before they were made public. This approach kept controversy to a minimum and defused partisanship, but it distressed consumer advocates and environmentalists, who felt excluded from the process. It also prompted remarks that the Senate had abandoned democracy. There were so many unanimous or near-unanimous votes in the Senate in 1993 that some House members joked that those senators who wanted to show dissent voted "aye" with their eyes closed.[21]

Bullock played a less active role during the 1997 session, after Republicans, for the first time since Reconstruction, had won a majority of Senate seats. He was strongly supportive of some key legislation, including a statewide water conservation and management plan, but he did little to promote a property tax relief effort that Governor Bush had made his highest priority for the session. One key element of Bush's proposal, an increase in state taxes as a partial trade-off for lower school district taxes, died primarily because of strong Senate opposition, which Bullock didn't try to defuse.

He was a legislator's legislator. Former Lieutenant Governor Bob Bullock, who retired in 1999 and died later that year, was often perceived to be more powerful than the governors with whom he served.

A few days after the 1997 session ended, Bullock surprised the Texas political community by announcing that he would not seek reelection in 1998. The former state leader, who had a history of health problems, was later diagnosed with lung cancer, and he died in June 1999.

After defeating Democrat John Sharp in a hard-fought race in 1998, former Agriculture Commissioner Rick Perry became Texas's first Republican lieutenant governor of modern times in 1999. Perry not only had to follow in Bullock's legendary footsteps, he also had to preside over the Senate during a session overshadowed by Governor George W. Bush's anticipated presidential race. The new lieutenant governor had the advantage, though, of entering the 1999 session with a $6 billion state budgetary surplus and a rare absence of emergencies. Perry lost one of his top priorities, a pilot project to allow students in low-performing public schools to use state-paid vouchers to transfer to private schools. But generally he received high marks for his performance during the session, from both Democrats and Republicans. As one senator observed, "He might not have used the Bullock style of cracking heads or the woodshed" to force legislative solutions. "He did effectively bring people together and kept us from having any meltdowns."[22] Perry was more low-key than Bullock, perhaps choosing to learn more about the Senate and its members before plunging into potential controversies. Nevertheless, he was credited with helping Republican and Democratic lawmakers negotiate a compromise on one of the key legislative packages of the session—a series of tax cuts, teacher pay raises, and other increased education spending.

Perry was elected to a lieutenant governor's term that wasn't to expire until January 2003. But in anticipation of Governor Bush's presidential race, the legislature in 1999 approved a constitutional amendment—which Texas voters later endorsed—to make it clear that Perry would have to give up the lieutenant governor's job in midterm if he were promoted to fill a vacancy in the governor's office. After Bush resigned the governorship in December 2000 to become president, Perry was promoted to governor. And, acting under the new constitutional amendment, senators elected state Senator Bill Ratliff, Republican of Mount Pleasant, to serve as lieutenant governor during the 2001 session.

Ratliff, a former chairman of the Senate Education and Finance committees, was businesslike in his role as presiding officer, and he generally received favorable reviews. He appointed the first African American, state Senator Rodney Ellis, Democrat of Houston, to chair the budget-writing Finance Committee. He also parted ways with most Republican senators and supported Ellis's bill to strengthen the state law against hate crimes, which passed that session. And Ratliff blocked a bill that would have removed state legal restrictions against Native Americans operating casinos on their reservations in Texas. At the end of the 2001 session, Ratliff announced that he would seek election to the lieutenant governor's post in 2002. But several days later, admitting he didn't have the stomach for the compromises often involved in a statewide race, he announced that he had changed his mind and would seek reelection to his Senate seat instead. "I do love policy-making, but I do not love politics," he said.[23] After winning reelection to the Senate in 2002 and serving during the regular and special sessions in 2003, Ratliff resigned in early 2004, expressing weariness after 15 years in the legislative arena.

Republican David Dewhurst won the 2002 lieutenant governor's race over Democrat John Sharp, who had narrowly lost the same office to Rick Perry in 1998. A wealthy businessman, Dewhurst had no legislative experience when he became the Senate's presiding officer in January 2003. His only experience in elected office had been his four previous years as state land commissioner, but he moved quickly to establish credibility

It's more than presiding. Lieutenant Governor David Dewhurst, elected in 2002 and reelected in 2006, presides over the Senate. Strongly independent and skillful in his use of the resources of his office, he has led the Senate on issues that have come into conflict with the speaker and governor.

as a leader. He appointed respected legislative insiders to key staff positions and spent many hours studying issues and meeting with individual senators. Although Republicans held a 19–12 Senate majority, he continued the tradition of appointing both Republicans and Democrats to leadership positions.

Dewhurst agreed with Governor Rick Perry and Speaker Tom Craddick that the legislature would bridge a $10 billion revenue shortfall and write a new state budget without increasing state taxes. But he and the Senate helped to minimize some of the spending cuts by insisting that lawmakers tap into nontax revenue, such as the state's "Rainy Day" savings account. On such budgetary details and other matters, including how quickly the legislature should move to improve the school finance system, Dewhurst sometimes differed with Perry and Craddick. Their differences stemmed partly from Dewhurst's independent nature, which was bolstered by the fact that he—not special interest groups—had largely funded his election to the state's powerful number two office. The Senate's rules also required the lieutenant governor to seek more consensus among senators than the speaker normally has to do in the House. Legislation traditionally wasn't approved in the Senate without the consent of two-thirds of the senators, which meant that the twelve Democratic senators had enough clout to force some budgetary concessions.

Dewhurst's leadership was severely challenged during the bitter partisan fight over congressional redistricting that took three special sessions in the summer and fall of 2003 to resolve. Democratic senators blocked a House-passed redistricting bill during the first special session by using a Senate tradition that required two-thirds of the senators to approve debate on any legislation. After Dewhurst announced that he would bypass that procedure—known as the "two-thirds rule"—to allow a redistricting bill to be passed on a simple majority vote during the second special session, eleven of the Senate's twelve Democrats fled to Albuquerque, N.M., where they remained for more than a month. Their flight, which received national media coverage, deprived the Senate of a quorum and the ability to conduct any business during the entire, 30-day second special session. It also severely damaged the Senate's tradition of personal and partisan cooperation. Democratic and Republican senators exchanged verbal attacks across state lines, with Dewhurst also catching much of the Democrats' anger. The ill feelings increased when Republican senators voted to impose sanctions, including thousands of dollars in fines, on the absentee Democrats. The boycotting senators eventually returned to Austin, and the legislature approved a congressional redistricting bill favoring Republicans during a third special session. The Republicans waived the fines, and Dewhurst immediately began working behind the scenes to restore the Senate's ability to conduct business in a civil, bipartisan fashion.

As noted earlier, Dewhurst was unable in 2005 to negotiate a compromise with Speaker Craddick over changes in the school funding system. But faced with the Texas Supreme Court order, he joined Craddick in backing the governor's tax trade-off proposal

A Voter ID Bill Suffers a Serious Senate Disease—and a Relapse in the House

Republicans had a strong majority in the Texas legislature during the 2007 session, but one of their top priorities—a bill that would have required Texas voters to produce a form of photo identification before casting ballots—died, thanks to the Senate's two-thirds "rule" and two ailing Democratic senators. An effort to revive the measure in 2009 failed as well, this time in the House.

Republicans said the voter ID bill was an essential protection against voter fraud, but Democratic opponents argued that it was an effort to discourage minority and elderly voters, who primarily vote for Democratic candidates, from going to the polls. The bill won easy approval in the Republican-dominated House in 2007 but ran aground in the Senate, where eleven Democratic senators, the minimum needed to block legislation, remained steadfast against it.

The Senate's rules, in effect, require two-thirds of the senators present to approve debate on any bill.

One of the Democrats, Senator Mario Gallegos of Houston, missed much of the session, recuperating from a liver transplant, and Republican Lieutenant Governor David Dewhurst could have won approval of the bill in Gallegos' absence. But Dewhurst agreed to give Gallegos advance notice and time to get to Austin before taking a vote on the controversial measure.

After Gallegos had returned to Austin, Dewhurst tried to win Senate approval of the bill one day when another Democratic senator, Carlos Uresti of San Antonio, was out of action (or so Dewhurst thought) with a stomach virus. Notified by other Democrats of the pending vote, Uresti rushed to the Senate chamber in time to cast a vote against the bill and then hurried to the senators' private lounge to vomit.[24]

Uresti soon recovered, but the voter ID bill didn't. During the 2009 session, Dewhurst and Republican senators bypassed the two-thirds rule to win Senate approval of another voter identification measure. The bill died in the House late in the session, thanks to parliamentary wrangling by Democratic legislators.

during the 2006 special session. Dewhurst was also instrumental in getting a teacher pay raise and other educational changes included in the legislation.

Dewhurst was successful in getting several legislative goals passed in 2007, but he lost one of his and fellow Republicans' top priorities, a bill that would have required Texas voters to have photo identification cards before voting. That bill, which sparked a major partisan fight, was approved by the House but died in the Senate, when Democratic senators used the two-thirds rule to block it. Then Dewhurst angered Democrats during the 2009 session when he and Republican senators bypassed the two-thirds rule—the second time in six years—to win Senate approval of the voter identification bill. But, ironically, the measure died in the House that session (see "A Voter ID Bill Suffers a Serious Senate Disease—and a Relapse in the House").

Dewhurst's insistence on winning approval of the voter ID bill, even to the point of changing the Senate's rules to do so, was widely viewed as political. He was believed to be considering a race for the U.S. Senate, anticipating that U.S. Senator Kay Bailey Hutchison would resign her seat to challenge Governor Rick Perry in the 2010 Republican primary.

INFLUENCE AND CONTROL OVER THE LEGISLATIVE PROCESS

The power of each presiding officer to appoint committees and determine which committee will have jurisdiction over a specific bill gives the speaker and the lieutenant governor tremendous influence over the lawmaking process.

The speaker and the lieutenant governor control the legislative process through the application of rules, including those set in the state constitution and those adopted by the House and the Senate. Each presiding officer is advised on procedures by a parliamentarian. The speaker and the lieutenant governor do not participate in House or Senate debate on bills and usually attempt to present an image of neutral presiding officers. Their formal powers, however, are further strengthened by their informal relationships with their committee leaders and interest groups. And, with the notable exceptions of the separate walkouts by House and Senate Democrats during the 2003 redistricting battle, the speaker and the lieutenant governor rarely lose control of the process.

In the Senate, the lieutenant governor can vote only to break a tie. The speaker can vote on any issue in the House but normally abstains from voting except to break a tie or to send a signal to encourage reluctant or wavering House members to vote a particular way on an issue.

The Leadership Teams

Traditionally, there has been no formal division along party lines or a formal system of floor leaders in either the Texas House or the Senate. The long-time, Democratic-dominated legislative system with the speaker's and lieutenant governor's control of committee appointments did not produce a leadership structure comparable to that of the U.S. Congress. The committee chairs constitute the speaker's and lieutenant governor's teams and usually act as their unofficial floor leaders in developing and building support for the leadership's legislative priorities. Most chairs are philosophically, if not always politically, aligned with the presiding officers.

THE COMMITTEE SYSTEM

The committee system is the backbone of the legislative process, and it is molded by the lieutenant governor and the speaker.[25] It is a screening process that decides the fate of most legislation.

The committee is where technical drafting errors and oversights in bills can be corrected and where compromise can begin to work for those bills that do eventually become law. Typically about a fourth of the bills proposed during a regular session win final legislative approval. (For example, this number equaled 1,742 of the 6,374 bills and constitutional amendments filed during the 2007 session.) Most that don't make it die in a Senate or a House committee, many without ever being heard. Rarely does a committee kill a bill on an outright vote because there are much easier, less obvious ways to scuttle legislation. A bill can be gutted, or so drastically amended or weakened, that even its sponsor can hardly recognize it. Or a bill can simply be ignored.

Committee chairs have considerable power over legislation that comes to their committees. They may kill bills by simply refusing to schedule them for a hearing. Or, after a hearing, a chair may send a bill to a subcommittee that he or she stacks with members opposed to the legislation, thus allowing the bill to die slowly and quietly in the legislative deep freeze. Even if a majority of committee members want to approve a bill, the chair can simply refuse to recognize such a motion. Most chairs, however, are sensitive to the wishes of the presiding officers. If the speaker or the lieutenant governor wants a bill to win committee approval or another measure to die in committee, a chair usually will comply.

Referral to a subcommittee doesn't always mean the death of a bill. Subcommittees also help committees distribute the workload. They work out compromises, correct technical problems in bills, or draft substitute legislation to accommodate competing interest groups.

It gets crowded in those small meeting rooms. On occasion, committees meet in the Senate chamber. Shown here is a meeting of the Senate Committee on State Affairs.

Standing Committees

The number and names of committees are periodically revised under House and Senate rules, but there have been relatively few major changes in the basic committee structure in recent years. During the 2009 session, the Senate had eighteen **standing committees**, varying in membership from five to fifteen. Additionally, there was the Committee of the Whole Senate. There were thirty-five standing committees in the House, with memberships ranging from five to twenty-seven (see Table 8–4).

TABLE 8–4   Senate and House Standing Committees, Eighty-First Legislature (2009)

Senate Committees	Number of Members
Administration	7
Agriculture and Rural Affairs	5
Business and Commerce	9
Committee of the Whole Senate	31
Criminal Justice	7
Economic Development	5
Education	9
Finance	15
Government Organization	7
Health and Human Services	9
Higher Education	5
Intergovernmental Relations	5
International Relations and Trade	7
Jurisprudence	7
Natural Resources	11
Nominations	7
State Affairs	9
Transportation and Homeland Security	9
Veteran Affairs and Military Installations	5

House Committees	Number of Members
Agriculture and Livestock	9
Appropriations	27
Border and Intergovernmental Affairs	9
Business and Industry	11
Calendars	13
Corrections	11
County Affairs	9
Criminal Jurisprudence	11
Culture, Recreation, and Tourism	9
Defense and Veterans Affairs	9
Elections	9
Energy Resources	9
Environmental Regulation	9
Federal Economic Stabilization Funding, Select	9
General Investigating & Ethics	5
Higher Education	9
House Administration	11

TABLE 8–4   *(Continued)*

Human Services	9
Insurance	9
Judiciary and Civil Jurisprudence	11
Land & Resource Management	9
Licensing and Administrative Procedures	9
Local and Consent Calendars	11
Natural Resources	11
Pensions, Investments & Financial Services	9
Public Education	11
Public Health	11
Public Safety	9
Redistricting	15
Rules and Resolutions	11
State Affairs	15
Technology, Economic Development, and Workforce	9
Transportation	11
Urban Affairs	11
Ways and Means	11

Source: Texas Legislature Online, *Legislative Reports for the 81st Legislature, Regular Session, 2009.*

Most of these committees are substantive. That is, they hold public hearings and evaluate bills related to their particular subject areas, such as higher education, natural resources, or public health. A few committees are procedural, such as the Rules and Resolutions Committee, which handles many routine congratulatory resolutions, and the Calendars Committee, which schedules bills for debate by the full House.

Some committees play more dominant roles in the lawmaking process than others, particularly in the House. The House State Affairs Committee, for example, handles many more major statewide bills than the Committee on Culture, Recreation and Tourism or the Committee on Agriculture and Livestock. The House Urban Affairs and County Affairs committees handle several hundred bills of importance to local governments each session. The importance of a committee is determined by the area of public policy over which it has jurisdiction or by its role in the House's operating procedure.

The House **Calendars Committee** historically has had more life-and-death power over legislation than any other committee because it sets the order of debate on the House floor. During each regular session, it kills hundreds of bills that have been approved by various substantive committees by refusing to schedule them for debate by the full House or scheduling them so late in the session they don't have time to win Senate approval. This committee traditionally works closely with the speaker and is one means by which the speaker and the speaker's team control the House. Although many legislators complain about the committee killing their priority bills, some lawmakers defend the panel as a means of keeping controversial legislation—on which many members would rather not have to cast votes—from reaching the House floor.

The state budget is the single most important bill enacted by the legislature because, through it, lawmakers determine how much money is spent on the state's public programs and services. In the House, the Appropriations Committee takes th in drafting state budgets, while the House Ways and Means Committee normally is responsible for producing any tax or revenue measures necessary to balance the budget.

The two most important committees in the Senate are the Finance Committee, which handles the budget and, usually, tax bills, and the State Affairs Committee, which, like its House counterpart, handles a variety of legislation of major, statewide importance.

Although committees have general subject areas of responsibility, legislative rules allow the lieutenant governor and the speaker some latitude in assigning bills. The presiding officer can ensure the death of a bill by sending it to a committee known to oppose it or can guarantee quick approval of a measure by referring it to a receptive, or friendly, panel.

Conference Committees

Legislation must be passed in exactly the same form by the House and the Senate. If one chamber refuses to accept the other's version of a bill, a **conference committee** can try to resolve the differences. Conference committees of five senators and five representatives are appointed by the presiding officers. A compromise bill has to be approved by at least three senators and three House members who serve on the conference committee before it is sent back to the full House and the full Senate for subsequent approval or rejection. Over the years, conference committees have drafted legislation in forms dramatically different from earlier versions approved by the House or the Senate. But since a conference panel is supposed to do no more than adjust the differences between the House and the Senate versions of a bill, both chambers have to pass a concurrent resolution to allow a conference committee to add significant new language.

Special Committees

Special or **select committees** are occasionally appointed by the governor, the lieutenant governor, and the speaker to study major policy issues, such as tax equity or school finance. These panels usually include private citizens as well as legislators, and they usually recommend legislation. Standing legislative committees also study issues in their assigned areas during the interims between sessions, and the presiding officers can ask them to conduct special investigations or inquiries pertaining to governmental matters.

RULES AND PROCEDURES ●

Laws are made in Texas according to the same basic process followed by the U.S. Congress and other state legislatures.[26] But, as the discussion of the committee system already has indicated, the rules that determine how and when legislation is considered are complex and loaded with traps where legislation can be killed. One often hears the remark around the capitol that "there are a lot more ways to kill a bill than to pass one." Legislators and lobbyists who master the rules can wield a tremendous amount of influence over the lawmaking process. The House and the Senate each has a detailed set of rules governing the disposition of legislation, and each has a parliamentarian to help interpret them.

The simplified outline of the process by which a bill becomes a law starts with the introduction of a bill in the House or the Senate and its referral to a committee by the presiding officer, which constitutes first **reading** (see Figure 8–2). That is the only reading that most bills will ever get.

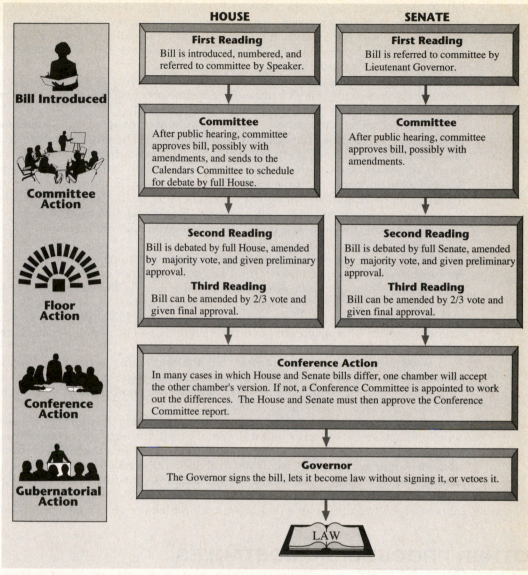

FIGURE 8–2 Basic Steps in the Texas Legislative Process.

A bill that wins committee approval can be considered on second reading by the full House or Senate, where it is debated and often amended. Some amendments are designed to improve a bill, whereas others are designed to kill it by loading it down with controversial or objectionable provisions that will prompt legislators to vote against it. Still other amendments that may be punitive toward particular individuals or groups are sometimes offered. Such an amendment, which may be temporarily added to a bill only to be removed before the measure becomes law, is designed to give a group or perhaps a local official a message that the sponsoring legislator expects his or her wishes to be heeded on a particular issue. Lawmakers also may offer amendments that they know have little chance of being approved merely to make favorable political points with constituents or interest groups.

If a bill is approved on second reading, it has to win one more vote on third reading before it goes to the other chamber for the same process, beginning with its referral to a committee.

If the second chamber approves the bill without any changes, or amendments, it then goes to the governor for signature into law or **veto**. The governor also can allow a bill to become law without his or her signature. This procedure is just the opposite of the pocket veto power afforded the president of the United States. If the president does not sign a bill approved by Congress by a certain deadline, it is automatically vetoed. If the governor of Texas does not sign or veto a bill by a certain deadline, it becomes law. A veto can be overridden and the bill allowed to become law by a two-thirds vote of both houses, although this process is rarely attempted given that the legislature has usually adjourned when the governor exercises most vetoes.

The governor has to accept or reject a bill in its entirety, except for the general **appropriations bill**, or state budget, from which the governor can delete specific spending proposals while approving others. This power is called a **line-item veto**. The budget or any other bill approved by the legislature that appropriates money has to be certified by the comptroller before it is sent to the governor. Texas has a pay-as-you-go state government, and the comptroller has to certify that there will be enough available revenue to fund the bill.

If the second chamber amends the bill, the originating house has to approve, or concur in, the changes or request a conference committee. Any compromise worked out by a conference committee has to be approved by both houses, without further changes, before it is sent to the governor.

All bills except revenue-raising measures can originate in either the House or the Senate. Tax bills must originate in the House, although the legislative leadership severely bent that rule to win approval in a special session in 1991 of a tax bill necessary to balance a new state budget. After the House had dismantled a $3.3 billion revenue bill recommended by its Ways and Means Committee and sent the Senate nothing but a $30 million shell, Lieutenant Governor Bullock and the Senate, in consultation with lobbyists, took over the writing of a new tax bill, which the House later approved.

OTHER PROCEDURAL OBSTACLES TO LEGISLATION

Pieces of legislation also encounter other significant procedural obstacles. In the House, there is the Calendars Committee, which was discussed earlier in this chapter. In the Senate, there is the two-thirds rule.

The **two-thirds rule** for debating bills on the Senate floor has been a strong obstacle to controversial bills because it means that only eleven senators, if they are determined enough and one is not absent at the wrong time, can keep any proposal from becoming law. This rule also is a source of the lieutenant governor's power. After a bill is approved by a committee, its sponsor can have it placed on the daily intent calendar. If the sponsor is recognized by the lieutenant governor, he or she will seek Senate permission to consider the bill. A sponsor can have majority Senate support for a measure but will watch it die if he or she cannot convince two-thirds of the senators to let the body formally debate it.

The two-thirds tradition also gives a senator the opportunity to vote on both sides of an issue. Sometimes a senator will vote to bring up a bill and then vote against the measure when it is actually passed, as only a majority vote is required for approval. This procedure enables the senator to please the bill's supporters, gives the sponsor a favor that can be repaid later, and, at the same time, tell the bill's opponents that he or she voted against the measure.

As noted earlier in this chapter, Lieutenant Governor David Dewhurst and Republican senators suspended the two-thirds rule to break a partisan impasse and win Senate approval of a Republican-backed congressional redistricting bill during a special session in 2003 and to win Senate approval of a voter identification bill in 2009. Although the procedure still enjoyed strong support among senators—a proposal to change it at the beginning of the 2007 session was defeated 30–1—there was increasing speculation that other efforts to suspend the two-thirds tradition on highly divisive, partisan issues may be more prevalent in the future.

The Senate rules also provide for **tags** and **filibusters**, both of which can be effective in killing bills near the end of a legislative session. A tag allows an individual senator to postpone a committee hearing on any bill for at least forty-eight hours, a delay that is often fatal in the crush of unfinished business during a session's closing days. The filibuster, a procedure that allows a senator to speak against a bill for as long as he or she can stand and talk, is usually little more than a nuisance to a bill's supporters early in a session, but it, too, can become a potent and ever-present threat against controversial legislation near the end of a session. Sometimes several senators will engage in a tag-team filibuster, taking turns speaking against a bill. Often, the mere likelihood of a senator speaking against a bill is sufficient to kill a measure. Late in a session, the lieutenant governor may refuse to recognize the sponsor of a controversial bill for fear a filibuster will fatally delay other major legislative proposals. State Senator Bill Meier of Euless spoke for forty-three hours in 1977 against a bill dealing with the public reporting of on-the-job accidents. In so doing, he captured the world's record for the longest filibuster, which he held for years.

Shortcuts, Obfuscation, and Confusion

Sponsors of legislation languishing in an unfriendly committee or subcommittee often try to resurrect their proposals by attaching them as amendments to related bills being debated on the House or Senate floor. Such maneuvers often are successful, particularly if opponents are absent or if the sponsor succeeds in "mumbling" his amendment through without challenge. Nevertheless, the speaker or the lieutenant governor must find that such amendments are relevant to the pending bill if an alert opponent raises a point of order against them.

To facilitate the passage of noncontroversial and local pieces of legislation, the House and the Senate have periodic local and consent or local and uncontested **calendars**, which are conducted under special rules that enable scores of bills to be routinely and quickly approved by the full House or Senate without debate. Bills of major statewide significance, even controversial measures, sometimes get placed on these calendars, but it takes only one senator or three representatives to have any bill st
Legislators will sometimes knowingly let a controversial bill slip by on a loca

Talking a bill to death. Full-fledged filibusters are rare, but the threat of a filibuster, especially during the final days of a legislative session, is often sufficient to win concessions or kill a bill. Former Senator Gonzalo Barrientos of Austin puts on comfortable shoes in anticipation of a lengthy filibuster.

without moving to strike it so as not to offend the sponsor or the presiding officer. But to protect themselves politically should the bill become an issue later, they will quietly register a vote against the measure in the House or Senate journal.

Compromises on controversial legislation often are worked out behind closed doors long before a bill is debated on the House or Senate floor or even afforded a public committee hearing. It can be argued that this approach to consensus building is an efficient, businesslike way to enact legislation. But it also serves to discourage the free and open debate that is so important to the democratic process.

Recent speakers also have discouraged the taking of **record votes** during House floor debate on most bills. A constitutional amendment approved by Texas voters in 2007 requires record votes on final House or Senate passage of all legislation, except local bills. But many important amendments in the House are decided with "division" votes, which are taken on the computerized voting machine but leave no formal record of how individual legislators have voted once the voting boards are cleared (see "Voting for a Dead Man"). This approach saves the taxpayers some printing costs and can give lawmakers some respite from lobby pressure. But it also serves to keep the public in the dark about significant decisions made by their elected representatives. The fewer the record votes legislators have to make, the more easily they can dodge accountability to their constituents.

Voting for a Dead Man

When record votes are taken, House rules prohibit members from punching the voting buttons on other members' desks, but the practice occurs regularly. Sometimes members will instruct their desk mates or other legislators to cast specific votes for them if they expect to be absent when the votes are called for. Other legislators make a habit of punching the voting buttons at all the empty desks within easy reach. This practice is normally challenged only in cases of close votes, when members of the losing side request a roll-call verification of the computerized vote, and the votes of members who do not answer the roll call are struck.

The House was embarrassed in 1991 when a dead lawmaker was recorded as answering the daily roll call and voting on several record votes. The legislator had died in his Austin apartment, but his body wasn't discovered for several hours. Meanwhile, colleagues had been pushing his voting button. This practice is not a problem in the Senate, where the secretary of the Senate orally calls the roll on record votes.

Often, legislators have their minds made up on an issue before the matter is debated on the floor. But there are many bills that most lawmakers will have little or no interest in and won't bother to study. When legislators are not familiar with a bill, they often simply vote the way the sponsor votes or the way the House or Senate leadership wants them to vote. Despite what tourists in the gallery may think, legislators who raise their fingers above their heads when a vote is taken are not asking the presiding officer for a rest break. They are signaling the way they are voting and encouraging other lawmakers to vote the same way. One finger means yes; two fingers mean no.

Partly because of the rules under which the legislature operates, partly because of the heavy volume of legislation, and partly because of political maneuvering, the closing weeks of a regular session are hectic. Legislators in both houses are asked to vote on dozens of conference committee reports they do not have time to read. With hundreds of bills being rushed through the legislature to the governor's desk, mistakes occur. Deliberate attempts are also made—often successfully—to slip in major changes in law through the confusion. For every surprise bill or special interest amendment that is caught, dozens slip through and become law.

THE EMERGING PARTY SYSTEM

Unlike the U.S. Congress, the Texas legislature is not organized along party lines, with rules that automatically give leadership positions to members of the majority party. The arrangement in Texas is due primarily to the absence of Republican legislators for many years and the more recent practice—before Republicans gained a House majority in 2003—of rural Democrats aligning themselves with a Republican minority to produce a conservative coalition. As recently as 1971, the year before a federal court declared urban, countywide House districts unconstitutional, there were only ten Republicans in the House and two in the Senate. As Republicans increased their numbers, they aligned themselves with conservative Democrats to attempt to control the policymaking process. This ideological coalition became increasingly important as single-member districts boosted not only the number of Republican lawmakers but also the number of moderate and liberal Democratic legislators elected from urban areas. It became a means of maintaining some legislative control for conservative Democrats as the base of power shifted in their own party.

Republicans and conservative Democrats formally organized the Texas Conservative Coalition in the House in the 1980s. The coalition remained a strong force in the 1990s, chaired for several years by Representative Warren Chisum of Pampa, who switched from the Democratic to the Republican Party in 1995. Chisum's mastery of the rules blocked many pieces of legislation on technicalities.

On occasion, liberal Democrats and conservative Republicans have formed "unholy alliances," but these coalitions were usually short-lived. During the controversy over the Sharpstown stock fraud scandal in 1971, liberal Democrats and Republicans formed a loose coalition called the "Dirty Thirty" that continually harassed House Speaker Gus Mutscher, who not only was a key figure in the scandal but also epitomized the rural conservative Democratic tradition of the statehouse.

The Growth of Partisanship

With the growth of the Republican Party in Texas in the 1980s, Speaker Gib Lewis, a conservative urban Democrat, appointed Republicans to major committee chairs in the House. But partisan divisions increased in 1987 when Lewis, Democratic Lieutenant Governor Bill Hobby, and Republican Governor Bill Clements fought over a new state budget in the face of a huge revenue shortfall. On one side of the debate were moderate and liberal Democratic legislators, including inner-city and South Texas minorities whose constituents had the most to gain from a tax increase and the most to lose from deep cuts in spending on human services and educational programs. On the other side were a handful of conservative, primarily rural Democrats and a number of Republicans with middle- and upper middle-class suburban constituents who insisted on fiscal restraint. Clements eventually gave in and supported a tax increase, but most of the House Republicans continued to fight the measure until it was approved in a summer special session.

In 1989, Republicans formed their first caucus in the House, and soon both parties had active caucuses in both the House and the Senate, which began to play key roles in marshaling legislative support on selected issues. They also became active in legislative races as Republicans began to mount aggressive, well-financed challenges of Democratic incumbents.

During the 1995 legislative session, when Democrats still held a majority of House and Senate seats, Lieutenant Governor Bob Bullock and Speaker Pete Laney, both Democrats, continued the practice of naming Republicans, as well as Democrats, to committee chairs. Bullock and Laney also were strongly supportive of Republican Governor George W. Bush's legislative priorities. All three leaders cooperated in making major changes in public education and juvenile justice and setting limits on civil liability lawsuits.

After many bitterly contested legislative races, Republicans won their first majority of the Senate in modern times during the 1996 elections and gained four seats in the House to narrow the Democratic majority in that body to 82–68. Bipartisanship still prevailed for the most part in the 1997 session. Bullock, the Democratic lieutenant governor, gave Republicans some new leadership positions in the Senate but named Democrats to chair most committees. But legislative fights with strong partisan overtones increased in 1997 and subsequent sessions over such issues as abortion, gay rights, and whether tax dollars should be spent to pay for private school tuition for some students.

Another partisan-charged issue in 1999 and 2001 was an attempt by some Democrats to strengthen the state law against hate crimes after three white men in East Texas were accused—and later convicted—of dragging an African-American man, James Byrd Jr., to death behind a pickup truck. Most of the Republican opposition to the bill was because it increased penalties for crimes motivated by prejudice against homosexuals as well as prejudice over race or religion. That provision was opposed by social conservatives and, in 1999, Governor George W. Bush—who did not want to anger conservatives on the eve of his race for the Republican presidential nomination—called the bill unnecessary. The measure, which sponsors named for Byrd, died in the Senate in 1999 but was passed in 2001.

Republicans Take Control

Aided by the redrawn legislative districts discussed earlier in this chapter, Republicans made major gains in the 2002 elections. They increased their majority in the state Senate to 19–12, captured an 88–62 majority in the Texas House, their first since Reconstruction, and elected Republican Tom Craddick of Midland as speaker. Those victories, plus Governor Rick Perry's election, gave Republicans control of all the points of power in the statehouse. They controlled the budget-setting process, making significant cuts in services to close a $10 billion revenue shortfall, enacted significant new restrictions on civil lawsuits, and won the contentious fight over congressional redistricting. Throughout the year, partisanship was stronger than it had been since the GOP became a competitive party in Texas.

Craddick and Dewhurst appointed Democrats, as well as Republicans, to chair committees and serve in other leadership positions. Democrats chaired six of the Senate's fifteen standing committees and thirteen of the forty-two committees in the House. Craddick also appointed a Democrat, state Representative Sylvester Turner of Houston, as speaker pro tempore. But Craddick stacked the key chairmanships and the membership of the budget-writing House Appropriations Committee with Republicans who clearly reflected his conservative viewpoint. After winning a change in House rules that removed seniority as a factor in appropriations appointments, the new speaker bumped from the panel three outspoken Democrats who opposed budget cuts.

Democrats regained some of their lost House seats in subsequent elections. By 2009, they had cut the Republican majority in the House to 76–74 and had helped Joe Straus, a less autocratic Republican, unseat Craddick as speaker. Sooner or later, Democrats likely will recapture majorities in both the House and the Senate. So, partisanship will remain part of the legislative process for the foreseeable future. Before too many more years, the legislature may even organize itself along the same partisan lines as the U.S. Congress—with distinct party positions, such as floor leaders, caucus leaders, and whips. If this were to happen, the legislative rules and powers of the presiding officers discussed earlier in this chapter would be significantly changed. But this development will depend on how long Republicans continue to dominate the statehouse, on how Democrats continue to react, and on the future leadership personalities that emerge in both parties. Another factor will be how well the two factions in the Republican Party—the traditional fiscal conservatives and the social conservatives—are able to accommodate each other's interests.

OTHER LEGISLATIVE CAUCUSES ————————————————●

Hispanic and African-American House members formed their own **caucuses** as their numbers began to increase in the 1970s in the wake of redistricting and creation of urban single-member districts. Their cohesive blocs of votes have proved influential in speaker elections and the resolution of major statewide issues, such as health care for the poor, public school finance, and taxation. Their ability to broker votes has won committee chairs and other concessions they may not otherwise have received (see "Gregory Luna and Irma Rangel, Champions of Education").

Some urban delegations, such as the group of legislators representing Harris County, the state's most populous county, have formed their own caucuses to discuss

Gregory Luna and Irma Rangel, Champions of Education

Gregory Luna and Irma Rangel made important contributions to young people, particularly minorities, in the legislature and other public forums.

Luna, whose father died when he was an infant, knew firsthand the difficulties that many Texas children faced in securing an education and a chance at a better life. He was only eleven years old when he got his first job as a busboy in a restaurant. After working as a police officer to help put himself through college and law school, Luna then devoted much of his adult life to improving civil rights and educational opportunities for Hispanics and all Texans.

As an attorney in San Antonio in 1968, Luna helped found the Mexican American Legal Defense and Educational Fund (MALDEF), which has waged successful courtroom fights for civil rights. MALDEF has forced school boards and other governments to redraw political boundaries to assure minority representation on governing bodies. In the 1980s, MALDEF filed a landmark lawsuit against the state that forced the Texas legislature to more equitably distribute state education dollars among wealthy and poor school districts.

Luna served in the Texas House from 1985 to 1992 and in the state Senate from 1993 until illness forced his resignation in September 1999. He died only a few weeks later of complications related to diabetes. He was 66.

Luna was chair of the Senate Hispanic Caucus and vice chair of the Senate Education Committee, and throughout his legislative career he fought for further reforms of school funding and for improved educational opportunities. His legislative style was usually low key, but he was effective. He knew what he had to do to accomplish a goal and quietly went about doing it.

"He was a monument of many, many people who were able to benefit from his efforts for a better education system for everyone," said the Reverend Virgil Elizondo. "He was in the ministry of public service."

Irma Rangel, a Democrat from Kingsville, was a schoolteacher and a prosecutor before becoming, in 1976, the first Hispanic woman elected to the Texas House. She chaired the House Higher Education Committee for several years and sponsored a state law to boost affirmative action by requiring Texas colleges and universities to automatically admit students who graduated in the top 10 percent of their high school classes. She also was instrumental in boosting state funding for higher education institutions along the border with Mexico.

Rangel was still a member of the House— its fifth most senior member—when she died of cancer in March 2003 at age 71. State Representative Pete Gallego, Democrat of Alpine, chairman of the Mexican American Legislative Caucus, called Rangel's life a "testament to everything that is good about public service."[27]

and seek consensus on issues of local importance. In Harris County's case, however, consensus is rarely found on major local controversies because of the political, ethnic, and urban-suburban diversity within the delegation. Twenty-five House members—one-sixth of the body's membership—represent various parts of Houston and Harris County, and seven senators have districts that are wholly within or include part of the county. On many occasions, debate in committees and on the House or Senate floor has bogged down into Houston fights over mass transportation, annexation, or fire and police civil service.

LEGISLATORS AND THEIR CONSTITUENTS ————————————————●

Although representative government is an essential component of American society, there are continued debates as to how people elected to public office should identify the interests and preferences of the people they represent.[28] Political theorists as well as legislators struggle with the problem of translating the will of the people into public policy. Most legislators represent diverse groups and interests in their districts. During a normal legislative session, there are thousands of proposed laws to consider, and legislators must constantly make decisions that will benefit or harm specific constituents.

Except for an occasional emotional issue—such as whether motorcycle riders should have to wear safety helmets or whether private citizens should be allowed to carry pistols—most Texans pay little attention to what the legislature is doing. That is why they often are surprised to discover they have to pay a few extra dollars to register their cars or learn that the fee for camping in a state park has suddenly been increased. Very few Texans—particularly in the large cities that are divided up among numerous lawmakers—can identify their state representatives or senators by name, and far fewer can tell you what their legislators have voted for or against. This public inattention gives a legislator great latitude when voting on public policies. It also is a major reason why most incumbent lawmakers who seek reelection are successful. Most legislative turnover is the result of voluntary retirements, not voter retribution.

Several Democratic incumbents, however, fell victim to redistricting that favored Republican challengers in 2002. Some were unseated at the polls, and others didn't seek reelection because of the redrawn district lines. And several incumbents of both parties have been unseated in their own party primaries in recent elections because of the controversy over Tom Craddick's speakership.

Media coverage of the legislature is uneven. The large daily newspapers with reporters in Austin make commendable efforts to cover the major legislative issues and players and provide both spot news accounts and in-depth interpretation of the legislature's actions. All too frequently, however, they are limited by insufficient space, and they rarely publish individual voting records or attempt to evaluate the performances of individual legislators. Most television and radio news shows provide only cursory legislative coverage.

Although legislators are aware of latent public opinion, they tend to be more responsive to the interest groups, or attentive members of the public, that operate in their individual districts or statewide.[29] People who are well informed and attentive to public policy issues are a relatively small portion of the total population, but they can be mobilized for or against an individual legislator. In some instances, these are community opinion leaders who, directly or indirectly, are able to communicate information to oth individuals about a legislator's performance. Or they may belong to public interest and special interest groups that compile legislative voting records on selected issues of importance to their memberships. Although these records are only sporadically disseminated by the news media to the general public, they are mailed to the sponsoring groups' members.

Many special interest groups contribute thousands of dollars to a legislator's reelection campaign or to the campaign of an opponent. But politically astute legislators duly take note of all the letters, phone calls, petitions, e-mail messages, and visits by their constituents—plus media coverage—lest they lose touch with a significant number of voters with different views on the issues and thus become politically vulnerable.

A favorite voter-contact tool of many legislators is a newsletter they can mail to households in their districts at state expense. These mailings usually include photos of the lawmaker plus articles summarizing, in the best possible light, his or her accomplishments in Austin. Sometimes, legislators also include a public opinion survey seeking constituent responses on a number of issues. Lawmakers also maintain websites on the Internet.

LEGISLATIVE DECISION-MAKING

In addition to the formal rules of each legislative body, there are unwritten rules, or **norms**, that shape the behavior of legislators and other actors in the lawmaking process.[30] The legislature is like most other social institutions in that its members have perceptions of the institution and the process as well as the way they are expected to behave or carry out their responsibilities. Other participants also impose their views and expectations on lawmakers.

The legislative process is designed to institutionalize conflict, and the rules and norms of the legislature are designed to give this conflict an element of civility. Debate is often intense and vigorous, and it may be difficult for some lawmakers to separate attacks on their positions from attacks on their personalities. But most legislators have learned the necessity of decorum and courtesy. Even if lawmakers believe some of their opponents in the House and Senate are deceitful, personal attacks on other legislators are considered unacceptable. Personal attacks, even to the point of fistfights, occasionally occur, but they are rare (see "How Legislators Are Supposed to Act").

With about 6,300 pieces of legislation introduced during a regular session—the level reached in 2007—no legislator could possibly read and understand each bill, much less the hundreds of amendments offered during floor debate. And despite moments of high drama when issues of major, statewide importance are being debated, most of the legislative workload is tedious and dull and produces little direct political benefit for most senators and representatives. Many of those bills contain hidden traps and potential controversies that can haunt a legislator later, often during a reelection campaign. So legislators use numerous information sources and rely on the norms of the process to assist them in decision-making.

To make the process work, legislators must accommodate the competing interests they represent and achieve reciprocity with their fellow legislators. An individual legislator will usually have no direct political or personal interest in most bills because much legislation is local in nature and affects only a limited number of lawmakers and constituents. A legislator accumulates obligations as he or she supports another lawmaker's bill, with the full expectation that the action will be returned in kind.

A number of other factors, however, help shape lawmakers' decisions on major legislation.[31] The wishes of constituents are considered, particularly if there is a

How Legislators Are Supposed to Act

Legislative "folkways" or norms refer to lawmakers' shared standards of conduct—what is regarded as appropriate behavior and what is expected of a legislator. Although they may be more important in some states than in others, most of the standards listed here are honored as part of the professionalism in nearly every state legislature. Mavericks occasionally violate the "rules of the game," but most newcomers to the state legislature soon discover these and similar norms and honor them.

- Treat your colleagues with respect. Do not make personal attacks on them or harass them.
- Serve an apprenticeship. Take some time to do your homework and go through a learning process before charging around acting like a "know-it-all."
- Don't be a publicity hound. Stay away from the microphone unless you really have something to say.
- Don't conceal the real purpose of a bill or purposely overlook some portion of it in order to assure its passage.

- Don't make a commitment on a vote until you are ready to be bound by it. Keep your word. Be reliable when you have made a commitment.
- Committee work is your punishment for getting elected. Effective legislators specialize enough in their subject areas to be able to advise their colleagues, especially those not on their committees.
- Reciprocate when you can. Support your friends and colleagues whenever possible so that they will support you whenever they can.
- Defend the legislature when it comes under attack from the press, the governor, or other critics. Institutional patriotism is much admired by your colleagues.
- Don't burn your bridges. Learn to get along with others. Remember, today's foe may be tomorrow's ally in a crucially close vote on some new matter. A policy of "no permanent enemies" usually works best.[32]

groundswell of dominant opinion coming from a legislator's district. Legislators also exchange information with other lawmakers, particularly with members of the same caucus, members who share the same political philosophy, and colleagues from the same counties or regions of the state. Lawmakers often take their cues from the sponsors of a bill or the speaker's and lieutenant governor's leadership teams. As the political parties develop more formal legislative structures, identifiable patterns of giving and taking cues are likely to emerge along party lines. (That process already has begun to a significant extent on budgetary, taxation, and redistricting issues, as was demonstrated during the 2003 sessions.)

A legislator's staff also assists in the decision-making process, not only by evaluating the substantive merits of legislation but also by assessing the political implications of a lawmaker's decisions. The Legislative Budget Board and the Legislative Council provide technical information and expertise that also can be weighed by legislators.

Interest groups are major sources of information and influence. Although an individual legislator will occasionally rail against a specific group, most lawmakers consider interest groups absolutely essential to the legislative process. Through their lobbyists, interest groups provide a vast amount of technical information and can signal the level of constituency interest, support, or opposition to proposed laws. A senator or representative can use interest groups to establish coalitions of support for a bill, and some legislators become closely identified with powerful interest groups because they almost always support a particular lobby's position.

The governor can also influence the legislature in several ways. He or she can raise the public's consciousness of an issue or need and can promote solutions through speeches and through the media. The governor can communicate indirectly to individual lawmakers through the governor's staff, party leaders, and influential persons in a lawmaker's district. The governor can also appeal personally to lawmakers in one-on-one meetings or in meetings with groups of legislators.

At the beginning of each regular session, the governor outlines his or her legislative priorities in a State of the State address to a joint session of the House and the Senate. Throughout the session, the governor usually has frequent meetings with the lieutenant governor and the speaker.

The governor may also visit the House or the Senate chamber in a personal show of support when legislation that he or she strongly advocates is being debated. Unlike most recent governors, Governor Ann Richards personally testified before legislative committees on several of her priorities, including ethics reform and government reorganization, during her first year in office. The severity of a governor's arm-twisting is often in the arm of the beholder, but it can include appeals to a lawmaker's reason or conscience, threats of retaliation, appeals for party support, and promises of a *quid pro quo*. The greatest threat that a governor can hang over a legislator is the possible veto of legislation or a budget item of importance to the lawmaker. In special sessions, the governor also can negotiate with a lawmaker over whether to add a bill that is important to the legislator to the special session's agenda, which is controlled by the governor.

Legislators also get information and support from other elected statewide officeholders, such as the attorney general, the comptroller, or the land commissioner. These officials and lawmakers can assist each other in achieving political agendas.

The news media provides information and perspective on issues in broader political terms. In part, the policy agenda is established by those issues the media perceives to be important.

The relative importance of any groups or actors on decision-making is difficult to measure and varies from lawmaker to lawmaker and from issue to issue (see "Some Influences on Legislators' Votes"). Outside influences can be tempered by a legislator's own attitude and opinion. On many issues, legislators get competing advice and pressure. As much as a lawmaker may like to be all things to all people, that cannot be. She cannot please a chemical lobbyist—who is seeking a tax break for a new plant on the Gulf Coast and also happens to be a large campaign contributor—and environmentalists who fear the facility would spoil a nearby wildlife habitat. He cannot please the governor promoting casino gambling as a new state revenue source and most of the voters in his district who have consistently voted against gambling. The ultimate decision and its eventual political consequences are the legislator's.

Should lawmakers cast votes on the basis of the specific concerns of their districts, their personal convictions, the position of political parties, or the wishes of the special interest groups that helped fund their campaigns? These criteria reflect complex relationships between the legislator and the people represented. And since the overriding

Some Influences on Legislators' Votes

- Personal political philosophies and policy interests
- Personal and political friends
- Other legislators
- Committee chairs
- Their staffs
- Interest groups and lobbyists
- The governor
- Other elected administrators and state agency heads

- Legislative leaders
- Party leaders
- Local elected officials
- The media
- Court decisions
- Regional blocs within the state
- County delegations
- Legislative caucuses
- National and state trends
- Programs that have worked in other states[33]

consideration for most lawmakers is to get reelected, the legislator must balance them carefully.

LEGISLATIVE STYLES

Some legislators become known for their commitment to producing good legislation. These "workhorses" spend endless hours developing programs and are repeatedly turned to by the presiding officers to handle tough policy issues. Other lawmakers tend to look to their leadership for direction and cues, further enhancing the power of leaders.

Other legislators earn reputations as grandstanders. Almost every legislator has shown off for the media or the spectators in the gallery at one time or another, but there are a number who develop a distinct reputation for this style of behavior. They appear to be more interested in scoring political points with their constituents or interest groups—with the objective of being reelected or seeking higher office—than with mastering the substance of legislation. Many of these lawmakers are lightweights who contribute little to the legislature's product. And, while they may introduce many bills during a session, they are not interested in the details of the lawmaking process and are unable to influence other legislators to support their legislation.

The legislature also has a number of opportunists, including members who pursue issues to produce personal or political benefits for themselves. They may sponsor legislation or take a position on an issue to curry favor with a special interest group or bring benefit to their personal businesses or professions. Legislative rules prohibit legislators from voting on issues in which they have a personal monetary interest, but individual lawmakers can interpret that prohibition as they see fit. Many lawmakers will try to cash in on their legislative experience by becoming lobbyists after they leave office at considerably higher pay than they received as legislators.

Still other legislators appear to be little more than spectators. They enjoy the receptions and other perks of the office much more than the drudgery of committee hearings, research, and floor debate. Some quickly weary of the legislative process and, after a few sessions, decide against seeking reelection.[34]

THE DEVELOPMENT OF LEGISLATIVE STAFF ●

The quality of a legislator's staff can help determine his or her success, and both the quality and quantity of legislative staffs have been significantly enhanced since the early 1970s.[35] This growth reflects an emerging professional approach to lawmaking and meeting the needs of an increasingly complex, urban state. During recent regular sessions, the House has had about 900 employees, including part-time workers, and the Senate about 800. These figures included Capitol and district office staff for individual senators and representatives, the committee staffs, assistants to the lieutenant governor and the speaker, and other support staff hired directly by the House and the Senate.

Additionally, there are permanent staff members assigned to the Legislative Budget Board, the legislature's financial research arm; the Legislative Council, which researches issues and drafts bills and resolutions for introduction by legislators; and the Legislative Reference Library, which provides resource materials for lawmakers, their staffs, and the general public. Other support staff are assigned to the Sunset Advisory Commission, which assists the legislature in periodic reviews of state agencies, and the state auditor, who is chosen by and reports to the legislative leadership.

Legislative staffers range from part-time secretaries and clerks to lawyers and other professionals who draft bills and provide research that result in major state laws. There are limits on the number of staff members and funds allocated for legislators' personal staffs. As a general rule, senators have larger staffs than House members. Staffing levels are usually reduced between sessions, and some members shut down their Capitol offices entirely. Most lawmakers, however, maintain offices both in Austin and in their home districts, even if their staffs function only to answer the phone.

A key support group in the House is the House Research Organization, which was organized as the House Study Group in the 1970s by a handful of primarily liberal lawmakers. The group's name was later changed, and its structure was reorganized to represent the entire House, but it still fills a strong research role. It is supported by funds from the House budget and is governed by a steering committee that represents a cross section of Democratic and Republican House members. During legislative sessions, its staff provides detailed analyses, including pro and con arguments, of many bills on the daily House calendar. During interims between sessions, it provides periodic analyses of proposed constitutional amendments and other issues. The Senate formed a similar organization, the Senate Research Center, in 1991.

The quality of other resources available to lawmakers also has improved in recent years. Legislators and their staffs can routinely check the status or texts of bills online, and so can the public. The Legislative Council maintains a website on the Internet that includes committee schedules, bill texts and analyses, and other legislative information. Private citizens also can use the website to identify their state representatives and senators.

LEGISLATIVE ETHICS AND REFORM ●

The majority of legislators are honest, hard-working individuals. But the weaknesses of a few and the millions of dollars spent by special interests to influence the lawmaking process undermine Texans' confidence in their legislature and their entire state

A Dubious Distinction

Texas state Senator Drew Nixon, Republican of Carthage, made history the hard way when he was sentenced to six months in the Travis County jail in 1997 for unlawfully carrying a weapon. He became the first Texas legislator to ever serve a jail sentence while in office. Nixon's sentence stemmed from his arrest during a prostitution sting in Austin during the 1997 legislative session. According to police, he was arrested for agreeing to pay a female undercover officer $35 for sex. A loaded pistol, which he was not licensed to carry, also was found under his car seat.

Nixon pleaded guilty to both charges but asked a Travis County jury for probation. He got probation and a $2,000 fine on the prostitution conviction. But jurors sentenced him to jail on the weapons violation because he had pleaded no contest to a similar charge in Dallas and got probation four years earlier, before he was elected to the Senate. Nixon served his sentence on weekends after the legislative session ended. He didn't seek reelection in 2000.

government (see "A Dubious Distinction"). Although legislators cannot pass laws guaranteeing ethical behavior, they can set strong standards for themselves, other public officials, and lobbyists and provide stiff penalties for those who fail to comply. Such reform efforts are periodically attempted, but, unfortunately, they usually are the result of scandals and fall short of creating an ideal ethical climate.

Fallout from the **Sharpstown stock fraud scandal** rocked the Capitol in 1971 and 1972 and helped produce some far-reaching legislative and political changes.[36] It involved banking legislation sought by Houston banker-developer Frank Sharp that was approved by the legislature in a special session in 1969, only to be vetoed by Governor Preston Smith. A lawsuit filed in 1971 by the federal Securities and Exchange Commission broke the news that Smith, House Speaker Gus Mutscher, Representative Tommy Shannon of Fort Worth, who had sponsored the bills, and others had profited from stock deals involving Sharp's National Bankers Life Insurance Company. Much of their stock was purchased with unsecured loans from Sharp's Sharpstown State Bank.

Mutscher, Shannon, and an aide to the speaker were convicted of conspiracy to accept bribes. Mutscher, who had consolidated power in the House and was often regarded as ironhanded and arbitrary, was forced to resign. Later, the House moved to limit the speaker's power through a modified seniority system for committee appointments. Subsequent speakers still exercised a great deal of power, but it was constrained by expectations that the speaker would be more responsive to the membership. The media also started giving greater scrutiny and coverage to the activities of the speaker.

Fallout from the Sharpstown scandal helped an outsider, Uvalde rancher Dolph Briscoe, win the 1972 gubernatorial race and helped produce a large turnover in legislative elections, one of the rare examples in Texas political history of "kicking the rascals out."

In 1973, the legislature responded with a series of ethics reform laws, including requirements that lobbyists register with the secretary of state and report their total expenditures in trying to influence legislation. State officials were required to file public reports identifying their sources of income, although not specific amounts.

Weaknesses in those laws, however, were vividly demonstrated in 1989, when wealthy East Texas poultry producer Lonnie "Bo" Pilgrim distributed $10,000 checks to senators in the capitol building while lobbying them on worker's compensation and the Travis County district attorney could find no law under which to prosecute him. There also were published reports that lobbyists had spent nearly $2 million entertaining lawmakers during the 1989 regular session without having to specify which legislators received the "freebies," thanks to a large loophole in the lobby registration law. News stories about lobbyists treating lawmakers to golf tournaments, ski trips, a junket to Las Vegas for a boxing match, and limousine service to a concert created an uproar.

Some senators had angrily rejected Pilgrim's checks on the spot, while others returned them after the media pounced on the story. But the very next year, Pilgrim— a long-time political contributor—again contributed thousands of dollars to several statewide officeholders and candidates. This time, the checks were more traditionally sent through the mail, and they were gratefully accepted.

Despite all the headlines over ethical problems, legislative turnover was minimal in 1990. But in early December, about a month after the general election, a Travis County grand jury began investigating Speaker Gib Lewis's ties to a San Antonio law firm, Heard, Goggan, Blair, and Williams. The firm had made large profits collecting delinquent taxes for local governments throughout Texas under a law that allowed it to collect an extra 15 percent from the taxpayers as its fee. For several years, it had successfully defeated legislation that would have hurt its business. The *Fort Worth Star–Telegram* reported that Heard Goggan had paid about half of a $10,000 tax bill owed to Tarrant County by a business that Lewis partly owned.[37] And the *Houston Chronicle* reported that the grand jury was also looking into a trip that Lewis had taken to a Mexican resort during the 1987 legislative session with four Heard Goggan partners and a lobbyist (all males) and six women (including a waitress from a topless nightclub in Houston).[38] The trip had been taken while a bill opposed by Heard Goggan was dying in a House committee.

On December 28, only twelve days before the 1991 regular legislative session was to convene and Lewis was to be reelected to a record fifth term as the House's presiding officer, grand jurors indicted Lewis on two misdemeanor ethics charges. He was accused of soliciting, accepting, and failing to report an illegal gift from Heard Goggan— the partial payment of the tax bill. Lewis insisted he was innocent and vowed to fight the charges. He said the tax payment was the settlement of a legal dispute. He also angrily accused Travis County District Attorney Ronnie Earle, who headed the prosecution and had been publicly advocating stronger ethics laws, of using the grand jury to "influence the speaker's election." Lewis said Earle was guilty of "unethical and reprehensible behavior."[39] Lewis won a postponement of his trial under a law that automatically grants continuances to legislators when they are in session. The grand jury investigation, which prosecutors said would include other legislators or former legislators, continued for several more weeks, but no more indictments were issued.

Meanwhile, Governor Ann Richards urged the legislature to pass a law imposing tougher ethical requirements on state officials and lobbyists. The Senate approved an ethics bill fairly early in the session, but the House did not act on its version until late in the session. The final bill was produced by a conference committee on the last night of the session in a private meeting and was approved by the House and the Senate only a few minutes before the legislature adjourned at midnight. There wasn't time to print and distribute copies, and very few legislators knew for sure what was in the bill.

Despite the secrecy and complaints that the bill wasn't strong enough, Richards signed it. She called the new law a "very strong step in the direction of openness and ethics reform in this state." The new law required more reporting of lobby expenditures and conflicts of interest between lobbyists and state officials, prohibited special interests from treating legislators to pleasure trips, prohibited lawmakers from accepting honoraria—or fees—for speaking before special interest groups, and created a new state Ethics Commission to review complaints about public officials.

But the new law did not put any limits on financial contributions to political campaigns, nor did it prohibit legislator-attorneys from representing clients before state agencies for pay. Moreover, it authorized the Ethics Commission to slap a bigger fine ($10,000) on someone who filed a frivolous complaint against a public official than the maximum fine ($5,000) that could be levied on an officeholder for violating the ethics law. That latter provision was viewed by many critics as an unreasonable effort to discourage citizen complaints. The new law also provided that complaints filed with the Ethics Commission would remain confidential unless the commission took action, a provision that would allow the commission to dismiss or sit on legitimate complaints without any public accounting.

In January 1992, Lewis announced that he wouldn't seek reelection to another term in the House. In a plea bargain later the same month, prosecutors dropped the two ethics indictments against Lewis in return for the speaker's "no contest" plea to two minor, unrelated charges. Lewis paid a $2,000 fine for failing to publicly disclose a business holding in 1988 and 1989, for which he had already paid a minor civil penalty to the secretary of state.

The legislature enacted other significant changes in ethics laws in 2003. The new provisions required officeholders and candidates to identify the occupations and employers of people who contribute more than $500, required financial reports to be filed with the Ethics Commission electronically, increased penalties for people who filed their reports late, and required—for the first time—officeholders and candidates for municipal offices in the large cities to file personal financial disclosure statements, similar to those already filed by state officeholders.

Also in 2003, Travis County District Attorney Ronnie Earle began a lengthy investigation of how corporate contributions were used to affect several legislative elections in the Republican takeover of the Texas House. Republicans accused Earle, a Democrat, of playing politics, but Earle said that he was investigating the possibility that corporate funds had been illegally spent on political activity.

The investigation produced several criminal indictments, including charges against Tom DeLay of Sugar Land, the then-powerful Republican leader of the U.S. House of Representatives, and the Texas Association of Business, one of the state's largest business groups. The business group was charged with illegally using corporate money to help Republicans win several Texas House races in 2002. For their part, DeLay and two associates were charged with money laundering and conspiracy relating to alleged improper campaign fundraising for Republican legislative candidates. DeLay and the other defendants said they were innocent of the charges, but the politically charged controversy raged for months. The 2002 legislative elections had been crucial because they not only gave Republicans a majority of the Texas House, they also gave Republicans enough clout to redraw congressional district lines in Texas, at DeLay's urging, to favor GOP candidates.

A state district judge dismissed charges against the business group and dismissed the conspiracy indictment against DeLay and his two associates, political consultants John Colyandro and Jim Ellis. But the judge let the money laundering charge against the three men stand. By mid-2009, no one had yet come to trial, but the Texas charges and ethical questions in Washington had taken a political toll on DeLay. He stepped down from his leadership position in January 2006 and resigned from Congress later that year.

SUMMARY AND CONCLUSIONS ●

1. Texas, the nation's second most populous state, has a part-time, low-paid legislature that operates under restrictions drafted by nineteenth-century Texans in the wake of the repressive Reconstruction era. There are serious questions about the legislature's ability to respond readily to modern needs and crises. Because lawmakers meet in regular session only every other year, emergencies sometimes require special legislative sessions.

2. On a continuum from a highly professional legislature to a citizen or amateur lawmaking body, the Texas legislature is somewhere in between. Turnover is moderate.

3. As recently as 1971, there were only a handful of African Americans, Hispanics, Republicans, and women in the 150-member House of Representatives and the thirty-one-member Senate. But political realignment and federal court intervention in redistricting, particularly the ordering of single-member House districts for urban counties in 1972, have significantly increased the number of women, ethnic minorities, and Republicans in the legislature. Republicans, at this writing prior to the 2010 elections, have a majority of both the Texas House and the state Senate.

4. Unlike the U.S. Congress, the Texas legislature is not organized along party lines and has only the tentative beginnings of an institutionalized leadership structure. The presiding officer of the House is the speaker, who is elected by the other House members. The presiding officer of the Senate is the lieutenant governor, who is elected by the voters statewide. Leadership in both the House and the Senate has been highly personal, centering on the presiding officers and their legislative teams.

5. The most significant powers of the speaker and the lieutenant governor are the appointment of House and Senate committees that screen and draft legislation and the assignment of bills to committees. The fate of most pieces of legislation is decided at the committee level. The presiding officers also play key roles in the development of major legislative proposals and, to a great extent, depend on their handpicked committee chairs to sell their legislative programs to House and Senate colleagues.

6. To be sent to the governor for signature into law, a bill must be approved on three readings in both the House and the Senate. Referral to committee is first reading, and that is as far as most bills get. Many are never scheduled for a hearing by the chairs of the committees to which they are assigned. Many others die in subcommittees.

7. Other hurdles to legislation are the Calendars Committee in the House and the two-thirds rule in the Senate. The Calendars Committee, composed entirely of speaker appointees, sets the schedule for floor debate in the House, and the two-thirds rule prohibits any bill from being debated on the Senate floor without the approval of two-thirds of the senators.

8. For those bills that survive the committee process, second reading is a crucial step. This is where most floor debate on legislation occurs and where many bills are further amended. If a bill is approved on second reading, it advances to third reading and, if approved again, then to the other legislative chamber, where it is referred to committee and has to repeat the process.

9. To become law, a bill has to be approved in exactly the same form by both chambers. A conference committee of House and Senate members often has to work out a compromise when the versions passed by the two chambers differ.

10. The governor can sign a bill, veto it, or let it become law without his or her signature. The governor can use the line-item veto to delete specific spending provisions from the general appropriations bill, or state budget. But all other bills have to be accepted or rejected in their entirety.

11. Tax bills must originate in the House. All other bills can originate in either chamber.

12. The legislative rules and heavy volume of bills considered sometimes enable lawmakers to sneak major, controversial proposals into law by adding little-noticed amendments to other bills.

13. The growth of Republican strength has increased partisan activity in the legislature and fueled speculation that, sooner or later, attempts may be made to organize the legislature along

the partisan lines of the U.S. Congress. Both major parties already have active legislative caucuses.

14. There is considerable diversity among legislators in style and work habits. Their decisions are influenced by a number of factors, including constituents, interest groups, colleagues, staff, the governor, and the media.

15. Although most legislators are honest, hardworking individuals, the weaknesses of a few and the millions of dollars spent by special interests to influence the lawmaking process serve to undermine Texans' confidence in state government. Lawmakers make periodic efforts to strengthen their ethical standards, but usually only after well-publicized scandals.

KEY TERMS

Institutionalization 232
Bicameral legislature 233
Regular legislative session 233
Special sessions 233
Redistricting 234
Speaker 242
Standing committees 254
Calendars committee 255

Conference committee 256
Select committees 256
Reading 256
Veto 258
Appropriations bill 258
Line-item veto 258
Two-thirds rule 258
Tags 259

Filibusters 259
Calendars 259
Record votes 260
Caucuses 264
Norms 266
Sharpstown stock fraud scandal 271

FURTHER READING

Articles

Anderson, Arthur J., "Texas Legislative Redistricting: Proposed Constitutional and Statutory Amendments for an Improved Process," *Southwestern Law Journal* 43 (October 1989), pp. 719–57.

Bickerstaff, Steve, "State Legislative and Congressional Reapportionment in Texas: A Historical Perspective," *Public Affairs Comment* 37 (Winter 1991), pp. 1–13.

Boulard, Garry, "Lobbyists as Outlaws," *State Legislatures* 22 (January 1996), pp. 20–25.

Edwards, Julie, "The Right to Vote and Reapportionment in the Texas Legislature," *Baylor Law Review* 41 (December 1989), pp. 689–730.

Freeman, Patricia K., "A Comparative Analysis of Speakers' Career Patterns in U.S. State Legislatures," *Legislative Studies Quarterly* 20 (August 1995), pp. 365–76.

Hamm, Robert, and Robert Harmel, "Legislative Party Development and the Speaker System: The Case of the Texas House," *Journal of Politics* 55 (November 1993), pp. 1140–51.

King, James D., "Changes in Professionalism in U.S. State Legislatures," *Legislative Studies Quarterly* 25 (May 2000), pp. 327–43.

Kubin, Jeffrey C., "The Case for Redistricting Commissions," *Texas Law Review* 75 (March 1997), pp. 837–72.

Moncrief, Gary F., Joel A. Thompson, and Karl T. Kurtz, "The Old Statehouse, It Ain't What It Used to Be," *Legislative Studies Quarterly* 21 (February 1996), pp. 57–72.

Mooney, Christopher Z., "Citizens, Structures and Sister States: Influences on State Legislative Professionalism," *Legislative Studies Quarterly* 20 (February 1995), pp. 47–67.

Books

Barber, James David, *The Lawmakers*. New Haven, CT: Yale University Press, 1965.

Barns, Ben, with Lisa Dickey, *Barn Burning, Barn Building: Tales of a Political Life, from LBJ through George W. Bush and Beyond*. Albany, TX: Bright Sky, 2006.

Deaton, Charles, *The Year They Threw the Rascals Out*. Austin, TX: Shoal Creek, 1973.

Fenno, Richard F., *Home Style: House Members in Their Districts*. Boston: Little, Brown, 1978.

Hellebust, Lyn, and Kristin Hellebust, *State Legislative Sourcebook, 2009*. Topkeka, KA: Government Research Service, 2009.

Herskowitz, Mickey, *Sharpstown Revisited: Frank Sharp and a Tale of Dirty Politics in Texas*. Austin, TX: Eakin, 1994.

Jewell, Malcolm E., and Samuel C. Patterson, *The Legislative Process in the United States*, 4th ed. New York: Random House, 1986.

Jones, Nancy Baker, and Ruthie Winegarten, *Capitol Women: Texas Female Legislators, 1923–1999.* Austin, TX: University of Texas Press, 2000.

Keefe, William J., and Morris S. Ogul, *The American Legislative Process: Congress and the States,* 8th ed. Englewood Cliffs, NJ: Prentice Hall, Inc., 1993.

Kingdon, John W., *Congressmen's Voting Decisions,* 2nd ed. New York: Harper & Row, 1981.

Kousser, Thad, *Term Limits and the Dismantling of State Legislative Professionalism.* New York: Cambridge University Press, 2005.

McNeely, Dave and Jim Henderson, *Bob Bullock: God Bless America.* Austin, TX: University of Texas Press, 2008.

Mayhew, David, *Congress: The Electoral Connection.* New Haven, CT: Yale University Press, 1974.

Rosenthal, Alan, *Engines of Democracy: Politics & Policymaking in State Legislatures.* Washington, DC: CQ Press, 2009.

———, *Legislative Life: People, Process and Performance in the States.* New York: Harper & Row, 1981.

———, *Governors and Legislatures: Contending Powers.* Washington, DC: Congressional Quarterly Books, 1990.

———, *The Decline of Representative Democracy: Process, Participation and Power in State Legislatures.* Washington, DC: CQ Press, 1998.

Texas House of Representatives, House Research Organization, *Term Limits: Tenure or Turnover,* Special Legislative Report No. 186 (February 4, 1994).

Websites

National Conference of State Legislatures   http://www.ncsl.org/   This bipartisan organization serves legislative institutions in the United States through its research, technical assistance, and opportunities for legislators to share ideas about pressing policy issues. Many of its reports are posted on its website and accessible to the general public.

Texas Legislature On-Line (TLOL)   http://www.capitol.state.tx.us/   In addition to providing links to other legislative websites such as the House, Senate, Legislative Budget Board, State Auditor, and the Sunset Commission, TLOL provides legislative histories, access to bills, amendments, and statutes affected by proposed legislation.

Texas Senate   http://www.senate.state.tx.us/   In addition to information from the lieutenant governor's office, biographical information, committee assignments, district data, and addresses are provided for each member of the Senate.

Texas House of Representatives   http://www.house.state.tx.us/   This website provides direct access to live broadcasts of legislative proceedings, information pertaining to the legislative process in the House, information from the speaker's office, and general information about the Capitol complex. Biographical information, committee assignments, district data, and addresses are provided for each member of the House.

Texas Legislative Council   http://www.tlc.state.tx.us/ The Texas Legislative Council (TLC) is a state agency within the legislative branch. The TLC drafts bills and other legislative documents, conducts legal and public policy research, and produces informational publications for the Senate and the House.

ENDNOTES

1. Rober T. Garrett, "Hands-off Speaker Gets Mixed Reviews—Straus Ends First Session with Republicans Split on His Style," *Dallas Morning News,* June 1, 2009, p. 1A.
2. For an extended discussion of legislative functions, see William J. Keefe and Morris S. Ogul, *The American Legislative Process,* 10th ed. (Upper Saddle River, NJ: Prentice Hall, 2001), pp. 21–44.
3. On the general concept of legislative institutionalization, see Nelson W. Polsby, "The Institutionalization of the U.S. House of Representatives," *American Political Science Review* 62 (March 1968), pp. 144–68. For a discussion of the emergence of the modern Congress, see Randall B. Ripley, *Congress: Process and Policy,* 4th ed. (New York: W.W. Norton, 1988), pp. 48–67.
4. Thomas R. Dye and Susan MacManus, *Politics in States and Communities,* 12th ed. (Upper Saddle River: NJ: Pearson Prentice Hall, 2007), pp. 209–212.
5. Council of State Governments, *Book of the States, 2007 Edition,* vol. 39 (Lexington, KY: 2007), Table 3.4.
6. See Article 3 of the Texas Constitution for the constitutional provisions pertaining to the structure, membership, and selection of the Texas Legislature.
7. Council of State Governments, *Book of the States, 2008 Edition,* vol. 40 (Lexington, KY: 2008), Table 3.9.
8. Dave McNeely, "Legislators' Recent Actions Fuel Public's Lack of Trust," *Austin American–Statesman,* June 11, 1991, p. A17.
9. For a comprehensive analysis of the literature on legislative recruitment and careers, see Donald R. Matthews, "Legislative Recruitment Careers," *Legislative Studies Quarterly* 9 (November 1984), pp. 547–85.
10. Gary F. Moncrief, Richard G. Niemi, and Lynda W. Powell, "Time, Term Limits, and Turnover: Trends in Membership Stability in U.S. State Legislatures," *Legislative Studies Quarterly* 29 (August 2004), p. 364.
11. Paul T. David and Ralph Eisenberg, *Devaluation of the Urban and Suburban Vote* (Charlottesville, VA: Bureau of Public Administration, University of Virginia, 1961).

12. Stephen Ansolabehere and James M. Snyder, Jr., *The End of Inequality: One Person, One Vote and the Transformation of American Politics* (New York: W.W. Norton, 2008), pp. 50–1.

13. *Baker v. Carr*, 369 U.S. 186 (1962); *Reynolds v. Sims*, 337 U.S. 533 (1964); and *Kilgarlin v. Martin*, 252 F. Supp 404 (S.D. Tex 1966).

14. *Georgia v. Ashcroft*, 539 U.S. 956 (2003).

15. *R.G. Ratcliffe*, "Stalemate Speaks to Hard Core—Neither Side Wants to Lose Face by Giving in on Remap Ruckus," *Houston Chronicle*, August 14, 2003, p. 27A.

16. Jane Elliott, "Unblinking Craddick Wins Again—Speaker Prevails in Remapping Fight, Other Battles," *Houston Chronicle*, October 12, 2003, p. 33A.

17. Garrett, "Hands-off Speaker Gets Mixed Reviews," p. 1A.

18. Ibid.

19. Ibid.

20. Fred Gantt, *The Chief Executive in Texas: A Study of Gubernatorial Leadership* (Austin, TX: University of Texas Press, 1964), p. 238.

21. Ross Ramsey and Cindy Rugeley, "Leaders of the Pack-Bullock, Laney Carry a Big Stick in State Legislature," *Houston Chronicle*, June 6, 1993, p. state, 1A.

22. State Senator Bill Ratliff, quoted in Kathy Walt, "Texas Legislature—Jobs Well Done—Senators Give Perry High Marks After Starting with Low Expectations," *Houston Chronicle*, June 6, 1999, p. 1E.

23. Clay Robison and R.G. Ratcliffe, "A Reversal of Course for Ratliff Lieutenant Governor Drops Plans to Run," *Houston Chronicle*, June 6, 2001, p. 1A.

24. Gary Scharrer, "Dewhurst: Voter ID Bill Most Likely Dead," *Houston Chronicle*, May 17, 2007, page 10B.

25. For a summary of the earlier scholarly work on legislative committees, see Heinz Eulau and Vera McCluggage, "Standing Committees in Legislatures: Three Decades of Research," *Legislative Studies Quarterly* 9 (May 1984), pp. 195–270.

26. See Malcolm E. Jewell and Samuel C. Patterson, *The Legislative Process in the United States* (New York: Random House, 1966), Chapter 11, for a summary of the function of legislative rules and procedures. See Barbara Sinclair's *Unorthodox Lawmaking*, 3rd ed. (Washington, DC: CQ Press, 2007) for an expanded discussion of rule changes in the U.S. Congress and their impact on policy formulation.

27. *Associated Press*, "Ex-Sen. Luna Remembered as a Champion of Education," as published in the *Houston Chronicle*, November 10, 1999, p. 32A; and Clay Robison, "House Veteran Rangel Dies of Cancer at Age 71," *Houston Chronicle*, March 19, 2003, p. 25A.

28. For a brief overview of the representative problem, see Neal Riemer, ed., *The Representative: Trustee? Delegate? Partisan? Politico?* (Boston: D.C. Heath, 1967). For a more comprehensive treatment of the subject, see Hanna F. Pitkin, *The Concept of Representation* (Berkeley: University of California Press, 1967).

29. For an excellent treatment of the relationship of U.S. legislators to their districts and constituencies, see Richard F. Fenno, Jr., *Home Style: House Members in Their Districts* (Boston: Little Brown, 1978).

30. There have been a number of studies of these informal norms within the legislative process. One is Donald R. Matthews, *U.S. Senators and Their World* (New York: Vintage, 1960). For the adaptation of this concept to state legislatures, see Alan Rosenthal, *Legislative Life: People, Process, and Performance of the States* (New York: Harper & Row, 1981).

31. The general concepts for this discussion are based on John W. Kingdon, *Congressmen's Voting Decisions*, 2nd ed. (New York: Harper & Row, 1981).

32. James MacGregor Burns, J. W. Peltason, Thomas E. Cronin, David B. Magleby, L. Tucker Gibson Jr., and Clay Robison, *Government by the People: Texas Version*, 2nd ed. (Upper Saddle River, NJ: Prentice Hall, 1998), p. 670.

33. Ibid, p. 675.

34. These legislative styles are similar to those developed by James David Barber, *The Lawmakers* (New Haven, CT: Yale University Press, 1965), Chapters 2–5.

35. For a general discussion of staff in state legislatures, see Alan Rosenthal, *Engines of Democracy: Politics and Policy-making in State Legislatures* (Washington, DC: CQ Press, 2007), pp. 185–89.

36. Richard Morehead, *50 Years in Texas Politics* (Burnet, TX: Eakin, 1982), pp. 236–37.

37. *Fort Worth Star-Telegram*, Dec. 4, 1990.

38. Bob Sablatura and Robert Cullick, "Lewis' Luxury Vacation at Mexico Resort Probed," *Houston Chronicle*, Dec. 12, 1990, p. 1A.

39. R.G. Ratcliffe, "Speaker Turns Himself in to Sheriff—Lewis Rips Indictment, Press," *Houston Chronicle*, Jan. 1, 1991, p. 1A.

The Texas Executive

Questions to Guide Your Reading

1. What are the advantages and disadvantages of the plural executive?

2. How does a governor use the informal resources of the office to compensate for the constitutional limits on the office's formal powers?

3. Of the contemporary governors, who do you perceive to have been the most successful in developing and implementing forward-looking public policies for the state?

4. Should Texas replace the plural executive with a cabinet similar to that of the U.S. president?

*The executive power of the State may with truth be said
to be represented by the Governor, although he enjoys but a
portion of its rights.*

—Alexis de Tocqueville[1]

*The Governor's office is not the primrose path of pleasure.
Every time you throw yourself in opposition to what somebody
wants, you immediately become the target for many a
poisoned arrow.*

—Governor Pat M. Neff[2]

I just love this job.

—Governor Ann Richards, on more than
one occasion soon after taking office.

The salary isn't bad, the fringe benefits are pretty good, and the job is very prestigious. One might definitely get a sense of power and influence from holding the position. And, if you thrive on publicity, it may be satisfying to have a pack of journalists following your every move and hanging on your every word. But sooner or later, the reporters will become a pain in the neck. It will be hard to get time to yourself and, if you are not careful, your efforts to relax may be subject to criticism. You will be authorized a large staff, but it will attempt to structure most of your waking hours. You can easily spend $30 million or $40 million—or even more—and a year's worth of sixteen-hour days winning the job and, in the process, be subjected to all kinds of ridicule and personal attacks. Once elected, you may catch all kinds of flak for developments over which you have little, if any, control. Finally, eight or ten other people will want your job and will be eager to make you look bad so they can challenge you when your term is up.

The office that usually comes to mind when people think of state government is the office of **governor**. It clearly is the most visible office in the state. But though the popular image of the office is one of power, those elected to it discover that the office is institutionally weak. The term "chief executive" is almost a misnomer, thanks to constitutional restrictions meant to ensure that no governor can repeat the oppressive abuses of the Reconstruction administration of Governor Edmund J. Davis.

Unlike the president of the United States, the governor of Texas has no formal appointive cabinet through which to impose policy on the governmental bureaucracy. Several other major state agencies are headed by independently elected officers, including such key players as the attorney general and the comptroller. The governor appoints hundreds of members of boards and commissions that set policy for numerous other state agencies. But most of those boards are structured in such a way that a new governor has to wait until halfway through his or her first term to appoint a majority of panel members.

All of this is not to suggest that the governor is merely a figurehead. The governor can veto legislation and has the exclusive authority to schedule special sessions of the legislature and set their agendas. Despite its limitations, the appointments power offers the opportunity to make a strong mark on state government. The high visibility of the office also offers a governor a ready-made public forum. So, though the state constitution limits the formal powers of the office, a governor's influence is shaped by his or her personality, political adroitness, staff appointments, and ability to define and sell an agenda that addresses broad needs and interests.

A HISTORICAL PERSPECTIVE ON THE EXECUTIVE FUNCTION IN TEXAS

The top executive officeholder in Texas has not always had such limited authority. In the 1836 Constitution of the Republic, the powers of the president of Texas "closely resembled the powers of the American president, except he was forbidden to lead armies without the consent of Congress."[3] The constitution adopted after Texas was annexed to the United States in 1845 continued the office of a strong single or unified executive and gave the governor significant powers, including the appointment of other executive officials.[4] When Texas adopted a revised constitution upon joining the Confederacy in 1861, there were only some minor reductions in the powers of the governor. The new charter called for the election of two other executive officeholders: the state treasurer and the comptroller of public accounts.[5]

The governor also retained extensive powers under the Constitution of 1866, written at the end of the Civil War. Although the treasurer and the comptroller remained elected, the legislative power of the governor was expanded through the line-item veto over budget bills, a power still retained today. The Constitution of 1866 was short-lived and replaced by the Constitution of 1869 to bring the state into compliance with the Reconstruction policies of the Radical Republicans who had taken over the U.S. Congress. The Constitution of 1869 was influenced by Jacksonian democracy, which led to the diffusion of the executive function among eight officeholders, six of whom were to be elected statewide.[6]

But Radical Reconstruction policies and the abuses of the Davis administration prompted Texans to put strict limits on the power of the governor in the Constitution of 1876, which still forms the basic framework of state government. The new constitution retained the **plural executive** structure of independently elected officeholders. The only executive officer the governor was given the power to appoint was the secretary of state. Terms of the governor and other elected members of the executive branch were limited to two years, their salaries were defined by the constitution, and the duties of each office were specified in great detail, thus limiting their discretionary powers. Restrictions also were placed on outside employment and holding any other office or commission.[7]

A few of the restrictions on the executive branch have been loosened over the years through constitutional amendments, but the changes have not significantly enhanced the governor's authority. In 1954, voters approved an amendment giving the legislature the authority to raise the governor's salary.[8] Another amendment, in 1972, expanded the term of office for the governor and most other statewide executive officeholders to four years. In 1980, the governor was given the power, with the approval of the state Senate, to remove persons from boards and commissions whom the governor had personally appointed.[9] But when Governor Ann Richards in 1991 tried to revive interest in giving the governor cabinet-style appointment powers over major state agencies, she met with only limited success.

THE STRUCTURE OF THE PLURAL EXECUTIVE

Article 4, Section 1 of the 1876 Constitution created the executive branch, which "shall consist of a Governor, who shall be the Chief Executive Officer of the State, a **Lieutenant Governor,** Secretary of State, Comptroller of Public Accounts, Treasurer, Commissioner of the

General Land Office, and Attorney General." Later added to the executive branch were the Agriculture Commissioner, the three-member Railroad Commission, and the fifteen-member State Board of Education. Only the secretary of state is appointed by the governor (see Figure 9–1). Members of the education board are elected from districts, and the other officeholders are elected statewide. The constitution requires most of these officials to be at least thirty years old and a resident of Texas for at least five years.[10]

Agencies headed by these officials are autonomous and—except for limited budgetary review—independent of the governor. In a confrontation with the governor over policy, agency heads can claim their own electoral mandates. For many years, there were only "scattered incidents of hostility within the executive branch," and elected officials generally "cooperated remarkably well with their chief executives."[11] This observation was based on a period in which Texas was a one-party Democratic state. Party politics were

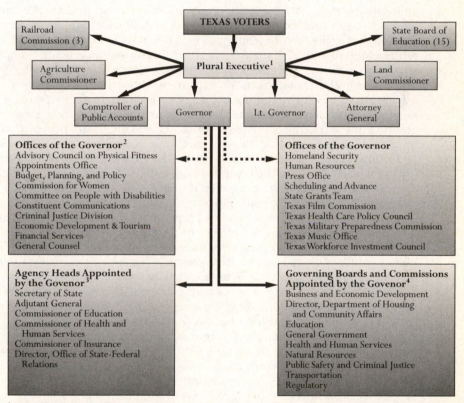

[1] Defined by the constitution or statutory law, the heads of these agencies are elected independently of the governor.
[2] The Offices of the Governor are created under statutory authority and serve to assist the governor in policy development, budgeting and planning, and coordination of policy among agencies and governments. Some 200 persons serve in these offices and are appointed by the governor.
[3] With the exception of the Secretary of State, which is authorized under the Texas Constitution, these administrative positions were created under statutory law giving the appointment authority to the governor.
[4] Some two hundred state agencies, including universities, are assigned by statutory law the responsibilities for the administration of public policy in these areas. The members of the governing bodies are appointed by the governor with the approval of the legislature. In turn, the agency executives are appointed by the governing boards.

FIGURE 9–1   Structure of the Executive Branch in Texas.

dominated by conservatives, and their interests were generally reflected by statewide elected officials, who believed it was in their own best political interests to cooperate with each other.

The potential for conflict between the governor and other executive officials increased as Texas became a two-party state, and conflict is likely to become more common in the future, even between officials within the same party. During Republican Governor Bill Clements's first term (1979–1983), the other elected officers in the executive branch were Democrats, including Attorney General Mark White, who frequently feuded with the governor and jockeyed for the political advantage that allowed him to unseat Clements in 1982.

In 2003, budgetary differences erupted between Republican Comptroller Carole Keeton Strayhorn and other Republican officeholders, including Governor Rick Perry. They resulted in the legislature's approval of a bill, signed by Perry, transferring two key programs from the comptroller's office to the Legislative Budget Board. The political animosity between Strayhorn and Perry intensified, and in 2006 the comptroller challenged the governor's reelection as an independent candidate. Perry ultimately won the election, but in the months leading up to it, official actions and pronouncements by both officeholders often had sharp political edges. Strayhorn, in particular, jumped on every opportunity to criticize her opponent. Despite the distraction, Perry called a special legislative session and won lawmakers' enactment of school finance changes necessary to meet a Texas Supreme Court deadline in a major education lawsuit. Performing her official duties, the comptroller certified the legislature's action, but she also repeatedly attacked the governor and second-guessed his priorities. She said the school property tax cuts approved by lawmakers and touted by the governor were inadequate, and she criticized Perry for endorsing higher state taxes to help pay for the local tax relief. (This dispute is discussed further in the section on the comptroller of public accounts later in this chapter.)

There can be conflict between any members of the executive branch. In 1994, for example, a coastal management plan promoted by Democratic Land Commissioner Garry Mauro was actively opposed by Perry, who then was agriculture commissioner.

One may argue that the effect of the plural executive on state politics and the governor's control of the executive branch is minimal because, for the most part, rancorous conflict among these elected officials still appears to be infrequent. But one also may argue that the governor, in an effort to avoid conflict with officials over whom he or she has no control, pursues policies that are not likely to be disruptive, innovative, or responsive to pressing contemporary issues.

It is difficult to develop coordinated policies if those holding office in a plural executive system have sharply different or competing agendas. But proponents of the plural executive contend that it does what it was intended to do: control and constrain the governor. Although collegial or collective decision making is often inefficient and potentially leads to deadlock, the advocates of the plural executive contend that democracy, in most instances, is to be preferred over efficiency.

The Governor of Texas in a Comparative Perspective

For more than thirty years, scholars have ranked the various state governors on their formal constitutional and legal powers, such as budgetary authority, appointment and veto powers, and term limitations.[12] From the earliest to the latest studies, the governor of Texas has ranked consistently with the weaker state governors (see Table 9–1).

TABLE 9–1   Comparison of the Formal Powers of Governors

Strong (4.0 and above)

Alaska (4.1)	Massachusetts (4.3)	New York (4.1)	West Virginia (4.1)
Maryland (4.1)	New Jersey (4.1)	Utah (4.0)	

Moderately Strong (3.5–3.9)

Arkansas (3.6)	Iowa (3.8)	Nebraska (3.8)	Tennessee (3.8)
Colorado (3.9)	Maine (3.6)	New Mexico (3.7)	Washington (3.6)
Connecticut (3.6)	Michigan (3.6)	North Dakota (3.9)	Wisconsin (3.5)
Delaware (3.5)	Minnesota (3.6)	Ohio (3.6)	
Florida (3.6)	Missouri (3.6)	Oregon (3.5)	
Illinois (3.8)	Montana (3.5)	Pennsylvania (3.8)	

Moderate (3.0–3.4)

Arizona (3.4)	Kansas (3.3)	South Carolina (3.0)
California (3.2)	Kentucky (3.3)	South Dakota (3.0)
Georgia (3.2)	Louisiana (3.4)	**Texas (3.2)**
Hawaii (3.4)	Nevada (3.0)	Virginia (3.2)
Idaho (3.3)	New Hampshire (3.2)	Wyoming (3.1)

Weak (2.9 and below)

Alabama (2.8)	North Carolina (2.9)	Oklahoma (2.8)	Vermont (2.5)
Mississippi (2.9)	Indiana (2.9)	Rhode Island (2.6)	

Source: Thad Beyle, "Gubernatorial Power," Table 7–5 Governors' Institutional Powers 2007, June 18, 2007, http://www.unc.edu/~beyle/tab7–5-InstPowers07.doc. Beyle's rankings are based on a six-point scale using the structure of the executive branch, tenure, appointment powers, budget powers, veto powers, and governor's party control. The governor of Texas ranks 35th using this scale.

QUALIFICATIONS AND BACKGROUNDS OF TEXAS GOVERNORS

The Texas Constitution has few requirements for a person who desires to run for governor. A governor must be at least thirty years old, a U.S. citizen, and a resident of Texas for at least five years. There also is a vague requirement that no individual can be excluded from office for religious beliefs, "provided he acknowledges the existence of a Supreme Being."[13] The constitution, however, doesn't spell out all the roadblocks to winning the office.

Until the election of Bill Clements in 1978, every governor since 1874 had been a Democrat (see Table 9–2). Clements served two terms (1979–1983 and 1987–1991). Republican George W. Bush was elected to the office in 1994 and again in 1998, and Republican Rick Perry was elected in 2002 and 2006, as Republican strength increased in Texas.

Most governors have been well-educated, middle-aged, and affluent white male Protestants. In many cases, their families were active in public life and helped shape their careers. No minorities and only two women have been elected to the office. Miriam A. "Ma" Ferguson, whose husband, James E. "Pa" Ferguson, had earlier been gover-

TABLE 9–2   Governors of Texas Since 1870

	Party Affiliation	Served
Edmund J. Davis	Republican	1870–1874
Richard Coke	Democrat	1874–1876
Richard B. Hubbard	Democrat	1876–1879
Oran M. Roberts	Democrat	1879–1883
John Ireland	Democrat	1883–1887
Lawrence Sullivan Ross	Democrat	1887–1891
James Stephen Hogg	Democrat	1891–1895
Charles A. Culberson	Democrat	1895–1899
Joseph D. Sayers	Democrat	1899–1903
Samuel W.T. Lanham	Democrat	1903–1907
Thomas Mitchell Campbell	Democrat	1907–1911
Oscar Branch Colquitt	Democrat	1911–1915
James E. Ferguson*	Democrat	1915–1917
William Pettus Hobby	Democrat	1917–1921
Pat Morris Neff	Democrat	1921–1925
Miriam A. Ferguson	Democrat	1925–1927
Dan Moody	Democrat	1927–1931
Ross S. Sterling	Democrat	1931–1933
Miriam A. Ferguson	Democrat	1933–1935
James V. Allred	Democrat	1935–1939
W. Lee O'Daniel	Democrat	1939–1941
Coke R. Stevenson	Democrat	1941–1947
Beauford H. Jester	Democrat	1947–1949
Allan Shivers	Democrat	1949–1957
Price Daniel	Democrat	1957–1963
John Connally	Democrat	1963–1969
Preston Smith	Democrat	1969–1973
Dolph Briscoe, Jr.**	Democrat	1973–1979
Williams P. Clements, Jr.	Republican	1979–1983
Mark White	Democrat	1983–1987
William P. Clements, Jr.	Republican	1987–1991
Ann Richards	Democrat	1991–1995
George W. Bush	Republican	1995–2000
Rick Perry	Republican	2000–present

*Only governor of Texas to be impeached and convicted.

**Prior to 1974, governors were elected for two-year terms of office.

Source: Texas State Library & Archives Commission, *Portraits of Texas Governors.*

served two terms (1925–1927 and 1933–1935), and Ann Richards served one term (1991–1995). By the time Richards became governor, only three women had ever been elected to statewide executive office in Texas. Richards, a Democrat, served two terms as state treasurer before being elected governor and was succeeded as treasurer by Republican Kay Bailey Hutchison. From 1919 to 1923, Annie Webb Blanton was state superintendent of schools, an elective office that no longer exists.

Miriam A. "Ma" Ferguson. She was the first woman to serve as governor of Texas (1925–1927 and 1933–1935). After her husband was denied a place on the ballot in 1924, she ran for governor under the slogan "two governors for the price of one."

With the rising costs of statewide political campaigns, a candidate's personal wealth or ability to raise large sums of money has taken on increased importance (see Chapter 7). Otherwise-qualified prospects are dissuaded from running for governor and other offices because of the difficult burden of fundraising. Former Governor Bill Clements and fellow Republican Clayton Williams, a Midland businessman who lost the 1990 gubernatorial race to Richards, spent millions of dollars out of their own pockets on gubernatorial races that were their first bids for elective office. Similarly, Democrat Tony Sanchez, a wealthy Laredo businessman, spent more than $50 million of his personal fortune on an unsuccessful race for governor in 2002. Their experience raises the possibility that personal wealth and the willingness to spend it on one's own election campaign will take on more importance in future races.

Modern campaigns are increasingly shaped by the mass media, particularly television, and media-driven campaigns usually are concerned more with image than substance. Some gubernatorial candidates have had difficulty utilizing or exploiting the mass media to their advantage. Candidates—no matter how qualified—who do not understand the electronic media are likely to be rebuffed in their efforts to win major statewide office.

Previous public service has provided gubernatorial aspirants with public visibility and linkages to party leaders, interest groups, and public officials around the state. Such relationships help candidates develop broad electoral support. Texas governors have previously served in local and statewide offices, the legislature, and Congress. Preston Smith (1969–1973) was a legislator and lieutenant governor prior to being elected governor. Dolph Briscoe (1973–1979) also served in the legislature. Mark White (1983–1987) served as secretary of state and then as attorney general. Ann Richards was a county commissioner and then state treasurer. Although he had never previously held elective office, Clements was a deputy U.S. secretary of defense prior to winning his first gubernatorial race. George W. Bush was elected governor in 1994 without any previous formal government experience. He had been an unofficial adviser to his father, former President George Bush. Rick Perry was a state representative, agriculture commissioner, and lieutenant governor before becoming governor.

IMPEACHMENT AND INCAPACITATION

A governor can be removed from office through impeachment proceedings initiated in the House of Representatives and conviction by the Senate in a trial of the impeachment charges (see "Impeaching a Governor"). Across the country, the most recent governor to be removed from office through the impeachment process was Rod Blagojevich of Illinois, who was voted out of office in early 2009 after being indicted on federal corruption charges in 2008.[14] Other states, such as California, can remove a governor through recall as well as impeachment. Through a process initiated by a petition of voters, a special election is held on the question of the removal of the governor. If the governor is removed by popular vote, a new governor is then elected. This occurred in late 2003 in California, when Democrat Gray Davis was recalled as governor and voters, in the same election, selected Arnold Schwarzenegger, a Republican, to replace him. Texas does not have the recall process for statewide officeholders.

If the governor dies, is incapacitated, is impeached and convicted, or voluntarily leaves office in midterm, the lieutenant governor replaces the governor until the next general election. In instances when the governor leaves the state, the lieutenant governor serves as acting governor.

Impeaching a Governor

Texas is one of only a few states that have removed a governor by impeachment. In 1917, a controversy erupted over Governor James E. "Pa" Ferguson's efforts to remove five University of Texas faculty members. The governor vetoed the university's appropriations, and when he called a special legislative session to consider other funding, he was immediately faced with articles of impeachment based primarily on the misuse of public funds. He ultimately was convicted and removed from office. But for two more decades, the husband-and-wife team of Ma and Pa Ferguson and the controversy that continued to surround them dominated a great deal of Texas politics.[15]

Impeachment politics. Governor James E. "Pa" Ferguson was the only governor (1915–1917) to be removed from office through the impeachment process. Ferguson was impeached and convicted during a controversy over his efforts to remove five University of Texas faculty members.

Torched. The 152-year-old Governor's Mansion, located across the street from the capitol building in Austin, was torched by an arsonist on June 8, 2008. The mansion, under renovation and unoccupied at the time, suffered extensive damage.

THE SALARY AND "PERKS" OF THE OFFICE

In 2009, the governor of Texas was paid $115,345. The state also provides the governor with housing, a security detail, travel expenses, and access to state-owned planes and cars. For many years, governors and their families lived in the Governor's Mansion in downtown Austin near the capitol. But that historic structure was severely damaged by an arsonist in 2008 while it was closed for renovations. Governor Rick Perry and his family already had relocated to a rental house elsewhere in Austin before the fire, and they remained there while state officials deliberated over how to rebuild the mansion.

THE POWERS OF THE GOVERNOR

There are competing views of the chief executive's functions, which have changed over time. Early state constitutions limited gubernatorial powers, and governors in many states found themselves in a subordinate position to their legislatures. Throughout the nineteenth century, those relationships were often redefined. At times, the governors' powers were increased and those of the legislatures reduced. During other periods, such as the era of Jacksonian democracy, the powers of both institutions were subjected to strong restrictions to assure greater responsiveness to the public. Reform movements of the early twentieth century, responding to political corruption, focused on management and efficiency in the governors' offices. In some states, the office of governor was restructured around the organizational principles of an executive cabinet. Events such as the Great Depression contributed to a further redefinition of executive leadership, with an emphasis in some states on policy initiatives, administrative control and coordination, and expanded political leadership.[16] The Texas Constitution of 1845, adopted when the state was admitted to the Union, modeled the governor's authority on the strong executive principle found in the U.S. Constitution. Later Texas constitutions reduced the powers of the office, however, reflecting apprehension of strong executive and political authority.

Texans, nonetheless, appear to have high expectations of their governor. Governors are evaluated in terms of their policy agendas and the leadership they exercise in achieving those goals. But how does a governor meet such expectations when the formal powers of the office are limited? The following discussion analyzes the formal powers and reviews the informal resources that the governor can use to complement them.

Legislative Powers

The governor has the opportunity to outline his or her legislative priorities at the beginning of each regular biennial session through the traditional "state of the state" address to the legislature. The governor also can communicate with lawmakers—collectively or individually—throughout the session. In this fashion, the governor can establish a policy agenda, recommend specific legislation, and set the stage for negotiations with legislative leaders, other state officials, and interest groups. The governor's addresses and other formal messages to the legislature are well covered by the media. They give the governor the opportunity to mobilize the public support that may be essential to the success of his or her initiatives.

The governor's effectiveness can be enhanced by the office's two major constitutional powers over the legislature—the veto and the authority to call and set the agenda for special legislative sessions.

The governor can call any number of special sessions, which can last as long as thirty days, and designate the subjects to be considered during the session. Sometimes, the mere threat of a special session can be enough to convince reluctant lawmakers to approve a priority program of the governor or reach an acceptable compromise during a regular session. Most legislators, who are paid only part-time salaries by the state, dread special sessions because they interfere with their regular occupations and disrupt their personal lives. Governor Bill Clements, who called two special sessions on workers' compensation reform in 1989, used the threat of a third to convince a handful of senators to break a year-long impasse and approve legislation backed by the governor, a majority of the House, and the business community. Governor Rick Perry called three special sessions in 2003 to win approval of a congressional redistricting bill that favored Republican candidates. The bill wouldn't have been passed without Perry's persistence (see Chapter 8).

There also are risks in calling special sessions. The governor's influence and reputation are on the line, and further inaction by the legislature can become a political liability. In some instances, the legislative leadership has liberally interpreted the subject matter of a governor's special session proclamation and considered bills not sought by the governor. Since the speaker and the lieutenant governor make the parliamentary rulings that determine whether a specific piece of legislation falls within the governor's call, the governor has to draft a proclamation setting a special session's agenda very carefully. Once a special session is called, the governor can increase his or her bargaining power by adding legislators' pet bills to the agenda in exchange for the lawmakers' support of the governor's program.

The governor of Texas has one of the strongest veto powers of any governor. When the legislature is in session, the governor has ten days (excluding Sundays) to veto a bill, sign it, or let it become law without his or her signature. A veto can be overridden by a two thirds vote of both the House and the Senate. During the past fifty years, Governor Clements was the only governor to have a veto overridden by lawmakers. It was a local bill related to game management that the Democrat-dominated legislature voted to override during the Republican governor's first term. The governor has twenty days after the legislature adjourns to veto bills passed in the closing days of a session. Such vetoes are absolute because the only way the legislature can respond is to have the bill reintroduced in the next session.

The governor also has line-item veto authority over the state budget. That is, the governor can strike specific spending items without vetoing the entire bill. All other bills have to be accepted or rejected in their entirety.

A governor may veto a bill for a number of reasons, including doubts about its constitutionality, objections to its wording, concerns that it duplicates existing law, or substantive differences with its policy. A governor's threat of a veto often is as effective as an actual veto because such threats can prompt legislators to make changes in their bills to meet a governor's objections.

Historic records on gubernatorial vetoes are not complete, but Governor Rick Perry is believed to have set a single-year record by vetoing 82 bills at the end of the 2001 legislative session. Those vetoes sparked a lot of anger from doctors, criminal justice reformers, state employees, advocates for the poor, and others. One veto, the striking down of a bill that would have banned the execution of mentally retarded convicts in Texas, received international attention. Although that veto was sharply criticized by death penalty opponents, it drew praise from crime victims' advocates. Perry attempted to milk the most favorable publicity that he could from the event by inviting more than a dozen relatives of people murdered by mentally retarded convicts to join him at a state capitol news conference to announce the veto.

Governor Dan Moody also was a frequent veto user. He vetoed 117 bills and resolutions between 1927 and 1931. Governor Richards vetoed thirty-six bills and resolutions in one regular and two special sessions in 1991 and allowed 228 bills to become law without her signature (see "The Governor's Leadership Resources").

Budgetary Powers

The governor of Texas has weaker budgetary authority than the governors of most states and the president of the United States. These budgetary constraints limit the governor's ability to develop a comprehensive legislative program. The budgetary process will be discussed in more detail in Chapter 13, but the legislature has the lead in budget-setting, with a major role played by the Legislative Budget Board (LBB), a ten-member panel that includes the lieutenant governor, the speaker, and eight key lawmakers. The LBB and the governor both make budgetary recommendations to the legislature, but lawmakers usually give greater attention to the LBB's product.

To meet emergencies between legislative sessions, the governor can propose the transfer of funds between programs or agencies, with the approval of the LBB. Or the LBB can recommend a funds transfer, subject to the governor's approval.

The Governor's Leadership Resources

Formal Constitutional Powers

- Veto legislation
- Exercise a line-item veto over the state budget
- Call and set the agenda for special legislative sessions
- Make recommendations on the budget
- Propose emergency budgetary transfers when the legislature is not in session
- Appoint hundreds of members of policy-making boards and commissions, subject to Senate confirmation
- Remove his or her own appointees from boards, with Senate approval
- Fill vacancies in U.S. Senate seats and certain elective state offices
- Proclaim acts of executive clemency, including stays of execution, for convicted criminals

- Mobilize the Texas National Guard to protect lives and property during natural disasters and other emergencies

Informal Resources

- Governor's electoral mandate
- A large staff to help develop and sell policy proposals
- Ability to communicate to the public through the mass media
- Public's perception and opinions about the governor's job performance
- The governor's political party and relationships with legislative leaders.
- Support and mobilization of interest groups

Appointive Powers

One indication of a strong governor is the power to hire and fire the persons responsible for implementing public policy. But as we discussed earlier in this chapter, the Texas governor's administrative authority is severely limited by the plural executive structure under which independently elected officeholders head several major state agencies.

Most of the remainder of the state bureaucracy falls under more than 200 boards and commissions that oversee various agencies created by state law. Most of these are part-time, unpaid positions whose occupants are heavily dependent on agency staffs and constituents for guidance. Although members of these boards are appointed by the governor and confirmed by the Senate, the structure creates the potential for boards and commissions to become captives of the narrow constituencies they are serving or regulating and reduces their accountability to both the governor and the legislature.

Most board members serve six-year **staggered terms**. That means it takes a new governor at least two years to get majorities favoring his or her policies on most boards. Resignations or deaths of board members may speed up the process, but a governor cannot remove a predecessor's appointees. A governor, with the approval of two-thirds of the Senate, can fire only his or her own appointees.

The governor appoints individuals to boards and commissions with approval of two-thirds of the Senate. **Senatorial courtesy**, an unwritten norm of the Senate, permits a senator to block the governor's nomination of a person who lives in that senator's district. The governor and staff members involved in appointments spend considerable time clearing potential nominees with senators because political considerations are as important in the confirmation process as a nominee's qualifications.

Individuals seek gubernatorial appointments for a variety of reasons, and the appointments process can be hectic, particularly at the beginning of a new governor's administration. Potential nominees are screened by the governor's staff to determine their availability and competence, political acceptability, and support by key interest groups. Although most governors would deny it, campaign contributions are also a significant factor. A number of Governor Clements' appointees had made substantial contributions to his campaign.[17] Governors Richards, Bush, and Perry also appointed major contributors to important posts. Governor Perry made the most controversial appointment of his first year in office, former Enron Corporation executive Max Yzaguirre as chairman of the Public Utility Commission, one day before receiving a $25,000 political donation from then-Enron Chairman Ken Lay in 2001. Perry insisted the timing was coincidental, but it generated much controversy after Enron filed for bankruptcy a few months later, prompting Yzaguirre's resignation from the post. Then, in 2003, less than one month after receiving a $100,000 contribution from homebuilder Bob Perry of Houston, Governor Perry appointed a top executive of the homebuilder's company to a new state commission charged with developing building performance standards. The commission had been created by the legislature to reduce consumer lawsuits against builders. Since June 1997, Bob Perry, who wasn't related to the governor, had contributed $580,000 to Rick Perry.[18] According to an analysis by the *Houston Chronicle*, Perry had accepted nearly $5 million in political donations from appointees through 2008. Nearly half of those donations came from individuals named to higher education governing boards.[19]

The governor appoints individuals to fill vacancies on all courts at the district level or above. If a U.S. senator dies or resigns, the governor appoints a replacement. When a vacancy occurs in another statewide office, except for the lieutenant governor, the governor also appoints a replacement. All of these appointees must later win election to keep their seats.

Governor Richards was particularly sensitive to constituencies that historically have been excluded from full participation in the governmental process and appointed a record number of women and minorities to state posts. About 41 percent of Richards' appointees during her four-year term were women, and about 33 percent were minorities. Her successor, Governor Bush, appointed women to 37 percent and minorities to 24 percent of the posts he filled during his first five years in office.[20] Bush appointed the first African American, Michael Williams, to the Texas Railroad Commission, and, at different times during his administration, appointed two Hispanics—Tony Garza and Alberto R. Gonzales—secretary of state. Bush later appointed Gonzales to fill a vacancy on the Texas Supreme Court. After Bush was elected president, he appointed Garza as U.S. ambassador to Mexico and Gonzales as White House counsel and later U.S. attorney general. Governor Perry appointed the first African American, Wallace Jefferson, to the Texas Supreme Court.

Judicial Powers

Texas has a seven-member Board of Pardons and Paroles, appointed by the governor.[21] This panel, which was reduced from eighteen members by a 2003 law, decides when prisoners can be released early, and its decisions do not require action by the governor. The governor, however, can influence the board's overall approach to paroles, as Governor Richards did when she convinced her appointees to sharply curtail the parole rate. This was done in response to citizen outrage over crimes committed by parolees (see Chapter 13).

The governor has the authority to grant executive clemency—acts of leniency or mercy—toward convicted criminals. One is a thirty-day stay of execution for a condemned murderer, which a governor can grant without a recommendation of the parole board. The governor, on recommendation of the board, can grant a full pardon to a criminal, a conditional pardon, or the commutation of a death sentence to life imprisonment.[22]

If a person flees a state to avoid prosecution or a prison term, the U.S. Constitution, under the extradition clause, requires that person, upon arrest in another state, to be returned to the state from which he or she fled. The governor is legally responsible for ordering state officials to carry out such extradition requests.[23]

Military Powers

The Texas Constitution authorizes the governor to function as the "commander-in-chief of the military force of the state, except when they are called into actual service of the United States."[24] The governor appoints the adjutant general to carry out this duty. Texas cannot declare war on another country, and the president of the United States has the primary responsibility for national defense. But when riots or natural disasters occur within the state, the governor can mobilize the Texas National Guard to protect lives and property and keep the peace. Should the United States go to war, the National Guard can be mobilized by the president as part of the national military forces. After the September 11, 2001 terrorist attacks on the World Trade Center and the Pentagon, some National Guard members from Texas were activated to temporarily bolster security at airports. Others went overseas to assist in the military operations in Afghanistan and Iraq. And some were assigned to support the U.S. Border Patrol along the U.S.–Mexico border after President George W. Bush ordered the National Guard's assistance in securing the border during political debate over illegal immigration.

INFORMAL RESOURCES OF THE GOVERNOR ————————●

Governors can compensate for the constitutional limitations on their office with their articulation of problems and issues, leadership capabilities, personalities, work habits, and administrative styles. Some governors want to get involved in the minutiae of building policy coalitions and give much of their personal time to effecting compromises and agreements. Other governors find such hands-on involvement distasteful, inefficient, and time-consuming and leave such detail work to subordinates.

As the most visible state official, the governor sometimes gets the credit that belongs to others but can just as readily be blamed for problems beyond his or her control. For example, a major factor in Governor Mark White's loss of his 1986 reelection bid was falling oil prices that had devastated the state's economy. White had no choice but to call the legislature into special session only a few months before the November election. Under the circumstances, he probably exercised the best leadership that he could in convincing lawmakers to cut the budget and raise taxes. But it wasn't the type of leadership appreciated by most voters.

The Governor's Staff

Nineteenth-century governors had only three or four individuals to assist them, but staffs have grown with the increased complexity of state government and the increased demands on the governor's time. By 1963, under John Connally, the governor's staff had grown to sixty-eight full-time and twelve part-time employees.[25] Under the administration of Dolph Briscoe in the 1970s, the staff expanded to more than 300, but staff sizes were smaller in most subsequent administrations. At one point in her term, Ann Richards had almost 300 people on her staff. The number decreased to about 200 under George W. Bush, but Bush approved higher salaries for some of his key staffers. Governor Perry also has about 200 employees.

The staff's organization reflects the governor's leadership style. Some governors create a highly centralized office with a chief of staff who functions to screen contacts and information going to the governor. Other governors want greater personal contacts with numerous staff members. But the critical question is whether the governor is getting sufficient information with which to make decisions that produce good public policy and minimize the potential for controversy, conflict, or embarrassment. Under ideal circumstances, the staff enhances the governor's political, administrative, and policymaking capabilities. There have been instances, however, when a governor has permitted his staff to insulate him by denying access to persons with significant information or recommendations.

Governors generally choose staffers who are loyal and share their basic political attitudes. Since communication with the governor's various constituencies is fundamental to success, some staffers are chosen for their skills in mass communications and public relations. Others are hired for their expertise in specific policy areas.[26] In many respects, staff members function as the governor's surrogates. Thus, if one makes a mistake, particularly a serious mistake, the public will perceive it as the governor's error.

The staff collects, organizes, and screens information, helps decide who sees the governor, and otherwise schedules the governor's time. Staffers also work on strategies to garner support for the governor's proposals from legislators, agencies, interest groups, and the public. Because the governor often lacks the time to conduct discussions and negotiations personally, key staff members often represent the governor in meetings and in lobbying lawmakers. Sometimes the governor gets involved personally, particularly if his or her participation is needed to break an impasse and effect a solution.[27]

The Governor and the Mass Media

The mass media help shape the political and policy options of the governor. Governors who have failed to understand the impact of the mass media have often courted disaster. A governor who is readily accessible to the media and understands the constraints under which the media operate is likely to develop a good working relationship with the press. But success with the media is more than being accessible and friendly.

Governors call press conferences to announce new policies or explain their positions on pending issues. They stage pseudo "news events," such as visiting a classroom to emphasize concern for educational quality or a high-tech facility to demonstrate a commitment to economic development. They or their staffers sometimes leak information to selected reporters to embarrass the opposition, put an action of the administration in the best possible light, or float a trial balloon to gauge legislative or public reaction to a proposal. Some governors spend political funds to purchase radio or television time to try to mobilize public opinion in support of pet proposals before the legislature. Overall, the timely use of the media can contribute significantly to the power and influence of a governor.

Periodic statewide public opinion polls commissioned by media organizations often include questions about the governor's performance. Those ratings are widely monitored by players in the political arena.

The Governor and the Political Party

Historically, the political factions within one-party Democratic Texas were somewhat ill-defined. Factionalism was often described in terms of liberal or conservative, but there were also complex urban–rural, regional, and economic differences. Democratic governors built policy coalitions around these factions, but there was little stability or continuity, and most governors derived only limited power from their position as party leader.

Under the two-party system, however, the political party is taking on more importance and may provide greater resources to the governor (see Figure 9–2). During his second term in the late 1980s, Bill Clements often had enough Republican votes in the House to thwart the will of the Democratic majority. After Republicans had gained legislative control, Rick Perry had strong support from Republican lawmakers and party officials during the budgetary and redistricting battles of 2003 (see Chapter 8).

Upon taking office in 1995, Republican Governor George W. Bush enjoyed the support of party leaders for his own priorities—efforts to improve education, restrict civil lawsuits, reform juvenile justice, and change the welfare system. Initially, he kept his distance from much of the agenda advocated by the social conservatives who had taken control of leadership positions in the Texas Republican Party in 1994. But in 1999, when he was preparing for a presidential race, Bush strengthened his antiabortion credentials with social conservatives by helping to convince the legislature to enact one of their major priorities—a law requiring parents to be notified before their minor daughters could have abortions. Governor Perry courted social conservatives from the beginning of his

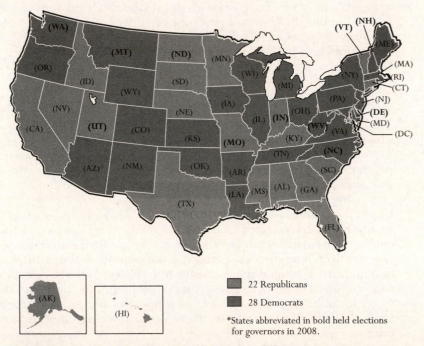

22 Republicans

28 Democrats

*States abbreviated in bold held elections for governors in 2008.

FIGURE 9–2   Party Control of the Governor's Office. *Source:* Democratic Governors Association, "Post Election Governors"; and Republican Governors Association, "2008 Gubernatorial Seats Up."

administration. He solidified their support for his 2006 reelection race with enactment of a state constitutional amendment banning same-sex marriages and a law that required parental approval, not just notification, for minors to get abortions. Perry, however, faced strong opposition from many conservatives in 2007 when he tried to order schoolgirls to be vaccinated against a virus linked to cervical cancer. Opponents said the governor was trying to interfere with parental rights.

The Governor and Interest Groups

Successful governors must be consummate political animals who continually nurture relationships throughout the political system. A gubernatorial candidate aggressively solicits the endorsements and contributions of various groups. These groups, in turn, develop stakes in gubernatorial elections and usually assume that the candidates they support will be responsive to their interests. A governor's policy initiatives often include legislation of benefit to key support groups, which maintain active roles throughout the policy process. Business groups, for example, were major contributors to Governor Rick Perry's successful election race in 2002, and the governor strongly supported their priorities, including additional limits on civil lawsuits, during the 2003 regular legislative session.

LEADERSHIP STYLES OF RECENT TEXAS GOVERNORS

Gubernatorial leadership styles have been as varied as the personalities that molded the chief executives' approaches to their jobs. Some governors have come to the office with well-defined policy agendas and attempted to exploit every resource available to them. Other governors have taken a more limited view of the office. They adopted an administrative or managerial posture and left policy initiatives to other institutions or elected officials. New programs, especially those with far-reaching tax or social implications, were pursued with considerable caution.

Some governors have thrived on the constant attention and political and social interactions that go with the office. They have worked long hours, continually engaged in public relations and coalition building. Strange as it may seem, however, there have been other governors who were introverted and apparently found many aspects of the office distasteful. They often insulated themselves from the public and other political officials through their staffs and seemed detached from the activities necessary to influence public policy.[28]

Bill Clements (1979–1983, 1987–1991)

Clements, a self-made multimillionaire who had founded an international oil-drilling firm, personally funded much of his first campaign in 1978, effectively using a sophisticated media strategy. The man who shocked the Democratic establishment by defeating John Hill by 17,000 votes had held no previous elected office. His only governmental experience had been as deputy secretary of defense under Presidents Richard Nixon and Gerald Ford. He was an outsider, a Republican, highly opinionated and blunt, and had a reputation for solid management skills. All the other elected statewide officials were Democrats, as were the vast majority of legislators, although many lawmakers shared Clements's conservative views.

A Republican in the Governor's Mansion. Bill Clements was the first Republican governor since Reconstruction and served during a period that coincided with the emergence of the two-party system in Texas.

On arriving in Austin, Clements did not understand the limitations of the powers of the governor.[29] In his election campaign, he had tapped a rather widely held view that state government was wasteful and had proposed that 25,000 state jobs be eliminated. He also appealed to popular notions of limited government and proposed that the Texas Constitution be amended to allow private citizens to propose laws through the initiative and referendum process. Gradually, however, he learned that he couldn't single-handedly run the statehouse and the bureaucracy the way he had the corporate boardroom, and he didn't accomplish either of those goals.

In an interview years later, Clements admitted that he didn't fully understand how state government worked when he first took office:

> Until I came to Austin and until I actually was in office and everything, I really didn't understand the detailed nuance of how the state government really functioned. I'd say it took me at least through that first legislative session. And, by the time that was over, well, I began to understand exactly how the state government works.[30]

Clements eagerly exercised his veto power. During his first legislative session in 1979, he vetoed a near-record fifty-one bills.[31] He also struck $252 million from the $20.7 billion state budget for 1980–1981.[32]

Clements generally received high marks for the quality of his staff and board appointments during his first term. Republicans, who for years had been shut out of appointments to boards and commissions, were appointed by the Republican governor. Yet Clements also appointed many conservative Democrats. In part, his appointment strategies were designed to convert conservative Democrats to the Republican Party, thus extending and consolidating Republican gains across the state. Clements made many judicial appointments during his two terms, including the first two women to the Texas Supreme Court and the first African American to the Court of Criminal Appeals.

Clements never developed effective public relations with the legislature, the news media, and the general public, and he often found himself at odds with other elected officials and interest groups, primarily because of his outspokenness. He was often portrayed as insensitive, as someone inclined to "shoot from the lip" and worry about the consequences later. After learning at a meeting at Texas A&M University that scuba diving by a pregnant woman could damage a fetus, he angered many women by saying, in jest, that diving could serve as a form of birth control. After an offshore Mexican oil well blew out and threatened Texas beaches in 1979, Clements advised coastal residents against "crying over spilt milk." The insensitive remark was compounded by revelations that SEDCO, the drilling firm he had founded, had leased the drilling equipment used on the blown-out well.

By the end of his first term in 1982, Clements's job performance rating had dropped, his image had suffered, and the Texas economy had begun to show signs of weakness. A revitalized Democratic statewide political effort helped Mark White unseat Clements in a bitterly fought campaign.

In 1986, Clements became only the second person in Texas history to regain the governor's office after losing it. And, though his motivations for staging a comeback effort weren't totally clear, it was widely believed that his main interest was revenge. His hostility toward White remained so intense that he snubbed White's offer of a handshake on Inauguration Day, a clear violation of the unwritten rules of American politics.

Clements spent his first six months back in Austin battling Lieutenant Governor Bill Hobby and Democratic legislators over the state budget. Clements insisted on deep service cuts that would have enabled him to keep a 1986 campaign promise against higher taxes, but he finally gave in during a summer special session in 1987 and signed a record $5.6 billion tax increase.

The public's opinion of Clements, meanwhile, was plummeting. Two-thirds of the respondents to the *Texas Poll* that summer said they disapproved of the governor's job performance.[33] Clements's negative ratings remained high throughout the remainder of his term. By the time he left the governor's office the second time, in 1991, he was widely viewed more as an obstructionist who would rather fight the Democratic majority in the legislature than as a leader who was ready to seek solutions to significant state problems.

After another standoff with the legislature over taxes in 1990, Clements again gave in and signed a $512 million tax increase. The revenue helped pay for a new school finance bill—which, ironically, was struck down as unconstitutional by the Supreme Court the next year—and met funding shortfalls in the Texas Department of Human Services and the Texas Department of Health. Clements, an avowed fiscal conservative, signed $6.1 billion in tax increases during his second term—more than any other governor in Texas history. The Texas economy was undergoing a painful transition in the wake of the oil bust, and state government's existing tax base was strained at a time of increasing budgetary demands.

Clements's two terms converged with the emergence of a two-party system in Texas, and his candidacy and elections contributed significantly to this historic development. By proving that a Republican could win the governorship, Clements made the party attractive to conservative Democrats, and many switched to the Republican Party.

There were only a handful of Republicans in the legislature and none in any other elected state offices when Clements was elected to his first term. After Clements had completed his second term in January 1991, Republicans held four of the nine seats on the Texas Supreme Court, two other statewide offices (in addition to a U.S. Senate seat), and more than one-third of the seats in the Texas House. They also had made major inroads in county and other local offices throughout the state.

In an interview in late 1990, Clements assessed his contribution to the development of a two-party system:

> The electorate out there breaks down into about one-third Democrats, one-third Republicans, and one-third independents. Well, that is a significant change in the political profile of Texas. That's a historic change, and I guess I'd like to say that I put a brick in place to bring that about.[34]

Ann Richards (1991–1995)

Taking her oath in January 1991, Governor Ann Richards attempted to convince the public that her election marked the emergence of a "New Texas." She invited supporters to join her in a march up Congress Avenue to symbolically retake the Capitol for "the people." And, hitting on the progressive Democratic themes of her campaign, she promised in her inaugural address a user-friendly, compassionate state government that would expand opportunities for everyone, particularly minorities and women. She promised to clean up the environment, improve education, attack crime, cut red tape, and boost ethical standards for public officeholders.

But the euphoria of the day was tempered by the reality of a $4 billion-plus potential deficit, a court order for school finance reform that could make the shortfall even greater, and a grand-jury investigation into legislative behavior that had further eroded public confidence in state government.

Richards moved quickly to establish herself as an activist governor. The day after her inauguration, she continued a campaign assault against high insurance rates by marching over to a meeting of the State Board of Insurance to speak against a proposed increase in auto insurance premiums. Unlike her recent predecessors, she also testified before House and Senate committees, ensuring that her legislative priorities would receive maximum media coverage. She also used the media to attack the state bureaucracy.

Richards also quickly fulfilled a campaign promise to appoint more women and minorities to key positions in state government. She appointed the first African American to the University of Texas System Board of Regents, the first African-American woman to the Texas A&M University governing board, and the first Hispanic to the Texas Court of Criminal Appeals. Twenty-five percent of the appointees during her first three months in office were Hispanic, 21 percent were African American, and 49 percent were women. Richards also named a disabled person to the Board of Human Services and a crime victim to the Board of Criminal Justice.[35]

With the state facing a revenue crunch, Richards took the lead in lobbying legislators for a constitutional amendment to create a state lottery. She failed to muster the necessary two-thirds vote in the House during the 1991 regular session, but finally prevailed in winning legislative approval in a special session that summer. The lottery was a relatively safe issue on which to stake a leadership claim because polls indicated it had the strong support of most Texans as a new source of revenue for state government.

Most other major issues before the legislature during Richards's first year in office, however, weren't so simple, and the new governor was less willing to strike specific policy positions on them. She preferred to support the initiatives of Democratic legislative leaders, or take the best bill they were willing to give her, rather than demand that legislators enact a specific plan. Richards, for example, outlined strong provisions for a new ethics law for legislators and other public officials, but ended up signing a much weaker bill rather than trying to force a showdown. Detractors would say Richards's

Increased role of women and minorities in state administration. Ann Richards was the second woman to be elected governor. She followed through on her campaign promises by increasing the number of women and minorities appointed to administrative positions.

leadership wilted in the heat of legislative battle. Supporters would say she was a pragmatist who knew the limits of her office and recognized the necessity of political compromise.

The progressive goals that Richards had outlined in her campaign were also tempered by the reality that Texas was a predominantly conservative state. Despite promoting a vision of a "New Texas" that offered more compassion for the poor, improved health care for the sick, and greater educational opportunity for all, Richards took pains to establish credentials for fiscal restraint. She opposed a proposal for a personal income tax, even though it could have provided a big boost in health and human services programs and education spending. She also eagerly launched a thorough review of state spending practices that helped reduce the size of the revenue and tax bill that she eventually signed during her first year in office.

Although Richards entered the 1993 legislative session with one of the highest public approval ratings of any governor in Texas history, she remained cautious during the entire session, apparently to save political capital for a 1994 reelection race. She joined Lieutenant Governor Bob Bullock and Speaker Pete Laney in insisting that a new state budget be written without an increase in state taxes. There was no tax bill, but the new budget didn't enable the legislature to give teachers a pay raise, which had been a Richards priority, and it didn't keep up with growing caseloads in health and human services.

In one of the most emotional issues of the session, Richards sided with police chiefs, mayors, physicians, and members of the clergy—and against a majority of the legislature—in killing a proposal to allow private citizens to legally carry handguns. (It was revived and approved under Governor George W. Bush two years later.) She successfully advocated an immunization program for children and actively promoted the legislature's efforts to meet a Texas Supreme Court order for a constitutional school finance system, but didn't propose a plan of her own.

Richards staked out a strong anti-crime position early in her term. In 1991, she ordered her appointees to the Board of Pardons and Paroles to sharply curtail a high rate of releases from state prisons, and she supported a huge prison expansion program. Richards also made economic development a major goal. She actively recruited companies to locate or expand in Texas and was instrumental in lobbying the U.S. Congress for approval of the North American Free Trade Agreement (NAFTA), even though NAFTA was bitterly opposed by organized labor, one of her long-time, key supporters.

Richards was a national figure who was readily welcomed on Wall Street, at Hollywood parties, and in corporate boardrooms throughout the country. Many analysts believed her role as Texas's chief ambassador was her greatest contribution, along with the appointments that opened up the state policymaking process to a record number of women, Hispanics, and African Americans.

Richards, who had no legislative experience, didn't seem to relish the often bloody give-and-take of the legislative process but obviously enjoyed her celebrity role as governor. During the 1993 session, Richards told reporters she wasn't the kind of leader who could force results. Instead, she said, she tried to contribute to "an atmosphere in which good things can happen."[36]

Although Richards was unseated by Republican George W. Bush in 1994, polls indicated she remained personally popular with her constituents. But most conservative, independent voters had never been comfortable with Richards politically. Her defeat coincided with voter discontent with the Democratic Party that swept the country that year. A number of other Democratic governors were also defeated, and Republicans captured control of both houses of the U.S. Congress. Richards's opposition to the handgun bill during the 1993 legislative session was another factor, particularly in key conservative areas of the state.

After leaving office, Richards was a lobbyist in Washington and remained in the public eye as a frequent television commentator. She died of cancer in 2006.

George W. Bush (1995–2000)

George W. Bush, son of former President George Bush, had never held public office before being elected governor, but he had gained valuable political experience campaigning for and serving as an unofficial adviser to his father. The younger Bush became Texas's second Republican governor in modern times by conducting an effective campaign for improvements in the public schools, tougher penalties for juvenile offenders, and reform of the welfare and civil justice systems. He succeeded in winning legislative approval of all four programs during the 1995 legislative session, the first of his term.

Bush's public style was low key. He seemed to go out of his way to avoid controversy during his first year in office. But he remained focused on his four primary goals, and he was assisted by conservative, Democratic legislative leaders who shared his views and sensed that public sentiment was on the governor's side. Although Democrats had majorities in both the House and the Senate in 1995, the Texas legislature was dominated by conservatives of both major parties, and work on some of the reforms the new governor wanted had already been initiated by Democratic officials.

While keeping a low public profile during his first legislative session, Bush actively worked with legislators behind the scenes, making minor compromises when necessary on his policy priorities. The governor had frequent private meetings with House and

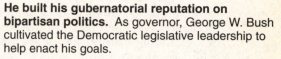

He built his gubernatorial reputation on bipartisan politics. As governor, George W. Bush cultivated the Democratic legislative leadership to help enact his goals.

Senate members and would sometimes drop by their capitol offices unannounced. He had weekly breakfast meetings with Lieutenant Governor Bob Bullock and Speaker Pete Laney, two Democrats whose work was crucial to the governor's program. "We disagree, but you'll never read about it," Bush said of his meetings with the two legislative leaders. "The way to forge good public policy amongst the leadership of the legislative branch and executive branch is to air our differences in private meetings that happen all the time. The way to ruin a relationship is to leak things [to the media] and to be disrespectful of meeting in private."[37]

Bush also believed his decisive victory in the 1994 election helped his cause in the legislature. "I won by 352,000 votes," he told reporters the day after the 1995 session adjourned. "And when you stand up in front of the legislature and outline a legislative agenda that was endorsed by the will of the people, that helps remind people that this is what Texans want."[38]

Unlike Governors White, Clements, and Richards before him, Bush did not face budgetary problems in state government that could have distracted lawmakers' attention from his priorities. Unlike Richards, Bush supported legislation that gave adult Texans the right to carry concealed handguns. The gun bill was not one of Bush's major priorities, but it had been an issue in his victory over Richards. Bush signed the gun bill approved by lawmakers in 1995.

Bush faced a tougher challenge during the 1997 legislative session, when he made school property tax reform a major goal. He proposed that state government assume a larger share of the cost of funding the public schools by lowering local school taxes by about $3 billion a year. To replace the lost revenue, he proposed an increase in the state sales tax, the enactment of a new business tax, and the transfer of $1 billion in state budgetary savings to the public schools. The House rejected most of Bush's proposal and approved a controversial tax trade-off that would have increased numerous state taxes in exchange for major cuts in local school taxes. Bush lobbied Republican legislators for the House plan and helped convince about half of the sixty-eight Republicans in the House to vote for it. Assured that Bush was actively backing the plan, Speaker Laney helped persuade a large number of Democratic House members to vote for it. The bipartisan balancing act was necessary because many Republican legislators had campaigned against higher taxes of any kind, and many Democratic lawmakers had previously been targeted by Republicans over the tax issue.

Despite the success in the House, the Senate, which had a Republican majority, refused to approve a large increase in state taxes. Bush remained mostly in the background while the Senate debated the issue. After it became obvious the House and the Senate were in a stalemate, legislative negotiators requested the governor's active participation once again. But Bush was unable to forge any compromise that raised state taxes. The governor managed to salvage only a modest amount of property tax relief—about $150 a year for the average homeowner—by convincing the legislature to increase homestead exemptions, a form of tax break that homeowners get on their school taxes. The legislature used $1 billion in state budgetary savings to repay school districts for the revenue they lost from the higher exemptions.

In failing to win more substantial property tax relief, Bush couldn't overcome two major obstacles. One was strong opposition from business lobbyists to the proposed state tax increases. The other was the absence of a state budgetary crisis that would have forced the legislature to increase taxes. "We have a budget surplus. How do you start with a surplus and turn that into a tax bill? It's pretty hard to explain," said state Senator John Whitmire, a Democrat from Houston.[39]

Bush said he wanted to lower property taxes because they had become so high they were making home ownership difficult for many Texans. Some Democrats said Bush had failed as a leader because he had been unable to convince the legislature to enact a more substantial property tax cut package, but the governor dismissed the criticism. "I think people are going to say this is a man who set a very bold agenda and acted boldly," he said.[40] He said the higher homestead exemption that the legislature did pass was important.

Bush easily won reelection over Democratic challenger Garry Mauro in 1998 and entered the 1999 legislative session amidst widespread speculation that he was preparing for a presidential race. With his pending White House campaign obviously on his mind, he convinced the legislature to enact some additional tax cuts and increase education spending. He also accepted a priority of Democratic lawmakers to give school teachers a $3,000-a-year pay raise. Bush's biggest legislative defeat in 1999 was the rejection of a pilot program to allow students from low-performing public schools to use tax-backed vouchers to attend private schools. However, in an effort to shore up support among religious and social conservatives in the Republican Party, Bush won approval of a law to require parents to be notified before their minor daughters could receive abortions. It was the most significant piece of abortion-control legislation to be passed by Texas lawmakers since the U.S. Supreme Court had legalized abortion 26 years earlier.

Bush officially launched a campaign for the 2000 Republican presidential nomination in June 1999. He was elected president in the 2000 election, resigned as governor in December and was succeeded by Rick Perry, the lieutenant governor.

Rick Perry (2000–)

Republican Rick Perry came to the governor's office with much more governmental experience than his immediate and more famous predecessor, George W. Bush. He had served six years as a state representative, eight years as state agriculture commissioner, and almost two years as lieutenant governor before succeeding Bush as governor in December 2000, after Bush had resigned to become president. But Perry wasn't blessed with Bush's politically powerful name or his popularity, and he hadn't been elected governor. He had inherited the job. Moreover, the 2001 legislative session, with which Perry immediately had to deal, promised to be contentious because of political redistricting and a worrisome budgetary outlook.

Perry, however, survived his first session mostly unscarred. He didn't have to sign or veto any redistricting bills because Republicans and Democrats in the legislature were unable to agree on new political boundaries for themselves or Texas's congressional delegation. The legislative impasse put legislative redistricting in the hands of the Legislative Redistricting Board and deferred congressional redistricting—for the time being, anyway—to a federal court. Lawmakers wrote a new state budget without having to raise taxes and, at Perry's urging, even found enough money to triple funding for a grant program to help thousands of young Texans from low-income families attend college.

The legislature also enacted one of Perry's criminal justice priorities, a law to give prison inmates the ability to obtain court-ordered DNA testing if they can demonstrate that there is a substantial possibility that the results will prove them innocent. But the governor didn't get his way on another criminal justice issue with significant political overtones. In one of the most emotional and partisan issues of the session, the legislature approved a bill, backed by most Democrats and opposed by most Republicans, to strengthen penalties for crimes motivated by hate or prejudice. It was a fight that had begun in earnest two years earlier, after three white assailants had dragged an African American, James Byrd, Jr., to death behind a pickup in East Texas. At one point, Perry convinced a Republican senator to help delay action on the bill because he opposed a provision that listed protected classes of people, including homosexuals, which was strongly opposed by social conservatives in the Republican Party. But after the measure won final legislative approval, Perry signed it within a few hours after it reached his desk. He said he still had doubts about it. "But I also believe that as governor, and as a Texan, I have an obligation to see issues from another person's perspective, to walk in another person's shoes," he said.[41]

Some legislators criticized Perry's mostly low-key style during the 2001 session and complained that he didn't let them know early enough and clearly enough what he wanted. Shortly after the legislative session had ended, however, Perry flexed his muscles and vetoed a record eighty-two bills, including a measure that would have banned the execution of mentally retarded convicts in Texas. Aware that international attention was focused on his decision, Perry invited relatives of murder victims to join him at a state

A long career in public service. Rick Perry served in the legislature, as agriculture commissioner, and as lieutenant governor prior to assuming the governorship when George W. Bush resigned to assume the presidency.

Capitol news conference announcing the veto. Crime victims' advocates praised the veto, but death penalty opponents criticized it. A year later, the United States Supreme Court, acting in a case from another state, prohibited the execution of mentally retarded inmates throughout the country.

Other vetoes drew sharp criticism from a range of people. During his first year as governor, Perry also had to dodge political fallout from the spectacular collapse of Enron Corporation, the Houston-based energy-trading giant, which had been a major source of political donations during his public career.

Despite his rural roots—Perry grew up in Paint Creek, a tiny town in West Texas—the governor was acutely aware of the clogged freeways that plagued the daily lives of urban and suburban Texans and, early on, sought to make improved transportation a signature issue of his administration. In early 2002, he proposed a massive $175 billion transportation network for Texas, which would include toll roads, railroads, and underground utility tunnels grouped in corridors stretching across the state. The plan, which Perry called the Trans Texas Corridor, would generate controversy for years.

Perry defeated Democratic nominee Tony Sanchez, a multimillionaire Laredo businessman, in a bruising campaign to win a full term in the governor's office in 2002. Perry's victory and the first Republican takeover of the Texas House in modern times put the GOP in undisputed control of state government, and Perry acted accordingly. The governor joined Republican legislative leaders in demanding that a $10 billion revenue shortfall be bridged by cutting spending, not raising state taxes, and Republicans prevailed. Advocates of health care programs and other services protested the spending reductions, and many of the state's daily newspapers editorialized for limited tax increases to help minimize the cuts in services. The legislature raised some state fees and enacted legislation to allow university governing boards to increase tuition, but Perry refused to budge on taxes, apparently convinced that most middle class Texans agreed with him. He also argued that the state's relatively low tax burden had to be protected to keep the state attractive to businesses looking for places to expand. Perry also won from the legislature a special economic development fund that could be used to provide financial incentives for business recruitment.

The governor also advocated and won significant new restrictions on medical malpractice claims and other civil lawsuits. He said the so-called tort reform changes were essential to easing a crisis in health care, particularly in rural areas, and improving the state's business climate, although opponents argued that they put unnecessary, new restrictions on consumers' access to the courts.

As was more fully discussed in Chapter 8, Perry also played a dominant role in a bitter, partisan fight over congressional redistricting in 2003. Perry fully supported an effort, initiated by U.S. House Majority Leader Tom DeLay of Sugar Land, to increase the number of Republicans elected to the U.S. House from Texas. Under a 2001 redistricting plan drawn by a federal court, Democrats still held a 17–15 majority in the Texas congressional delegation, despite recent Republican sweeps of all statewide offices and Republican majorities in both the Texas House and the state Senate. DeLay, Perry, and other GOP leaders argued that the congressional delegation should more accurately reflect the state's Republican strength. A bill that would have redrawn the congressional districts to favor more Republican candidates died during the 2003 regular session after more than 50 Democratic members of the Texas House fled to Ardmore, Oklahoma, to break a quorum and keep the House from acting on the measure. Using one of his strongest constitutional powers, Perry then called the legislature back into special session that summer to try again. Eventually it took three special sessions to complete the task, but Perry was persistent. He even waited out a second Democratic boycott, when eleven Democratic senators flew to Albuquerque, New Mexico, to hold out for more than a month and shut down the Senate during the entire second special session. A redistricting bill that the Republican-dominated legislature finally passed during the third special session gave Republicans a majority in the Texas congressional delegation after the 2004 elections, with several incumbent Democrats losing their seats.

Perry's job approval ratings were subpar during most of that term, partly because of the controversy over redistricting and partly because he and legislative leaders failed repeatedly during 2004 and 2005 to agree on a plan for cutting school property taxes, which the governor had vowed to do during his 2002 election campaign. Finally, in the fall of 2005, Perry enlisted the help of former Comptroller John Sharp, an old friend from his college days at Texas A&M, but more recently a political rival whom Perry had defeated in a hard-fought race for lieutenant governor in 1998. He appointed Sharp, a Democrat, to chair a study commission to make recommendations for restructuring the state tax system and reducing local property taxes. Within a few weeks of the appointment, the Texas Supreme Court, in a widely anticipated ruling, held that the school finance system was unconstitutional because of a heavy reliance on local property taxes.

In early 2006, Sharp's commission recommended an expanded business tax and an increase in the cigarette tax to help pay for reductions in local school taxes. Perry endorsed the plan, solicited widespread support from the business community for it and called the legislature into special session in April. This time, faced with a court deadline, Perry and Republican legislative leaders worked closely together and were successful in getting the plan passed. Democrats and educator groups criticized the tax trade-off because it didn't significantly increase funding for education, and Perry also was accused of overstating the significance of the property tax cuts for most Texans. But the plan satisfied the court order.

Perry, meanwhile, had strengthened his support among conservative Republican voters in preparation for his 2006 reelection race. In 2005, he advocated a state constitutional amendment banning same-sex marriage, which Texans overwhelmingly approved with strong support from fundamentalist churches. He also backed a new state law to require minors to have their parents' permission before obtaining an abortion. Perry also courted national conservatives, prompting speculation that he was trying to open the door to a vice presidential invitation on the 2008 Republican ticket. If he was, he was unsuccessful.

Perry attracted three high-profile reelection opponents, an unusually high number, in 2006. They included Democratic nominee Chris Bell, a former congressman and former city councilman from Houston, and independents Carole Keeton Strayhorn, the state comptroller, and Kinky Friedman, an author–musician whose campaign was punctuated with satirical one-liners. Strayhorn, who had openly feuded with Perry on budgetary matters, ran as an independent because she knew she couldn't unseat the governor in the Republican primary. Perry was reelected, but with only 39 percent of the vote.

That low margin probably contributed to the rocky relationship the governor had with many lawmakers, including Republicans, during the 2007 and 2009 legislative sessions. In 2007, Perry infuriated many conservatives by issuing an executive order to require schoolgirls to be vaccinated against a virus linked to cervical cancer. Perry said his order was an important health care initiative. But opponents said it interfered with parental rights and questioned the governor's authority to issue it. With Republicans taking the lead, legislators overwhelmingly approved a bill to rescind it. Many Republican

Secession Is Not an Option

The Civil War may have determined that a state cannot withdraw from the Union, but secession remains a popular word with many disgruntled American citizens, including some conservative Republican primary voters whom Governor Rick Perry was trying to impress in preparation for his 2010 reelection campaign.

Seeking to bolster his image as a Washington "outsider" and distinguish himself from a popular potential opponent, U.S. Senator Kay Bailey Hutchison, Perry courted right-wing voters by attending a handful of antitax "tea parties" in April 2009. But he stirred up more controversy than he intended when a reporter in Austin asked him about the "secede" signs that were held aloft by some participants in the events.

"Texas is a unique place," the governor replied. "When we came into the Union in 1845, one of the issues was that we would be able to leave if we decided to do that."

"My hope is that America, and Washington in particular, pays attention," he added. "We've got a great Union. There's absolutely no reason to dissolve it. But if Washington continues to thumb their nose at the American people, you know, who knows what might come out of that? But Texas is a very unique place, and we're a pretty independent lot, to boot."[42]

Although Perry didn't endorse secession, he didn't strongly repudiate it either, and that failure sparked a political firestorm. Democrats criticized him, late-night TV hosts joked about him and experts corrected him. The terms under which Texas was admitted to the Union didn't allow for secession. They instead gave Texas the option of dividing into as many as five states.

After several weeks of trying to downplay the controversy, Perry finally took steps to try to repair the damage. In letters to Texas newspapers, he attacked the expansion of the federal government but took pains to also note that he would never advocate secession.

And in an interview with the *Los Angeles Times*, he said: "We live in a great country. I'm not in favor of Texas seceding."[43]

---

lawmakers, particularly from rural areas, also fought the governor over the expanded use of toll roads, an important, but controversial, part of Perry's transportation plan. Several toll road projects were allowed to continue, but lawmakers placed new limits on privately financed toll projects.

Perry's relationship with the Republican-led legislature deteriorated even further in 2009. The Senate rejected one of his appointees to the Board of Pardons and Paroles as unqualified for the job and rejected his choice for chairman of the State Board of Education following complaints that the chairman tried to impose his religious beliefs on educational policies. The Texas Department of Transportation, headed by Perry appointees, again came under legislative attack. Perhaps the biggest disagreement between the governor and many legislators, however, was Perry's refusal to accept $555 million in extra federal unemployment compensation money under the economic recovery stimulus package championed by President Barack Obama. Perry argued that the federal money came with too many "strings attached," including a requirement that Texas make more jobless workers eligible for benefits. The Senate passed a bill to make the changes required by the federal government so the state could accept the money, but the measure died in the House in the face of a likely Perry veto. By rejecting the money, the governor was seeking to strengthen his support among conservative Republican voters in anticipation of a reelection challenge from U.S. Senator Kay Bailey Hutchison in the 2010 Republican primary. Perry's anti-Washington rhetoric became so inflamed that he received national attention for failing to repudiate secession at an antitax protest rally (see "Secession Is Not an Option").

In addition to winning the fight over the unemployment money, Perry claimed several other victories at the end of the 2009 session, including tax cuts for small business owners, replenishing his economic development funds and helping convince lawmakers to leave about $9 billion in the state's Rainy Day Fund (money set aside for emergencies). But several proposals backed by the governor, which were important to conservative Republicans, failed, including legislation to require voters to show more identification when casting ballots and to require women to have ultrasounds before undergoing abortions.

In the face of Perry's opposition, the 2009 Legislature also refused to expand the Children's Health Insurance Program, although Texas had more children without health insurance than any other state.

OTHER OFFICES OF THE EXECUTIVE BRANCH ———●

Lieutenant Governor

The lieutenant governor is the second highest–ranking official in the state, but the executive powers of this office are limited. Were the governor to die, be incapacitated, removed from office, or voluntarily leave office in midterm, the lieutenant governor would become governor. That eventuality has occurred only four times. In 1917, William P. Hobby replaced James E. Ferguson, who was impeached. Governor W. Lee O'Daniel resigned in 1941 to enter the U.S. Senate and was succeeded by Coke Stevenson. Governor Beauford Jester died in office in 1949 and was replaced by Allan Shivers. And, George W. Bush resigned in December 2000 after being elected president and was succeeded by Rick Perry.

In Texas, the office of lieutenant governor is primarily a legislative office. Because of the lieutenant governor's key legislative role and statewide constituency, many experts consider this position the most powerful office in state government. The lieutenant governor, who need not belong to the same party as the governor and is elected independently of the governor, is the presiding officer of the Senate and traditionally has been given enormous power over the legislative process by the Senate rules. The legislative powers and prerogatives of the office far exceed those of the vice president on the federal level. The lieutenant governor also chairs the Legislative Budget Board, which plays a key role in the state budgetary process.

Democrat Bill Hobby, son of the former governor, served a record eighteen years as lieutenant governor before retiring in 1991. He was succeeded by Bob Bullock, a former state comptroller and one of the most influential state officials in recent history. Bullock, who chose not to seek reelection in 1998 and who died the next year, was succeeded by Republican Rick Perry, a former state agriculture commissioner.

Perry presided over the Senate for only one session, 1999, before succeeding Bush as governor after the 2000 presidential election. State senators then elected state Senator Bill Ratliff, Republican of Mt. Pleasant, to complete Perry's term as lieutenant governor and preside over the Senate during the 2001 session. Republican David Dewhurst was elected lieutenant governor in 2002. The former state land commissioner had no legislative experience but made a quick, yet thorough, study of major issues and legislative procedures (see Chapter 8). He was reelected to a second term in 2006.

Attorney General

As the state's chief legal officer, the attorney general is called upon to defend state laws enacted by the legislature and orders adopted by regulatory agencies. The office also enforces the state's antitrust and consumer protection laws and helps collect child-support payments from delinquent noncustodial parents. Recent attorneys general have been kept busy defending the state or negotiating settlements in federal and state court actions challenging the constitutionality of state prisons, the public school finance system, the method of selecting state judges, and other major policies. The attorney general also gives opinions on the legality of actions of other state and local officials and is at the center of the policymaking process.[44]

Unlike counterparts in the federal government and some other states, the Texas attorney general is primarily a civil lawyer. Except for representing the state in the appeals of death penalty cases and assisting local prosecutors, the position has relatively little responsibility for criminal law enforcement. Many candidates for the office like to campaign on tough law-and-order platforms, but responsibilities for criminal prosecution are vested in locally elected county and district attorneys (see Chapter 12). Reacting to the times, however, Attorney General Greg Abbott created a "cyber crimes unit," which went online to crack down on sexual predators prowling Internet chat rooms, posing as teenagers, to lure young victims into personal meetings. His unit, with the assistance of local law enforcement officers, has made numerous arrests.

Dan Morales, a former Democratic state representative from San Antonio, was elected attorney general in 1990, becoming the second Hispanic elected to statewide office in Texas. He won reelection in 1994 but chose not to run for a third term in 1998.

The state's chief legal officer. Former Texas Supreme Court Justice Greg Abbott, a Republican, was elected attorney general in 2002 and reelected in 2006.

He was succeeded by former Texas Supreme Court Justice John Cornyn, Texas's first Republican attorney general in modern times. Cornyn was elected to the U.S. Senate in 2002 and was succeeded by Abbott, a Republican and another former Texas Supreme Court justice. Abbott was reelected in 2006.

In a major policy decision made independently of the governor, the legislature, and other state officials, Morales in 1996 filed a multibillion-dollar damage suit against tobacco companies, seeking reimbursement for public health care costs associated with smoking (see Chapter 13). Some other state officials supported Morales' decision, although others had reservations about the state jumping into the tobacco controversy. But Morales acted within his authority as the state's chief legal officer. The decision was his alone to make, and it resulted in a $17.3 billion settlement for the state. The tobacco suit also sparked a controversy over legal fees that, several years after Morales had left office, resulted in him being sentenced to federal prison for four years for mail fraud and filing a false income tax return.

Comptroller of Public Accounts

The comptroller is the state's primary tax administrator, accounting officer, and revenue estimator. Texas functions under a **pay-as-you-go** principle, which means that the state cannot adopt an operating budget that exceeds anticipated revenue. The comptroller is responsible for providing the revenue estimates on which biennial state budgets are drafted by the legislature. A budget cannot become law without the comptroller's certification that it falls within the official revenue projection. The comptroller's office produces a revenue estimate of all projected state income for the two-year budget period by using sophisticated models of the state's economy.[45] If the revenue estimate is below the legislature's budget proposals, appropriations must be reduced or taxes must be raised. In a volatile, changing economy, it is difficult to accurately project revenues two years in the future. In the mid-1980s, then-Comptroller Bob Bullock had to adjust his revenue estimate downward several times to account for plunging oil prices.

The comptroller's powerful role in budgetary affairs was enhanced by the legislature in 1990 with the additional authority to conduct management audits of local school districts, and again in 1991 with similar oversight authority over other state agencies. Through this process, Comptroller John Sharp and his successor, Republican Carole Keeton Strayhorn, identified billions of dollars' worth of potential savings for legislative budget writers and local school boards.

Strayhorn, who changed her name from Rylander after marrying in early 2003, was a strong supporter of—and reaped favorable publicity from—the management audits. But the legislature, in a 2003 special session, transferred those programs to the Legislative Budget Board after the comptroller had become involved in a series of budgetary disputes with legislators and other Republican leaders. Always outspoken and widely viewed as politically ambitious, Strayhorn had surprised the governor and the Legislature with a larger-than-anticipated revenue shortfall of $10 billion at the beginning of the 2003 regular session. Strayhorn later threatened—but only briefly—not to certify the new state budget drafted by lawmakers. Finally, to make matters worse, she announced that the no-new-taxes budget about which the governor and Republican lawmakers had bragged actually included $2.7 billion in higher fees to be paid by millions of Texans. Strayhorn blamed Governor Rick Perry for the decision to strip the management audit programs from her agency. The governor's office denied the allegation,

Keeping the numbers straight. Comptroller Susan Combs, a former state legislator and agricultural commissioner, was elected in 2006. In addition to providing revenue estimates required to balance the biennial budget, the comptroller is the state's primary tax administrator and accounting officer.

but Perry had signed the bill. As noted earlier in this chapter, Strayhorn was so angry—or ambitious—that she unsuccessfully challenged Perry's reelection in 2006 as an independent candidate.

Republican Susan Combs, a former agriculture commissioner, was elected comptroller in 2006.

Commissioner of the General Land Office

Texas retains ownership, including mineral rights, to approximately 22 million acres of public lands, which are managed by the state land commissioner. Revenues generated by mineral leases and other land uses are earmarked for education through the Permanent University Fund and the Permanent School Fund. This agency also is responsible for the Veterans Land Program, which provides low interest loans to veterans for the purchase of land and houses.

Land, lots of land. Republican Jerry Patterson, a former state senator, was elected land commissioner in 2002 and reelected in 2006. Texas owns some 22 million acres of land, including mineral rights, which are administered by this office.

During sixteen years in office, Land Commissioner Garry Mauro, a Democrat, developed several environmental initiatives, including beach cleanup efforts and a program for cleaning up oil spills off the Texas coast. Mauro also took the lead in developing a coastal zone management plan to coordinate environmental protection efforts along the coast. After Mauro unsuccessfully ran for governor in 1998, the next land commissioner, Republican David Dewhurst, a businessman from Houston, continued the beach cleanup efforts. Dewhurst also won legislative approval of a program to replenish beaches and protect them from erosion. Dewhurst was elected lieutenant governor in 2002 and was succeeded as land commissioner by Jerry Patterson, a former state senator from Harris County. Patterson's priorities also included beach protection as well as development of new nursing homes for veterans and new veterans' cemeteries. He was reelected to a second term in 2006.

Commissioner of Agriculture

This office, created by statute rather than by the constitution, is responsible for carrying out laws regulating and benefiting the agricultural sector of the state's economy. In addition to providing support for agricultural research and education, the agency is responsible for the administration of consumer protection laws in the areas of weights and measures, packaging and labeling, and marketing. Republican Rick Perry aggressively promoted Texas agricultural products during two terms as commissioner. Republican Susan Combs, a former state representative from Austin, was elected to the office in 1998 after Perry ran for lieutenant governor. She also urged Texans to buy more produce grown in the Lone Star State. After Combs ran for comptroller in 2006, she was succeeded by Republican Todd Staples, a former state senator from Palestine.

Secretary of State

The secretary of state, the only constitutional official appointed by the governor, has a variety of duties, including granting charters to corporations and processing the extradition of prisoners to other states. The primary function of this office, however, is to administer state election laws. That responsibility includes reviewing county and local election procedures, developing statewide policy for voter registration, and receiving and tabulating election returns.

Elected Boards and Commissions

Only two—the Texas Railroad Commission and the State Board of Education—of the more than 200 boards and commissions that head most state agencies are elected.

Texas Railroad Commission.   This body was originally designed to regulate intrastate (within Texas) operations of railroads. It also regulated intrastate trucking for many years, but it lost its trucking responsibilities and most of its railroad regulation to the federal government. It still has some oversight over rail safety and regulates oil and natural gas production and lignite mining in Texas.

The commission includes three elected members who serve six-year, staggered terms and rotate the position of chair among themselves. The oil and gas industry has historically focused much attention on this agency and made large campaign contributions to commission members. Many critics claim the commission is a prime example of a regulatory body that has been co-opted by those interests it was created to regulate.

In recent years, the Texas Railroad Commission has become a staging area for opportunistic politicians who seek election to the commission primarily as a stepping-stone to higher office. A commissioner doesn't have to resign in the middle of his or her six-year term to seek another office and, as an incumbent regulator, has little trouble collecting large contributions from the oil and gas industry that can be used to further political ambitions. Both Democrat John Sharp and Republican Carole Keeton Strayhorn used seats on the commission to strengthen their political bases for successful races for state comptroller in 1990 and 1998, respectively. Other recent commission members haven't been as successful, but not because they didn't try. Between 1980 and 2002, fifteen people served on the three-member commission, and only four actually completed a full six-year term. One recent commissioner, Tony Garza, resigned in midterm to accept President George W. Bush's appointment as ambassador to Mexico.

The game of musical chairs has prompted calls in recent years for the commission to be abolished and its duties transferred to other agencies appointed by the governor, including the Public Utility Commission, which already has oversight over electric utilities, and the Texas Commission on Environmental Quality, the state's main environmental protection agency. Democrat Hector Uribe, a former state senator, ran for the commission in 1996, promising to work to abolish it. But Strayhorn, his Republican opponent, argued that the agency was important and needed to be retained. Strayhorn defeated Uribe for a six-year term on the commission, but two years later she ran for and won election to the comptroller's office.

State Board of Education. Since the early settlers declared their independence from Mexico, public education has been a major policy issue in Texas. In recent years, it has probably attracted more attention than ever before. The debate has focused not only on educational quality and financing, but also on how best to carry out and manage public education programs. The state has bounced back and forth between an elected state education board and an appointed one.

Prior to educational reforms enacted in 1984, the State Board of Education was made up of twenty-seven members elected from congressional districts across the state. At the urging of reformers dissatisfied with student performance, the legislature provided for a new education board of fifteen members to be appointed by the governor and confirmed by the Senate. The idea was to reduce the board's independence while new education reforms ordered by the legislature were being carried out. But the law also provided that the board would again become an elected body within a few years. Some state leaders later proposed that the board remain appointive and put the question to the voters, who opted for an elected board in 1986. The present board has fifteen members elected from districts established by the legislature.

Philosophical and partisan bickering on the board in recent years prompted the legislature to reduce its powers. The panel's main remaining duties include investment of education dollars in the Permanent School Fund and some oversight over textbook selection and curriculum standards.

But the day-to-day administration of the Texas Education Agency, the agency responsible for public education, is under the direction of the commissioner of education, who is appointed by the governor.

SUMMARY AND CONCLUSIONS

1. Although it is the most visible office in state government and the public believes it has considerable power, the office of governor is weak in formal powers. Unlike the president of the United States, the governor of Texas has no formal cabinet that serves at his or her pleasure. Texas has a "plural executive," which includes several independently elected statewide officeholders. This arrangement was a reaction to the abuses of the Davis administration during the Reconstruction era, but reform advocates argue that it diminishes the ability of the executive branch to respond to modern problems.

2. Administrative responsibilities are further fragmented through 200-plus boards and commissions authorized by statutory law. Although the governor appoints individuals to these boards, the governor's control is diluted by board members' staggered terms, the need for senatorial approval of the governor's appointments, and legal requirements relating to the composition of these boards.

3. A governor's cabinet has long been advocated by some critics of state government as a solution to the fragmentation of the executive branch. But the legislature has been reluctant to expand the governor's power in this fashion.

4. Besides appointments, the governor's main formal powers are the veto of legislation, line-item veto authority over the budget, and the authority to call and set the agenda for special legislative sessions.

5. Potentially, the governor has a number of informal resources that can be used to shape public policy. Governors have used their staffs, their access to the mass media, their party roles, and their relationships to key interest groups to influence the legislature and other elected officials.

6. Other elected officeholders in the executive branch are the lieutenant governor, the attorney general, the comptroller, the land commissioner, the agriculture commissioner, the three members of the Texas Railroad Commission, and the fifteen members of the State Board of Education. The top appointed official in the executive branch is the secretary of state. Although the lieutenant governor is part of the executive branch, the duties of that office are primarily legislative.

KEY TERMS

Governor   279
Plural executive   280
Lieutenant governor   280
Staggered terms   290
Senatorial courtesy   290
Attorney general   308

Comptroller of public
 accounts   309
Pay-as-you-go   309
Commissioner of the General
 Land Office   310

Commissioner of
 Agriculture   311
Secretary of state   311
Texas Railroad Commission   311
State Board of Education   312

FURTHER READING

Articles

Fairbanks, James David, "The Textbook Governor," *Texas Journal of Political Studies* 6, (Fall–Winter 1983), pp. 54–63.

Thompson, Pat, and Steven R. Boyd, "Use of the Line Item Veto in Texas, 1940–1990," State and *Local Government Review* 26 (Winter 1994), pp. 38–45.

Books

Anderson, Ken. *You Can't Do That, Dan Moody: The Klan Fighting Governor of Texas.* Austin, TX: Eakin, 1998.

Beyle, Thad L., "Being Governor," in *The State of the States,* 3rd ed., edited by Carl E. Van Horn. Washington, DC: CQ Press, 1996, pp. 77–107.

Beyle, Thad L., "Governors: The Middlemen and Women in Our Political System," in Politics in *the American States: A Comparative Analysis,* 6th ed., edited by Virginia Gray and Herbert Jacob. Washington, DC: CQ Press, 1996, pp. 207–52.

Davis, J. William, *There Shall Also Be a Lieutenant Governor.* Austin, TX: Institute of Public Affairs, University of Texas, 1967.

Dickson, James D., *Law and Politics: The Office of Attorney General in Texas.* Austin, TX: Sterling Swift, 1976.

Frederick, Douglas W., "Reexamining the Texas Railroad Commission," in *Texas Politics: A Reader,* edited by Anthony Champagne and Edward J. Harpham. New York: W. W. Norton, 1997, pp. 67–76.

Gantt, Fred, Jr., *The Chief Executive in Texas: A Study of Gubernatorial Leadership.* Austin, TX: University of Texas Press, 1964.

Hendrickson, Kenneth E., *Chief Executives of Texas: From Stephen F. Austin to John B. Connally, Jr.* College Station, TX: Texas A&M Press, 1995.

Ivans, Molly, and Lou Dubose. *Shrub: The Short but Happy Life of George W. Bush.* New York: Random House, 2000.

Lipson, Leslie, with an introduction by Marshall E. Dimock, *The American Governor from Figurehead to Leader.* Chicago: University of Chicago Press, 1939.

Morris, Celia, *Storming the Statehouse: Running for Governor with Ann Richards and Dianne Feinstein.* New York: Charles Scribner's Sons, 1992.

Paulissen, May Nelson, and Carl McQueary. *Miriam: The Southern Belle Who Became the First Woman Governor of Texas.* Austin, TX: Eakin, 1995.

Prindle, David, *Petroleum Politics and the Texas Railroad Commission.* Austin, TX: University of Texas Press, 1981.

Reston, James, Jr., *The Lone Star State: The Life of John Connally.* New York: Harper & Row, 1989.

Rosenthal, Alan, *The Governor and the Legislature.* Washington, DC: CQ Press, 1988.

Sabato, Larry, *Goodbye to Good-Time Charlie: The American Governorship Transformed,* 2nd ed. Washington, DC: CQ Press, 1983.

Shropshire, Mike, and Frank Schaeffer, *The Thorny Rose of Texas: An Intimate Portrait of Governor Ann Richards.* New York: Birch Lane, 1994.

Texas General Land Office, *The Land Commissioners of Texas.* Austin, TX: Texas General Land Office, 1986.

Tolleson-Rinehart, Sue, and Jeanie R. Stanley, *Claytie and the Lady.* Austin. TX: University of Texas Press, 1994.

Weaver, Jacqueline Lang, *Unitization of Oil and Gas Fields in Texas: A Study of Legislative, Administrative and Judicial Politics.* Washington, DC: Resources for the Future, Inc., 1986.

Welch, June R., *The Texas Governors.* Dallas, TX: Yellow Rose Press, 1988.

Wiggins, Charles, Keith E. Hamm, and Howard Balanoff, "The Gubernatorial Transition in Texas: Bolt Cutters, Late Trains, Lame Ducks, and Bullock's Bullets," in *Gubernatorial Transitions: The 1982 Elections,* edited by Thad L. Beyle. Durham, NC: Duke University Press, 1985.

Websites

Governor of Texas   http://www.governor.state.tx.us/ The governor's website offers up-to-date and archived news releases and speeches, ongoing initiatives, the governor's budget, and information about the structure and responsibilities of the governor's office. Links are provided to the important divisions or sections of the governor's office as well as to other state agencies.

State of Texas   http://www.state.tx.us/   This is the state's official webpage, *Texas Online-Official Portal of the State of Texas,* which provides links to more than 200 state agencies. Most of the state agencies have their own sites, with detailed information about their organizational structure, programs, budgets, reports, and recent activities.

Office of the Comptroller   http://www.cpa.state.tx.us/ In addition to providing links to other state agencies, the website of the comptroller's office provides a wide array of information pertaining to state taxes, management and accounting systems, and performance reviews of state operations and agencies.

National Governors Association (NGA)   http://www.nga.org/   This bipartisan organization provides information on "Key State Issues" and monitors and analyzes the progress of important state policy issues. Information on the governors of all fifty states is also available.

ENDNOTES

1. Alexis de Tocqueville, *Democracy in America* with an introduction by Joseph Epstein (New York, NY: Bantam Dell, 2000), p. 94.
2. Pat M. Neff, *Messages of Pat M. Neff* (Austin, TX: A. C. Baldwin, 1921), pp. 34–35.
3. Fred Gantt, Jr., *The Chief Executive in Texas* (Austin, TX: University of Texas Press, 1964), p. 24.
4. Ibid., pp. 24–25.
5. Ibid., p. 27.
6. Ibid., pp. 27–32.
7. Ibid., pp. 32–36.
8. Ibid., p. 37.
9. Charles F. Cnudde and Robert E. Crew, *Constitutional Democracy in Texas* (St. Paul, MN: West, 1989), p. 90.
10. Texas Constitution, Art. 4, Sec. 4.
11. Gantt, *The Chief Executive in Texas,* p. 116.
12. Joseph A. Schlesinger, "The Politics of the Executive" in *Politics in the American States,* 2nd ed., edited by Herbert Jacob and Kenneth N. Vines (Boston: Little, Brown, 1971), Chapter 6; and Thad L. Beyle "The Governors, 1988–89," in *The Book of the States, 1990–1991* (Lexington, KY: Council of State Governments, 1990), p. 54.

13. Texas Constitution, Art. 1, Sec. 4.

14. Ray Long and Rick Pearson, Impeached Illinois Gov. Rod Blagojevich Has Been Removed from Office, *Chicago Tribune,* January 20, 2009.

15. Fred Gantt, Jr., *The Chief Executive in Texas* (Austin, TX: University of Texas Press, 1964), pp. 229–30.

16. For an excellent treatment of the American governor through the Depression years, see Leslie Lipson, *The American Governor from Figurehead to Leader* (Chicago: University of Chicago Press, 1939).

17. Wayne Slater, "Clements Puts Stamp on Panels, Minorities, Women Neglected, Critics Say," Dallas *Morning News,* April 27, 1987, p. 1A.

18. Janet Elliott, "Perry Homes Executive Named to Commission—Houston Builder Governor's Top Contributor," Houston *Chronicle,* September 30, 2003, page 15A.

19. Matt Stiles, "Appointees Gave Perry $5 Million," *Houston Chronicle,* May 4, 2009, p. 1A.

20. Peggy Fikac, "Bush Appointing Many Females, Minorities—Record 'Very Good for a Republican,'" an *Antonio Express—News,* July 9, 2000, p. 14A.

21. Texas Constitution, Art. 4, Sec. 11.

22. Wilbourn E. Benton, *Texas Politics: Constraints and Opportunities,* 5th ed. (Chicago: Nelson-Hall, 1984), pp. 164–66.

23. Ibid., pp. 166–67.

24. Texas Constitution, Art. 4, Sec. 7.

25. Gantt, *The Chief Executive in Texas,* pp. 90–107.

26. Robert S. Lorch, *State and Local Politics,* 3rd ed. (Englewood Cliffs, NJ: Prentice Hall, 1989), pp. 115–16.

27. Ibid., pp. 116–19.

28. See James E. Anderson, Richard W. Murray, and Edward L. Farley, *Texas Politics,* 6th ed. (New York: HarperCollins, 1991) for an excellent analysis of the leadership styles of Governors Shivers, Daniel, Connally, Smith, and Briscoe.

29. *Fort Worth Star–Telegram,* January 1, 1980.

30. Clay Robison, "The Clements Years," *Houston Chronicle,* December 2, 1990, *Texas Magazine,* p. 6.

31. *Houston Post,* June 17, 1979.

32. Austin *American–Statesman,* June 16, 1979.

33. *Texas Poll,* Summer 1987, conducted for Harte-Hanks Communications, Inc., by the Public Policy Resources Laboratory at Texas A&M University.

34. Robison, "The Clements Years," p. 6.

35. *Texas Government Newsletter,* 19 (February 25, 1991), p. 1.

36. Clay Robison, "Richard's Caution Saves Precious Political Capital," Houston *Chronicle,* June 2, 1993, p. 1A.

37. R. G. Ratcliffe, "Away from the Spotlight, Governor Makes His Mark," *Houston Chronicle,* April 15, 1995, p. 1A.

38. R. G. Ratcliffe, "Legislature Fulfills Most Bush Promises," *Houston Chronicle,* May 31, 1995, p. 1A.

39. Clay Robison, "Poor Timing Hurt Bid for Property Tax Relief," *Houston Chronicle,* May 27, 1997, p. 1A.

40. Sam Attlesey and Wayne Slater, "Democrats Call Bush and Ineffective Leader," *Dallas Morning* News, June 4, 1997, p. 29A.

41. Jane Elliott, "77th Texas Legislature," *Houston Chronicle,* May 12, 2001, p. 1A.

42. Anna M. Tinsley, "At Rally, Perry Says Secession is on Minds of Many in the State," *Fort Worth Star–Telegram,* April 16, 2009, p. B1.

43. Mark Z. Barabak, "In Texas, Even Taking Sides Is Bigger," *Los Angeles Times-Washington Post News Service,* May 18, 2009.

44. Daniel Elazar, "The Principles and Traditions Underlying State Constitutions," *Publius: The Journal of Federalism* 12 (Winter 1982), p. 17.

45. Texas Comptroller of Public Accounts, *Fiscal Notes* (December 1990), p. 9.

CHAPTER 10

The Bureaucracy and Policy Implementation

Questions to Guide Your Reading

1. What are the functions or roles of administrative agencies of state and local governments?

2. Do administrative agencies play a key role in the development of public policy?

3. Some have asserted that bureaucracies are undemocratic. But do the Texas Legislature, city councils, and other policy bodies have the resources and ability to keep administrative agencies responsive and responsible to Texas citizens?

4. What is a merit system, and would Texans be better served by a unified system that covered all state employees?

Public service is a public trust. As public servants we take pride in the service we provide for our fellow citizens.

— **Texas Governor's Office**[1]

Government is going to be seen as bigger, dumber and slower than ever before if we don't become smaller, smarter and faster.

— **Carole Keeton Strayhorn, State Comptroller, 2003**[2]

Citizens across Texas rely on the routine services public employees provide, often with little understanding or appreciation of the importance these people play in our daily lives. We take it for granted that the water flowing through our taps will not cause dysentery. The garbage is picked up regularly, with most of us giving little thought to what happens to it. Most of us have no idea where wastewater goes or how it is treated. We have little sense of the complex administrative structures required to maintain streets, public libraries, and many other public services. Although most of us have attended public schools, we know little, or nothing, about the diverse workforce required to make them work.

Most Texans know someone who works for a government. They are our friends, neighbors, members of our churches, and club members with whom we share common interests. We tend to have positive perceptions of public employees whom we know or with whom we interact. But we also have much ambivalence toward public employees and the agencies for which they work.

In a more general sense, bureaucrats and **bureaucracies** are even pejorative terms for many Texans. They convey an image of inefficiency, indifference, or incompetence in the delivery of public services and are often associated with "red tape." Many people associate governmental agencies with waste or the irresponsible use of taxes, and some citizens believe that public agencies are undemocratic or unaccountable. Many candidates for elected office campaign on promises to reduce governmental waste and spending, streamline government, and reduce the number of people on public payrolls. Such bureaucrat bashing plays well with most voters, and it provides few liabilities for political candidates. But, once elected, public officials soon realize that governments do not run on rhetoric but on the work of the same public employees, or bureaucrats, against whom they campaigned.

Moreover, government employees are not exempt from the regulations, programs, and policies they administer. They do not have special privileges because they are public employees. They are also subject to the same taxes as the general public (see Reality or Myth?).

Over the past two decades, the number of people working for the federal government has declined as many of their functions have been contracted out to private companies, without significant savings to taxpayers or evidence of improvement in services. The number of Texas state and local employees in 2007, meanwhile, increased to the equivalent of 1.3 million full-time workers. Some 290,000 people work full-time for the state, and 1,053,991 for local governments in Texas. Several hundred thousand more work part-time.

But state agencies have an aging workforce with many workers nearing retirement, and the task of replacing them has been made more difficult by the long-standing pattern of bureaucrat bashing that has convinced many young people that a career in the public sector is undesirable. Effective administration of public services requires competent employees, but some scholars argue that we have created an environment in which governments at all levels will have a difficult time recruiting new employees who are among the best and the brightest of their generation.

Reality or Myth?

Distorted views or myths about public employees and bureaucracies shape our perceptions and attitudes about government, often leading to public opposition to new programs, particularly those that serve some of the more vulnerable people in our society. How do we address these myths to help us be more effective in our relationships with governments?

Bureaucracies are excessively wasteful. It is quite common for Texans to make broad claims that bureaucrats are wasting taxpayers' money. These claims tend to be reinforced with anecdotes about the four or five persons working to fill a pothole, unnecessary or poorly constructed projects, long lines at the tax office when some helpers seem to be available, a police car parked at a restaurant, and a myriad of other perceptions. But problems of waste, duplication, and ineffectiveness cannot be singularly assigned to public employees. One theme of this book has been the constitutional fragmentation of authority and responsibility, and when we apply this to the executive branch and the administration of state programs, this leads to "duplicated functions, overlapping responsibilities, inadequate communication, and inconsistent goals—making it difficult for government to implement efficient and effective policies."[1]

A "performance review process" was authorized by the Texas Legislature in 1991 and initially implemented by the Office of the Comptroller. Texas was perceived to be at the forefront of the "reinventing government" movement, and when Vice President Al Gore led the National Performance Review in 1993, many components of the process were drawn from the Texas experience. In the 2008 Government Performance Project report sponsored by the Pew Center on the States, Texas, which has used performance-based management for many years, was given an A– for its varied uses of information technology for management, finances, and communicating with the public. And while the national average was a C+, Texas received a B for its personnel practices.[2]

Many of the performance recommendations that target waste have been adopted by the legislature and state agencies, but the long term,

and sometimes immeasurable, results are just as significant. The reports provide more information about state agencies, what they are doing, and how well they are doing it. The ongoing process affects the attitudes and behavior of public employees, with improvements in agency responses to citizens.

There has been runaway growth in the number of government employees. The state's population was 11.1 million in 1970. By 2008, the population had grown to 24.3 million, an increase of 117 percent. The total number of government employees in 1972 was a little more than 500,000. By 2007, the number had increased to more than 1.3 million, an increase of 166 percent. State employees increased by 133 percent. Total local government employment increased by 177 percent. Employment in city governments increased by 89 percent; county government increased by 258 percent; school districts' employment grew by 209 percent; and special districts grew by 109 percent. One might conclude from these figures that growth in public employment has been excessive, but there are other perspectives on this issue.

With the complex dimensions of population growth and increased public expectations, there has been a significant increase in programs and services at all levels of government. New problems or issues, such as pollution abatement and long-term care for the indigent elderly, have arisen, and governments are called on to address them. There is an array of federal mandates—special education, bilingual education, welfare, to name a few— that require additional state expenditures and government employees. There are federal court orders as well, such as those that dealt with conditions in state jails and prisons, that have required additional state funding and public personnel.

Business is so much more efficient and cost effective, so let's privatize. Privatization appeals to many Texans, partly because of the strong conservative values in the state. Government employees don't have to compete for business, but private companies do, and competition, it is believed, can produce greater efficiency and cut costs.

The local presence of state agencies. Although we tend to associate state government with Austin, most state employees work in other areas throughout the state. State prison and jail facilities, such as the Walls Unit in Huntsville, are dispersed in counties throughout the state.

But many studies comparing the efficiency of government with the private sector in providing trash collection, health care, education, transportation, food services, utility services and running jails have produced mixed results.[3] Charles Goodsell, a longtime student of bureaucracies, studied much of this literature and concluded: " In short, there is much evidence that is ambivalent. The assumption that business always does better than government is not upheld. . . . When you add up these study results, the basis for the mantra that business is always better evaporates."[4]

Notes

[1] Texas Comptroller of Public Accounts, *Texas Performance Review: Disturbing the Peace*, vol. 1, Appendix 1, p. 9.
[2] Barrett, Katherine, and Richard Greene, "Grading the States 2008: The Mandate to Measure," *The Pew Center on the States*, March 2008, p. 87.
[3] Douglas J. Amy, "The Case FOR Bureaucracy," *Government is Good: An Unapologetic Defense of a Vital Institution*, A web project of Douglas J. Amy, Professor of Politics at Mount Holyoke College, 2007, http://www.governmentisgood.com/articles.php?aid=20&p=1.
[4] Charles Goodsell, *The Case for Bureaucracy: A Public Administration Polemic*, 4th ed. (Washington, DC: CQ Press, 2004), pp. 6, 54.

The sheer size of state government and the fragmented structure of the executive branch (see Chapter 9) also contribute to problems in the state bureaucracy. No single, elected official is ultimately responsible for the quality of public services performed by thousands of state workers. A loosely connected and often confusing network of more than 200 state agencies and universities is responsible for carrying out programs and policies approved and funded by the legislature and the governor. Programs often are developed and agencies established with little thought for policy coordination between departments. The organization of many agencies also is influenced by interest groups, which believe agencies should serve their needs, not those of the general public.

Fragmentation also extends to local governments. With thousands of school districts, cities, counties, and special districts in Texas—many with overlapping jurisdictions—people often are confused about where to turn for help with public services.

The legislature and the governor develop and enact the broad outlines of public policy, but the hundreds of state agencies and local governments must transform those policies into specific programs, based on standard operating procedures. As noted in previous chapters, the legislature meets in regular session only five months every other year; and the systematic review and oversight of every state agency is impossible. Moreover, the governor has only limited administrative control over most of the agencies in the executive branch. Unlike the president of the United States, who has the Office of Management and Budget to assist in legislative clearance, the review of regulations prepared by agencies, and management review, the governor has no comparable resource.[3] The part-time boards and commissions that oversee most state agencies can exercise considerable independence in interpreting policies and determining the character and the quality of public services. Many boards, moreover, are heavily dependent on the guidance of veteran administrators and career bureaucrats within their agencies.

Bureaucracies and bureaucratic behavior have been debated intensely for more than 100 years. The debate has not been conclusive, but it has been instructive. There is general agreement that modern, interdependent societies require large bureaucracies to provide the range of services demanded by citizens. There are inherent nondemocratic aspects in the hierarchical structure of bureaucracies, but bureaucracies, through the uniform application of rules and procedures, contribute to the maintenance of a democratic society. Unlike people in other political systems in which bribery is widespread, we have come to expect that we have rights to public services without having to slide money under the table, and there are laws providing strong criminal penalties for bribery. The power and influence of agencies and bureaucrats must be checked by aggressive review and oversight by the legislature. There is some abuse and malfeasance in governmental agencies, but most agencies effectively carry out the policy mandates of legislative bodies.

DEFINING BUREAUCRACY ●

Max Weber, a German sociologist writing in the early part of the twentieth century, regarded bureaucracies as efficient means of organizing large numbers of people to carry out the required tasks for accomplishing specific goals.[4] Bureaucratic structures are inevitable in large, complex societies that have a great deal of individual and group interdependence. To a large extent, these complex organizations are "superior to other methods of organizing people to perform tasks."[5]

Scholars have identified a number of characteristics of bureaucracies, the first of which is size. Whether defined in terms of the number of employees, size of budgets, or number of programs administered, size suggests complex relationships among the people working for an organization. Employees of some large state agencies are scattered among many cities, and both the size and geographic dispersion of these agencies contribute to their organizational hierarchy.[6]

Within governmental organizations, specific positions are assigned specific responsibilities or given specific authority in a hierarchical arrangement. Most agency staffs have one individual at the top, with the organization divided into bureaus, divisions, field offices, or other units. The organization develops rules for supervision, management, and reporting of activities.

Bureaucracies require a division of labor among employees and encourage the development of expertise based on experience and education. State agencies break down the responsibilities given to them by the legislature into narrowly defined tasks for their employees. Thousands of workers become specialists in a limited number of activities.

The specialization and division of labor in large organizations require rules and procedures to coordinate the activities of many individuals. Rules reduce the need for continued supervision of employees, and they lay the foundation for standardized behavior.[7] Rules define how tasks are to be carried out, who is responsible for carrying them out, and who qualifies for the organization's or agency's services.

Contemporary bureaucracies also are characterized by impersonal relationships, which is why people often complain about having to deal with "faceless" bureaucrats. Responsibilities within an agency are assigned to positions, which can be held by several workers who are supposed to be able to provide the requested service. When you get a voter-registration card or have your driver's license renewed, the name of the person assisting you should make no difference. People come and go in large organizations, and the ongoing functions of organizations are not dependent on specific individuals.[8]

THE GROWTH OF GOVERNMENT EMPLOYMENT IN TEXAS

In 1972, there were 504,000 full-time state and local government employees in Texas.[9] Thirty-five years later, there were two-and-one-half times that many (see Table 10–1). By 2008, the state had 662 full-time state and local government employees per 10,000 residents, but Texas had only 153 state employees per 10,000 people, forty-second among the states. With 509 local government workers per 10,000 people, Texas ranked eighteenth.[10] Local governments have a larger number of public employees per capita

TABLE 10–1   Employment by Type of Government, 1972– 2007

Unit of Government	Full-Time Equivalent Employees				
	1972	**1982**	**1992**	**2002**	**2007**
State	124,560	175,660	238,974	269,674	290,451
Total Local	380,038	557,082	744,325	979,164	1,053,991
Counties	37,302	67,228	94,145	120,885	133,722
Municipalities	93,107	127,794	147,812	172,846	175,635
School Districts	223,646	335,855	460,212	634,589	690,712
Special Districts	25,983	26,205	42,156	50,844	53,922
Total for Texas	504,598	732,742	983,299	1,248,838	1,344,442

Source: U.S. Department of Commerce, Bureau of the Census, *Census of Governments, 1972,* vol. 3, no. 2, table 14; *Census of Governments, 1982,* vol. 3, no. 2, table 13; *Census of Governments, 1992,* vol. 3, no. 2, table 14; *Census of Governments, 2002,* vol. 3, table 9; and *Government Employment and Payroll Data,* 2007, http://www.census.gov/govs/apes/ (latest Texas data via Build-a-Table).

because they are responsible for a wide range of services. The number of employees at all levels of government has increased along with the state's population, but per capita local government employment does not come close to states such as Alaska, Kansas, Nebraska, and New York.

There also has been more privatization of government over the past two decades. Governments continue to raise taxes, but they contract with private companies to carry out some services. Contractors' employees aren't public employees and aren't counted in the public employment census data. Supporters of privatization say it can reduce governmental costs by promoting efficiency. Critics, however, argue that contracting out governmental functions can be more costly. It also can result in less public scrutiny and control.

There has been a substantial expansion of programs at all levels of government in recent years. State spending during the 2000–2001 biennium was $98.1 billion and, ten years later, the legislature appropriated $182 billion for the 2010–2011 biennium. Between 2000 and 2010 alone, state spending almost doubled, while the population grew by 17 percent in the first eight years of the decade. Although some argue that state spending is out of control, Texas still ranks low in per capita expenditures. Texas was last among the states in per capita spending by state government alone—$3,831 per person—in 2007. When combined state and local spending was compared, Texas's ranking rose slightly, thanks partly to the large share of public school costs borne by local taxpayers. In such key areas as per capita state spending on public health, education, and welfare, Texas ranked below many other states.[11]

Privatization Hits a "Black Hole"

The legislature in 2003 ordered a controversial restructuring of Texas's health and human services agencies with an eye toward privatizing some functions, such as screening applicants for public assistance, which had previously been done by state employees. Republican state leaders predicted the changes would promote efficiency and save money for taxpayers, but the reorganization and privatization got off to a rough start. Within a few years, thousands of children had been dropped from Medicaid and the Children's Health Insurance Program (CHIP), to the dismay of health care advocates who blamed the problem on changes in eligibility rules and problems with the transition to private contractors.

Accenture LLP—a company given an $899 million state contract to screen applicants for children's health coverage and other welfare benefits—came under fire from legislators and advocates angry that Texans in need were losing benefits because of inadequate staffing and training at private call centers operated by the company. Eventually, the contract was terminated.

In 2006, the *Houston Chronicle* reported that for three months dozens of documents from applicants seeking food stamps and other public assistance in Texas were mistakenly routed to a fax machine in a warehouse in Seattle, Washington, because a wrong phone number had been listed on an information memo. The applicants thought they were sending their faxes, which included personal financial information, to the Texas Health and Human Services Commission or to its private contractor in Midland.

"There was a black hole in Seattle, Washington," a clerk at the warehouse told the newspaper. "People send us check stubs. They send us bills. We've gotten letters from people asking why they haven't been approved for food stamps yet. They were faxing in their personal information."[12]

TABLE 10–2   State and Local Employment by General Functions, 2007

Service or Function	State Employees	County Employees	City/Town Employees	School District Employees	Special District Employees
Education	**39.8%**	1.0%	3.0%	100.0%	0.1%
Social Services	**25.4%**	**30.2%**	4.8%		**52.5%**
Public Safety and Corrections	**17.0%**	**33.2%**	**38.4%**		0.7%
Transportation	5.5%	7.5%	9.0%		3.1%
Government Administration	6.1%	**22.6%**	**14.1%**		0.1%
Environment/Housing	4.0%	2.1%	8.9%		**14.1%**
Utilities		0.1%	**15.6%**		**28.0%**
All Other Functions	2.3%	3.4%	6.3%		1.4%
Total Number of Employees	**290,451**	**133,722**	**175,635**	**690,712**	**53,922**

*Top three functions highlighted for each level of government.

Source: U.S. Department of Commerce, Bureau of the Census, *Government Employment & Payroll*, 2007, http://www.census.gov/govs/apes/ (latest Texas data via Build-a-Table).

Efforts to curtail government growth and spending have met with only marginal success. Texas citizens have come to expect a wide range of public services, and these expectations increase as the population grows. The federal government also has imposed mandates on state and local governments that require additional expenditures and personnel. And the success of interest groups in winning approval of new programs adds to the growth of public employment. The legislature reduced spending on many programs to help bridge a $10 billion revenue shortfall in 2003. And that same year, it ordered a major reorganization of health and human services agencies, with the goal of privatizing some services (see "Privatization Hits a 'Black Hole'"). But state spending continued to grow with the population.

Eighty-two percent of state government employees work in higher education, public safety and corrections, and social services (see Table 10–2). Eighty-six percent of county government employees work in three areas: social services, public safety and corrections, and general governmental administration. About 38 percent of city employees are engaged in fire and police protection, and another 30 percent work for city utilities and in housing, sanitation, parks and recreation, and natural resources departments. Elementary and secondary school teachers are employees of local school districts. Almost thirty percent of the employees of special districts work in utilities, and more than 50 percent work in social services, including public hospitals.

BUREAUCRATS AND PUBLIC POLICY ●

The bureaucracy does more than carry out the policies set by the legislature. It is involved in virtually every stage of the policymaking process. The legislature usually broadly defines a program and gives the affected agency the responsibility for filling in the details.[13] Administrative agencies can sometimes interpret a vaguely worded law differently from its original legislative purpose. Although the legislature can use oversight committees and the budgetary process to control the bureaucracy, agencies often have resources and political influence that protect their prerogatives. Many appointed agency heads have political ties to interest groups affected by the work of their agencies, and these officials help develop policy alternatives and laws because legislators depend on their technical expertise.

Policy Implementation

Implementation is the conversion of policy plans into reality.[14] Although one state agency may be primarily responsible for translating legislative intent into a specific program, other governmental bodies are also involved. The courts, for example, shape the actions of the bureaucrats through their interpretation of statutes and administrative rules. And there may be jurisdictional and political battles between different agencies over program objectives. Such conflicts often result from Texas's plural executive system of government, in which the governor and several other statewide officials are elected independently of each other and numerous other agencies are headed by appointed boards and commissions (see Chapter 9).

In some cases, a new agency may have to be organized and staffed to carry out the goals of a new law. More often, however, the new responsibilities are assigned by the legislature to an existing agency, which develops the necessary rules, procedures, and guidelines for operating the new program. Additional employees are hired if the legislature provides the necessary funding. If not, responsibilities are reassigned among existing personnel. Sometimes tasks are coordinated with other agencies. Ultimately, all this activity translates into hundreds of thousands of daily transactions between governmental employees—or an agency's private contractors—and the public.

Establishing rules and standards at the agency level for carrying out programs enacted by the legislature is a complex process that also involves the legislative sponsors, interest groups, sometimes specific businesses, and other interested parties. Rules and procedures are not just hatched in a vacuum. The task is highly political, is subject to intense negotiations, and is often contentious. It often requires a lot of political adroitness by administrators to assure a program's success.

Almost everyone has heard horror stories about persons who have suffered abuse or neglect at the hands of public employees and agencies. Whether they involve an indigent family that fell through the cracks of the welfare system or a county jail prisoner who was lost in the administrative process of the judicial system, these stories tend to reinforce the suspicion and hostility that many people have toward bureaucracies and public employees. Unquestionably, such abuses deserve attention and demand correction, yet thousands of governmental programs are successfully carried out with little or no fanfare and are consistent with the purpose of the authorizing legislation.

Most public employees take pride in what they do and attempt to be conscientious in translating policy objectives into workable public services. They are citizens and taxpayers who also receive services from other state and local agencies. A complex, interdependent state with more than 24 million people depends on the effectiveness and efficiency of governmental agencies. That activity appears, on the whole, to be mutually satisfactory or beneficial to most parties.

Obstacles to Policy Implementation

When things go wrong in state government and problems go unresolved, there is a tendency to blame the bureaucrats for excessive red tape, inefficiency, mismanagement, or incompetence. Bureaucrat bashing plays well politically, and many candidates for public office run on such campaigns. But in many cases they are unfairly blaming government employees for complex problems that policymakers have been unable—or unwilling—to resolve. One high profile issue is the perennial struggle to improve the quality of the public education system. Some of the criticism directed at educational bureaucrats has been justified, but the legislature and the governor are ultimately responsible for the enactment of sound educational policies and the development of a sufficient and equitable system of paying for them.

Some legislative policies may be misdirected, with little potential for producing the intended results. Or economic and social conditions may change, making programs inappropriate. Administrators also may find that approaches different from those outlined by the legislature would have worked better. The legislature also frequently fails to fund programs adequately. In some cases, those charged with carrying out a new policy may not have the know-how or the resources to make it work.[15] Finally, programs often produce unanticipated results.[16]

The accountability and responsiveness of state and local agencies are also affected by other factors, including the influence of special interests. Thanks to the clout of special interest lobbyists with the legislature, regulatory agencies are often headed by boards that include a majority of members from the professions or industries they are supposed to regulate. Many taxpayers may feel this system is merely a legalized way of letting the foxes guard the henhouse. It is an extension of the "iron triangles" concept (see Chapters 4 and 13), whereby special interests seek to influence not only the legislators responsible for enacting laws but also the agencies responsible for enforcing them.

Appointment to State Agencies

Business and professional groups argue that their professions can be effectively regulated only by individuals knowledgeable of them. Although that argument has some validity, it also increases the potential for incestuous relationships that mock the regulatory process. There is always the possibility—and often the likelihood—that industry representatives serving on boards or commissions will be inclined to protect their industries against the best interests of consumers. This pattern of influence and control is often referred to as **co-optation**, underscoring the possibility that agencies may be captured by the industries they are supposed to regulate. Licensing agencies also may seek to adopt unfair regulations designed to restrict new competitors from entering an industry.

Historically, many nine-member state regulatory boards included only industry representatives. But under the sunset review process, discussed in more detail later in this chapter, laws have gradually been changed to turn over some positions on most of those boards to public members. The Sunset Advisory Commission has concluded:

> Boards consisting only of members from a regulated profession or group affected by the activities of an agency may not respond adequately to broad public interests. This potential problem can be addressed by giving the general public a direct voice in the activities of the agency through representation on the board.[17]

The "fox in the henhouse" approach to state regulation was highlighted when Governor Ann Richards demanded that the Texas Department of Health crack down on deplorable conditions in some nursing homes. It was revealed that state inspectors had repeatedly found unsanitary conditions in three nursing homes partly owned by a member of the Texas Board of Health. The board member, an appointee of former Governor Bill Clements, denied any allegations of improper care but resigned after moving to another state.[18] Texas law then required that one member of the eighteen-member health board be involved in the nursing home industry, while other members included other health care professionals. The board has since been restructured.

POLITICAL CONTROL AND THE RESPONSIVENESS OF THE BUREAUCRACY

Legislative Budgetary Control

Every two years, the legislature has traditionally set the budgets for state agencies and then provided little scrutiny over how effectively the money was actually spent, unless there was a financial crisis that required a special legislative session or an emergency transfer of funds by the governor and the Legislative Budget Board. Perhaps the most control that lawmakers exercise over agency spending, besides setting the bottom line, is their approval of a number of line items in agency budgets that restrict portions of the budget to specific programs (see "How to Control Bureaucrats").

How to Control Bureaucrats

Taking a cue from political scientist Robert Lineberry, Texas policymakers can use several strategies to control bureaucracies and help ensure that policies are carried out as intended:

- Change the law or make legislation more detailed to reduce or eliminate the discretionary authority of an agency.
- Overrule the bureaucracy and reverse or rescind an action of an agency. With the independence of many agencies, boards, and commissions at the state level, the governor can reverse few agency decisions. So this step often requires legislative action.
- Transfer the responsibility for a program to another agency through administrative reorganization.
- Replace an agency head who refuses to or is incapable of carrying out program objectives.

But there are only a few agencies over which the governor can directly exercise such authority in Texas.

- Cut or threaten to reduce the budget of an agency to force compliance with policy objectives.
- Abolish an agency or program through sunset legislation.
- Pressure the bureaucracy to change, using legislative hearings and public disclosures of agency neglect or inadequacies.
- Protect public employees who reveal incompetence, mismanagement, and corruption through whistleblower legislation.
- Enact revolving-door restrictions to reduce or eliminate the movement of former state employees to industries over which they had regulatory authority.[19]

Performance Reviews

Facing a large revenue shortfall in 1991, the legislature directed Comptroller John Sharp to conduct unprecedented performance reviews of all state agencies to determine ways to eliminate mismanagement and inefficiency and save tax dollars. Sharp recommended $4 billion worth of spending cuts, agency and funds consolidations, accounting changes, some minor tax increases, and increases in various state fees to more accurately reflect the costs of providing services. Pressure from special interests killed many of the recommendations, but the legislature adopted about $2.4 billion of them. Sharp produced follow-up reports in 1993, 1995, and 1997, and his successor, Carole Keeton Strayhorn, continued the performance reviews after she took office. At the beginning of the 2003 session of the legislature, she made 64 recommendations for further restructuring of state agencies and their operations, some of which were adopted by lawmakers. The comptroller also has similarly reviewed the operations of a significant number of local school districts.

The performance reviews generally have been considered instrumental in improving administrative practices. But after a series of budgetary disputes in 2003, the legislature, with Governor Rick Perry's approval, transferred the work from the comptroller's office to the Legislative Budget Board (see Chapter 9). The move was criticized by those who believed the reviews should have remained under the oversight of an independently elected officeholder, but it remained to be seen what the ultimate effect of the transfer would be.

Sunset Legislation

Although Texas has been slow to modernize its budgetary process and other key functions of state government, it was one of the first states to require formal, exhaustive reviews of how effectively agencies are doing their jobs. The sunset process enacted in 1977 was so named because most agencies have to be periodically re-created by the legislature or automatically go out of business.[20] Relatively few agencies—except for a number of inactive ones like the Pink Bollworm Commission and the Stonewall Jackson Memorial Board—have been abolished. But the obligatory review has produced some significant structural and policy changes in the state bureaucracy that the legislature may not have otherwise ordered. It also has expanded employment opportunities for lobbyists because special interest groups have much to win or lose in the sunset process. In many cases, special interests have succeeded in protecting the status quo.

Each agency is usually up for **sunset review** every twelve years under a rotating order set out in the sunset law. The review begins with the Sunset Advisory Commission, which includes four state representatives appointed by the speaker of the House, four senators appointed by the lieutenant governor, and two public members, one named by the speaker and the other by the lieutenant governor. The commission employs a staff that studies each agency up for review during the next regular, biennial legislative session and reports its findings to the panel, which makes recommendations to the legislature.

In a few cases, the commission will propose that an agency—usually a minor one—be terminated or consolidated with another agency. In most cases, however, the commission recommends the continuation of an agency but outlines suggested changes in its organizational structure and operations. The future of the agency is then debated by the full legislature. If lawmakers fail to approve a sunset bill for any agency by September 1 of the year the agency is scheduled for review, the agency will be phased out of existence over the next year. It will be terminated abruptly on September 1 if the legislature refuses to approve a new budget for the agency. In recent years, however, the legislature has postponed controversial sunset decisions by passing special laws to allow some agencies to stay open past their review dates.

The Texas Higher Education Coordinating Board is subject to sunset review, but individual universities are not. Also exempted from sunset review are the courts and state agencies created by the constitution, such as the governor's office, the attorney general, the comptroller, and the General Land Office.

The sunset process hasn't reduced the size of the state bureaucracy. By 2007, there were some 300,000 state employees, compared to about 164,000 in 1977, the year the sunset law was approved. Although more than sixty agencies have been terminated or merged, others have been created (see Table 10–3). But Bill Wells, the Sunset Advisory Commission's former executive director, said the statistics didn't tell the full story. He believed the sunset process had served to slow down the creation of new agencies. "You can't say how many [new agencies] would have been created if sunset hadn't heightened the awareness of the fact that we've got maybe too many agencies now," he said. "There is a heightened awareness of the fact that you need to go a little slower, and you need to really have a problem before you create an agency."[21]

The sunset review process has helped rid state government of some deadwood, modernized some state laws and bureaucratic procedures, and made some agencies more responsive and accountable to the public. Under a sunset policy discussed earlier in this chapter, public members have been added to the boards of numerous small regulatory agencies that previously had included only representatives of the professions or industries that they regulated.

The largest agencies and those with influential constituencies are usually the most difficult to change because special interests are working overtime and making large political contributions to protect their turf. In 1993, for example, the insurance lobby succeeded in weakening some regulatory reforms in the Department of Insurance sunset bill. In another case that year, there was such a high-stakes battle involving telephone companies, newspaper publishers, electric utilities, and consumers over the Public Utility Commission sunset bill that the legislature postponed action on PUC sunset for two years. The lobby's influence over the 1993 sunset bills prompted Governor Ann Richards and some legislators to suggest that the sunset process should be changed or repealed because it was being abused by special interests. But consumer advocates, who value the sunset process, blamed the problem on legislators who had difficulty saying no to special interest lobbyists.

TABLE 10–3   Sunset Action from 1979 to 2009, 66th to 81st Legislative Sessions

Actions Taken by Commission	Total	Percent
Agencies Reviewed	423*	
Agencies Continued	337	84%
Agencies Abolished Outright	35	8%
Agencies Abolished and Functions Transferred	23	5%
Agencies Consolidated	12	3%
Agencies Separated	2	1%

*Some agencies reviewed were not subject to continuation or abolishment or had their Sunset date removed. Total also includes other special reviews and projects.

Source: Texas Sunset Advisory Commission, Summary of Sunset Legislation, 81st Legislature.

Since major state agencies have to be re-created in some form, they can be held hostage by legislators for any number of purposes during their review year. In 1989, Governor Bill Clements and other foes of Agriculture Commissioner Jim Hightower used the sunset process to trim Hightower's influence. Unlike most other statewide, elected offices, the agriculture commissioner's post wasn't created by the state constitution. It is statutory, which made it vulnerable when the Department of Agriculture had to pass sunset review. Hightower, a liberal Democrat, had cultivated the enmity of conservative agricultural producers and the chemical industry by, among other things, proposing tighter restrictions on the use of pesticides and more protection for agricultural workers. Clements, a Republican who opposed most of Hightower's politics, backed efforts to change the law to replace Hightower's job with a commissioner or multimember commission appointed by the governor. Hightower had strong support in the Senate, which then had a Democratic majority, for keeping his post elective. But he had trouble in the House, where one-third of the members were Republicans and many rural, conservative Democrats shared a dim view of his policies and politics. Hightower had survived attacks in previous legislative sessions, but this time, with the future of the agricultural agency at stake, he was forced to accept a compromise. His job remained elective, but he had to share his authority to regulate pesticides with a new, appointive board created in the sunset law. Hightower's political troubles were so deep that he was unseated the next year by Rick Perry, one of the legislative sponsors of the pesticide regulation compromise.

The Revolving Door

Over the years, many regulatory agencies had become training grounds for young attorneys and other professionals taking their first jobs out of college or law school. They would work for state agencies for a few years for relatively low pay while gaining valuable experience in a particular regulatory area and making influential contacts in the state bureaucracy. Then they would leave state employment for higher-paying jobs in the industries they had regulated and would represent their new employers before the state boards and commissions for which they had once worked. Or they would become consultants or join law firms representing regulatory clients. Former gubernatorial appointees to boards and commissions—not just hired staffers—also participated in this **revolving-door** phenomenon, which raised ethical questions about possible insider advantages.

An early step in restricting the revolving door was part of the 1975 law that created the Public Utility Commission (PUC). This law prohibited PUC members and high-ranking staffers from going to work for regulated utilities immediately after leaving the agency. An ethics reform law in 1991 expanded the restrictions to other agencies.

WHISTLEBLOWING ●

Governmental agencies make mistakes that can be very costly to the public in terms of financial waste or regulatory neglect, which may endanger the public's health or safety. Because agencies spend huge sums of money for supplies, construction, and basic services, there also is the potential for public officials or employees to be offered kickbacks or bribes to influence decisions that would benefit particular vendors or contractors.

Texas has a **whistleblower** protection law, which is designed to protect public employees who report wrongdoing within their agencies to their supervisors. If an employee is subjected to retaliation after having come forward, the law permits the worker to file a lawsuit against the offending agency.

A major test of the law's effectiveness was brought by George Green, an architect for the Texas Department of Human Services. Green complained of shoddy construction on agency facilities, kickbacks, and noncompliance with contracts and said his supervisors refused to take action against the offending contractors. After he went public with his charges, Green was fired for allegedly abusing sick-leave time and making one unauthorized call on his state telephone—a thirteen-cent call to his father. Criminal charges were brought against him, and although they were eventually dropped, he spent $130,000 in legal fees, could not find a job, and depleted his personal assets.

Green sued the state under the whistleblower law and won a $13.6 million judgment from a Travis County jury in 1991. The amount included $3.6 million in actual damages that Green had suffered and $10 million in punitive damages to punish the state for the way he had been treated. The state appealed, dragging out a resolution of the case, until the judgment eventually was upheld by the Texas Supreme Court in 1994. But the legislature was not in session that year, and state leaders said there was no money in the state budget to pay Green. So he had to wait for the legislature to convene in 1995. Green, meanwhile, was still unemployed and living off the generosity of friends and family and a personal loan he had made against a portion of his judgment.

By the time the legislature convened in 1995, Green's judgment, with interest, had grown to almost $20 million, and interest continued to grow at the rate of more than $4,500 a day. The case was receiving considerable media attention nationally, as well as in Texas. But many legislators, particularly in the House, did not want to pay him the full amount, which they considered excessive. They particularly objected to the $10 million the jury had awarded as punitive damages and pointed out that taxpayers would ultimately have to pick up the tab. Green refused to accept an amount smaller than the judgment and interest, and the 1995 session ended in late May without Green receiving any payment.

Legislators, however, took steps to assure there never would be such a large whistleblower judgment again. They changed the law to limit all whistleblower suit damages against the state to $250,000. Critics of the change warned it would seriously curtail whistleblower suits and undermine an important taxpayer protection because the best lawyers, whose fees are based on the size of a judgment, would quit taking whistleblower cases.

Finally, in November 1995, Green reached a compromise with legislative leaders. The Legislative Budget Board (LBB), which can transfer funds when the full legislature is not in session, approved a $13.8 million settlement, which Green accepted. Part of the money went to lawyers and a lobbyist who had helped Green collect payment, and $1 million of the total went to an investor who had loaned Green money during his battle. Lieutenant Governor Bob Bullock, who chaired the LBB, apologized to Green and called his ordeal a "black mark on the history of Texas."[22]

Even then, Green's story continued. A former consultant sued Green for allegedly failing to pay him for helping Green collect the judgment from the state. In December 1996, another Travis County jury awarded the former consultant more than $600,000 in actual and punitive damages against Green.

Green's experience speaks to a major problem. Few public employees can afford to be subjected to this type of retaliation, and few have the resources to fight state government. Although the original intent of the law was to protect whistleblowers and to encourage their inside information, most state and local employees may have received a different message from the Green case and the legislature's decision to weaken the law (see "Options Available to Public Employees").

Options Available to Public Employees

Public employees appear to have five options when they encounter wrongdoing within their agencies:

1. They can simply remain silent and not rock the boat for fear of possible recriminations.
2. They can work through the normal operating procedures of the organization to try to influence or change the actions of other employees.
3. They can leak information to the news media and hope that external, public pressure will force changes.
4. They can leave the organization and then attempt to go public to prompt changes.
5. Or they can simply go away and find employment elsewhere.

REGULATION

The legislature delegates much authority for carrying out state policy to regulatory agencies, and regulation, in turn, takes many forms. There is economic regulation, which affects the prices that some businesses can charge for their services. Major state regulators in this area include the Department of Insurance, which has oversight over rates that can be charged for automobile and homeowners insurance, and the Public Utility Commission, which has authority over rates charged for some telephone services and over electric rates charged by some utilities. City governments regulate selected areas of the local economy.

A second regulatory function is the **licensing** of professions and franchising of corporations. Under state law, some occupations require formal training, testing, and subsequent licensing from a state agency. These include doctors, nurses, accountants, lawyers, and a host of other professions. Individuals and companies also must have state charters or licenses to open a state bank, a funeral home, or a nursing home. Licensing implies regulation, and the acceptance of a license implies a willingness to comply with state controls. On the local level, contractors are required to meet building codes established by city councils.

State agencies also regulate the allocation of natural resources and safeguard their quality. The Texas Commission on Environmental Quality enforces state laws protecting air and water. Disputes over the use of water from the underground Edwards Aquifer in the San Antonio area prompted state intervention; and a drought in the mid-1990s convinced the legislature to order the development of a statewide water conservation and management plan (see Chapter 13). In another crucial conservation area, the Texas Railroad Commission establishes the rate at which a well can pump oil from the ground.

State and local governments also can regulate by providing operating subsidies to businesses, including tax breaks that are subject to limitations imposed by the legislature. These incentives usually are offered for specified periods to encourage businesses to locate or expand in a specific community. In return, the businesses may agree to conditions imposed on them by the participating government. Cities grant franchises to cable television systems, which agree to provide a specific level of service in return for the operating rights.

State agencies also regulate companies for fairness and competition. Although there are many federal laws dealing with price fixing, monopolies, and unfair competition, there also are state statutes relating to the competitiveness of the state's economy. Additionally, the state is involved in what some writers call social regulation.[23] This type of

How We See It | Negotiating Bureaucracies

Despite all the rhetoric for shrinking government, historical evidence shows that state and local governments have expanded in response to a growing population and increased demands for public services. Although some people promote privatization as a solution to big government, privatization simply replaces a public bureaucracy with a private bureaucracy. Indeed, trying to resolve a problem by negotiating the complex administrative structures of private companies often is no less frustrating for the consumer or taxpayer than dealing with governmental red tape.

This book's authors have both studied the actions of bureaucracies for more than thirty years, and one served on the Civil Service Commission of the City of San Antonio. Like many other people, we have had to negotiate their complexities to resolve issues that personally affected us. In so doing, we have concluded that the best defense is a good offense. That is, learn how an agency works and then develop the appropriate strategy and tactics to achieve your objective. To this end, we have compiled some rules for "working the bureaucracy."

- **Remember you are dealing with people.** Bureaucracies are comprised of individuals, most of whom want to do a good job. Many of them are overworked, but most take pride in what they do and strive to be successful in carrying out their tasks. Approach them in a cooperative spirit, not as if you are looking for a fight.
- **Find the right agency and the right person or persons authorized to provide solutions.** Bureaucracies also operate under organizational structures that divide responsibilities among employees. Standard operating procedures describe what each person is authorized to do. The first person you call or meet in an agency may not be the person who can deal with your issue. You may feel you are "getting the run around" if you are transferred from person to person or agency to agency. But you can save yourself some time and frustration by making clear your needs or request in your first encounter with a governmental employee. That will enhance the chances of your request being assigned promptly to the right person or office.
- **Be patient.** Employees of large organizations often don't know everything their agencies do. Most public workers are specialists. They have specific areas of responsibility and specific tasks and often know little about other offices or divisions within their agency.
- **Be tenacious.** Dealing with bureaucracies can be frustrating, but persistence is imperative. The more questions you ask, the more you are going to understand the organization and the quicker you are going to find someone who can help you.
- **Know your rights and act on them:** Governments exist for you. You do not exist for governments. The more you learn about governmental procedures, the more likely you are to be successful. If an employee of a state agency dismisses your inquiry or claim in a cavalier manner, go above that person's head to the next person in the chain of command. If the obstruction persists at the higher levels of the agency, call your legislator's office with a detailed summary of what occurred. (It also will help to know which state representative and which state senator represent

you.) Not all legislators will respond to your complaint, particularly if you have dealt with the agency erratically. But many will, and agencies normally respond to inquiries from legislators, who set their budgets and pass the laws under which the agencies operate.

- **Occasionally, you may have to be adversarial.** Sometimes, unfortunately, governmental agencies and their employees misinterpret the law or refuse to do what the law requires. In those cases, your only recourse may be filing a lawsuit against the agency. Corporations and well-organized interest groups usually have the financial resources for such a fight. Most citizens, however, don't. So, concentrate on the above steps, and do everything you can to avoid getting to this one.

regulation is much broader than the economic regulation just described. Social regulations affect "the conditions under which goods and services are produced and the physical characteristics of products that are manufactured."[24] While the federal government has preempted many state policies in these areas, there are state agencies involved in regulating workplace safety and consumer protection.

MERIT SYSTEMS AND PROFESSIONAL MANAGEMENT

Earlier in Texas history, public employees were hired on the basis of **political patronage,** or the personal relationships and friendships they had with elected or appointed public officials. Little consideration was given to their skills, competence, or expertise. There were few rules concerning terms of employment, advancement, or the rights or conduct of public employees, and there were wide variations in wages and salaries from agency to agency. There also were high rates of employee turnover.

To better serve the public and state workers, some reform advocates pushed for a **merit employment system** based, in part, on the Civil Service Commission created by the federal government for its workers in 1883. Although other states have developed comprehensive, statewide employment or personnel systems administered by a single agency, the reform movement in Texas has not been as successful. Improvements have been made, but state government in Texas continues to function under a decentralized personnel system.[25]

Merit-based public employment was inconsistent with the individualistic views of government, politics, and public administration evolving from the dominant political subcultures of Texas (see Chapter 1). The plural executive system worked against efforts to centralize and coordinate personnel policies because the various elected, executive officeholders jealously guarded their prerogatives to hire and fire the people who worked for them.

Governmental functions have expanded in modern times, and carrying out public policy has become more complex and technical.[26] Many programs require highly specialized skills, not political hacks who have no formal training or expertise for technical jobs. Furthermore, the public has gradually developed higher expectations of its government and reacts unfavorably to incompetent public workers. Additional pressure for merit employment has come from the federal government. Since the 1930s, numerous federal grants have required the state to enact a merit system for state employees administering them. In more recent years, federal laws prohibiting hiring discrimination on the basis of sex, age, disability, race, or ethnicity have been extended to state and local governments. These requirements, in turn, have forced Texas government to pay more attention to employment practices (see "Is There a Job in Public Service in Your Future?").[27]

Even so, politics has not been totally eliminated in the hiring and promotion of public employees. State government's personnel "system" is not a merit system but a highly fragmented system with different agencies assigned various personnel responsibilities. Ultimately, the legislature has the legal authority to define personnel practices, and the biennial budget is the major tool used by legislators to establish several hundred job classifications and corresponding salary schedules. The technical work on the state's classification schedule is assigned to the State Classification Office, a division of the State Auditor's Office. This is an agency of the legislature, not the executive branch, supervised

Is There a Job in Public Service in Your Future?

Governments across the nation and in Texas are facing a potential shortage of the skilled workers necessary for technical and professional jobs.[1] Almost half of the employees of state and local governments in Texas are forty or older, and many of those are eligible to retire with full benefits or are near retirement age. Proportionally, governments have far fewer employees under thirty than the general work force.[2]

According to the Texas Auditor's 2007 annual report on full-time state employees, there were approximately 290,000 employees working for the state. Half of these employees worked for institutions of higher education, and the other half worked for all the other state agencies.[3] In recent years, the annual turnover rate for state employees has ranged from 14 percent to more than 17 percent, including voluntary and involuntary separations as well as retirements.[4]

Government employees are, on the whole, better educated than the general population. More than half of government employees have at least a bachelor's degree, compared to 25 percent of all Texans 25 and older. With the increased complexity of government programs and services, skills now required of government employees are knowledge and information based. More than half of government employees are "knowledge workers"—engineers, teachers, health care workers, systems analysts, urban planners, finance specialists, legal professionals, managers, to name a few. But only 31 percent of the general workforce is classified as such.[5]

Studies also indicate significant career possibilities in government for women and some minorities. Women comprise 56 percent of the state's employees, a significantly higher percentage than in the civilian workforce. Across all general job categories, women approximate or exceed the proportions found outside of government. This also is true for the state's African American employees. By contrast, the proportion of Hispanic employees in state government is lower in all categories than in the private sector.[6]

There is a tendency to associate public employment with low pay, but the compensation is surprising if consideration is given to the entire employment package rather than just the stated salary. State employees earned 13 percent less in base pay than employees in the private sector, and local employees, 18 percent less. Among the ten largest states, "Texas showed the greatest differential between private sector and state government workers and the second greatest differential between private and local government workers."[7] But the real question is, "What is the total package, including benefits?"

If one includes total benefits, such as health insurance, retirement contributions, vacation and leave pay, and replacement and longevity pay, compensation for state employees is much more competitive. The average state employee was paid $37,365 in 2008, but when benefits were calculated, the total compensation package was $55,468, or $26.67 per hour, a figure comparable to the private sector.[8]

States and local governments have begun to respond to the pending employment crisis, but many governments do not have the financial resources to attract highly qualified individuals. Nor is the problem so acute that it has become a high priority.

As state and local governments lose a significant number of high-performing, highly skilled, and experienced employees, they will have to become more aggressive in recruiting younger people of comparable education and skills to maintain and improve the quality of public services. But many potential employees have no knowledge of the career opportunities in government, and many governments have not taken advantage of the recruiting tools and strategies used by employers in the private sector.

Many public employees find a great deal of satisfaction in what they do because they are essentially responsible for bringing "policy ideas to life."[9]

Notes

[1] U.S. Government Accountability Office, "Older Workers: Federal Agencies Face Challenges, but Have Opportunities to Hire and Retain Experienced Employees," April 30, 2008; and Stuart Greenfield, "Public Sector Employment: The Current Situation," *Center for State & Local Government Excellence*, 2007, http://www.slge.org.

[2] Stuart Greenfield, "Personnel Predicament: The Coming Human Resource Crisis in Texas Government," *Texas Business Review*, August 2003, p. 1.

[3] Texas State Auditor, "A Summary Report on Full-Time Equivalent State Employees for Fiscal Year 2007," November 2007.

[4] Texas State Auditor, *Annual Report on Classified Employees Turnover* (for fiscal years 2000–2008).

[5] Texas State Auditor, A Summary Report on Full-Time Equivalent State Employees for Fiscal Year 2007," November 2007.

[6] Texas Workforce Commission, Civil Rights Division, "Equal Employment: Opportunity and Minority Hiring Practices Report," January, 2009.

[7] Greenfield, "Personnel Predicament," p. 4.

[8] Texas State Auditor's Office, "A Report on State Employee Benefits as a Percentage of Total Compensation," Report No. 09–704, February 2009, p. i.; and U.S. Department of Labor, Bureau of Labor Statistics, *News*, June 16, 2009.

[9] Donald F. Kettl and James W. Fesler, *The Politics of the Administrative Process*, 3rd ed. (Washington, DC: CQ Press, 2005), p. xx.

by the Legislative Audit Committee. The legislature also establishes policies on vacations, holidays, and retirement.

Within this highly decentralized personnel system, the primary responsibility for carrying out personnel policies is still delegated to the various state agencies. An administrator can develop specific policies for an agency as long as the agency works within the general framework defined by the legislature. Some agencies have developed modern personnel plans—including employee grievance procedures and competitive examinations for placement and advancement—while others have not.

All state job openings are required to be listed with the Texas Workforce Commission. Agencies also advertise for workers through the mass media and college placement centers. But many jobs still are filled as a result of friendships, personal contacts, and the influence of key political players.

Higher and public education employees are subject to different employment policies, which are determined by individual university governing boards and local school districts. Unlike state government, many cities across Texas have adopted centrally administered merit systems organized around the accepted principles of modern personnel management. Their personnel departments include independent civil service commissions that have some rule-making authority and hear appeals of personnel matters. These changes, which resulted from the urban reform movement (see Chapter 12), were designed to recruit quality employees and to insulate them from external political pressures. They have led to a high level of professionalism in some cities. Large metropolitan counties also have tried to structure their employment systems on the basis of merit, but the partisan election of county officials thwarts the full implementation of merit systems.

SUMMARY AND CONCLUSIONS

1. Despite a historical ambivalence, if not animosity, toward government, Texans have come to expect good roads and schools, safe drinking water, and a host of other public programs to meet their needs and interests. Consequently, government has grown with the population. More than 1.3 million Texans are now employed either full or part-time by state and local governments. Collectively, we refer to them and the agencies for which they work as the bureaucracy.

2. The bureaucracy has the primary responsibility of carrying out public policies adopted by the legislature and the local governing bodies. Administrative agencies are also involved in virtually every stage of the policymaking process. Legislators depend on administrative agencies for counsel and advice when they draft public policies, and they rely on them to help assess the success or failure of policies.

3. When things go wrong and problems go unresolved, there is a tendency to blame bureaucrats. But, often, government employees are unfairly blamed for complex problems that elected policymakers have been unwilling or unable to resolve. The fragmented structure of the executive branch of state government is, in itself, a major obstacle to the efficient, responsive delivery of public services. There also is the potential for agencies headed by appointed boards to become unaccountable to the voters and susceptible to the influence of special interest groups.

4. Through sunset legislation, Texas became one of the first states to require formal reviews of how effectively state agencies are doing their jobs. Most agencies are subject to periodic review and reauthorization by the legislature. The process has not reduced the size of the bureaucracy, but it has helped rid state government of obsolete agencies and produced greater accountability. The legislature also has empowered the Legislative Budget Board to conduct performance reviews of state programs to promote efficiency and reduce waste. In addition, Texas has adopted revolving-door restrictions that prohibit former board members and key employees of regulatory agencies from going to work for regulated companies within a certain period after leaving their state posts.

5. Although many local governments have adopted merit employment systems, state government functions under a decentralized personnel system. It is highly fragmented, with each agency largely free to set its own personnel policies.

KEY TERMS

Bureaucracy   317
Co-optation   325
Sunset review   327

Revolving door   329
Whistleblower   329
Licensing   331

Political patronage   333
Merit employment system   333

FURTHER READING

Articles

Barrett, Katherine, and Richard Greene, "Grading the States 2008: The Mandate to Measure," The Pew Center on the States, March 2008.

Campbell, Brett, "Killing the Messenger: Did DHS Retaliate Against a Whistleblower?" *Texas Observer,* July 12, 1991, pp. 8–11.

Curry, Landon, "Politics of Sunset Review in Texas," *Public Administration Review* 50 (January–February 1990), pp. 58–63.

Frederick, Douglas W., "Reexamining the Texas Railroad Commission," in *Texas Politics: A Reader,* edited by Anthony Champagne and Edward J. Harpham. New York: W.W. Norton, 1997, pp. 67–76.

Molina, Mario, and Patricia M. Shields, "The Treatment of Bureaucracy in Texas Government Textbooks," Department of Political Science, Texas State University, Faculty Publications, 1998.

Books

Beal, Ronald L., *Texas Administrative Practice and Procedure.* Charlottesville, VA: Michie, 1998.

Gosling, James J., *Budgetary Politics,* 2nd ed. New York: Garland, 1997.

Johnson, William C., *Public Administration.* Long Grove, IL: Waveland, 2004.

Kettl, Donald F. and James W. Fesler, *The Politics of the Administrative State,* 3rd ed. Washington, DC: CQ Press, 2005.

Schultz, David A., and Robert Maranto, *The Politics of Civil Service Reform.* New York: Peter Lang, 1998.

Sunset Advisory Commission, *Guide to the Texas Sunset Process, 2008* (Austin, TX: 2008).

Van Wart, Montgomery, *Changing Public Sector Values.* New York: Garland, 1998.

Websites

Texas State Auditors Office   http://www.sao.state.tx.us/ Under the jurisdiction of the legislature, the auditor's office manages the State Classification Plan and provides support to state agency and higher education human resources offices.

Office of the Comptroller   http://www.cpa.state.tx.us/ In addition to providing links to other state agencies, the comptroller's office provides a wide array of information pertaining to state taxes, management and accounting systems, and earlier performance reviews of state operations and agencies.

ENDNOTES ●

1. Texas Governor's Office of Budgeting and Planning, "Strategic Planning and Budgeting in the 'New Texas,'" in *Case Studies in Public Budgeting and Financial Management,* 2nd ed., edited by Aman Khan and W. Bartley Hildreth (Boca Raton, FL: CRC Press, 2003).

2. Carole Keeton Strayhorn, "Limited Government, Unlimited Opportunity: Recommendations of the Texas Comptroller," *Window on State Government,* January 2003, http://www.window.state.tx.us/etexas2003/.

3. Donald F. Kettl and James W. Fesler, *The Politics of the Administrative Process,* 3rd ed. (Washington, DC: CQ Press, 2005), pp. 127–8.

4. See Max Weber, "Bureaucracy," in *Max Weber Essays in Sociology,* edited by H. H. Gerth and C. Wright Mills (New York: Oxford University Press, 1971), pp. 196–244.

5. Jeffrey D. Straussman, *Public Administration* (New York: Longman, 1990), p. 65.

6. The following discussion is based on Dennis Palumbo and Steven Maynard-Moody, *Contemporary Public Administration* (New York: Longman, 1991), pp. 26–31; and Straussman, *Public Administration,* pp. 63–64.

7. Melvin J. Dubnick and Barbara S. Romzek, *American Public Administration* (New York: Macmillan, 1991), p. 248.

8. Ibid, pp. 248–49.

9. The U.S. Census Bureau conducts a census of all U.S. governments every five years. In compiling employment data, part-time and full-time employees are counted. There were a total of 1,386,524 persons working for the state and local governments in 2002. Using payroll data, this total is recalculated as "full-time equivalent" employees.

10. U.S. Bureau of Labor Statistics, "State Government Employees per 10,000 Population, 2008," *Governing: State and Local Sourcebook,* http://sourcebook.governing.com/subtopicresults.jsp?ind=681.

11. U.S. Bureau of the Census, *Statistical Abstract of the U.S.: 2006* (Washington, DC: 2005), Tables 440 and 441.

12. Polly Ross Hughes, "Needy Texans' Applications Faxed into a Black Hole," Houston Chronicle, June 2, 2006, p. 1A.

13. Theodore J. Lowi, *The End of Liberalism,* 2nd ed. (New York: W.W. Norton, 1979), p. 274.

14. Larry N. Gerston, *Making Public Policy* (Glenview, IL: Scott, Foresman, 1983), p. 95.

15. Palumbo and Maynard-Moody, *Contemporary Public Administration,* p. 304.

16. Straussman, *Public Administration,* p. 246.

17. Texas Sunset Advisory Commission, *Texas Sunset Advisory Commission Report,* October 1991, http://www.lib.utexas.edu/taro/tslac/40063/tsl-40063.html.

18. Lee Hancock, "Nursing Homes Under Fire - Ex Official Defends his Facilities, *Dallas Morning News,* October 24, 1991, p. 1A.

19. Robert Lineberry, *American Public Policy* (New York: Harper & Row, 1977), pp. 84–85.

20. Colorado was the first state to adopt sunset legislation in 1976. See Straussman, *Public Administration,* p. 39.

21. Associated Press, (not available to autors) *Dallas Times Herald,* August 14, 1983.

22. Clay Robison, "Long Wait for Justice Pays Off/$13.8 Million Goes to Whistle Blower," *Houston Chronicle,* November 16, 1995, p. 1A.

23. Straussman, *Public Administration,* p. 286.

24. William Lilley III and James C. Miller III, "The New Social Regulation," *Public Interest,* 47 (Spring 1977), p. 53.

25. Council of State Governments, *The Book of the States, 1990–1991,* vol. 28 (Lexington, KY: Council of State Governments, 1990), p. 346.

26. For a summary of the merit system movement, see Palumbo and Maynard-Moody, *Contemporary Public Administration,* pp. 165–74.

27. Office of the Governor, Division of Planning Coordination, *Quality Texas Government, 1972.* Much of this discussion is based on this report.

CHAPTER 11

The Judicial System in Texas

Questions to Guide Your Reading

1. Does the structure of the state's judicial system assure residents fair and speedy trials?

2. Should a judge be required to recuse or excuse himself from hearing a case in his court if any of the parties has made a contribution to his election campaign?

3. Would the appointment or nonpartisan election of state judges improve the quality of justice in Texas?

4. Is execution by lethal injection a "cruel and unusual" punishment?

The Texas (judicial) system is a hodgepodge of courts.

—**Anthony Champagne**[1]

I am concerned by the public's perception that money in judicial races influences outcomes. This is an area where perception itself destroys public confidence.

—**Texas Supreme Court Chief Justice Wallace B. Jefferson**[2]

Although most people would like to think that justice in Texas is blind, so that everyone has a level playing field in the state's courts, it is not. Litigation, whether civil or criminal, is expensive, and many Texans do not have the resources to pay for legal assistance. Most judges try to be fair, but, even so, their decisions are molded by their political and ideological views, life experiences, ethnicity, and gender. In recent years, moreover, Texas courts have been beset by a series of controversies that have severely strained the notion that the scales of justice are weighed in an atmosphere that is above reproach. Large campaign contributions to elected state judges from lawyers who practice before them and from other special interests fuel an ongoing high-stakes war for philosophical and political control of the judiciary, raising questions in the media and many advocacy groups about whether Texas courtrooms are "for sale."

Minorities and women remain underrepresented among the ranks of Texas judges. Even the basic structure of the judicial system—an assortment of about 2,600 courts of various, often overlapping, jurisdictions—is so outdated that many experts believe it should be overhauled. But change doesn't come easily, and some influential people have a vested interest in maintaining the status quo.

State courts resolve civil disputes over property rights and personal injuries. They also determine guilt or innocence and set punishment in criminal cases involving offenses against people, property, and public institutions. To a more limited extent than the federal judiciary, they help set policy by reviewing the actions of the executive and legislative branches of government. A civil dispute may stem from something as simple as a tenant breaking an apartment lease to something as complex and potentially expensive as a manufacturer's liability for defective tires that contribute to the deaths or injuries of dozens of motorists. Criminal cases range from traffic offenses, punishable by fines, to capital murder, for which the death penalty can be imposed.

Some streamlining of Texas's judicial processes, especially at the appellate level, was accomplished in 1981. But the Texas judiciary, particularly in urban areas, has become overloaded by criminal cases and an increasingly litigious approach to civil disputes. It can take months to get a civil or a criminal case—one that isn't settled out of court or in a plea bargain with prosecutors—to trial.

STATE COURTS IN THE FEDERAL SYSTEM ●

Like people in every state, Texans are subject to the jurisdiction of both state and federal courts. The federal judiciary, created by Article III of the United States Constitution, has jurisdiction over violations of federal laws, including criminal offenses that occur across state lines, and over banking, securities, and other activities regulated by the federal government. Federal courts have also had major effects on state government policies and Texas's criminal justice system through interpretations and applications of the U.S. Constitution and federal laws, including the Bill of Rights.

Although Texas has a bill of rights in its constitution, the federal courts have taken the lead in protecting many civil and political rights, as when the U.S. Supreme Court declared the white primary election unconstitutional in *Smith v. Allwright* in 1944. Federal court intervention continues in the redistricting of legislative and congressional district lines.[3] The federal judiciary also ordered far-reaching improvements in the state prison system (see Chapter 13). And when police officers read criminal suspects their rights, the officers are complying with constitutional requirements determined by the U.S. Supreme Court in the Miranda case.[4]

Nevertheless, it is estimated that more than 95 percent of all litigation is based on state laws or local ordinances. Thus anyone involved in a lawsuit is likely to be found in a state rather than a federal court.

THE LEGAL FRAMEWORK FOR THE JUDICIAL SYSTEM

The United States and Texas constitutions form the basic legal framework of the Texas court system. Building on that framework, the Texas legislature has enacted codes of criminal and civil procedure to govern conduct in the courtroom and statutory laws for the courts to apply.

Most criminal activities are defined and their punishments established in the Texas **Penal Code**. In criminal cases the state, often based on charges made by another individual, initiates action against a person accused of a crime. The most serious criminal offenses, for which prison sentences can be imposed, are called felonies. More minor offenses, punishable by fines or short sentences in county jails, are called misdemeanors. Many property crimes and drug offenses are classified as state jail felonies and are punishable by community service work or time in a state jail, a prison-like facility operated by the state.

Civil lawsuits, which can be brought under numerous statutes, involve conflicts between two or more parties—individuals, corporations, governments, or other entities. Civil law governs contracts and property rights between private citizens, affords individuals an avenue for relief against corporate abuses, and determines liability for personal injuries. Administrative law includes government enforcement powers over many aspects of the state's economy.

An individual with a grievance has to take the initiative of going to court. A person can be having problems with a landlord who refuses to return a deposit, a dry cleaner that lost a suit, or a friend who has borrowed and wrecked a car. But in a civil dispute, there is no legal issue to be resolved unless a lawsuit is filed. An injured person filing a lawsuit is a plaintiff. Because even the most minor disputes in the lowest courts can require professional assistance from a lawyer, a person will soon discover that the pursuit of justice can be very costly and time consuming.

Statutes and constitutional laws are subject to change through legislative action and popular consent of the voters, and over the years there have been significant changes in what is legal or illegal, permissible or impermissible. At one time, for example, state law provided for a potential life prison sentence for the possession of a few ounces of marijuana. Small amounts are now considered a misdemeanor punishable by a fine. The legal drinking age was lowered to 18 for a few years but was reestablished at 21 after parents and school officials convinced the legislature that the younger age had helped increase alcohol abuse among teenagers.

THE STRUCTURE OF THE TEXAS COURT SYSTEM

There are five levels of Texas courts, but some courts at different levels have overlapping authority and jurisdiction (see Figure 11–1). Some courts have only **original jurisdiction**; that is, they try or resolve only those cases being heard for the first time. They weigh the facts presented as evidence and apply the law in reaching a decision, or verdict. Other courts have only **appellate jurisdiction**. They review the decisions of lower courts to determine if constitutional and statutory principles and procedures were correctly interpreted and followed. Appellate courts are empowered to reverse the judgments of the lower courts and to order cases retried if constitutional or procedural mistakes were made. Still other courts have both original and appellate jurisdiction.

At the highest appellate level, Texas has a **bifurcated court system** with the nine-member Texas Supreme Court serving as the court of last resort in civil cases and the nine-member Texas Court of Criminal Appeals functioning as the court of last resort in criminal cases. Only one other state, Oklahoma, has a similar structure.[5]

Unlike federal judges, who are appointed by the president to lifetime terms, state judges, except for those on municipal courts, are elected to limited terms in partisan elections. Midterm vacancies, however, are filled by appointment. Vacancies on the justice of the peace and county courts are filled by county commissioners courts, whereas vacancies on the district and appellate benches are filled by the governor.

Courts of Limited Jurisdiction

Municipal and Justice of the Peace Courts.   The lowest ranking courts in Texas are **municipal courts** and **justice of the peace courts**. You or someone you know probably has appeared before a judge in one of these courts because both handle a large volume of traffic tickets. Some of these courts are big sources of revenue for local governments, and they are often accused of subordinating justice and fairness to financial considerations.

Some 913 municipal courts are established under state law, including some with multiple judges.[6] The qualifications, terms of office, and method of selecting municipal judges are determined by the individual cities, but they are generally appointed by the city council. Municipal courts have original and exclusive jurisdiction over city ordinances, but most of these courts are not courts of record, where a word-for-word transcript is made of trial proceedings. Only very rudimentary information is officially recorded in most of these courts, and any appeal from them is heard *de novo* by the higher court. That is, the second court has to conduct a new trial and hear the same witnesses and evidence all over again because no official record of the original proceedings was kept. The informality of these proceedings and the absence of a record add to the confusion and cost of using the system.[7] In response to these problems, the legislature in recent years has created municipal courts of record for some cities.

Each county in Texas is required to have one justice of the peace court, and each county government in the larger metropolitan areas may create sixteen. There are 821 of these courts in Texas. Justices of the peace are elected to four-year terms from precincts, or subdivisions of the county, drawn by the commissioners court, which also sets their salaries. Justices of the peace are not required to be licensed attorneys, a situation that has generated much criticism of these courts.

Although their duties vary from county to county, justice of the peace courts, with certain restrictions, have original jurisdiction in civil cases when the amount in dispute is $10,000 or less, and they have original jurisdiction over criminal offenses that are

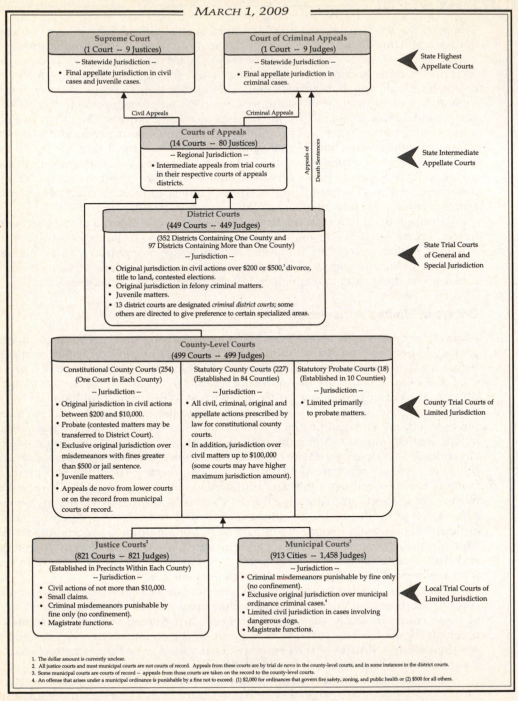

FIGURE 11–1   Court Structure of Texas.   *Source:* Texas Office of Court Administration.

Limited, but important jurisdiction. Justice of the Peace Courts have limited jurisdiction in civil and criminal matters, such as small claims, evictions, or Class C misdemeanors. Judge Monica Caballero presides over JP Court 1, Place 1 in Bexar County.

punishable by fines only. In some areas of criminal law, they have overlapping jurisdiction with municipal courts. Justices of the peace also sit as judges of small claims courts, and in many rural counties they serve as coroners. They also function as state magistrates with the authority to hold preliminary hearings to determine if there is probable cause to hold a criminal defendant.

These are not courts of record, and cases appealed from them are tried *de novo* in county courts, county courts-at-law, or district courts. Each justice court has an elected constable to serve warrants and perform other duties for the court.

County Courts.   If there is confusion about the authority and jurisdiction of municipal and justice of the peace courts, it is compounded by the county courts. They were created by the Texas Constitution to serve the needs of the sparsely populated, rural society that existed when the charter was written in 1875. But population growth and urbanization have placed enormous demands on the judicial system, and rather than modernize the system, the state has added courts while making only modest changes in the structure and jurisdiction of the existing courts.

Each county has a **constitutional county court**. The holder of this office, the county judge, is elected countywide to a four-year term. This individual is the chief executive officer of the county and presides over the county commissioners court, the policymaking body of county government (see Chapter 12). Most urban county judges do not perform judicial duties, but county judges in many rural counties perform both executive and judicial functions, a dual responsibility that some experts believe is inconsistent with the Texas Constitution's separation of powers doctrine. Although a large number of county judges are lawyers, they are not required to be. They are required only to be "well informed in the law" and to take appropriate courses in evidence and legal procedures.

The constitutional county court shares some original civil jurisdiction with both the justice of the peace and district courts. It has original criminal jurisdiction over misdemeanors punishable by fines of more than $500 and jail sentences of one year or less. These courts also probate wills and have appellate jurisdiction over cases tried originally in justice of the peace and municipal courts.

Over the years, the legislature also has created 245 **statutory county courts**, or county courts-at-law, in more than ninety counties. Some specialize in probate cases and are called probate courts. These courts were designed to deal with specific local problems and, consequently, have inconsistent jurisdictions. Judges on these courts are elected countywide and have to be lawyers, but the authority of a particular court is defined by the legislation creating it. Some cannot hear civil disputes involving more than $2,500, while others can hear disputes involving as much as $100,000. Drunken driving cases are the primary criminal cases tried before these courts, but some also hear appeals *de novo* from lower courts.

County courts across the state disposed of more than 824,000 civil and criminal cases during the 2008 fiscal year but saw more than 880,000 cases added to their dockets. At the end of the year, more than 930,000 cases were pending before the county courts.[8]

Courts of General Jurisdiction

The primary trial court in Texas is the **district court**. Although there is some overlapping jurisdiction with county courts, district courts have original jurisdiction over civil cases involving $200 or more in damages, divorce cases, contested elections, suits over land titles

The Court is now in session. Judge Phillip A. Kazen presides over a murder case in the 227th District Court in Bexar County, Texas. While there is some overlapping jurisdiction with county courts, the state district courts have general jurisdiction in both civil and criminal matters.

and liens, suits for slander or defamation, all criminal felony cases, and misdemeanors involving official misconduct. In recent years, the legislature has created district courts with specialized jurisdictions over criminal or civil law or over such specialties as family law—divorces and child custody cases. In some large metropolitan counties that have numerous district courts, the jurisdictions of the respective courts are determined by informal agreements among the judges. District court judges are elected to four-year terms, must be at least twenty-five years old, and must have practiced law or served as a judge of another court for four years prior to taking office.

The Texas Constitution gives the legislature the responsibility to define judicial districts, and as the expanding population produced greater caseloads, new district courts were created. In 1981, there were 328 district courts. In 2009, there were 449. A single county may be allocated more than one district court with overlapping geographical jurisdiction. Harris County, the state's most populous county, has fifty-nine district courts, each covering the entire county. By contrast, one rural district court may include several counties. As these courts evolved, there was little systematic consideration of the respective workloads of individual courts, and there are now great disparities in the number of people that district courts serve.

Many urban counties suffer from a heavy backlog of cases that can delay a trial date in civil lawsuits and even some criminal cases for months or years. The district courts disposed of 846,606 civil and criminal cases during the 2008 fiscal year, but new cases were added, and the courts began 2009 with 901,224 pending cases.[9]

Delays in criminal cases have prompted a widespread use of **plea bargains**. In plea bargaining, a criminal defendant, through a lawyer, negotiates with prosecutors a guilty plea that will get a lesser sentence than he or she could expect to receive if convicted in a trial. The process saves the state the time-consuming expense of a full-blown trial and has become an essential tool in clearing urban court dockets.

Former District Attorney John B. Holmes, Jr., estimated that 90 percent of the thousands of felony cases filed in Harris County (Houston) each year were disposed of through plea bargains. Without plea bargains, the caseload would simply overwhelm the twenty-two Harris County district courts that handle criminal cases.

Harris County's civil district courts disposed of more than 97,000 lawsuits—divorces, personal injuries, tax disputes, and others—in fiscal year 2008 but left more than 86,000 other cases pending.[10] Many civil lawsuits are resolved through negotiations between the opposing parties, but those that are tried and appealed can take several years to be resolved.

The wide disparities in populations and caseloads of the various district courts prompted the adoption of a constitutional amendment in 1985 that created the Judicial Districts Board. That panel was responsible for redrawing judicial districts with an eye toward a more equitable distribution of the workload. But in 1994, yielding to pressure from incumbent judges who did not want to lose their offices, it issued recommendations that primarily preserved the status quo. Extensive changes by the legislature were considered unlikely.

Although the district court is the state's primary trial court and the state pays the district judges' base salaries, the counties pick up virtually all the other district court expenses. The counties provide courtrooms, pay the courts' operating expenses, and supplement the judges' state pay.

The Appellate Courts

Intermediate Courts of Appeals.   There are fourteen intermediate **Courts of Appeals** covering thirteen multicounty regions that hear appeals of both civil and criminal cases from the district courts. Two courts, the First Court of Appeals and the Fourteenth Court of Appeals, are based in Houston and cover the same area. The Texas Constitution provides that each court shall have a chief justice and at least two other justices, but the legislature can add to that number and has done so for most courts. Each Houston court has nine judges, and the Fifth Court of Appeals in Dallas has thirteen judges. Five of these intermediate courts, however, have only three members. Appellate judges are elected to six-year terms. They must be at least thirty-five years old and have at least ten years of experience as an attorney or a judge on a court of record.

All Courts of Appeals combined disposed of more than 11,000 cases during fiscal 2008. Approximately 8,000 other cases were still pending on their dockets at the end of that year, with criminal cases accounting for more than half of the unfinished business.[11] Disparities, nevertheless, exist in the number of caseloads between individual courts, with those in Houston and Dallas handling the lion's share. The Texas Supreme Court partially balances the load by transferring cases among courts. The Courts of Appeals normally decide cases in panels of three judges, but an entire court can hear some appeals *en banc*.

The Highest Appellate Courts.   The creation of separate courts of last resort for civil and criminal cases was part of the effort by the constitutional framers of 1875 to fragment political power and decentralize the structure of state and local government. It was also based on the rationale that criminal cases should be handled more expeditiously, and the way to accomplish this was through a separate appellate court.[12]

Cases on appeal. Civil cases reach the Texas Supreme Court on appeal from the lower courts and are argued on points of law. The justices read briefs and listen to oral arguments from opposing attorneys. Justices can interrupt and query an attorney at any time.

Although it decides only civil appeals, the **Texas Supreme Court** is probably viewed by most Texans as the titular head of the state judiciary, and it has been given some authority to coordinate the state judicial system.[13] The Supreme Court is charged with developing administrative procedures for the state courts and rules of civil procedure. It appoints the Board of Law Examiners, which is responsible for licensing attorneys, and has oversight of the State Bar, the professional organization to which all lawyers in Texas must belong. The Supreme Court also has disciplinary authority over state judges through recommendations of the State Commission on Judicial Conduct.

The Texas Supreme Court includes a chief justice and eight justices who serve staggered, six-year terms. Three members are up for election every two years on a statewide ballot. Members must be at least thirty-five years old and must have been a practicing attorney, a judge of a court of record, or a combination of both for at least ten years.

The **Texas Court of Criminal Appeals**, which hears only criminal cases on appeal, includes a presiding judge and eight other judges elected statewide to staggered, six-year terms. The qualifications for members of this court are the same as those for the Supreme Court.

Under the federal system, some decisions of the Texas Supreme Court and the Texas Court of Criminal Appeals can be appealed to the U.S. Supreme Court. Those cases have to involve a federal question or a constitutional right assured under the U.S. Constitution.

JUDICIAL REFORM, A DIFFICULT TASK

Judicial reform has been a recurring issue in Texas politics. Small, incremental changes have been made since the 1970s, but many jurists and scholars continue to push for an overhaul of the structure and jurisdiction of state courts. In September 1989, Texas Supreme Court Chief Justice Thomas R. Phillips requested an in-depth study of the Texas judiciary by the Texas Research League, a privately financed, nonprofit organization specializing in studies of state government.

The League concluded that the court system was fundamentally flawed and sorely in need of an overhaul. It made twenty-seven recommendations, including one that the legislature rewrite the judiciary article of the state constitution to provide a fundamental framework for a unified court system.

Despite a series of similar studies and reports, however, reform of Texas courts has been difficult. The public may have a lot to gain from judicial restructuring, but the primary stakeholders—the judges, the attorneys, the court administrative personnel, and litigants who benefit from delays, confusion, and inefficiency—have resisted change. Unless there is a spontaneous popular demand for reform, there will be few structural changes in the judiciary until some or all of these participants perceive some advantages from reform.[14]

COURT PERSONNEL

Texas Judges

Many judges on the intermediate and highest appellate courts previously served on lower courts. Most district judges came to their offices from private law practice or from a prosecutor's office.

With the partisan realignment of Texas, Republicans saw election gains and more appointments to judicial vacancies. A number of judges also switched from the Democratic

Party. By 2003, almost two-thirds of the judges at the district court level and higher were Republicans, but by 2006 Democrats were making a comeback. Democrats swept all judicial races on the ballot in Dallas County that year and made a strong showing in Harris County two years later. In 2009, however, Republicans still held all nine seats on the Texas Supreme Court and all nine seats on the Texas Court of Criminal Appeals.

Most Texas judges are white males. More women, Hispanics, and African Americans are entering the legal profession and running for judicial offices, but they are still disproportionately underrepresented in the judiciary. As will be discussed later in this chapter, advocates for minorities have pressed for changes in the judicial selection process to enhance their chances to serve on the bench.

Judicial elections have been diluted by a large number of appointments to judicial vacancies. The governor appoints judges to fill midterm vacancies on the district and appellate courts. County commissioners courts fill midterm vacancies on county court-at-law and justice of the peace courts. Appointees are required to run for office in the next general election to keep their seats, but their incumbency can enhance their election chances.

Other Participants in the State Judiciary

County and district clerks, both elected offices, are custodians of court records. Bailiffs are peace officers assigned to the courts to help maintain order and protect judges and other parties. Other law enforcement officers play critical roles in the arrest, detention, and investigation of persons accused of crimes (see "Tulia: A Miscarriage of Justice").

County attorneys and district attorneys are responsible for prosecuting criminal cases. Both positions are elected (see Chapter 12). Some counties don't have a county attorney. In those that do, the county attorney is the chief legal advisor to county commissioners, represents the county in civil lawsuits, and may prosecute misdemeanors. The district attorney prosecutes felonies and, in some counties, also handles misdemeanors. The district attorney exercises considerable power in the criminal justice process by deciding which cases to take to a grand jury for an indictment, whether to seek the maximum penalty for an offense, or whether to plea bargain with a defendant for a reduced sentence. The office represents one county in metropolitan areas and several counties in less populated areas of the state.

Tulia: A Miscarriage of Justice

What began as a drug sting in Tulia, a small town in the Texas Panhandle, quickly escalated into one of the biggest miscarriages of justice in recent Texas history. After belated, but intense, media coverage, help finally arrived for thirty-five victims, but not before they had paid a high price.

In July 1999, forty-six Tulia residents, including thirty-nine African Americans, were arrested on drug charges. Thirty-eight of the defendants were later convicted, all on the testimony of Tom Coleman, the sole undercover officer and only prosecution witness against them. After the *Texas Observer* newspaper, followed by other media, focused attention on the arrests and raised questions about whether they were racially motivated, special evidentiary hearings into the drug sting were convened in March 2003. Retired state District Judge Ron Chapman of Dallas presided over the hearings, during which Coleman's testimony was discredited, and recommended that the Texas Court of Criminal Appeals overturn all thirty-eight convictions. In a separate proceeding, Coleman was later indicted on three counts of perjury stemming from his testimony before Chapman.

The Texas legislature then stepped in, passing a law that allowed fourteen Tulia defendants who were still in prison to be released on bond while the Court of Criminal Appeals considered their cases. And, finally, Governor Rick Perry pardoned thirty-five of the defendants in August 2003, more than four years after the arrests. "Questions surrounding testimony from the key witnesses in these cases, coupled with recommendations from the Board of Pardons and Paroles, weighed heavily in my final decision," the governor said. "Texans demand a system that is tough but fair. I believe my decision to grant pardons in these cases is both appropriate and just," he added. Perry's office said three of the Tulia defendants weren't eligible for pardons.[15]

Jeff Blackburn of Amarillo, an attorney for the Tulia defendants, also filed a civil lawsuit in federal court, seeking damages against a regional drug task force and several local government officials in Swisher County, where Tulia is located. Will Harrell, executive director for Texas of the American Civil Liberties Union, said systemic flaws in the criminal justice system, such as police misconduct, abuse of authority and inadequate legal representation of the poor, still needed to be addressed.

The Jury Systems

Other important players in the judicial process are the private citizens who serve on juries, of which there are two kinds—grand juries and trial, or petit, juries. Although there is some debate about the competency of a jury of ordinary citizens to make reasonable decisions on complex and technical civil and criminal matters, no acceptable alternatives have been found.

The Grand Jury. The **grand jury**, in theory, functions to ensure that the government has sufficient reason to proceed with a criminal **prosecution** against an individual. It includes twelve persons selected by a district judge from a list proposed by a jury commission appointed by the local district judge or judges. Although the grand jury evolved to protect the individual against arbitrary and capricious behavior by governmental officials, a district attorney can exercise great control over a grand jury through deciding which evidence and which witnesses jurors will hear. There have been allegations over the years that grand juries over-represent the interests of upper social and economic groups and under-represent minorities. Grand jury meetings and deliberations are conducted in private, and the accused is not allowed to have an attorney present during grand jury questioning.

A grand jury usually meets on specified days of the week and serves for the duration of the district court's term, usually from three to six months. If at least nine grand jurors believe there is enough evidence to warrant a trial in a case under investigation, they will issue an **indictment**, or a "true bill," a written statement charging a person or persons with a crime. A grand jury investigation also may result in no indictment, or a "no bill" (see "A Grand Jury Challenges the DA").

In some cases, grand juries will issue indictments alleging misdemeanors. That often happens after an investigation fails to produce a strong enough case for a felony indictment. Most misdemeanors, however, aren't handled by grand juries. They are handled by the district or county attorney, who prepares an information—a document formally charging an individual with a misdemeanor—on the basis of a complaint filed by a private citizen.

A Grand Jury Challenges the DA

No one was injured, but the damage was extensive after a fire broke out in June 2007 at the suburban Houston home of Texas Supreme Court Justice David Medina. The justice's house and a neighbor's home were destroyed, and a third house was damaged. Medina wasn't home when the fire started, but his wife, Francisca, and one of their children were. Investigators, who spent several months on the case, determined the fire was intentionally set. Medina was called to testify before a grand jury, but he said neither he nor any member of his family had done anything wrong. Harris County District Attorney Chuck Rosenthal said the justice wasn't a suspect in the arson.

Although district attorneys normally have a lot of influence over grand juries, Rosenthal and this grand jury soon parted company, sparking a politically charged controversy and allegations of a "runaway grand jury." In January 2008, the grand jury indicted Francisca Medina on an arson charge and David Medina on a charge of tampering with evidence. Within hours, Rosenthal said he would move to have the charges dismissed due to "insufficient evidence."

A judge dismissed the charges the next day, angering grand jurors and raising allegations of political favoritism. Rosenthal and Medina were both Republicans.

For several more weeks, controversy continued to dog Rosenthal, a strong, law-and-order advocate whose office had sent more convicts to death row than any other prosecutor's office in the country. No sooner had the Medina dispute started to subside when Rosenthal became embroiled in a controversy over the public disclosure of office e-mails that included some sexually explicit and racist content.

Under increasing pressure, Rosenthal resigned in February 2008, saying a combination of prescription drugs had impaired his judgment. The publicity over the e-mails also had taken a toll on his family, he said.

"I am hopeful that, in my retirement, the media will accord my family the privacy we need to heal," Rosenthal said.[16]

The Petit Jury.   The jury on which most people are likely to be called to serve is the trial, or **petit jury**. Citizens who are at least eighteen years old and meet other minimal requirements are eligible for jury duty, and anyone refusing to comply with a jury summons can be fined for contempt of court (see "Paying a Big Price for Skipping Jury Duty"). Persons older than seventy, individuals with legal custody of young children, and fulltime students are exempted from jury duty.

The legislature in 1991 increased the likelihood of an individual's being called to jury duty by providing that county and district clerks prepare jury summonses from lists of Texans holding driver's licenses or Department of Public Safety identification cards. Previously, prospective jurors were chosen from voter registration lists, and it was believed that some Texans had not been registering to vote in order to avoid jury duty.

Six persons make up a jury in a justice of the peace or county court, and twelve in a district court. Attorneys for both sides in a criminal or civil case screen the prospective jurors, known as **veniremen**, before a jury is seated. In major felony cases, such as capital murder, prosecutors and defense attorneys may take several days to select a jury from among hundreds of prospects.

Paying a Big Price for Skipping Jury Duty

Probably no one knows for sure, but Douglas Maupin, a masonry contractor, may have paid the biggest penalty ever—eighty-three days in jail—for missing jury duty. Maupin was stopped by police in Collin County on February 15, 2009, for speeding. He was jailed when police discovered a warrant had been issued against him for failing to appear for jury duty six years earlier. Maupin, thirty-four, who couldn't afford to pay his $1,500 bond and said a jail clerk had rebuffed his attempt to get a public defender, was released only after a newspaper, the *Dallas Morning News*, learned of his plight.

"He should not have spent that much time. This is unacceptable," said District Judge Chris Oldner, after ordering Maupin's release in May. "I don't know why the process failed to notify us."

The judge who signed the original warrant against Maupin in 2003 had retired. Oldner said he hadn't known that Maupin was in jail until after Maupin had written a letter to the newspaper about his confinement. The judge ordered an investigation.

In addition to the jury duty warrant, Maupin faced seven charges for failing to pay tolls. Five of those cases were dropped by the court in March, and the other two were dismissed for time served in April. He also had two outstanding warrants for a speeding ticket and driving without insurance in Arlington, but a municipal judge agreed to drop those charges and allow him to be released on time served.

"I understand I am partially responsible, but I just want my day in court," Maupin said. "I do know I have the right to due process and a speedy trial. I've had neither. It's not right."[17]

Attorneys for each side in a criminal case are allowed a certain number of peremptory challenges, which allow them to dismiss a prospective juror without having to explain the reason, and an unlimited number of challenges for cause. In the latter case, the lawyer has to state why he or she believes a particular venireman wouldn't be able to evaluate the evidence in the case impartially. The judge decides whether to grant each challenge for cause but can rule against a peremptory challenge only if he or she believes the prosecutor is trying to exclude prospective jurors because of their race, such as keeping African Americans off a jury that is to try an African-American defendant. If that happens, the defendant is entitled to a new group, or panel, of prospective jurors.

In civil cases, attorneys for both sides determine whether any persons on the jury panel should be disqualified because they are related to one of the parties, have some other personal or business connection, or could otherwise be prejudiced. For example, a lawyer defending a doctor in a malpractice suit probably would not want to seat a prospective juror who had been dissatisfied with his own medical treatment. Such potential conflicts are discovered by attorneys' careful screening and questioning of veniremen.

Unanimous jury verdicts are required to convict a defendant in a criminal case. Agreement of only ten of the twelve members of a district court jury and five of the six on a county court jury, however, are necessary to reach a verdict in a civil suit. In a criminal case, jurors have to be convinced "beyond a reasonable doubt" that a defendant is guilty before returning a guilty verdict.

JUDICIAL PROCEDURES AND DECISION-MAKING

Civil litigants and criminal defendants (except those charged with capital murder) can waive their right to a jury trial if they believe it would be to their advantage to have their cases decided by a judge. Following established procedures, which differ between civil and criminal cases and are enforced by the judge, the trial moves through the presentation of opening arguments by the opposing attorneys, examination and cross-examination of witnesses, presentation of evidence, rebuttal, and summation. Some trials can be completed in a few hours, but the trial of a complex civil lawsuit or a sensational criminal case can take weeks or months. Convicted criminal defendants or parties dissatisfied with a judge or jury's verdict in a civil lawsuit can then appeal their case to higher courts.

The procedure in the appellate courts is markedly different from that in the trial courts. There is no jury at the appellate level to rehear evidence. Instead, judges review the decisions and the procedures of the lower court for conformance to constitutional and statutory requirements. The record of the trial court proceedings and legal briefs filed by attorneys are available for appellate judges to review.

Most civil and criminal appeals are initially made to one of the fourteen intermediate Courts of Appeals. Parties dissatisfied with decisions of the Courts of Appeals can appeal to the Texas Supreme Court or the Court of Criminal Appeals.

Cases reach the Texas Supreme Court primarily on **petitions for review**, usually filed by the losing parties, claiming that legal or procedural mistakes were made in the lower courts. The petitions are divided up among the nine justices for review. The justices and their briefing attorneys then prepare memoranda on their assigned cases for circulation among the other court members. Meeting in private conference, the court decides which petitions to reject outright—thus upholding the lower court decisions—and which to schedule for attorneys' oral arguments. A case won't be heard without the approval of at least four of the nine justices.

Oral arguments, in which lawyers present their perspectives on the legal points that are at issue in their cases and answer questions from the justices, are presented in open court. The responsibility for writing the majority opinions that state the court's decisions is determined by lot among the justices. It often takes several months after oral arguments before a decision is issued. Legal points and judicial philosophies are debated among the justices behind the closed doors of their conference room. But differences sometimes spill out for public view through split decisions and strongly worded dissenting opinions.

Most cases taken to the Texas Supreme Court on appeal are from one of the Courts of Appeals, but occasionally the Supreme Court receives a direct appeal from a district court. In recent years, the court has been hearing about 10 percent of the petitions for review it receives.

The Texas Supreme Court also acts on petitions for **writs of mandamus**, or orders directing a lower court or another public official to take a certain action. Many involve disputes over procedure or evidence in cases still pending in trial courts.

The Texas Court of Criminal Appeals has appellate jurisdiction in criminal cases that originate in the district and county courts. Death penalty cases are appealed directly to the Court of Criminal Appeals. Other criminal cases are appealed first to the intermediate Courts of Appeals. Either the defendant or the prosecution can appeal the Courts of Appeals' decisions to the Court of Criminal Appeals by filing **petitions for discretionary review**, which the high court may grant if at least four judges agree. The court sets one day a week aside for lawyers' oral arguments in the cases it agrees to review. The task of writing majority opinions is rotated among the nine judges.

JUDICIAL CONCERNS AND CONTROVERSIES

For more than twenty years, Texas courts have been beset with conflict and controversy. Large campaign contributions from lawyers and other special interests to judges and judicial candidates periodically raise allegations that Texas has the best justice that money can buy. With millions of dollars at stake in crucial legal decisions, the Texas Supreme Court has been a philosophical and political battleground. Meanwhile, minorities, who hold a disproportionately small number of judicial offices, continue to press for greater influence in electing judges. And lengthy ballots, particularly in urban areas, make it increasingly difficult for most voters to choose intelligently among judicial candidates (see "Long Ballots Produce Election Day Surprises").

Long Ballots Produce Election Day Surprises

Like most other candidates for the Texas Court of Criminal Appeals, Houston attorney Steve Mansfield received little publicity when he began a campaign in 1994 to unseat Democratic Judge Charles Campbell, a twelve-year incumbent. Running as a crime victims' advocate, Mansfield first defeated an equally unknown attorney for the Republican nomination. He then got more publicity than he wanted—all of it negative. In the middle of his general election campaign, Mansfield was found to have lied about his personal and political background and exaggerated his legal experience. He was primarily an insurance lawyer with little experience in criminal law. Still, he unseated Campbell, thanks to heavy straight-ticket Republican voting in a GOP landslide.

Bad publicity continued to dog Mansfield, even after he took office. Texas Republican Party officials shunned him at a party fundraiser, and the Board of Law Examiners investigated the circumstances under which he had obtained a Texas law license, which he needed to serve on the court.

At his swearing-in ceremony in January 1995, Mansfield promised to be a hard-working judge, and he spent his first year in office living up to his promise by authoring thirty-three opinions, slightly more than the court average. It was unknown how much of the actual research and

writing could be credited to Mansfield and how much to the experienced staff he inherited from Campbell and was wise enough to retain. But, as he had promised during his campaign, Mansfield usually sided with the prosecution.

Several months after Mansfield took office, the State Bar publicly reprimanded him for his campaign lies. But the Board of Law Examiners did not challenge his law license, which cleared the way for him to remain on the court for his full six-year term. Many judges, prosecutors, and other state officials considered Mansfield's election an embarrassment and a good argument for appointing, rather than electing, judges. Despite the controversy, Mansfield enjoyed his new job. "It's certainly been the greatest challenge I've ever faced. I've worked very hard to live up to the trust the people of Texas put in me," he said.[18]

Mansfield didn't seek reelection in 2000 and left the court after six years. Attempting a comeback, he ran for another Court of Criminal Appeals seat in the 2002 Republican primary but lost.

Although these issues and concerns may seem unrelated, they all share one important characteristic: They cast a cloud over the Texas judiciary. Each, in its own way, undermines public confidence in the state courts and makes many Texans question how just their system of justice is.

Judicial Activism

In earlier chapters, we noted the historical domination of state politics and policies by the conservative, business-oriented establishment. That domination also applied to the judiciary, as insurance companies, banks, utilities, and other large corporate entities became accustomed to favorable rulings from a Democratic, but conservative, Texas Supreme Court.

Establishment-oriented justices, usually elected with the support of the state's largest law firms, tended to view their role as strict constructionists. They believed the legislature had the authority to enact public policy and that the courts were to narrowly interpret and apply the law. Judges were not to engage in setting policy but were to honor legal precedent and prior case law, which in general had favored the interests of corporations over those of consumers, laborers, and the lower social classes.

The establishment began to feel the first tremors of a philosophical earthquake in the 1970s. The Texas Trial Lawyers Association, whose members represent consumers in lawsuits against businesses, doctors, and insurance companies, increased its political activity. And, in 1973, the legislature, with increased minority and female membership from single-member House districts ordered by the federal courts, enacted the Deceptive Trade Practices–Consumer Protection Act, which encouraged injured parties to take their grievances to court. Among other things, the new law allowed consumers to sue for attorneys' fees as well as compensatory and punitive damages.

Trial, or plaintiffs', attorneys, who usually receive a healthy percentage of monetary damages awarded their clients, began contributing millions of dollars to successful Texas Supreme Court candidates, and judicial precedents started falling. A revamped court issued significant decisions that made it easier for consumers to win large judgments for medical malpractice, faulty products, and other complaints against businesses and their insurers. The new activist, liberal interpretation of the law contrasted sharply with the traditional record of the court.

The business community and defense lawyers accused the new court majority of exceeding its constitutional authority by trying to write its own laws. Some business leaders contended the court's activism endangered the state's economy by discouraging new businesses from moving to Texas, a fear that was soon to be put to partisan advantage by Republican leaders.

Judicial Impropriety

Controversy over the Texas Supreme Court escalated into a full-blown storm in 1986 when the Judicial Affairs Committee of the Texas House investigated two justices, Democrats C. L. Ray and William Kilgarlin, for alleged improper contact with attorneys practicing before the court. The two justices denied the allegations, made largely by former briefing attorneys, but never testified before the legislative panel. Both justices had consistently sided with plaintiffs' lawyers and had received considerable campaign support from them, and they contended the investigation was politically motivated and orchestrated by defense lawyers and corporate interests opposed to their judicial activism.

The committee eventually concluded its investigation without recommending any action against the justices. But in June 1987, the State Commission on Judicial Conduct issued public sanctions against both. Ray was reprimanded for seven violations of the Code of Judicial Conduct, including the acceptance of free airplane rides from attorneys practicing before the court and improper communication with lawyers about pending cases. Kilgarlin received a milder admonishment because two of his law clerks had accepted a weekend trip to Las Vegas from a law firm with cases pending before the court. Both justices were cited for soliciting funds from attorneys to help pay for litigation the justices had brought against the House Judicial Affairs Committee and a former briefing attorney who testified against them.

Later in 1987, the Texas judiciary, particularly the Texas Supreme Court, received negative publicity on a national scale when the high court upheld a record $11 billion judgment awarded Pennzoil Company in a dispute with Texaco Inc. Several members of the Texas Supreme Court were even featured on a network television program that questioned whether justice was "for sale" in Texas.

The record judgment was awarded to Pennzoil after a state district court jury in Houston had determined that Texaco had wrongfully interfered in Pennzoil's attempt to acquire Getty Oil Company in 1984. Texaco, which sought protection under federal bankruptcy laws, later reached a settlement with Pennzoil, but it also waged a massive public relations campaign against the Texas judiciary.

In a segment on CBS-TV's program, *60 Minutes*, correspondent Mike Wallace pointed out that plaintiff's attorney Joe Jamail of Houston, who represented Pennzoil, had contributed $10,000 to the original trial judge in the case and thousands of dollars more to Texas Supreme Court justices. The program also generally criticized the elective system that allowed Texas judges to legally accept large campaign contributions from lawyers who practiced before them. The program presented what already had been reported in the Texas media, but after the national exposure, Governor Bill Clements and other Republicans renewed attacks on the activist, Democratic justices. And some Texas newspapers published editorials calling for changes in the judicial selection process.

Campaign Contributions and Republican Gains

Supreme Court Chief Justice John L. Hill, a former attorney general who had narrowly lost a gubernatorial race to Clements in 1978, had been a strong supporter of electing state judges and had spent more than $1 million winning the chief justice's seat in 1984. As did his colleagues on the court, he accepted many campaign contributions from lawyers. But in 1986, Hill announced that the "recent trend toward excessive political contributions in judicial races" had prompted him to change his mind.[19] He now advocated a so-called **merit selection** plan of gubernatorial appointments and periodic retention elections. But the other eight Supreme Court justices—like Hill, all Democrats—still favored the elective system, and the legislature ignored pleas for change.

Hill resigned from the court on January 1, 1988, to return to private law practice and lobby as a private citizen for changing the judicial selection method. His resignation and the midterm resignations of two other Democratic justices before the 1988 elections gave Republicans a golden opportunity to make historic inroads on the high court. And they helped the business community regain control of the court from plaintiffs' attorneys.

Party realignment and midterm judicial appointments by Clements had already increased the number of Republican judges across the state, particularly on district court benches in urban areas. But only one Republican had ever served on the Texas Supreme Court in modern times. Will Garwood was appointed by Clements in 1979 to fill a vacancy on the court but was defeated by Democrat C. L. Ray in the 1980 election.

GOP leaders had already been planning to recruit a Republican slate of candidates for the three Supreme Court seats that normally would have been on the ballot in 1988. Now, six seats were contested, including those held by three new Republican justices appointed by Clements to fill the unexpected vacancies. Even though a full Supreme Court term is six years, the governor's judicial appointees have to run in the next election to keep their seats. Clements appointed Thomas R. Phillips, a state district judge from Houston, to succeed Hill and become the first Republican chief justice since Reconstruction.

The competing legal and financial interests in Texas understood that the six Texas Supreme Court races on the 1988 ballot would help set the philosophy of the court for years to come. Consequently, these were the most expensive court races in Texas history, with the twelve Republican and Democratic nominees raising $10 million in direct campaign contributions. Much of the money was spent on television advertising.

Contributions to the winners averaged $836,347. Phillips, one of three Republican winners, spent $2 million, the most by a winning candidate. The smallest amount spent by a winner was $449,290. Some individual donations to candidates were as large as $65,000.[20] Reformers argued that such large contributions created an appearance of impropriety and eroded public confidence in the judiciary's independence.

But the successes of Republicans and conservative Democrats in the 1988 races probably hindered, more than helped, the cause of reforming the judicial selection process. The business and medical communities, which had considerable success fighting the plaintiffs' lawyers under the existing rules with large campaign contributions of their own, were pleased with the election results. "I'm a happy camper today," said Kim Ross, lobbyist for the Texas Medical Association, whose political action committee had supported two conservative Democratic winners and the three Republican victors.[21] In several key liability cases over the next few years, the Supreme Court began to demonstrate a rediscovered philosophy favoring business defendants over plaintiffs.[22]

Republicans won a fourth seat on the Texas Supreme Court in 1990 and a fifth in 1994, to give the GOP a majority for the first time since Reconstruction. Republican challengers in 1994 also unseated nineteen incumbent Democratic district judges in Harris County in strong straight-party voting. Republicans completed their sweep of the high court in 1998. Justice Rose Spector, one of two remaining Democratic justices, was unseated by Republican Harriet O'Neill, and Democrat Raul A. Gonzalez retired in midterm and was replaced by Alberto R. Gonzales, an appointee of Governor George W. Bush who later would follow Bush to the White House.

Phillips, the chief justice since 1988, resigned in midterm in 2004 to accept a temporary appointment as a visiting professor at the South Texas College of Law in Houston (see "How I See It: Arguments for Retention Elections in Texas"). He later reentered private law practice. Phillips believed the court's reputation had been enhanced during his tenure; but, as his predecessor had done on stepping down sixteen years earlier, he criticized the money-driven, partisan election system for judges. He said it "creates great instability in the judiciary and erodes public confidence in the fairness of our decisions."[23]

Wallace B. Jefferson, who succeeded Phillips as chief justice, also has called for replacing partisan judicial elections with appointments and retention elections.[24]

How I See It | Arguments for Retention Elections in Texas

Thomas R. Phillips was chief justice of the Texas Supreme Court from 1988–2004. He now practices law in Austin. The following comments are excerpts from Phillips' State of the Judiciary speech delivered to the Texas legislature in March 2003.

Our partisan, high-dollar judicial selection system has diminished public confidence in our courts, damaged our reputation throughout the country and around the world, and discouraged able lawyers from pursuing a judicial career. I urge you to submit a constitutional amendment at the earliest possible date to allow the people to decide whether they would prefer another election method.

Today, long ballots, partisan sweeps, and big money campaigns have completely negated the original intent of judicial elections. Most other states have concluded that the goals of an independent, qualified and accountable judiciary can better be achieved by treating judicial races differently. Many states have chosen retention elections, which require every judge to run on a nonpartisan—yes or no—ballot at the end of each term.

All current Supreme Court, Court of Criminal Appeals, Courts of Appeals and district court justices and judges would stand for retention elections at the end of their terms. When a vacancy occurs, whether by death, resignation, removal, defeat, or new court creation, the governor would appoint a successor. Although the new judge would take office immediately, his or her appointment would be subject to Senate confirmation before the first retention election.

Retention elections would preserve most of the good of electing judges while alleviating most of the bad. Far from diluting the democratic process, retention elections would actually give most voters more control over their judges than they now enjoy. Today, most Texas judicial races are unopposed. With retention elections, every judge would face his or her employers, the people, at regular intervals.

Because retention elections are nonpartisan, they will encourage a more deliberate vote. Since 1980, nearly one-third of all state judges who were opposed in a general election were defeated. Most of these defeats, I submit, were more about party label than competence or qualifications. Retention elections will also minimize the need for most judges to amass million-dollar war chests and hire image consultants. Millions of people worldwide now believe that politics has compromised the rule of law in Texas courts.

Advocate of retention elections. Texas Supreme Court Chief Justice Thomas R. Phillips, the first Republican to serve as chief justice since Reconstruction, resigned in 2004. Like his predecessor, he was critical of the impact of campaign contributions on the state's partisan election system.

Legislative Reaction to Judicial Activism

The business community had also moved its war against the trial lawyers to the legislature, which in 1987 enacted a so-called "**tort reform**" package that attempted to put some limits on personal injury lawsuits and damage judgments entered by the courts. (A *tort* is a wrongful act over which a lawsuit can be brought.) Insurance companies, which had been lobbying nationwide for states to set limits on jury awards in personal injury cases, were major proponents of the legislation. They were joined by the Texas Civil Justice League, an organization of trade and professional associations, cities, and businesses formed in 1986 to seek similar changes in Texas tort law. The high-stakes campaign for change was enthusiastically supported by Governor Bill Clements but was opposed by consumer groups and plaintiffs' lawyers, who had been making millions of dollars from the judiciary's new liberalism.

Cities, businesses, doctors, and even charitable organizations had been hit with tremendous increases in insurance premiums, which they blamed on greedy trial lawyers and large court awards in malpractice and personal injury lawsuits. Trial lawyers blamed the insurance industry, which, they said, had started raising premiums to recoup losses the companies had suffered in investment income after interest rates had fallen.

Among other things, the 1987 tort reform laws limited governmental liability, attempted to discourage frivolous lawsuits, and limited the ability of claimants to collect damages for injuries that were largely their own fault. They also set limits on punitive damages, which are designed to punish whoever caused an accident or an injury and are often awarded in addition to an injured party's compensation for actual losses.

Other limits on lawsuits were enacted in later legislative sessions, including 1995 and 2003. The 1995 changes, major priorities of then-Governor George W. Bush, imposed even stricter limits on punitive damages and limited the liability of a party who is only partially responsible for an injury. The 2003 legislation, actively sought by Governor Rick Perry and a new Republican majority in the Texas House, set new restrictions on class action lawsuits—which are brought on behalf of large groups of people—and imposed new limits on money that could be awarded for noneconomic damages—such as pain, suffering or disfigurement—in medical malpractice cases. Lawsuits—or the threat of lawsuits—had been blamed for rising premiums for medical malpractice insurance, which some doctors and other advocates of civil justice changes had characterized as a "crisis" in health care in Texas.

A leading proponent for the civil justice restrictions in 2003 was Texans for Lawsuit Reform (TLR), a Houston-based business group whose political action committee gave more than $1 million to successful legislative candidates during the 2002 campaigns.[25] The group, which has given the lion's share of its contributions to Republicans, experienced some noteworthy reversals in the 2006 elections. TLR contributed $3.8 million, primarily in highly contested legislative races, including $2.7 million to candidates who lost.[26]

Winners and Losers

In a study released in 1999, Texas Watch, a consumer advocacy group, said that doctors, hospitals, and other business-related litigants had been big winners before the Texas Supreme Court during the previous four years and that consumers had fared poorly. The group studied more than 625 cases in which the court had written opinions between January 1, 1995, and April 14, 1999. That was a period during which most court members had received substantial campaign funding from doctors, insurers, and other business interests. And most of the opinions were issued after the Texas legislature had enacted tort reform laws setting limits on civil lawsuits. The study determined that physicians and hospitals had won 86 percent of their appeals, most of which involved medical malpractice claims brought by injured patients or their families. Other consistent winners were insurance companies (73 percent), manufacturers (72 percent), banks (67 percent), utilities (65 percent), and other businesses (68 percent). Insurance policyholders, injured workers, injured patients, and other individual litigants won only 36 percent of the time.[27] The report covered only cases in which the Supreme Court had written opinions.

Hundreds of other cases in which the high court upheld lower courts without issuing its own opinions weren't studied. "Individuals are the lowest link in the legal food chain that ends in the Texas Supreme Court," said Walt Borges, who directed the study. "The study raises a question about the fairness of the Texas Supreme Court and state law," he added.[28]

CBS-TV's *60 Minutes,* which had turned the national spotlight on plaintiffs' lawyers and their political contributions to Texas judges in 1987, revisited the Texas judiciary in a follow-up program in 1998. Noting that the partisan system of electing judges had remained unchanged, the new *60 Minutes* segment suggested that justice may still be for sale in Texas, but with different people—the business community—now wielding the influence. The Texas legislature in 1995 had imposed modest limits on campaign contributions to judges and judicial candidates and restricted the periods during which judges and their challengers could raise funds. A judge, however, could still receive as much as $30,000 from members of the same law firm and as much as $300,000 in total contributions from special interests through political action committees. The 1996 races for the Texas Supreme Court—the first conducted under the new law—demonstrated how weak the new reforms were. Four Republican incumbents still raised a combined $4 million, easily swamping fundraising efforts by their unsuccessful challengers.

Texas Watch, the consumer advocacy group, issued a follow-up report on the Supreme Court's 2000–2001 term, which found that consumers were beginning to fare better in some court decisions. But the group determined that businesses, insurance companies and other defendants still won 52 percent of cases pitting consumers against businesses. Consumers won 41 percent of the cases, and the remaining decisions were split, according to the new study.[29] Some observers attributed the moderating influence to appointments Governor George W. Bush had made to midterm vacancies on the court in the late 1990s. As some of those justices began to leave the court, however, consumer advocates complained of another philosophical shift against plaintiffs. Texas Watch issued still another report in October 2006, noting that the Supreme Court had ruled for business defendants and against workers and other consumers in about 80 percent of the cases it had decided during the previous twelve months.[30]

Minorities Fight for Representation

As the high-stakes battles were being waged over the Texas Supreme Court's philosophical and political makeup, minorities were actively seeking more representation in the Texas judiciary. But instead of pouring millions of dollars into judicial races, Hispanics and African Americans filed lawsuits to try to force change through the federal courts.

Throughout Texas history, Hispanics and African Americans have had difficulty winning election to state courts. The high cost of judicial campaigns, polarized voting along ethnic lines in the statewide or countywide races that are required of most judges, and low rates of minority participation in elections have minimized their electoral successes. The first Hispanic was seated on the Texas Supreme Court in 1984 and on the Court of Criminal Appeals in 1991. The first African American was seated on the Texas Court of Criminal Appeals in 1990 and on the Texas Supreme Court in 2001.

Another factor limiting minority participation is a proportional shortage of minority attorneys, from whose ranks judges are drawn. State leaders' efforts to increase the number of minority lawyers were thwarted for several years by an antiaffirmative action federal court ruling in 1996 and a related state attorney general's opinion, which prohibited Texas law schools and universities from giving preferential treatment to minorities in admissions, student aid, and other programs. Those restrictions were eased in 2003, when the U.S. Supreme Court ruled that college admissions policies could include race as a factor, provided racial quotas weren't established.

As of February 1989, a few months before a major lawsuit went to trial over the issue, only 35 of 375 state district judges were Hispanic, and only seven were African American. There were only three Hispanics and no African Americans among the eighty judges on the fourteen intermediate Courts of Appeals. Although they constituted at least one-third of the Texas population, African Americans and Hispanics held only 11.2 percent of the district judgeships and less than 4 percent of the intermediate appellate seats.[31]

Three African American judges in Dallas, who had been appointed by Governor Mark White to fill judicial vacancies, had been unseated in countywide elections. One was Jesse Oliver, a former legislator who had won election to the Texas House from a district within Dallas County but couldn't win a 1988 judicial race countywide. Oliver, a Democrat, had overwhelming African-American support but lost about 90 percent of Dallas's white precincts.[32]

In a lawsuit tried in September 1989 in federal district court in Midland, attorneys for the League of United Latin American Citizens (LULAC) and other minority plaintiffs argued that the countywide system of electing state district judges violated the federal Voting Rights Act by diluting the voting strength of minorities. This case, *League of United Latin American Citizens et al. v. Mattox et al.,* took almost five years and two appeals to the United States Supreme Court to resolve. It didn't change Texas's judicial selection system, but a summary of the case and its bumpy journey through the judicial process highlights the political stakes involved in the issue.

In November 1989, U.S. District Judge Lucius Bunton ruled that the countywide system was illegal in nine of the state's largest counties—Harris, Dallas, Tarrant, Bexar, Travis, Jefferson, Lubbock, Ector, and Midland. Those counties elected 172 district judges, almost half of the state's total, but had only a handful of minorities serving on the district courts. Bunton did not order an immediate remedy but strongly urged the legislature to address the issue in a special session. After the legislature failed to act, Bunton the next year ordered judges in the nine counties to run for election from districts in nonpartisan elections. But the state won a stay of Bunton's order from the Fifth U.S. Circuit Court of Appeals, and partisan, countywide judicial elections were held as scheduled in 1990.

Ironically, one minority judge was outspoken in his opposition to district elections. State District Judge Felix Salazar of Houston didn't seek reelection in 1990, at least in part because he disliked the prospect of having to run from a district rather than countywide. A Democrat, Salazar lived in a predominantly non-Hispanic, white Houston neighborhood and in previous elections had been endorsed by a diversity of groups. He claimed that small districts could work against the interests of minorities because a judge from a conservative Anglo district could feel political pressure to sentence minority criminal defendants more harshly than whites. "The judge will have to espouse the feeling of the community. His district may think that's all right, and it will be hell unseating him," he told the *Houston Chronicle.*[33]

Other opponents of district elections argued that districts could also put undue pressure from minority communities on judges. But Jesse Oliver, the former African-American legislator and judge who had been unseated in a countywide race in Dallas, didn't agree that judicial districts would distort the administration of justice any more than countywide elections. "For one thing, if the community does exert pressure, then the white community is exerting all the pressure now because they are electing the judges in Dallas County," he said.[34]

Ruling on the Texas case and on one from Louisiana in June 1991, the U.S. Supreme Court held that the Voting Rights Act applied to elections for the judiciary. But the high court didn't strike down the at-large election system. "We believe that the state's interest in maintaining an electoral system—in this case, Texas's interest in maintaining the link between a district judge's (countywide) jurisdiction and the area of residency of his or her voters—is a legitimate factor to be considered" in determining whether the Voting Rights Act has been violated, the court wrote. The court also emphasized that the state's interest was only one factor to be considered and didn't automatically outweigh proof of diluting minority votes.[35]

The U.S. Supreme Court returned the Texas lawsuit to the Fifth U.S. Circuit Court of Appeals for more deliberations, and in January 1993, a three-judge panel of the Fifth Circuit ruled 2–1 that countywide elections illegally diluted the voting strength of minorities in eight counties—Harris, Dallas, Bexar, Tarrant, Jefferson, Lubbock, Ector, and Midland.

Under pressure from minority legislators, Attorney General Dan Morales agreed to a settlement with the plaintiffs that would have required district elections for most of the judges in those counties and a ninth, Travis County. The settlement was endorsed by Governor Ann Richards, Democratic legislative leaders, and Democratic majorities in the Texas House and Senate. But it was opposed by Texas Supreme Court Chief Justice Thomas R. Phillips and state District Judges Sharolyn Wood of Houston and Harold Entz of Dallas, Republican defendants in the lawsuit.

The full Fifth Circuit rejected the settlement in a 9–4 vote in August 1993, holding that the "evidence of any dilution of minority voting power (in countywide judicial elections) is marginal at best."[36] The Fifth Circuit said partisan affiliation was a more significant factor than ethnicity in judicial elections. Then in January 1994, the U.S. Supreme Court brought the lawsuit to an end by upholding the Fifth Circuit's opinion.

That left the issue of judicial selection in the hands of the Texas legislature, which for years had refused to change the elective system. State Senator Rodney Ellis, a Houston Democrat and a leading proponent of district elections, called the decision "devastating" and said it amounted to a "wholesale assault on civil rights." State District Judge Sharolyn Wood, a Houston Republican who had fought district elections, had a different reaction. "Hooray for Texas!" she said.[37]

By 2008, according to the most complete data available, about 13 percent of the state judges at the county court level and higher were Hispanic and about 3 percent were African American.[38]

MINORITY JUDICIAL APPOINTMENTS

Democratic Governor Mark White appointed the first Hispanic, Raul A. Gonzalez, the son of migrant workers, to the Texas Supreme Court in 1984 to fill a vacancy created by a resignation. Gonzalez made history a second time in 1986 by winning election to the seat and becoming the first Hispanic to win a statewide election in Texas. A native of Weslaco in the Rio Grande Valley, Gonzalez had been a state district judge in Brownsville and had been appointed to the Thirteenth Court of Appeals in Corpus Christi by Republican Governor Bill Clements in 1981.

Despite his background, Gonzalez, a Democrat, was one of the most conservative members of the Supreme Court during his tenure. Consequently, he came under frequent attack from trial lawyers and, ironically, from many of the constituent groups within his own party who advocated increasing the number of minority judges. Gonzalez's reelection race in 1994, one of the most bitterly contested Supreme Court races in recent memory, proved that ethnicity can quickly take a back seat to judicial philosophy and partisanship.

Gonzalez defeated a strong challenge in the Democratic primary from Corpus Christi attorney Rene Haas, who was supported by trial lawyers, women's groups, consumer advocates, several key Democratic legislators, and a number of African-American and Hispanic leaders in the Democratic Party. Gonzalez drew heavy financial support from business interests, insurance companies, and defense attorneys. He had angered many Democrats by siding with the Republican justices in a 5–4 decision upholding a Senate redistricting plan that favored Republicans in the 1992 elections. And he angered many women and trial lawyers by voting with the court majority in two cases overturning damages awarded women who had complained of being emotionally and physically abused by men.

Raul Gonzalez resigned from the Supreme Court in midterm in late 1998 and was replaced by Alberto R. Gonzales, a Republican appointee of Governor George W. Bush and only the second Hispanic to serve on the high court. As had Raul Gonzalez, Alberto Gonzales came from a modest background. His parents were migrant workers when he was born in San Antonio, but they soon moved to Houston, where his father became a construction worker. The young Gonzales, one of eight children, joined the Air Force after graduating from high school and earned degrees from Rice University and Harvard Law School. He had never been a judge before Governor Bush named him to the Supreme Court. But he had been a partner in one of Houston's largest law firms, had been Bush's top staff lawyer, and had served under Bush as Texas secretary of state.

Alberto Gonzales's appointment came at a time when Governor Bush was actively trying to increase the Republican Party's appeal to Hispanics, and Bush acknowledged that it was important to him that Gonzales was Hispanic. "Of course, it mattered what his ethnicity is, but first and foremost what mattered is, I've got great confidence in Al. I know him well. He's a good friend. He'll do a fine job," Bush said.[39] Bush's confidence in Gonzales continued after Bush became president in 2001. He appointed Gonzales White House counsel and later United States attorney general.

On succeeding Bush, Republican Governor Rick Perry named minorities to the first two vacancies he had the opportunity to fill on the Texas Supreme Court in 2001. One was Wallace Jefferson, an appellate lawyer from San Antonio who became the first African American to serve on the high court. Perry named Jefferson to succeed Alberto Gonzales, who had resigned to take the White House job. Jefferson, a Republican, was the great-great-great grandson of a slave. Later the same year, Perry appointed Xavier Rodriguez, a San Antonio labor lawyer, to the Supreme Court to succeed former Justice Greg Abbott, who had resigned to run for Texas attorney general. Rodriguez became the third Hispanic to serve on the court, but he was unseated in the 2002 Republican primary by Austin lawyer Steven Wayne Smith, an Anglo. Jefferson was elected in 2002 to keep his seat on the high court, and a second African American, Republican Dale Wainwright, a state district judge from Houston, was elected to an open Supreme Court seat the same year. Perry appointed another Hispanic, David M. Medina, to the Supreme Court in 2004.

Governor Ann Richards appointed the first Hispanic, Fortunato P. Benavides, to the Texas Court of Criminal Appeals to fill a vacancy in 1991. Benavides had been a justice on the Thirteenth Court of Appeals and a district judge and a county court-at-law judge in Hidalgo County. But Benavides's tenure on the statewide court was short-lived. He was narrowly unseated in 1992 by Republican Lawrence Meyers of Fort Worth, an Anglo, who became the first Republican elected to the criminal court. Benavides later was appointed by President Clinton to the Fifth U.S. Circuit Court of Appeals.

Governor Bill Clements appointed the first African American, Louis Sturns, a Republican state district judge from Fort Worth, to the Texas Court of Criminal Appeals on March 16, 1990. Because the vacancy that Sturns filled had occurred after the filing deadline for the 1990 party primaries, the State Republican Executive Committee put Sturns on the general election ballot as the GOP nominee for the seat. The State Democratic Executive Committee nominated another African American, Morris Overstreet, a county court-at-law judge from Amarillo. Overstreet narrowly defeated Sturns in the November general election to become the first African American elected to a statewide office in Texas. Overstreet served on the court until 1998, when, instead of seeking reelection, he lost a race for the Democratic nomination for Texas attorney general.

WOMEN IN THE JUDICIARY

The first woman to serve as a state district judge in Texas was Sarah T. Hughes of Dallas, who was appointed to the bench in 1935 by Governor James V. Allred and served until 1961, when she resigned to accept an appointment by President John F. Kennedy to the federal district bench. Ironically, Hughes is best known for swearing a grim-faced Lyndon B. Johnson into office aboard Air Force One on November 22, 1963, following Kennedy's assassination in Dallas.

Ruby Sondock of Houston was the first woman to serve on the Texas Supreme Court. She had been a state district judge before Governor Bill Clements named her to the high court on June 25, 1982, to fill a vacancy temporarily. Sondock chose not to seek election to the seat and served only a few months. She later returned to the district bench. Barbara Culver, a state district judge from Midland, became the second female Supreme Court justice when Clements appointed her in February 1988 to fill another vacancy. Culver also served less than a year. She was unseated by Democrat Jack Hightower in the 1988 general election.

Democrat Rose Spector, a state district judge from San Antonio, became the first woman elected to the Texas Supreme Court when she defeated Republican Justice Eugene Cook in 1992. She was unseated in 1998 by Republican Harriet O'Neill.

In 1994, Republican Sharon Keller, a former Dallas County prosecutor, became the first woman elected to the Texas Court of Criminal Appeals, and she became the first female presiding judge of the court in 2001. Four women, including Keller, were serving on the nine-member court in 2009. And more than 260 women were judges at the county court level or higher in Texas.[40]

THE DIFFICULT SEARCH FOR SOLUTIONS

The debates and lawsuits over judicial elections and representation in Texas emphasize the significant role of the courts in policymaking as well as day-to-day litigation. The composition of the courts makes a difference. Although some may argue that the role of a judge is simply to apply the law to the facts and issues of a specific case, judges bring to the courts their own values, philosophical views and life experiences, and these factors serve to filter their interpretations of the law—and determine the shape of justice for millions of people.

An emerging pattern of women jurists. In 2009, four women, including Sharon Keller, the presiding judge, served on the state's highest court for criminal appeals.

There is no one simple solution to all the problems and inequities in the judicial system. Stricter limits on the amount of campaign funds that judges and judicial candidates could raise from lawyers and other special interests, for example, could reduce the appearance of influence-peddling in the judiciary and temper the high-stakes war between the trial lawyers and the business community for philosophical control of the courts. Campaign finance reform also could help build or restore public confidence in the impartiality of the judiciary. Such reform, however, may not improve opportunities for more minorities to win election to the bench. Nor would it shorten the long election ballots that discourage Texans from casting informed votes in judicial races.

The same shortcomings could be anticipated with nonpartisan judicial elections or a merit selection system—two frequently mentioned alternatives to Texas's system of partisan judicial elections. In nonpartisan elections, judges and judicial candidates would not run under Democratic, Republican, or other party labels. This would guard against partisan bickering on the multimember appellate courts and eliminate the possibility that a poorly qualified candidate could be swept into office by one-party, straight-ticket voting.

Under the merit selection plan (sometimes referred to as the "Missouri Plan"), the governor would appoint judges from lists of nominees recommended by nominating committees. The appointed judges would have to run later in **retention elections** to keep their seats, but they wouldn't have opponents on the ballot. Voters would simply decide whether a judge should remain in office or be removed—to be replaced by another gubernatorial appointee.

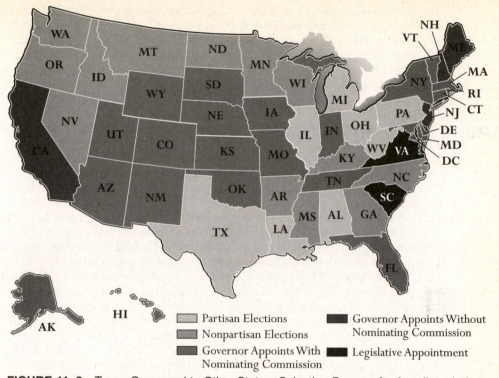

FIGURE 11–2 Texas Compared to Other States: Selection Process for Appellate Judges. There is no uniformity in the manner states select judges. In an effort to reduce the impact of politics and campaign contributions, many states have moved toward nonpartisan elections or gubernatorial appointments with retention elections. With the exception of municipal judges, Texas selects judges by partisan election. This map shows how states select their appellate judges.

Source: American Judicature Society, "Judicial Selection in the States: Appellate and General Jurisdiction Courts."

Texas was one of only eight states in 2009 with a partisan election system for judges (see Figure 11–2). Thirteen states had nonpartisan judicial elections, and half used some form of judicial nominating commission, usually in conjunction with a gubernatorial appointment. Only sixteen states, however, combined the use of nominating commissions with retention elections, as provided in the Missouri Plan. Each alternative has its advantages, but none would necessarily eliminate undue political influences on the judiciary.[41]

Under a merit selection system, interest groups could still apply pressure on the governor and the members of the committees making recommendations for appointments. Although a merit selection plan could be written to require the nominating panels to make ethnically diverse recommendations to the governor, that wouldn't answer the question of how to structure the retention elections. Minority appointees could still be at a disadvantage in retention elections if they had to run countywide, rather than in smaller geographic districts. Despite their popularity among minorities, district elections for judges are still viewed by many decision makers as a form of **ward politics** that may be appropriate or desirable for legislative seats but not for judges. Judges, they argue, don't represent a particular constituency.

Attempts have been made in recent years to overhaul the judicial selection process, but they have failed. In 1995, as discussed earlier in this chapter, lawmakers set modest limits on campaign contributions to judges and judicial candidates and restricted the periods during which judges and judicial candidates can accept political donations.

CRIME AND PUNISHMENT

Under both the United States Constitution and the Texas Constitution, a person charged with a crime is presumed innocent until the state can prove guilt beyond a reasonable doubt to a judge or a jury. The state also has the burden to prosecute fairly and to follow principles of procedural due process outlined in constitutional and statutory law and interpreted by the courts. Even persons charged with the most heinous crimes retain these fundamental rights. Although there is often a public outcry about "coddling" criminals, the process is designed to protect an individual from governmental abuses, to lessen the chance that an innocent person will be wrongly convicted of a crime.

In Texas, as well as in other states, these rights have sometimes been violated. Over the years, however, the federal courts in particular have strengthened their enforcement. Through a case-by-case process, the U.S. Supreme Court has applied the Bill of Rights to the states by way of the "due process of law" and the "equal protection of law" clauses of the Fourteenth Amendment to the U.S. Constitution. The failure of police or prosecutors to comply with specific procedures for handling a person accused of a crime may result in charges against an individual being dropped or a conviction reversed on appeal.

Arrested suspects must be taken before a magistrate—usually a justice of the peace or a municipal court judge—to be formally informed of the offense or offenses with which they are charged and told their legal rights. Depending on the charges, a bond (bail) may be set to allow them to get out of jail and remain free pending their trials. They have the right to remain silent, to consult with an attorney and have an attorney present during questioning by law enforcement officers or prosecutors, and to be warned that any statement they make can be used against them in a trial. Defendants who cannot afford to hire a lawyer must be provided with court-appointed attorneys at taxpayer expense. Many of these protections were extended to the states by the U.S. Supreme Court in the landmark **Miranda ruling** in 1966.

All criminal defendants have the right to a trial by jury but—except in capital murder cases—may waive a jury trial and have their cases decided by a judge. Defendants may plead guilty, not guilty, or *nolo contendere* (no contest). Prosecutors and defense attorneys settle many cases through plea bargaining, a process described earlier in this chapter. The trial judge doesn't have to accept the plea bargain but usually does. When defendants choose to have their guilt or innocence determined by a judge, the judge also determines the punishment if they are convicted. A jury can return a guilty verdict only if all jurors agree that the defendant is guilty beyond a reasonable doubt. If the jury cannot reach a unanimous verdict—even after lengthy negotiations and prodding from the judge—the judge must declare a mistrial. In that case, the prosecution has to seek a new trial with another jury or drop the charges. In a jury trial, a defendant may choose to have the punishment set by the jury. If not, it is determined by the judge.

In 1991, the Texas Court of Criminal Appeals took the major step of ordering, for the first time, an official definition of "reasonable doubt" that was to be submitted to every jury deciding a criminal case. According to the definition, evidence against a criminal defendant must be so convincing that jurors would be willing to rely upon it "without hesitation" in the most important events in their own lives.[42] But, reflecting a change in philosophy, a more conservative Court of Criminal Appeals eliminated that definition in 2000, to the dismay of some criminal defense lawyers. "We find the better practice is to give no definition of reasonable doubt at all to the jury," said the new opinion written by Judge Mike Keasler.[43]

Jury trials are required in **capital murder** cases, which are punishable by death or life in prison without parole. Executions in Texas used to be carried out by electrocution at the state prison unit in downtown Huntsville. Some 361 individuals were executed in Texas from 1924 to 1964, when executions were suspended because of legal challenges. In 1972, the U.S. Supreme Court halted executions in all the states by striking down all the death penalty laws then on the books as unconstitutional. The high court held that capital punishment, as then practiced, violated the constitutional prohibition against cruel and unusual punishment because it could be applied in a discriminatory fashion. Not only could virtually any act of murder be punished by death under the old Texas law, but so could rape and certain other crimes.

In 1973, the Texas legislature rewrote the death penalty statute to try to meet the Supreme Court's standards by defining capital crimes as murder committed under specific circumstances. The list was expanded later and now includes the murder of a law enforcement officer or firefighter who is on duty, murder committed during the course of committing certain other major crimes, murder for hire, murdering more than one

"Old Sparky." Prior to the practice of execution by lethal injection, this now-retired electric chair was used in Huntsville to carry out executions.

person, murder of a prison guard or employee, murder committed while escaping or attempting to escape from a penal institution, or murder of a child younger than six.

A jury that has found a person guilty of capital murder must answer certain questions about the defendant before choosing between death or life imprisonment, the only punishments available. Jurors are required to consider whether a convicted murderer will be a continuing danger to society as well as mitigating circumstances, including evidence of mental retardation, before deciding punishment.[44]

The first execution under the 1973 Texas law was carried out in 1982. By then the legislature, acting in 1977, had changed the method of execution from the electric chair to the intravenous injection of a lethal substance. By 2009, more than 300 men and two women had been executed in Texas by lethal injection. Karla Faye Tucker, the first woman executed in Texas since the Civil War, was put to death in 1998 for killing two people with a pickax almost fifteen years earlier. The second woman was executed in early 2000 for the murder of her husband.

After considerable controversy in Texas and other states, the U.S. Supreme Court in June 2002 banned the execution of mentally retarded convicts. Death penalty opponents had argued that before the high court ruling Texas had executed at least six inmates who were demonstrably retarded. The Texas legislature, in its first session after the Supreme Court ban, failed to revise its death penalty statute to comply with the court's order, requiring defense attorneys to continue the battle, case by case. Some feared that, without new

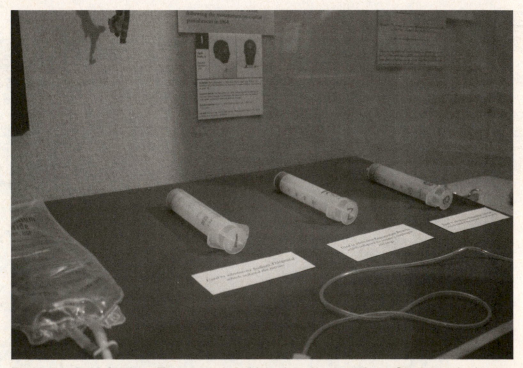

Tools of lethal injection. Texas uses lethal injections for executions. Condemned prisoners are strapped to a gurney, two needles are inserted, and the inmate is injected with three solutions which produce an anesthetic overdose and respiratory and cardiac arrest.

state guidelines for evaluating and trying convicts, additional mentally retarded people would be executed in Texas, despite the Supreme Court's ban.[45]

In 2008, the nation's high court, deciding two appeals from Kentucky, ruled that the chemicals used in lethal injections did not amount to cruel and unusual punishment and did not violate the U.S. Constitution. Death penalty opponents had argued that the chemicals may cause the condemned to feel intense pain. Texas uses the same chemicals as Kentucky (see "Shutting the Court Door on a Condemned Inmate's Last-Gasp Appeal").

Shutting the Court Door on a Condemned Inmate's Last-Gasp Appeal

Despite the controversy it provokes, the death penalty still has strong political support in Texas, which has executed more than 300 convicts by lethal injection—more than all other states combined—since 1982. And few, if any, public officials in Texas are stronger supporters of the death penalty than is Sharon Keller, presiding judge of the Texas Court of Criminal Appeals, which upholds the vast majority of the death sentences it reviews. However, in the view of many lawyers and other Texans as well, Keller went too far when she cut off a condemned inmate's attempt to file a last-gasp appeal only a few hours before he was executed.

Lawyers for Michael Richard, a convicted murderer and rapist, attempted to halt his execution by lethal injection on September 25, 2007, following the United States Supreme Court's decision earlier that day to accept two Kentucky cases challenging the constitutionality of chemicals used for lethal injection. Death penalty opponents had argued that the execution method may amount to cruel and unusual punishment, prohibited by the U.S. Constitution, because the condemned may feel intense pain as the mixture of drugs is administered. Texas uses the same chemicals as Kentucky.

Richard's attorneys tried to get a stay of execution for their client until the nation's high court decided the Kentucky cases, but computer problems at one lawyer's office slowed the preparation of their appeal. When they asked the Court of Criminal Appeals for more time, Keller ordered the court clerk's office to close at the normal time,

5 P.M. Richard's lawyers didn't have time to file his appeal, and he was executed later that evening.

After the controversy over Keller's decision erupted during subsequent days, three other judges on the nine-member court said they had been available for work on the evening of Richard's execution and could have handled his appeal had they known about it. Twenty lawyers from across Texas, including many prominent names, later filed a formal complaint against Keller with the State Commission on Judicial Conduct. The complaint accused the judge of violating the constitutional due process of a condemned man, stating that "Judge Keller's actions denied Michael Richard two constitutional rights, access to the courts and due process, which led to his execution."

Keller blamed Richard's lawyers. "I think the question ought to be why didn't they file something on time. They had all day," she said.[46]

A few weeks later, the Court of Criminal Appeals announced it would accept emergency e-mail filings of appeals in death penalty cases in an effort to avoid something like the Richard's case from occurring again.

In 2008, the State Commission on Judicial Conduct filed misconduct charges against Keller over her handling of the Richard's case. The charges, if upheld, could have led to Keller's removal from the bench, but the case hadn't been resolved by mid-2009. A resolution in the Texas House calling for her impeachment fell short.

After capital murder, the most serious criminal offense is a first degree **felony** (e.g., aggravated sexual assault or noncapital murder), punishable by a prison sentence of five to ninety-nine years or life. Second-degree felonies, such as burglary of someone's home and bribery, are punishable by two to twenty years in prison. Third-degree felonies, including intentional bodily injury to a child and theft of trade secrets, are punishable by two to ten years in prison. State jail felonies, which include many property crimes such as burglary of an office building and drug offenses, are punishable by up to two years in a state-run jail or time in a community corrections program, each of which is supposed to emphasize rehabilitation as well as punishment.

The most minor crimes are classified as Class A, B, or C **misdemeanors**. Crimes such as public lewdness and harboring a runaway child are examples of Class A misdemeanors and are punishable by a maximum $4,000 fine and one year in a county jail. The unauthorized use of television cable decoding equipment and falsely claiming to be a police officer are examples of Class B misdemeanors and carry a maximum sentence of 180 days in a county jail and a $2,000 fine. Class C misdemeanors include illegal gambling and the issuing of bad checks. They are punishable by a maximum $500 fine.

People convicted of crimes can be sentenced to **probation** (also called community supervision). That means they are not sent to prison but must meet certain conditions, such as restrictions on where they travel and with whom they associate. Except for those

Opposition to executions. Death penalty opponents outside the state Capitol protesting a 2008 U.S. Supreme Court ruling that death by lethal injection does not violate the federal Constitution's prohibition against cruel and unusual punishment.

under the death penalty and some capital murderers serving life sentences, convicted felons sentenced to prison can become eligible for **parole**—early release under supervisory restrictions—after serving a portion of their sentences. Capital murderers sentenced to life in prison before a significant change in state law in 2005 can be considered for parole after serving 40 years. Those sentenced after the 2005 law, which imposed life without parole for capital murderers who aren't sentenced to death, cannot be paroled. Parole decisions are made by the Board of Pardons and Paroles, which is appointed by the governor.

A landmark federal court order in 1980 forced the state to spend billions of dollars expanding and improving its prison system and forced the legislature to reevaluate the punishment of some criminals (see Chapter 13).

THE POLITICS OF CRIMINAL JUSTICE

The Texas Court of Criminal Appeals must try to balance the constitutional rights of convicts against the public welfare—a role that puts the court at the center of major philosophical and political battles.

The combatants on one side of the debate are the prosecutors—the elected district and county attorneys—who don't like to see the convictions they have won reversed, partly because too many reversals could cost them reelection. Judges of the trial courts, who also must periodically face the voters, are also sensitive to reversals. So are the police and sheriff's departments that arrest the defendants and provide the evidence on which criminal convictions are based (see "A Crime Lab Scandal").

On the other side of the debate are defense attorneys, who have an obligation to protect the rights and interests of their clients and who in their appeals often attack procedures used by police, prosecutors, and trial judges. Also on this side are civil libertarians, who insist that a criminal defendant's every right—even the most technical—be protected,

A Crime Lab Scandal

Recent scientific advances can improve the administration of justice, as demonstrated by a growing number of criminal cases in which DNA samples have been used to help convict or clear suspects. Texas Governor Rick Perry has issued pardons for several men after DNA evidence proved they had been wrongfully convicted of crimes. One man was pardoned after serving 18 years in prison after being wrongfully convicted of aggravated sexual assault.

Convictions in a number of other cases were thrown into question with the exposure of errors in the work of some crime labs, particularly the crime lab operated by the Houston Police Department. The Houston lab's DNA division was shut down in 2002 because of serious problems, which were reported in numerous articles by the *Houston Chronicle*.[47] Independent investigators later discovered errors in the handling of DNA, body fluids, controlled substances, and other evidence in hundreds of cases. Poor training and inadequate standards contributed to the problems. By 2006, two men had been released from prison, with one receiving a pardon from the governor, after it was determined the lab had mishandled evidence in their cases, and the investigation continued.

The controversy also prompted the legislature to create the Texas Forensic Science Commission to oversee crime labs. The new commission had the power to investigate allegations of misconduct or negligence.

and minority groups, which have challenged the conduct of trials in which minorities have been excluded from juries weighing the fate of minority defendants.

Throughout much of its early history, the Texas Court of Criminal Appeals was accused of excessive concern with legal technicalities that benefited convicted criminals.[48] The court reversed 42 percent of the cases appealed to it during the first quarter of the twentieth century, when Texas and many other states had a harsh system of criminal justice that often reflected class and racial bias. By 1966, the reversal rate had dropped to 3 percent. But changes in the court's makeup and changes in political attitudes produced fluctuations in that record in subsequent years.

The court signaled a shift toward a conservative philosophy after the 1994 elections of Judges Sharon Keller and Steve Mansfield had increased the number of Republicans on the court to three. During the first thirteen months the new judges were in office, for example, the court ordered the reinstatement of two death sentences it had reversed before Keller's and Mansfield's arrival.

The court's conservatism was solidified with a Republican sweep of all three court seats on the 1996 ballot. A 6–3 Democratic majority had become a 6–3 Republican majority, the first GOP majority on the court since Reconstruction. Republicans increased their majority to 7–2 in 1997, when long-time Presiding Judge Mike McCormick, one of the court's most conservative members, switched from the Democratic to the Republican Party. The Republican takeover of the court was completed in 1998, when Democrats lost their last two seats on the panel. McCormick did not seek reelection in 2000 and was replaced as presiding judge by Sharon Keller, a former prosecutor.

After the GOP takeover, the Court of Criminal Appeals quickly began compiling a strong, pro-prosecutorial record, particularly in death penalty cases. The court upheld a number of death sentences that later were overturned by federal courts. In one case, later reversed by a federal court, it affirmed a capital conviction even though the defendant's attorney had slept through part of his trial. In another case, it upheld a death sentence despite the fact that a prosecution witness had argued improperly that the defendant was a future danger to society partly because he was Hispanic. That ruling prompted then–Texas Attorney General John Cornyn, a Republican and strong law-and-order advocate, to admit to the United States Supreme Court that the prosecution had committed reversible error in the case. Such rulings prompted defense lawyers and civil libertarians to heap much criticism upon the court. "They're so far gone they're barely even a court anymore," lawyer Jeff Blackburn of Amarillo said in an interview with the *Houston Chronicle*.[49]

INCREASED POLICY ROLE OF THE STATE COURTS

The federal judiciary has traditionally had more influence than the state courts in molding public policy. Over the years, it has been at the center of political debate over the proper role of the judiciary in the policymaking process. This debate, often framed in terms of judicial activism versus judicial restraint, attempts to address the question of where judicial interpretation of the law and the Constitution ends and legislating from the bench begins. It's a question often answered only in terms of subjective, political philosophy. Much of the Texas Supreme Court's time is spent refereeing disputes between trial lawyers and insurance companies. But in recent years, this court has increasingly played an active role in shaping broader public policies and addressing significant constitutional issues.

The Courts and Education

In one of its most significant and best-known rulings, the Texas Supreme Court, in the Edgewood school finance case in 1989, unanimously ordered major, basic changes in the financing of public education to provide more equity between rich and poor school districts (see Chapter 13). The lawsuit was brought against the state by poor districts after years of legislative inaction against a property tax–based finance system that had produced huge disparities in local resources and the quality of local schools.

The unanimity of the opinion, written by then-Justice Oscar Mauzy, a Democrat, surprised many legislators and school officials because two of the three Republican justices on the court at that time had been appointed by Governor Bill Clements, who had insisted that the courts had no business trying to tell the legislature what to do about school finance. The decision, which held that the school finance law violated a constitutional requirement for an efficient education system, obviously was the product of considerable compromise among the nine justices.

Compliance with the school finance order did not come easily, however. A 1990 school finance law failed to meet the court's standards. So the court issued another order in 1991 and a third order in 1992, after the legislature had again come up short. The court lost its unanimity on the third order, which struck down a 1991 law that had established special county education districts with a minimum property tax. In a challenge brought this time by wealthy school districts, a 7–2 court majority ruled that the tax was a statewide property tax prohibited by the Texas Constitution. Mauzy and fellow Democratic Justice Lloyd Doggett sharply dissented.

The legislature responded with still another school finance law in 1993. This law gave the wealthiest school districts several options for sharing revenue with poor districts, and it was challenged by both rich and poor districts. The rich districts objected to sharing their property wealth, while the poor districts argued that the new law was inadequately funded and did not sufficiently reduce the funding gap between rich and poor districts. The Texas Supreme Court upheld the law in a 5–4 decision in January 1995. By that time a majority of the court's members were Republicans. In the majority opinion, Justice John Cornyn, a Republican, wrote:

> Children who live in property-poor districts and children who live in property-rich districts now have substantially equal access to the funds necessary for a general diffusion of knowledge. . . . It is apparent from the court's [previous] opinions that we have recognized that an efficient system does not require equality of access to revenue at all levels.[50]

But Republican Justice Craig Enoch, who dissented, wrote that the state had failed to adequately provide for the public schools. He said the new law contributed to further "constitutional tensions" by promoting continued use of local property taxes.

By 2003, the school finance law was under attack again, this time from school districts contending that the share-the-wealth requirement and inadequate state aid were forcing many districts to raise local school maintenance tax rates to the maximum $1.50 per $100 valuation. They argued that amounted to an unconstitutional statewide property tax. In the fall of 2005, the Texas Supreme Court, in a subsequent decision, agreed. This time, the court gave the state until June 1, 2006, to correct the problem, which the legislature did in a special session that spring. Lawmakers enacted Governor Rick Perry's plan to cut school maintenance tax rates by as much as one-third over the next two years, replacing the lost revenue with money from a budgetary surplus, an expanded business tax, a $1 per pack increase in the cigarette tax and tightened collections of sales taxes on used cars.

In 1992, a state district judge in Brownsville ruled that the state's system of funding higher education was also unconstitutional because it shortchanged Hispanics in South Texas. However, the Texas Supreme Court reversed that decision and upheld the higher education system.[51]

In another education case with major implications, the Texas Supreme Court in 1994 upheld the right of Texas parents to educate their own children. Ending a ten-year legal battle, the court overturned a Texas Education Agency ruling that home schools were illegal. The court held that a home school was legitimate if parents used books, workbooks, or other written materials and met "basic education goals" by teaching basic subjects.[52]

The Courts and Abortion Rights

In 1998, dealing with another controversial issue, the Texas Supreme Court upheld $1.2 million in damages against antiabortion protesters who had staged massive demonstrations at Houston abortion clinics during the 1992 Republican National Convention. Some clinics had been vandalized and patients harassed. The high court also upheld most of the restrictions a lower court had set on demonstrations near the clinics and the homes of several doctors who performed abortions. The court said it was trying to balance free speech rights with the rights of the clinics to conduct business, the rights of women to have access to pregnancy counseling and abortion services, and privacy rights of physicians. The court prohibited demonstrators from blocking access to clinics, intimidating patients, and engaging in other forms of aggressive behavior.[53] In a case from Florida, the U.S. Supreme Court had ruled in 1994 that judges could limit demonstrations near abortion clinics but that restrictions on protestors had to be strictly limited.[54]

The Texas Supreme Court became embroiled in the abortion issue again in 2000 after a state law went into effect requiring parents to be notified by the doctors before their minor daughters could have abortions. The law included a "judicial bypass" provision, giving a young woman who didn't want her parents to be told an opportunity to convince a judge that she was mature and well-informed enough to make an abortion decision by herself or that notifying her parents would be harmful. Acting on several early cases, the Texas Supreme Court set guidelines for district judges to follow in making bypass decisions.

In another abortion case, decided in 2002, the Texas Supreme Court held that the state's refusal to pay for medically necessary abortions for poor women didn't violate the Texas Constitution. The court ruled that the restriction on funding abortions for women on Medicaid didn't discriminate by gender and advanced a legitimate governmental interest of favoring childbirth over abortion.[55]

The Courts and Gay Rights

Deciding still another controversial issue, the Texas Supreme Court in 1996 ruled against the Log Cabin Republicans, a gay GOP group that had been denied a booth at the Republican State Convention in San Antonio. The court said the group had no grounds to sue for deprivation of rights under the Texas Constitution because the Republican Party was not a governmental agency.[56]

SUMMARY AND CONCLUSIONS ⟶ ●

1. Texas has a confusing array of courts, many with overlapping jurisdictions. It is one of only two states with a bifurcated court system at the highest appellate level. The Texas Supreme Court is the court of last resort in civil cases, and the Texas Court of Criminal Appeals in criminal cases.

2. This judicial system is particularly inadequate in urban counties, where thousands of criminal cases each year are disposed of through plea bargains negotiated by prosecutors and defendants, and where it can take years to resolve civil disputes that aren't settled out of court.

3. State judges, except those on municipal court benches, are elected in partisan elections. In practice, however, Texas has a mixed judicial selection system because many judges quit or retire in midterm, allowing the governor or a county commissioners' court to appoint their successors.

4. Grand juries are supposed to ensure that the government has sufficient evidence to proceed with a criminal prosecution against an individual. Petit, or trial, juries hear evidence and render verdicts in both civil and criminal cases. Litigants in civil cases and most criminal defendants can waive a jury trial and have their cases decided by a judge.

5. Cases can be appealed to appellate courts, where there are no juries. Appellate courts review the decisions and procedures of trial courts for conformity to constitutional and statutory requirements.

6. Judges who espouse strict construction believe they are supposed to narrowly interpret and apply the laws enacted by the legislature. Judicial activists take a more expansive view of the law and often offer broad policy interpretations in their decisions.

7. The Texas Supreme Court became a battleground in the 1980s between trial lawyers who represent injured parties—or plaintiffs—in damage lawsuits and the businesses, doctors, and insurance companies they sue. After trial lawyers began contributing millions of dollars to successful Supreme Court candidates, judicial precedents that had favored the corporate establishment began to fall, and it became easier for plaintiffs to win huge damage awards. The business and medical communities retaliated by winning some legislative changes in the procedures under which lawsuits are tried and by increasing their own contributions in judicial races.

8. Party realignment increased the number of Republican judges on trial courts in the 1980s and soon gave Republicans, with support from the business and medical communities, their first majority on the Texas Supreme Court in modern times.

9. Only a handful of women and minorities have ever served on the state's highest courts, and historically they have been underrepresented on the lower court benches as well. In a lawsuit in 1989, the countywide system of electing judges in nine of the state's largest counties was found to violate the Voting Rights Act by diluting the voting strength of minorities. That ruling was reversed by the U.S. Supreme Court in 1994.

10. The philosophical battles, the underrepresentation of minorities, and long ballots that discourage urban voters from learning the qualifications of judges and judicial candidates have increased pressure to reform the judicial selection process. But the legislature has been reluctant to change it. Possible alternatives are nonpartisan elections, elections from geographic districts, or a merit selection plan. Under the latter plan, the governor would appoint judges from lists of nominees recommended by experts. Judges would have to run later in retention elections to keep their seats, but they wouldn't have opponents on the ballot. Although each of these alternatives has supporters, none alone would resolve all the problems and controversies affecting the judiciary.

11. The Texas Court of Criminal Appeals is at the center of philosophical and political disputes as it weighs the constitutional rights of convicted criminals against the public's concern about crime. In recent years, the court has developed a strong record in support of prosecutors, particularly in death penalty cases.

12. The federal judiciary has traditionally had more influence than the state courts in molding public policy. But in recent years the Texas Supreme Court has increasingly played an active role in addressing significant constitutional issues, such as school funding and abortion.

KEY TERMS ─────────────────────────────●

FURTHER READING ─────────────────────●

Articles

Burka, Paul, "Trial by Technicality," *Texas Monthly,* April 1982, pp. 126–31, 210–18, 241.

Champagne, Anthony, "Campaign Contributions in Texas Supreme Court Races," *Crime, Law and Social Change,* 17 (1992), pp. 91–106.

———, "Judicial Selection in Texas: Democracy's Deadlock," in *Texas Politics: A Reader,* edited by Anthony Champagne and Edward J. Harpham (New York: W. W. Norton, 1997).

———, "The Role of Personality in Judicial Reform," *State Constitutional Commentaries and Notes* 2 (Winter 1991), pp. 5–8.

———, "The Selection and Retention of Judges in Texas," *Southwestern Law Journal* 40 (May 1986), 53, pp. 95–99.

Champagne, Anthony, and Greg Thielemann, "Awareness of Trial Court Judges," *Judicature* 74 (February–March 1991), pp. 271–76.

Chapman, Ronald W, "Judicial Roulette: Alternatives to Single-Member Districts as a Legal and Political Solution to Voting-Rights Challenges to At-Large Judicial Elections," *SMU Law Review* 48 (January–February 1995), pp. 457–84.

Cooper, Lance A., "A Historical Overview of Judicial Selection in Texas," *Texas Wesleyan Law Review* 2 (Fall 1995), pp. 317–333.

Hardberger, Phil, "Juries Under Siege," *St. Mary's Law Journal* 30 (1998), pp. 1–142.

Hill, John, "Taking Texas Judges Out of Politics: An Argument for Merit Election," *Baylor Law Review* 40 (1988).

Books

Horton, David M., and Ryan Kellus Turner. *Lone Star Justice: A Comprehensive Overview of the Texas Criminal Justice System.* Austin, TX: Eakin, 1999.

Parrish, James R., *A Two-Headed Monster: Crimes and Texas Prisons.* Austin, TX: Eakin, 1989.

Reamy, Gerald S., *Criminal Offenses and Defenses in Texas.* Suwane, GA: Harrison, 2000.

Reamy, Gerald S., and Walter W. Steele, Jr., *Texas Criminal Procedure.* Dallas, TX: Academia Press, 2004.

Texas Judicial Council, Office of Court Administration, *Texas Judicial System, 77th Annual Report, 2006.* Austin, TX: 2006.

Texas Research League, *Texas Courts: A Proposal for Structural-Functional Reform,* Report 2. Austin, TX: 1991.

———, *The Texas Judiciary: A Structural–Functional Overview,* Report 1. Austin, TX: 1990.

Websites

Texas Courts Online   http://www.courts.state.tx.us/ Site provides access to state court system, judicial administrative agencies, and links to other judicial sites.

Texas Bar Association   http://www.texasbar.com/ This site provides access to a wide range of information relevant to the legal profession.

Texas Department of Criminal Justice   http://www.tdcj. state.tx.us/   This agency is responsible for the administration of the state's prison/jail system. Organizational data can be found at this site, along with statistics and reports on the prison population, prison sites, paroles, and programs designed to prevent recidivism.

Texas Juvenile Probation Commission   http://www.tjpc.state.tx.us/   This agency works with local juvenile probation departments to rehabilitate juvenile offenders. This site provides information about state funding, standards, training, certification, and monitoring of caseworkers, and statistics on juvenile offenders.

Texas Youth Commission   http://www.tyc.state.tx.us/ The Texas Youth Commission is responsible for "secure care, custody and control of juveniles who

are committed to state custody" for criminal behavior. This site includes information on facilities, programs, correctional treatment, and juvenile crime in Texas.

Bureau of Justice Statistics   http://www.ojp.usdoj.gov/bjs/   The Bureau of Justice Statistics is the primary source for criminal justice statistics in the United States.

ENDNOTES

1. Anthony Champagne, "Judicial Selection in Texas: Democracy's Deadlock," in *Texas Politics: A Reader,* edited by Anthony Champagne and Edward J. Harpham (New York: W. W. Norton, 1997), p. 97.
2. Chief Justice Wallace B. Jefferson, "The State of the Judiciary in Texas," presented to the 81st Legislature, February 11, 2009.
3. *Smith v. Allwright,* 321 U.S. 649 (1944).
4. *Miranda v. Arizona,* 384 U.S. 436 (1966).
5. Texas Research League, *The Texas Judiciary: A Structural-Functional Overview,* Report 1 (Austin, TX: 1990).
6. The number of courts will change from year to year as a result of legislative action or actions of local governments.
7. Allen E. Smith, *The Impact of the Texas Constitution on the Judiciary* (Houston: University of Houston, Institute for Urban Studies, 1973), p. 45.
8. Office of Court Administration, *Annual Statistical Report for the Texas Judiciary, Fiscal Year 2008* (December 2008), pp. 39–40.
9. Ibid., pp.33–34.
10. Ibid., pp. 33–34; "District Courts: Case Activity by County," September 1, 2007 to August 31, 2008).
11. Ibid., p. 27.
12. Smith, *The Impact of the Texas Constitution on the Judiciary,* p. 28.
13. Ibid., p. 31.
14. Texas Research League, Texas Courts: A Proposal for Structural-Functional Reform, pp. 1–15.
15. Polly Ross Hughes, "Perry Pardons 35 in Tulia Sting," *Houston Chronicle,* August 23, 2003, p. 1A.
16. Peggy O'Hare, Brian Rogers, Bill Murphy, Terri Langford, Rosanna Ruiz, Todd Ackerman, and Janet Elliott, "Rosenthal Quits, Cites Prescription Drugs," *Houston Chronicle,* February 16, 2008, page 1A.
17. Katie Fairbank, "83 Days–for Missing Jury Duty–Collin Man's Case Fell Through Cracks After He Was Jailed on '03 Warrant," *Dallas Morning News,* May 9, 2009, p. 1A.
18. Clay Robison, "Board Won't Act on Mansfield/Judge's Veracity Questioned," *Houston Chronicle,* June 28, 1995, p. 17.
19. *Houston Post,* May 18, 1986.
20. Anthony Champagne, "Campaign Contributions in Texas Supreme Court Races," *Crime, Law and Social Change* 17 (1992), pp. 91–106.
21. *Houston Post,* November 10, 1988.
22. Bruce Hight, "Texas Supreme Court Sides with Business," *Austin American–Statesman,* December 9, 1993. p. E1.
23. Clay Robison, "Texas' Chief Justice Resigning–Longtime Foe of State's System of Electing Judges to Teach Law," *Houston Chronicle,* April 30, 2004, p. 1A.
24. Jefferson, "The State of the Judiciary in Texas."
25. Clay Robison, "Memo Alleges Rep. Nixon Said Lobby OK'd Him," *Houston Chronicle,* August 21, 2003, p. 24A.
26. Texans for Public Justice, "Voters Rebuked Texas' Biggest PAC," *Lobby Watch,* January 11, 2007.
27. Texas Watch, *The Food Chain: Winners and Losers in the Texas Supreme Court, 1995–1999* (Austin: 1999).
28. Texas Watch press release, May 3, 1999.
29. Texas Watch, *Access Denied: The Texas Supreme Court in 2000–2001* (Austin, TX: 2001).
30. Armando Villafranca, "Report: State High Court Favoring Corporations Voting Alliances Hurt Consumers, Group Says," *Houston Chronicle,* September 18, 2002, p. 25A.
31. Samuel Issacharoff, *The Texas Judiciary and the Voting Rights Act: Background and Options* (Austin, TX: Texas Policy Research Forum), pp. 2, 13.
32. *Texas Lawyer,* September 18, 1989.
33. Jim Simon, "Judicial Election Plan Brings Quick Jockeying," *Houston Chronicle,* December 24, 1989, p. 1B.
34. *Texas Lawyer,* September 18, 1989.
35. *League of United Latin American Citizens, et al. v. Mattox, et al.,* 501 U.S. 419 (1991); *Chisom v. Roemer,* 501 U.S. 380 (1991).
36. *League of United Latin American Citizens v. Clements,* 999 F2d 831 (1993).
37. Clay Robison, "Ruling on Judge Elections Slaps Dems, Minorities," *Houston Chronicle,* January 19, 1994, p.1A.
38. Office of Court Administration, *Annual Statistical Report for the Texas Judiciary, Fiscal Year 2008,* p. 13.
39. Clay Robison, "Bush Names Gonzales for High Court," *Houston Chronicle,* November 13, 1998, p. 1A.
40. Office of Court Administration, *Annual Statistical Report for the Texas Judiciary, Fiscal Year 2008,* p. 13.
41. American Judicature Society, "Judicial Selection Methods in the States," 2008.

42. *Texas Lawyer,* November 11, 1991.

43. *Paulson v. State,* Texas Court of Criminal Appeals, October 4, 2000.

44. *Texas Lawyer,* June 3, 1991.

45. Rachel Graves, "Retarded on Death Row in Legal Limbo," *Houston Chronicle,* May 11, 2003, p. 1A.

46. R. G. Ratcliffe and Polly Ross Hughes, "Questions Raised on Sept. 25 Execution—Lawyers Say Appellate Judge Violated Rights of Condemned Man," *Houston Chronicle,* October 11, 2007, page 1A; and R. G. Ratcliffe, "Court Says It Will Take e-filings in Death Cases," *Houston Chronicle,* November 7, 2007, page 1A.

47. Renee C. Lee, "Mumphrey's Pardon Ends 'Miscarriage of Justice,'" *Houston Chronicle,* March 18, 2006, p.1A; Roma Khanna and Steve McVicker, "Police Lab Tailored Tests to Theories, Report Says," *Houston Chronicle,* May 12, 2006, p. 1A; and Roma Khanna, "Forensic Panel Still 3 People Shy of Completion," *Houston Chronicle,* January 24, 2006, p. 4B.

48. Paul Burka, "Trial by Technicality, *Texas Monthly,* April, 1982, pp. 126–31, 210–18, 241.

49. Rick Casey, "Tulia 35 Escape High Court Horror," *Houston Chronicle,* August 27, 2003, p. 23A.

50. *Edgewood v. Meno,* 893 S.W.2d 450 (1995).

51. *Richards v. LULAC,* 868 S.W.2d 306 (1993); and Wendy Benjaminson, "Home Schools Win Court Fight," *Houston Chronicle,* June 16, 1994, p. 1A.

52. *Texas Education Agency v. Leeper,* 893 S.W.2d 432 (1994).

53. *Operation Rescue—National v. Planned Parenthood of Houston and Southeast Texas, Inc.,* 975 S.W.2d 546 (1998). See also Clay Robison, "Anti-abortion Protesters Lose '92 Case Ruling," *Houston Chronicle,* July 4, 1998, p. 1A.

54. *Madsen v. Women's Health Clinic, Inc.,* 512 U.S. (1994).

55. *Charles E. Bell v. Low Income Women of Texas,* 95 S.W.3d 253 (2002).

56. *Republican Party of Texas v. Dietz,* 924 S.W.2d 932 (1996).

CHAPTER 12

Local Government in Texas
Cities, Towns, Counties, and Special Districts

Questions to Guide Your Reading

1. Should all Texas cities, regardless of size, be given home rule authority to choose whatever form of government deemed appropriate by citizens?

2. Does the election system used by a city or special district make any difference as to how power or influence is distributed?

3. How might county government be reorganized to improve its ability to respond to increased urbanization and policy demands by an ever-growing population?

4. How do you account for proliferation of special districts throughout the state?

The best school of democracy and the best guarantee of its success is the practice of local self-government.

—James Bryce[1]

The American system, which divides the local authority among so many citizens, does not scruple [hesitate] to multiply the functions of the town officers.

—Alexis de Tocqueville[2]

Texans have an affinity for local government, but the mosaic of local governments with overlapping jurisdictions is confusing to many citizens. There are more than 4,800 local governments, of all sizes, across the state. Some operate with a handful of employees and budgets of $100,000 or $200,000 a year, while others have tens of thousands of employees with billion dollar-plus budgets. Their governmental structures range from the simple to the complex. Some special districts perform one basic function, while cities perform any number of services that are limited only by budgetary and legal restraints. Some counties have fewer than 1,000 people, but Harris County has more than 3.9 million residents. One school district in West Texas has only nineteen students, while the Houston Independent School District has approximately 200,000. Three of the ten largest cities in the United States are in Texas, but many cities across the state have fewer than 1,000 residents.

As we tackle the issues of local government, we can only scratch the surface. The key to understanding local governments in Texas is to understand what responsibilities have been assigned to them by the Texas Constitution and statutory law. Once the institutional structures and functions of local governments have been studied, attention will be directed to a number of core problems confronting them and their political capacities to address these issues. Two themes underlie this analysis: what changes can make local governments more effective, and is it possible or desirable to reduce the fragmentation in local governments?

A tradition of localism is rooted in the fabric of our political history. Since the founding of the nation, Americans have expressed a strong belief in the right to local self-government.[3] In many areas of the young country, local governments existed long before there was a viable state or federal government. Early communities had to fend for themselves and had limited expectations of services or protections to be provided by state or federal governments.

This history of local self-help has led to the popular notion that local governments have fundamental rights based on the concept of local sovereignty, or ultimate power. Thomas Jefferson, for example, developed a theory of local government, designed in part to strengthen the powers of the states, in which local sovereignty was rooted in the sovereignty of the individual. Local governments, which he termed wards, would have a wide range of responsibilities, including education, police, roads, caring for the poor, conducting elections, some minor judicial functions, and a semblance of a militia to maintain local defenses.[4]

In light of the expanded role of state and federal governments, we might find Jefferson's view rather romantic, outdated, and naive. Nonetheless, the concept has permeated American attitudes toward government and continues to shape citizen responses to government initiatives. Some people suggest that this cultural legacy persists in grassroots politics, the flight to suburbia, the creation of neighborhood organizations and gated communities, and the persistence of distrust of the national and state governments. Today, it is common to hear the argument that local government is closest to the people and best represents their interests and desires.[5]

Although this view is widely held, the prevailing constitutional theory on the relationship of local governments to the state is the unitary system that was discussed in Chapter 3. Simply stated, this theory holds that local governments are the creations of the state. The powers, functions, and responsibilities that they exercise have been delegated or granted to them by the state government, and no local government has sovereign powers. There have been numerous court cases enunciating this principle, which is referred to as the **Dillon rule**, but the best summary is derived from an Iowa case in which a court held the following:

> The true view is this: Municipal corporations owe their origin to, and derive their powers and rights wholly from, the legislature. It breathes into them the breath of life, without which they cannot exist. As it creates, so it may destroy. If it may destroy, it may abridge and control. Unless there is some constitutional limitation on the right, the legislature might by a single act, if we can suppose it capable of so great a folly and so great a wrong, sweep from its existence all of the municipal corporations in the State, and the corporations could not prevent it. We know of no limitation on this right so far as the corporations are concerned. They are so to phrase it, the mere tenants at will of the legislature.[6]

The Dillon rule is now the prevailing theory defining the relationships of states and local governments, and it is applicable to local governments in Texas. In short, local governments are fundamentally the administrative subdivisions of the state and have no rights except those granted to them by the state.

LOCAL GOVERNMENTS IN THE TEXAS POLITICAL SYSTEM

Local governments—counties, cities, school districts, and special districts—are created by the state and operate under limits set by the Texas Constitution and the legislature. They have found their capabilities and resources increasingly burdened by the pressing needs of a growing, urban state. Some of this pressure has come from the state and federal governments ordering or mandating significant improvements in environmental, educational, health, and other programs, but letting cities, counties, and school districts pick up much of the tab. Prior to the state's commitment to an extensive prison construction program in the 1990s, for example, the Texas government forced counties to spend millions of local taxpayer dollars to house state prisoners in county jails because it had failed to adequately address a criminal justice crisis. Local school districts and their property-tax payers also are at the mercy of the legislature, which has ordered expensive educational programs and has raised classroom standards without fully paying for them. Cities, too, find their budgetary problems exacerbated by state mandates. Local governments are the governments closest to the people, but they have to shoulder much of the responsibility—and often take much of the public outrage—for policy decisions made in Austin and in Washington.

Although the legal position expressed by the Dillon rule subordinates local governments to the state, there are practical and political limitations on what the state can do with local governments.[7] More importantly, the state relies on local governments to carry out many of its responsibilities.

Texas granted cities home rule authority in 1912. Home rule cities, discussed in more detail in this chapter, have considerable authority and discretion over their own local policies, but within limits set by state law. Texas voters approved a constitutional amendment in 1933 that also gave counties home rule authority, but no county established home rule government before the amendment was repealed in 1969. In principle, the amendment was quite progressive, but it was subject to contradictory interpretations, and procedures for a county to adopt home rule were excessively restrictive and difficult to comply with.[8] County home rule proposals were again introduced in the 1997 and 1999 legislative sessions by lawmakers from several urban areas, but these were defeated by opposition from a variety of state and local interests. As a general observation, Texas has given its home rule cities considerable discretionary powers permitting them to provide public services not specifically defined by state statutes. By contrast, the discretionary powers of counties are limited.[9]

The states vary considerably in the major responsibilities assigned to different levels of government. Texas, like most other states, assigns the primary responsibility for public education to local school districts while retaining the primary responsibility for highways, public welfare, and public health at the state level. Police and fire protection, water and sanitation services, parks, recreation, and libraries are the primary responsibility of city governments. Public hospitals are a shared function of the state, counties, and special districts.[10] Texas counties share with the state a primary responsibility for the courts and criminal justice system. Altogether, there are more than 4,800 local governments in Texas (see Chapter 3, Table 3–1).

URBAN TEXAS

Despite popular images of wide-open spaces dotted with cattle and oil wells, Texas is an urban state. Some areas, particularly in West Texas, still offer much room to roam, but more than eighty percent of Texans live in cities or urban areas. First-time visitors to the state often express surprise at the size and diversity of Houston and Dallas and the more relaxed charm of San Antonio, whose riverwalk reminds many tourists of some European cities. Austin, the seat of state government and location of a world-class university, is highly attractive to young professionals and high-technology businesses.

When the Texas Constitution was adopted in 1876, the state was rural and agrarian. Less than 10 percent of the population lived in cities. According to the 1880 census, Galveston was the largest city with a population of 22,248, followed by San Antonio with 20,550. Dallas, a relatively new settlement, had 10,358 residents, and Houston, 16,513. For most of the period from 1880 to 1920, San Antonio was Texas's largest city, but since the 1930 census, Houston has held that distinction.[11] In 1940, only 45 percent of Texans lived in urban areas, but by 1960, some 60 percent of the population resided in cities. Since the 1970 census, eight of every ten Texans have been living in cities. More recent data indicate that more than 83 percent of Texans live in urban areas.

Houston, San Antonio, and Dallas are among the ten largest cities in the United States. According to 2007 estimates, Houston had a population of 2,046,792; San Antonio, 1,284,332; and Dallas, 1,240,044. Six additional Texas cities—El Paso, Fort Worth, Austin, Corpus Christi, Arlington, and Plano—each had more than 250,000. Growth rates, however, have varied widely from city to city, thanks to differences in economic expansion, **annexation** policies, in-migration from other areas, and fertility and mortality rates. In some instances, the growth rate for the central city has been relatively modest, while growth in surrounding suburban areas has been quite high, reflecting continued urban sprawl.

Compared with many other parts of the country, Texas cities have a relatively low ratio of population to incorporated area. Texas cities are relatively young and had a lot of inexpensive land available to them during their early development. So, unlike older cities in other states, they tended to expand outward rather than upward. Texas cities also have used liberal annexation powers granted by the legislature to block the development of nearby, small municipalities that would curb their expansion. Houston covers approximately 540 square miles, the largest land mass of any city in the state, and has a **population density** of approximately 4,000 persons per square mile. Population density affects policy and budgetary issues relating to virtually every public service provided by the city. Land use, zoning laws, police and fire protection, the location of libraries and parks, and the development of water and sanitation systems are all related to the density of a city's population.

The racial and ethnic composition of Texas cities also is a major factor in urban diversity. Plano, located north of Dallas, reported in the 2007 population estimates a combined minority population of 33 percent with the Hispanic and Asian populations of similar size (see Table 12–1). By contrast, El Paso had a combined minority population of 84 percent, with 80 percent of the population identified as Hispanic. Eight of Texas's ten largest cities have minority populations exceeding 50 percent. Along the Texas–Mexico border, Laredo is 95 percent Hispanic; Brownsville, 92 percent; McAllen, 81 percent; and Harlingen, 74 percent. In 2007, the African-American population in Dallas was 23 percent. Houston's African-American population was 25 percent, and Fort Worth's, 18 percent. But the African-American population in El Paso was less than 3 percent; in Corpus Christi, 4 percent; and San Antonio, 6.5 percent.[12]

The more than 1,200 incorporated municipalities in Texas are diverse, and urban life, politics, and government have developed different styles across the state. The basic forms of city government are defined by statutory and constitutional law, but cities vary in their demographic makeup, their economies, the historical experiences that shaped their development, and their quality of life. There are local differences in economic development, public safety, public education, health and environmental quality, housing, transportation, culture, recreation, and politics.[13]

THE CITIES AND THE STATE

Although Texas became an urban state in 1950, a rural-dominated legislature was slow in redrawing House and Senate districts to reflect the population changes. Urban areas did not receive a fair share of legislative seats until the 1970s, when the federal courts finally forced the state to redistrict using the principle of "one man, one vote." So, historically, state public policy and expenditures were tilted toward rural areas and interests, while urban areas were often neglected. The early neglect contributed to many of the problems now confronting cities, although recent policies enacted by a more urban-oriented legislature have been more responsive to cities' concerns.

The state has granted cities—unlike counties and special districts—a wide range of discretionary power over organizational structure and local public policy. Texas, in fact, ranks high among the states in that regard, but cities still are strongly affected by state laws and policies. Cities, therefore, actively lobby the legislature and other state officials on numerous issues. The Texas Municipal League (TML) is supported by member cities

TABLE 12–1   Select Characteristics of the Ten Largest Cities in Texas, 2007

City	Total Population in 2007	Over 65 (%)	Under 18 (%)	Median Age	African American (%)	Hispanic (%)	Asian (%)	Median Household Income 2007	Persons below Poverty Level 2007 (%)	Children below Poverty Level 2007 (%)
Houston	2,046,792	8.7%	26.4%	32.9	24.9%	41.1%	5.4%	$40,856	20.7%	31.3%
San Antonio	1,284,332	10.4%	27.8%	32.5	6.9%	60.7%	2.1%	$41,593	18.2%	26.2%
Dallas	1,240,044	8.3%	27.2%	31.9	23.0%	43.4%	2.6%	$40,986	21.1%	32.3%
Austin	749,659	6.4%	23.2%	31.4	8.0%	34.8%	5.7%	$48,966	17.5%	23.8%
Fort Worth	650,613	8.3%	28.5%	31.7	18.0%	33.5%	3.3%	$47,104	16.2%	22.3%
El Paso	605,410	11.5%	30.2%	32.2	2.8%	80.1%	1.2%	$35,646	27.4%	38.6%
Arlington	359,365	7.4%	27.3%	31.4	18.0%	26.9%	6.4%	$50,447	13.0%	19.1%
Corpus Christi	290,010	11.0%	27.4%	33.8	3.9%	58.3%	1.5%	$41,416	18.8%	28.3%
Plano	263,663	7.7%	26.7%	35.7	6.3%	14.0%	12.9%	$84,492	5.9%	7.6%
Garland	230,429	8.9%	26.2%	34.2	12.9%	37.1%	9.4%	$48,558	13.4%	23.2%
State Totals	23,904,380	10.0%	27.7%	33.2	11.4%	36.0%	3.4%	$47,548	16.3%	23.2%

Source: U.S. Census Bureau, *2007 American Community Survey.*

and maintains a full-time staff in Austin to monitor the activities of the legislature and state agencies. Many of the larger cities also designate staff members to serve as legislative liaisons, or they retain professional lobbyists. In the larger cities, there usually is a legislative committee of the city council that works with the city staff, community leaders, and civic organizations to establish a legislative agenda. Houston, Dallas, and San Antonio have the potential for considerable impact on the state legislature when their legislative delegations share common interests or goals. But often there are sharp differences among local delegations.

Increasingly, state legislators from numerous central city areas are collaborating on issues that affect all Texas municipalities.[14] Hundreds of pieces of legislation that could affect cities are introduced during each legislative session. TML's highest priority is to block "bad legislation" that it believes is adverse to the interests of Texas cities.[15]

GENERAL LAW AND HOME RULE CITIES ─────────────●

The Texas Constitution provides for two general categories of cities: general law and home rule. **General law cities** have fewer than 5,000 residents and have more restrictions in organizing their governments, setting taxes, and annexing territory than do **home rule cities**. They are allowed only those powers specifically granted to them by the legislature. Most Texas cities—approximately 875—are general law cities.[16]

A city with more than 5,000 inhabitants can adopt any form of government its residents choose, provided it does not conflict with the state constitution (Article XI, Sections 4, 5) or statutes. This option is called home rule and is formalized through the voters' adoption of a **city charter**, which is the fundamental document—something like a constitution—under which a city operates. A charter establishes a city's governing body, the organization of its administrative agencies and municipal courts, its taxing authority, and procedures for conducting elections, annexing additional territory, and revising the charter (see "Is This Any Way to Change a City Charter?"). As of 2006, there were 334 home rule cities in Texas.[17]

Is This Any Way to Change a City Charter?

Boerne, Texas, which is just northwest of San Antonio, held a special election in May 2002 to amend its charter to bring it in line with a law recently enacted by the Texas legislature. The new law permitted local governments to purchase items valued at $25,000 or less without seeking bids. Prior to its enactment, the limit was $15,000, and the charter of Boerne included this figure. To permit the city to follow the state law and to anticipate future increases in the cap, a charter amendment would have permitted the city council to change spending caps each year as allowed by state law.

In a cliffhanger election in which only 57 of 4,836 registered voters participated, the charter amendment was defeated, 29–28. The election occurred when there were no city or school board elections to draw voters to the polls. Few voters apparently were even aware the issue was on the ballot, and some just didn't care or believe the issue was important to them.[18]

(Continued)

Struggling to stay ahead of the curve. Boerne, Texas, a small city approximately thirty miles from San Antonio, has seen its population increase by approximately 50 percent since the 2000 census. As with many suburban cities, it is faced with new issues that challenge its resources and generate political conflict over its future development.

What happened in Boerne occurs throughout the state in charter elections. Just as is true for changes to the state constitution, all too often a small minority of a city's voters decide on changes in its fundamental law. Although we have no empirical evidence, it might be argued that most changes are well-intentioned and necessary. It is evident, however, that a few individuals can use charter elections for their own self-interests.

FORMS OF CITY GOVERNMENT IN TEXAS ———●

Most Texas cities have functioned under more than one form of government. Changes in city charters often follow periods of crises, intense political conflict, or an inability of those in government to address long-term problems. Proposed changes in governmental structures and elections often threaten groups and interests that have a stake in the way business is currently being conducted, and charter revisions have a tendency to polarize a community.

Many of the larger cities in Texas have gone through a succession of different forms of governments—the mayor–council, the commission, and council-manager. There is a history behind the changes in city government, but citizens, elected officials and those who study local governments continue to raise the question: Does the form of city government make any difference as to how a city is run, how responsive it is to its citizens, to its ability to address current issues and anticipate future issues, and to its overall efficiency and effectiveness?

According to the Texas Municipal League, there were 1,211 municipal governments in Texas in 2006. More than 900 cities operated with some variation of the mayor–council form; approximately 280 used some form of council–manager or commission–manager government; and only a handful used the commission form of government.[19]

Mayor–Council

The mayor–council, the most common form of municipal government in Texas, was derived from the English model of city government. The legislative function of the city is vested in the city council, and the executive function is assigned to the mayor. This type of government is based on the separation of powers principle, which also characterizes the state and federal governments. In terms of power, however, there are two distinguishable forms of mayor—the **weak mayor** and the **strong mayor**—and in most Texas cities, the mayor is weak.

The city charter determines a mayor's strength. The weak mayor has little control over policy initiatives or implementation. The mayor's power may be constrained by one or more of the following: limited or no appointment or removal power over city offices, limited budgetary authority, and the election of other city administrators independently of the mayor (see Figure 12–1). Under these circumstances, the mayor shares power with the city council over city administration and policy implementation, and "is the chief executive in name only."[20] These restrictions limit both the political and administrative leadership of the mayor. Although it is possible for a mayor to use personal or political resources to influence the city council and other administrators and to provide energetic leadership, there are formidable obstacles to overcome.[21]

A strong mayor has real power and authority, including appointive and removal powers over city agency heads. Such appointments often require city council approval,

The strong mayor combines political leadership with policy initiatives and administrative responsibilities. Bill White, a lawyer, businessman, and former Deputy Secretary of Energy of the United States, was elected to his third term in 2007 as Houston's mayor.

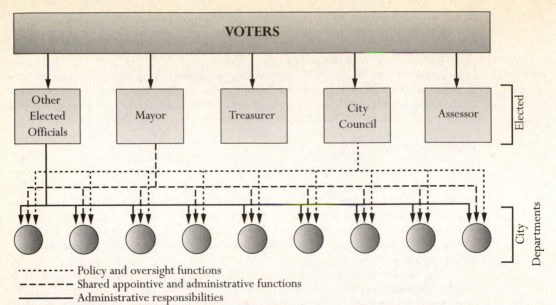

FIGURE 12–1   The Weak Mayor Form of Government. Mayors have limited budget and administrative power under the weak mayor form of government.

but the appointees are responsible to the mayor and serve at mayoral discretion. The mayor has control over budget preparation and exercises some veto authority over city council actions. This form of city government clearly distinguishes between executive and legislative functions.

The strong mayor form of government is found in many of the larger American cities, but it now is used by only one major city in Texas—Houston (see Figure 12–2). El Paso functioned under this form of government until 2004, when the city changed to council–manager government. This form may be unpopular in the state because the strong mayor often was associated with urban political machines, ward politics, and political corruption. Moreover, the fragmentation of authority and responsibility in local government parallels that found in state government and is another reminder of the deep distrust of government that Reconstruction produced in Texas. Finally, the state's individualistic and traditionalistic subcultures (see Chapter 1) reinforce hostile attitudes toward governmental institutions that are potentially more responsive to lower socioeconomic groups.

As might be expected, the salaries of the mayor and council members in a strong mayor city are generally higher than in cities with other forms of city government. In many cities, mayors and council members receive little or no pay or only modest reimbursements for services. But the mayor of Houston earned $176,762 in 2009, and each council member, $51,337.[22]

City Commission

The commission and council–manager forms of government are products of the twentieth century. Both reflect, in part, efforts to reform city governments through

Organization Chart

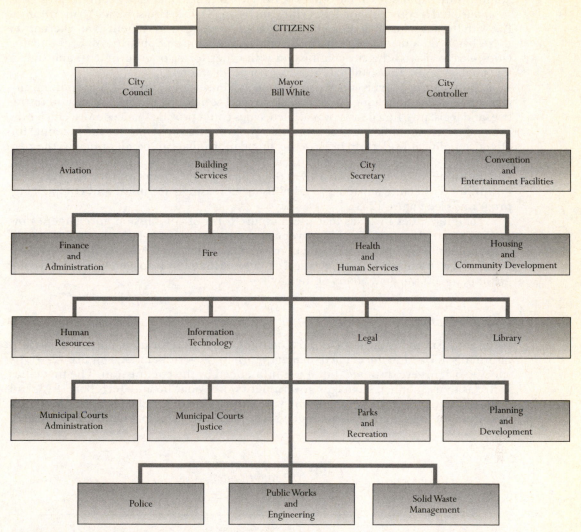

FIGURE 12–2 Organizational Chart of the City of Houston. Houston is the only large Texas city that uses the strong mayor form of government in which the mayor has major day-to-day administrative responsibilities.

administrative efficiency, the reduction of partisan conflict, and the adaptation of a businesslike approach to running city government.

The origin of the **city commission** usually is traced to the Texas island city of Galveston. After a hurricane and subsequent flooding devastated most of the city in 1900, the government then in office proved incompetent and incapable of responding. The crisis prompted a group of citizens to win the legislature's approval of a new form of government designed to be more responsive by combining the city's legislative and administrative functions in the offices of five city commissioners. City commissions were soon adopted by other major Texas cities, including Dallas, Houston, and San Antonio. But with the subsequent development of council–manager government as an alternative, there has been a marked decline in the city commission's popularity. All of the major cities have replaced the city commission with other forms of government, and only a few small cities in Texas still have this form of government.

Initially, the commission was supported as a businesslike approach to running city government. By eliminating partisan elections and combining the executive, administrative, and legislative functions, it was argued, cities could provide services more efficiently. But critics have identified several problems. The commission minimizes the potential for effective political leadership because no single individual can be identified as the person in charge. Moreover, there is minimal oversight and review of policies and budgets. Commissioners are elected primarily as policymakers, not administrators, and there are downsides to electing amateurs to administer increasingly technical and complex city programs (see Figure 12–3).

The few cities in Texas that use the pure form of commission government now generally have three members—a mayor and two commissioners—who are each assigned responsibilities for specific city functions, such as water, sanitation, and public safety. Some of the commission cities now use a city administrator or manager, hired by the commission, to run the daily affairs of the city.

Council–Manager

After enthusiasm for the city commission waned, urban reformers, both in Texas and nationally, looked to the **council–manager** form of government (see Figure 12–4). Its specific origins are disputed, but it was influenced by the commission. The first cities in Texas to use council–manager government were Amarillo and Terrell in 1913, and it soon became popular among home rule cities. Nine of the state's ten largest cities now function under council–manager government. Its principal characteristics are a

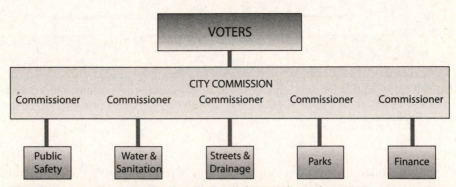

FIGURE 12–3   City Commission Form of Government. Commissioners combine policy and administrative functions under the commission form of government developed in Galveston after the 1900 hurricane. Few Texas cities use this form of government, and many that do have added a manager.

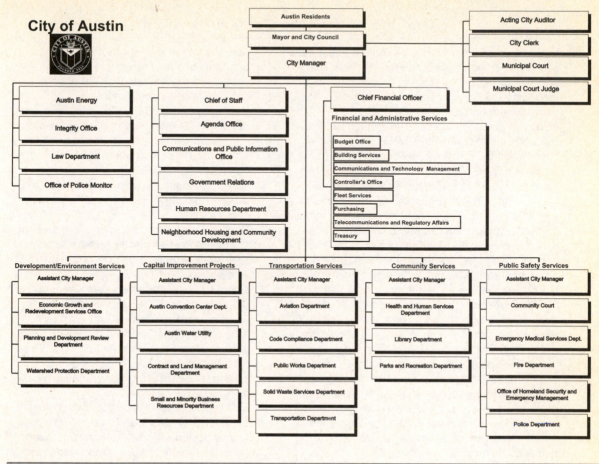

City of Austin

Austin Residents

Mayor and City Council

City Manager

Acting City Auditor

City Clerk

Municipal Court

Municipal Court Judge

Austin Energy

Integrity Office

Law Department

Office of Police Monitor

Chief of Staff

Agenda Office

Communications and Public Information Office

Government Relations

Human Resources Department

Neighborhood Housing and Community Development

Chief Financial Officer

Financial and Administrative Services

Budget Office

Building Services

Communications and Technology Management

Controller's Office

Fleet Services

Purchasing

Telecommunications and Regulatory Affairs

Treasury

Development/Environment Services

Assistant City Manager

Economic Growth and Redevelopment Services Office

Planning and Development Review Department

Watershed Protection Department

Capital Improvement Projects

Assistant City Manager

Austin Convention Center Dept.

Austin Water Utility

Contract and Land Management Department

Small and Minority Business Resources Department

Transportation Services

Assistant City Manager

Aviation Department

Code Compliance Department

Public Works Department

Solid Waste Services Department

Transportation Department

Community Services

Assistant City Manager

Health and Human Services Department

Library Department

Parks and Recreation Department

Public Safety Services

Assistant City Manager

Community Court

Emergency Medical Services Dept.

Fire Department

Office of Homeland Security and Emergency Management

Police Department

Effective 8/202009

Communications and Public Information Office – (512) 974-2220

FIGURE 12–4   Organizational Chart for the City of Austin.   *Source:* http://www.ci.austin.tx.us/help/downloads/

professional city management, nonpartisan city elections, and a clear distinction between policymaking and administration. In recent years, however, it has become evident that this policy-administration distinction has been modified by the increased roles of mayors and city council members in the day-to-day operations of city government.

In some council–manager cities, the mayor is chosen by the city council from among its membership to preside over council meetings and fulfill a primarily symbolic role. In other cities, the mayor is elected citywide, an arrangement that enhances the political position of the office without necessarily giving it formal legal authority. The mayor is usually a voting member of city council but has few other institutional powers. The mayor does, however, have the opportunity to become a visible spokesperson for the city and has a forum from which to promote ideas and programs.

The Job of the City Council Member

Regardless of the form of government, most city councils in Texas are small, with five to fifteen members elected for two-year terms. Most council seats are elected at-large, or citywide, and council elections are nonpartisan. Council members in most cities can serve for an unlimited number of terms. Recent referenda on term limitations, however, have been held in several Texas cities. San Antonio limits its council members and mayor to four two-year terms, and Houston, three two-year terms.

In most cities, a council office is part-time with little or no compensation, and although some large cities (e.g., Houston, Austin, and Dallas) have recently increased salaries significantly, many council members do not consider their pay to be commensurate with the time spent on the job. Council members in San Antonio are still paid $20 per meeting. Low salaries were part of the early urban reform tradition. The idea was that people would run for office out of a sense of civic duty rather than to advance themselves financially.

The frequency of council meetings varies. In many small towns, councils may meet for only a few hours each month; but councils in large cities meet much more frequently, usually weekly, with meetings lasting several hours. Cities are dealing with a wider range of complex issues than ever before, and demands on a council member's time are great. In addition to their policymaking roles, council members in large cities are faced with increased demands for constituent services. Many council members are finding that public service is extremely costly in terms of time lost from their families and the jobs or professions that provide their livelihoods.

Council members often complain that they had no idea how much time the public would demand of them and no idea of the personal costs of public service. Yet public service has its rewards, and these rewards often come from a sense that one has made a significant contribution to the future well-being of his or her city. And there are some prescriptions for effectiveness:

1. Learn all you can about your city—its history, its operations, its finances, and those responsible for carrying out the policies of the council. But recognize that change occurs in political institutions and the political climate of a community.

2. Don't let honest differences of opinion with other council members or staff degenerate into personality conflicts. Remember that "there are no permanent friends or permanent enemies in politics."

3. Take the budget and budgetary process seriously. The budget is at the heart of all policy decisions.

4. Don't be misled by the strong demands of special interest groups that want action now, their way. Remember, you represent the whole city.

5. Listen to what your constituents, your fellow council members, and staff have to say. Don't give quick answers until you are confident that you understand the issue. Keep your constituents informed and encourage citizen participation. Balancing interests among your constituents can produce breakthroughs in city policies.

6. Don't spring surprises on your fellow council members or staff. Spend time before a public discussion soliciting information, ascertaining interests in your issue or concerns, and soliciting others' perspectives.

7. Don't bypass the system and don't let others bypass the system. Procedures, when used appropriately, assure openness and consistency in decision-making and policy implementation.

8. Recognize that in some situations there will be winners and losers.

9. Develop a vision for the future of your city, along with short-term and long-term goals.

10. Celebrate when good things—of which you have been a part—happen. Let the public share in these successes. Your constituents often hear only about the problems of the city, which, in turn, contributes to negative attitudes toward government.[24]

Most aren't this large or ornate. City councils vary in size, and so do the chambers in which they meet, but all have the basic responsibility of establishing city policies. Many of the councils across the state have very modest and informal facilities. By contrast, the San Antonio City Council meets in the renovated lobby of a historical bank located in the central business district.

The city council is primarily responsible for developing public policy (see "The Job of the City Council Member"). It creates, organizes, and restructures city departments, approves the city budget, establishes the tax rate, authorizes the issuance of bonds (subject to voter approval), enacts local laws (ordinances), and conducts inquiries and investigations into the operations and functions of city agencies.[23]

The council hires a full-time city manager, who is responsible for administering city government on a day-to-day basis. The manager hires and fires assistants and department heads, supervises their activities, and translates the policy directives of the city council into concrete action by city employees. The city manager is also responsible for developing a city budget for council approval and then supervising its implementation. Professionalism is one of the key attributes of the council–manager form of government. Initially, many city managers were engineers, but in recent years there has been a tendency for managers to become generalists with expertise in public finance. City managers are fairly well paid. In 2009, the city manager of Dallas was paid $278,000. San Antonio's city manager was paid $315,000, with scheduled increases to $335,000 over the next three years, and the city manager of Austin earned $242,000, along with other benefits. The city manager of even a small city such as Seguin (population 28,000) received $150,560.[25]

At one time in the not too distant past, the salaries of mayors and council members serving in council-manager cities were very low, but there has been a trend in recent years to increase salaries in response to the expanded workload. Annual salaries of the mayor and city council members in Austin are $53,000 and $45,000, respectively. Until recently, the mayor and council members in Dallas received $50 per meeting, but voters approved a charter amendment in 2001 to raise the mayor's pay to $60,000 a year and council members to $37,500.[26] By contrast, San Antonio's council members and mayor currently earn $20 per meeting and the mayor an additional $3,000 per year.[27] There have been discussions about increasing their pay, but such changes would require an amendment to San Antonio's charter.

There is a delicate line between policymaking and administration, and a city manager is, in principle, supposed to be politically neutral. The overall effectiveness of city managers depends on three main factors: their relationships with their city councils; their ability to develop support for their recommendations within the council and the community at large without appearing to have gone beyond the scope of their authority; and the overall perception of their financial and managerial skills (see "Is This Any Job for a Woman?"). In the real world of municipal government, city managers play a central role in setting policy as well as carrying it out. Managers' adroit use of their resources and their sensitivity to political factions and the personal agendas of elected officials are key to determining their success.

Is This Any Job for a Woman?

When the council–manager form of government was first adopted, there was a general perception that the job of the city manager required an engineer or someone from a related field of training to address the basic infrastructure problems of a city. At that time, city officials concentrated most of their work on basic services—streets, water systems, wastewater treatment plants, utilities, public safety, and other public facilities. Budgets were relatively modest, and few cities provided what we now call "social services." So, city councils tended to hire

Mary K. Suhm. Dallas City Manager.

Sheryl Sculley. San Antonio City Manager.

engineers who understood the development and maintenance of infrastructures, and in those days engineering was almost exclusively a male career.

Over the years, as city populations increased and demands for public services became more complex, budgetary and management skills came to be perceived as more critical for a city manager than engineering, and the next generation of city managers was trained in finance and budgeting. Yet, until recently, it was still a male-dominated career.

But urban management in Texas has undergone a sea change over the past two decades. Women, especially those with training in finance and budgeting, began to work their way up the ranks of city agencies. As the older generation of city managers retired or moved on, these women established their own reputations for management and leadership.

In 2009, the city managers of three of Texas's largest cities—San Antonio, Dallas, and El Paso—were women. Two—Sheryl Sculley (San Antonio) and Joyce Wilson (El Paso)—were recruited from other cities. Mary K. Suhm worked her way up through the ranks of Dallas government. Their

Joyce Wilson. El Paso City Manager.

undergraduate degrees were in the liberal arts or business, and all had master's degrees in public administration. As have many of their recent male counterparts, they had considerable experience in public finance and budgeting.[28]

The three, appointed to their current positions in 2004 or later, have worked effectively in the rough and tumble world of city management and politics.

MUNICIPAL ELECTION SYSTEMS

Nonpartisan City Elections

Virtually every city in Texas elects its council members in **nonpartisan elections**. Claiming that there was "no Democratic or Republican way to pave a street," city reformers who were part of the nonpartisan movement (1920s to 1950s) expressed a strong aversion to political parties and particularly to the urban political machines. To enforce separation of city elections from party politics, most municipal elections are held at times other than the party primaries or the general election.

The nonpartisan ballot—combined with at-large, citywide elections—has historically benefited higher social and economic groups. Parties and party labels normally serve as cues for voters. When they are eliminated in city elections, voters are forced to find alternative sources of information about candidates. Many local newspapers, which endorsed candidates and decided how much coverage to give them, had ties to the dominant urban elites. Candidates from lower socioeconomic groups had few contacts with the influential civic and business organizations that recruited, supported, and endorsed candidates. Although no longer in existence, San Antonio's Good Government League and Dallas's Citizens Charter Association controlled the recruitment and election of candidates in those two cities for several decades. Both organizations drew members from the Democratic and the Republican parties, but they reflected and pursued the interests of higher socioeconomic groups, often to the detriment of lower-income and minority populations.

Despite the nonpartisan characteristics of city election systems, partisanship and party affiliation can play a role in city elections. Party labels are still excluded from the ballot, but some city council candidates are beginning to be identified by their party affiliations through news stories, endorsements by party organizations, and campaign advertisements. In the 2001 and 2003 city elections in Houston, for example, party affiliations of major candidates were widely known, and national party committees contributed money to some of the campaigns. Areas that are Republican in partisan orientation are likely to support indivi-duals with Republican attributes, and, conversely, areas that vote Democratic in general elections are likely to support candidates with Democratic leanings. These developments clearly challenge the nonpartisan traditions of many cities throughout Texas.

At-Large Elections

Another notable feature of city politics in Texas is the general use of citywide or at-large elections. In 1992, the latest year for which comprehensive data are available from the U.S. Census Bureau, there were 6,409 individuals elected to the governing bodies of 1,171 cities and towns in Texas. Some 5,649, or 88 percent, were elected at-large. Only 12 percent were elected from single-member districts, discussed in the following section.[29] Of the 1,204 Texas cities in 2002, some 207, or 14 percent, used single-member districts.[30]

In an at-large election, all of a city's voters participate in the selection of all the members of the city council. In a pure at-large system, every candidate runs against every other candidate. If there are eight candidates running for five positions on the city council, the candidates with the five highest vote totals are the winners.

A variation of the at-large system is the place system. Candidates file for a specific council seat and run citywide for places, or positions. Cities using the place system may require that the winning candidate receive a simple plurality of votes (more votes than any other candidate running for the same position) or an absolute majority of votes (more than half of the votes cast). If a city requires the latter and there are more than two persons in a race, **runoff elections** between the two highest vote getters are often required.

Single-Member Districts

An alternative to at-large elections is the **single-member district**, or ward. Under this system, a city is divided into separate geographic districts, each represented by a different council member. A candidate must live in and run for election from a specific district, and voters can cast a ballot only in the race for the council seat that represents their district. A person elected from a single-member district can, depending on the city's charter, be elected by a plurality or an absolute majority of votes.

Legal Attacks on At-Large Elections

Election systems are not politically neutral (see "The Debate over Electoral Systems"). At-large systems have historically benefited the nonminority, high-income areas of a city, while single-member districts tend to be more inclusive of all groups and areas of a city.

The Debate over Electoral Systems

There has been much debate over what is the most desirable form of city elections. Advocates of at-large, nonpartisan elections often warn of ward politics and the potential relationship of single-member districts to political machines, bosses, partisan conflict, corruption, and mismanagement. Even without corruption, they argue, council members elected from districts are concerned primarily with the interests of their own neighborhoods and may be more susceptible to trade-offs, swapping votes for programs and services that would benefit small segments of the community rather than benefiting the entire city. It also has been argued that district elections divide communities along racial, ethnic, or economic lines, resulting in high levels of political conflict. Moreover, proponents of at-large elections argue that their system produces higher caliber candidates, results in more media exposure for political campaigns, and permits a voter to participate in the selection of the entire city council rather than just one member.

But, on the other hand, critics of the at-large system believe that single-member districts make elected officials more responsive to the needs and interests of specific constituencies. They also argue that at-large elections discriminate against African Americans and Hispanics because of racially polarized voting and the dilution of the impact of minority voting strength. Furthermore, citywide election campaigns, especially in the larger cities, are much more expensive than district campaigns, thus adversely affecting the electoral chances of candidates from low-income, often minority, areas. It also has been argued that single-member districts produce a more diverse group of elected officials and ensure that a city council considers more diverse views and interests. At-large elections, critics say, permit a small group of individuals—the city's elites—to control the electoral process and the council by recruiting and financially supporting candidates to protect their interests.[31]

At-large elections are still considered constitutional and are permitted under the state's election code, but their use is most prevalent in smaller cities with small minority populations. Many local governments across Texas now use single-member districts. The extended legal battles over election systems have resulted in a significant increase in Hispanics and African Americans elected to office throughout the state.

Hispanics and African Americans, through various advocacy groups such as the National Association for the Advancement of Colored People, the Mexican American Legal Defense and Educational Fund, Texas Rural Legal Aid, the G.I. Forum, and the Southwest Voter Registration and Education Project, have challenged in federal courts the election systems used by numerous Texas cities. From the small East Texas town of Jefferson to El Paso, Houston, and Dallas, minority groups have, with considerable success, proved the inequities of at-large elections and forced city governments to adopt electoral plans with districts that give minorities a better chance of electing candidates to city councils. The ethnic and racial composition of city councils has changed dramatically over the past twenty years, with a marked increase in Hispanics and African Americans elected to these governing bodies (see Chapter 7).

CITY REVENUES AND EXPENDITURES

Despite a growing number of expenses, Texas cities have limited financial options. Unlike counties and school districts, they receive no state appropriations. City governments are disproportionately dependent on **regressive taxes**, such as property taxes and a one-cent

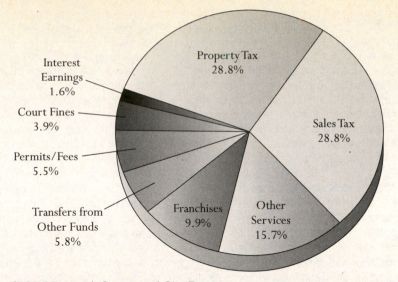

Interest Earnings 1.6%

Court Fines 3.9%

Permits/Fees 5.5%

Transfers from Other Funds 5.8%

Property Tax 28.8%

Sales Tax 28.8%

Franchises 9.9%

Other Services 15.7%

FIGURE 12–5 Sources of City Revenues. *Source: Texas Town and City* 97 (January 2009), p. 22.

sales tax (see Figure 12–5). Other revenue sources include franchise fees, court fines, hotel occupancy taxes, taxes on amusements, fees on various permits, and transfers from funds generated by locally owned utilities.[32]

Texas cities have been given considerable discretion to determine what taxes they will impose, and to a large extent the state has not depended on the cities to fund state programs. Nevertheless, cities are continually threatened by legislative proposals to place caps or other restrictions on their taxing authority.[33] Through their associations and lobbyists, cities work hard to thwart such restrictions.

The state limits the property tax rate a city can impose and permits citizens to petition their city council for a **rollback election** to nullify any tax increase of more than 8 percent in a given year. Although there have been few rollback elections in recent years, the potential for such citizen initiatives serves to constrain policymakers. A proposal to lower the cap on annual increases in property appraisals, a key element in determining property tax bills, was defeated in the legislature in 2005.[34]

City revenues tend to track the state's economy. When the economy is robust and expanding, city revenues usually grow. Revenue from property taxes increases with the construction of new homes and businesses. Rising property values also result in higher tax appraisals and increased revenue. Sales tax revenue increases as retailers sell more products. When the economy weakens, however, cities are forced to raise property taxes, increase fees, lay off city workers, freeze the hiring of new employees, or reduce services.[35]

Texas was beginning to experience recessionary conditions—higher unemployment and underemployment, decreases in manufacturing and sales and declines in housing values—by early 2009. The state comptroller reported in July that sales tax allocations to local governments had decreased.[36] And, in a Texas Municipal League survey, more than 20 percent of Texas cities said they anticipated lower revenues in 2009 and 2010. Approximately one-third of the cities said they had increased property taxes

So near to power and influence but so far away. Poor neighborhoods stand in sharp contrast to the nearby high-rise office buildings and hotels of downtown San Antonio.

and more than 60 percent indicated they had increased fees. And, as has been frequently the case over the past twenty years, capital improvements were put on hold.[37]

Although cities are required by law to balance their operating budgets, many municipal construction projects are financed by loans through the issuance of **general obligation bonds**, which are subject to voter approval. These bonds are secured by the city's taxing power. The city pledges its full faith and credit to the lender and, over a number of years, repays the bonds with tax revenue. Cities also fund various projects through **revenue bonds** that are payable solely from the revenues derived from an income-producing facility maintained by the city. And, with a significant pent-up demand for improving infrastructure (streets, waste disposal systems, libraries, and other facilities), cities had entered an era of bond financing radically altered by the performance of Wall Street and changes in state and federal tax laws.[38] However, it is more difficult to raise money during recessions, a prospect cities faced in 2009.

Cities and towns share responsibilities for providing services with other local governments, but their primary functions are police and fire protection, streets and roads, solid waste management, sewer treatment and drainage, water supply, parks and recreation, public transportation, and libraries. Some Texas cities provide electricity and natural gas, but those services are provided by private utilities in other communities. Cities often contract services out to private corporations, but the legal authority for such functions remains with the city or town. In some cases, special districts, which are independent of the cities, have been established within the boundaries of a city to provide specific services.

URBAN PROBLEMS IN TEXAS ————————————————————————●

During the 1970s and through the early 1980s, Texas cities were key participants in the dramatic economic growth of the state. Many of the older cities of the country—particularly in the East and the Midwest—"looked at their Texas counterparts and envied their capacity to attract population and business."[39] Texas cities had low taxes, a probusiness tradition, few labor unions with significant economic clout, an abundant work force, proximity to natural resources, and governing bodies that favored economic growth and development. At the beginning of the twenty-first century, however, many Texas cities are confronted with some of the problems associated with the older urban areas outside Texas.

Graying of Texas Cities

The Texas population is aging, or graying. Americans are living longer, and older age groups are among the fastest growing segments of the population. As the population ages, additional pressures are placed on city governments for public services. The local property tax, a major source of revenue for city governments, is stretched almost to its limits. Moreover, many Texas cities have granted, in addition to the standard **homestead exemption**, additional property tax exemptions for individuals older than sixty-five. As more and more people become old enough to claim these exemptions, younger taxpayers will be called upon to shoulder the burden through higher tax rates. There is also the looming possibility that older citizens on fixed incomes will be much more reluctant to support bond issues if they result in significant property tax increases.

"White Flight"

The population characteristics of Texas cities have changed over the past five decades. Major metropolitan areas experienced a "white flight" to the suburbs, a dramatic increase in the growth rate of minority populations, and small growth rates among Anglos in the central cities.[40] Income levels for most minority Texans have always been lower than those of Anglos, and a larger proportion of the minority population falls below the poverty level (see Chapter 1). The increased concentration of lower-income people in the central cities increases pressure for more public services, while a declining proportion of affluent property owners weakens the local tax structures that pay for the services.

Declining Infrastructures

There has been much concern across Texas and the United States about the declining infrastructures of local governments. In its 2008 "Report Card for American Infrastructure," the American Society of Civil Engineers gave Texas a mediocre score of C.[41] This survey mirrored a number of federal agency studies of the state's infrastructure problems. The message seems clear. Public facilities must be constantly maintained or expanded to support a growing population. Governments at all levels must plan for growth, allocate funds, and build facilities as this growth occurs. When they don't, infrastructure problems compound with the potential costs exceeding the capacity of governments to pay for them. It has been projected that Texas will have to invest some $173 billion for water systems over the next 50 years. Many Texas cities already are out of compliance with federal standards for treating water and sewage and disposing of solid waste and are risking fines. Costs for these upgrades over the next ten years alone are estimated at $25 billion.[42]

Some capital improvements are paid out of current operating budgets; but a more common practice is for cities to borrow money to improve roads, streets, water systems, and the like. These bonds are repaid from taxes on property. When property values decline—as they did in the late 1980s—cities are restrained—by the constitution and statutes—in how much indebtedness they can incur to support needed improvements. A construction boom that began in the 1990s and continued through much of the first decade of the twenty-first century added a significant new tax base. However, a growing population increased the demand for roads, utilities, water and wastewater systems, and an array of other capital needs. Cities are having trouble keeping up with these new demands.

Crime and Urban Violence

Crime is a major problem facing Texas cities and counties, just as it is in many other parts of the country. Although crime rates in most offense categories declined in the 1990s and through the early years of the twenty-first century, many Texans continue to believe that crime is on the rise. Much of the problem is related to drug abuse, gang violence, and juvenile crime. These perceptions also are shaped, in part, by anecdotal information, local news coverage that often focuses on "blood and guts," and political candidates who emphasize crime in their campaigns. Political candidates and elected officials often propose expansion of law enforcement, but many city and county budgets cannot absorb the costs.

State- and Federal-Mandated Programs

As we discussed in Chapter 3, both federal and state governments have increasingly used mandates in recent years to implement public policy. A **mandate** is a law or regulation enacted by a higher level of government that compels a lower level of government to carry out a specific action. In simpler terms, it is a form of "passing the buck." Federal mandates cover a wide range of governmental functions, including transportation, education for the disabled, water and air quality, and voter registration. States, meanwhile, have shifted much of the cost of public education to local governments.

Despite a decrease in federal funding for many urban problems since the 1980s, there has been an increase in federal mandates on the states, counties, and the cities and an increase in state mandates on local governments, often with no financial support. In some cases, the state simply passes the responsibility for—and the costs of—carrying out federal mandates to local governments. Congress enacted a law in 1995 to restrict unfunded mandates, but the law applied only to future, not existing, mandates. Such restrictions can still be circumvented if Congress chooses.

Although this practice may seem unfair and illogical, it is politically attractive to federal policymakers because they can "appease a large and vocal interest group that demands an extensive program without incurring the wrath of their constituents." While they get the credit for such programs, they do not get the blame for their costs.[43] Cities and other local governments across Texas claim that these unfunded requirements are excessively expensive, force them to rearrange their priorities, and limit local initiatives dealing with their most pressing issues. If local governments do not comply with mandates, they can be subject to litigation and face the prospects of losing federal or state funds. If they comply with mandates, they are then likely to reduce other services or seek alternative sources of funding now denied them.

Environmental Issues

Texas is one of the most polluted states in the nation. Petrochemical industries generate a large amount of pollutants as by-products in processing fossil fuels or in manufacturing chemicals. The indiscriminate disposal of much of this waste in years past has produced toxic waste dumps in many cities, often in low-income, minority neighborhoods. Heavy automobile traffic and coal-burning power plants spew tons of pollutants into the air, while fertilizers and herbicides threaten local water supplies. Cities are frequently on "ozone alert" days, which could trigger additional federal and state requirements to contain the problems.

Some cities are addressing these issues through "smart growth" programs, and more recently, "sustainability" and "green city" programs. After the administration of President George W. Bush made little effort to deal with the problem of global warming, many Texas cities joined other local governments with a wide array of environmental initiatives.

Public Employment

As the baby boom generation begins to retire, governmental agencies are beginning to face serious personnel issues. For more than three decades, bureaucrat bashing by political candidates, legislators, think tanks, and the media has helped increase public hostility toward government. This, in turn, has discouraged many highly skilled young people from seeking careers in public service.

Retiring public employees also have accumulated expensive pensions, including health care benefits, that many cities may have trouble paying. Local governments often made commitments to provide retirement benefits without allocating sufficient funds to assure that all benefits will be paid.

COUNTY GOVERNMENT IN TEXAS

Prior to Texas independence, local government was organized both under Spanish and Mexican law around the municipality. This unit consisted of large land areas with "presidios for military protection, missions established by the Catholic Church, and settlements established by various colonists and impresarios."[44] There were twenty-three such municipalities at the time of independence, and they became the first twenty-three counties organized under the Texas Constitution of 1836.

Texas now has 254 counties, more than any other state. The Constitution gives the legislature the power to create, abolish, or alter counties. But it prescribes certain requirements for a new county, including its size and the proximity of its boundaries to the county seat of the county from which it is created. The last county created was Kenedy in 1921.[45]

Counties are administrative subunits of the state that were developed initially to serve a predominantly rural population. Created primarily to administer state law, they possess powers delegated to them by the state, but they have relatively few implied powers.[46] Unlike home rule cities, counties lack the basic legislative power of enacting ordinances. They can carry out only those administrative functions granted them by the state. Counties administer and collect some state taxes and enforce a variety of state laws and regulations. They also build roads and bridges, administer local welfare programs, aid in fire protection, and perform other functions primarily local in nature.[47] All Texas counties function under the same constitutional restrictions and basic organizational structure, despite wide variations in population, local characteristics, and public needs.

The Diversity of Counties

According to 2008 population estimates, Loving County, the state's least populous, had only 62 residents, compared to 3.9 million in Harris County, the most populous (see Table 12–2). Rockwall County includes only 147 square miles, while Brewster County covers 6,204 square miles. Some 58 percent of the state's population lives in the ten most populous counties.[48]

Motley County, with a population of about 1,465, had a 2008 budget of $737,978 and paid its county judge $16,226 a year and each of its commissioners, $11,786. Dallas County had a $741 million budget and paid its county judge $153,853 and each commissioner $126,802 a year. Harris County's 2008 budget was $2.3 billion. Its county judge was paid $152,856, and each of its commissioners received $145,212.[49] Although there is an obvious relationship between the population of a county and salaries paid to its officials, the county's tax base is also a significant factor.

The Structure of County Government

The organizational structure of county government is highly fragmented, reflecting the principles of Jacksonian democracy and the reaction of late-nineteenth century Texans to Radical Reconstruction. The governing body of a county is the **commissioners court**, but it shares administrative functions with other independently elected officials (see Figure 12–6). Moreover, the name commissioners court is somewhat misleading because that body has no judicial functions.

TABLE 12–2   Ten Largest and Ten Smallest Texas Counties, 1980–2008

	1980 Population	1990 Population	2000 Population	2008 Population
Harris County	2,409,547	2,818,199	3,400,578	3,922,115
Dallas County	1,556,390	1,852,810	2,218,899	2,377,477
Tarrant County	860,880	1,170,103	1,446,219	1,716,365
Bexar County	988,800	1,185,394	1,392,391	1,593,859
Travis County	419,573	576,407	812,280	956,901
El Paso County	479,899	591,610	679,622	749,721
Collin County	144,576	264,036	491,675	749,590
Hidalgo County	283,229	383,545	569,463	725,978
Denton County	143,126	273,525	432,976	627,725
Fort Bend County	130,846	225,421	354,452	523,339
Glasscock County	1,304	1,447	1,406	1,208
Sterling County	1,206	1,438	1,393	1,192
Terrell County	1,595	1,410	1,081	1,005
McMullen County	789	817	851	859
Roberts County	1,187	1,025	887	842
Kent County	1,145	1,010	859	816
Borden County	859	799	729	696
King County	425	354	356	355
Kenedy County	543	460	414	351
Loving County	91	107	67	62

Sources: U.S Census Bureau, *U.S. Censuses, 1980, 1990, 2000*; Texas State Data Center, *Total Population Estimates for Counties, 2008.*

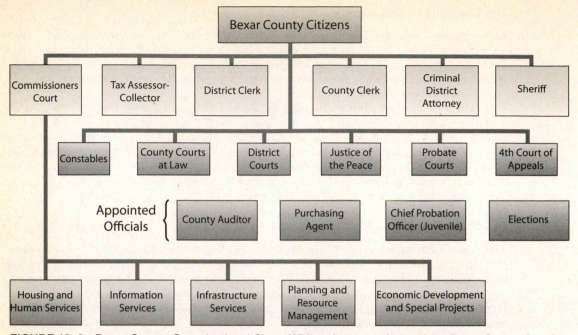

FIGURE 12–6   Bexar County Organizational Chart. While urban counties such as Bexar County function with many employees and provide a wide array of services, all counties in Texas function under a similar structure, which provides for the election of many officials and fragments authority among them.

Commissioners Court and County Judge.   The commissioners court includes a **county judge**, who is elected countywide, and four county commissioners, who are elected from a county's four commissioners precincts. Like other elected county officials, the judge and the commissioners serve four-year terms and are elected in partisan elections.

Until the 1960s, there were gross inequities in the population distributions among commissioners precincts in most counties. This issue of malapportionment came to a head in the 1968 case of *Avery v. Midland County*. Ninety-seven percent of the county's population, which lived in the city of Midland, elected only one commissioner, and the remaining three percent of the county's residents elected the other three. Similar inequities were prevalent all over the state, but the U.S. Supreme Court applied the "one man, one vote" principle to the counties and required that districts be equally apportioned.[50] Subsequently, Congress placed Texas under the Voting Rights Act in 1975, and counties were required to consider the interests of minority populations in drawing the boundaries for commissioners precincts. African Americans and Hispanics across the state have challenged county electoral systems and have increased minority representation on county commissioners courts. After the 2000 census, most Texas counties quickly redistricted their commissioner precincts in compliance with state and federal law.

The county judge presides over commissioners court, participates in the court's deliberations, and votes on issues before it. If there is a vacancy among the commissioners, the county judge appoints a replacement. If the county judge vacates his or her office, the commissioners choose a replacement.

It has become a full-time job. The problems and complexities of governments in urban counties have transformed the responsibilities of the county judge and commissioners into full-time jobs. County Judge Nelson Wolff, a former mayor of the city of San Antonio, a city council member, a state legislator, and a delegate to the 1974 constitutional convention, presides over the Bexar County Commissioners Court, which generally meets at least once a week.

The Texas Constitution also gives the county judge some judicial responsibilities but does not require the officeholder to be a lawyer. Most urban counties have county courts-at-law that relieve the county judge of judicial duties. However, county judges in some rural counties perform a judicial as well as an executive role, combining two sets of duties in one office.

The commissioners court fills midterm vacancies in other county offices (see Table 12–3). It also has authority over the county budget, which permits the court to exercise some influence, if not control, over other elected officeholders.[51] The court sets the annual tax rate, which is limited by the Texas Constitution, approves the tax roll, and supervises all expenditures of county money. Other county officials must obtain the court's authorization for personnel positions, salaries, and office expenses. Consequently, the budgetary process often sparks political disputes and other conflicts.

Historically, county road construction and maintenance were primary functions of commissioners court. The Optional Road Law of 1947 gave counties the authority to create a consolidated road system under the supervision of a county engineer, who relieved

TABLE 12–3 **Major Duties of the Commissioners Court**

1. Set tax rate and adopt county budget.
2. Appoint county officials authorized under statutory law and hire personnel.
3. Fill county elective and appointive vacancies.
4. Administer elections, including the establishment of voting precincts, the appointment of an election administrator, the appointment of precinct judges, the calling of county bond elections, and the certification of election returns.
5. Let contracts and authorize payment of all county bills.
6. Build and maintain county roads and bridges.
7. Build, maintain, and improve county facilities, including jails.
8. Provide for libraries, hospitals, and medical care for the indigent.
9. Provide for emergency relief and civil disaster assistance.
10. Provide for fire protection and sanitation.

Source: Texas Commission on Intergovernmental Relations, *An Introduction to County Government* (Austin, TX: 1985), p. 9.

commissioners of road maintenance and construction headaches. But the importance of roads to the commissioners and their constituents can still generate political disputes.

County Clerk.   The constitution provides for an elected **county clerk** to serve as the clerk of the commissioners court, the clerk of the county courts, and, in the smaller counties, the clerk of the district court. Over the years, the legislature has enacted hundreds of statutory provisions defining specific responsibilities of the office, prompting one writer to describe the office as the "dumping ground for miscellaneous functions" of the county.[52] The office is the depository of a county's vital statistics, such as birth and death records and documents related to real estate transactions. It issues marriage licenses and various other licenses required by state law.[53] The county clerk also serves as a county's chief elections administrator if commissioners court has not created a separate elections administrator's office.[54]

District Clerk.   This position, also elected countywide, assists a county's district court or courts by maintaining custody of court documents and records.[55] In small counties, the county clerk is authorized to double as the district clerk, and sixty-two counties combined these two offices in 2008.[56]

County and District Attorneys.   The state's legal interests in both civil and criminal matters are represented at the local level by one of three officers—the **county attorney**, the **district attorney**, or the criminal district attorney. The legislature has enacted numerous provisions for legal departments that vary from county to county. Some counties have no county attorney but have a criminal district attorney. Under state law, others are authorized both a county attorney and a district attorney. Additionally, there are inconsistencies in the specific functions and responsibilities of the offices from county to county.[57] District attorneys prosecute the more serious cases, usually felonies, in the district courts, while the county attorneys prosecute lesser offenses, primarily misdemeanors, in the county courts.[58]

These officers can also provide legal advice and opinions to other county officials and give legal counsel to public officials or employees who have been sued for acts committed in carrying out their official duties. Upon request of the commissioners court, the district attorney or county attorney may initiate lawsuits on behalf of the county. Various other laws charge these attorneys with protecting the public health, assisting the attorney general in cases involving deceptive trade practices, enforcing the state's election laws, collecting delinquent taxes, and even enforcing the Texas Communist Control Act of 1951.[59]

Tax Assessor–Collector.   The property tax is the primary source of revenue for counties. Although the commissioners court sets property tax rates, the **county tax assessor–collector**, another elected officer, has the task of ascertaining who owns what property, how much tax is owed on that property, then collecting the tax. In counties with fewer than 10,000 people, these responsibilities are assigned to the sheriff, unless voters decide to create a separate tax assessor–collector office. Thirteen counties, mainly those below 5,000 in population, continue to let the sheriff handle the job.[60]

Prior to reforms enacted in the 1970s, the tax assessor–collector also was responsible for appraising property or determining its value. This process was often steeped in politics because the higher the value of a piece of property, the more taxes its owner has to pay. Lowering property values for selected friends or supporters gave those holding this office considerable power, which often was abused. In an effort to move toward greater consistency across the state and to enhance the professionalism of tax appraisals, the legislature now requires each county to create an **appraisal district** that is separate from the tax office.[61] The appraisal district, whose members represent other local governmental units, now determines the value of all property in the county. The district also certifies the tax rolls, and other governmental units are required by law to use its appraisals.[62]

County Law Enforcement.   **Sheriffs** and **constables**, a county's law enforcement officers, are part of an old tradition under the Anglo-Saxon legal system. Each county has one sheriff with countywide jurisdiction, but the number of constables can vary. In counties with fewer than 18,000 residents, the commissioners court can designate the entire county as a single justice of the peace precinct or can create as many as four precincts, with each precinct assigned one constable. In the large counties, as many as eight justice of the peace precincts can be created with a constable assigned to each. Most larger counties have four constables.[63]

In a small rural county, the sheriff is the primary law enforcement officer for the entire county. But in the urban counties, city police departments generally assume exclusive jurisdiction in the incorporated municipal areas, leaving the sheriff jurisdiction over the unincorporated areas. Most sheriffs have considerable discretion in the hiring, promotion, and firing of deputies and other employees, although some counties have adopted a merit employment system for the sheriff's office. The sheriff also serves as the administrative officer for the district and county courts.

Constables are authorized to patrol their precincts, make arrests, and conduct criminal investigations, but their primary function is to serve as administrative officers of the justice of the peace courts. They are responsible for serving subpoenas, executing judgments of the court, and delivering other legal documents.[64]

County governments are responsible for constructing and staffing county jails, which are managed in most counties by the sheriff and in some counties by a jail administrator. During the late 1980s and early 1990s, counties across the state pursued an aggressive policy of jail construction in response to court decisions, increased crime rates, and a shortage of state prison space. Jail construction was a "growth" industry during this period,

How would you like to spend a few days here? Prior to federal court intervention, many local governments maintained aging jails that were small, crowded, and unsanitary. Most counties have replaced their aging jails, but Blanco County still utilizes the jail that was constructed in 1893 while awaiting completion of a new facility.

but by the mid-1990s some counties found that they had overextended their finances to construct these jails. They also were left with excess jail capacity after the state built new prisons. To compensate for these problems, several counties contracted with other states to house their prisoners in Texas jails.

All counties are authorized to create an office of medical examiner. This individual is appointed by commissioners court and determines the cause of death of murder victims or others who die under suspicious or unusual circumstances. In counties that do not have a medical examiner, the justice of the peace is charged with conducting an inquest to determine if there are conditions to merit an autopsy.

Counties, either individually or as part of multicounty judicial districts, are required to provide facilities for a criminal probation office. Probation standards are set by the state. Funded by the state, the chief adult probation officer of a county is chosen by the district judges, who supervise the office.

County Auditor. All counties with 10,000 or more population are required to have a county auditor, and smaller counties may have one if the commissioners court chooses. Two counties with fewer than 25,000 residents may jointly agree to hire an auditor to serve both counties. The **county auditor** is appointed by the district judges of the county for a two-year term. He or she is primarily responsible for reviewing every bill and expenditure of a county to assure its correctness and legality. Such oversight can, in effect, impose budgetary restrictions on commissioners court and produce political conflict with other county officers.

The role of the auditor varies from county to county. In counties with more than 225,000 people, the auditor is the budget officer who prepares the county budget for submission to commissioners court unless an alternative has been authorized by the legislature.[65] In smaller counties, the commissioners court prepares the budget, based on estimates provided by the auditor.

County Treasurer. This officer is responsible for receiving and disbursing county funds. Although this office has existed since 1846, its primary functions are now carried out by the county auditor, and constitutional amendments eliminated this office in nine counties.

CRITICISMS OF COUNTY GOVERNMENT

The structure of county government in Texas, designed for a rural state, has inhibited efforts of urban counties to respond to growing needs for public services. The state has experimented with county home rule, but the provisions were so poorly written, confusing, and contradictory that local home rule at the county level was never given a real chance. Efforts were made in the 1997 and 1999 sessions of the legislature to amend the constitution to once again allow counties to adopt home rule, but there was limited statewide support for this change.

Even though the county functions primarily as an extension, or administrative subdivision, of state government, there is little supervision of the counties by the state and wide disparity in the way counties interpret and administer their functions. Some counties do a very good job; others have a dismal record. The fragmentation represented by several independently elected officers always poses the potential for jurisdictional conflict, administrative inefficiency, and even government deadlock.

Like other local governments in Texas, counties rely heavily on the property tax for revenue but cannot exceed tax rate limits set by the state constitution. Those limits reflected a general apprehension about government when they were initially set in 1876. They now further restrict the counties' ability to provide services.

Historically, county courthouses have been associated with political patronage and the **spoils system**. Victorious candidates have claimed the right to appoint personal and political friends to work for them, and state courts have held that elected county officials have wide discretion in the selection of their employees. Reformers have advocated a civil service system for county employees based on merit and competitive examinations and offering job security from one election to the next. A 1971 law allows counties with more than 200,000 population to create a **civil service system**, but it excludes several county offices, including the district attorney. An elected public official retains considerable control over the initial hiring of employees through a probationary period of six months.[66]

SPECIAL DISTRICTS IN TEXAS

Every day, Texans utilize the services of municipal utility districts (MUDs), water conservation and improvement districts (WCIDs), hospital districts, and a host of other local governments, which have been deemed by some as the "invisible governments" of the state.[67] There are approximately 3,400 such governmental units across Texas classified as **special districts**, and every year additional ones are created. These include drainage districts, navigation districts, fresh water supply districts, river authorities, underground water districts, sanitation districts, housing authorities, and soil conservation districts. School districts are also considered a form of special district.

Functions and Structures

Special districts are units of local government created by the state to perform specific functions. Wide variations in their functions, taxing and borrowing authority, governance, and performance limit generalizations about them. Most special districts are authorized to perform a single function and are designated single-purpose districts. But some are multipurpose districts because the laws creating them permit them to provide more than one service to constituents. For example, in addition to providing water to people in their service areas, MUDs may assume responsibility for drainage, solid waste collection, firefighting, parks, and other recreational facilities.[68] Some districts, such as hospital districts, normally cover an entire county. Others, such as MUDs, cover part of one county, while still others, such as river authorities, cover a number of counties.

A special district is governed by a board, either appointed by other governmental units or elected in nonpartisan elections. The board members of hospital districts are appointed by county commissioners courts; city housing authority boards are appointed by mayors or city councils. Many of these districts have taxing and borrowing authority, but others have no taxing powers and are supported by user fees or funds dedicated to them by other governmental agencies. Many special districts are eligible for federal grants-in-aid.

Special districts exist for a variety of reasons. Independent school districts were created, in part, to depoliticize education and remove the responsibility for it from county and city governments. Reformers in the late nineteenth and early twentieth centuries argued that the governance of schools had to be autonomous and insulated from partisan politics. That goal could be accomplished only by the creation of districts that had their own governing bodies and tax bases. Similar arguments also have been made about other specialized governmental functions.[69]

In some cases, existing governments are unwilling or unable—because of state restrictions on their tax, debt, or jurisdictional authority—to provide essential services to developing communities. Counties are particularly limited by state law and the constitution and do not have the authority to provide many of the services now demanded by their citizens. So special districts were created to fill the gap. Since many districts can be created by statute, it has been far easier to create an additional layer of government than change the authority or powers of existing governments by constitutional amendment.[70]

The cost of providing a particular governmental service is another reason for the growth of special districts. By creating a special district that includes a number of governmental units and a larger population and tax base, the costs can be spread over a wider area. Special districts often are promoted by individuals, groups, or corporations for selfish gains (see "The Ambitious Little Water District"). Builders, for example, sometimes develop plans for large tracts of land in the unincorporated areas of a county and then get local governments or the legislature to create municipal utility or water districts to provide water and sewer services.[71]

Some special districts have been designed to serve specific geographical areas. River basins that extend for thousands of square miles and cover ten or twenty counties

The Ambitious Little Water District

Most Texans have never heard of sparsely populated Roberts County, which sits over the Ogallala Aquifer in the Texas Panhandle. And it is highly unlikely that they have heard of Roberts County Water District #1, a "fresh water supply district" approved in 2007 by voters owning land in the eight square miles comprising the district. Yet, high-stakes politics over water supplies and private property rights are being played out in the district's organization.

Communities throughout the Southwest are facing severe water shortages that, if not cured, will limit their abilities to continue to grow and prosper. There also has been a quiet effort by some wealthy individuals, including oilman T. Boone Pickens of Dallas, to fill their needs and reap profits by purchasing water rights in sparsely populated areas that have access to underground water.

Roberts County Water District #1 sits over land to which Pickens has water rights and is the vehicle he has designed to pump water from the Ogallala through a pipeline to Dallas, some 300 miles away. He also may build transmission lines to transmit power from wind farms to metropolitan areas in the central part of the state.

Pickens initially tried to organize this water district in 2002 but was rebuffed by a group of Roberts County residents who initiated a plan for a countywide water district over which he would have little control. So Pickens pursued another strategy.

During the 2006 election cycle, he gave $1.2 million to political candidates and political committees, including sixteen state senators and one-third of the members of the Texas House. Pickens also spent some $1 million on lobbyists working the Texas legislature in 2007.

During that session, the legislature enacted changes in state law to give Pickens virtual carte blanche to organize a special district with wide-ranging powers. The law pertaining to special districts was modified to permit people who owned property within the district but lived elsewhere to vote in the organization election. At the same time, lawmakers resisted efforts to make substantive changes in eminent domain laws, which give governments the power to take private property for public use. Consequently, the water district contemplated by Pickens would have eminent domain powers extending hundreds of miles beyond the small district's boundaries.

There was no doubt what the outcome of the election on the district's creation in November 2007 would be. Only five voters owned land in the district, and all had business relationships with Pickens. The oilman had sold them small parcels of his huge holdings shortly after the end of the 2007 legislative session and before the November election. Two were residents of Roberts County, and three lived hundreds of miles away from the district.

As Pickens' plans for pumping water from the Ogallala unfold, it may become evident how a special district can be used by individuals or corporations to advance their own economic interests.

Pickens' water supply district will provide him with a wide range of legal powers to expedite the delivery of water to customers hundreds of miles away. Using the so-called "right of recapture" (access to water under one's own property), Pickens anticipates pumping 200,000 acre feet of water out of the aquifer each year, which could place additional stress on the primary water source of West Texas. Using the power of eminent domain, he can force landowners to sell him access to their land for a pipeline. And if his plans for a wind farm materialize, he could also use those easements to build power lines. What is significant for the present are the actions of the legislature that weakened the public's control over the organization and governance of special districts. This opened the way for individuals or corporations to pursue actions that could be potentially harmful to a large number of Texans.[72]

have presented a particular problem. Because no existing governments had jurisdiction over the use of water resources in these basins, river authorities with multicounty jurisdictions were created.[73]

Consequences of Single-Purpose Districts

From one perspective, special districts compensate for the fragmentation and limited authority of local government that exists throughout Texas. But, ironically, these districts also contribute to further fragmentation and delay the more difficult development of comprehensive, multipurpose governmental units that could more efficiently provide public services.

A special district has been called a "halfway house between cityhood and non-cityhood, between incorporation and nonincorporation."[74] Residents of a developing community or subdivision may not want to create a new city or become part of a nearby existing city, but they need certain basic services, such as water, electricity, and fire protection, some of which could be provided through the creation of special districts.

Many special districts are small operations with limited financial resources and few employees. Salaries often are low, and some districts have difficulty retaining the licensed technical people required to perform daily operations. In some cases, record keeping and management operations are shoddy and amateurish, and the costs of providing services by many of these operations may actually be higher than what similar services cost in larger governmental systems. Special districts may also use outside legal and professional assistance, which can be very costly, and many districts lack the expertise to maximize their investments or borrowing potential.[75]

Some special districts expand their functions beyond the original purpose for which they were created. The metropolitan transit authority in San Antonio, for example, authorized under state law to impose a 1 percent sales tax for public transportation, became involved in building the Alamodome, a multipurpose convention and sports facility. As governments expand their functions, there is a greater potential for intergovernmental rivalry, conflict, deadlock, and duplication of costs.

Except for the 1,000-plus independent school districts and a small number of other highly visible districts, such as river authorities, most special districts operate in anonymity. The public has only limited knowledge of their jurisdiction, management, operations, or performance. Many taxpayers may not be aware they pay taxes to some of these entities, nor do they have any concept of the districts' indebtedness. There is little media coverage of their work, few individuals attend their board meetings, and turnout for their elections is extremely low. In the case of the governing boards that are appointed by other governmental agencies, the appointment process is often dominated by a small number of individuals or groups who also dominate the activities of the special district. This domination is probably the most damning indictment of special districts.

INDEPENDENT SCHOOL DISTRICTS ●

The current controversies over educational quality and equity in Texas have roots in the early organization and governance of the public schools. Education was an issue in the Texas independence movement, but it was the Reconstruction period that set the stage for many of the long-term issues of school finance and governance. During Reconstruction, the Radical Republicans attempted to centralize the education system at the state level. But with the end of Republican control prior to the constitutional convention of 1875, the centralized system was eliminated and the control and financing of public education were transferred to the counties.

Instead of an orderly, comprehensive system that assured public education to every child in the state, community schools were created. They could be formed by any group of parents petitioning the county judge, who had considerable influence and control over the schools. County judges could appoint trustees nominated by the organizing parents and distribute money from the state's Available School Fund to the organized schools within their respective counties. This produced marked differences in the availability, funding, and quality of public education across the state. Community schools also were self-selective. People who initiated the creation of a school could decide which children could attend. Consequently, there was racial and economic segregation, and the children of Texans with limited political clout were denied access to an adequate public education. These characteristics dominated public education in Texas at the end of the nineteenth century, and vestiges remained until 1909.

The **independent school district**, currently the basic organizational structure for public education in Texas, had its origins in the Constitution of 1876. Cities and towns were allowed to create independent school districts and to impose a tax to support them. Initially, the city government served as the school board, but in 1879 a school district was

School days, school days. School boards, such as the East Central Independent School District Board shown here, are responsible for policy and budgeting, leaving day-to-day management of a school district to the superintendent.

permitted to organize independently of the city or town, elect its own board of trustees, and impose its own school tax. But residents of rural areas, where most nineteenth-century Texans lived, were denied these powers and had only the option of forming community schools. So, in effect, Texas operated under a dual school system, with the majority of students subject to the discretionary and often arbitrary powers of county governments.

Inequities in the Public Education System

From the very beginning, the inequities in such a school system were clear to many parents, elected officials, and educators, and there were early efforts to reform and modernize public schools. Most were linked to national education reform movements funded by northern philanthropists after the Civil War to promote public education in the South. George Peabody of Massachusetts created the Peabody Education Fund in 1867 to be followed by others, including John D. Rockefeller, who established the General Education Board. These organizations provided financial aid and technical support to leaders of state reform movements during the early part of the twentieth century.

There has been an ongoing saga of educational reform efforts in Texas. Early initiatives focused on the accessibility of schools to children in rural areas, compulsory school attendance, funding, recruiting teachers, and teacher training. Schools were segregated, and school revenues were tied to local property taxes. Subsequent reforms were directed at the structure and governance of local school districts. The diverse and fragmented structure of Texas schools has been modified over the years through consolidation, greater uniformity in the organization of school districts, the extension of the independent school district to virtually every community in the state, and the expansion of the authority of the Texas Education Agency.

Texas now has more than 4.6 million children in public schools and a host of new issues, including bilingual and special education, graduation rates, student performance, and mandated testing for progress and accountability (see Chapter 13).

Differences among School Districts

Although regulation and coordination are provided on a statewide level through the State Board of Education (SBOE) and the Texas Education Agency (TEA), public education is now administered through approximately 1,050 local school districts, which include some 7,800 schools. In the 2007–2008 school year, some of the smallest, rural school districts had fewer than 75 students. The largest, the Houston Independent School District, had 198,000 students. The sixteen largest districts—with more than 50,000 students each—enrolled approximately 1.3 million or 28 percent of the 4.6 million students attending pre-kindergarten through grade 12. By contrast, 433 rural districts, most serving fewer than 500 students each, enrolled 144,000 students. Students from minority ethnic or racial groups constituted 65 percent of the public school population in Texas in 2007–2008, and their numbers are projected to increase.[76]

As might be expected, school districts also vary in financial resources, facilities, graduation rates, and other performance measures.

Local School Governance

School districts are governed by **school boards**, ranging in size from three to nine members; most have seven. Trustees are elected in nonpartisan elections for terms that vary from two to six years, with most serving three-year terms. By 2008, 161 of the 1,000-plus school districts elected their boards from single-member districts.[77] School districts with significant minority populations have shifted from at-large elections to single-member districting, primarily as a consequence of lawsuits or the threats of lawsuits by minority plaintiffs under the Voting Rights Act.

Most school board elections are held on the first Saturday in May, the same day most cities hold their elections. School board election turnouts are low, usually less than 10 percent of registered voters. But turnout increases when there are highly visible issues, such as the firing of a superintendent or a dramatic increase in taxes. One unanticipated consequence of single-member districts has been a general decline in voter turnout for school board elections.

Recruiting qualified candidates for school boards often is difficult, and many elections are uncontested. Individuals are asked to run by the superintendent, other members of the board, or key community leaders, many of whom point out that it is difficult to find people who are willing to give the required time and energy. Individuals often have little knowledge of what school board members do, and because many trustees serve for only one term, some boards have high turnover rates. Moreover, there is no way for a potential trustee to anticipate the amount of time it will take for briefings by the superintendent and staff, preparing for and participating in board meetings, and taking phone calls from parents and taxpayers. A board member must also deal with the political aspect of the job, including attendance at community functions and major school programs and meeting with teachers and taxpayer groups. Board members receive no salaries but are reimbursed for travel related to board business.

The most important decision that a school board makes is the hiring of a **school superintendent**. In organization and management structure, the school district is similar to the council–manager form of government used by many cities. The board hires a superintendent, who is in charge of the district's day-to-day operations. Although the board has the primary policymaking responsibility for a district, part-time board members are often dominated by the superintendent and the superintendent's staff. School trustees and superintendents tend to talk about "keeping politics out of education," and superintendents often attempt to convey the impression that they serve simply to carry out the will of their boards. In most instances, however, a school board's agenda is established by the superintendent, and the board members depend on the superintendent and other professional staff members for information and policy recommendations. Very few board members have much time to give to the district, and most have only limited knowledge of the many laws affecting education. State law, in fact, restricts the intrusion of board members into the daily management and administration of a district. An excessively politicized school board that becomes involved in day-to-day administration can be called to task by the Texas Education Agency. In an extreme case, the TEA can even take over the management of a school district.

SOLUTIONS TO THE PROBLEMS OF LOCAL GOVERNMENTS

Privatization of Functions

As local governments have juggled their financial problems with increased demands for public services, they have resorted to contracting out some services to private companies. Many governments believe **privatization** can reduce costs through businesslike efficiency, and they consider it an attractive alternative in the face of voter hostility toward higher taxes. Cities, for example, are contracting for garbage pickup, waste disposal, towing, food services, security, and a variety of other services. Privatization also provides a way for local governments that have reached their limit on bonded indebtedness to make new capital improvements by leasing a facility from a private contractor. A civic center or school facility can be constructed by a private contractor and leased back to the government for an extended period.

Annexation and Extraterritorial Jurisdiction

Population growth in the areas surrounding most large Texas cities has forced municipalities and counties to wrestle with urban sprawl. El Paso, for example, included 26 square miles in 1950 but had expanded to 248 square miles by 2009. Houston grew from 160 square miles in 1950 to 596 square miles in 2009, with its extraterritorial jurisdiction encompassing 1,312 square miles, excluding the cities that lie within this area.[78]

The cities' ability to expand their boundaries beyond suburban development derives from their annexation powers and **extraterritorial jurisdiction** over neighboring areas. With the Municipal Annexation Act of 1963, the legislature granted cities considerable discretionary authority over nearby unincorporated areas. Specific annexation powers and extraterritorial jurisdiction vary with the size of a city and the charter under which it functions. Generally, cities have extraterritorial jurisdiction over unincorporated areas within one-half mile to five miles of the city limits, making development in those areas subject to the city's building codes, zoning and land use restrictions, utility easement requirements, and road and street specifications. This authority restricts the use of unincorporated land and requires those building outside of the city to build according to at least minimal standards. Later, when those areas are annexed by the city, they are less likely to quickly degenerate into suburban slums that will require a high infusion of city dollars for basic services.

Residents and businesses outside of a city's corporate limits also benefit from access to public and private facilities and services in the city. It is argued that they should "share the tax burden associated with constructing and maintaining those facilities and services."[79]

Cities can annex areas equivalent to 10 percent of their existing territory in a given year, and if this authority is not exercised in one year, it can be carried over to subsequent years. Annexation usually does not require a vote of those people who are to be incorporated into the city. However, within two and a half years, a city is required to provide annexed areas with services comparable to those provided in its older neighborhoods. Otherwise, individuals living in these newly annexed areas can exercise an option to be de-annexed, a situation that rarely occurs.

Cities have even annexed thin strips of land, miles from urban development, along major roads and arteries leading into them. Since a city's extraterritorial jurisdiction extended as far as five miles on either side of the strip that was annexed, this practice has enabled a city to control future development in a large area. In San Antonio, these annexation policies have often been referred to as "spoke annexation," and it has taken more than thirty years for much of the territory brought under the city's jurisdiction to be developed and annexed by the city.[80]

The aggressive use of annexation has permitted most large cities in Texas to expand geographically with population growth. Texas cities have been able to share in the benefits of growth in the areas surrounding them and limit the development of small suburban towns that would potentially limit future expansion.[81]

For more than thirty years after the enactment of the Municipal Annexation Act, the state legislature did little to restrict the annexation powers of the cities, but in recent legislative sessions, many lawmakers have demonstrated, along with their constituents, an anti-city sentiment with proposals that would have eroded municipal authority, reduced municipal revenues, and imposed costly new mandates. Of particular concern to cities were attacks on annexation powers. The Seventy-Fifth Legislature in 1999 enacted a major overhaul of annexation authority, including a provision that requires cities to outline their annexation plans three years in advance. But cities felt that they were able to obtain, through their lobbying efforts, a relatively "well-balanced" law.[82] The legislature in 2001 continued to reflect growing suburban-rural hostility toward the central cities. It enacted a law that modified the extraterritorial jurisdiction of cities by requiring city-county agreements on the regulation of subdivisions.[83]

Modernization of County Government

City governments provide most basic public services in urban areas, and as cities expand to county boundaries and beyond, there is increased overlapping jurisdiction of county and city governments and a reduction of county services in the annexed areas. Counties, nevertheless, still play an important role in Texas. Rural Texans, in particular, continue to rely on counties to provide a number of services, and demands on counties will increase. Recommendations to modernize county government include another attempt at county home rule, granting counties some legislative or ordinance-making authority, modernizing county information and communications systems, and creating an office of county administrator, appointed by commissioners court, to run the departments now assigned to commissioners. Another recommendation is to extend the civil service system to smaller counties and to all county employees.[84]

Economic Development

Historically, cities have collaborated with the private sector to stimulate local economies. Private sector initiatives have come from chambers of commerce or economic development foundations, corporations, other groups, or individuals, and city governments have participated. Cities also are using a variety of new financing techniques to assist in economic development, including development impact taxes and fees, user charges, creation of special district assessments, tax increment financing, and privatization of governmental functions.[85]

A state law was enacted in 1989 to permit cities, with the approval of local voters, to impose a 0.5 percent sales tax for local economic development.[86] By 2005, voters in more than 500 Texas cities had approved this tax option.

Texas cities, as well as some counties, aggressively court American and foreign companies to relocate or develop new plants or operations in their communities. Cities and local chambers of commerce sponsor public relations campaigns touting local benefits and attractions. Local governments offer **tax abatements**—exemptions from property taxes on a business for a specified period—to encourage a company to locate or expand in a particular Texas city. Other financial incentives to companies being courted include lowered utility bills and assistance in obtaining housing for employees. Many cities have established relationships with "sister cities" in foreign countries, and state government has assisted cities by establishing trade and commerce offices in a few key foreign cities. The city of San Antonio aggressively wooed Toyota to locate a new manufacturing plant in South Texas, and the coordinated efforts of the city, the state, and the private sector resulted in a decision in 2003 to bring the new plant to the city. State and local officials predicted the facility would be a major economic generator and help transform the city's economy. By 2006, the plant was in production and had built several thousand trucks by the end of the year.

The legislature has permitted counties to form industrial development corporations or enterprise zones and to relax state regulatory policies to encourage the redevelopment of depressed areas. Portions of a county may be designated as reinvestment zones, in which tax abatements can be offered to attract new businesses. Counties also can create county boards of development, civic centers, foreign trade zones, and research and development authorities.[87]

A wide range of federal programs for local economic development also are available. Most depend on local initiatives in the planning and application process and require a political commitment by elected officials and a demonstrated rationale for the receipt of federal dollars.

Interlocal Contracting

Because many small governments have limited tax bases and staffs, they enter into contracts with larger governments for various public services. In 1971, the legislature, following a constitutional amendment, enacted the Interlocal Cooperation Act, which gave cities, counties, and other political subdivisions rather broad authority for such contracts.[88] The law has been amended several times to expand the scope of these agreements, and local governments are now contracting with each other for services in at least twenty-five functional areas, ranging from aviation to water and wastewater management.[89] Contracting is not an alternative to consolidation of local governments, but it does hold out some promise for improving the quality of local services and reducing their costs.

Metro Government and Consolidation

In the metropolitan areas of the state's ten largest counties, there are more than 1,100 cities, school districts and special districts providing public services. In Harris County (Houston) alone, there are 487 separate governmental units (see Table 12–4). Legislators, scholars, and reform groups have extensively studied the duplication and other problems produced by such proliferation and fragmentation and have made numerous recommendations over the years. There have been a variety of proposals designed to eliminate duplication and overlap, including city-county consolidation and various forms of **metro government**. Efforts initiated by San Antonio and Bexar County to obtain constitutional authority to propose city-county consolidation to voters in the county failed in the 1997 legislative session. Other metropolitan areas joined Bexar County and San Antonio in an expanded effort to obtain this authority from the legislature in the 1999 session, but again it failed. Without such authority, county-city collaboration is more likely to take the form of increased intergovernmental contracting and the informal cooperation that local governments develop out of necessity and mutual self-interest.[90]

Public Improvement Districts

Under one state law, property owners in a specific area of a city or its extraterritorial jurisdiction can petition the city to create a special **public improvement district**. These districts can undertake a wide range of improvements—landscaping, lighting, signs,

TABLE 12–4   Local Governments in the Ten Largest and Ten Smallest Texas Counties, 2007

	Population (2007)	Total	County	Municipal	School Districts	Special Districts
State	**23,904,380**	**4,835**	**254**	**1,209**	**1,081**	**2,291**
Harris	3,891,420	487	1	28	24	434
Dallas	2,364,853	63	1	25	16	21
Tarrant	1,699,919	67	1	34	18	14
Bexar	1,579,414	51	1	22	16	12
Travis	947,215	79	1	15	8	55
El Paso	747,477	36	1	6	10	19
Hidalgo	719,940	77	1	22	16	38
Collin	731,350	51	1	24	15	11
Denton	615,019	69	1	33	11	24
Fort Bend	510,868	138	1	16	5	116
Glasscock	1,219	4	1		1	2
Sterling	1,202	5	1	1	1	2
Terrell	1,005	4	1		1	2
McMullen	860	5	1		1	3
Roberts	848	4	1	1	1	1
Kent	815	5	1	1	1	2
Borden	700	2	1		1	
Kenedy	364	2	1		1	
King	356	3	1		1	1
Loving	61	2	1			1

Sources: U.S. Census Bureau, *Census of Governments, 2007, Government Organization;* and Texas State Data Center, *2007 Total Population Estimates for Texas Counties, October 2008.*

sidewalks, streets, pedestrian malls, libraries, parking, water, wastewater, and drainage facilities. Public improvement districts do not have the same autonomy as other special districts. They are created solely through the discretionary powers of the city and are funded by assessments on property within their boundaries.[91] Although their budgets and assessments must be approved by the city, they can be operated and managed by private management companies or by the citizens themselves. Fort Worth created a special improvement district for its downtown area in 1986, and other cities have considered the option.

SUMMARY AND CONCLUSIONS

1. Local governments in Texas are the creations of the state and have only those powers granted to them by the state constitution and statutes. With limited discretionary authority but a great deal of responsibility, local governments often find it difficult to respond effectively to the needs of their citizens.

2. More than 83 percent of the state's population lives in urban areas. Texas cities have highly diverse social structures, economies, and historical traditions and,

subsequently, there are marked differences in urban politics across the state. Eight of the ten largest cities have more than 50 percent minority populations, contributing to a long-standing controversy over urban electoral systems.

3. Texas cities with fewer than 5,000 people are designated general law cities and are limited as to what form of government they can use. Cities with more than 5,000 people can function as home rule cities, choosing a form of government that satisfies community needs as long as it does not conflict with the state constitution or statutes. Over the state's history, Texas cities have experimented with three forms of government—mayor-council, commission, and council–manager. The choices reflect complex political dynamics, and as social, economic, and political environments change, cities often change their form of government.

4. A notable feature of city politics in Texas is the widespread use of nonpartisan, at-large elections. In homogeneous communities, these election systems appear to work quite well. But in communities with highly diverse racial, economic, and social groups—in which voting is polarized—at-large elections adversely affect key segments of the population. Prompted by legal attacks on at-large elections under the Voting Rights Act, many cities, as well as special purpose districts, have adopted single-member districts, thus increasing minority representation on local governing bodies.

5. County governments, initially created to serve a rural population, function primarily as the administrative subdivisions of the state. Much like state government, county government is highly fragmented with administrative powers shared by a variety of elected officials.

6. Thousands of special-purpose districts provide numerous public services and add to the fragmentation of local government. Most people know little about their jurisdiction, structure, functions, and leadership, making them the "invisible governments" of Texas.

7. Texas has approximately 1,050 independent school districts, which are working to improve the quality of education against a backdrop of social, cultural, and financial problems.

8. Federal and state governments have imposed additional requirements on the cities through mandates and preemptions that are increasingly straining local resources.

9. Texas cities are now facing many of the same problems of the nation's older cities. Increased population, urban sprawl, white flight, an increase in the aging and low-income populations and inadequate, declining infrastructures require cities to look for solutions that will avert a decline in urban living conditions.

10. Local governments are using a variety of strategies to deal with their problems. Cities have used their annexation powers and extraterritorial jurisdiction to expand their tax bases and exercise limited controls over development in adjacent areas. Cities are also using public improvement districts to permit targeted areas to impose additional taxes for needed services. Both counties and cities are privatizing governmental functions to decrease costs and increase efficiency. Interlocal contracting permits governments to provide services to each other on a contractual basis, and many counties and cities are engaged in aggressive economic development programs. Some people advocate governmental consolidation, but there is limited support for this alternative in Texas.

KEY TERMS

Dillon rule   381
Annexation   382
Population density   383
General law cities   385
Home rule cities   385
City charter   385
Weak mayor   387
Strong mayor   387
City commission   389

Council–manager government   390
Nonpartisan elections   395
At-large elections   396
Runoff elections   396
Single-member districts   396
Regressive taxes   397
Rollback election   398
General obligation bonds   399

Revenue bonds   399
Homestead exemption   400
Mandate   401
Commissioners court   403
County judge   404
County clerk   406
County attorney   406
District attorney   406
County tax assessor–collector   407

FURGER READING ⎯⎯⎯⎯⎯⎯⎯⎯⎯⎯⎯⎯⎯⎯⎯⎯⎯⎯⎯⎯⎯⎯⎯ ●

Articles

Davidson, Chandler, and Luis Ricardo Fraga, "Slating Groups as Parties in a Nonpartisan Setting," *Western Political Quarterly* 41, (June 1988), pp. 373–90.

Jones, Laurence, Curtis Hawk, and Delbert A. Taebel, "Political Changes and Partisanship in Texas County Government," *Texas Journal of Political Studies* 11 (Spring–Summer 1989), pp. 28–42.

Thomas, Robert, "City Charters and Their Political Implications," in *Perspectives on American and Texas Politics,* edited by Donald S. Lutz and Kent L. Tedin. Dubuque, IA: Kendall/Hunt, 1987.

Reynolds, Morgan O., "General Ordinance-Making Powers for County Governments in Texas," Special Report, Texas Real Estate Research Center, College Station, TX: College of Agriculture, Texas A&M University, August 1985.

Rice, Bradley R., "The Galveston Plan of City Government by Commission: The Birth of a Progressive Idea," *Southwestern Historical Quarterly* 78 (April 1975), pp. 36–48.

Zax, Jeffrey S., "Election Methods and Black and Hispanic City Council Membership," *Social Science Quarterly* 71 (June 1990), pp. 339–55.

Books

Bridges, Amy, *Morning Glories: Municipal Reform in the Southwest.* Princeton, NJ: Princeton University Press, 1997.

Brooks, David B., *Texas Practice: County and Special District Law,* vols. 35 and 36. St. Paul, MN: West, 1989.

Bullard, Robert D., *Invisible Houston: The Black Experience in Boom and Bust.* College Station, TX: Texas A&M University Press, 1987.

Burns, Nancy, *The Formation of American Local Governments.* New York: Oxford University Press, 1994.

De Leon, Arnoldo, *Ethnicity in the Sunbelt: A History of Mexican Americans in Houston.* Houston, TX: University of Houston Press, 1989.

Domhoff, G. William, *Who Really Rules? New Haven and Community Power Reexamined.* Santa Monica, CA: Goodyear Publishing Company, Inc., 1978.

Feagin, Joe R., *Free Enterprise City: Houston in Political–Economic Perspective.* New Brunswick, NJ: Rutgers University Press, 1988.

Hanson, Russell L., ed., *Governing Partners: State-Local Relations in the United States.* Boulder, CO: Westview, 1998.

Hawley, Willis D., *Nonpartisan Elections and the Case for Party Politics.* New York: John Wiley & Sons, 1973.

Herzog, Lawrence A., *Where North Meets South: Cities, Space and Politics on the United States–Mexico Border.* Austin, TX: University of Texas Press, 1990.

Johnson, David R., John A. Booth, and Richard J. Harris, eds., *The Politics of San Antonio: Community, Progress, and Power.* Lincoln, NE: University of Nebraska Press, 1983.

McComb, David G., *Houston: A History.* Austin, TX: University of Texas Press, 1981.

Marando, Vincent L., and Robert D. Thomas, *The Forgotten Governments: County Commissioners as Policy Makers.* Gainesville, FL: University Presses of Florida, 1977.

Miller, Char, and Heywood T. Sanders, eds., *Urban Texas.* College Station, TX: Texas A&M University Press, 1990.

Orum, Anthony M., Power, Money and the People: *The Making of Modern Austin.* Austin, TX: Texas Monthly Press, 1987.

Perrenod, Virginia Marion, *Special Districts, Special Purposes: Fringe Governments and Urban Problems in the Houston Area.* College Station, TX: Texas A&M University Press, 1984.

Perry, David C., and Alfred J. Watkins, eds., *The Rise of the Sunbelt Cities.* Beverly Hills, CA: Sage, 1977.

Polsby, Nelson, *Community Power and Political Theory,* 2nd ed. New Haven, CT: Yale University Press, 1980.

Syed, Anwar Hussain, *The Political Theory of American Local Government.* New York: Random House, 1966.

Thometz, Carol Estes, *The Decision-Makers: The Power Structure of Dallas.* Dallas, TX: Southern Methodist University Press, 1963.

Thrombley, Woodworth G., *Special Districts and Authorities in Texas.* Austin, TX: University of Texas, 1959.

Wolff, Nelson W., *Mayor: An Inside View of San Antonio Politics, 1981–1995.* San Antonio, TX: San Antonio Express-News, 1997.

Young, Roy E., *The Place System in Texas Elections.* Austin, TX: Institute of Public Affairs, University of Texas, 1965.

Websites

State of Texas   http://www.state.tx.us/   This site provides access to websites for all counties in Texas as well as the Councils of Government. Select cities have developed web pages that can also be accessed through this site. Information varies, with some sites providing more comprehensive information than others.

Texas Association of Counties   http://www.county.org/ This association serves county governments throughout the state. Links to related organizations can be found here, as well as information on recent legislation and laws pertaining to counties, support services, news releases, and educational programs for county officials.

Texas Municipal League   http://www.tml.org/   This organization provides a range of services to Texas cities. In addition to providing links to affiliate organizations, this site provides information on the association's publications, programs, and services, including its legislative policy program.

Texas Association of School Boards   http://www.tasb.org/ The Texas Association of School Boards serves the 1,000-plus state school districts through policy advocacy and support services. This site includes links to many of the school districts as well as information pertaining to services, programs, and publications.

ENDNOTES

1. James Bryce, *Modern Democracies,* vol. 1 (New York: Macmillan, 1921), p. 133.
2. Alexis de Tocqueville, *Democracy in America* with an introduction by Joseph Epstein (New York: Bantam Dell, 2004), p. 75.
3. Anwar Hussain Syed, *The Political Theory of American Local Government* (New York: Random House, 1966), p. 27.
4. Ibid., pp. 38–52. Syed presents a summary of Jefferson's theory of local government.
5. Roscoe C. Martin, *Grass Roots* (Tuscaloosa, AL: University of Alabama Press, 1957), p. 5; and Robert C. Wood, *Suburbia* (Boston: Houghton Mifflin, 1958), p. 18.
6. *City of Clinton v. The Cedar Rapids and Missouri River Railroad Co.,* 24 Iowa 455 (1868).
7. Roscoe C. Martin, *The Cities in the Federal System* (New York: Atherton, 1965), pp. 28–35.
8. David B. Brooks, *Texas Practice: County and Special District Law,* vol. 35 (St. Paul, MN: West, 1989), pp. 41–46. A good part of the materials presented on county government rely on this comprehensive work.
9. Advisory Commission on Intergovernmental Relations, *Measuring Local Government Discretionary Authority,* Report M–131 (Washington, DC: ACIR, 1981).
10. Advisory Commission on Intergovernmental Relations, *State and Local Roles in the Federal System* (Washington, DC: ACIR, 1982), pp. 32–33.
11. For an excellent overview of urban development in Texas, see Char Miller and David R. Johnson, "The Rise of Urban Texas," in *Urban Texas: Politics and Development,* edited by Char Miller and Heywood T. Sanders. (College Station: Texas A&M University Press, 1990).
12. U.S. Census Bureau, *American Community Survey, 2007.*
13. See Richard L. Cole, Ann Crowley Smith, and Delbert A. Taebel, with a foreword by Marlan Blissett, *Urban Life in Texas: A Statistical Profile and Assessment of the Largest Cities* (Austin. TX: University of Texas Press, 1986), for an example of rankings of larger Texas cities on various dimensions measuring aspects of urban quality of life.
14. Randy Cain, "TML and Large Cities Approach Legislature Together," *Texas Town and City,* 79 (January 1991), pp. 18–19.
15. "Seventy-fifth Texas Legislature Adjourns," *Texas Town and City,* 84 (June 1997), p. 10; and "Texas Legislature Adjourns," *Texas Town and City,* 88 (June 1999), p. LV1.
16. Texas Municipal League, telephone conversation with research staff, July, 2006.
17. Ibid.
18. Zeke MacCormack, "Boerne Rejects Charter Change," *San Antonio Express–News,* May 7, 2002, p. 5B.
19. Ibid.; and Texas Municipal League research staff, telephone conversation, June 2004.
20. Murray S. Stedman, *Urban Politics,* 2nd ed. (Cambridge, MA: Winthrop, 1975), p. 51.
21. Beryl E. Pettus and Randall W. Bland, *Texas Government Today,* 3rd ed. (Homewood, IL: Dorsey, 1984), p. 347.
22. Telephone call to Office of Human Resources, City of Houston, July 10, 2009.
23. Wilbourn E. Benton, *Texas Politics,* 5th ed. (Chicago: Nelson-Hall, 1984), p. 260.
24. Ernie Mosher, "Suggestions for Public Service," *Texas Town and City 92* (June 2005): 14–16; and Nelson Wolff, "How I See It: Lessons for Leadership," in *Government and Politics in the Lone Star State: Theory and Practice,* 6th ed., edited by L. Tucker Gibson and Clay Robison, (Upper Saddle River, NJ: Prentice Hall, 2008), pp. 397–98.
25. Greg Jefferson and Kelly Guckian, "Fire Department's Overtime is Highest," *San Antonio Express–News,* January 25, 2009; City of Dallas and Human Resources Office budget staff, telephone conversation, July, 2009.
26. City of Austin and City Dallas budget staffs, telephone conversations, December 30, 2003.
27. See the city charter of San Antonio, Article II, Sections 6 and 9.
28. City government websites.
29. Bureau of the Census, *1992 Census of Government,* Table 11.

30. Texas Municipal League research staff, telephone conversation, May 2002.

31. Tom Albin, et al., *Local Government Election Systems* (Austin, TX: Local Government Election Systems Policy Research Project, University of Texas, 1984), p. 2.

32. "Where Do Texas Cities Get Their Money?," *Texas Town and City* 92 (January 2005), pp. 20–21.

33. Ibid,; Frank Sturzl, "The Courses of Municipal Revenue," *Texas Town and City* 93 (June 2006), pp. 14–16.

34. Karen Brooks, "For Uphill Battle, Legislator Was Up to Challenge," *Texas Town and City* 92 (July 2005), pp. 14–15.

35. "Municipal Fiscal Conditions are Improving," *Texas Town and City* 92 (March 2005), pp. 10–13.

36. Texas Comptroller of Public Accounts, "Comptroller Susan Combs Distributes Monthly Sales Tax Revenue to Local Governments," Press Release, July 10, 2009.

37. "Fiscal Conditions Survey Shows Troubling Times Ahead," *Texas Town and City* 96 (March 2009), pp. 22–24, 35.

38. Lawrence E. Jordan, "Municipal Bond Issuance in Texas: The New Realities," *Texas Town and City,* 79 (December 1991), pp. 12, 25.

39. Miller and Sanders, *Urban Texas: Politics and Development,* p. xiv.

40. *Texas Almanac,* 1992–1993 (Dallas, TX: A.H. Belo, 1991), pp. 137–38; and U.S. Census, 2000.

41. American Society of Civil Engineers, "Report Card for American Infrastructure: Texas," September 2008.

42. Jennifer Stowe, "The Emerging Need for Water and Wastewater Affordability Programs," *Texas Town and City* 96 (May 2009), pp. 10–11.

43. Frank Sturzl, "The Tyranny of Environmental Mandates," *Texas Town and City* 79 (September 1991), pp. 14–15, 32, 65–66.

44. Brooks, *Texas Practice: County and Special District Law,* vol. 35, p. 2.

45. Ibid., p. 14.

46. For a sample of Texas court decisions that affirm the general principle of the Dillon rule, that the county can only perform those functions allocated to it by law, see Robert E. Norwood and Sabrina Strawn, *Texas County Government: Let the People Choose,* 2nd ed. (Austin, TX: Texas Research League, 1984), pp. 11–12.

47. Ibid., p. 9.

48. Texas State Data Center, *Estimates for Total Populations of Counties and Places in Texas for July 1, 2007 and January 1, 2008.*

49. Texas Association of Counties, *2008 Salary Survey* (Austin, TX: Texas Association of Counties, 2008).

50. *Avery v. Midland County,* 88 S. Ct. 1114 (1968).

51. Norwood and Strawn, *Texas County Government,* p. 22.

52. Brooks, *Texas Practice: County and Special District Law,* vol. 35, p. 331.

53. Texas Commission on Intergovernmental Relations, *An Introduction to Texas County Government* (Austin, TX, 1980), p. 10.

54. Brooks, *Texas Practice: County and Special District Law,* vol. 35, pp. 392–93.

55. David C. Brooks, *Texas Practice: County and Special District Law,* Vol. 36 (St. Paul, MN: West, 1989), pp. 104–05.

56. Texas Association of Counties, *2005 Salary Survey.*

57. Brooks, *Texas Practice: County and Special District Law,* vol. 36, pp. 4–8.

58. Ibid., pp. 49–50.

59. Ibid., pp. 18–49.

60. Texas Association of Counties, *2008 Salary Survey.*

61. Norwood and Strawn, *Texas County Government,* p. 24.

62. Brooks, *Texas Practice: County and Special District Law,* vol. 35, p. 495.

63. Brooks, *Texas Practice: County and Special District Law,* vol. 36, pp. 122–23.

64. Texas Commission on Intergovernmental Relations, *An Introduction to County Government,* p. 22.

65. Norwood and Strawn, *Texas County Government,* p. 27.

66. Brooks, *Texas Practice: County and Special District Law,* vol. 35, pp. 273–74.

67. Virginia Marion Perrenod, *Special Districts, Special Purposes: Fringe Governments and Urban Problems in the Houston Area* (College Station, TX: Texas A&M University Press, 1984), p. 4.

68. Ibid.

69. Woodworth G. Thrombley, *Special Districts and Authorities in Texas* (Austin: Institute of Public Affairs, University of Texas, 1959), pp. 17–18.

70. Benton, *Texas Politics: Constraints and Opportunities,* p. 282.

71. Perrenod, *Special Districts, Special Purposes,* p. 18.

72. Jim Landers, "T. Boone Pickens to Import Water, Wind Power to North Texas," *Dallas Morning News,* April 18, 2008, p. 3D; and Texans for Public Justice, "Watch Your Assets: T. Boone Pickens Land Grab," October 4, 2007.

73. Thrombley, *Special Districts and Authorities in Texas,* p. 13.

74. Robert S. Lorch, *State and Local Politics,* 3rd ed. (Englewood Cliffs, NJ: Prentice Hall, 1989), p. 246.

75. Ibid., p. 247.

76. Texas Education Agency, *Snapshot 2007–2008: School District Profiles.*

77. Texas Association of School Boards, Membership Services, telephone conversation, April 22, 2008; Summary documents of board electoral systems provided by the TASB.

78. "Houston: City/Community Information," http://www.texasbest.com/houston/houston.html.

79. City of San Marcos, Texas, "Annexation Policies," http://www.ci.san-marcos.tx.us/Annexation-Policies.htm.

80. For a more detailed discussion of annexation authority, see Wilbourn E. Benton, *Texas Politics,* pp. 264–66.

81. Scott N. Houston, "Municipal Annexation in Texas," Texas APA-Southmost Section, McAllen, Texas, November 2004, p. 10.

82. "Texas Legislature Adjourns," *Texas Town and City,* 86 (July 1999), p. 10.

83. "Texas Legislature Adjourns," *Texas Town and City,* 89 (July 2001), p. 11.

84. Norwood and Strawn, *Texas County Government,* pp. 75–81.

85. Joel B. Goldsteen and Russell Fricano, *Municipal Finance Practices and Preferences for New Development: Survey of Texas Cities* (Arlington, TX: Institute of Urban Studies, University of Texas at Arlington, 1988), pp. 3–11.

86. Bill R. Shelton, Bob Bolen, and Ray Perryman, "Passing a Sales Tax Referendum for Economic Development," *Texas Town and City* 79 (September 1991), 10.

87. Brooks, *Texas Practice: County and Special District Law,* vol. 36, pp. 229–42.

88. Tom Adams, "Introduction and Recent Experience with the Interlocal Contract," in *Interlocal Contract in Texas,* edited by Richard W. Tees, Richard L. Cole, and Jay G. Stanford (Arlington, TX: Institute of Urban Studies, University of Arlington, 1990), p. 1.

89. Tees, et al., Interlocal Contract in Texas, pp. B1–B7.

90. Vincent Ostrom, *The Meaning of American Federalism* (San Francisco: Institute for Contemporary Studies, 1991), p. 161. Ostrom suggests that advocates of metropolitan government often overlook the "rich and intricate framework for negotiating, adjudicating, and deciding questions" that are now in place in many urbanized areas with multiple governmental units.

91. Ann Long Diveley and Dwight A. Shupe, "Public Improvement Districts: An Alternative for Financing Public Improvements and Services," *Texas Town and City* 79 (September 1991).

CHAPTER

Contemporary Public Policy Issues in Texas

Questions to Guide Your Reading

1. Does the policymaking process constrain the ability of some groups or sectors of Texas to get governments to respond to their problems?

2. If there is general agreement that most taxes in Texas are regressive, why is there so much opposition to a state income tax, a progressive tax?

3. What are some of the more difficult problems facing Texans in the efforts to improve the state's educational system?

It's as big as the House and Senate want to make it, and it's as big as the needs of Texas are. I mean, goodness gracious, how long is a piece of string? How do we rank (in spending)? How do we look, compared to other states throughout the country?

—**Lieutenant Governor Bob Bullock**[1]

At the beginning of the twenty-first century, Texas's problems with poverty, pollution, crime, education, a clogged transportation system, and an outdated tax structure were similar to challenges faced by other states. In Texas, as elsewhere, identifying a policy problem was easier than forging a political solution, as the state's new Republican leadership learned. With much difficulty, Texas had survived the collapse of its traditional oil-based economy and then the collapse of its real estate industry in the 1980s. As the economy diversified, state government also had spent billions of taxpayer dollars on major improvements in prisons and mental health facilities and a more equitable distribution of public education dollars. However, the work of addressing public needs is never completed, and the political controversy involved in setting policy is never stilled, as our discussion of selected, major issues in this chapter will show. These issues represent enduring problems, and the policy decisions made in recent years are part of a long sequence of actions and inactions by state officials.

THE POLICY PROCESS

Political scientists and policy analysts spend a lot of time defining public policy and all its critical elements. We will use the definition developed by Thomas Dye, who defined public policy as "whatever governments choose to do or not to do."[2]

Except for an occasional federal judge, individuals acting alone haven't forced many changes in public policy. The political power necessary to shape policy is exercised through groups and, as we have pointed out throughout this book, some groups or interests have been more influential than others. Before we discuss specific policy changes, we will attempt to outline the concepts involved in the process.

The Elements of Public Policy

Setting public policy usually involves questions of costs and benefits. The ultimate political problems to resolve are who will benefit from specific policy decisions and who will pay the bill.[3] Certain groups, businesses, or individuals receive direct benefits from governmental decisions—benefits that are paid for by other individuals through taxes. In this process there is, in effect, a transfer of money from one segment of the population to another. Critical decisions must be made on the allocation of the tax burden, which will inevitably produce intense political conflict.

Public policies also provide indirect benefits. Although low-income Texans may receive the direct benefits of welfare assistance, job training programs, and subsidized housing and health care, the entire population eventually stands to gain if the poverty cycle is interrupted. Similar arguments can be made for funding equity between poor and rich school districts. The state's economic growth and future prosperity will be adversely affected and its crime rate will rise if serious problems of illiteracy and school dropouts aren't successfully addressed now.

Public policy also includes regulation of the private sector. Indiscriminate use of land, water, and other natural resources has been curtailed by environmental policies seeking to protect the best interests of the state as a whole. But those policies often conflict with property rights and spark angry responses from some businesses and other private property owners, who threaten political retaliation against public officeholders.

Additionally, public policy affects the governmental process itself. Decisions on political redistricting, revisions in election laws, and changes in the structure and organization of state and local governments ultimately address the issue of how power is distributed. They help determine how many people will be able to achieve their personal and collective objectives and improve their lives.

Another dimension of public policy is rooted in the notion of the general good of the community. Related to the concept of indirect benefits, it reflects the values upon which a political culture is based. Whether defined in terms of "it's the right thing to do" or a more systematic theory of the bonds that create the political community, there are elements of public policy that reflect the common needs or interests of those who live in the state.

The Stages of the Policy Process

There are many activities in the private sector that bear on public policy, such as a decision by a large corporation to close its operations in a city. But the following discussion focuses on the governmental institutions that make binding and enforceable decisions affecting all those who live in the state.[4]

A number of scholars have approached policymaking as a sequential process (Table 13–1). Although this approach may suggest artificial start and stop points, the process is dynamic and continuous.

People have to identify a problem before they can expect the government's help in resolving it.[5] Subsequent steps in the policymaking process include gaining access to public officials, getting a solution drawn up and adopted, seeing it carried out, and evaluating its effectiveness.

TABLE 13–1   Stages of the Policy Process

Stages of the Process	Actions Taken
Identification and Formation of an Issue	Defining a common problem and building coalitions to force the issue on the public agenda.
Access and Representation	Gaining access to elected or administrative officials and getting them to see the problem.
Formulation	Getting those in government to initiate action on the problem by sifting through alternative solutions.
Adoption or Legitimation	The government's specific solution to the problem, including the authorization of programs and allocation of funds.
Implementation	The application of the government's policy to the problem.
Evaluation	Assessing the effects of the policy and determining if its objectives were achieved.

Sources: Charles O. Jones, *An Introduction to the Study of Public Policy,* 2nd ed. (North Scituate, MA: Duxbury, 1977); and James E. Anderson, David W. Brady, Charles S. Bullock III, and Joseph Stewart, Jr., *Public Policy and Politics in America,* 2nd ed. (Monterey, CA: Brooks/Cole, 1984).

People in a particular neighborhood, for example, may experience an increase in respiratory problems. Right away, they suspect a nearby chemical plant, and their suspicions are reinforced every time winds blow across the neighborhood from the direction of the plant. After complaints to the plant manager bring no satisfaction—or relief—the unhappy neighbors turn to government. To make sure they are heard, they identify others affected by the same problem and join forces in a citizens' group. Such groups are central to the policymaking process. By banding together, people increase their financial resources, leadership capabilities, and political strength.

Their next step is to find the governmental body or agency that can address the problem and then convince it to do so. They may first approach the city council, only to learn that state laws and regulations govern emissions from the plant. They may then turn to the Texas Commission on Environmental Quality, which may determine that the plant is violating its state permit and may impose an administrative fine or seek legal action by the attorney general. Or the commission may find its hands tied by a loophole in the state's antipollution laws. In that case, the concerned citizens need help from the legislature, where they have to convince their elected representatives to translate their concerns into a change in policy.

Simply identifying a problem and getting a large number of other people to share your concerns is not a solution. Solutions must be developed and enacted through specific laws, regulations, or other policy changes. Philosophically, there is little disagreement that every child in Texas should have access to a quality education. But what does that mean in practical political terms? Proposed solutions have been extremely diverse. Legislative staffs, blue ribbon committees, independent research organizations, academicians, and consultants from various points on the political spectrum have all contributed studies and opinions. The resolution of their differences is essentially a political process. In the final analysis, "successful policy formulations must deal with the question of selecting courses of action that can actually be adopted."[6]

The legislature is primarily responsible for sifting through proposed alternatives and setting policy at the state level. But the separation of powers doctrine under which our government operates gives the judiciary important scrutiny over legislative action—or inaction. In recent years, several major federal and state court decisions have forced the legislature to make far-reaching changes in education, criminal justice, and mental health and mental retardation programs. Those court orders have prompted some lawmakers and other critics to complain that the judiciary overstepped its authority and was attempting to preempt the legislature. Others believe, however, that the legislature had neglected its responsibilities and needed some prodding.

Virtually every public policy has a cost. It is not enough for the legislature to create a program. Programs have to be funded, or they are meaningless. Sometimes, the legislature requires local governments to pick up the tab, but most programs have to compete with hundreds of other programs for a limited number of state tax dollars. Thus, the state's complex budgetary process is at the heart of policymaking and is closely monitored by individuals and organizations interested in policy development. Conflicts over the budgetary process can be very intense.

Once legislation has been enacted and funded, its specific provisions must be implemented, or carried out. Much of this activity is the responsibility of state and local agencies that have been created to carry "a program to the problem."[7] Earlier political scientists referred to this stage of the policy process as public administration, and much of it falls within the domain of administrative agencies and departments. But government bureaucrats aren't the only ones involved in carrying out policy. So are legislators, judges, interest groups, and nonprofit organizations. The activities in this implementation phase include:

- **Interpretation**—the translation of program language into acceptable and feasible directives.
- **Organization**—the establishment of organizational units and standard operating procedures for putting a program into effect.
- **Application**—the routine provision of services, payments, or other agreed-upon program objectives or instruments.[8]

Governments spend a lot of time evaluating the effects of public policy. In Texas, this is called performance review (see Chapter 10). An enormous amount of information is gathered to determine if programs have met stated goals and, if not, what changes or adjustments are required. Legislative committees, in their oversight function, demand information from agencies to help determine whether to continue to fund programs, expand them, or change them. With an eye on future funding, agencies also spend considerable resources assessing the impact of their own activities and performance. Program evaluation also is part of the broader issue of accountability of public officials and their responsiveness to the needs, demands, and expectations of their constituents. Interest groups, think tanks, scholars, and the news media also actively participate in this phase of the policy process.

Program assessment and evaluation become the basis for future policy and funding decisions. We have found some comprehensive solutions to a limited number of problems, including some diseases, but most governmental policy produces only limited or partial solutions. Problems and issues are ongoing, and policymakers often have to adjust or redirect their efforts at problem-solving. A solution enacted today can produce additional problems requiring further attention tomorrow. As we will discuss later in this chapter, for example, recent changes in public education policies and funding are part of a long history of efforts to improve the quality of education in Texas.

Iron Triangles and Issue Networks

There are thousands of players in the policy arenas of state and local governments, including bureaucrats, the courts, interest groups, businesses, the news media, and policy specialists. Although some of these have a broad perspective on state policy and a wide range of policy interests, most have narrow and highly specialized interests. One way to think about the relationships among policy participants is to "identify the clusters of individuals that effectively make most of the routine decisions in a given substantive area of policy."[9]

At the state level, these clusters—sometimes referred to as iron triangles of government—include members of the House and the Senate and their staffs; high-level bureaucrats; and representatives of interest groups. Both houses of the legislature are divided into standing committees, which have jurisdiction over specific policy areas, and key committee members usually form one leg of each triangle. There are hundreds of these subsystems in state government, although the use of this concept to explain policy development does not always identify all of the critical players or explain the complexity of the process.

Political scientist Hugh Heclo argues that "the iron triangle concept is not so much wrong as it is disastrously incomplete," and he offers a more complex model—**issue networks**—for mapping out the relationships inherent in the policy process.[10] This concept acknowledges the key roles of the iron triangle players but also takes into account other factors, including the increased interdependence of state and local governments on the federal government. Specialists from all three levels of government are frequently involved in developing specific policies. And, groups such as the National Governors' Association, the Council of State Governments, and the U.S. Conference of Mayors actively seek to influence federal policies that affect state and local governments.

The policy process also is increasingly dominated by specialists who may be identified with interest groups, corporations, legislative committees, or administrative agencies. These experts, or "technopols," understand the technical nature of a problem and, more importantly, the institutional, political, and personal relationships of those involved in trying to solve it.[11]

The number of actual participants in policy development will vary, of course, from issue to issue. Sometimes, only a few individuals are involved in shaping a specific policy. But on other occasions, when changes are being considered in tax law, health care, or public education, for example, there is a "kaleidoscopic interaction of changing issue networks."[12]

In the following discussion of contemporary state policies, you will see some practical applications of these concepts.

THE BUDGETARY PROCESS ━━━━━━━━━━━━━━━━━━━━━━━━━●

Balancing a new state budget in the face of a $10 billion revenue shortfall was the legislature's most difficult task in 2003, and that regular session of the legislature was the most difficult budgetary session in a dozen years. With Republicans in charge of the statehouse, the new budget was written without increasing state taxes, but fees for numerous state services were increased and funding was cut for health care and many other important programs. Lawmakers for the first time also allowed university regents to raise tuition without legislative approval, and the costs of attending public universities in Texas soon began to soar. The Republican approach to bridging the revenue shortfall differed from how the legislature had resolved the most significant, previous budgetary crisis in 1991, when Democrats still held the governor's office and a majority of both legislative houses. The legislature balanced the 1991 budget with some cuts and other cost-savings steps plus a $2.7 billion package of tax and fee increases. The legislature, with voter approval, also created the Texas lottery that year as a future revenue source. Texas lawmakers wrote state budgets in 1993, 1995, 1997, 1999, 2001, 2005, 2007 and 2009 without raising state taxes, but they put more stress on an already strained budget and tax system. Moreover, it took several billion dollars in federal economic stimulus funds to help lawmakers avoid higher state taxes or significant cuts in services in 2009.

Like most other states and unlike the federal government, Texas operates on a pay-as-you-go basis that prohibits **deficit financing**. The comptroller must certify that each budget can be paid for with anticipated revenue from taxes, fees, and other sources. And, like other states, Texas greatly increased its spending on state government programs in the 1970s, 1980s, and 1990s. Population growth and inflation were major factors, in addition to federal mandates and court orders for prison and education reforms.

The biggest share of state expenditures (including federal funds appropriated by the legislature) is for education, which accounted for approximately 41 percent of the 2010–2011 budget. Health and human services, which has seen a significant boost in recent years from increased Medicaid spending but suffered other cuts in the 2003 session, was second at 33 percent. Business and economic development accounted for 11 percent (see Table 13–2).

The two-year 2010–2011 state budget totaled $182 billion, an increase of about $94 billion over the 2000–2001 budget. Legislative budget experts say increases in federal programs and mandates and federal court orders have accounted for much of the recent increase in state spending.

Two-Year Budgets

The Texas legislature's budget-writing problems are compounded by the length of the budget period and the structure of the budget itself. Since the Texas Constitution provides that the legislature meet in regular session only every other year, lawmakers must write two-year, or biennial, budgets for state government. That means state agencies, which begin preparing their budget requests several months before a session convenes, have to anticipate some of their spending needs three years in advance. Critics, including many legislators and agency directors, say two-year budgets require too much guesswork and cause inadequate funding of some programs and wasteful spending in other areas. They believe that Texas, which is the nation's second most populous state and has a wide diversity of needs in a changing economy, should have annual budget sessions of the legislature, a change that would require a constitutional amendment.

The governor and legislative leaders have the authority between legislative sessions to transfer funds between programs and agencies to meet some emergencies. The governor proposes transfers to the Legislative Budget Board (LBB), a ten-member panel that includes the lieutenant governor, the speaker, and eight key legislators. The LBB can accept, reject, or modify the governor's proposal and can propose budgetary changes to the governor.

Agencies submit their biennial appropriations, or spending, requests to the Legislative Budget Board. After its staff reviews the requests, the LBB normally recommends a budget that the full legislature uses as a starting point in its budgetary deliberations.

TABLE 13–2 State Appropriations for 2010–2011 Biennium (All funds)

FUNCTION	Funds Appropriated (in millions)	Total (%)
General Government	4,077.3	2.2%
Health and Human Services	59,616.6	32.7%
Education	75,437.1	41.4%
Judiciary	669.2	0.4%
Public Safety and Criminal Justice	10,759.6	5.9%
Natural Resources	3,447.9	1.9%
Business and Economic Development	20,713.6	11.4%
Regulatory	892.1	0.5%
General Provisions	666.6	0.4%
Legislature	354.9	0.2%
Federal Stimulus Funds	5,675.5	3.1%
TOTAL FOR ALL FUNCTIONS	**182,310.3**	**100.0%**

Source: Legislative Budget Board, Summary of Conference Committee Report for Senate Bill 1, May 2009.

Dedicated Funds

The legislature's control over the budget-setting process is further restricted by legal requirements that dedicate or set aside a major portion of state revenue for specific purposes, leaving legislators with discretion over only about one-half of total appropriations. The remainder includes federal funds earmarked for specific purposes by the federal government or monies dedicated to specific uses by the state constitution or state law. The state treasury has more than 500 separate funds, including many that are dedicated to highways, education, parks, teacher retirement, and dozens of other specific purposes. These restrictions hamper the legislature, particularly during lean periods. But the dedicated funds are jealously guarded by the interest groups that benefit from them, and many funds have become "sacred cows" that most legislators dare not try to change.

One of the major **dedicated funds** is the Highway Trust Fund, which automatically gets three-fourths of the revenue from the motor fuels tax. Under the Texas Constitution, revenue in that fund can be spent only to purchase right of way for highways or to construct, maintain, and police highways. The remainder of the motor fuels tax revenue goes to public education. Any legislative proposal to tap into the highway fund for other state needs would be fought by a strong lobbying effort from highway contractors as well as business leaders, mayors, and county judges with local road projects they wanted completed.

Other major dedicated funds include the Permanent School Fund and the Permanent University Fund, land- and mineral-rich endowments that help support the public schools and boost funding for the University of Texas and Texas A&M University systems. In 1991, the legislature, working with the comptroller, began consolidating and eliminating many funds, but constitutionally dedicated funds cannot be changed without voter approval.

STATE TAXES ●

The legislature enacted a hybrid corporate income tax in 1991, but Texas entered the twenty-first century as one of only nine states without a personal income tax, and public and political opposition to that revenue source remained high.[13] Each budgetary crisis had seemingly stretched the existing tax structure to the breaking point, only to see the legislature come up with another patch. Critics compared the tax structure to an ugly patchwork quilt that had been stitched together over the years to accommodate various special interest groups and cover an assortment of emergencies. Senator Carl Parker, a Port Arthur Democrat, argued in Senate floor debate in 1991: "They [existing taxes] hit the poor people worse than they do rich folks. They let some people off scot-free, while they tax others heavily. And the direction we seem to be going is worse, not better."[14]

The Regressive Tax System

A 2003 study by Citizens for Tax Justice and the Institute on Taxation and Economic Policy ranked Texas's tax system among the ten most regressive in the country. Texas's system is based largely on the sales tax, the local property tax, and fees that consume a larger portion of the incomes of the poor and the middle classes than the upper class (Table 13–3). Based on this study's calculations, state and local governments in Texas taxed poor families at 11.4 percent of their incomes and middle-class families at 8.4 percent. By contrast, the wealthiest Texans (the richest 1 percent of the families) paid only

TABLE 13–3   The Ten Most Regressive State Tax Systems

State	Taxes as a Percentage of Income on		
	Poorest 20%	Middle 60%	Top 1%
Washington	17.6%	11.2%	3.3%
Florida	14.4%	9.8%	3.0%
Tennessee	11.7%	8.9%	3.4%
South Dakota	10.0%	8.4%	2.3%
Texas	**11.4%**	**8.4%**	**3.5%**
Illinois	13.1%	10.5%	5.8%
Michigan	13.3%	11.2%	6.7%
Pennsylvania	11.4%	9.0%	4.8%
Nevada	8.3%	6.5%	2.0%
Alabama	10.6%	9.6%	4.9%

Note: States are ranked by the ITEP Tax Inequality Index. The ten states in the table are those whose tax systems most increase income inequality after taxes compared to before taxes.

Source: Who Pays? A Distributional Analysis of the Tax Systems of All 50 States, 2nd ed. (Washington, DC: Institute on Taxation and Economic Policy.)

3.5 percent of their incomes in state and local taxes. Political leaders have long touted Texas as a low-tax state, but, according to this study, that is only from the perspective of wealthy Texans.[15]

Sales Taxes

In 1961, the legislature, over the objections of then-Governor Price Daniel, enacted the state's first **sales tax**. Its initial rate was 2 percent of the cost of purchased goods. The rate has since been increased several times, and the tax now produces about one-fourth of all state revenue. In 2009, the statewide sales tax rate of 6.25 percent was tied with California and Massachusetts for tenth highest in the nation. An 8.25 percent rate is charged in most Texas metropolitan areas, where city and mass transportation authority taxes of 1 percent each are added to the state tax, a practice that many other states follow.[16] The sales tax generated $ 21.6 billion in 2008, 25 percent of the state's tax revenues.[17]

With each financial crisis, it becomes more difficult politically for the legislature to raise the sales tax rate. And even though groceries and medicine are tax exempt, critics charge that the sales tax is regressive because it affects low-income Texans disproportionately more than wealthier citizens. Moreover, the sales tax is heavily weighted toward products and leaves many services—including legal and medical fees and advertising— untaxed. Thus sales tax revenue doesn't automatically grow with the state's economy because the Texas economy is becoming more and more service-oriented.

Business Taxes

The franchise tax, which was overhauled in 1991 and became a hybrid corporate income tax, for many years was the state's major business tax. It applied only to corporations, which were taxed on their income or assets, whichever was greater. The tax didn't cover partnerships or sole proprietorships and was paid by fewer than 200,000 of the state's

2.5 million businesses. At the urging of Governor Rick Perry, the legislature in a special session in 2006 replaced the **franchise tax** with a broader-based business tax, which applied not only to corporations but also to professional partnerships, such as law firms, for the first time. The new business tax, which produced $4.5 billion in 2008, was part of a trade-off for lower school property taxes and was enacted in response to a Texas Supreme Court order for a new way of paying for public education. Although the smallest businesses were exempted from the tax, the new levy still raised taxes for many companies that had been paying little, if any, taxes under the franchise tax. So, the legislature in 2009 raised the exemption even more.

Property Taxes

The biggest source of taxpayer dissatisfaction and anger in Texas in recent years has been the local property, or ad valorem, tax, the major source of revenue for 3,800 cities, counties, schools, and special districts. Total property tax levies have increased by 254 percent in the twenty-year period between 1988 and 2007, from $10.5 billion to $35.1 billion, according to the state comptroller's office.[18] The heaviest increases have been in local school taxes, which have been significantly raised to pay for state-mandated education reforms and school finance requirements, including a law ordering the transfer of millions of dollars from wealthy to poor school districts.

Severance Taxes

Oil and gas severance taxes helped the legislature balance the budget with relative ease when oil prices were high in the 1970s. But energy-tax revenue slowed considerably after the energy industry crashed in the 1980s. Severance taxes accounted for 28 percent of state tax revenue in 1981, but only 5 percent in recent years.[19]

Other Taxes

State government also has several volume-based taxes, such as taxes on cigarettes, alcoholic beverages, and motor fuels. They have set rates per pack or per gallon and don't produce more revenue when inflation raises the price of the product. These taxes, particularly the so-called "**sin taxes**" on cigarettes and alcohol, have been raised frequently over the years and produced $2.2 billion in revenue in 2008.[20] The legislature raised the cigarette tax from 41 cents per pack to $1.41 per pack in 2006, giving Texas one of the highest rates in the country.

Gambling on New Revenue

For years, Texas government maintained a strong moralistic opposition to gambling. Charitable bingo games were tolerated and eventually legalized. But the state constitution prohibited lotteries, and horse race betting was outlawed in the 1930s. After the oil bust in the 1980s, however, many legislators began to view gambling as a financial opportunity rather than a moral evil, and in key elections most Texas voters indicated they agreed.

In a special session in 1986, when spending was cut and taxes were raised to compensate for lost revenue from plummeting oil prices, the legislature legalized local option, pari-mutuel betting on horse and dog races. Voters approved the measure the next year. In 1991, under strong pressure from Governor Ann Richards, the legislature approved a constitutional amendment to legalize a state **lottery**, which voters also endorsed that year. Limited casino gambling on cruise ships operating off the Texas coast also has been legalized by the legislature.

Gambling, however, has not been a panacea for the state's financial needs. Years after pari-mutuel betting had been approved, the horse and dog racing tracks still had not produced any significant revenue for the state treasury.

The lottery jumped off to a much more impressive start. It became the first lottery in the United States to sell more than $4 billion worth of tickets in its first two years of operation, and it reached that milestone in twenty-two months. By late 1997, however, lottery sales had begun to lag behind projections, and even supporters of the game warned that the lottery couldn't necessarily be depended upon as a reliable, long-term revenue source. Lawmakers for the first time in 1997 dedicated lottery revenue to public education but also ordered that shortfalls in school funding from the lottery be made up with tax dollars.[21] The lottery generated $1.6 billion for public education in 2008.[22]

All but two states permit some form of public or legalized gambling, which includes commercial casinos, Indian casinos, pari-mutuel wagering, racetrack casinos, lotteries and charitable gaming. Some thirty years ago, gambling was legal in only three states, but over the last three decades, states, including Texas, have come to view taxes on gambling as a means to ease some of their budget problems.[23] As noted already, Texas has a state lottery and permits pari-mutuel wagering. The state also permits charitable gaming, but

Gambling on New Revenue. Texans approved a lottery in 1991, and by 2008, lottery sales produced $1.6 billion for public education.

casino gambling remains a contentious issue. There are no commercial casinos in the state, and the efforts of the state's three Native American tribes to run casinos on their reservations have been challenged by state officials (see Chapter 1).

But there is a risk in relying on taxes on gambling. Money people spend on gambling is discretionary, and in economic hard times, there is a high probability of a reduction in personal funds spent on gambling, thus producing a reduction in tax revenues. In budgeting, this contingency must be included in budget estimates to obtain a realistic assessment of available tax revenues.

Bonds: Build Now, Pay Later

Although the Texas Constitution has a general prohibition against state government going into debt, the state had about $31.2 billion in state bonds outstanding at the end of fiscal 2008. About $2.8 billion of the total would have to be paid off with tax dollars, while approximately $28.4 billion of the state debt was in the form of self-supporting revenue bonds.[24] Taxpayer-supported debt ballooned during tight budgetary periods when the legislature, prompted by federal court orders, used **general obligation bonds**, which are backed by state taxes, to finance the construction of prisons and mental health and mental retardation facilities. These expenses were submitted to the voters for approval in the form of constitutional amendments.

Some legislators have become increasingly uneasy about loading up the additional tax liability on future taxpayers. Interest on bonds can double the cost of a construction project, experts say. Debt service paid from taxes totaled $1.27 billion in the 2006–2007 biennium, according to the Legislative Budget Board.[25] Bond issues, however, have been widely supported by Democrats and Republicans, liberals and conservatives alike. In promoting a prison bond issue in 1989, then-Governor Bill Clements said, "If there ever was anything that was proper for us to bond, it's our prison system, where those facilities will be on-line and in use for a twenty-five or thirty-year period."[26]

Over the years, the state also has issued hundreds of millions of dollars in bonds for such self-supporting programs as water development and veterans' assistance. Those programs use the state's credit to borrow money at favorable interest rates. The state lends that money to a local government to help construct a water treatment plant or to a veteran to help purchase a house, and the debt is repaid by the loan recipients, not by the state's taxpayers.

Alternatives to Finding New Revenues

State leaders throughout the country have been reexamining their delivery of public services to assure taxpayers they were getting the best possible return on their dollars. Texas was in the forefront of these efforts.

In 1991, the Texas legislature, facing a large revenue shortfall, instructed the state comptroller to supervise periodic performance reviews of all state agencies and programs with an eye toward eliminating inefficiency and mismanagement and producing savings. The comptroller also reviewed the budgets and operations of some local school districts. Billions of dollars in potential savings were identified over the next several years, and a number of the comptroller's recommendations were adopted by the legislature and school boards.

The legislature transferred those programs from the comptroller's office to the Legislative Budget Board in 2003 after a series of budgetary disputes with Comptroller Carole Keeton Strayhorn (see Chapter 9). Along with the sunset process, performance reviews continue to be used by the legislature for cutting the budget.

The Income Tax: An Alternative to a Regressive Tax System?

Various liberal legislators and groups seeking more funding for state services have long advocated a state **income tax**. But until fairly recently no major officeholder or serious candidate for a major office dared even hint at support for such a politically taboo alternative. Finally, in late 1989, then–Lieutenant Governor Bill Hobby broke the ice for serious discussion of the issue in a speech to the Texas Association of Taxpayers, whose members included executives of many of the major businesses in Texas. Hobby, who had already announced that he wouldn't seek reelection in 1990, proposed that a personal and corporate income tax be enacted, coupled with abolition of the corporate franchise tax and reductions in property and sales taxes. Hobby also told his audience that it would take the business community to convince the legislature to pass an income tax.

Lieutenant Governor Bob Bullock then shocked much of the political establishment by announcing in March 1991, less than two months after succeeding Hobby, that he would actively campaign for a state income tax. Bullock, a former state comptroller, said it was the only way to meet the state's present and future needs fairly and adequately while also providing relief from existing unpopular taxes. Bullock proposed making local school property taxes deductible from the income tax, and he recommended the repeal of the franchise tax. "I personally dislike—and I imagine most Texans do—any type of new taxes. But I also know deep down in my heart, deep down in my heart, that it's the right thing to do for Texas," he said.[27]

Although other surveys indicated there was still widespread opposition to an income tax among Texans, the *Texas Poll* published that spring signaled that Bullock had struck a favorable chord with many property taxpayers. Half of the poll's 1,003 respondents said they would favor a 5 percent state income tax if it enabled local property taxes to be cut in half, and 54 percent said they would support an income tax to pay for public schools if property taxes were greatly reduced.[28]

Bullock, however, didn't receive much support from lobby groups. The Texas House, which initiates legislative action on tax bills, also remained strongly opposed to an income tax, as did the governor, Democrat Ann Richards.

Eventually, the legislature that year changed the corporate franchise tax to include the hybrid corporate income tax described earlier in this chapter, while holding the line against a personal income tax. A blue-ribbon task force appointed by the governor and legislative leaders to study revenue options recommended that the legislature enact both corporate and personal income taxes in 1993. The recommendation, believed to have been engineered behind the scenes by Bullock, came over the objections of the task force chairman, former Governor John Connally. Connally argued that an income tax would raise too much money and encourage excessive spending by the legislature. And, he added, "The people don't want it."[29]

During the 1993 legislative session, Bullock pulled another surprise and proposed a constitutional amendment, which won easy legislative approval, to ban a personal income tax unless the voters approved one. Bullock probably had more than one reason for his apparent about-face. One obvious factor was that his 1994 reelection date was approaching, and he needed to defuse any political problems caused by his endorsement of an income tax two years earlier. Moreover, Governor Richards and most legislators still strongly opposed an income tax. Some observers also believed that Bullock viewed his new proposal as a way to eventually win Texans' approval of a personal income tax. His constitutional amendment provided that an income tax would have to help fund public education and be accompanied by a reduction in unpopular school property taxes, provisions similar to his 1991 income tax plan.

Whatever Bullock's motivations, the amendment was overwhelmingly approved by Texas voters in November 1993, leaving many people convinced that a major revenue option had been removed from the state's budget picture for years to come.

Texas is one of only a handful of states without a personal income tax. And whenever the legislature does decide to try to sell one to voters, support from the business community will be crucial. The sales tax was first adopted after the business lobby got behind it, and business interests remain influential today. State government's ability to provide quality education, highways, and other public support systems is essential to the business community's long-term success. A personal income tax also would offer businesses the opportunity to transfer more of their tax load to consumers. That, ironically, could produce a conflict with some of the more liberal, long-time supporters of an income tax. A likely solution would be the enactment of generous tax exemptions for low-income Texans.

EDUCATIONAL POLICIES AND POLITICS ●

Public Education: A Struggle for Equity and Quality

More tax dollars are spent on education than any other governmental program in Texas. In 1949, the legislature enacted the Gilmer–Aikin law, which made major improvements in the administration of public education and significantly boosted funding for public schools, but it was soon outdated. By the 1970s, it was obvious that quality and equity were lacking in many classrooms. Thousands of functional illiterates were being graduated from high school each year, and thousands of children in poor school districts were being shortchanged with substandard facilities and educational aids.

Public elementary and secondary education in Texas is financed by a combination of state and local revenue, a system that produced wide disparities in education spending among the state's approximately 1,050 school districts. The only local source of operating revenue for school districts is the property tax. Districts with a wealth of oil production or expensive commercial property had high tax bases that enabled them to raise large amounts of money with relatively low tax rates. Poor districts with low tax bases, on the other hand, had to impose higher tax rates to raise only a fraction of the money that the wealthy districts could spend on education.

While poor districts had to struggle to maintain minimal educational programs, rich districts could attract the best teachers with higher pay, build more classrooms, purchase more books and computers, and, in some cases, have enough money left over to put AstroTurf in their football stadiums and construct indoor swimming pools. The glaring inequities didn't exist only between different counties or regions of the state. In many cases, educational resources varied greatly between districts within the same county (see "School Consolidations versus Community Identity"). Many of the poorest districts were also in heavily Hispanic South Texas, and ethnicity became a significant factor in a protracted struggle between the haves and the have-nots. Hispanic leaders played major roles in the fight to improve the futures of their children.

In 1968, a group of parents led by Demetrio P. Rodriquez, a San Antonio sheet metal worker and high school dropout, filed a federal lawsuit (*Rodriguez v. San Antonio Independent School District*) challenging the system. The plaintiffs had children in the Edgewood Independent School District, one of the state's poorest. A three-judge federal panel agreed with the parents and ruled in 1971 that the school finance system was unconstitutional. But the state appealed, and the U.S. Supreme Court in 1973 reversed

School Consolidations versus Community Identity

There were more than 5,000 school districts in Texas in 1947, and that number was greatly reduced over the next several years. Despite potential savings, however, efficiency in school administration and the more equitable distribution of tax dollars, consolidations have been relatively rare in recent years, with districts now numbering approximately 1,050. In many small towns, the school district is not only a major employer, it is also the center of social activities and the heart of the community itself. Be it rich or poor, local residents don't want to give up the hometown school.

The *Houston Chronicle* vividly illustrated that point at the beginning of the 1990–1991 school year with a visit to sparsely populated Cochran County in West Texas. The Whiteface Consolidated School District, which sits atop an oil field, had a tax base of $1.3 million per student and a tax rate of only 46 cents per $100 valuation. It had an indoor swimming pool that the entire community of 450 people shared, and it paid its teachers,

on the average, about $3,500 a year more than the neighboring Morton Independent School District did. Morton, the county seat, is a slightly larger town only twelve miles away, but the oil field ends somewhere between the two communities. With a tax base of only $73,400 per student, Morton was one of the state's poorest school districts, and its tax rate was 96.5 cents per $100 valuation. Nevertheless, Morton Superintendent Charles Skeen said consolidation was no more popular with the people of Morton than it was with their neighbors in Whiteface.

"When you have two communities and you take the school out of one of them, the people fear they will lose their town," Skeen said. Whiteface Superintendent David Foote said virtually the same thing: "A lot of people live in this town so their children can go to a small school. They know that if a community loses its school, where the school is the center of the community, the community dies.[30]

the lower court decision. The high court said that the Texas system of financing public education was unfair but held that it didn't violate the U.S. Constitution. Its consciousness raised, the legislature started pumping hundreds of millions of dollars in so-called "equalization" aid into the poorer school districts. But lawmakers didn't change the system, and the inequities persisted and worsened.

By the early 1980s, there was a growing concern among Texas leaders over not just the financing of public education but also the quality of education. Their concerns were shared by leaders in other states in the wake of a national study called *A Nation at Risk* that had sharply criticized the nation's educational systems as inadequate. In 1983, newly elected Governor Mark White tried to raise schoolteachers' salaries to keep a campaign promise to the thousands of teachers who had been instrumental in his election. When the legislature refused to increase taxes for higher teacher pay without first studying the educational system with an eye toward reform, White joined Lieutenant Governor Bill Hobby and House Speaker Gib Lewis in appointing the Select Committee on Public Education. Computer magnate Ross Perot of Dallas—who several years later would become better known as an independent candidate for president—was selected to chair it. In an exhaustive study, the panel found that high schools were graduating many students who could barely read and write and concluded that major reforms were necessary if the state's young people were to be able to compete for jobs in a changing and highly competitive state and international economy.

A long, arduous battle for equity. The Edgewood Independent School District, with an extremely limited tax base, was an early leader in efforts to produce greater equity in funding public education throughout the state. Perales Elementary School is just a few blocks from the residence of the lead plaintiff in the case of *Rodriquez v. San Antonio Independent School District.*

With Perot spending some of his own personal wealth on a strong lobbying campaign, the legislature in a special session in 1984 enacted many educational reforms in a landmark piece of legislation known as **House Bill 72** and raised taxes to boost education spending. The bill raised teacher pay, limited class sizes, required prekindergarten classes for disadvantaged four-year-olds, required students to pass a basic skills test before graduating from high school, and required school districts to provide tutorials for failing students. It also replaced the elected State Board of Education, viewed as antireform by state leaders, with a new panel appointed by the governor. The new board became an elected body four years later, after the appointed panel had time to oversee the initial implementation of the new law.

The two most controversial provisions in the 1984 education reform law, however, were a literacy test for teachers and the so-called **no pass, no play** rule, both of which were to contribute to White's reelection defeat in 1986. Most teachers easily passed the one-time literacy—or competency—test, a requirement for keeping their jobs, but many resented it as an insult to their abilities and professionalism. The no pass, no play rule, which prohibited students who failed any course from participating in athletics and other extracurricular activities for six weeks, infuriated many coaches, students, parents, and school administrators, particularly in the hundreds of small Texas towns where Friday night football was a major social activity and an important source of community pride. Education reformers, however, viewed the restriction as an important statement that the first emphasis of education should be on the classroom, not on the football field or the band hall.

The 1984 law, however, still didn't change the basic, inequitable finance system, and the state was soon back in court over that issue. This lawsuit (*Edgewood v. Kirby*) was filed in state district court in Austin, and it contended the inequities violated the Texas Constitution. It was initially filed in 1984, shortly before the enactment of House Bill 72, by the Edgewood Independent School District, twelve other poor districts, and a number of families represented by the Mexican American Legal Defense and Educational Fund (MALDEF). Dozens of other districts and individuals joined the case as plaintiff-intervenors, and, in 1987, state District Judge Harley Clark of Austin ruled the school finance system violated the state constitution.

The Third Court of Appeals reversed Clark in December 1988. But the Texas Supreme Court, in a unanimous, landmark decision in October 1989, struck down the finance system and ordered lawmakers to replace it by May 1, 1990, with a new law that gave public school children an equal opportunity at a quality education. The bipartisan opinion, written by Democratic Justice Oscar Mauzy, a former chairman of the Senate Education Committee, didn't outline a specific solution. In an obvious effort to reach consensus among all nine justices, it was purposefully vague in some areas. But the court said the existing finance system violated a state constitutional requirement for an efficient system of public education. It warned the legislature that merely increasing the amount of state education aid wasn't enough. The decision concluded that "a Band-Aid will not suffice; the system itself must be changed."[31] The Texas Supreme Court cited glaring disparities among school districts' abilities to raise revenue from property taxes because of wide differences in taxable wealth. "The amount of money spent on a student's education has a real and meaningful impact on the educational opportunity offered that student," the court wrote. "High-wealth districts are able to provide for their students broader educational experiences including more extensive curricula, more up-to-date technological equipment, better libraries and library personnel, teacher aides, counseling services, lower student–teacher ratios, better facilities, parental involvement programs, and dropout prevention programs. They are also better able to attract and retain experienced teachers and administrators."[32]

Funding Problems Persist

Governor Bill Clements called the legislature into special session in February 1990 to address the Texas Supreme Court order. But the issue was so divisive it took four special sessions and an extension of the court's deadline for the governor and the legislature to agree on a new finance plan, which included a small increase in the state sales tax to boost funding to poor districts. But the Edgewood plaintiffs called the new law inadequate and promptly took the state back to court.

After a trial on the new law, state District Judge Scott McCown of Austin, who had taken over jurisdiction of the lawsuit after Harley Clark retired, agreed. Although he allowed the new law to remain in effect for the 1990–1991 school year, McCown ruled in September 1990 that the plan was, like its predecessor, unconstitutional because it didn't narrow the huge gap in wealth between rich and poor school districts. The Texas Supreme Court agreed.

A legislative solution still remained difficult, and lawmakers had to enact two more school finance plans before finally meeting the Supreme Court's approval. Acting in 1993, the legislature approved a law, signed by Governor Ann Richards, that gave wealthy school districts several options for sharing revenue with poor districts. It was challenged both by rich districts, which objected to the requirement that they share their property wealth, and by poor districts, which argued that the new law was inadequately funded and didn't sufficiently reduce the funding gap between rich and poor districts.

The Texas Supreme Court upheld the 1993 law in a 5–4 decision in January 1995. In the majority opinion, Justice John Cornyn, a Republican, wrote that children from poor and wealthy school districts "now have substantially equal access to the funds necessary for a general diffusion of knowledge." But Republican Justice Craig Enoch, who dissented, said the state had failed to adequately provide for public education and warned of more funding problems because of the continued heavy reliance on local property taxes.[33]

In the late 1990s, the legislature increased funding for public education but failed to keep up with the increasing needs of a growing school enrollment. The property tax burden continued to increase, and by 2006 local property taxes were paying for about 60 percent of public education costs (see Table 13–4). The school finance system also was under attack again in court. A number of school districts had joined a suit in state district court, arguing that the 1993 law was unconstitutional because many districts had been forced to raise their property tax rates to or near the limit allowed by the state for school maintenance and operations, $1.50 per $100 valuation. The districts argued that the situation amounted to, in effect, a state property tax, which was prohibited by the Texas Constitution. The districts also sought more state aid.

Ruling in the latest lawsuit in 2005, the Texas Supreme Court held that the heavy reliance on property taxes for school funding amounted to an unconstitutional statewide property tax and gave the state until June 1, 2006, to correct the problem. Governor Rick Perry called the legislature into special session and won approval of a proposal to cut school maintenance tax rates by as much as one-third over the next two years. To replace the lost revenue, legislators used part of a budgetary surplus, enacted the new, broad-based business tax described earlier in this chapter and raised the state cigarette tax by $1 per pack. The Legislature, however, didn't increase state funding for the public schools, and the local school tax savings touted by Perry soon were eroded by rising property values. As property values increased, tax bills increased without any change in the tax rate.

Other Issues Affecting the Public Schools

Teacher Pay and Working Conditions.   The school districts' financial problems and other work-related stresses were taking their toll on schoolteachers. Thirty-eight percent of teachers were seriously considering quitting the profession in 1994, according to a survey by the Texas State Teachers Association (TSTA). Teachers complained of low pay, excessive paperwork and other administrative hassles, and poor student discipline.[34]

TABLE 13–4   Sources of Funding for Public Education in Texas, 2005–2006

Funding Source	Receipts	Percent of Total
Local*	$18,610,805,437	53.0%
State	12,142,141,203	34.6%
Federal	1,202,862,841	3.4%
Other Local and Intermediate*	1,249,417,499	3.6%
Equity Transfers among Districts*	1,323,012,429	3.7%
Other Resources	556,348,194	1.6%
Total	**$35,084,587,603**	100%

*Funds from local sources comprise 60.5% of funds generated from within the state.

Source: Texas Education Agency, *2005–2006 Budgeted Financial Data.*

The legislature raised the minimum teacher salary in 1995 and gave teachers an across-the-board pay increase in 1999. However, according to the National Education Association, Texas still ranked only thirty-second in the country, with average teacher pay of $39,232 in 2001–2002.[35]

The legislature in 2001 gave teachers a $1,000 annual allotment for health care insurance but cut that payment in half two years later to help balance a new state budget without raising state taxes. According to the American Federation of Teachers, the national average pay for teachers in 2006–2007 was $51,009, but the average pay of Texas teachers was $45,392, twenty-ninth in the country.[36] Lawmakers in 2006 gave teachers an across-the-board $2,000 pay raise, but teacher pay in Texas still lagged behind the national average.

Standardized Tests and "Accountability." For years now, students in the public schools have been required to take standardized tests to be promoted to higher grades, graduate from high school and help measure a school's effectiveness. But the tests—most recently called the Texas Assessment of Knowledge and Skills (TAKS)—and the so-called school "accountability" system to which the results of these tests contributed have been controversial. There have been accusations that teachers were pressured to concentrate on teaching students how to pass the test in order to attain a favorable rating for their schools rather than present a more enriching educational curriculum. The testing and accountability systems have been revised several times, including in 2009, as legislators and educators struggled to balance political and educational concerns.

A solution for low-performing students? Charter schools such as the KIPP Aspire Middle School, located in central San Antonio, were authorized and funded under the leadership of George Bush in 1995 to provide alternatives to the public schools for low-performing students.

Charter Schools.   Upon taking office in 1995, Governor George W. Bush advocated more innovation for local schools and less red tape for teachers and administrators. The legislature responded with a major rewrite of the education law to allow school districts and other groups to create charter schools that would be free of some state regulations. The charter school movement got off to a mixed start. Several had financial problems or were mismanaged and had to shut down after brief periods of operation. Others flourished, strongly supported by parents and students who believed their innovative techniques enhanced the learning experience. By 2008, there were 374 charter schools operating in Texas.

Virtual Charter Schools.   The growth of Internet use sparked interest in putting schools online, but the concept encountered strong opposition in Texas from teachers' groups, who argued that the state should raise teacher pay and make other improvements in public school classrooms before diverting tax dollars for programs that, at least initially, would benefit only a limited number of students. Legislation that would have authorized a pilot online education program was defeated by Texas lawmakers in 2003. That same year, more than 120 virtual schools were operating in other states.[37]

Private School Vouchers.   For several years, a number of legislators, primarily Republicans, have advocated a voucher program that would allow some public school children to attend private schools at state expense. The idea, supporters say, is to allow disadvantaged children from failing schools to have a chance at a quality education. But opponents, including public education groups, say such a program would unfairly divert money from the public schools at a time when public classrooms need more funding. Voucher bills have failed during several recent legislative sessions.

Home Schools.   In 1994, the Texas Supreme Court upheld the right of parents to educate their own children at home, ending a ten-year legal battle over the home school issue in Texas. The court said a home school was legitimate if parents met "basic education goals" and used a curriculum based on books, workbooks, or other written materials. It was reported at the time that nearly 1 million American families, including 100,000 in Texas, educated their children at home.[38] The U.S. Department of Education reported that there were 1.5 million homeschooled students in 2007, and while it is difficult to verify state-by-state data, the number of children homeschooled in Texas continued to increase.[39]

Higher Education: The Quest for Excellence and Equity Continues

Texas has thirty-five state-supported, general academic universities; eight medical schools and health science centers; four public law schools; fifty community (or junior) college districts; and four campuses of the Texas State Technical College System. These institutions of higher learning serve more than one million students. They are governed by numerous policy-setting boards appointed by the governor or, in the case of community colleges, elected by local voters. The Texas Higher Education Coordinating Board, which is appointed by the governor, has oversight over university construction and degree programs.

The state makes no pretense that all its universities were created equal. The University of Texas at Austin and Texas A&M University at College Station are the state's largest universities, have higher entrance requirements than other schools, fulfill important research functions and, thanks to a constitutional endowment, have some of the state's best educational facilities. They receive revenue generated by the land- and mineral-rich **Permanent University Fund (PUF)**. The University of Texas receives two-thirds of the money in the Available University Fund, which includes dividends, interest, and other income earned by the PUF, and Texas A&M receives one-third. University of Texas and Texas A&M regents can also pledge revenue to back bonds issued for land acquisition, construction, building repairs, purchase of capital equipment, and purchase of library materials for other campuses within the two university systems. Universities outside the two largest systems shared a separate building fund to which the legislature appropriated about $175 million a year.

Responding to a federal desegregation lawsuit, the state in the 1980s made a commitment to improve higher educational opportunities for minority students and employment opportunities for minority faculty members. More funding was provided for predominantly African-American Texas Southern University in Houston and Prairie View A&M University in nearby Waller County. Prairie View, which is part of the Texas A&M System, was guaranteed a special share of Available University Fund revenue in a constitutional amendment adopted in 1984. Texas agreed to a five-year desegregation plan with the U.S. Department of Education in 1983 and subsequently created the Texas Educational Opportunity Plan, under which traditionally Anglo schools, including the University of Texas at Austin and Texas A&M, increased minority recruitment efforts.

Residents of heavily Hispanic South Texas, however, challenged the state's distribution of higher education dollars. In a lawsuit filed in state district court in Brownsville

The state's future depends on it. There is general agreement that the state's future economic growth is tied directly to its ability to expand its institutions of higher learning. In addition to the creation of new universities across the state, many institutions, including the University of Texas at San Antonio shown here, now have multiple campuses.

in 1987, several Hispanic groups and individuals represented by the Mexican American Legal Defense and Educational Fund contended the state's higher education system discriminated against Mexican American students by spending less on universities in the border area. The plaintiffs pointed out that there were no state-supported professional schools south of San Antonio and only one doctoral program—in bilingual education at Texas A&I University in Kingsville.

After the lawsuit was filed, Texas A&I, Laredo State University, and Corpus Christi State University were made part of the Texas A&M System, and Pan American University campuses in Edinburg and Brownsville were added to the University of Texas System. But efforts to negotiate a settlement of the suit failed, and it went to trial in late 1991 as a class action on behalf of all Mexican Americans who allegedly suffered or stood to suffer discrimination in higher education in the Mexican border area of Texas. In January 1992, state District Judge Benjamin Euresti, Jr., of Brownsville ruled the higher education funding system unconstitutional because it discriminated against South Texas, but his ruling later was overturned by the Texas Supreme Court.[40]

Hopwood: A Temporary Setback to Affirmative Action

Texas's efforts to increase minority enrollments in its universities suffered a setback in 1996 when the Fifth U.S. Circuit Court of Appeals in New Orleans ruled that a race-based admissions policy previously used by the University of Texas School of Law was unconstitutional. The U.S. Supreme Court refused to grant the state's appeal and let the appellate court's decision stand. The so-called "Hopwood case" was named after lead plaintiff Cheryl Hopwood, one of four white students who sued after not being admitted into the law school.[41]

Then–Texas Attorney General Dan Morales held in 1997 that the Hopwood ruling went beyond the law school and prohibited all universities in Texas from using race or ethnicity as a preferential factor in admissions, scholarships, and other student programs. Morales's opinion was attacked as overly broad by many civil rights leaders and minority legislators, but it had the force of law.[42] The Texas legislature, meeting in 1997, attempted to soften the blow to affirmative action by enacting a new law that guaranteed automatic admissions to state universities for high school graduates who finished in the top 10 percent of their classes, regardless of their scores on college entrance examinations. The law was designed to give the best students from poor and predominantly minority school districts an equal footing in university admissions with better prepared graduates of wealthier school districts. The new law also allowed university officials to consider other admissions criteria, including a student's family income and parents' education level.

There was little change in minority enrollments at many Texas universities after the Hopwood decision because many universities hadn't used race as a factor in admissions anyway. But the two largest—the University of Texas at Austin and Texas A&M University—did. The drop-off in minority enrollment was particularly troubling at the UT law school the first year after the Hopwood restrictions went into effect. The first-year law class of almost 500 students in the fall of 1997 included only four African Americans and twenty-five Hispanics. There had been thirty-one African Americans and forty-two Hispanics in the previous year's entering class. And the more flexible admissions standards set by the legislature applied only to entering undergraduate students, not to those seeking admission to law school and other professional schools.[43]

Many higher education administrators and civil rights leaders said it was wrong to dismantle affirmative action programs that had been designed to improve educational and professional opportunities for minorities, who had historically suffered from segregation and were still overrepresented among the nation's poor. They said it was particularly short-sighted to de-emphasize minority recruitment efforts at a time when Hispanics and African Americans were only a few years away from making up a majority of the Texas population.

Morales urged university officials to redouble their efforts to recruit disadvantaged students of all races. "We must express to young Texans the reality that in this country one is capable of rising as high as his or her individual talents, ability, and hard work will allow," he said.[44]

Finally, in 2003, the U.S. Supreme Court, ruling in a case from Michigan, effectively repealed Hopwood by holding that universities can use affirmative action programs to give minority students help in admissions, provided that racial quotas weren't used. The University of Texas, among other institutions, then began steps to develop new, race-based admissions criteria. Some legislators, meanwhile, wanted to put limits on the number of students who could be admitted to a university under the 10 percent law because it was restricting admissions options at the University of Texas at Austin, consuming a large percentage of each year's freshman class. After refusing for several years to change the law, the legislature in 2009 imposed some restrictions.

Tuition Deregulation: The Price of Admission Goes Up

With tax dollars becoming increasingly tight, University of Texas officials successfully lobbied the legislature in 2003 for a new law that, for the first time, gave individual university governing boards the freedom to set tuition rates independently of legislative action. Within three years, tuition and fees at state-supported universities had jumped an average 39 percent, while state appropriations for student financial aid increased by only 15 percent during the same period, according to figures compiled by the Texas Higher Education Coordinating Board. But even with the higher tuition, Texas universities still remained a bargain and weren't out of line with college costs in other states, Governor Rick Perry said. University officials said higher tuition was necessary to help pay for the increasing cost of higher education.[45]

CRIMINAL JUSTICE

Texas did away with public hangings on the courthouse square years ago but retained a frontier attitude toward crime and criminals, an attitude that produced a criminal justice system based more on revenge than rehabilitation (see "Witnessing Executions"). Politicians were elected to the legislature on tough, anticrime promises to "lock 'em up and throw away the key." Once in office, they passed laws providing long sentences for more and more offenses and built more prisons. Eventually, the system was overwhelmed by sheer numbers, and crime became a bigger problem than ever.

Legislators and most other state policymakers ignored deteriorating prison conditions until U.S. District Judge William Wayne Justice of Tyler declared the prison system unconstitutional in 1980 in a landmark lawsuit brought by inmates (*Ruiz v. Estelle*). He cited numerous problems, including overcrowded conditions, poor staffing levels, inadequate medical and psychiatric care for prisoners, and the use of so-called "building tenders"—inmates who were given positions of authority over other prisoners, whom they frequently abused. Justice ordered extensive reforms with which the state agreed to comply, and he appointed a monitor to help him supervise what was then known as the Texas Department of Corrections and is now the institutional division of the Texas Department of Criminal Justice.[46]

Witnessing Executions

After executions were resumed in Texas in 1982, they were witnessed by only a limited number of public officials plus as many as five people designated by the condemned, if he wished to have family members or friends present. Lobbying by crime victims' advocates convinced the Texas Board of Criminal Justice in 1995 to expand the witness list to include as many as five relatives or friends of the condemned's murder victim or victims. Survivors said watching their loved ones' killers be put to death could help bring "closure" to their ordeal. The witness viewing area in the small death chamber in Huntsville was partitioned to separate the condemned's witnesses from those of the victim.

The first execution to be witnessed by the victims' loved ones was that of Leo Ernest Jenkins on February 9, 1996. Jenkins had been sentenced to die by lethal injection for the August 1988 murders of Mark Brandon Kelley, 26, and his sister, Kara Denise Kelley Voss, 20, during a robbery of their family's pawn shop in Houston. The execution was witnessed by the victims' parents, Linda and Jim Kelley; their sister, Robin Amanda Kelley; their grandmother, Angie Kelley; and Mark Kelley's widow, Lisa.

"This is justice in a big way. Believe me, justice was served tonight," Linda Kelley, the victims' mother, said. "I was angry. I was angry at him [Jenkins] when he died."[47]

One key order by Justice limited the population of prison units to 95 percent of capacity to guard against a recurrence of overcrowding and to allow for the housing of inmates according to their classifications, which were designed to separate youthful, first-time offenders from more hardened criminals and those with special needs from the general prison population.

Crowded Prisons Prompt Reforms

The prison population limit and an increase in violent crimes in the 1980s helped produce a criminal justice crisis that lasted for several years. By the time the *Ruiz* lawsuit was settled in 1992 and the state given more flexibility over its prison operations, Texas had spent hundreds of millions of dollars building new prisons but still couldn't accommodate all the offenders flooding the system. Thousands of convicted felons were backlogged in overcrowded county jails because there wasn't enough room in the prisons. And hundreds of dangerous criminals were being paroled early to endanger and outrage law-abiding Texans.

Many of the convicts overloading the system were nonviolent, repeat offenders—among them alcoholics and drug addicts who continued to get in trouble because they were unable to function in the free world. Experts believed that alcoholism, drug addiction, or drug-related crimes were responsible for about 85 percent of the prison population.[48] At the urging of Governor Ann Richards in 1991, the legislature created a new alcoholism and drug abuse treatment program within the prison system, which planners hoped would reduce that recidivism.

In settling the *Ruiz* lawsuit in 1992, the state agreed to maintain safe prisons, and the federal court's active supervision of the prison system ended. Then, in 1993, the legislature enacted a major package of criminal justice reforms, including the first overhaul of the penal code in twenty years. The plan doubled the minimum time that violent felons would have to serve in prison—from one-fourth to one-half of their sentences—before becoming eligible for parole. To reserve more prison space for the most dangerous criminals, however, the legislature lowered the penalties for most property crimes and drug offenses. These nonviolent offenders were diverted to community corrections programs or a new system of state-run jails, to which they could be sentenced for a maximum of two years. To build 20,000 new state jail beds and additional prison units, the legislature and Texas voters also approved a $1 billion bond proposal in 1993. It was the fourth bond authorization, for a total of $3 billion, mostly for prison construction, that voters had approved in six years.

Senator John Whitmire of Houston, then-chairman of the Senate Criminal Justice Committee and an architect of the changes, said the new plan would not only be tough but also "smart" against crime. The changes were supported by some district attorneys, but other prosecutors and some law enforcement officers feared that the lighter penalties for many drug dealers and property criminals would boost the crime rate and make their jobs more difficult.

After taking office in 1991, Governor Richards directed her appointees to the Board of Pardons and Paroles to sharply curtail a parole rate that had been releasing several hundred inmates a week, including murderers and other violent offenders who sometimes killed and raped again. Richards credited the reduction in paroles with a drop in the state's crime rate; but it also increased the backlog of convicted felons in many county jails to dangerously high levels. By early 1994, there were 30,000 state convicts packed into county jails because there was no room for them in state prisons, and several jails had erupted in prisoner disturbances.

The legislature authorized doubling the size of the prison system during the 1994–1995 budget period, and a construction boom was soon underway. Although prisons had traditionally been located in East Texas, new prisons were built throughout the state. Small cities and rural counties, seeking to recover from the recession of the 1980s and eager for the new jobs that prisons would provide, offered the state free land and other considerations in an intense lobbying frenzy. Private contractors also lobbied the Board of Criminal Justice, which chose the sites and granted the contracts.

More Trouble Ahead?

By the late 1990s, Texas had room for more than 150,000 inmates in its prisons, state jails, and substance abuse facilities, and the backlog of convicted felons in county jails was temporarily eliminated. But criminal justice experts warned the state would soon need even more prison space if the legislature didn't enact additional sentencing and parole reforms and attack crime among juveniles. And, sure enough, within a few years the prisons were full again. By the middle of 2008, 173,000 persons were incarcerated in prisons and jails in Texas (see Table 13–5). The state's prison population is overwhelmingly male. Men comprise 92 percent (or 159,000) of the prison population while there are only 14,000 women, or eight percent of the population. To partially address the problem of overcrowding, the State Board of Pardons and Paroles relaxed its rules to speed up the release of convicts who had been returned to prison for minor violations of their paroles, such as not reporting to their parole officers on time.

Is this the only solution to reducing crime rates in Texas? Second only to California, Texas incarcerates some 170,000 people in its prisons and state jails, such as the Fabian Dale Dominquez unit in San Antonio.

TABLE 13–5   Comparison of State Prison Populations, 2008

State	Male Inmates	Female Inmates	Total Inmates	2008 Population Estimates	Incarceration Rate*
California	161,713	11,607	173,320	36,756,666	471
Texas	158,950	14,282	173,232	24,326,974	669
Florida	93,529	6,965	100,494	18,328,340	535
New York	59,520	2,691	62,211	19,490,297	322
Georgia	50,457	3,559	54,016	9,685,744	563
Ohio	47,255	3,905	51,160	11,485,910	442
Michigan	48,384	2,098	50,482	10,003,422	499
Pennsylvania	43,721	2,592	46,313	12,448,279	365
Illinois	42,921	2,754	45,675	12,901,563	N/A
Virginia	36,200	3,024	39,224	7,769,089	490
All 50 States	**1,307,145**	**102,297**	**1,409,422**	**304,059,724**	**506**

*Prisoners per 100,000 persons; includes federal and state prisoners.

Source: U.S. Department of Justice, Bureau of Justice Statistics, "Prison Inmates at Midyear 2008," March 2009; and *Sourcebook of Criminal Justice Statistics Online.*

A Woman's Execution

Most of the more than 300 executions that have been carried out in Texas since executions were resumed in 1982 have received only routine attention in the news media. But the scheduled execution of the 145th inmate—a woman and professed born-again Christian—attracted worldwide attention and renewed debate over the death penalty.

Karla Faye Tucker, 38, was sentenced to die for her role in the pickax murders of two Houstonians in 1983, two of the most gruesome murders in the city's history. As her execution date approached, she appealed for clemency on the basis that she had undergone a religious conversion and been rehabilitated while in prison. She won support from influential religious leaders and even from a former prosecutor involved in her case. But crime victims' advocates strongly supported her execution. The courts rejected her appeals, and the Texas Board of Pardons and Paroles refused her plea to have her death sentence commuted to life in prison. The particularly horrible nature of her crime apparently was a factor in the board's decision.

Tucker was put to death by lethal injection on February 3, 1998, in Huntsville. She was the first woman executed in Texas since the Civil War and only the second woman put to death in the United States since the resumption of the death penalty.

Another woman, Betty Lou Beets, a 62-year-old great-grandmother, was executed in Texas on February 24, 2000. She was put to death for the 1983 murder of Dallas firefighter Jimmy Don Beets, her fifth husband. Prosecutors said she shot him to death to collect his $110,000 pension and life insurance package.

The Death Penalty: Still Popular in Texas

Texas continues to lead the nation in executions. More than 300 men and two women have been put to death in Texas since executions resumed in 1982 (see "A Woman's Execution"). Death penalty opponents took advantage of Governor George W. Bush's presidential race in 2000 to focus international attention on the issue, but most Texans continued to support capital punishment.

According to a Scripps Howard *Texas Poll* conducted during the 2000 presidential race, 73 percent of Texans supported the death penalty, even though 57 percent of the respondents said they believed that innocent people had been executed. Nearly nine out of ten respondents said that death row inmates should have the right to obtain free DNA testing to try to prove their innocence.[47]

HEALTH AND HUMAN SERVICES

This area is where state government weighs compassion against the cold realities of its budget, and Texas has historically been stingy. Texas has traditionally spent less money per capita on health and welfare than most states. Even in the 1970s, when the oil industry was still pumping a healthy amount of tax revenue into the state treasury, Texas was slapped with two federal court orders for providing inadequate care to the mentally ill and the mentally retarded in state institutions. Perhaps the tight-fisted attitude springs from the legacy of frontier colonists standing on their own two feet to fight adversity and win a better life. This view has been perpetuated by countless politicians claiming that Texans could prevail in hard times by pulling up their bootstraps and hanging tough. But this perception ignores the reality that many people in modern Texas cannot pull their bootstraps because they don't have any boots. According to the 2007 American Community Survey, approximately 16.3 percent of Texans—approximately one of every six—lived in poverty. Particularly hard hit were children, the elderly, and minorities (see Chapter 1).

Welfare Reform: Unimpressive Results

By the late 1990s, welfare changes designed to break the cycle of poverty were major priorities of both state and federal governments. New laws emphasized education and job training for welfare recipients and put limits on how long they could collect benefits. The Texas legislature in 1995 enacted a law that required recipients of public assistance to sign responsibility agreements and participate in educational or job training programs in order to receive benefits. It also imposed limits of one to three years on the time a person could collect welfare. The federal government enacted a more sweeping welfare reform law in 1996 that put a five-year lifetime limit on welfare benefits for most recipients and required able-bodied adults to go to work within two years of receiving assistance. The U.S. Congress abolished the Aid to Families with Dependent Children (AFDC) program, which had provided federal funds for every eligible welfare recipient since the 1930s. In its place, the states were given broad authority to design their own welfare programs with fixed amounts of federal money. The new federal law also gave the states quotas to meet in finding jobs for welfare recipients and eliminated most welfare benefits for immigrants.

It will take years to fully evaluate the effectiveness of the welfare changes, but early results in Texas were mixed. State officials reported that more than 100,000 people left Texas's welfare rolls during the first half of 1997 alone. But most of them were children, and not all of the adults quickly found jobs—or at least the kind of employment that would remove them from poverty. About half of the adults who left the welfare rolls had found new jobs, while 10 percent were earning more money from existing jobs, according to an October 1997 survey by the Texas Legislative Council. The legislative researchers said that state and federal welfare reforms had helped, but they concluded that the state's strong economy was the main reason former welfare recipients were finding jobs.[48]

The state agency primarily responsible for moving people from welfare to work was the Texas Workforce Commission, which coordinated job training programs for low-income Texans. Supporters credited the agency with helping reduce the state's welfare rolls by thousands of people. Critics, however, said the agency was training too many people for menial, minimum-wage jobs that didn't pay enough to permanently remove them from poverty. They said the commission needed to offer more training for higher paying jobs that offered a more secure future. But state officials said the economy and private employers—not the government—determined the type of jobs available.[49]

The state's welfare reform law also required poor people to attend state-run classes on how to get a job before they could receive welfare payments. "The class had no textbook and no test," wrote a newspaper reporter who attended one of the early classes conducted by state work counselors in Austin. "But the lesson was clear: Texas expects you to try to get a job before asking for welfare."[50]

More than 275,000 Texas families had left the welfare rolls by 2000, and, according to a study released that year, health care coverage had become a major problem for many of them. This report, by Families USA, a Washington-based advocacy group that supports universal health coverage, determined that 100,000 low-income Texas parents had lost Medicaid coverage since 1996. That was a 46 percent drop in adult Medicaid enrollees in Texas and the second-largest decline among the fifteen states that account for most of the country's uninsured people. Medicaid is a government-sponsored health insurance program for the poor. Although the study didn't determine whether people who left Medicaid had other health insurance, advocates for the poor said many of the people who left Medicaid were probably former welfare recipients who had taken low-paying jobs that didn't offer health insurance. "Only a small minority are lucky enough to land jobs that include an employer-paid health benefit," said Anne Dunkelberg, a health policy analyst at the Center for Public Policy Priorities, an Austin-based advocacy group for low- and middle-income people. "It's an unfortunate shortcoming of welfare reform that we can't guarantee folks that full-time work will get them access to health insurance."[51] State officials said some former welfare recipients could still be eligible for Medicaid but didn't know how many.

By 2006, ten years after the welfare reform law was passed, the number of families receiving welfare in Texas had decreased from 275,000 families to 150,000. Nevertheless, the number of Texans in poverty increased.

Health Insurance for Children

Another critical health care need in Texas is insurance coverage for children. Nearly one-fourth of Texas's 5.8 million children in 1999 didn't have health insurance, ranking Texas next to last among the states in that category. The legislature responded that year by creating the Children's Health Insurance Program, or CHIP, to provide low-cost health coverage to children of the working poor, those families who earned too much to qualify for Medicaid but couldn't afford insurance on their own. The program was open to children younger than nineteen whose families' annual income was no more than twice the poverty level, or $34,100 a year for a family of four. Legislators budgeted $179.6 million for the program in the 2000–2001 state budget, with each dollar the state spent drawing as much as $3 in federal matching funds.[52] In the 2001 legislative session, $122 million was appropriated to simplify and facilitate coverage of children eligible for Medicaid. Even so, thousands of children lost health insurance after the legislature in 2003 reversed course and imposed stricter rules for CHIP coverage to help close a $10 billion shortfall in the state budget. Within only a few months, enrollment had dropped by about 50,000, and it dropped by thousands more within the next two years.

Also by 2003, Texas led the nation in the percentage of uninsured residents, with one in four people, children and adults, lacking health insurance.[53] Critics said state legislators, in cutting back on CHIP coverage, were short-sighted because many children unable to receive preventive health care will end up in the emergency rooms of public hospitals, where treatment for serious, but preventable, illnesses will cost taxpayers even more. The legislature restored some of the CHIP cuts in 2007 but, facing opposition from Governor Rick Perry, refused additional expansion of the program in 2009. That proposal would have made health coverage available to about 80,000 additional children by raising eligibility for CHIP to 300 percent of poverty, or a maximum income of about $66,000 a year for a family of four.

Reorganizing Health and Human Services

The legislature in 2003 also ordered a major reorganization of the state's health and human services agencies. The goal of the most sweeping overhaul of social services in modern Texas history was to make state government smaller and save tax dollars through administrative changes and some privatization. Republican leaders who backed the changes predicted they would benefit both the needy recipients of state services and the taxpayers footing the bill. But advocates for the poor were skeptical. It would take several years to complete the consolidation of twelve agencies into five and assess the results, but the reorganization caught the immediate attention of the business community. Several dozen companies submitted bids for consulting contracts to help the state carry out the privatization effort, but it got off to a rough start.

Accenture, a Bermuda-based company, was given an $899 million state contract to operate call centers to determine applicants' eligibility for public benefits. But soon the company's work was embroiled in controversy, with many applicants complaining of delays in processing claims and lost paperwork. At one point, some applicants even faxed confidential financial and health information to a warehouse in Seattle, Washington, because a wrong phone number had been printed on an information sheet (see "Privatization Hits a Black Hole" in Chapter 10). In late 2006, state officials announced Texas was cutting the contract by $356 million and ending it two years early. Under the changes, Accenture was left primarily with the responsibility for data entry, leaving state employees to screen applicants' qualifications for food stamps, Medicaid and other assistance. "We didn't draw the line between vendor work and state work in the right place," said Health and Human Services Commissioner Albert Hawkins. "As we rebalance the roles between the state and the vendor, we will be drawing that line in a different place."[54]

A Big Payoff from Tobacco

In a major health-related initiative, then–Texas Attorney General Dan Morales sued the tobacco industry in 1996, seeking billions of dollars in reimbursement for tax money spent to treat smoking-related illnesses. The suit also sought restrictions on tobacco companies' marketing and advertising that Morales said were targeting children.

Shortly before Texas's suit was scheduled to go to trial in early 1998, Morales and the tobacco industry negotiated a $17.3 billion settlement. Tobacco companies agreed to pay Texas and its county hospitals the huge sum over twenty-five years and end all their advertising on billboards and public transportation facilities in the state. The agreement called for Texas's first-year proceeds from the settlement, or about $1.2 billion, to be spent on antismoking and health care programs, mostly for children. Morales believed those expenditures were particularly important because health care had traditionally been underfunded in Texas and he considered the antitobacco suit a health care issue. The legislature agreed. Part of the money was used to fund the new Children's Health Insurance Program, described earlier in this section, and most of the remaining funds were used to create numerous health care–related endowments for medical schools and to establish an antismoking education program at the Texas Department of Health.

The way the legislature structured the antismoking education program, however, was controversial. Lawmakers put $200 million of the tobacco funds into an endowment, which budget writers said would ensure the most effective use of the money for years to come. Most health care providers and advocates supported that approach. But the American Cancer Society of Texas, the American Lung Association's Texas division, and the Campaign for Tobacco Free Kids objected because the $200 million endowment initially would generate only about $10 million a year that could actually be spent. The dissenting groups said that amount was woefully inadequate for developing effective antismoking programs in a state as large as Texas.

An even larger controversy, meanwhile, raged over $3.3 billion in legal fees awarded to a team of private plaintiffs' lawyers that Morales had hired on a contingency contract to represent the state in the tobacco suit. The fees were to be paid by tobacco companies, not by the state, over an undetermined number of years. And Morales insisted that the state couldn't have won the huge settlement without the lawyers' help. But then-Governor George W. Bush and other critics complained that the legal fees were excessive.

Texas wasn't the only state to sue tobacco companies. Mississippi, Florida, and Minnesota also negotiated separate out-of-court settlements with the industry. And, after Texas reached its settlement in 1998, cigarette companies negotiated a national $246 billion settlement with the remaining states.

ENVIRONMENTAL PROBLEMS AND POLICIES ——————●

Texas is blessed with an abundance of fragile natural resources that can no longer be taken for granted. But efforts to impose environmental regulations are difficult for a number of reasons. For one, Texas still has a large share of the nation's oil refining and chemical manufacturing industries, despite the 1980s oil bust. And while efforts have been made to reduce environmental risks, state policymakers are influenced by economic considerations because those same industries employ thousands of people and pump billions of dollars into the economy and the state treasury. Compounding the problem are the desire to attract new industries, a legacy that emphasizes individual property rights, and Texans' love for their automobiles, pickups, and sport utility vehicles.

Dirty Air

In a national environmental survey in 1992, *City & State* magazine ranked Texas forty-eighth of the fifty states in the quality of governmental programs protecting natural resources. "This is a state that will do what it can to attract and keep business, even if that means a price must be paid with increased pollution," the magazine said.[55] Texas received some additional notoriety in 1999 when Houston beat out Los Angeles for the unwanted title of the nation's "dirtiest air" city. Specifically, the Houston metropolitan area led the nation that year in the number of days—fifty-two—in which the city's air violated the national health standard for ozone, the main ingredient in smog. Los Angeles ended the year with forty-two violation days. Ozone, which contributes to respiratory health problems, is formed when various pollutants in the air mix in sunlight, and it can be a major problem on sunny, summer days. Some progress has been made since then. For one thing, Los Angeles reclaimed its "dirtiest air" standing. Los Angeles recorded 49 days of smog reaching unhealthy levels in 2002, compared to 26 in Houston, that city's fewest number of days in 15 years.[56] But problems persist.

Unlike large cities in many other states, Texas cities have been slow to develop local rail transportation systems. Dallas and Houston only recently built the state's first two, and Austin was following suit with a limited rail system of its own. But automobiles have increasingly clogged streets and freeways and spewed tons of pollutants into the air. State officials responded with antipollution restrictions only after being forced to do so by the federal government. To meet federal Clean Air Act standards for smog reduction, the state now requires motorists in the Houston, Dallas-Fort Worth, and certain other metropolitan areas to have special emissions inspections of their cars. And, speed limits on freeways and highways in metropolitan areas have been lowered to 55 miles per hour. In 2003, the legislature—to avoid losing millions of dollars in federal highway funding—also enacted a plan for raising state funds to pay for the emission reduction effort. The plan, among other things, increased the costs of auto title transfers and imposed surcharges on some large diesel equipment.

Many state political leaders also have preferred to encourage industries to voluntarily reduce pollution, rather than impose strict cleanup requirements. Then-Governor George W. Bush, for example, convinced the legislature in 1999 to enact a voluntary cleanup program for many of the old industrial facilities in Texas that still hadn't been brought into compliance with federal clean air standards. These facilities had been built before 1971 and had initially been "grandfathered" by lawmakers that year from the higher emission-control standards placed on new industrial plants. Environmentalists complained that many of the old facilities were major polluters and urged the legislature to require them to upgrade their equipment. But state lawmakers required only "grandfathered" power plants operated by utility companies to be upgraded while continuing voluntary compliance for the older plants in other industries. Legislators raised state emissions fees on the biggest polluters as an incentive for them to comply, but environmentalists complained that the higher fees would apply to only a handful of plants.[57]

Global Warming

The debate over global warming has escalated in Texas in recent years, as it has internationally. Some state officials have tried to ignore global warming, others have tried to downplay its potential significance, and others have said they don't believe a growing body of scientific evidence that emissions of climate-changing gases were taking a toll on the environment. Despite the political debate, scientists at Texas A&M University issued a report in 2009 emphasizing that not only was global warming real but that, in the not-too-distant future, it would pose a potentially devastating threat to the Gulf Coast region of Texas. These scientists predicted that global warming would cause sea levels to rise, spawn more intense hurricanes, and result in more coastal flooding. Damage to coastal communities from hurricanes would more than triple by the 2080s. The study, funded by the National Commission on Energy Policy, a bipartisan research and advisory group, assumed the storms would be more intense and produce higher sea levels because of human-induced global warming.[58]

An Endangered Water Supply

Population growth and a drought in the mid-1990s increased public concern over Texas's water supply. Much of the attention of environmentalists, farmers, ranchers, and government officials initially was focused on the underground Edwards Aquifer, the sole source of water for San Antonio and its rural neighbors. A major legal battle began in 1991, when the Sierra Club sued the federal government, contending the U.S. Interior Department had violated the Endangered Species Act. The environmentalists said the department had failed to guard against excessive pumping from the underground reservoir, which could endanger salamanders that live in the aquifer or aquifer-fed springs.

The lawsuit angered many San Antonians and farmers and ranchers. Nevertheless, U.S. District Judge Lucius Bunton of Midland ruled in favor of the Sierra Club, warning that overpumping not only threatened endangered species, but also posed a contamination threat to the aquifer itself. Bunton eventually ordered San Antonio and several smaller cities to reduce pumping from the aquifer, but his order was blocked in 1996 by the Fifth U.S. Circuit Court of Appeals in New Orleans.[59] In 1993, the Texas legislature created the regional Edwards Aquifer Authority with the power to regulate pumping from the aquifer and to protect the reservoir from pollution. The Texas Supreme

Court upheld the state law in 1996, despite the objections of landowners who contended the state was ignoring their rights.[60]

Advocates of landowners' rights argued that any pumping limitations could damage the livelihoods of farmers and ranchers and adversely affect the San Antonio economy. Emotions ran high. Maurice Rimkus, a Uvalde County farmer, said of the Sierra Club: "It's a loose nut that's been cross-threaded on the bolt. They're a bunch of idealists living in a dream world."[61]

Environmentalists argued that more than salamanders were at stake. The future of San Antonio and the entire region was dependent on protecting water levels in the aquifer, they said. "San Antonio and the agricultural users have been in a state of denial for a number of years about the seriousness of the situation," said Ken Kramer, director of the Lone Star Chapter of the Sierra Club.[62] After the drought worsened in 1996, the legislature approved a comprehensive, statewide water conservation plan in 1997.

Another water issue also has begun to attract attention. State Land Commissioner Jerry Patterson has proposed leasing state lands to private companies, which would pump groundwater for sale to cities or other entities that needed it. Patterson said such leases could raise more money for public education, but critics questioned how much water a growing state could afford to sell.

Centralized Regulation

The legislature in 1993 centralized most of state government's environmental protection efforts into one agency, the Texas Natural Resource Conservation Commission, which consolidated separate agencies that had specialized in protecting water, air, and other selected resources. Both industrial interests and environmentalists generally preferred the new commission, later renamed the Texas Commission on Environmental Quality, over the fragmented regulatory system that it replaced. Some environmental leaders, however, complained that the agency, in deciding the fate of new industrial permits, all too often favored economic development over environmental protection.

SUMMARY AND CONCLUSIONS ●

1. The political power necessary to shape policy is exercised through groups, and some groups are more influential than others. Setting public policy also usually involves questions of costs and benefits. The ultimate political problem is who will benefit from specific policy decisions and who will pay the bill.

2. "Iron triangles" of state government—key legislators and their staffs, high-level bureaucrats, and interest group lobbyists—are at the center of the policymaking process. They also can be part of larger "issue networks" that reflect the increased interdependence of state and local governments on the federal government and the heightened role of issue specialists.

3. The legislature is primarily responsible for setting policy at the state level, but the separation of powers doctrine gives the judiciary important scrutiny over legislative action—or inaction. In recent years, federal and state court decisions have forced the legislature to make major changes in education, criminal justice, and mental health and mental retardation programs. These developments have compounded a state budgetary process already made difficult by a two-year budget cycle, a changing economy, and outdated tax and budgetary structures.

4. Although Texas recently spent billions of dollars on an unprecedented prison expansion program, most state leaders realize that new prisons alone won't solve the crime problem. More crucial in the

long run will be the state's efforts to improve quality in the public schools, and develop equity in school financing, because many failures in the public school system soon enter the criminal justice system. State officials also recognize the importance of alcohol and drug abuse treatment programs in fighting criminal behavior.

5. Texas historically has been stingy in spending on health and human services programs, reflecting the individualistic political view that has long been dominant in the state. New federal and state laws require state officials to move thousands of poor people off the welfare rolls and into jobs, but welfare reform is a difficult task.

KEY TERMS

Issue networks   430
Deficit financing   430
Dedicated funds   432
Sales tax   433
Franchise tax   434
Property tax   434

Sin tax   434
Lottery   434
General obligation bonds   436
Income tax   437
House Bill 72   440
No pass, no play   440

Edgewood v. Kirby   441
Permanent University Fund
  (PUF)   445
Ruiz v. Estelle   447

FURTHER READING

Articles

Burka, Paul, "You Lose Again!" *Texas Monthly* 26 (March 1998), pp. 108, 114–117.

King, Michael, "Who's Poisoning Texas: Part I?" *Texas Observer* 90 (April 24, 1998), pp. 8–12.

———, "Who's Poisoning Texas: Part II?" *Texas Observer* 90 (May 8, 1998), pp. 8–13.

Mandell, Jeff, "Privatizing Hopwood," *Texas Observer* 90 (January 16, 1998).

Somma, Mark, "Institutions, Ideology, and the Tragedy of the Commons: West Texas Groundwater Policy," *Publius* 27 (Winter 1997), pp. 1–13.

Walters, Jonathan, "Did Somebody Say Downsizing?" *Governing* 11 (February 1998), pp. 17–20.

Books

Anton, Thomas J., *Federalism and Public Policy: How the System Works.* New York: Random House, 1989.

Cochran, Clarke E., Lawrence C. Mayer, T. R. Carr, and N. Joseph Cayer, *American Public Policy: An Introduction,* 8th ed. Belmont, CA: Thomson Wadsworth, 2006.

Dye, Thomas R., *Understanding Public Policy,* 12th ed. Upper Saddle River, NJ: Prentice Hall, 2008.

Heclo, Hugh, "Issue Networks and the Executive Establishment," in *The New American Political System,* edited by Anthony King. Washington, DC: American Enterprise Institute, 1978.

Harpham, Edward J., "Welfare Reform and the New Paternalism in Texas," in *Texas Politics: A Reader,* edited by Anthony Champagne and Edward J. Harpham. New York: W. W. Norton, 1997.

Sharp, John, Texas Comptroller of Public Accounts, *A Report from the Texas Performance Review: Behind the Walls—The Price and Performance of the Texas Department of Criminal Justice.* Austin: Texas Comptroller of Public Accounts, 1994.

———, Texas Comptroller of Public Accounts, *Breaking the Mold: New Ways to Govern Texas: A Report from the Texas Performance Review,* 2 vols. Austin, TX: Texas Comptroller of Public Accounts, 1991.

Thomas, Clark D., "Education Reform in Texas," in *Texas Politics: A Reader,* edited by Anthony Champagne and Edward J. Harpham. New York: W. W. Norton, 1997.

Weinstein, Bernard L., "Taxes in Texas," in *Texas Politics: A Reader,* edited by Anthony Champagne and Edward J. Harpham. New York: W. W. Norton, 1997.

Websites

Center for Public Policy Priorities   http://www.cppp.org/ The center focuses on public policies affecting low- and middle-income people, including health care, child care, human services funding, welfare reform, and nutrition.

Common Cause of Texas   http://www.commoncause.org/site/pp.asp?c=dkLINK1MQIwG&b=4846323 Common Cause is a nonpartisan, nonprofit citizens organization committed to "honest and accountable government." Reports, policy positions, and legislative alerts can be found at this site.

Consumers Union http://www.consumersunion.org/ This is an independent, nonprofit "testing and information organization serving only consumers." The organization's advocates testify before federal and state legislative and regulatory bodies on policies affecting consumers. The organization's communications and policy positions can be found at this site.

Sierra Club http://www.texas.sierraclub.org/ The Sierra Club has been actively involved in a number of statewide environmental issues. In addition to providing links to other sites, this site has policy reports and action alerts.

Texas Association of Business http://www.txbiz.org/ Committed to serving business interests in Texas, this site provides information on the organization's legislative program, legislative updates, and links to other legislative sources.

Texas Taxpayers and Research Association http://www.ttara.org/ This is an association of businesses and individuals interested in state fiscal policy and other public policy issues.

ENDNOTES

1. Lieutenant Governor Bob Bullock, January 31, 1991, responding to a reporter's question about how big a tax bill he believed the legislature would have to enact that year.

2. Thomas R. Dye, *Understanding Public Policy,* 12th edition (Upper Saddle River, NJ: Prentice Hall, 2008), p. 1.

3. This section draws primarily from L. L. Wade and R. L. Curry, Jr., *A Logic of Public Policy: Aspects of Political Economy* (Belmont, CA: Wadsworth, 1970), Chapter 1.

4. Ibid. This same chapter is an excellent introduction to the definitional issues and approaches to public policy analysis.

5. The following discussion is organized around the general stages presented by James E. Anderson, David W. Brady, Charles S. Bullock, III, and Joseph Stewart, Jr., *Public Policy and Politics in America,* 2nd ed. (Monterey, CA: Brooks/Cole, 1984); and Charles O. Jones, *An Introduction to the Study of Public Policy,* 2nd ed. (North Scituate, MA: Duxbury Press, 1977).

6. Anderson, et al., *Public Policy and Politics in America,* p. 8.

7. Jones, *An Introduction to the Study of Public Policy,* pp. 138–39.

8. Ibid., p. 139.

9. Randall B. Ripley and Grace A. Franklin, *Congress, the Bureaucracy, and Public Policy,* 3rd ed. (Homewood, IL: Dorsey, 1984), p. 10.

10. Hugh Heclo, "Issue Networks and the Executive Establishment," in *The New American Political System,* edited by Anthony King (Washington, DC: American Enterprise Institute, 1978), p. 88. Much of this section is based on this article.

11. Ibid., p. 107.

12. Ibid., p. 104.

13. Federation of Tax Administrators, "State Individual Income Taxes, 2008." New Hampshire and Tennessee tax income from dividends and interest but not salaries or wages.

14. Clay Robison, "Taxes in Crisis—Tax 'Quilt' is Bursting at Seams—Lawmakers Facing Inequitable Tax Bite," *Houston Chronicle,* April 22, 1991, p. 1A.

15. Michael P. Ettlinger, Robert S. McIntyre, Elizabeth A. Fray, John F. O'Hare, Julie King, and Neil Miransky, *Who Pays? A Distributional Analysis of the Tax Systems in All 50 States,* 2nd ed. (Washington, DC: Citizens for Tax Justice and the Institute on Taxation and Economic Policy, 2003), p. 9.

16. Federation of Tax Administrators, "State Sales Taxes," January 2008.

17. Texas Comptroller of Public Accounts, "Texas Net Revenue by Source for Fiscal 2008." www.window.state.tx.us/taxbud/revenue.html.

18. Texas Comptroller of Public Accounts, *Annual Property Tax Report—Tax Year 2007,* Ch. 1, p. 4. www.window.state.tx.us/taxinfo/proptax/annual07/index.html.

19. Texas Comptroller of Public Accounts, "Revenue by Source for Fiscal Year 2008." (cited above in footnote 17).

20. Ibid.

21. R.G. Ratcliffe, "Lottery Names Latest Director–$248 Million Expected Shortfall to Schools Seen" *Houston Chronicle,* December 17, 1997, p. 37A.

22. Texas Comptroller of Public Accounts, "Revenue by Source for Fiscal Year 2008." (cited above in footnote 17.

23. Kava Peterson, "48 States Raking in Gambling Proceeds," *Stateline,* May 23, 2006, www.stateline.org/live/details/story?contentId=114503; and American Gaming Association, "Industry Information: States with Gaming." www.americangaming.org/Industry/factsheets/general_info_detail.cfv?id=15.

24. Texas Bond Review Board, "Debt Affordability Study," February 2009, p. 3. www.brb.state.tx.us/pub/bfo/DAS2009.pdf.

25. Ibid., p. 38.

26. R. G. Ratcliffe, "Texas Trend Relies on Bonds to Build Now," *Houston Chronicle,* January 16, 1989, p. 1A.

27. Clay Robison, "Bullock Backs State Income Tax—Richards, Lewis Dubious," *Houston Chronicle,* March 7, 1991, p. 1A.

28. *The Texas Poll,* April 21, 1991, conducted for Harte-Hanks Communications, Inc., by the Public Policy Resources Laboratory of Texas A&M University.

29. Clay Robison, "Task Force Urges State Income Tax—Panel's Proposal Not Expected to Pass During Special Session," *Houston Chronicle,* June 30, 1991, p. 1A.

30. Clay Robison, "Separate and Unequal—Two School Districts Differ by 12 Miles, Lots of Money," *Houston Chronicle,* August 19, 1990, p, 1 State.

31. *Edgewood Independent School District, et al. v. William Kirby, et al.,* 777 S.W. 2d 391 (1989).

32. Ibid.

33. *Edgewood Independent School District, et al. v. Lionel Meno, et al.,* 893 S.W. 2d 450 (1995).

34. Associated Press, "38% of Teachers Thinking of Calling it Quits," *Houston Chronicle,* April 30, 1994, p. 36A.

35. National Education Association, news release, May 21, 2003.

36. American Federation of Teachers, *Survey and Analysis of Teacher Salary Trends, 2007* (Washington, DC, 2007).

37. *Associated Press,* November 4, 2003.

38. Wendy Benjaminson, "Home Schools Win Court Fight/Ruling Backs Right to Teach Their Own Children," *Houston Chronicle,* June 16, 1994, p. 1A.

39. U.S. Department of Education, National Center for Education Statistics, "1.5 Million Homeschooled Students in the United States in 2007," *Issue Brief,* December 2008.

40. *Ann Richards, et al. v. League of United Latin American Citizens, et al.,* S.W. 2d 306 (1993).

41. *Hopwood, et al., v. State of Texas, et al.,* 78 F.3d 932 (1996).

42. Lydia Lum, "UH Won't Award Scholarship Pending Review of AG Ruling," *Houston Chronicle,* February 7, 1997, p. 20A.

43. Lydia Lum, "The Hopwood Effect/Minorities Heading Out of State for Professional Schools," *Houston Chronicle,* August 25, 1997, p. 1A.

44. Lum, "UH Won't Award Scholarship Pending Review of AG Ruling," p. 20A.

45. Clay Robison, "Since Deregulation, College Tuition Costs 39% More than 3 Years Ago—Appropriations for Financial Aid Have Not Kept Pace," *Houston Chronicle,* September 24, 2006, p. A1

46. *Ruiz v. Estelle,* 503 F.Sup. 1265 (1980).

47. Lee Hancock, "Victims' Relatives Watch Execution in 1st for Texas," *Dallas Morning News,* February 10, 1996, p. 1A.

48. Clay Robison, Julie Mason, and Jim Zook, "Building of Prisons under Gun—2 Legislators Say It's up to County," *Houston Chronicle,* September 8, 1991, p. 25A.

49. The Scripps Howard *Texas Poll,* Scripps Howard Data Center, June 2000.

50. Polly Ross Hughes, "Job Aid Drop in Welfare Rolls—Poll Responses Raise Concern," *Houston Chronicle,* October 19, 1997, p. 1A.

51. Bill Minutaglio, "State Workforce Commission Falls under Increased Scrutiny—Critics Doubt Long-term Effects; Supporters Tout Welfare Numbers," *Dallas Morning News,* December 14, 1997, p. 1A.

52. Denise Gamino, "Welfare 'Students' Find Job Class Dull, but Attendance is Required," *Austin American–Statesman,* December 6, 1997, p. B1.

53. *Dallas Morning News,* June 20, 2000, p. 1A.

54. Christopher Lee, "Applicants Flock to Health Plan—More than 23,000 Families Seek Low-Cost Insurance for Children," *Dallas Morning News,* April 8, 2000, p. 33A.

55. Polly Ross Hughes, "Rule Changes Push Thousands of Children off Insurance Rolls," *Houston Chronicle,* November 12, 2003, p. 1A

56. Janet Elliott, "State Social Services Contract–Accenture Deal to be Reduced by $356 Million, End 2 Years Early over Backlog, Errors," *Houston Chronicle,* December 22, 2006, p. A1.

57. *City & State,* July 13, 1993, pp. SG2, SG6.

58. Dina Cappiello, "Houston Avoids Title of Smoggiest U.S. City," *Houston Chronicle,* September 24, 2003, p. 23A.

59. Bill Dawson and Clay Robison, "76th Legislature—Compromise Will Urge Older Plants to Reduce Emissions Voluntarily," *Houston Chronicle,* May 31, 1999, p. 26A.

60. Matthew Tresaugue, "Global Warming Warning for Texas Coastal Damage Could Triple by 2080s," *Houston Chronicle,* June 2, 2009, p. 3B.

61. Ralph K. M. Haurwitz, "Court Blocks Order to Trim Use of Water," *Austin American–Statesman,* September 11, 1996, p. B1.

62. Associated Press, *Dallas Morning News,* June 29, 1996.

63. Ralph K.M Haurwitz, "Judge Could Shut the Tap on Aquifer's Users," *Austin American–Statesman,* June 13, 1994, p.A1.

64. Ibid.

Glossary

Absentee (or early) voting A period before the regularly scheduled election date during which voters are allowed to cast ballots. With recent changes in election law, a person does not have to offer a reason for voting absentee.

Activists A small segment of the population that is engaged in various political activities.

Agenda building The process of groups or individuals identifying problems or issues that affect them and keeping pressure on policymakers to develop and implement public policy solutions.

Agenda setting A theory that the media's choice of which news events and issues to cover helps define what is important for the public to know and what issues to think about.

Agriculture, commissioner of An elected state official responsible for administering laws and programs that benefit agriculture.

Annexation The authority of cities to add territory, subject to restrictions set by state law.

Appellate jurisdiction The authority of a court to review the decisions of lower courts to determine if the law was correctly interpreted and legal procedures were correctly followed.

Appraisal district County-wide tax office that appraises the value of property and certifies the tax rolls used by every taxing authority in the county.

Appropriations bill A legislative action authorizing the expenditure of money for a public program or purpose. A general appropriations bill approved by the legislature every two years is the state budget.

Attorney general The state's chief legal officer. He or she represents the state in lawsuits, is responsible for enforcing the state's antitrust, consumer protection, and other civil laws, and issues advisory opinions on legal questions to state and local officeholders. This elected official has little responsibility for criminal law enforcement.

Bicameral legislature A law-making body, such as the Texas legislature, that includes two chambers.

Bifactionalism The presence of two dominant factions organized around regional, economic, or ideological differences within a single political party. For much of the twentieth century, Texas functioned as a one-party system with two dominant factions.

Bifurcated court system Existence of two courts at the highest level of the state judiciary. The Texas Supreme Court is the court of last resort in civil cases, and the Court of Criminal Appeals has the final authority to review criminal cases. Texas and Oklahoma are the only two states that use this system.

Block grants Federal grants of money to states and local governments for broad programs or services rather than narrowly defined programs. These grants give state and local governments more discretion over the use of the funds.

Bureaucracy The agencies of government and their employees responsible for carrying out policies and providing public services approved by elected officials.

Calendar The agenda or the list of bills to be considered by the House or the Senate on a given day.

Campaign consultant A professional expert who helps political candidates plan, organize, and run their campaigns.

Capital murder Murder committed under certain circumstances for which the death penalty or life in prison must be imposed.

Capitol press corps Representatives of Texas newspapers, television and radio stations, and wire services who are assigned to Austin full time to report on state government and politics.

Categorical grants-in-aid Grants of federal money that can be spent only for specific programs or purposes. This is the source of most federal assistance to state and local governments.

Caucus A group of legislators who band together for common political or partisan goals or along ethnic or geographic lines.

City charter A document, defined or authorized by state law, under which a city operates. In Texas home rule cities, local voters may choose among several forms of city government.

City commission A form of city government in which elected commissioners collectively serve as a city's policy-making body and individually serve as administrative heads of different city departments. Although once popular, this form of government is rarely used in Texas today.

City, general law Texas cities with fewer than 5,000 residents are allowed to exercise only those powers specifically granted to them by the legislature. Most cities in Texas are classified as general law cities.

City, home rule Texas cities with more than 5,000 residents can adopt any form of government residents choose, provided it does not conflict with the state constitution or statutes. Home rule powers are formalized through local voters' adoption of a city charter spelling out how the city is to be governed.

Civil lawsuit A noncriminal legal dispute between two or more individuals, businesses, governments, or other entities.

Civil Service system (*see Merit Employment System*).

Commissioner of the General Land Office An elected official who manages the state's public lands and administers the Veterans Land Program, which provides low-interest loans to veterans for the purchase of land and houses.

Commissioners court The principal policy-making body for county government comprised of four commissioners and the county judge. It sets the county tax rate and supervises expenditures.

Committee, Calendars A special procedural committee in the Texas House of Representatives that schedules bills that already have been approved by other committees for floor debate.

Committee, conference A panel of House members and senators appointed to work out a compromise on a bill if different versions of the legislation were passed by the House and the Senate.

Committee, select A special committee—usually appointed by the governor, the lieutenant governor, and the speaker—that studies a specific issue and makes recommendations to the legislature. This panel usually includes private citizens as well as legislators.

Committee, standing A legislative committee that specializes in bills by subject matter. A bill has to win committee approval before it can be considered by the full House or Senate.

Comptroller of Public Accounts The state's primary tax administrator and revenue estimator. It is an elective position.

Concurrent powers Powers shared by both the national and state governments.

Confederation (confederacy) A system in which each member government is considered sovereign, and the national government is limited to powers delegated to it by its member governments.

Constable An elected law enforcement officer assigned as an administrative officer in a justice of the peace precinct. He or she is responsible primarily for executing court judgments, serving subpoenas, and delivering other legal documents. Constables also are authorized to patrol their precincts, make arrests, and conduct criminal investigations.

Constitution Legal structure of a political system, establishing government bodies and defining their powers.

Constitutional Convention of 1974 The last major attempt to write a new Texas constitution. Members of the legislature served as delegates and failed to overcome political differences and the influence of special interests.

Constitutional county courts The Texas Constitution provides for 254 courts with limited jurisdiction and held by an elected county judge.

Contract theory The view that governments originated from the general agreement among and consent of members of the public to address common interests and needs.

Cooperative federalism Policies emphasizing cooperative efforts among the federal, state, and local governments to address common problems and provide public services to the citizens.

Co-optation Influence over state regulatory boards by the industries they are supposed to regulate, often to the detriment of the general public.

Council-manager government A form of city government in which policy is set by an elected city council, which hires a professional city manager to head the daily administration of city government.

County attorney An elected official who is the chief legal officer of some counties. He or she also prosecutes lesser criminal offenses, primarily misdemeanors, in county courts.

County auditor An officer appointed by the district judges of the county. This person is primarily responsible for reviewing every bill and expenditure of a county to assure it is correct and legal. All counties with 10,000 or more residents are required to have an auditor, and smaller counties may have one if commissioners court chooses. In counties with more than 225,000 people, the auditor is also the budget officer who prepares the county budget for consideration by commissioners court.

County chair The presiding officer of a political party's county executive committee. He or she is elected countywide by voters in the party primary.

County clerk The chief record-keeping officer of a county.

County court, constitutional (*see Commissioners Court*).

County court-at-law, statutory A court created by the legislature that exercises limited jurisdiction over criminal and/or civil cases. The jurisdiction of these courts varies from county to county.

County executive committee A panel responsible on the local level for the organization and management of a political party's primary election. It includes the party's county chair and each precinct chair.

County judge The presiding officer of a county commissioners court. This office also has some judicial authority, which is assumed by separate county courts-at-law in most urban counties.

County tax assessor-collector An elected official who determines how much property tax is owed on the different pieces of property within a county and then collects the tax. This officeholder acts on the basis of property values determined by the county appraisal district and a tax rate set by county commissioners court.

County treasurer An elected officer who is responsible for receiving and disbursing county funds. The office's primary functions are now carried out by the county auditor, and the office has been eliminated in a number of counties.

Court of Appeals An intermediate-level court that reviews civil and criminal cases from the district courts.

Court of Criminal Appeals, Texas A Texas nine-member court with final appellate jurisdiction over criminal cases.

Davis, Governor Edmund J. Unpopular Republican governor (1870–1874), whose highly unpopular policies contributed to the decisions of the Constitutional Convention of 1875 to limit and fragment the powers of the governor.

Dealignment A view that the party system is breaking up and the electoral influence of political parties is being replaced by interest groups, the media, and well-financed candidates who use their own media campaigns to dominate the nomination and election process.

Dedicated funds Constitutional or statutory requirements that restrict some state tax or fee revenues to spending on specific programs.

Deficit financing Borrowing money to meet operating expenses. It is prohibited by the Texas constitution, which provides that state government operate on a pay-as-you-go basis.

Delegated powers These are powers specifically assigned to the national, or federal, government by the U.S. Constitution, including powers to tax, borrow and coin money, declare war, and regulate interstate and foreign commerce.

Denied powers Powers that are denied to both the states and national government. The best known restrictions are listed in the Bill of Rights.

Devolution Return of powers assumed by the federal government to the states.

Dillon rule A principle holding that local governments are creations of state government and their powers and responsibilities are defined by the state.

District attorney An elected official who prosecutes the more serious criminal offenses, usually felonies, before state district courts.

District court Court with general jurisdiction over criminal felony cases and civil disputes.

Economic diversification   The development of new and varied business activities. New businesses were encouraged to relocate or expand in Texas after the oil and gas industry, which had been the base of the state's economy, suffered a major recession in the 1980s.

Edgewood v. Kirby   A lawsuit in which the Texas Supreme Court in 1989 declared the Texas school finance system unconstitutional because of wide disparities in property wealth and educational opportunities between school districts.

Editorial autonomy   The freedom of a local newspaper or television station to set its own news policies independently of absentee owners who may run a chain of media outlets throughout the country.

Election, at-large   A system under which city council members or other officeholders are elected by voters in the entire city, school district, or single-purpose district. Many of these election systems have been struck down by the federal courts or by the U.S. Justice Department under the Voting Rights Act as discriminatory against minorities.

Election, general   An election for state, federal, and county offices held in November of even-numbered years. The ballot includes nominees of the two major political parties plus other candidates who meet certain legal requirements.

Election, local   An election for city council, the school board, and certain other local offices. Most of these are nonpartisan.

Election, nonpartisan   Local elections where candidates file for place, position, or district with no political party label attached to their names.

Election, primary   An election in which the Democratic or Republican party chooses its nominees for public offices. In presidential election years, the primary also plays a key role in selecting Texas delegates to the parties' national nominating conventions.

Election, retention   Elections in which judges run on their own records rather than against other candidates. Voters cast their ballots on the question of whether the incumbent judge should stay in office.

Election, rollback   An election in which local voters can nullify a property tax increase that exceeds 8 percent in a given year.

Election, runoff   This is required if no candidate receives an absolute majority of the votes cast in a primary race. The runoff is between the top two vote-getters.

Election, special   An election set by the legislature or called by the governor for a specific purpose, such as voting on constitutional amendments or filling a vacancy in a legislative office. Local governments can also call special elections.

Elitism   The view that political power is primarily held by a few individuals who derive power from leadership positions in large business, civic, or governmental institutions.

Establishment, The   In the days of one-party Democratic politics in Texas, it was a loosely knit coalition of Anglo businessmen, oilmen, bankers, and lawyers who controlled state policymaking through the dominant, conservative wing of the Democratic party.

Extradition   A process by which a person in one state can be returned to another state to face criminal charges.

Extraterritorial jurisdiction   The power of an incorporated city to control development within nearby unincorporated areas.

Fat cat   An individual who contributes a large amount of money to political candidates.

Federalism   A system that balances the power and sovereignty of state governments with the national government. Both the states and the national government derive their authority directly from the people, and the states have considerable autonomy within their areas of responsibility.

Felony   A criminal offense that can be punished by imprisonment and/or a fine. This is a more serious offense than a misdemeanor.

Filibuster   A procedure that allows a senator to speak against a bill for as long as he or she can stand and talk. It can become a formidable obstacle or threat against controversial bills near the end of a legislative session.

Full faith and credit   A provision in the U.S. Constitution (Article IV, Section 1) that requires states to recognize civil judgments and official documents rendered by the courts of other states.

General obligation bonds   A method of borrowing money to pay for new construction projects, such as prisons or mental hospitals. Interest on these bonds, which require voter approval in the form of constitutional amendments, is paid with tax revenue.

Gerrymandering   The drawing of political districts in such a way as to reduce the effect of voting by members of an ethnic or political minority.

Globalization of the economy   Increased interdependence in trade, manufacturing, and commerce between the United States and other countries.

Governor   The state's top executive officeholder.

Grand jury   Panel that reviews evidence submitted by prosecutors to determine whether to indict, or charge, an individual with a criminal offense. A grand jury can hear witnesses, but all its meetings are in private.

Grange   An organization formed in the late nineteenth century to improve the lot of farmers. Its influence in Texas after Reconstruction was felt in constitutional provisions limiting taxes and government spending and restricting banks, railroads, and other big businesses.

Grant, formula   A federal grant based on specific criteria such as income levels or population.

Grant, project   A federal grant for a defined project.

Grassroots   A term used to describe a wide range of political activities designed to organize and mobilize the electorate at the local level. While modern campaigns are increasingly dominated by the campaign consultants, such support can prove crucial for political candidates, particularly for those with limited financial resources.

Homestead exemption   Provision of the law that permits a person who owns a home and is living in it to claim an exemption to reduce the property taxes on the house.

House Bill 72   A landmark school reform law enacted in 1984. Among other things, it reduced class sizes, required teachers to pass a literacy test to keep their jobs, and imposed the no pass, no play rule, which restricts failing students from participating in extracurricular activities.

Hyperpluralism   The rapid expansion of interest groups that serves to disrupt and potentially deadlock the policy-making process.

Implied powers   Although not specifically defined by the U.S. Constitution, these are powers assumed by the national government as necessary in carrying out its responsibilities.

Independent school district   A specific form of special district that administers the public schools in a designated area. It is governed by an elected board of trustees empowered to levy local property taxes, establish local school policies, and employ a school superintendent as its chief administrator.

Indictment   A written statement issued by a grand jury, charging a person or persons with a crime or crimes.

Individualism   An attitude, rooted in classical liberal theory and reinforced by the frontier tradition, that citizens are capable of taking care of themselves with minimal governmental assistance.

Individualistic subculture   A view that government should interfere as little as possible in the private activities of its citizens while assuring that adequate public facilities and a favorable business climate are available to permit individuals to pursue their self-interests.

Information age   A reference to the contemporary era where there has been an explosion of information available through new information technologies.

Initiative   A petition and election process where voters propose laws or constitutional amendments for adoption by a popular vote.

Institutionalization   The complex process of institutional change and adaptation in the organization and operations of the legislature.

Interest group   A group of people with common goals who are organized to seek political results they are unable to achieve by themselves.

Interstate compacts   Formal, long-term cooperative agreements among the states dealing with common problems or issues and subject to approval of the U.S. Congress.

Iron rule of oligarchy   A theory developed by Robert Michels, a European sociologist, that all organizations inevitably are dominated by a few individuals.

Iron triangles   Relationships among the interest groups, the administrative agencies, and the legislative committees involved in drafting the laws and regulations affecting a particular area of the economy or a specific segment of the population.

Issue networks Term coined by Hugh Heclo to describe the complex institutional and political relationships in the policy-making process.

Issue-attention cycle A pattern in which public interest in an issue or problem is heightened by intensive media coverage. Media attention and public interest will wane after government takes steps to address their concerns, but most issues or problems are never permanently resolved. Another crisis, perhaps years later, will restart the cycle.

Jim Crow laws Legislation enacted by many states after the Civil War to limit the rights and power of African Americans.

Justice of the peace court A low-ranking court with jurisdiction over minor civil disputes and criminal cases.

Licensing A key regulatory function of government that seeks to ensure that individuals and companies providing critical professional services to the public are properly trained or qualified.

Lieutenant governor The presiding officer of the Senate. This officeholder also becomes governor if the governor dies, becomes incapacitated, or is removed from office.

Limited government The constitutional principle restricting governmental authority and spelling out personal rights.

Lobbying An effort, usually organized and using a variety of strategies and techniques, to influence the making of laws or public policy.

Lottery A form of gambling, conducted by many states, in which participants purchase tickets that offer an opportunity to cash in on a winning number or set of winning numbers. Voters legalized a state lottery in Texas in 1991.

Mandates Federal laws or regulations that require state or local governments to take certain actions, often at costs that the federal government doesn't reimburse. The state government also imposes mandates on local governments.

Maquiladora Program Economic program initiated by Mexico to increase manufacturing and the assembly of goods.

Matching funds Money that states or local governments have to provide to qualify for certain federal grants.

Mayor, strong A form of city government that gives the mayor considerable power, including budgetary control and appointment and removal authority over city department heads.

Mayor, weak A form of city government in which the mayor shares authority with the city council and other elected officials but has little independent control over city policy or city administration.

Media bias A perception—sometimes real, sometimes imagined—that reporters and news organizations slant their news coverage to favor one side or the other in particular issues or disputes.

Media, controlled Paid advertising in the media whose content and presentation are determined by a political candidate or campaign.

Media event An event staged by an officeholder or political candidate that is designed to attract media—especially television coverage.

Merit employment system A personnel system under which public employees are selected for government jobs through competitive examinations and the systematic evaluation of job performance.

Merit selection A proposal under which the governor would appoint state judges from lists of potential nominees recommended by committees of experts. Appointed judges would have to run later in retention elections to keep their seats but wouldn't have opponents on the ballot. Voters would simply decide whether a judge should remain in office or be replaced by another gubernatorial appointee.

Metro government Consolidation of city and county governments to avoid duplication of public services. This approach has been tried in several other parts of the country but so far has attracted little interest in Texas.

Miranda ruling A far-reaching decision of the U.S. Supreme Court that requires law enforcement officers to warn a criminal suspect of his right to remain silent and have an attorney present during questioning.

Mischief of factions Term coined by James Madison to describe the complex relationships among groups and interests within the American political system and the institutional arrangements that potentially balance the power of groups.

Misdemeanor A minor criminal offense punishable by a fine or a short sentence in the county jail.

Moralistic subculture A view that government's primary responsibility is to promote the public welfare and should actively use its authority and power to improve the social and economic well-being of its citizens.

Motor voter registration Term referring to federal and state laws that allow people to register to vote at offices where they receive their driver's licenses.

Municipal court Court of limited jurisdiction that hears cases involving city ordinances and primarily handles traffic tickets.

Myths (*see Political Myths*).

Negative television advertisements Television commercials in which political candidates attack their opponents, sometimes over a legitimate issue, but more often over an alleged flaw in their opponent's character or ability to hold office. Many such ads are deliberately misleading or outright false.

New federalism A term used to describe recent changes in federal-state relationships. Used primarily by conservative presidents, it suggests a devolution or return of power to the states and a decreased role of the federal government in domestic policy.

No pass, no play rule A student failing a course is restricted from participating in extracurricular activities.

Nolo contendere A plea of no contest to a criminal charge.

Norms (*legislative*) Unwritten rules of institutional behavior that are critical to the stability and effectiveness of the institution.

North American Free Trade Agreement (NAFTA) Treaty signed in 1993 to lower trade barriers among the United States, Mexico, and Canada and to create a common economic market. It is widely referred to as NAFTA.

One-party system The domination of elections and governmental processes by a single party, which may be split into different ideological, economic, or regional factions. In Texas, the phrase is used to describe the period from the late 1870s to the late 1970s, when the Democratic party claimed virtually all elected, partisan offices.

Open meetings and public information records acts Laws that require state and local governmental bodies to conduct most of their actions in public and maintain records for public inspection.

Original jurisdiction The authority of a court to try or resolve a civil lawsuit or a criminal prosecution being heard for the first time.

Parole The early release of an inmate from prison, subject to certain conditions.

Party activist Member of a political party involved in organizational and electoral activities.

Pay-as-you-go principle A constitutional prohibition against state government borrowing money for its operating budget.

Penal code A body of law that defines most criminal offenses and sets a range of punishments that can be assessed.

Permanent University Fund A land- and mineral-rich endowment that benefits the University of Texas and Texas A & M University systems, particularly the flagship universities in Austin and College Station.

Petit jury A panel of citizens that hears evidence in a civil lawsuit or a criminal prosecution and decides the outcome by issuing a verdict.

Petition for review Petition to Texas Supreme Court that legal or procedural mistakes were made in the lower court, thus meriting a hearing before the court.

Platform A set of principles or positions on various issues adopted by a political party at its state or national convention.

Plea bargain A procedure that allows a person charged with a crime to negotiate a guilty plea with prosecutors in exchange for a lighter sentence than he or she would expect to receive if convicted in a trial.

Plural executive A fragmented system of authority under which most statewide, executive officeholders are elected independently of the governor. This arrangement, which is used in Texas, places severe limitations on the governor's power.

Pluralism   Theories holding that a diversity of groups—and people—are instrumental in the policy-making process, and no one group is able to dominate the decisions of government.

Political action committee   Often referred to as PAC, this is a committee representing a specific interest group or including employees of a specific company that raises money from its members for distribution to selected officeholders and political candidates.

Political culture   A widely shared set of views, attitudes, beliefs, and customs of a people as to how their government should be organized and run.

Political myths   Generally held views rooted in the political culture that are used to explain the common historical and cultural experiences.

Political party   A group that seeks to elect public officeholders under its own name.

Political patronage   The hiring of government employees on the basis of personal friendships or favors rather than ability or merit.

Political socialization   The process that begins in early childhood whereby a person assimilates the beliefs, attitudes, and behaviors of society and acquires views toward the political system and government.

Poll tax   A tax that Texas and some other states used to require people to pay before allowing them to vote. The purpose was to discourage minorities and poor whites from participating in the political process. The tax was declared unconstitutional in the 1960s.

Popular sovereignty   The constitutional principle of self-government; the belief that the people control their government and governments are subject to limitations and constraints.

Population density   Number of persons residing within a square mile.

Precinct   A specific, local voting area created by county commissioners court. The state election code outlines detailed requirements for drawing up these election units.

Precinct chair   A local officer in a political party who presides over the precinct convention and serves on the party's county executive committee. Voters in each precinct elect a chair in the party's primary election.

Preemptions   Federal laws that limit the authority or powers of state and local governments.

Privatization   Government contracting with private companies to provide some public services.

Privileges and immunities   The right of a resident of one state to be protected by the laws and afforded the legal opportunities in any other state he or she visits. Certain exceptions, however, have been allowed by the courts, including the right of states to charge nonresidents higher college tuition or higher hunting and fishing license fees.

Probation   A procedure under which a convicted criminal isn't sent to prison if he or she meets certain conditions, such as restrictions on travel and with whom he or she associates.

Prosecution   The conduct of legal proceedings against an individual charged with a crime.

Public Improvement District   Specific area of a city in which property owners pay special taxes in return for improvements to streets and other public facilities in their neighborhood.

Public interest groups   Groups that are primarily concerned with consumer or environmental protection, the promotion of strong ethical standards for public officials, or increased funding for health and human services programs. Since they often are poorly funded, grassroots, volunteer efforts are crucial to their success.

Public opinion polling   The scientific compiling of people's attitudes toward business products, public issues, public officeholders, or political candidates. It has become a key ingredient of statewide political campaigns and is usually conducted by telephone using a representative sample of voters.

Radical Reconstructionists   The group of Republicans who took control of Congress in 1866 and imposed hated military governments on the former Confederate states after the Civil War.

Railroad Commission, Texas   A three-member, elected body that regulates oil and natural gas production and lignite mining in Texas.

Reading   Bills are required to go through three readings in both houses of the legislature. The first reading occurs with the introduction of a bill in the House or the Senate and its referral to a committee by the presiding officer. The second reading is the initial debate by the full House or Senate on a bill that has been approved by a committee. The third occurs with the final presentation of a bill before the full House or Senate.

Realignment A major shift in political party support or identification, which usually occurs around a critical election. In Texas, this was a gradual transformation from a one-party system dominated by Democrats to a two-party system in which Republicans became the dominant party statewide.

Record vote A vote taken in the House or the Senate of which a permanent record is kept, listing how individual legislators voted. By contrast, there are voice votes where legislators simply voice ayes or nays on an issue without being permanently recorded.

Redistricting The process of redrawing legislative and other political district boundaries to reflect changing population patterns. Districts for the Texas House, state Senate, and U.S. Congress are redrawn every ten years by the legislature.

Referendum An election, usually initiated by a petition of voters, where an action of a legislative body is submitted for approval by the voters.

Regressive tax A tax that imposes a disproportionately heavier burden on low-income people than on the more affluent.

Regular legislative session The 140-day period in odd-numbered years in which the legislature meets and can consider laws on any issue or subject.

Religious Right An ultraconservative political faction that draws considerable support from fundamentalist religious groups and economic conservatives.

Republic A political system in which sovereign power resides in the citizenry and is exercised by representatives elected by and responsible to them.

Reserved powers Powers given to state governments by the Tenth Amendment. These are powers not delegated to the national government nor otherwise prohibited to the states by the Constitution.

Revenue bonds Bonds sold by governments that are repaid from the revenues generated from income-producing facilities.

Revenue sharing A program begun under President Nixon and later repealed in which state and local governments received federal aid that could be used for virtually any purpose the recipient government wanted.

Revolving door The practice of former members of state boards and commissions or key employees of agencies leaving state government for more lucrative jobs with the industries they used to regulate. It raises questions of undue industry influence over regulatory agencies.

Right-to-work law Law prohibiting the requirements of union membership in order to get or hold a job.

Ruiz v. Estelle A lawsuit in which a federal judge in 1980 declared the Texas prison system unconstitutional and ordered sweeping, expensive reforms.

School board Governing body of a public school district.

School superintendent Chief administrator of a school district hired by the school board.

Secretary of state Administers state election laws, grants charters to corporations, and processes the extradition of prisoners to other states. This officeholder is appointed by the governor.

Senatorial courtesy An unwritten policy that permits a senator to block the confirmation of a gubernatorial appointee who lives in the senator's district.

Separation of powers The division of authority among three distinct branches of government—the legislative, the executive, and the judicial—which serves as checks and balances on each other's power.

Session, regular This is the 140-day period in odd-numbered years in which the legislature meets and can consider and pass laws on any issue or subject.

Session, special A legislative session that can be called at any other time by the governor. It is limited to thirty days and can consider only subjects or issues designated by the governor.

Sharpstown stock fraud scandal After rocking state government in 1971 and 1972, it helped produce some far-reaching legislative and political changes. It involved the passage of banking legislation sought by Houston financier Frank Sharp and quick profits that some state officials made on stock purchased in an insurance company owned by Sharp with unsecured loans from Sharp's Sharpstown State Bank.

Sheriff An elected official who is the chief law enforcement officer of a county. In urban areas, his or her jurisdiction usually is limited to the unincorporated areas of a county, while local police departments have jurisdiction over incorporated cities.

Shield law A law that protects a news reporter from having to disclose confidential sources of information to a court. A number of states have such laws, and Texas enacted a shield law in 2009.

Single-issue group A single purpose or highly ideological group that promotes a single issue or cause with only limited regard for the views or interests of other groups. Such groups often are reluctant to compromise.

Single-member district A system in which a legislator, city council member, or other public official is elected from a specific geographic area.

Social contract (*see Contract Theory*).

Sound bite A short, quotable phrase by a public official or political candidate that may sound good on television or radio but lacks depth and is often meaningless.

Speaker The presiding officer of the House of Representatives.

Special district A unit of local government created by the state to perform a specific function or functions not met by cities or counties, including the provision of public services to unincorporated areas.

Spin The presentation of information in the best possible light for a public official or political candidate. It usually is provided by a press secretary, campaign consultant, or another individual representing the officeholder or candidate.

Spoils system Practice, usually identified with machine politics, of rewarding public jobs to one's political friends or supporters with little regard to abilities or skills.

Staggered terms A requirement that members of state boards and commissions appointed by the governor serve terms that begin on different dates. This is to assure that a board maintains a level of experience by guarding against situations where all board members leave office at the same time.

State Board of Education A fifteen-member body, whose members are elected by districts, that oversees the administration of public education in Texas.

State chair and vice chair The two top state leaders of a political party, one of whom must be a woman. They are selected every two years by delegates to the party's state convention.

State executive committee The statewide governing board of a political party. It includes a man and a woman elected by party members from each of the thirty-one state senatorial districts and the state chair and vice chair.

Statutes Laws enacted by a legislative body.

Statutory law (*see Statutes*).

Suffrage The right to vote.

Sunset review The process under which most state agencies have to be periodically reviewed and re-created by the legislature or go out of business.

Supremacy clause A provision of the U.S. Constitution that says federal law prevails in conflicts between the powers of the states and the national government.

Supreme court, Texas A nine-member court with final appellate jurisdiction over civil lawsuits.

Tag A rule that allows an individual senator to postpone a committee hearing on any bill for at least forty-eight hours, a delay that can be fatal to a bill during the closing days of a legislative session.

Tax abatements Device used by governments to attract new businesses through the reduction or elimination of property taxes for a specific period of time.

Tax, franchise The state's major business tax. It is applied only to corporations and, until changed by the legislature in 1991, was based on a business's assets. Now it is a hybrid corporate income tax that is based on a corporation's income or assets, whichever would produce the highest payment to the state.

Tax, income   A tax based on a corporation's or an individual's income. Texas has a hybrid corporate income tax but is one of only a few states without a personal income tax.

Tax, property   A tax on homes, businesses, and certain other forms of property that is the main source of revenue for local governments. The tax is based on the assessed value of the property.

Tax, sales   A tax charged as a set percentage of most retail purchases and many services. It is the main source of tax revenue for state government and an important source of revenue for many cities and metropolitan transit authorities.

Tax, sin   A common nickname for a tax on tobacco or alcoholic beverages.

Third party   A minor political party. There have been many in Texas over the years, but none has had significant success on a statewide level.

Ticket splitting   The decisions of voters to divide their votes among candidates of more than one political party in the same election.

Tort reform   Changes in state law to put limits on personal injury lawsuits and damage judgments entered by the courts.

Traditionalistic subculture   A view that political power should be concentrated in the hands of a few elite citizens who belong to established families or influential social groups. Public policy basically serves the interests of this small group.

Transnational regionalism   The expanding economic and social interdependence of South Texas and Mexico.

Two-party system   A political system that has two dominant parties, such as that of the United States.

Two-thirds rule   A rule under which the Texas Senate has traditionally operated that requires approval of at least two-thirds of senators before a bill can be debated on the Senate floor. It allows a minority of senators to block controversial legislation.

Unicameral   A single-body legislature.

Unitary system   A system in which ultimate power is vested in a central or national government and local governments have only those powers granted to them by the central government. This principle describes the relationship between the state and local governments in Texas.

Urbanization   The process by which a predominantly rural society or area becomes urban.

Venireman   A person who has been called for a jury panel.

Veto   The power of the governor to reject, or kill, a bill passed by the legislature.

Veto, line-item   The power of the governor to reject certain parts of an appropriation, or spending, bill without killing the entire measure.

Voting Rights Act   A federal law designed to protect the voting rights of minorities by requiring the Justice Department's approval of changes in political districts and certain other electoral procedures. The act, as amended, has eliminated most of the more restrictive state laws that limited minority political participation.

Ward politics   Term, often with negative connotations, that refers to partisan politics linked to political favoritism.

Whistleblower   A government employee who publicly reports wrongdoing or unethical conduct within a government agency.

White primary   A series of state laws and party rules that denied African Americans the right to vote in the Democratic primary in Texas in the first half of the twentieth century.

Writ of mandamus   Court order directing a lower court or another public official to take a certain action.

Photo Credits

Chapter 1   Page 1: Texas State Preservation Board; 6: Northern Illinois University; 6: Texas State Library and Archives Commission; 8: Tucker Gibson; 8: Tucker Gibson; 12: Tucker Gibson; 13: Texas State Library and Archives Commission; 15: The Institute of Texan Cultures; 17: Courtesy of the Office of Representative Hubert Vo; 18: Tucker Gibson; 23: Courtesy of the Office of Governor Rick Perry; 23: Courtesy of the Office of Governor Rick Perry.

Chapter 2   Page 34: Texas State Library and Archives Commission; 40: Tucker Gibson; 41: Tucker Gibson; 43: Tucker Gibson; 45: Tucker Gibson; 46: Texas State Library and Archives Commission; 51: Courtesy of Rick Noriega; 55: Texas Senate Media Services.

Chapter 3   Page 64: Tucker Gibson; 88: Tucker Gibson; 92: Immigration and Customs Enforcement Website (July 9, 2009).

Chapter 4   Page 99: Tucker Gibson; 115: Courtesy of Jack Gullahorn; 122: Tucker Gibson.

Chapter 5: Page 128: Tucker Gibson; 137: Courtesy of Jim Hightower and Associates; 149: Tucker Gibson; 151: Tucker Gibson.

Chapter 6   Page 158: Tucker Gibson; 167: Texas State Library and Archives Commission; 169: Senator John G. Tower Library, Southwestern University; 175: Tucker Gibson; 181: Courtesy of Fred Tawil; 184: Tucker Gibson.

Chapter 7   Page 192: Tucker Gibson; 198: Courtesy of the family of Mrs. G. R. Arnett; 203: University of Texas at El Paso; 204: Institute of Texan Cultures.

Chapter 8   Page 229: Texas State Preservation Board; 236: Texas State Preservation Board; 238: Tucker Gibson; 244: Tucker Gibson; 246: Courtesy of the Office of the Speaker, Texas House Media Services; 248: Texas Senate Media Services; 250: Courtesy of the Office of Lt. Governor David Dewhurst; 253: Texas Senate Media Services; 260: Texas Senate Media Services.

Chapter 9   Page 278: Courtesy of the Office of Governor Rick Perry; 285: Texas State Preservation Board; 286: Texas State Preservation Board; 287: Tucker Gibson; 296: Texas State Preservation Board; 299: Texas State Preservation Board; 301: Texas State Preservation Board; 303: Courtesy of the Office of Governor Rick Perry; 308: Courtesy of the Office of Attorney General Greg Abbot; 310: Courtesy of the Office of Comptroller Susan Combs; 310: Courtesy of the Office of Land Commissioner Jerry Patterson.

Chapter 10   Page 316: Texas State Preservation Board; 319: Tucker Gibson; 332: Tucker Gibson.

Chapter 11   Page 338: Tucker Gibson; 343: Tucker Gibson; 344: Tucker Gibson; 346: Courtesy of Oslo McCarthy, Texas Supreme Court; 353: *Houston Chronicle*; 357: Courtesy of Thomas R. Phillips; 364: Bob Daemmrich/Bob Daemmrich Photography, Inc.; 367: Tucker Gibson; 368: Tucker Gibson; 370: Tucker Gibson.

Chapter 12   Page 379: Tucker Gibson; 386: Tucker Gibson; 387: Courtesy of the Office of Mayor Bill White, Houston; 393: Tucker Gibson; 394: Courtesy of the City of San Antonio; 394: Courtesy of the City of Dallas; 395: Courtesy of the City of El Paso; 399: Tucker Gibson; 405: Tucker Gibson; 408: Tucker Gibson; 413: Tucker Gibson.

Chapter 13   Page 425: Tucker Gibson; 435: Tucker Gibson; 440: Tucker Gibson; 443: Tucker Gibson; 445: Tucker Gibson; 450: Tucker Gibson.

Index

A

A. H. Belo Corp., 148
Abatements, tax, 417
Abbott, Greg, 308, 362
Abortion
   protests and marches and, 121
   Religious Right and, 182
   Texas judicial system and, 374
Abrader, Andres Manuel Lopez, 92
Absentee ballots, 201
Absolute majority of votes, primaries and, 197
Accenture, 322
Accountability, partisan, 186
Activists
   judicial, 354
   party, 185, 186
   political, 223
Advertising, political. *See also* Mass media
   "buying" elections and, 134
   free air time and, 134
   local elections, 213–214
   name identification and, 213–214
   negative, 135, 214
   paid commercials, 134
   recent gubernatorial races and, 135–138, 214–215
   susceptibility of young adults to, 134
   thirty-second spots and, 214
Advertising tax, 142
Affirmative action, 112, 446–447
African Americans. *See also* Political suffrage
   affirmative action programs and, 446–447
   at-large election systems and, 396–397
   demographics of, 13–14, 383
   educational attainment and, 25
   educational discrimination and, 446
   1875 Constitutional Convention and, 46
   elected officials (1974–2002), 209
   electoral equity and, 170
   historical experiences of, 7
   income and, 22–23
   interest groups and, 104, 111–112
   Jim Crow laws and, 165, 241
   judicial appointments and, 348
   legislative caucuses and, 264
   political gains by, 209, 224
   political participation and, 224, 236–237, 240
   political parties and, 176–177
   political power and, 14
   restrictive registration law, 203
   right to vote and, 44
   in Texas legislature, 237
   voting exclusions and, 51

Age
   demographics in Texas cities, 400
   intergenerational obligations and, 20
   median age, 20
   party identification and, 176
   political participation and, 196–197, 224
   property tax exemptions and, 400
   retirement benefits, 235
   voting differences and, 175
Agenda building, 131
Agenda setting, 130–131, 164
Agricultural interest groups, 113–114
Agriculture Commissioner, 286, 310, 311
Aid to Families with Dependent Children (AFDC),
   75–76, 78, 452
AIDS issue, 5
Air pollution, 455–456
Alamo, 2, 6, 40
Alamodome, 412
Albin, Tom, 397
Alliance for Better Campaigns, 135
Allred, James, 166, 363
Amendments, constitutional, 37, 53–54, 58
American Federation of State, County, and Municipal
   Workers, 113
American Independent Party, 177
Americans Disabled for Attendant Programs Today
   (ADAPT), 111, 122
Americans with Disabilities Act (1990), 77
Anglos
   classification of, 15
   demographics and, 15–16
   educational attainment and, 24–25
   income and, 23
   migration into Texas, 15–16
   political participation and, 224
Animal rights groups, 121
Annexation, 41, 382–383, 416–417
Anti-Catholicism, 165
Anti-labor sentiment, 114
AOL–Times Warner merger, 149
Appellate courts, 345–347
Appellate jurisdiction, 341
Application of public policy, 429
Appointive powers, governor, 290–291
Appraisal districts, 407
Appropriations, state, 431. *See also* Budgetary process
Appropriations bills, 258
Armbrister, Ken, 238–139, 241
Armstrong, Bob, 171
Arnold, Ann, 135
Articles of Confederation, 69